BLACK AMERICAN MUSIC:

Past and Present

Second Edition

BLACK AMERICAN MUSIC:

Past and Present

Second Edition

Hildred Roach

KRIEGER PUBLISHING COMPANY
MALABAR, FLORIDA
1992

Second Edition 1992

Printed and Published by
KRIEGER PUBLISHING COMPANY
KRIEGER DRIVE
MALABAR, FLORIDA 32950

Library of Congress Cataloging-in-Publication Data

Roach, Hildred.
Black American music : past and present : pan-African composers thenceforth and now / by Hildred Roach. — 2nd ed.
p. cm.
Includes bibliographical references and index.
ISBN 0-89464-580-3 (acid-free paper)(cloth)
ISBN 0-89464-766-0 (paperback)
1. Afro-Americans—Music—History and criticism. 2. Blacks—Music—History and criticism. 3. Music—United States—History and criticism. I. Title.
ML3556.R58 1991
780'.89'96073—dc20 91-2398
CIP
MN

10 9 8 7 6 5 4 3 2

CONTENTS

APPENDIXES

ILLUSTRATIONS

MUSICAL EXAMPLES

PREFACE TO THE SECOND EDITION

The purpose of this second edition remains the same as that of the first: to pay tribute to Pan-African composers and their music; to introduce beginning scholars to the music; and to reiterate a "call to remembrance" of the specific factors which bear links to clear identity not only to African-American music, but to all American music. This book is also designed to perpetuate the historical tradition already started by other writers and to preserve a part of the rich cultural heritage by helping to build a strong consolidation of the truth. Hopefully, the current revisions and additions will further the cause for such ideals, and the merger of two volumes into one will make the book easier to use.

Black American Music: Past & Present was a direct result of the recent cultural revolution which sought to develop new philosophical positions of change, challenge and command, and which sought to proclaim the true story of a proud legacy. Such books as this which were written during the "Second Renaissance" of the exciting 1960's–1970's were meant to fill the void which existed in the works which dared place William G. Still and thirteen others like him in a footnote while Stephen Foster commanded the page, and which intentionally omitted the contributions of Black composers. Such books as *Black American Music: Past & Present* were also written as statements that discounted untrue propaganda and disbelief about the quality, quantity and quotas of this music. At such a time, books which should have squelched the awful fallacies were either out of print or simply ignored and never really widely distributed for the benefit of world culture. The scholastic productivity of these recent documentations were encouraging signs of a new era which hopefully would eliminate the practice of omission or lack of attention to the important subject of Black music.

When, in 1973, it was a miracle to find books delivering even the names of Pan-African composers, we educators were alone in establishing new courses to deal with the fascinating saga of Pan-African music. No set curriculum guidelines as to teaching materials, resource documents, or otherwise were available to standardize information, and few were willing to work harder to discover the real essence of the studies.

Since that time, however, much has improved. New books and revisions to standard books have evidenced a change, and more scholars now find that the information within their own compounds agrees with the data compiled by others, and that the direct force felt from the recent cultural renaissance is emblazoned into more minds than ever before. The progress is heartening, refreshing, and clearly a step in the right direction toward more truthful revelations about the histories of all American music.

Today, critical years after the release of *Black American Music: Past and Present*, and the publication of Eileen Southern's *The Music of Black Americans*, marks an era of change—change mandated by generations of people bewildered, befuddled, and anguished over the state of modern education which dared misguide and miseducate, thereby leaving the search for real answers to chance. Books long since written about legendary composers in our midst should have been more readily available, should have been required reading, and should have been loudly applauded for their apt timing. Instead, research by minorities was generally discounted, abandoned, or unknown, at least in North America. And the perpetuation of basking in the "security" of educational foundations of Europe blinded Americans who failed to append to the historical "tree" prideful new accomplishments of their own.

During the past few years, the subject of music by these composers has mushroomed so rapidly that the body of information seems much more monumental than ever before imagined. In addition, several new centers (such as those at Yale, Cornell, and the University of Michigan) have sprung forth to assist with wider dissemination of information and to encourage scholarship in this area. Concomitant with these openings have been the releases of several important recordings such as the Columbia Records "Black Composers Series"; a massive and informative dictionary of Black musicians by Eileen Southern; the related score-record set by Willis Patterson and the University of Michigan; and new viewpoints discussed in several new books about the subject of this music or specific personalities. Outstanding, too, were the associations which, along with the Association for the Study of Negro Life and History and the National Association of Negro Musicians, also helped promote the study and performance of this music by setting up symposiums and citing achievements. Committees on Cultural Diversity in Performance, Friends of Kennedy Center, the Afro-American Creative Society, Opera Ebony, and the Black Caucus of Music Educators were among those whose constituents continually demanded more from leaders and legacies.

Although it is true that much has been done, it is equally clear that the job is not yet finished. More institutions, administrators, faculty, and students must be made aware of the importance of better budgets to support new courses, better preparedness in presenting the facts of the new courses, and decidedly better philosophies to identify the study of cultural heritages with the study of Self. Apathy, self-consciousness, and negativism have no place in this new era.

Not enough work has been done in teaching the information relative to composers in various parts of the world, such as in Saudi Arabia or even in places as close to North America as Brazil. Not enough work has been completed on the relationship between the music of the Indians and the Africans, especially in cases such as the sixteenth century meeting of Brazilian Indians and African slaves who were surprised to find similarities in their instrumentations and musical presentations. Neither have the recent discoveries by Ivan Van Sertima about ancient Blacks in Mexico (*National Leader News*, June 2, 1983) nor the pre-colonial African inhabitants been clearly connected to the musical contributions of the Americas in general. And more importantly, certainly not enough work has been done to disseminate and impart this knowledge within new courses, to expand standard course syllabi to include the new eras and new ideas, or to increase an understanding of not only the correlations in the music of Americans but in the music of the world.

The "second cultural awakening" has begun a revolution of political and scholastic beliefs, permitted the establishment of relevant curricula, and has promoted a study of the positive contributions of Pan-Africans to world culture. Now, therefore, is the perfect time for reassessing the impetus set into motion by a few and generating expanded excitement for many. Additionally, now is the time for appraising three and one-half centuries of achievements by Pan-African composers in America, and far more centuries of achievements in the history of the western world.

Whenever it seems that a person has singlehandedly accomplished such a feat as the completion of a book, it must be considered that the production has really been brought about by many background supporters and well-wishers rather than by the author alone. Many educators, students, friends, publishers, composers, and institutions supplied me with information, photographs, constructive criticisms, and moral support. I am indebted to the many publishers and composers who granted me permission to use excerpts of selected works for illustrative purposes, and to the persons whose materials and interests were meaningful. Although the author takes the responsibility for any errors in reporting, certainly the support "cast" played a grand role in whatever the book has become.

The following are also eligible for honors, accolades, and acknowledgments forever:

Clergymen: Ministers A. Knighton Stanley, Susan Newman, Rubin Tendai, Peoples Congregational Church; John Johnson of the United Methodist Church, New York; Father Nathaniel Porter of the Episcopal Church; and Father Joseph Lapauw of the Missionhurst-CICM.

Organizations and Other Firms: Judith Still of Still Music, AGM International, Motown, Columbia, and Epic Records, Frances Murphy of *Afro-American News*, Bill O'Leary of the *Washington Post News*, Adrienne Rhodes and staff of the United Negro College Fund, Verna Bolton of Morehouse Alumni Affairs, Lance Bowling of Cambria Records, Johnson Publications, African-American Forum; Harry Andrews of the Wilmington Board of Music Education; Camille Taylor of the Black Music Caucus of MENC; Sola Soile, Publishing Manager of the University of Ife Press, Ltd.; ASCAP, Peer-Southern and Wendy Eisenberg; Charlotte Klein Associates; Aykut Gorkey and Beverley Furman of Atlantic Records; Jean Riggins of Capital Records; Macmillan Books, Niani Kilkinney of Smithsonian; Charles Lourie of Blue Note; Wayne Coleman of Amistad Research Center; Gary Johnson of Casio, Inc.; Brazeal Dennard of the National Association of Negro Musicians; Antoinette Handy-Miller of the National Endowment For the Arts; Bernice Reagon from Smithsonian; Archie Bufkins of the National Committee on Cultural Diversity in Performance; Pan-American Organization, especially Efrain Paesky; the Belgian Centre for Music Documentation, especially Anna Van Steenbergen; Ed Hardy of Dale Music; Theodore Presser; Fantasy/Milestone; Capital; Tower Record Shop; Epic Records; Rusty Bogart of Ohlsson's Books; and Dr. V. Melnick from the Center of Applied Research at the University of D.C.

Chairmen of Music Departments: Doris McGinty and Raymond Jackson of Howard University; Malcolm Breda, Xavier University; Georgia Ryder, Norfolk State University; and William Moore, University of the District of Columbia, for critical readings.

Embassies in Washington D.C.: Ghana; Congo; Nigeria, especially Anna Ekam; Brazil, especially Cybele Magro; Haiti; Kenya; Dominican Republic; and Belgium, especially Myra Lawley.

Foreign Language Consultants: John Butler, Marie Racine and Janet Hampton from the University of the District of Columbia; and José and Nito Sanchez from Panama.

Libraries and Staff: Yvonne Stephenson and Lerett Tettford of the

University of Guyana; Maria Rievera of University of P.R.; Dennis Oettinger, Mary Parrish, and Riisa Rymer of St. Thomas; The Shomburg Collection, New York; Marcie Bracey, Jo Ellen Price El-Bashir, Deborra Richardson, Esme Bhan, and Karen Jefferson of the Moorland Room of Howard University; the Library of Congress, especially Clarence Williams, Wayne Shirley, Elmer Booze, and Thomas Jones; the University of the District of Columbia, especially Ulysses Cameron, Barbara Quinnam, Albertine Johnson, Lucretia Jackson, Gemma Parks, and Clemment Goddard; Tuskegee Institute, especially Danny Williams; and my friend from the Library of Congress, Michael Green, who was exceptional in assisting with tasks from reading to research.

Educators: Don Lee White for his files; Brazeal Dennard from NANM of Detroit; Edith Work of Fisk; Rebecca Cureau and Jeanne Johns Adkins; Betty Leonard; Leon Thompson; Hale Smith; Noel Da Costa and T. J. Anderson; J. Kwabena Nketia; Delores Lewis; William Burres Garcia; Evelyn Davidson White; Lorraine Faxio; Clyde Parker; Booker T. Felder, Wanda Brown, Vada Butcher, Marion Cumbo, William McDonald, Samuel Akpabot, and Akin Euba.

Colleagues and Students of the University of the District of Columbia: virtually all of my colleagues and students who constantly "lent me their ears," expertise, and materials, especially José Gil, Robert Felder, Marva Cooper, Janette Harris, Calvin LeCompte, Charlotte Hollomon, Percy Gregory, James Palmore, Anne Burt, Judith Korey, Frank Staroba, Sanders Milligan, George Edwards, Vijaya Melnick and the CARUP staff; Pearl Williams-Jones (for the critical readings), Harvey Van Buren, Jr., Calvin Jones, Arthur Dawkins, William Mandle, and all my students such as Montague Smith, Owilda Curtis, Marjorie Stith, Jesse Crews, Constance Qualls, Reginald Bondurant, Christopher Redding, research assistants Cynthia Blalock, Cherylrene Loftland and Astrid Baxter, and Christopher Fisher (who reworked the music examples).

Caribbean Educators, Librarians, and Consultants: In Guyana, William Pilgrim and Sister Rose Magdalene from the Ministry of Culture; Edith Pieters from Ministry of Education; Yvonne Stephenson, Lerett Tettford from the University of Guyana Library; Attorneys Sheila and Ananda Chapman; Enid Housty, and Enid Medas who gave invaluable advice; in Trinidad, Muriel Donowa-McDavidson, Louise McIntosh, Clarissa Alleyne, Christopher Boynes, Rocky McCollins, Felix Roach, Desmond and Mary Bullah, Desmond Guyton, Margaret Rouse-Jones and Claudette Modeste; and Bertriana Gramsaul and Rabia Ramogan at the University of West Indies; in Puerto Rico, Hector Vega Druet and Maria Rievera of the University of P.R.; and in St. Thomas, Dennis Oettinger, Mary Parrish, Riisa Rymer and Lorna Richards.

Family and Friends: Ma Pearl, the Twins and Mark, Marlene Brooks, Ruth and Bernard Colner, Louis Ford, the Thomas Clyburns, Jacqueline Sadler, Patricia Adams, Attorneys Claiborne Chavers, Spencer Boyer, and Gabriel Christian; Donna Donaldson, Will Carter, Shirley Moore, Margaret Welch Wilson, and Simona A. Allen.

Others: William Gottlieb, photographer; typists Gwendolyn Davis, Peggy Shorter, Marilyn Millstone, and Tawana Spivey; readers Constance Liser and Patricia Maida from the University of D.C.; Roberta Morausky from Western Connecticut State College; and editor Mary Roberts from

Krieger Publishing Company, who was far more than just a reader and who sent materials and support.

Special acknowledgments are also in order for the publisher of this book, Robert E. Krieger. It goes without saying that the future of our common American heritage depends upon the commitments of such astute publishers who direct their expertise, excellence, and energies toward the preservation and dissemination of information. Their search for Truth and for the preservation of wisdom, worth, and wit will emblazon their names in world history for years to come.

PREFACE TO THE FIRST EDITION

The need to survey African-American composers and their music is real and immediate. This book is intended to meet this need and present a balanced view of the involvement of Blacks in various types of music. An interrelationship will be demonstrated between African musical sources and North American composers. Also, a logical conclusion is to show that some Black music influenced, and was influenced by, European music.

Outstanding among the many persons and organizations who deserve my sincere gratitude for their inspirations and contributions are: pioneers of Black Studies Margaret Wilson, Maud Hare, Benjamin Brawley, Alain Locke, John Work III, Margaret Butcher, Edgar Toppin, Langston Hughes, Lerone Bennett and John Franklin; composers Hale Smith, Ulysses Kay, John Carter, Noel DaCosta and others who supplied invaluable research information in addition to highlights of their own careers; publishers and consultants: Edward B. Marks, Oliver Daniel of Broadcast Music and J. K. Nketia of the University of Ghana; family, friends and colleagues Altona Johns, Dr. Vivian McBrier, Antoinette Handy-Miller, Geneva Southall, Maurice Strider, Roger Askew, Nathaniel Williams, Mrs. John W. Work III, Mildred Ellis, Harvey and Florence Van Buren, William and Shirley Moore, Cheryl Moulton, Joseph Gathings, Jeanne McRae, Annie W. Roberts, Susie Graham, Adelaide P. Wicks and Attorney H. Carl Moultrie; librarian Ulysses Cameron; clerical assistants Raymond Jones, Carl Roach and Dianne Spann; photographers Scott and Merceron of Scurlock Studios; and Ruby Roach Satterwhite, who sketched instruments and planned rough designs associated with the text.

I am greatly indebted to Dr. Oscar Henry of Fisk University for his criticism and reading of the book in its earliest form, and to Ruth and Bernard Colner for their proofreading assistance. My thanks are also extended to Edward Owens, editor, and to Robert Bell of Crescendo Publishers for their patience and appraisals. My Mother, Pearl, constantly encouraged the completion of this project, and to her I give the highest praise of all: the dedication of this book.

Since each facet of this music cannot be examined here, composers and musical forms are stressed rather than performers, the latter being discussed only where they serve to classify anonymous composer-performers of a significant era or style. This book covers aspects of Black music which are usually omitted from standard music history books. Therefore, it should supplement such established works. It is, then, a recall of Black developments to be placed alongside other proud assets of fellow Americans.

Black American Music: Past and Present may be used for courses in Black music or with books of introduction, listening or analysis of music. Teachers and students should find the contents helpful as a guide to composers and their music, and the general public may find it useful as source material to correlate with any field or specific knowledge. Hopefully, this work will promote a necessary identity among Blacks universally, as well as inform others of a proud and genuine heritage of these contributions not only in American music, but in American history.

The author suggests that the readers make full use of the materials found in the list of musical terms, the list of composers and publishers of the music discussed and the additional readings and recordings. All efforts must be made to promote the listening, performing and understanding of the music that is Afro-American.

PART ONE

THE BEGINNING (1619–1870's)

I

SLAVE ERA: THE BLACK MAN IN COLONIAL AMERICA

The first shiploads of Black slaves to America were Africans. This slave trade together with the Civil War and Reconstruction served as the background for the earliest musical contributions by anonymous Blacks.

By the process of either bargaining or stealing, Africa became the prime source of American slaves. Although taken from various areas of the country, the greatest numbers of Africans were gathered from points nearest the Gulf of Guinea. One of the strongest and most famous of these West African areas was Ashanti (modern Ghana) whose magnificent coasts along Tema, Accra, Winneba, Cape Coast and Elmina became common ports of call. However, many parts of Africa remained untouched by European traders, and certain distant locations from the coast, such as Egypt, supplied only a small number of slaves, as the journey prevented large numbers from surviving the ordeal of the desert.

The original home of the Africans was considered backward and uncivilized by White Americans, and Blacks were made to believe this. However, Africa was a country of many languages, cultures and world foundations. Even within a small radius, thousands of tribal constituencies such as Ashanti, Wa, Twi, Akan, Ga, Ewe, Kwa, Yoruba, Mandingo, Tshi and Ibo evidenced this variety. This factor must have contributed to the difficulty in communicating not only with the slave traders, but with fellow Africans as well. There were also several social, political and religious practices found among the African Christians, Moslems and native religions which further delayed immediate comradeships among Africans and which helped to perpetuate slavery even more.

However diverse, each tribe had some things in common. Individually, each had practiced a long history of social organization, politics, teaching, learning and general development. Each had boasted a populace of chieftains, architects, craftsmen, doctors, warriors, scientists and musicians and each had planned its own mores, religion, government and social commitments. Each was more geographically linked than modern politics now indicate.

Africans populated Abyssinia (Ethiopia) with its regal splendor and strong lineage; Egypt, with the spectacular pyramids; and Mali, which boasted not only Timbuktu as a famous center of learning, but its famous patron kings and court musicians. If we are to believe historians Herodotus and others, Africa also served as a spawning ground for related theories fused into ancient western civilizations identified with Greece and Rome; these theories ironically built upon the best customs of those who eventually became subjects to the western world.

Had the Black man been taught the value of his heritage, he might have had a stronger ego, full of pride for himself and his brother, and an adequate regimen of satisfactions in the accomplishments of his people.

He might have developed a love for the strength of his culture, his craftsmanship, and his music. However, he was forced to leave this heritage and begin anew in a world where his ideas of music and art were little known and yet to develop. Little did he know that his musical nature and spiritual stimuli would be so important in the development of the New World.

Since tribal roots and other cultural associations of Africa were eventually banned, the older heritage meant nothing to those whose majority of melodies sprang from beneath the level of human society. Having been reduced to rank and status of pigs and horses, they were termed "chattel." Denied the education common to Whites, African languages and structures were soon forgotten.

During slavery, mistreatment and deprivations which accompanied these conditions were constant. Although slavery had existed in Africa and other parts of the world wherein Whites had also been enslaved, nowhere did reports seem to outdo the mountain of wrongs enforced upon the Blacks as in America. But American slavery is not the real question here. The point of this discussion is to bring out these elements of society whose intense bitterness within oppression produced the multiplicity of passions that became the basis of Black music and to show the general conditions under which an art may grow. These elements must be considered for a valid understanding of some characteristics common to Black music.

Guardian Figure Mask, West Africa. Courtesy of Fisk University.

In early 1619, Black slaves entered Virginia, according to John H. Franklin (who named them "indentured servants"). They were then transported to other parts of America (see maps). Slaves became concentrated in the southern states mainly because of the economic importance of cotton. And even though slaves were also maintained in northern states, they were not in great number. Therefore, the majority of the earliest musical endeavors emanated from the geographical areas of the South.

Slave narratives written by Frederick Douglass and Sojourner Truth show that because slave owners were suspicious and fearful of insurrections which had occurred both on ship and land, slaves were "forced" to sing their songs so that it could be assumed that they were not planning other incidents. Consequently, such music was often molded from inhuman experiences of slavery, and was used to forget the conditions under which they worked. Music also relieved the burden of their problems, both physical and spiritual, and at times, served as a signal to amuse themselves.

To sing and play were not new to the Africans, whose functional art was interwoven into their everyday life. Yet to perform under such conditions was an experience to which they were not accustomed. Nevertheless, the strength of their character and their natural talents surfaced under circumstances that might have destroyed weaker men. They poured their emotions into the music that told a part of the American story which now provides a basis for the cultural awakening of Blacks in our time.

Early slave music consisted of many human passions derived from oppression. Spirituals, blues, hollers and work songs were some examples which echoed emotional despair as well as jubilation and optimistic yearning for a Utopia—a better place without a master, without auction blocks and without conditions of servitude. These songs, both simple and complicated, had grown out of the duties and the drudgery associated with bondage and had served for work, worship and play. Many such creative influences were vestiges of their own Africa.

No doubt, many of the earliest songs were sad. It is incorrect to assume, however, that all were of this nature, for within a span of some 200 years, slaves knew both sadness and happiness. Revealing the functional categories of African music, many songs collected during Reconstruction reflected individual and collective thoughts of diverse situations of life and emotion. For example, those Africans toiling under burdensome circumstances undoubtedly composed one way while those treated more humanely naturally composed another. Likewise, music used for funerals differed from that used for entertainment. Thus, slave texts referred to a gamut of emotions.

Even though commenting on only one musical form, Frederick Douglass, born and educated as a slave, was of the opinion that all spirituals seemed sad. In his autobiography, *My Bondage and My Freedom*, he wrote:

> I did not, when a slave, fully understand the deep meaning of those rude and apparently incoherent songs. . . . They breathed the prayer and complaint of soul overflowing with the bitterest anguish. . . . The remark . . . that slaves were the most contented and happy laborers in the world . . . was a mistake . . . to suppose. . . . The songs represented their sorrows, rather than their joys.
>
> Slaves were expected to sing as well as to work . . . [as] a means of telling the overseer, in the distance, where they were and what they were about . . . those commissioned to the Great House farm were peculiarly vocal. . . . While on the way they would make the grand old woods for miles around reverberate with their wild and plaintive notes. They were indeed both merry and sad. Child as I was, these wild songs greatly depressed my spirits.

Many have used his statements to assume that all slave songs were sad, without first considering that not all spirituals were sad. Nor were the countless other songs experienced within 200 years completely sad. For one thing, some Blacks had managed a share of the material goods before the Civil War and were pleased with their possessions. Others were either too young to comprehend the situation or were too happy to have escaped hopeless conditions of serfdom and indebtedness at home. Still others, like the Black cowboys or a very few nomads, were without many of the cares of southern slavery. In addition, many songs of joy arose from the Black populace once Emancipation appeared imminent or when a slave successfully escaped.

It was not entirely the music, then, but the slavery itself which described the real sorrow that Douglass must have felt, and which penetrated the environment around which all such songs were created. Music was wrongly accused, for music had the power to induce boundless happiness. By soothing the souls and healing the sick, it could create an aesthetic quality of mind beyond recall. It could quench hate, develop a mock peace and pronounce a man "free" from the cares of slavery and Reconstruction.

All this was the power of the music composed by Blacks. For theirs was a practical art which lived as they lived. More important than the fact that the songs later served as historical data, is the realization that these songs directly functioned in the plans and survival of the Blacks from the era of Nat Turner to that of Martin Luther King. The strong characteristics and inbred qualities found in the African people and their songs prepared them for the coming transition in building a new way of life, their own language and a new music.

Elmina Castle, a slave fort in Ghana, West Africa.

Ganvie Sea Village, Cotonou, Dahomey.

II

AFRICAN HERITAGE: AN INFLUENCE IN MUSICAL TRADITION

In order to define Black American music, we must first consider Africa as the source of the talents developed in compositions from the earliest to the present. For throughout slavery, the proofs of an African heritage were evident in the elements of early African-American music. As the slaves steadily produced successive generations of offspring, the influence of their African characteristics and those of Europe merged to create the modern era of Americanism. Consciously or subconsciously, Old Africa, the Mother Country of civilization, remained the most important source of originality for Blacks, and eventually for many musical attempts in American nationalism.

In order to further comprehend this African spirit within an artistic realm of Afro-American music, we must seriously study Africa in relation to its people and its culture. For example, one could recall the multi-tribal complexities which enhanced the African social systems. This fact alone assured that great varieties of musical substance would exist in early slave music. When compounded, these innumerable features defined the music as a distinctive collection of sounds marked by diverse improvisation in performance with melismatic or ornamental melodies, exciting dances, complex rhythms, unique harmonies, scales, forms, titles and textures.

The definition of African music represented the core of Black music in America. In Africa, the soul of music evolved from an inseparable combination of the sister arts of music with drama and dance, and became expertly woven into the language and customs of the people. These elements blended according to the event, appropriateness of the vernacular, age, sex and status of the participants. Yet neither instrument, form, peer group, text, dance, nor musical elements could be taken out of the context of the event for which the music was planned. Neither could any of these elements or media be mixed unless prescribed by tradition.

African instruments, costumes, accessories and dramatic reactions were dictated by the correlation of the composite arts of music, drama and dance and one would be meaningless without the other. Seen in various activities, this correlation weighed heavily on the importance of speech and life itself. For example, a dramatic play or story could include the spontaneous interpolation of music and dance and could be based on actual experiences such as hunting or harvesting. A master drummer would begin a pattern based on word derivatives, inspiring dancers to sing and to act out words with a life-like reality and emotion. A funeral would require appropriate costuming, instruments, textual references to the decedent's history, dirges, specific peer characters, appropriate prayers and dances. All of the above demonstrated necessary elements of cohesiveness.

African music generally involved a close relationship between performers and the community. For example, the funeral mentioned could begin with dirges and prayers from the family members, and gradually include members of the total community or village. Singers were answered by a communal response, a technique referred to as "call and response" which was later reflected in religious sermons, jazz and other forms of the Afro-American.

The method of oral tradition was greatly responsible for the maintenance of the samples of African heritage which miraculously survived the centuries. Because of the illiteracy of most Blacks (at least in the English language) and because of the diversity of African languages, a process of rote teaching was instrumental in sustaining the legends and music of old Africa. Although some Africans had composed their own symbols to represent language sounds, the oral tradition was still by far the most common practice in Africa for decades, and remained the most effective method of reaching the thousands of slaves in America.

Oral tradition must be held responsible for one of the most exciting aspects of African and Afro-American performance—that of improvisation, or improvised variation. When passed orally, music was subject to change in its generation, transportation, and reception. The ornamentation of melodic tones, song forms, and accompanying body movements involved spontaneity and change from singer to singer, verse to verse, and from locale to locale. In speaking of African music, A. M. Jones pointed to this identical characteristic of improvisation, as have Ware, Allen and Garrison in their transcriptions of *Slave Songs*. This practice of variation marked almost each performance and was often suggested at the will of the master drummer or the lead singer. It must be understood that, in African music, this freedom to vary the structure depended upon the basic underlying form and that only specific points within the pieces were used for addition or alterations. Melodic alteration, however, was more liberal, as is seen in African-American music.

Words, Rhythm, and Dance

The most important factor of African music seems always to have been the text. African languages themselves were musical in the spoken dialogue

Young girls from Fanti village await signal to dance. Dancer receives cue from master drummer.

and demanded that pitches be relatively perfect for correct communication. One notes a similarity between this and the "sing-song" speech of southern Blacks. Even drum idioms attempted high and low imitations of speech intonations when they were performed on female and male instruments whose small and large sizes denoted levels of pitch sounds. Therefore, the "talking drums" were capable of sending out vital messages which were clearly understood by the population. So important were the words that they served as the basis around which were formulated the remaining musical elements of melody, harmony, rhythm, form and timbre. According to J. K. Nketia, Professor at the University of Ghana, the words could be realized by modern musical transcriptions as in Example 1, and could suggest to a composer the actual elements of music.

Ex. 1. A representation of textual influence in African music.

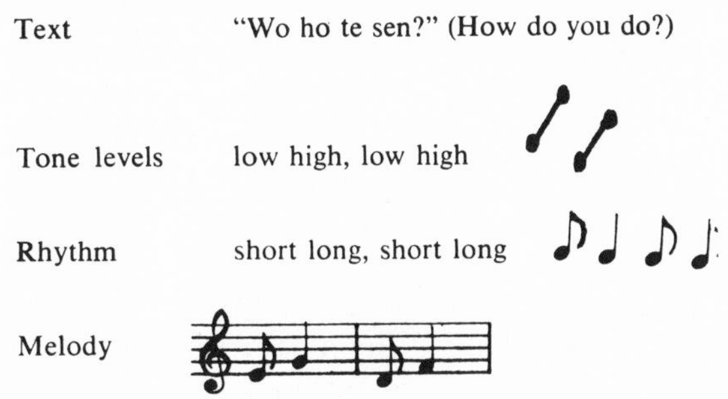

Because of its impact upon the total American population, rhythm, or movement, was considered a most basic characteristic of African music, and essentially made it unique from any other parts. Much like the principle used in liturgical chants of western music, rhythm was dictated by the flow of words and generally reflected African life styles. From the city markets to the countryside villages, rhythm imitated the movements of the various lingual and human activities, whether fast or slow. When transcribed into western terminology, traditional African compositions showed life's constancy and tribal diversities through both complex and simple rhythms of time, space, energy and change.

Although duple and triple rhythms could be detected, actual beats within transcribed measures were not restricted to strong or weak beats, as in western music, but rather to word emphasis. Nor were the measures always in even numbers of four, eight or sixteen. While not composed in the same symmetry of design, this employed a freedom of "over the bar phrases" as felt in the music of J. S. Bach, or even a feeling of non-measure. Thus the odd numbers of measures were balanced by a more correct representation with emphasis on speech. These resulting designs of three, five or seven measures, while common to contemporary music, were nevertheless somewhat strange to the ears of the early Euro-Americans.

Because of the complexities of simultaneous rhythms or poly-rhythms, the overall metric patterns showed changes within sections, or denoted measures which could be interpreted as either three or six beats, or as two triple beats. That is, a 3/4 meter could sometimes be interpreted as 6/8, and 6/8 could easily be felt as 2/4. Often during the course of a piece, such metric obscurity would smoothly shift from duple to triple time, as in Example 2. Since music was generally of the oral tradition, the metric complexities were not compositionally planned for the manuscript in western terms. However, modern transcriptions of traditionalism do indicate such findings.

Ex. 2. Polyrhythm and metric combinations in obscurity.

Another composition collected by A. M. Jones for his second volume of *Studies in African Music*, the *Agbadza*, a social dance, reveals more combinations of sounds which travel in polyrhythms scored for seven parts. In addition to the instruments represented on the printed score, it is also noted that accompanying rhythms from dancers would also become a part of the already complicated transcription seen in Example 3.

In general, rhythm patterns ♪♪♩ or ♪ ♩ were favored. Many of these rhythmic idioms were found within compositions of the New World, from spirituals and hollers to jazz. The following chart of rhythms shows traditional African patterns which were inherited by the Afro-Americans. Taken from melodies transcribed from African sources, it shows multimeters, delays, prolongations, offbeats or additives, triplets and smaller beats. Words and rhythms were copied by the human body in the dances which almost invariably accompanied the music. Through the medium of dance, Africa spoke in intricate movements of joys and sorrows, religion, love, abandonments and war. Among other events, dance was used at celebrations, recreations, marriages, youth rituals, worship and funerals. When used in worship, dance was not considered sacrilegious, but only as worshipful as the 150th Psalm which encouraged one to "Praise Him with

Ex. 3. *Agbadza Dance* (Social Dance), from *Studies in African Music* (Vol. 2), by A. M. Jones (Oxford University Press). Used by permission.

timbrel and dance." When otherwise used, dance was as natural an accompaniment to the songs as were the overpowering drums.

Ex. 4. Chart of African rhythms.

Triplets	[illegible]	[illegible]	[illegible]	[illegible]
(Additives) Syncopation	[illegible]	[illegible]	[illegible]	[illegible]
Offbeat & Rythmic Delays	[illegible]	[illegible]	[illegible]	[illegible]
Multi - Meters	3 4 [illegible]	6 8 [illegible]	[illegible]	[illegible]
Prolongation	[illegible]	[illegible]	[illegible]	[illegible]

In America, dance also occurred at various events, both secular and sacred. Afro-Americans inherited African features of ornamentation or variation upon the basic language of all dance—from complex improvising in walking, running and jumping, to formations of circular, linear or spiraling movements. One dance, the religious shout, was similar to the frenzied dances of fetish chiefs or warriors and was evidently used at both religious and secular outings. The ring games of children and later, the popular dances of the stage also included many effects which were inherited from African recreation. Still others of African background included the calinda, habanera rhythms, mabunda and various voodoo derivatives along with the bamboula, a hybrid version of which is shown in Example 5.

Ex. 5. *The Bamboula*

Melody and Harmony

Melody was suggested by the rise and fall of vocal inflections. When polylinear tones (many melodies) were combined in African music, the resulting combination became harmony. Melody and harmony were both planned by tribal practices which varied from a mixture of Asian and African elements in the Eastern region to strict African ornamentations in the West. Quite frequently African harmony appeared to grow melodically, either as overlapping melodies, or as melodic calls with harmonic answers. The latter technique was simulated in early Afro-American spirituals and hollers, etc.

An important feature of African melody was its constant change and variation, or ornamentation. Similar to western characteristics of vocal religious chants from the middle ages, vowels were extended over several different notes, complete with pitch waverings resembling trills or vibrato. These vowels involved quarter tones, which are somewhat smaller than half steps, and much like the Asian scale which is constructed on the sitar. Other ornaments also common to African melodies were the glissando, slides and grace notes. Not only were the melismatic melodies under constant ornamentation, but modern transcriptions show variations in actual repeats of verses or refrains. Coptic music reflects such chants.

Further melodic analysis suggested common harmonies and depending on local practice, African melodies made use of many scales, intervals and other combinations which westerners call modal. Each scale often had varieties of tone patterns which could lend themselves to either diatonic, chromatic or quarter tone movements. Simple harmonic accompaniments sometimes used thirds, fourths and fifths, but were usually conceived as polymelodies. In his *Studies in African Music*, A. M. Jones has demonstrated these points by the use of scientific diagrams depicting melodic and speech patterns of various locales.

Even though some African elements were also common to periods of western music, the total performance indicated a difference between European music and early Afro-American music. This was particularly true of both the ornamental variation in Black performances, the characteristic accompaniments and the overall manner of presentation. The following Example 6 represents some features listed above which continued during the early American days.

Western concepts of harmonic progressions and strict rules of tonal centers were not evident in African music, although they later became adopted by African-Americans. The duration of notes was also not as strict, as in western cadential or sectional endings. Songs could terminate on long or short notes such as the eighth or sixteenth, and harmonies could step or skip about in parallel movements of sixths. Consonances generally characterized the overall harmonic strength, as shown above. If West African music approached the idea of a standard cadence, it was through the frequent use of the downward interval of a third (Example 6c), a characteristic feature also seen in terminating phrases in Afro-American blues.

Ex. 6. Melodic and harmonic characteristics of African music

a. Ornaments: trill, slide and grace note.
b. Scales: a heptatonic, hexatonic and pentatonic type.
c. Intervals and harmonies.

Form

The form or structure of African compositions represented the end product of improvised or planned music. Its shape contained an overview of harmony, melody and rhythm. Form was also dependent upon the text around which it was constructed. By its title, form implied the media for performance, such as the instrumentation, sex and approximate age group. In general, these forms were represented at incidental, occasional or recreational events. Into the first group went songs for work, games, storytelling and the like. Occasional music included that usually reserved for the royal houses, for festivals, special groups and ceremonies. Recreational music implied music used in groups for both young and old and centered around events.

Some African songs were complex in organization and performance, sometimes involving a return to the beginning of the song as in the western *"dal segno,"* or of alternating at intervals between one, two or three lead singers and chorus. Binary form was used, and this two-part structure also influenced Afro-American blues. Variations and suites were common as were verses with refrain, or strophic form, being spontaneously composed according to the whims of the lead singers. Whatever the form, dancers, instrumentalists and singers were all limited by the lingual framework, as suggested in the formal examples given below.

Adowa: Music and dance for mixed group; suite of eight movements, with order depending upon direction of master drummer. Used for funeral or band music; sometimes with short sections and closing refrain.

Kundum: Series of warrior dances forming a suite; expressed spirit and sentiments of Nzema and Ahanta people during festivals; showed bravery, thanks for harvest, prowess and endurance.

Akom: Suite of dances performed by fetish priests which served to bring the priest out of a trance; contained both secular and religious elements.

Fontonfrom: Series of warrior dances forming a suite; motions symbolic of combat; 77 proverbs uttered on drum and followed by dancer.

Nnwonkoro: Intended for women, mainly adults; this form was sung for entertainment; having various themes of loved ones, one or two cantors alternated with chorus, clapping and swinging in place.

Timbre

The characteristic sound peculiar to any instrument or voice is its timbre. African instruments which included winds, strings and percussion,

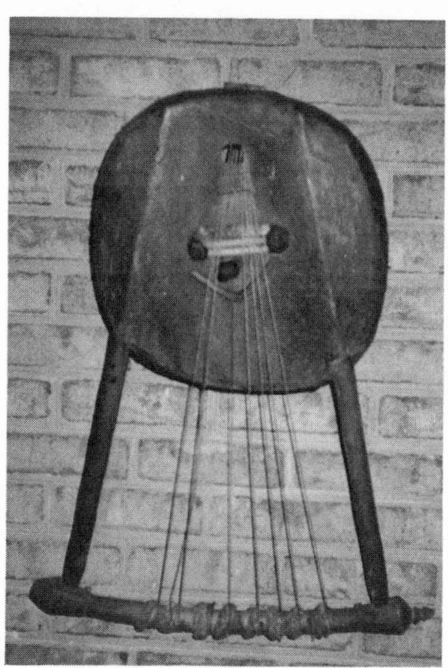

African lyre. Spencer Boyer Collection.

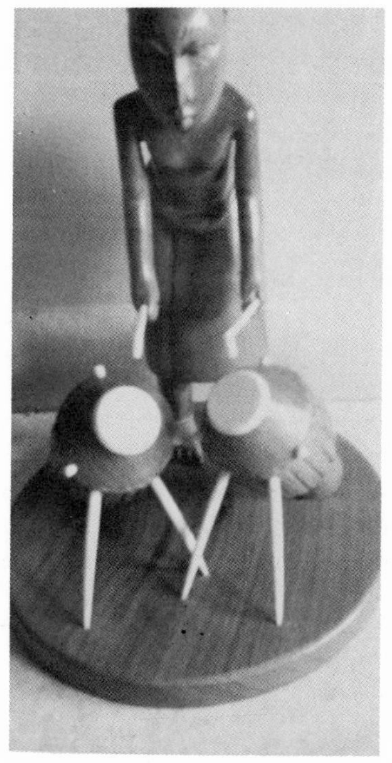

Wooden figure playing pair of spider (atumpan) drums. Percussion instruments (left to right): single bell, talking drums (bommaa), double bell, apentemma drum.

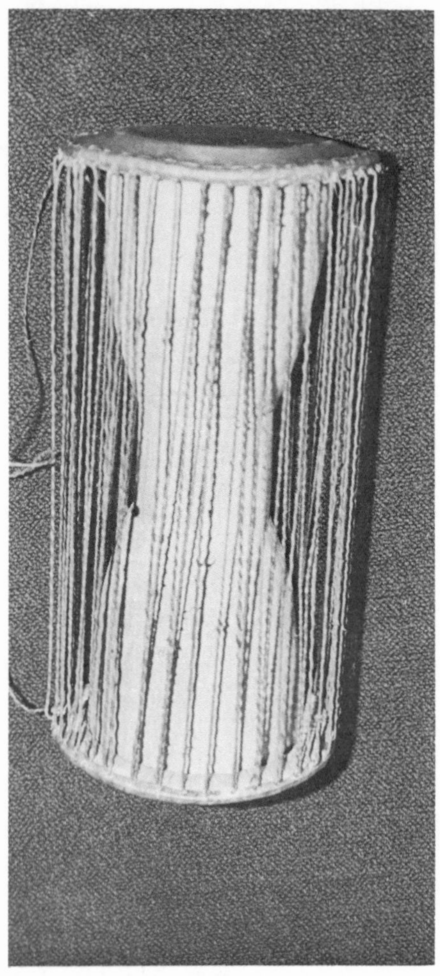

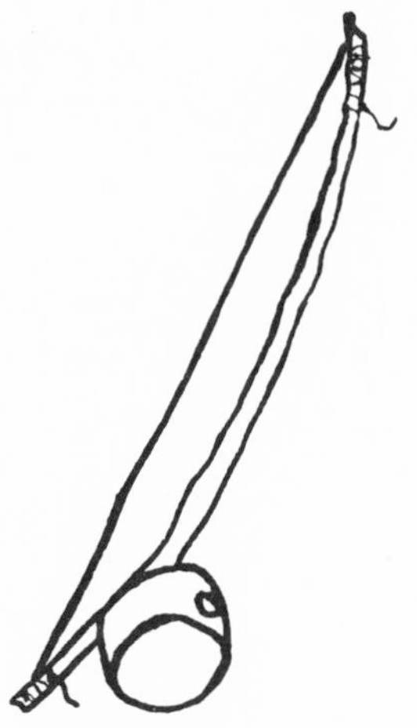

Donno drum with stick. Pressure or hourglass drum is placed under arm and is squeezed to make high and low pitches. Stringed instrument with gourd amplifier, sometimes played by plucking while partly resting in the mouth (musical bow).

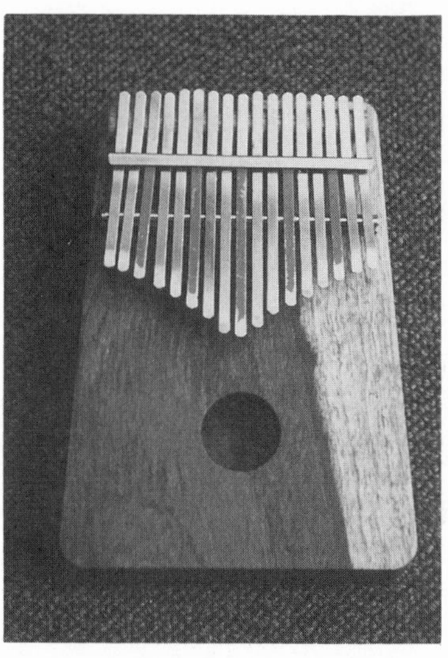

Mbira (thumb piano).

Wooden replica of oboe. Spencer Boyer Collection.

were handmade of materials at hand. A drum constructed from a membrane gave a dull or low timbre when relaxed, or a sharp, exciting clash when tightened. The voice could be nasal or throaty, depending upon the choice of the locale, and much like the blues singers in America, could not be justly appraised by western standards of singing, or even by groups from another African locale. Also dictated by taste, African timbres were further expanded by additions of spider webs, tassles, jingles, paper and other objects which, when attached to instruments, were capable of enhancing their tone qualities.

Egyptian art and Biblical psalm texts revealed a great deal about types of instruments used in ancient Africa. African instrumentation, according to historians Curt Sachs, Donald Grout and Robert Stevenson, provided much of the background for western timbres developed in ancient Greece and Rome, as well as in Asia. African history also points to the fact of distant travels by kings and court musicians, or griots, who were responsible

Beaded gourd, usually shaken by women. Stringed instrument: gonje with bow.

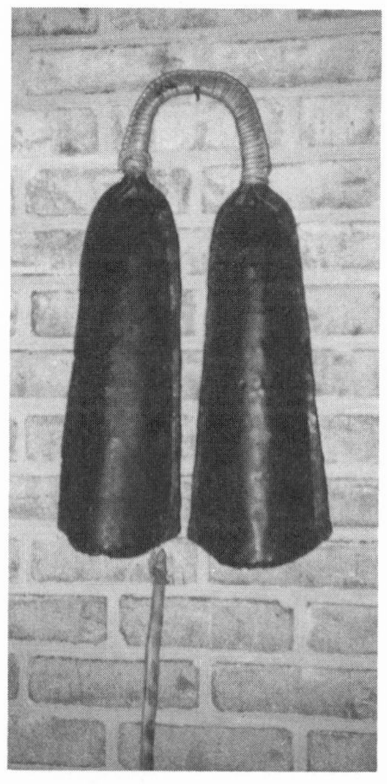

Double bell. Spencer Boyer Collection.

for some of the exchanges and influences of musical ideas long before the middle ages and early Biblical references.

Some instruments seen in Africa today are the same types as those described in documents written by explorers centuries ago, well before the ominous year of 1619. Traditionally, these instruments were carefully sculptured and reflected grace, beauty, intricacy of design and practicality. This craft was carefully or sometimes crudely copied in America by Africans who remembered the original, and who produced products from the gut-bucket, bones and gourds to the banjo.

In America, instruments from Europe were delivered which bore marks of greater refinements in construction. These mingled in pleasant interchanges with their counterparts of African ancestry. Around the fifteenth century, Africans had earlier bargained with peaceful European explorers for western-made violins. They encountered the violin in America some decades later and continued using it. Some of the African products which had influenced the history of instruments are listed below:

Winds: Flutes; single and double reeds; wia, chivoti, auleru, odurogya. Trumpets and horns (shells, calabash, ivory, wood, elephant tusks); Makondere, magwala, nyele, hieni, ntahera, awe.

Strings: Harp, lyre, lute, zither: Tongoli, ndongo, kundi, ko, kora, ntongoli, litungu, thum, ekakira, kono, gonje, ligombo, tobo.

Percussion: Drums, bells, gongs, jingles, xylophone: gourds, atumpan, atsimevu, donno, apentemma, kidi, nnawuta, frikyiwa, adenkum, ntara, kende, ngelenge.

Because of their great variety, and their dominant positions within the musical practices of Africa, drums were decidedly most important. In im-

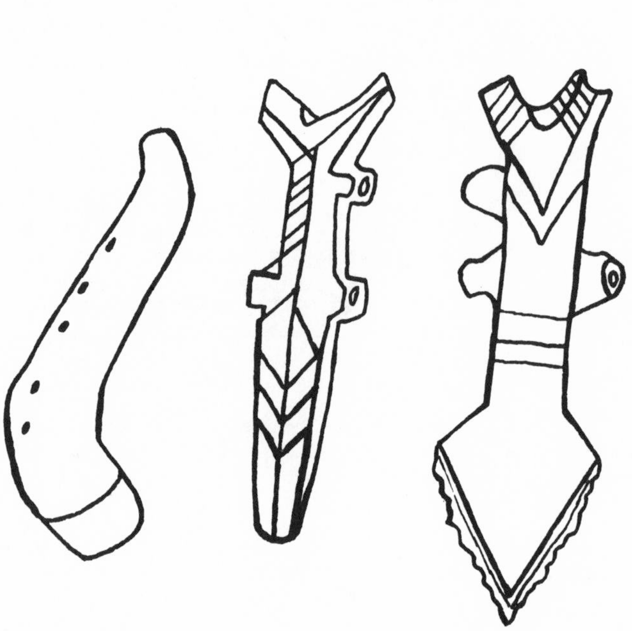

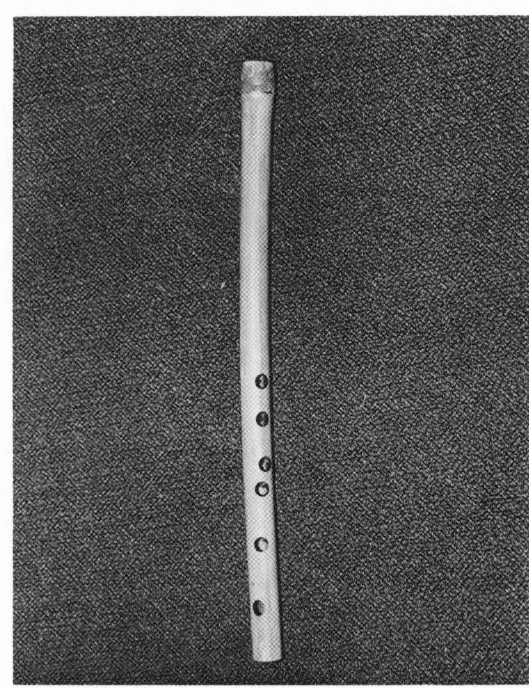

Wind instruments: ivory horn, two notched wooden flutes (wia). Wind instrument: bamboo flute.

itation of the percussive throb of the human body, drums characterized the rhythmic flow of the strength which must have accompanied the original Africans to America.

Texture

As seen earlier, melodic and homophonic elements together with polymelodies and polyrhythms were generally common and could be produced by the following: a melodic sound of a leader, or two lead singers, followed by the vertical sounds of a chorus. The chorus could also produce polyphony or countermelodies, rather than homophony. Varieties of this music overlapped, but not in strict imitation. Monody, homophony and polyphony have been used to describe these textures.

One overlapping texture was termed "hocket" by musicologists of the modern era. Performed on instruments possessing a limited range, the tones required to sound a piece were shared among several instruments which took turns playing at the proper time. Generally, the notched flutes with approximately three notes each would perform such melodies together, or other instruments would develop a total composition by the same process. Although involving time and precision, "hocket" as used here did not refer to the rhythmic principle of western music in the middle ages. Texture was made up of timbre, melody, harmony and rhythm, and denoted the total product of these elements.

Well versed in songs for every occasion, African tribes had used music as a practical art which reflected all facets of everyday living. Each tribe had insisted that its members enjoy the art of music-making. Having learned it at infancy and having retained the love of this music, many Africans were accomplished musicians upon arrival in America. It is correct to conclude that this tradition as practiced by Africans was passed on to the early Afro-Americans. To the Afro-Americans, the idea of functional music was real. The varieties of compositional techniques were utilized in the early slave songs and in more recent forms. Many composers became true pioneers in their love for this new music and reinforced the tradition of their forefathers.

III

EARLY FOLK MUSIC

Early folk music flourished from the time of the Baroque and Classical periods of western music to the era of the Romantic period, spanning the lives of the European composers from Frescobaldi to George Bridgetower, Samuel Coleridge-Taylor and Frédéric Chopin. (See Chapter XV, European section.) During the first agonizing days, the multi-functional music was more African than American, gradually transforming itself into Afro-American sacred and secular forms.

Inspired by the same environmental roots and conditions, secular songs grew alongside religious songs with an interrelationship that was often indistinguishable. That is, the subject of a call or holler could well be addressed to the same God of the spirituals discussed in Chapter four. This uniqueness was caused by the fact that, unlike African traditionalism which restricted its music to appropriate functions and events, slaves were not allowed to freely participate in all aspects of life common to African customs. Consequently, worship, work and relaxation were often performed under identical surroundings. Because of this unfortunate arrangement, neither could the strict definition nor the traditional practice of African music in correlation with other arts always be maintained. Thus, many elements of dance, instrumentation and other responses were necessarily abandoned in America.

Nevertheless, early folk songs occasionally consisted of instrumental, dance and vocal music, despite the fact that modern transcriptions were not able to capture many authentic accompaniments. Yet since the majority of Africans were generally commanded to work at a rapid pace, it is possible that much of the music was vocal, or was vocal with percussive sounds of working tools. Unless the slaves were regularly hired out to other plantations as professional performers, the Black population was generally restricted to these vocal developments. To sponsor the serious study of a western instrument for a Black person was rare, although this was certainly the case in a few instances since posters announcing runaway slaves indicated that they might try to pass themselves off as free orchestra players, and since some others such as Elizabeth Greenfield did indeed excel as concert artists.

Calls, Cries, Hollers, and Shouts

The earliest of songs—the field or street calls, cries, hollers, shouts, work songs and play songs—were among those virtually spontaneous examples whose charm and naivety of materials served as foundations for both innocent and complex organizations for successive decades. According to Webster, a "call" was defined as a "loud tone, a shout, an announcement, summon or signal." This definition was exactly the way in which the call was used during slavery; that is, a high-pitched or subdued yell or chant to somewhere or somebody, for the purpose of commanding attention or emoting individual expressions of relief, abandonment or sorrow. Sometimes relaxing, complaining, or sometimes ostentatious show-offs resembling an auctioneer or square dance caller, the tunes were used for various functions from expressing love to shouting out directions to fellow workers.

Calls were sometimes used interchangeably with other forms. Harold Courlander, in his *Songs From Alabama*, listed titles of *Hey Rufus*, *Father's Field Call*, *Children's Field Call*, *Woh Hoo* and others, while B. A. Botkin recorded *Mississippi Sounding Call*, *Unloading Rails*, *Tamping Ties* and *Heaving the Lead Line*. Even blues collected by Alan and John Lomax, Lewis Jones and John Work revealed editions of camp hollers which related directly to the call. The titles of calls, hollers and cries therefore represented similarities in function, but not necessarily in general structural make-up.

The "cry" was equivalent to either a wail as in pain, anger, religion, fright or sorrow. When used in the street for selling wares, it was simply a synonym for "call." The verses, however, generally were clever gimmicks commanding attention to the announcement. To holler was also to yell or shout, as in a call. Whites often referred to those slaves "hollering in the fields." Although a synonymous relationship was seen in the like definitions, the terms could also imply dynamics of expression such as a more frantic sound for the holler, versus the lower subtlety of a cry. Some cries collected by Arna Bontemps and Langston Hughes showed poems similar to those used in minstrelsy as *Watermelon Vendor's Cry*, *Waffle Man's Cry*, *Oyster Man's Cry*, *Six Negro Market Songs of Harlem* and *Street Chef*.

Strangely enough, "shout" also implied a loud voice as in a yell or call. But more importantly, it referred to a frenzied, trance like dance of spiritual joy. Inherited from African religious dances, these physical reactions to the word of God and salvation were accompanied by verbal whoops of joy, and were performed seriously or whimsically, both inside and outside of Protestant churches. Dances other than the shout were discussed in Chapter two and were further reflected in the paintings of James Cloney and William Sidney Mount.

Work and Play Songs

Work and play songs were action pieces which required body movements. Lyrics of work songs dealt with railroad building, wood chopping, hauling bales, and pulling barges, while play songs dealt with counting games, hiding, riding and other dramatic play. More so than field hollers, the messages of the work songs were accompanied by the rhythmic swinging of a hammer as in *Steel Laying Holler*, *Rock Island Line* or *I've Been Working on the Railroad*.

Play songs, on the other hand, were lighter pieces inspired by comedy and cheerful recreation rather than drudgery and toil. Consequently, being less restrictive allowed for running in circles, stooping, rising and imaginary flying as suggested in the lyrics of *Little Sallie Walker*, or in zigzag motions as in *All Hid*. *Little Sallie Walker*, one of the most familiar of the play songs (see example 7), was sung by a ring of players encircling a single person who acted out the words of the song, and who finally chose his successor by a properly directed "shake":

Little Sallie Walker, (A music)
Sittin' in the saucer.
Rise, Sallie, rise, and
Wipe ya' weeping eyes, and
Fly to the east, and
Fly to the west, and
Fly to the very one that you love the best! (B music)

Chorus
Put'cha han' on ya' hip and
Let'cha backbone slip!
Shake it to the east, and
Shake it to the west, and
Shake it to the very one that you love the best!

It is significant to note that with the exception of the play songs, all of the early folk forms discussed here were associated with work. Even though it is true that calls, cries and hollers contained many different kinds of lyrics, their main purpose was to sustain one during his labor and to assist in selling or issuing directions. For the Blacks, the emphasis in early American life was placed on work, not play. Nevertheless, the origins of these songs did not preclude the fact that some were later used in minstrel performances as clever comic tunes or as stump recitations.

Text and Technique

Originally, work pieces consisted of actual African texts or lyrics with music, not necessarily in rhyme. Later, slaves set European dialect to African music, or vice versa, much like the two examples below which were taken from Arna Bontemps' and Langston Hughes' *The Book of Negro Folklore,* entitled *Cala Vendor's Cry* and *Street Chef*:

Tout chaud [all hot] madame,
Git 'em while they're hot! Hot Calas! (*Cry*)

Ah'm a natu'al bo'n cook
An' dat aint no lie,
Ah can fry po'k chops
An' habe a lo-down pie. . . . (*Chef*)

The text of play songs showed the abandonment and carefree attitude of children at play. Sung in upward and downward intervals of thirds, or partly intoned in approximate pitches, *All Hid* was an example:

Five, ten, fifteen, twenty,
Twenty-five, thirty, thirty-five, forty,
Forty-five, fifty, fifty-five, sixty. . . . (*etc.*)
All Hid? (Ready or not, here I come!)

Textual phrases were sometimes half sung, half spoken or moaned. They became vocal techniques of syllabic, sporadic or ornamental styles which were passed on from composition to composition and were found in blues and spirituals as well as in many modern-day styles. In addition to the conventional poetry above, other sounds, both African and European were used, including prolongations of "ah," "oo," "ummm," "ee," "heh," "Lordy," "oh," "Jesus," "woh hoo," and "yeh." A single word could form an entire song through such elongations, or words could be interpolated between lines of other poetic structures to indicate an emotion or to ornament the music.

Characterized by short, sporadic, or long melodic lines, the forms and styles of these compositions ranged from simple to highly ornamental techniques. Variation, stanza without refrain and binary were common to the structures. According to present-day transcriptions, slides, grace notes, chromatics and ranges from seconds to sixths were plentiful, although occasional octaves and other intervals were also used. If most transcriptions of these were correct, they represented more complex ornamentations than were shown in the spirituals of that period. Yet modern transcriptions could not always denote actual performances since these compositions were both changed constantly and difficult to score. Just as in African music, cadences were not strict and pieces could terminate on any note of the scale. Example 7 shows some of these features along with some of the short forms which were common in early America.

Ex. 7. Techniques and forms of early folk music. *Juba*. Reprinted by permission of Harvard University Press from *On the Trail of Negro Folk—Songs* by Dorothy Scarborough. Copyright 1925 by Harvard University Press; 1953 by Mary McDaniel Parker.

a. Chromatics, modes, word prolongation.
b. Slide, thirds, ornamentation and approximations; cadences.
c. Ballads: *Juba* (Reprinted by permission of Harvard University Press from *On The Trail Of Negro Folk-Songs* by Dorothy Scarborough, Copyright 1925 by Harvard University Press; 1953 by Mary McDaniel Parker); *Musieu Bainjo* from *Slave Songs* by Allen, Garrison and Ware and play song, *Little Sallie Walker* (traditional).

Like the spirituals and blues which they greatly influenced, these basic songs were usually in duple meter. This was true of street cries, work songs and play songs. However, many were also of free style rhythms emphasizing words or syllables. The connection of these small, unsophisticated forms cannot be discounted in the continual quest for a definition of Afro-American music, its origin, performance, history and technical styles.

Composers

Among the many composers of these small secular songs were both anonymous persons as well as some named in chapters VI and IX. As difficult as it was to identify slave composer-performers, certain records did fortunately surface from time to time indicating the status and worth of certain talents. One such individual was "Blind Billy" Armistead, listed in the Lynchburgers Club booklet, *Ambassadors of Goodwill*, as a fife player who "was said to have been the only Negro concert artist during slave days to appear in concert halls of Virginia." It was "not proper to have a party without Billy," and it was also understood that his *Wandering Willie* was performed "with such pathos that it bought tears to the eyes of his audience." No birth date was given, but he died in 1855.

IV

SPIRITUALS

Having been born somewhere between African voyages of the 1600's and American Reconstruction, spirituals were the end products of calls and hollers developed during early colonialism. Their exact origin cannot be established. Yet these anonymous songs have continually served as sources of inspiration for African Americans in their urgent quest for identity, heritage and a homeland.

Variously called jubilee, minstrel, religious, slave or folk songs, spirituals covered a wide range of subjects both religious and secular. They fell into a broad, all-inclusive definition as recorded in Webster's Dictionary: "of the spirit or the soul, often in a religious or moral aspect, as distinguished from the body; . . . concerned with intellect . . . showing much refinement of thought and feeling; spiritualistic or supernatural; a spiritual thing or concern . . . " The Old Testament inspired many of the themes.

The words "often of a religious or moral aspect" generally did represent the feeling of the songs, but "often" did not imply "always." Despite the overabundance of Biblical words used in the majority of songs called spirituals, their functions were not purely religious. They were constantly used in the search of freedom, in religious services, to teach, gossip, scold, signal, or to delight in the telling of tales. Like work songs, calls and hollers, spirituals developed simultaneously in appeasement of the curiosity of the overseers who required a knowledge of the whereabouts or location of slaves. They also relieved the minds and bodies of the enslaved and they served more significantly as a practical means of informing the slaves of their own affairs, i.e., social politics, deliverance, escape or satire. As Webster has defined, the spirituals were also "concerned with the intellect" and were most refined in both "thought and feeling."

H. T. Burleigh called the spirituals the "spontaneous outbursts of intense religious fervor which had their origin chiefly in camp meetings, revivals and other religious exercises." Others have also conceded that spirituals resulted from the "introductions" of Christianity to slaves in America—a tactic intended to establish docility among chattel.

While Christianity was perhaps instrumental in the use of a large number of words, it seems dogmatic to assume this in each case. In fact, not every such song preserved contained the elements of religion, nor was each used for only one purpose. There was much more ambiguity in designs, origins and functions than has generally been assumed. For example, *Who Dat Comin' Over Yonder?*, *Git on Board, Little Chillen'*, *I Know de Udder Worl' Is not Like Dis*, *Die in de Fiel*, and *Same Train* (below) may or may not have been composed with any religious spiritualism in mind.

Same train, same train, same train carry my mother, [sister]
Same train, same train, same train carry my mother,
Same train be back tommorrer, same train, same train.

Same train a-blowin' at de station, same train, same train,
Same train a-blowin' at de station,
Same train be back tommorrer, same train, same train.

Christian kingdoms existed in Africa much earlier than slavery in America. However, some Africans were nevertheless introduced to Christianity by American colonists. Even though it is difficult to state their exact influence, it is safe to say that the collective experiences of both Africa and America served to produce the spirituals, and that the centuries of American mixtures resulted in the refined products as sung by the Fisk Jubilee Singers at Reconstruction.

Early collections of Black music contained more spirituals than other small forms. This indicated an importance attached to these songs. The earliest of these collections were compiled by Whites. In 1867, W. F. Allen, Charles Ware and Lucy M. Garrison published a collection entitled *Slave Songs in the United States*, and because of the geographic source of the islands off the coast of Georgia and South Carolina, their transcriptions were considered more traditional in dialect and performance than others collected within the city. Since that time, collections by Black composers James Weldon and J. Rosamond Johnson, John W. Work III, H. T. Burleigh, Hall Johnson, Nathaniel Dett and many more have followed.

Understandably, none of these could denote the exact dates of the compositions. Although such songs as *No More Auction Block for Me* must well suggest the era of Emancipation, this could be speculative reasoning as the origin of the song could also border on implications of death, love conditions or social solidification against slavery. Consequently, the best solution as to the dates of composition were those by W. E. B. DuBois and Benjamin Brawley who, in their books, *The Souls of Black Folk* and *The Negro Genius*, pointed out general periods of the following songs:

Early Period: *See Fo' and Twenty Elders on Deir Knees; You May Bury Me in de East; Nobody Knows; Swing Low, Sweet Chariot*

Middle Period: *March On; Bright Sparkles; I've Been A-Listenin' All de Night Long; Steal Away* (attributed to Nat Turner)

Late Period: *(Bright Sparkles); Dust, Dust and Ashes, My Mother Took Her Flight; I Hope My Mother Will Be There in That Beautiful World on High.*

Content and Purpose

Spirituals covered the history, thoughts and treatment of the Black Man. They pondered his fate, his everyday life, emotions and freedom. If some of the African-American history resembles that of the Jewish people, it was because of two main factors. First, Biblical events pinpointed Egypt as the site where the Jews were held in captivity and Ethiopia as the place where the Black Queen of Sheba gave birth to Solomon's son. The facts were therefore real to history. Second, if we are to believe the records of West African explorers from Europe, the captivity of Blacks, some of whom were Egyptians, caused them to assume a natural kinship. Where once the captors of the Jews had been their enemy, they now had become as brothers. Part of this history was unwittingly related in a folktale version of *Joshua Fit de Battle* or *When Israel Was in Egypt Land*:

Ex. 8. *When Israel Was in Egypt Land.* Traditional.

When Israel was in Egypt Land, Let My People Go,
Oppressed so hard they could not stand, Let my people go;
Go down, Moses, way down in Egypt land,
Tell ole Pharaoh, Let my people go.

Because they functioned as practical tools for emotional and physical escape, multifold purposes were assigned to the spirituals from religious expression to communication (by code). Many topics therefore reflected the diverse purposes and concerns of this era. From a hymn-style comment of *There's a Man Goin' 'Round Takin' Names* to an oral folktale version of *Old Noah, He Built Himself an Ark*, the spirituals were composed with allegorical or supernatural flavor, with deep expressions of mystical and religious emotions, or as with the gossip-like quality of *The Hypocrite and the Concubine*.

A. M. Jones states that African songs were "full of allusions and hidden meanings" and could not be translated without the help of an African, despite a knowledge of African words in definition. Even play songs or fishing songs could speak of a tale other than that understood by the words alone, without benefit of the interpreted message. If we accept the possibility that at least some of the spirituals retained an African heritage, then it would be easier to conclude that the following songs possibly contained various symbolic interpretations and connotations: *Steal Away*; *Good News, Member, I Heard From Heaven Today*; *Wade in de Water*; *You Go, I'll Go With You*; *I'll Meet You at the Station When the Train Comes Along* and *Ain't I Glad I Got Out of the Wilderness*.

Spirituals were further laden with obsessions about "freedom land", "home," utopias, "Jesus," "deliverer," or "Saviour." Some ambiguity or dual meaning could have pointed to "Jesus" or "Savior" as either the God of Christianity, Ntoa, the supernatural spirits of ancestors, or to a Harriet Tubman of the Underground Railroad. Canaan may have depicted a Heaven, a better life to the north, or freedom after Emancipation. "Home" could have meant either Heaven or Africa. In any case, the slaves were eventually forced to resort to the use of words and actions of a significance contrary to that outwardly spoken or suggested. This fact alone implied a sound knowledge of English and prearranged communications among the slaves.

Melody and Harmony

Spirituals were sung in major, minor, modal or mixtures of scales. While a great majority could be analyzed within a major mode, they could also include both minor or modal scales simultaneously. Some already harmonized with western harmonies in modern transcriptions could be explained within scales common to Africa as well. For example, DuBois pointed to *Nobody Knows de Trouble I've Seen* and *Steal Away* as examples from the early period. Even though they both blended well with the major transcriptions, it was a fact that specific tones of the major scale were omitted in the original melodies, thereby generally reflecting the pentatonic scales. *Steal Away* has been attributed to Nat Turner.

Some melodies of both the western and African systems agreed upon the predominant use of thirds, fifths and octaves. Consequently, the Afro-American examples fell into the same aural confines. Whereas African melodies of various tribes used thirds, fourths, sevenths and octaves as harmonies, the spirituals did not regularly employ many large skips in the linear or melodic intervals, but were more vocally diatonic and highly ornamented.

Some keys and chords were clearly outlined and confirmed by the melodies used, and others were not. For example, *Steal Away* and *Nobody Knows* implied a tonic chord at the beginning and ending. The following Example implies both tonic and dominant seventh chords in its melodic line.

Ex. 9. *Nobody Knows, Steal Away,* scale outlines. Traditional.

Ex. 10. *Rock O' My Soul.* Traditional.

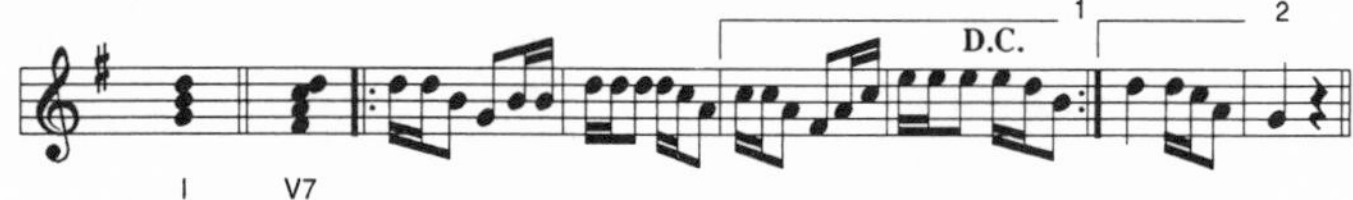

Rock O' My Soul in the bosom of Abraham; (Three times)
O Rock o' my soul!

Although the chords were not as problematic to Western analysis as were the keys because of the agreement of consonances, keys remained a mystery for some time. In western music, most keys could be determined by cadential endings, though some have ended on the dominant or simply in another key from that found at the beginning. In African music, pieces could end on almost any note of the scale. As already discovered by Maud Hare, John Work and others, some spirituals used African concepts in arrangements of melodic tones, but generally concluded with western cadential patterns.

Melodic endings in songs of work, play or blues moved up or down a third toward a tonal center. Common endings in spirituals descended scalewise from three to one. Certain others ended a fourth, a second, or third below, or from a third above, as in Example 11. The melodic outlines could easily be harmonized using I, IV, and V, the customary chordal basis for confirming tonal centers in western music. Such harmonies were indeed eventually adopted by the Blacks who later assimilated things American.

Ex. 11. Melodic techniques of spirituals.

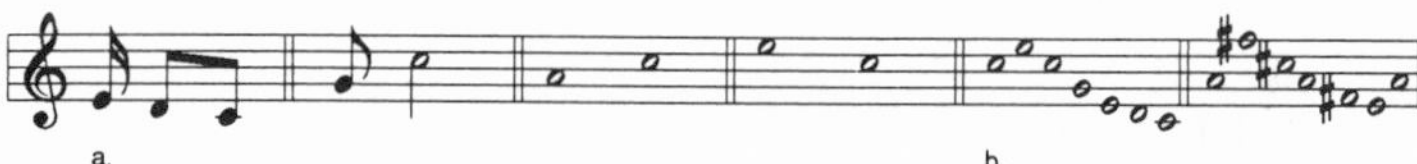

a. Endings
b. Melodic ranges: *No Man Can Hinder Me; Just Been to the Fountain.*

According to documents by Ware, Allen, Garrison and others, the use of parts was spontaneous, and as there were no set rules, would occur at any given time during the performances. Examples ranged from several voices to a lead singer in alternation with other voices. Sometimes the solo voice was used as an improvised upper melody (obligato) over a chorus of harmony.

In general, frequent usage of consonances could be sustained by the common chords of the period (I, IV, V). These were in keeping with the broader, theoretical practices found in both folk and art music inherited from Europe. Even though the bass outlines (lowest overall melody) were not always sung as in western practices, most of the spirituals transcribed from live performances during Reconstruction showed strict use of these common chords. No doubt, as in some African music, many chords of the sixth were employed (having the third as the lowest tone of a chord) as well as alternate harmonies. However, these chords without roots as lowest tones were probably derived more from intervals than from any key concept at the beginning, and only later adapting to the customary key nomenclature of western music.

African melodies and scales had used a variety of tunes which were changed by lowering and raising tones one-half step, or even a quarter tone. This was not a change in the scale, but simply a variation from one manner of rendering tones "straight." For that reason, a heptatonic scale (altered) could make use of the lowered sixth, seventh, or third. This idiom has consistently lasted in the spirituals, and has further influenced the history of jazz and other Black music. Although these features of jazz scales will be discussed at a later time, it is yet interesting to note that those scales of the spirituals discussed by African scholars and those shown in David Baker's and John Mehegan's jazz studies are quite similar in concept. Some of these melodic variants brought from Africa were preserved in the spirituals shown in Example 12.

Ex. 12. *Come Go With Me* (transposed) and *The Hypocrite and the Concubine*, from *Slave Songs*, Allen, Garrison and Ware.

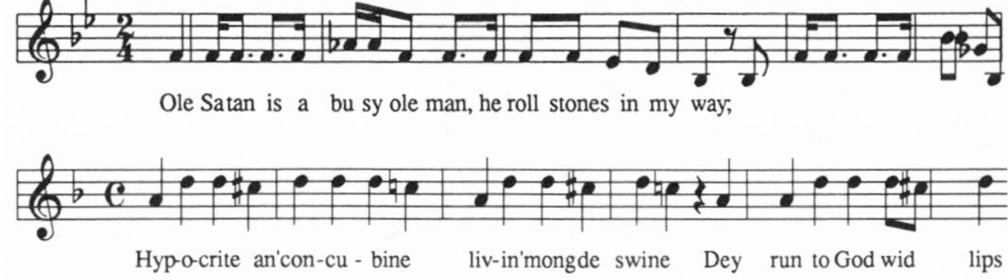

H. E. Krehbiel and others have explored the ranges of several spirituals. In some respects, certain of the spirituals were instrumental in character, departing from diatonicism and other vocal idioms in general. Some of the greatest intervalic leaps were found in *I Just Been to the Fountain*, *No Man Can Hinder Me* and *O'er the Crossing* (Ex. 11). The slaves were naturally influenced by remnants of the practices of their own ancestors, some of whose songs contained melodic ranges at least as wide as octaves. Coupled with the highly ornamental performance of an African heritage, these collections indicated a history of great talent.

Texture

Original spirituals were not created in the same manner as the tonal concert arrangements so familiar today, complete with brilliant piano accompaniments. The oldest of spirituals were often vocal, with or without instrumental accompaniment, depending upon the occasion. They were either melodic compositions performed by a single soloist, or were harmonies composed at random with a melody begun by a leader. Harmony was improvised by singers at hand, and consisted of an amalgamation of African and European sounds. Undoubtedly, this resulted in both homophonic and polyphonic compositions. The homophonic types were similar in style to hymns, having two to four parts. This style contained a leader whose main melody was supported by two and/or four-part harmony.

Afro-American compositions were also quasi-polyphonic or imitative in style. Performances of such pieces were the results of antiphonal or "call and response" singing between solo and chorus or between ensemble and ensemble. The same themes or different melodies altogether were sung by the choruses, and alternations of the phrases sometimes overlapped. This polyphony was close to "canons" or other small pieces of the early Baroque, but were not as strictly imitative as those of the later Baroque period.

Not only was polyphony realized by vocal timbres, but accompanying instruments added to this complexity of overlapping sounds. With their many varieties of rhythms in contrapuntal style, they developed a definitive position of African polyphony. Examples 13a and 13b show an African example in contrast to an example of Afro-American music.

Ex. 13a. African and American polyphony. *Osenyee bobuo ee* (Condolences), No. 28, *Folk Songs* by J. K. Nketia. Used by Permission of African Institute, University of Ghana at Legon.

Ex. 13b. *Sittin' Down Beside O' The Lamb*, taken from *American Negro Songs and Spirituals*, edited by John W. Work. © 1940 by John W. Work. Used by permission of Crown Publishers, Inc.

Ornamentation in Spirituals

The body of spirituals contained a wide variety of ornaments derived from African vocal music. Just as Africans had decorated their bodies for dance and their instruments for effects, so had they maintained a continuous tradition of vocal decoration. Early explorers wrote of this fascinating aspect of African music before American colonialism, and the practice did not end with the arrival of Africans in America. Aside from rhythmic influence, improvised inflections of African origin have influenced American music more than any other element.

Although some transcriptions did not reflect ornaments (such as the *Slave Songs* by Ware, etc.) Harold Courlander gave clearer insight into the traditional manner of performance. Since Blacks have seemingly always had a tradition of improvising an innocent melody, the Courlander collection, *Negro Songs from Alabama* showed how vocal approximations must have been sung. E. A. McIlhenny, who claimed to have copied his harmonies as Blacks sang them, gave his information about ornamentation in his collection of *Befo' de War Spirituals*. Reared in America and having observed the singing of slaves as a child, McIlhenny frequently sat in church where the songs were performed. He wrote:

> It is almost impossible to get exact wording of spirituals for even the same singer never sings one twice exactly the same. The singer will vary the words, lines and melody every time. . . . Stanzas never occur twice in the same order, but are sung as they come to the mind of the singer, and as the singer will improvise . . . the number of stanzas . . . is unlimited. . . . There is also great variation . . . begins with a simple sweet melody, but as the singer becomes more . . . uplifted and enthused by oft repeated lines, all sorts of quavering notes and melodious expression will be improvised.

One characteristic style governed by an emotional state, boasted the art of "hitting" a note from each side by sliding into and away from it, thereby not exacting a given pitch. A difficult technique within itself, this manner of singing resembled a wavering or trill-like technique, and in other situations, a slide or approximation at best. Some have recorded the same techniques in examples of African music, thus providing examples of African ornamentation.

Rhythmic groups such as triplets, dotted figures and sixteenth notes also served to ornament the vocal line. Turns (e.g. notes sung above and below the main notes, but not necessarily changing tones as in western music), auxiliary tones and other additions were sung using these rhythmic groups. *Job, Job*, and *Preach My Gospel*, of the Harold Courlander collection, *Poor Mourner's Got a Home at Last* and *This Is a Sin-Tryin' World* of the John W. Work collection and various African counterparts from the Nketia and Jones' collections demonstrate the traditions of added notes and vocal inflections. One of these, *Preach My Gospel*, strongly resembles the highly melismatic style of certain ancient western Gregorian chants in that the vocal line is so ornamented that a great distortion of the words results in the extension of syllables. Some of the rhythmic ornaments are seen in Example 14, but as in the case of other musical elements, should be considered as approximate.

Ex. 14. Ornaments in spirituals.

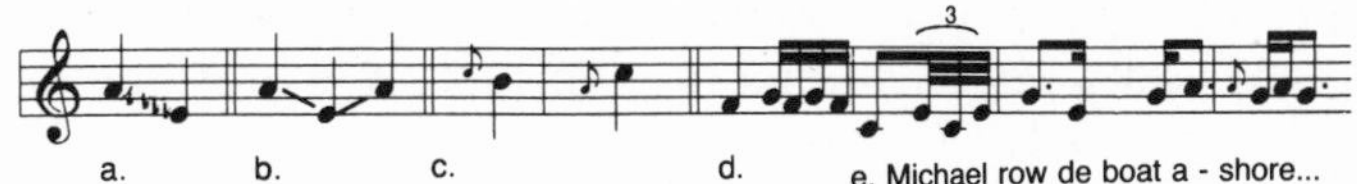

Due to oral tradition which allowed differences in numerous versions of the same song, the use of ornaments and improvisation resulted in still other versions. The familiar *Nobody Knows, Were You There?* and *Go Down Moses* were but three songs which could be heard as follows:

Ex. 15. Variations in spirituals.

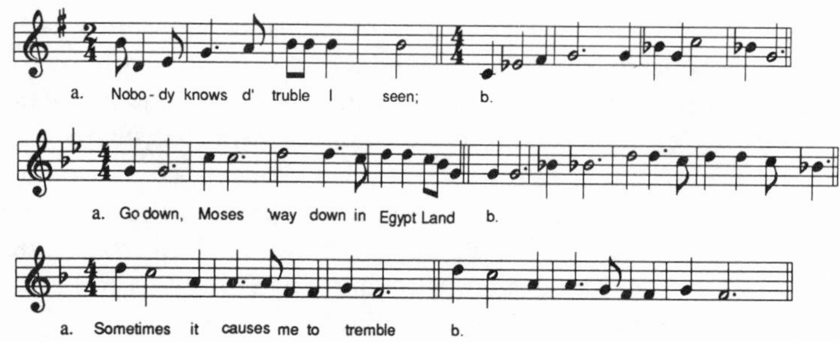

a. Versions I: *Nobody Knows; Go Down, Moses; Were You There?*
b. Versions II: Alternates of same compositions.

Rhythm

One of the most direct influences of Africa was found in the diverse and difficult rhythms of spirituals. Based upon the rhythms of drum and dance as well as emotional spontaneity, they spun into movements which encouraged foot reactions similar to the contagion of jazz as well as vocal communion among the slave population. Inherent within the spirituals were such dance rhythms as the shout, the bamboula and both religious and secular influences. Depending upon the spirits of the people, these rhythms were either heavy and somber, or gay and carefree. Although a few of the meters were transcribed into triple rhythm, the majority of the spirituals were performed in the duple meter of the shout. The rhythm of a spiritual as shown in Example 16 incorporates both the movement of the shout and of the glorious spirit within the song.

Ex. 16. *Shout on Chil'en* from *Slave Songs* by Allen, Garrison & Ware.

Shout on, chil'en, you never die; Glory hallelu!
You in de Lord, an' de Lord in you; Glory hallelu!

Although simple, regular meters did exist in the collections mentioned, the bulk were irregular or uncommon combinations of six and two together, or of three and two. Most of the meters in duple time did not affect syncopations, short and long phrases of rhythmic sequences, or alternations from six to three, etc.

Unlike the African examples of rhythm which were governed by the text and generally changed when words differed, American songs were more repetitive in their renditions. Many American versions were repetitive for two reasons: First, many songs were created on the spot without much time for serious or formal alterations; second, there was the problem of a limited vocabulary in a foreign tongue. Yet the popularity of some songs had to depend partly on simplicity and their ability to be learned quickly. On the other hand, some of the more sophisticated, refreshing examples of story-telling spirituals were more verbose, indicating that many had been composed during leisure hours or over long periods of time. Such examples could also suggest a talented, educated leader or trained musician.

As in African music, the text was the significant element in the effect of Afro-American music. Yet the newer texts created some problems of juxtaposition with the music and therefore the text eventually lost the original fluidity and natural beauty of the African languages. The harder sounds of emerging dialects of European languages replaced the soft, fluid and musical quality inherent in the African languages. Consequently, inflections of new words in the melodic line were lost due to rhythmic awkwardness.

Tempos were fast, moderate and slow, depending on the emotions emitted by the text. However, one tempo was not necessarily "reserved" for a religious piece as opposed to one for a secular text. Depending upon the function and the mood of both the group and the situation at hand, tempos would change to meet the event. In such cases, tempos were as relative or as obscure as an "allegro" or an "adagio" of western examples. They were learned and performed according to the whims of the leader, and varied from performance to performance.

Rhythmic cadences ended either on long or short notes suggested by the mood and character of the pieces. *God Got Plenty of Room, Rock O' Jubilee, Tell My Jesus Mornin', No Man Can Hinder Me* and others represented in the *Slave Songs* by Ware, Garrison and Allen, indicate short endings. The majority of spirituals, however, used the traditional endings of western music. The following spirituals reveal African-American rhythms and when compared with the chart of African rhythms found in Chapter II, encompass many of the characteristics seen in the preceding discussion.

Ex. 17. Rhythm in spirituals.

I Got a home up in-a that Kingdom, (Ain't-a That Good News!)

(I Got Shoes;) You got shoes; All-a God's Chil'en got shoes!
When I get to Heaven, gonna put on m'shoes an' gonna shout
all over God's Heaven!

Fier, my Saviour, fier; Satan's Camp A-fire;
Fier, believer, fier, (Satan's Camp A-fire).

Form

The most common poetry was shaped into four lines with a refrain. Four to six lines or more were also seen. There was the ballad form, variation form, binary form (as seen in *Lonesome Valley* and *Praise Member*), ternary form, strophic and other patterns of altered forms. There were also pieces which appeared to be through-composed.

Spirituals sometimes resembled blues or ballads and could be distinguished by the text and manner of spirit. For example, some blues contained from three to six or more lines of poetry while the spirituals customarily contained four lines. Some similarities in poetic construction were seen in *I Wish to God, Steady, Jesus Listenin'* and the others compared as follows:

I. Four lines (Blues)	(Spiritual)
I wish to God that train would come, I wish to God that train would come, I wish to God that train would come, To take me back where I come from.	Steady, Jesus listenin', Steady, Jesus listenin', Steady, Jesus listenin', You must be born again.

II. Three lines (Blues)	(Spiritual)
I rushed down there, but a little too late, I rushed down there, but a little too late, Thief had got my chickens and made it for the gate.	Dere's no rain to wet you, Oh yes, I want to go home. Want to go home.

In particular, the call and response technique of the leader and chorus influenced almost all of the spirituals. Few were composed, according to available sources, without leaders. The chorus responded in repetitious phrases, leaving a soloist free to compose words as the song progressed. As a definite feature of African formations, one or two singers could lead the chorus into any of the following alternatives:

I.	Call and Response Techniques			
Verse:	Solo	First Line	or:	Solo I
	Chorus	Second Line		Solo II
	Solo	Third Line		Solo I
	Chorus	Fourth Line		Solo II
Refrain:		Tutti		Tutti

II.	Call and Response Techniques			
Verse:	Chorus	First Line	or:	Tutti
	Solo	Second Line		Solo
	Chorus	Third Line		Chorus
	Solo	Fourth Line		Chorus
Refrain:	Tutti			Solo

Example 18 gives both African and Afro-American techniques which further point to the frequency of the call and response:

Ex. 18. Call and response in Africa and America.
Ayirem obi barima, No. 4, from *Folk Songs of Ghana* by J. K. Nketia.
Used by permission of the composer.

Oh Mary, O Martha, Traditional.

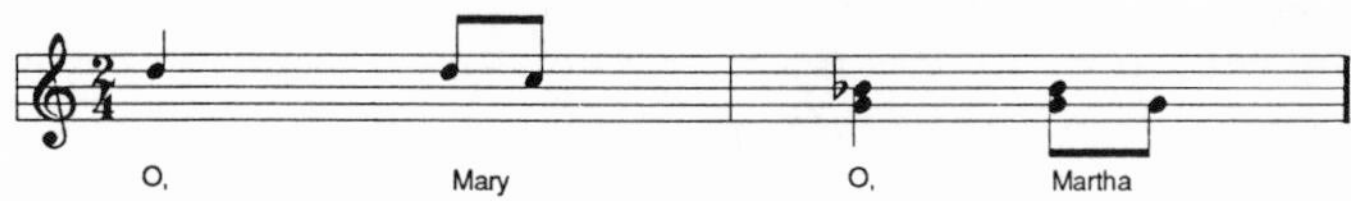

Timbre

Since tradition consisted of vocal and instrumental ensembles along with dancing, there is reason to believe that many varieties of instrumental timbres existed, even if not as frequently practiced as in African concepts. Unquestionably, spirituals mainly represented a vocal style of great emotion.

A rarity in print is an instrumental version of a song entitled *Prayer*, which follows in the style of vocal spirituals. This clever example was found in Alabama and reveals a genuine spirit of a by-gone era.

Ex. 19. *Prayer*, No. 8, from *Negro Songs from Alabama* by Harold Courlander, author and collector; transcribed by John Benson Brooks. Used by permission.

Originality of Spirituals

The originality of spirituals by Blacks has been the subject of much scrutiny and criticism as well as commendation. In 1863, Frederick Ritter stated the "merit" of the songs. Still others felt that they consisted of too much borrowing and were therefore not original at all. Dr. Richard Wallenschek, in *An Inquiry into the Origin and Development of Music, Songs, Instruments, Dances and Pantomimes of Savage Races*, voiced the opinion that "Negro songs were very much overrated" and that they were "mere imitations of European compositions which the Negroes had picked up and served up again with only slight variation".

A statement so misleading as both the title and the thought should not go unchallenged, for any composer has always deserved the right to use elements which he has heard. The art of musical composition has frequently consisted of borrowing from generations long ago to the era of television commercials today. The practice of using another composer's material for thematic inspiration and improvisation has been noted throughout the history of both classical and popular music. Popular melodies once served as "cantus firmi", or principal melodies around which other parts were woven to create religious works. Other examples have occurred in the theme and variations form from Handel to Brahms and imitative pieces of Bach. The borrowed melody was often altered or so changed or interwoven until detection was almost impossible. These classical ideas and their use and variation were the tools of the master artist.

While it was true that some elements of White songs of America influenced early Black composers, it was equally true that African-Americans borrowed from their own native land to provide themselves with materials. It was also a fact that in their process of alteration there resulted a complete change in the music, as discussed above, and such improvisation rendered the songs quite unique. This was particularly true in cases where African texts were translated into English or French, or where examples were altered by additions or rhythmic excitements. The late John Work III, a noted teacher-composer, staunchly defended this right to provide, produce and reproduce. He also proved how much the final result differed from the originals.

As it was noticed that American slaves were great imitators of the music about them, so did Ware, Allen and Garrison, in the preface of their *Slave Songs*, write that a few of the slave songs recorded in their book became established favorites among Whites as well. They noted that hardly a Sunday passed at the church on St. Helena without the use of *Gabriel's Trumpet, I Heard from Heaven Today* or *Jehovah Hallejah*. However, the songs undoubtedly took on a contrary meaning to Whites and were not the same as when sung by Blacks. For it was a fact that the burdens, hardships and inconveniences reflected in many of the songs could not possibly have been realized to their fullest extent by those who had not suffered the same injustices.

History has also shown that White composers have borrowed Black materials from African concepts of performance and construction from minstrelsy to jazz and from tin pan alley to popular. Stephen Foster, Dan Emmett, Thomas Rice, George Gershwin and a host of others used materials lifted directly from the ballads and life patterns of Blacks for use in their own compositions. Part III will discuss other kindred materials during the contemporary era, consisting of composers such as Aaron Copland, Igor Stravinsky and Darius Milhaud. Those who once criticized Blacks so harshly of borrowing melodies hardly ever wrote of this reverse fact, and books since that time which failed to reflect the history of Black contributions to American and other music have committed a "sin of omission" by unwittingly omitting facts as to the roots of some American music.

In addition to the above anonymous "composers" of untrained skills, it must be realized that there were a few exceptions of Blacks who were capable of composing thoughtful works of art. Some Black concert artists performed music of all kinds at an early time and were capable of reading music. They traveled in America and in Europe, along with those in America who were either free men or slave plantation performers. At a later time, those Blacks located around larger cities as New Orleans were better able to read and write music at an earlier age than were the most unsophisticated field hands. There were doubtless several of these who were musicians as talented as the Anglo-African violinist and composer, George Bridgetower, whose concert associations with Ludwig Beethoven were favorable and real.

Influence of the Spirituals

Spirituals became artistic forms during the era of Reconstruction and were made famous by the pioneer performances of the Fisk Jubilee Singers. Unable to appreciate the worth of the songs, they were at first reluctant to promote the excellence of compositional techniques with emotion. Could the Afro-Americans have been ashamed to sing songs to the God of their oppressors? Or had they not been freed by the same God? Was this an intellectual rebuff against the hateful conditions of slave art, or disgust for the circumstances? And finally, why could these songs serve them in slavery but not at the time of their release?

Art had always been practical for the African, and it was partly so for the Afro-American. It was not something separate and opposite from life, an object away from his being as afforded only by the elite, erudite and rich. His idea of the functioning art was perhaps responsible for the fact that certain of his songs were buried and forgotten after Emancipation, having outgrown their purpose. He no longer felt the need for *Steal Away* in quite the same way as had Nat Turner, the minister-insurrectionist, and perhaps the composer of the song. Now the Afro-American wished to retain only that which was free—free of anything peculiar to the illusions and institutions of slavery.

Fortunately, the Fisk Singers were finally persuaded to sing the spirituals in order to raise funds for the school, not then a university. The sincere desire for the continuation of their education inspired them to abandon former prejudices against the spirituals and to promote the depths of emotions found within these long rejected compositions. Since then, spirituals enlightened the world to their messages and emotions, becoming the penetrating force in both popular and classical music of the modern period.

One of the more popular spirituals, *No More Auction Block For Me (Many Thousand Gone)* was paraphrased in the song *We Shall Overcome*, a protest form of the 1960's. Arrangements and adaptations of spirituals have also been recorded in abundance for concert solo and choral ensembles, having been promoted since the era of the Jubilee Singers by composers Nathaniel Dett, John W. Work III, Eva Jessye, Margaret Bonds, William Dawson, Undine Moore, the Johnsons, Clarence C. White and many others. Symphonies and other compositions have been written utilizing the character-

Jubilee Singers. Courtesy of Fisk University.

istics of these songs. It was Burleigh's singing of spirituals, for instance, that gave way to the inspirations for the Czech composer, Anton Dvorak, to complete his *New World Symphony*. Other composers such as William Grant Still and William Dawson have composed music based on spirituals.

In turn, Whites in America have also studied and used elements of spirituals in search of Americanism. Inspired by Dvorak's *Symphony*, they pursued indigenous music of the American Indian and the Black American in hopes of capturing the spirit of American nationalism in music, popular during the late nineteenth century. Indeed, the wealth of melodic intricacies and rhythmic motives fascinated most American composers at one time or another. The influence of spirituals is found in the following compositions which represent but a sample of their power, a fundamental basis for many styles to come:

Afro-American Suite, Undine Moore, for flute, cello, piano
Afro-American Symphony, William Grant Still, for orchestra
Bandanna Sketches, C. C. White, for violin, piano
Cantata, John Carter, for soprano, piano
Go Down Moses (Northern Windows), Hampton Hawes, for jazz combo
Go Down Moses, Fela Sowande, for organ
In His Own Soul (Bible Vignettes), R. N. Dett, for piano
Negro Folk Symphony, William Dawson, for orchestra
Scuppernong Suite, John Work, for piano
24 Negro Melodies, Samuel Coleridge-Taylor, for piano
Troubled Water, Margaret Bonds, for piano

Many writings have been published about spirituals and their strengths. But at least one writer, George Pullen Jackson—who perhaps should not be mentioned in the same list with the most important of these—doubted their authenticity and worth, and felt that they were more influenced by other music than they were themselves influential.

John W. Work III wrote articles which supported the premise that Black gospel music was a direct outgrowth of the spirituals, being changed by the "rhythmic piano." Also tracing the common vocal "rhythms" of long and short meters, these were important to the phase which was shaped by the simultaneous developments of ragtime, blues and early jazz. By far the most comprehensive and voluminous findings, however, were set forth by John Lovell, Jr. in *The Black Song: The Forge and the Flame*. Published in 1972, it contained information about the origin, development and international influence of the spirituals, and was immediately cited as perhaps the most authoritative of all.

PART TWO

THE AWAKENING (1800's–1950's)

V

MODERN PERIOD: THE EMERGENCE OF BLACK PROFESSIONALS

African-Americans emerged in the late 1800's as professionals in many areas from scientific research to artistic achievements. Although greatly experimental, strides were nevertheless made in publishing and performance, academic and business ventures and in status changes. Having gained momentum from the days of Nat Turner, this era boasted some brilliant leaders whose philosophies and general contributions helped shape the music and the lives of Black people for successive generations. Of considerable influence were the philosopher-educators W. E. B. DuBois, Frederick Douglass, Marcus Garvey and Booker T. Washington. Their collective theories showed the Black position as it existed then and denoted needs and goals to be met.

By 1920, America produced many scholars in philosophy, poetry, science, art and music. Some of the most illuminating of such poets were found in Harlem, New York—Langston Hughes, James Weldon Johnson and Countee Cullen. Countless musicians such as Louis Armstrong and Duke Ellington also contributed to the era. Their accomplishments were referred to as the "Black Renaissance" and were designed to point out, defend and promote the talents and worth of the Black man and his culture.

Erupting out of the violent slave era, this second stage of brave development was formed against the transition from the European Romantic period, American Reconstruction and Africanism to the dilemmas of the World War, Modernism and Black assimilation. Affected by the psychological, physical and social elements of the society which prevailed in a segregated society, these Americans were little better off in "knowing their place" of race and class status than they were previously. This colored the conditions within which the music was composed, and confused natural growth of emotional reactions. Thus all did not run smoothly for these recently freed slaves regardless of this professionalism.

Leroi Jones' in *Blues People* stated that the earliest part of Black American history reflected a shout and an expression of the blues, so did these more modern problems of economics, social errors, poverty and power struggles also sustain the "blue" ingredients of life. Perhaps the requirements of urban living over rural life, or the almost complete relocation of the New Orleans musicians contributed to the everpresent complexities of an overcrowded profession. Eventually, countless musicians moved into the larger cities from many localities. They were either able to "sell their wares" more readily, or were not able to sell them at all.

The blues followed them into urban environments as faithfully and persistently as spirituals followed slaves to the plantation. Nowhere was there a hiding place. The great congregations of people who had moved from the south lured by northern opportunities in technology as well as in the arts, were frequently the last to be hired and the first to be fired. Jobs were hard to find, and hard to keep, and the social plights were equally unjust. Consequently, many had to work under the precarious conditions of the speakeasy, and at the whims of racketeers. In addition, jobs were not fairly distributed among Blacks and Whites, thus eliminating or limiting the rapid growth of Black professionalism in the arts.

Some blues related the sadness found in the treatment and conditions of Blacks. *I'm Tired of Bein' Jim Crowed, Cloudy in the West* and other blues which depicted poverty, depression and despair were found in abundance, and stressed the downhearted facts of life from "I spent my last nickel in a subway train.." to "I gave up my room, could not pay the rent; went down to the Welfare and didn't get a cent".

No matter that they did not find the economic security which they so desperately needed, the majority of these professionals ultimately profited by remaining in an urban setting. Many found fame in publishing and recording, radio appearances, night clubs and concert halls. Musicians also found limited but supportive aid from the Works Progress Administration (WPA), a federal organization established during the depression which helped supply jobs for many urban citizens.

Not only were American cities advantageous to the musician, but concepts and studies abroad in such cities as Paris were possible. These deeper commitments to the music produced a better prepared individual who grew to achieve popular notoriety in swing, bebop and other jazz styles as well as that of the classical arts.

The history of Black professionalism in America rested heavily upon the musical experiences which they had inherited and practiced for innumerable decades. According to Robert Stevenson, their African ancestors had perfected the art of music in their societies as early as the seventh century, and had traveled to share their findings with nearby Asian and European countries. In America, Blacks had also performed as slaves and free men dating back to the 1700's and possibly before. However, there had been little or no gain economically, as many slaves had been hired out by the lure of mere trinkets for themselves while their "masters" received the money. Paid Blacks were few indeed. This new era in the history of such professionalism therefore marked the time when more significant numbers of Blacks generally outlined their own careers and participated in commercial undertakings for the benefit of their own fame and fortune.

VI

BLACK MINSTRELS

The history of Black minstrels began in Africa and descended into Afro-American lifestyles of early colonial times. Many of the characteristics observed in early Black minstrelsy were similar to those from Europe, while others were quite different. In the *Harvard Dictionary of Music*, Apel defined minstrels as "professional musicians of the Middle Ages, especially those who were employed in a feudal household" and "of show business activities and the music thereof." These European-based minstrels, called minnesingers, troubadours, trouveres or jongleurs, performed as jugglers, acrobats, poetic debaters, tricksters and musicians.

Particularly since the publishing of Frank Snowden's book, *Blacks in Antiquity*, we now know that some of those minstrels who performed in ancient Europe were Africans. In fact, the idea of such minstrels was also found in Africa long before the Middle Ages and decidedly long before our American roots were established. A report of West African minstrels, called "griots" by D. T. Niane, showed similarities to those in Europe. Found in *Sundiata, An Epic of Old Mali*, it outlined duties of the traveling griots whose oral tradition ranged from preserving and verbalizing historical records, recalling lineages and engaging in the counseling of kings to playing magical tricks and musical instruments.

Blacks served as traveling minstrels in America before 1800. Particularly after Reconstruction, many minstrels participated in shows which traveled from city to city in search of money and fame. Alternating their acts with songs, dances, jokes, dialogues and clowning, they differed from earlier jesters in that the painted face represented that of the Black American. Unlike the clown who mixed his colors to depict emotions of comic gaity and distortion, and unlike the African who used his colors to similate colors with human emotions (white, for example, denoted joy) this use of the charcoal color was not for similar ceremonies.

Colored faces eventually became a compulsory rule for the American minstrel shows. An obnoxious practice begun by Whites and subsequently demanded by audiences of both races, many Blacks were forced to continue it for the sake of popularity. This cyclic force of the White man painting his face to resemble a despised Black was therefore copied by the Black man himself, an irony of comedy personified.

Judging a blackface as a performer in imitation of a Black man was ludicrous in itself. Taking another view, it was excruciatingly painful and humiliating to enjoy a living while enduring that predicament. However, even if Blacks felt themselves "traitors" in bowing to unkind demands, who could blame them for a sense of economic justice in the quest for an honest living? And who could blame them for claiming a share of a fame so readily available?

Music, on the other hand, was an artistic expression which was not always looked upon as something as evil as the society in which it grew. For one thing, some minstrels proved to be as talented, skillful and enjoyable as their competitors, and secondly, their shows were hilariously comical. Because comedy and talent were in command of the audiences, Black minstrels soon learned to subdue the uncomfortable realities and to smile through the medium of song. Consequently, music eventually overcame the demeaning sneers and coerced the performers to laugh with the audience.

Origins of American Minstrelsy

Because American minstrelsy was a type of staged production which flourished from early 1800 to early 1900, it was one of the oldest settings for Black professionals. Its commercial authority embraced the life of Stephen Foster (1826–1864) and terminated near the death of a famous Black counterpart, James Bland (1854–1911). Even though the late Alain Locke, philosopher and writer, divided minstrelsy into two parts (1850–1875 and 1875–1895), it is obvious that the fact functioned well outside these dates, having begun with early colonial life and eventually directed toward vaudeville, burlesque, extravaganza, or the "tin pan" varieties of modern music.

Legend and fact showed that Blacks were responsible for the embryonic stages of American minstrelsy, and that many were involved in musical contributions as to form, style, instrumentation and performance practices. Ever since slaves were commanded to "make a noise" in the field or were invited to perform at plantation revelries, their skills have inspired subjects and patterns for secondhand presentations among Whites. Blacks, however, could not claim the credit for American commercialism of the art, since exploitation of their ideas first benefited others.

Although the origins of American minstrelsy were not generally recorded as having been contributed by Blacks, the popular story about Thomas Rice (1808–1860) did confirm that he had imitated on stage a song and dance routine which he had copied from a deformed Black. Also printed in Christy's *Minstrel Songster*, it stated in part:

Come listen all you gals and boys,
I'se just from Tacky Hoe,
I'm goin' to sing a little song;
My name's Jim Crow! (*Several verses*)

Chorus
Wheel about an' turn about an' do jus' so;
Ebry time I wheel about I jump Jim Crow!

Little did that Black man know that he would jump Jim Crow for so long thereafter, for not only was this JC routine carried out on stage but offstage as well. "Jim Crowism" became a sensational act to be repeated time and time again, with thunderous applause from a separated society. And little did America know that the Black man's deformity would shape the disfigurement of the Nation for so long a time. It was significant that "Jim Crow" was later used to describe segregation in all of its manifestations. Thus, minstrel also implied segregation, in spite of the joy of its musical worth.

Media and Minstrel Participants

Much as in opera, instruments were used for introductions, interludes, postludes and accompaniment. The familiar solos, duets and choruses joined with the banjo, piano, guitar, gongs, tambourines, and other percussions and winds. Later, the band instrumentation was developed into small ragtime ensembles.

Near 1800, a poster of the era listed the following instruments required: tuba, banjo, violin, clappers, bass and viola. No doubt, there was not a set instrumentation, as performances were accorded by both taste and available instruments. The same poster read:

Needed:

1. musician to double band and orchestra; bass drummer who reads; trombone, baritone, all must double.
2. wanted: bass singer for quartette, doubling comedy, etc., strong cornet player . . .
3. one strong colored cornet player . . . salary must be low (!)

Minstrel participants depended upon the instruments to support their actions from beginning to end. These participants ranged from the announcer or interlocutor who was frequently interrupted with spasmodic chords from the band, to the end men or blackface comedians. The stump speakers, Tambo and Mr. Bones, were also an expected part of the show since they alternately fed each other ridiculous, and sometimes ribald, jokes along with the "brer rabbit" type stories. Other characters were arranged as soloists, choruses and other small ensembles with dances assembled on stage.

Form

The overall form of the show resembled an operetta in that its main elements of dance, spoken dialogue and song were similarly written. While the operetta was most related to the opera because of its quality of music drama, the minstrel show was not necessarily a story, but rather a series of events arranged into scenes and acts. It was a variety show whose unsophisticated presentations covered the activities of the south, with particular emphasis upon southern Blacks. One example of a show was seen in *Dusky Clouds* by Nahaves and Lippmann, whose program of events was:

1. Overture (instrumental)
2. Opening chorus
3. Song (solo with chorus)
4. *Carry Me Back to Old Virginny* (dance music by J. Bland)
5. Song (male quartet)
6. Song (waltz, ballad)
7. Song (company)
8. Scarf dance (specialty)
9. Song (solo with chorus)
10. Finale (company)

Some forms within the shows included European dances such as the waltz. There were also early Afro-American routines such as the cake-walk, an elaborate strutting effect; the shuffle, the buck and wing, the clog, the jig, the pigeon wing and others. Later, there were tap dances, rags, camel walk, turkey trots, grizzly bear and the lame duck, which became popular even in vaudeville shows. Still others represented in song forms were the airs, ballads, blues and hybrid forms, the most important of which are discussed in the following sections.

Ballads, Blues, and Hybrids

Two of the most popular song forms of Black minstrelsy were the ballad and the blues. The ballad, a romantic or sentimental song, told a story or expressed an emotion in short, simple stanzas, and was quite similar to the earlier European poetry depicting romance and exciting adventures. The blues reflected despair and sadness, but really contained commentaries of several moods from depression and self-pity to love and cynicism. Generally a style of either verse with refrain, or verse without refrain, it could also contain humorous words similar to those of some ballads. Both types used an ABAB structure with choral refrains ABAC and ABAB repeated, and they occurred with verses and refrains reversed. Many varieties existed as simple airs, or even as "da capo". Some ballads were also AABB with refrain or in ABA form. Both forms were tonal structures, in keeping with nineteenth century practices (also see chapter VIII).

The ballad spoke of the same subjects as the blues—love, places, people and things. Its words, however, were generally happier in content, outlook and presentation, and contained close styles with the European songs. Not always sophisticated, ballads were apt to use euphemism in their expressions, were more verbose and frequently through-composed. On the other hand, blues were more often concerned with the raw and real bluntness of life, and would state messages with unsophisticated earthiness. The blues form was generally repetitious in its texts, even though the shape and structure were not always of the classic twelve-bar type. A similarity of ideas is seen in the comparison of the ballad and blues tests below, as well as a difference in word formations:

Ballad:
Carry me back to ole Virginny.
There's where the cotton and
'tatoes grow . . .
There's where this ole darkey's
heart am long'd to go.

Blues:
I've got those Vicksburg blues
and I'm singin' it every-
where I please.
Now, the reason I'm singin' it
is to give my poor heart
some ease.

Some ballad texts not necessarily composed for the minstrel shows were nevertheless influential. Some were of the mixed blues-ballad types, or hybrids. Others were free varieties such as catchy ditties of the street or playground. One such example was *Hard to Be a Nigger*:

Naught fer naught, figger fer figger,
Figger fer de white man, Naught fer de nigger!

Another example was *Short'nin Bread*:

Two little niggers lyin' in bed,
One of 'em sick an' de odder mos' dead.
Call fer de doctor an' de doctor said,
Feed dem darkies on short'nin' bread.

While ballads resembled blues, some of the words also were related to spirituals and other songs. One verse used in the shows came from *When de Good Lord Sets You Free*, whose likeness was akin to *Shortnin' Bread*:

Big Black nigger, lyin' on de log,
Finger on de trigger, eye on de hog.
Gun say bump! Hog say bip!
Nigger jumped on him with all his grip.

The chorus of the same song was less secular in its text, and reflected the religious elements so typical in the songs of Black folks: "Oh mourner, you shall be free . . . "

Hybrid ballads were further influenced by the spirituals. The following song shows religious and secular texts in *Cornfield Medley*:

Well I heard a mighty rumblin' an' I didn't know from where,
From way down yonder in the cornfiel'.
T'was only brother Gabriel just a-combin' out his hair
From way down yonder in the cornfiel'.

Chorus:
Tra la la la la la la (*repeat*)
Oh sinners, it won't be long,

Solo:
Till you hear brother Gabriel go up in the cloud and say . . .

Chorus:
Peter, go ring dem bells (*repeat*)
I heard from heav'n to hail, hail, hail, Jerusalem, hail!
Maha, ha, Hail, Jerusalem, Hail. . . . etc.

In addition to resembling one of the songs listed in *Callender's Original Minstrel Songsters*, the above also had representations from the spiritual, *Dere's a Meetin' Here Tonight.*

Early Composer-performers

Composers of minstrelsy were most often performers. Therefore, the history of performance involved the art of composition, whether or not it was transcribed. Frequently, the oral tradition was used to preserve Black compositions because neither Blacks nor Whites could notate the music exactly. Consequently, many bards went unrecorded in history, since few manuscripts carried the name of the Black composer. One such musically inclined person sought to correct this injustice by partially identifying himself:

Ef anybody ax you who writ dis song,
Tell 'im 'twuz a dark-skinned nigger
Wid a pair o' blue duckins on,
A-lookin' for a home,
Jes a-lookin' for a home.

Many tunes actually composed by Blacks were written down by Whites. The work of Thomas Rice was one example. Other Whites who served as 'keepers of records' were Stephen Foster, whose *Ring, Ring de Banjo, Old Black Joe* and *My Kentucky Home* were inspired by Black subjects, and Dan

Emmett, whose *Ethiopian Walk-Around* was later adopted by Confederate Whites as their *Dixie*.

Perhaps the first noteworthy Black writer of popular ballads was Samuel Lucas (1848–1916). His *Grandfather's Clock Is Too Tall for the Shelf* (which has also been attributed to H. C. Work), and his *Carve Dat Possum* were favorites among the people. Along with Billy Kersands and James Bland, he was considered among the greatest of "comedian-writers." At that time, composers, comedians, dancers etc. were expected to double in their performances; thus earning that title. Most, however, did not necessarily carry the title of composer or singer during early minstrelsy, since the word "minstrel" was inseparable from the various other duties of composer-performer.

Many composers of minstrelsy were represented in early jazz in some reports, e.g., A. J. R. Connor, composer of *My Cherished Hope, My Fondest Dreams, American Polka Quadrilles, New York Polka Waltz* and others; Gussie Davis, composer of *In the Baggage Coach Ahead, Do the Old Folks Miss Me, My Creole Sue, Down in Poverty Row, The Fatal Wedding, The Light House by the Sea, When Nelly Was Raking the Hay, Wait 'Til the Tide Comes In, The Cabin on the Mississippi Shore*; Nathan Bivens, composer of *It Makes no Dif'rence What You Do, Get the Money*; Will Accooe, composer of *'Cause I'se in Society Now, A Trip to Coon Town*; and George Milburn, composer of *Listen to the Mocking Bird*. As in the case of the latter composer, many writers sold their rights to the songs which they composed, thus contributing to the difficulty in tracing their origins.

THOMAS (BLIND TOM) BETHUNE (1849–1908)

Thomas Bethune, composer-pianist, was born a slave near Columbus, Georgia. One of the most colorful of the early writers, he was a child prodigy variously described as "a genius with unerring memory" or an eccentric. There were some who claim that he was either autistic to some degree, or an example of an idiot savant, perhaps mainly because of his daily physical exercises which must have resembled Yoga, and because of the self-punishment inflicted upon his eyes in an attempt to gain his eyesight—a practice which sometimes resulted in the success of capturing glimpses of obscurred images and light. No one can ridicule, however, the documented writings which speak of his largely self-taught ability and inspiration to excel on a near-miracle level of achievement.

A widely acclaimed concert pianist, he was early tested by professional musicians and discovered to be a most brilliant musician with perfect pitch who could duplicate perfectly on the piano any music which was played for him. His owner exhibited his talents in concerts throughout the United States, Africa and Europe, where his performances included nearly 5,000 catalogued pieces from Chopin and Beethoven to his own original works. The Moorland Room at Howard University houses written attestations to these facts of his "profound sensationalism" and the Azalia Hackley Room at Detroit supports these facts through various newspapers and exhibitions of his published works.

Of a tonal style which reflected the theoretical practices of the nineteenth century and salon-type descriptions of the natural resources around him, his compositions included *Rainstorm* and *The Battle of Manassas* (reprint/Hinshaw; tape/G. Southall, Minn.; PBS video through BEEM).

JAMES BLAND (1854–1911)

One of the most famous, talented, entertaining and exciting of the early Black composer-performers was James Bland. Born in Flushing, New York, Bland spent much of his life in Philadelphia and Washington, attending Washington public schools. According to his biographer, John Daly, he enrolled at Howard University for a short time, studied theory with a Professor White and later abandoned his education in order to join with the Haverly Colored Minstrels who were performing in Baltimore. A newspaper article found in the Azalia Hackley Collection Room in Detroit's Public Library, however, stated that Bland graduated from Howard. He then left America for Europe where he became quite famous and lived well above his means. Squandering his money and neglecting his health led to his decline. By the time he returned to America, he was forgotten and was not offered adequate work to maintain his expenses.

According to John Daly, Bland was credited with making the "Bland Banjo," a five-stringed instrument thought to be a combination of African derivation plus the violin fingerboard. However, Bland was not the originator of the banjo, according to John Tasker Howard. He credited its creation to another Black, Joel Walker Sweeney (1813–1860) who, in imitation of the gourd banjo used by the slaves, stretched some skin across a cheesebox and placed five strings on it. Howard pointed out that many believed this to be a myth. However, it was a fact that the history of the African "gonje" (a gourd with strings) and the harp or any of the stringed instruments common to Africa testified to the credibility of this matter. In fact, to make such an instrument would not have been difficult for the

James Bland. Courtesy of Virginia State Library.

slaves. Bland was nevertheless significant in making improvements upon the original banjo, no matter who created it.

Like Stephen Foster, his white counterpart, Bland wrote over 700 songs, many of which were not recorded and were consequently lost, stolen, or sold. As was the case in art music, both publishers and composers of the day were dishonest, careless and impractical in the matter of copyrights, and were generally unprofessional. Also like Foster, Bland was born into a well-to-do family, whose father was the first Black to hold the position of Examiner in the United States Patent Office. Both Foster and Bland were said by Daly to have led wild and reckless lives, and both were rather young when they died. Neither was a good business man, and each allowed his money to slip away.

Among the most famous of the songs which Bland wrote were *Carry Me Back to Ole Virginny*, adopted by the State of Virginia in 1940 as the State Song, and *Oh Dem Golden Slippers*, both themes of which are shown below. It is also significant that *Carry Me Back to Ole Virginny* is found in the old *Christy Minstrel Songster* as a song composed by another Black, Charles White. However, it is seemingly similar in title only. Words have been revised during the recent decades.

Ex. 20. *Carry Me Back to Ole Virginny* and *Oh Dem Golden Slippers*. Permission granted by Theodore Presser Company.

His other pieces were various types of ballads, musicals and airs. His writing was similar to that of Foster, especially as to the subject of texts, the general emotional styles and his use of basic chord structures. Sometimes through-composed pieces, they were mostly strophic form, having verses with choral refrains, or vice versa. In part, his list of compositions included: *Close Dem Windows, Hand Me Down My Walking Stick, Listen to the Silver Trumpet, Dancing on De Kitchen Floor, Oh, Lucinda, The Homestead, Father's Growing Old, Missouri Hound Dog, Hot Time in Our Town, In the Evening by the Moonlight, Pretty Little Caroline Rose, De Golden Wedding, You could have Been True, Gabriel's Band, The Old Fashion-Cottage, The Farmer's Daughter, Christmas Dinner, You Gotta Stop Kicking My Hound Around, Dandy Black Brigade, There's a Long, Long, Trail, Heaven Is My Harbor, In the Morning by the Bright Light, Listen to the Silver Trumpets, Keep Dem Golden Gates Wide Open* and a musical, *Sporting Girl.*

Later Composers

Black composers of the 1900's made more sophisticated effects, drawing from the experiences of the rag and other existing varieties and utilizing in jazz more complex harmonies as demonstrated by Charles Ives and the traditional European contributions of Brahms and Debussy. Even though popular songs remained basically tonal, i.e. key oriented, the tendency was to add more sevenths. Thus, the beginning of jazz was again reflected in the earlier forms. Yet the simpler style of the old harmonies was never really completely abandoned for the newer ones.

As minstrelsy aged, personalities who distinguished themselves more as composers than performers were Hubert (Eubie) Blake, Robert Cole, Will Cook, H. T. Burleigh, and J. Rosamond Johnson. While many persons also wrote in art music styles, depending upon the circumstances and educational advantages, most composers like Fats Waller, W. C. Handy and Duke Ellington were almost always connected with jazz and similar forms. On the other hand, some like Burleigh ultimately became standard names in art songs and spirituals.

WILL MARION COOK (1869–1944)

Will Marion Cook, a native of Washington D.C., was a talented musician of many styles. Educated at the Hochschule in Berlin, he later studied at Oberlin College and the National Conservatory of Music. A violinist of repute, he teamed with Bert Williams, William Moore, H. B. Smith, Cecil Mack, James Weldon Johnson, Alex Rogers and others to create some of the best musicals of that time. He also found the time to write classical and popular music, although his recognition was gained mostly through popular music.

Cook wrote tonal music consisting of ballads and the music of show business, as well as various arrangements of folk tunes and original compositions. His music was written for several types of instrumental and vocal forms. Among them were stage scores for *In Dahomey, Abyssinia* and *Banana Land*; *Springtime, Bon Bon Buddy, Creole Dance, Down de Lover's Lane, Exhortation* (Negro Sermon), *An Explanation, Fas' Fas' World, A Little Bit of Heaven Called Home, The Little Gypsy Maid, Love Is the Tend'rest of Themes, Manny, Red Red Rose, Sing Along, Mandy Lou, Mammy Lasses Candy Chile, On Emancipation Day, Rain Song, Until Then, Wid de Moon, Moon, Moon, Clorindy* and *Who Dat Say Chicken in This Crowd.*

Will Marion Cook. Moorland-Spingarn Research Center, Howard University.

Ex. 21. *Lift Ev'ry Voice and Sing*, by J. Rosamond and James Weldon Johnson. Copyright, Edward B. Marks Music Corporation. Used by permission.

list - 'ning skies, Let it re - sound loud as the roll - ing sea.
wear - y feet Come to the place for which our fa - thers sighed?
to the light, Keep us for - ev - er in the path, we pray.
Sing a song full of the faith that the dark past has taught us
We have come ov - er a - way that with tears has been wa - tered
Lest our feet stray from the pla - ces, our God, where we met Thee
pp
rall. e molto cresc.
allargando
Sing a song full of the hope that the pres-ent has brought
We have come, tread - ing our path thro' the blood of the slaugh -
Lest our hearts, drunk with the wine of the world, we for - get
mp
sfz
rall. e molto cresc.
allargando
ff Tempo I
us: Fac - ing the ris - ing sun of our new day be -
tered, Out from the gloom - y past, Till now we stand at
Thee; Shad-owed be - neath Thy hand, May we for - ev - er
Tempo I
ff
sfz

JOHN ROSAMOND JOHNSON (1873–1954)

John Rosamond Johnson, brother of James Weldon, was born in Jacksonville, Florida. His wide range of experiences consisted of study at the University of Atlanta and the New England Conservatory with David Bispham. A pianist-singer, he toured America and Europe in programs of spirituals, and in *Porgy and Bess*.

During the "Black Renaissance", Johnson teamed with both James Weldon Johnson and Robert Cole to produce a large quantity of highly popular songs used in musicals and variety shows. With his brother, he wrote the "Negro National Anthem," *Lift Ev'ry Voice and Sing*, as seen in Example 21.

Other songs published with his brother were the *American Negro Spirituals, Rolling Along in Song*, a history of "Negro music" with 85 arrangements and a host of other songs for the minstrel and stage shows. Johnson also wrote: *African Drum Dance* (ballet), *I Told My Love to the Roses, Morning,*

John Rosamond Johnson. Theodore Presser Company.

James Weldon Johnson. Moorland-Spingarn Research Center, Howard University.

Noon, and Night, Now Let Me Fly, O, Southland, Little Gal, Since You Went Away, I Ain't Going' Study War No More, Go Chain de Lion Down, and *My Castle on the Nile.*

JAMES TIM BRYMN (1881–1946)

J. Tim Brymn, composer, conductor and arranger, was born in Kinston, North Carolina. Educated at Christian Institute, Shaw University and the National Conservatory of Music in New York City, he was well qualified to serve as music director of the Clef Club, and to function in the grand manner of the minstrel-jazz composers.

Brymn led the orchestra in Reisenweber's Jardin de Dance, Ziegfeld Roof and other places. During World War I, he served as the leader of the musical unit, 350 Field Artillery, AEF. Often using Chris Smith and Clarence Williams as collaborators, he wrote the following works: *Please Go Way and Let Me Sleep, La Rhumba, Shout, Sister, Shout, Josephine, My Joe, Camel Walk, Look Into Your Baby's Face and Say Goo-goo, My Pillow and Me,* and many others.

FORD DABNEY (1883–1958)

Ford Dabney, a Washingtonian who eventually settled in New York, was another composer engaged in the area of early jazz and minstrelsy. A member of ASCAP in 1937, he was educated at the Armstrong Manual Training School. He also studied with his father, Charles Dach, William Walddecker, Samuel Fabian and others. As the official court musician for the President of Haiti in 1904, Dabney was competent, but was not as publicized as other composers.

When Dabney returned to the United States in 1907, he led his own quartet, conducted the Ziegfeld Midnight Frolics orchestra for eight years, created the original dance numbers for the Vernon Castles, the famous dancers, and organized the Tempo Club, a Negro talent bureau. He participated in the musical activities of the day by writing for films, vaudeville theatres, composing and touring. Among his compositions were: *Porto Rico* (Rag Intermezzo), *Reach for the Ceiling, Rang Tang* (broadway stage score), *That Minor Strain, Oh You Devil* and *Shine.*

J. HUBERT (EUBIE) BLAKE (1883–1983)

J. Hubert Blake, an early ragtime pianist-composer of renown, was active as a performer and composer. Born in Baltimore, Maryland, he later traveled to New York and became associated with the Harlem Renaissance while mainly developing a reputation as a composer of musicals.

While performing as pianist and organist at local cafes, vaudeville shows, and other places of entertainment, he later returned to his studies around 1950 as a student of the Schillinger method of composition. With Noble Sissle, he was a member of the vaudeville team which composed and performed the musicals *Shuffle Along* and *Chocolate Dandies.* Once the assistant conductor to Jim Europe of the Clef Club, he toured with the musical show organized by Europe for the United States Infantry.

Blake was honored with other musicians at the New World Symphony Orchestra Dinner held on October 5, 1969, in New York. In addition to other lectures and concerts, he has also appeared on such television shows as David Frost and other talk shows. The inimitable ragtime composer-pianist and Broadway musical figure of the Tin Pan Alley collaborators, represented a century of pioneer developments and brilliant accomplishments. A chief exponent of the piano style which influenced so many forms

Eubie Blake. The composer of more than one thousand songs was 100 years old when this photo was taken at a salute to him at the Kennedy Center. The salute, EUBIE BLAKE: A CENTURY OF MUSIC, was produced as a public television special by WQED/Pittsburgh. Photo Credit: WQED. Courtesy of Charlotte Klein Associates.

and fashions, Eubie, a gift to American music and its archives of achievements and a lively enrichment to this decade, was only just beginning to show the world anew that which had made him a living legend in the first place. He performed on television, at Yale University, the Kennedy Center, the Tribute for Josephine Baker, and at the Brass Conference (Kleinsinger concert) where he was also awarded the Louis Armstrong Medal (*down beat* and *Post News*); at ninety-one, he was a topic of a March 1974 television special, "Eubie Blake, Ragtime Legacy" where he was interviewed by Carol Randolph and on which he performed as soloist and as accompanist to blues singer Edith Wilson.

As the 1980 recipient of an honorary doctorate from Fisk University in Nashville, Tennessee, he was presented with a citation from President Walter Leonard which read: "Man of charm as commentator with wit and humor on the human condition; a musician of style and verve as entertainer, combing the varied themes and tempi of traditional forms with the African syncopation of ragtime." One of his albums proclaimed him as "Wizard of Ragtime," Leonard Feather named him a "pioneer of vaudeville and ragtime," and an article in *Newsweek* (February 22, 1971) captioned him as "Mr. Ragtime" at age eighty-eight and listed his planned appearances for Los Angeles, Toronto, St. Louis, and other towns. Max Morath, in the preface of his *Giants of Ragtime* piano collection, called Eubie a "pace-setter for most of his century" and included therein his *Tricky Fingers, Troublesome Ivories*, and *Dictys on Seventh Avenue*. During 1982, a revival of the Broadway show, *Eubie*, toured several cities, including Washington D.C., once again revealing the uniqueness of *I'm Just Wild About Harry* and other songs. Other captions from this decade were "The Comeback Kid: Eubie Blake is Wowing Them Again at the Age of 90" (*Wall Street Journal*, October 23, 1973) and "Good Times and Eubie Blake" (*Washington Post*, 1980).

At the age of ninety-seven, Eubie was honored by the U.S. Army, among other institutions and associations. Several spectaculars paid him homage in his 100th year. Major artists coordinated by the Charlotte Klein Associates and Ron Abbott, producer, performed a salute to Eubie at the Kennedy Center in Washington D.C., in January 1983. Entitled "Eubie Blake: A Century of Music," the special was shown on public television station WQED soon thereafter. Another of the most tremendous tributes ever rendered any person was the sensational 100th birthday celebration held at St. Peter's Church in New York on February 6, 1983, while Eubie lay ill. Scheduled for twenty-four hours of music given by the most talented among the jazz artists, the jazz marathon hailed Eubie as one who "significantly influenced the course of the American musical theatre" and as one who had "written three thousand tunes in his century" of life. The event highlighted his rags, *Tricky Fingers* and *Dictys on Seventh Avenue*, the latter of which, Patti Hagan pointed out, was used for his graduation piece for a bachelor's degree earned from New York University in 1950 (*New Yorker*, February 28, 1983).

Blake's list of works included the following: *Charleston Rag, You Were Meant for Me, Shuffle Along, Chocolate Dandies, Baby Mine, Love will Find a Way, Loving You the Way I Do, Memories of You, My Handy Man Ain't Handy Anymore, That Lindy Hop, You're Lucky to Me, Swanee Home, Roll Jordan, Tricky Fingers, Troublesome Ivories, Dictys on Seventh Avenue, Fizz Water* and *The Chevy Chase*. Eubie's legacy to the world is partly seen in the numerous recordings of his pieces: *Shuffle Along* (in *Recorded Anthology of American Music*, New World Records/NW260); *Fizz Water* (on *Classic Rags*, Columbia 12974); *Sounds of Africa* (*Jazz Odyssey: The Sound of Harlem*/Columbia); *Eighty-Six Years of Eubie Blake* (Columbia/C2S-847); *Troublesome Ivories* (Keith Nichols, piano, One-Up/2035); and others on Biograph, Smithsonian, EMB, etc. Scores published by Shapiro: *Blackbirds of 1930*; by Berlin: *Dear Li'l Pal* fox-trot, *Don't Love Me Blues* fox-trot, *Messin Around*; by Witmark: *I'm Just Wild About Harry*; by Handy: *Truckin' on Down* (with Porter) and *We Are Americans Too* (with Razaf & Cooke); easy arrangements of *Memories of You* (Schaum piano pieces); in *Afro-America Sings* (Ollie McFarland, Detroit public schools); *Charleston Rag, Sincerely* (E. B. Marks) and others.

Other Composers

The list of Black involvement in later minstrelsy is so long that it would not be practical to review it all. While some composers who practiced minstrelsy will also be discussed in early jazz, a considerable number of other Blacks connected with early music are excerpted in a list compiled by W. C. Handy in 1937: Cecil Mack, *Teasing*; Joe Trent, *Muddy Waters*; Maceo Pinkard, *Mammy O' Mine, Sweet Georgia Brown, Congratulations* and *Mammy*; J. C. Johnson, *Believe It, Beloved, Old Fashioned Love*; Will Vodery, *Tomorrow*; Henry Creamer, *Way Down Yonder in New Orleans* and *After You're Gone*; Porter Grainger, *Cotton*; Clarence Muse, *Sleepy Time Down South*; Perry Bradford, *Crazy Blues*; Peter Bocage, *Mama's Gone Goodbye*; Charles Warfield, *Baby, Won't You Please Come Home*; Spencer Williams, *Everybody Loves My Baby* and *I've Found a New Baby*; King Oliver, *Sugar Foot Stomp*; Bennie Benjamin, *I Don't Want to Set the World on Fire* and *When the Lights Go on Again All Over the World*; Shelton Brooks, *Some of These Days*; Lucky Roberts, *Moonlight Cocktail*; Ernest Hogan, *All Coons Look Alike to Me*; Al John, *Go Way Back and Sit Down*; and the Spikes Brothers and Benny Carter, *Some Day Sweetheart*.

The Influence of Black Minstrelsy

As in the case of other early Black music, the growth of minstrel songs paralleled Baroque, Classical and Romantic periods. While contemporary with some of the early Euro-American composers as Billings, Mason, Hopkinson, McDowell, Carpenter and Paine, minstrelsy was well aware of slave music.

As songs of the minstrel shows were developed with an intermingling of European and African developments transplanted to America, they, in turn, influenced music being written in Europe. The dances enlivened the music of Coleridge-Taylor (1875–1912), an Anglo-African. Claude Debussy (1862–1918) was a European composer who used elements of minstrelsy in his compositions, such as in Golliwog's *Cakewalk*, which made use of cake-walk dance rhythms—quick notes alternating with slow notes (♪ ♩ ♪ ♪ ♩). Another musician who was greatly affected by such music was the concert pianist Louis Gottschalk (1829–1869). Born in New Orleans of French-Spanish or possibly Jewish-Creole ancestry, his fame was international. Songs heard during his childhood experiences were in his compositions *Banjo, Bamboula, Savane* and others, which used not only minstrel styles but African contributions as well. Gottschalk's constant association with these musical forms is recorded as practical historical information. Born before Dvorak, he was not given due credit for having pioneered indigenous music in quest of American nationalism.

As a total entity, the minstrel show also served as the basis for vaudeville, burlesque and other musicals of the tin pan variety. The instrumentation found in minstrelsy was vital in supplying gems for early jazz ensembles and in developing characteristic instrumental idioms used in all the popular forms. Fortunately, the offspring of minstrelsy fared better than the blackface era in bringing to the world an acceptance of its musical style and performance.

VII

JAZZ: ITS DEFINITIONS, HISTORY, AND INFLUENCE

Derived mainly from American folk sources, jazz is America's most complicated, most highly developed indigenous music. Jazz is intellectual or relaxed; classical or popular; base or lofty; delicate, sincere or hilarious. Primarily an instrumental style, it has been strongly influenced by vocal music; because of an early overlapping of work and praise, it has also been influenced by the sacred and the secular.

Because the Afro-American has been most responsible for formation and its major developments, there is no doubt that jazz consists of the summation of the Black man's experience as well as a review of his culture. There is no music which encompasses more of Black lifestyle.

There is no other music which tells more of Americanism than jazz, or more of the kindred spirits of its makers. The synthesis of African and European inventions reflects the melding of cultures through its improvisation, its art forms and its messages.

Definition

Jazz has been defined as improvisation, blues, ragtime, soul or rhythm. Perhaps stemming from "jazz," the sexual term from Creole patois applied to the Congo dances of New Orleans, the derivatives and synonyms also included "razz," meaning to "tease, ridicule or heckle." Jazz, razz, jass and rag, as well as jig and shout have long since been constituents and associated terms.

However, jazz was not only blues, or a shout, a jig or a clog. Yet it was greatly influenced by all of these elements, from the movement of a "shout" to the dotted rhythm of a jig. Jazz emerged from each of their developments, but neither form alone was jazz itself.

Nor was jazz just improvisation alone, as this would have denied the written melody, harmony and rhythm, and would have restricted jazz to a definition of spontaneity. Jazz was not just rhythm, although rhythm was the most characteristic aspect of Africanism and excitement, and was seemingly the most outstanding feature of many related forms.

Jazz, then, was a collective term implying many features. In general, it was a combination of blues, ragtime, jubilee songs, shouts, jigs, clogs, coon songs and African-American primitivism, i.e., old, ancient or early, and not crude or "uncivilized"—a group which contained both secular and religious forms, including idioms of both popular and classical music. Specifically, jazz was also a verb, meaning to improvise by additions of tones or by the dotting of rhythms. And like the definition of African music, jazz was a correlation of speech with music and dance, wherein instruments "spoke" the sounds of an intense system while inspiring the listeners to participate.

Jazz was to folk music what a fugue was to art music, but without the strictness of a fugue. As a compositional technique, both could be incorporated into a musical work and could be readily recognized, and both became a culmination of previous forms upon which they were based. To some, jazz eventually became the "classical music of the Blacks" because of its origins and its ultimate accomplishment as an art form, and even more so because European-based art music also began from similar origins of popularism (see Chapter XV).

Jazz originally differed from art music in its function. Although jazz partly sprang from church, its purpose was for dance and entertainment, and not for intellectual deliberation. Black musicians of the Awakening Period were not allowed free access to either ballrooms, clubs or concert halls. Therefore, jazz was relegated to cheap dance halls and the like. Partly because of unfair unions, segregation and "Jim Crow" laws, and partly because Whites in art music felt that Blacks were inferior in mind and in mastering a skill, jazz was further distinguished by the fact that its audience was mainly Black. Blacks bought blues recordings, enjoyed jazz in the clubs and cafes, and developed their own rules for participation. Its popularity, financial possibilities and excitement eventually attracted Whites.

Most significantly, jazz further differentiated itself from traditional art music and most smaller popular forms in that it made use of changing harmonies such as the seventh chords in one period and a mixture of sevenths with altered chords from the mid-1900's onward. Early forms used triads (chords with three notes) while using sevenths, ninths and altered chords less frequently. In addition, jazz rhythm was one of its more characteristic aspects with its daring syncopations and cross rhythms not as commonly noted in art music. With each decade, definitions expanded.

History

The birthplace of jazz is speculative. At first, historians and the publishing media ignored the art and relegated the responsibility of its promotion mainly to chance. Because similar musical activities began in Kansas, St. Louis, Chicago, New Orleans and New York, it is inaccurate to say that the center of greatest activity was developed in New Orleans, or that New Orleans was the birthplace of jazz. Eubie Blake indicated that he heard jazz at an early age, and Duke Ellington also stated that he heard jazz in Washington when only a child. Jazz participants included musicians of many other towns who performed in classical and popular orchestras, at church picnics and in the streets and parks, usually to the appropriately accompanying rhythms and shouts of the dancers. Original instruments were most often homemade or of modern western origin, depending on availability.

Jazz was publicized in the media around 1900. But the popularity of jazz and its origins must be distinguished. Its popularity reached a peak in the 1900's and drew the attention of more of the total populace than ever before. Speculation has since arisen concerning the originators of the name "jazz"; none is conclusive. Unlike the spirituals, the name just happened and no one could say who was responsible. Interviews printed by Rudi Blesh in *They All Played Ragtime* indicated that Blacks themselves named the music before newspapers began to use the term. Jelly Roll Morton also claimed to have originated the term "jazz," in spite of the work of his immediate predecessors.

As to the origin, Samuel Charters published *Jazz: New Orleans* in which he presented letters speculating on the subject. In some 1919 editions of the New York Dramatic Mirror, they stated that any of the following legends might have been responsible for the name:

1. Bert Kelly and his "Jas" Comedy Band";
2. A boy from New Orleans, "Stalebread," and his "Spasm Band";
3. The jazz effects of "Right at Em's Razz Band"; or
4. The various names of the "Negro" orchestras of New Orleans who played at picnics, outings and funerals.

Through evolutionary stages, jazz must surely be older than ninety years. Its origins in blues, spirituals, ballads, coon songs, shouts, jigs and rags were performed long before the title of jazz was given. The forms were definitely perpetuated within minstrel shows and similar places and the religious and secular emotions had long since been a part of the music of minstrelsy, from whose bands jazz was partly derived.

For a long time, there have been diverse opinions about the exact historical periods of jazz, an argument not easily resolved and certainly not intended to be solved here. Yet it is important to know that ın *Jazz: Its Evolution and Essence,* Hodeir categorized jazz into several sections: Primitive (beginning at approximately 1900); Oldtime, Pre-Classical, Classical and Modern, (the latter beginning in 1945). In the *Harvard Dictionary* of *Music,* Willi Apel divided the periods into some five discussions covering stylistic trends of ragtime in 1890, blues, jazz, hot jazz, sweet, boogie (and contrapuntal types, etc.); swing from 1935, and modern. John Mehegan designated 1875 as the beginning of an Archaic period. Tanner and Gerow in their *Jazz,* traced European and African heritages while indicating periodic styles and techniques of basic blues (although they unfortunately do not use blues in the chronological development of jazz). They also discussed jazz from dixieland to third stream. The general disarray of the lists taken from various books, the lack of conformity in describing eras, together with the disagreement of dates, stem both from individual interpretations of the data, and from personal accentuation.

Jazz did not begin suddenly in 1880 if we depend upon the foregoing discussions and include the opinions of musicians and letters of documentation. Its advances were evolutionary. Therefore, the "archaic," "primitive" or ancient origins of jazz should probably cover the earliest roots developed in slavery and minstrelsy. Using African inheritance as the primary source, this first era would overlap with that of minstrelsy and early folk forms, for those minstrels before 1830 used those folk forms and continued to do so after the Civil War. For example, W. C. Handy and Willie (the Lion) Smith related to Leonard Feather the same facts as Eubie Blake. They stated that the music which they heard as children was the same jazz which they improved upon later. The "jazzy" strains of Louis Gottschalk also indicate that he must have heard similar music which influenced him some forty years before Handy and Smith were born.

The second stage of jazz, then, could well begin around Reconstruction when many more Black professionals emerged on stage as performers in their own right, and performed that which they had both heard and practiced themselves. This would be the era of Handy and Smith, George Milburn, James Bland, and Sam Lucas, the latter three of whom were already involved in composing and performing the minstrel-style music which was to directly influence the performance and compositional aspects of jazz.

Eventually others began emphasizing jigs, clogs, shouts, blues, coon songs and ragtime.

By early 1900, a third stage began whose era of achievements and personalities included Louis Armstrong, Duke Ellington, the Johnsons, the Smiths and older musicians who molded jazz into an independent and recognized art form. They practiced dixieland blues and swing styles while continuing to improve upon the rags and other smaller forms.

The span of the 1940's and 1950's saw Charlie Parker, Lionel Hampton, Thelonius Monk, Coleman Hawkins and others who made significant changes in melodic, harmonic and other elemental structures, and who further developed jazz into a more sophisticated type of music. Some of the dance characteristics subsided and gave way to faster tempos and challenging timbres and techniques. However, the 1950's introduced cool, progressive and other modern styles which revolted against the trends of tempos and literal loquaciousness of bop and other forms, while retaining the difficulty of form, timbres and harmonic concepts.

The Influence of Jazz

Once a totally Black involvement, jazz developed a reputation for being loud, bawdy, untamed and low-class. Yet Jazz influenced orchestrations, harmonic outlines, rhythms, forms and titles of both European and American music. Its polyrhythmic, improvisational and constantly syncopated elements also filtered into "chance music" as well as art music and other popular tin pan forms. From the use of the saxophone, the banjo, the expanded ranges and techniques found in some classical symphonic compositions to the characteristic emotions, melodies and harmonies, jazz influenced greatly. Itself influenced by classical music, jazz has reciprocated, encountered, reacted and emerged into a body of sound almost indistinguishable from art music. Some composers of many nationalities who were directly or indirectly influenced by jazz are listed below. As further proof of the jazz influence, Aaron Copland's book, *New Music*, directly shows the scope of this fact during the entire modern period by illustrating certain compositions where jazz is contained and by including himself as one of those influenced by jazz.

Composers and Compositions Influenced by Jazz Elements

Bernstein, Leonard (1918–1990)	*Mass; West Side Story; Concerto for Piano*
Gottschalk, Louis (1829–1869)	*Banjo; Bamboula*
Satie, Erik (1866–1925)	*Parade* (ballet); *Ragtime du Paquebot*
Ravel, Maurice (1875–1937)	*Violin Sonata; Piano Concerto in G*
Stravinsky, Igor (1882–1971)	*Histoire du Soldat; Piano Rag Music; Ragtime for Eleven Instruments*
Milhaud, Darius (1892–1974)	*Scaramouche; La Création du Monde*
Still, William Grant (1895–1978)	*Afro-American Symphony; Three Rhytmic Spirituals*
Gershwin, George(1898–1937)	*Rhapsody in Blue; Porgy and Bess; Three Preludes; Concerto in F*
Chavez, Carlos (1899–1978)	*Fox Blues*
Copland, Aaron (1900–1990)	*Concerto* for piano and orchestra
Krenek, Ernst (1900–)	*Johnny Spielt Auf*
Weill, Kurt (1900–1950)	*Three Penny Opera*

Work, John III (1901–1967)	*Sassafras; Appalachia*
Bonds, Margaret (1913–1972)	*I Got a Home In-a That Rock*
Carter, John (1937–)	*Cantata*
Roldán, Amadeo (1900–1939)	*Rítmicas V y VI; Poema Negro*
Garcia-Caturla, Alejandro (1906–1940)	*Dos Poemas Afro-Cubanos; Danza Negra; Bombe*
Villa-Lobos, Heitor (1887–1959)	*Danzas Africanas*
Carpenter, John Alden (1876–1951)	*Krazy Kat*
Smith, Hale (1925–)	*Nuances; Comes Tomorrow*
Kay, Ulysses (1917–)	*Four Inventions*
Baker, David (1931–)	*Catholic Mass for Peace*
Perkinson, Coleridge-Taylor (1932–)	*Thirteen Love Songs in Jazz Settings*
Da Costa, Noel (1930–)	*Five Verses with Vamps*
Tillis, Frederick (1930–)	*Three Plus One for Guitar, Clarinet and Tape; Sequences and Burlesque*
Anderson, T. J. (1928–)	*Blues* (from *Bagatelles*)
Cunningham, Arthur (1928–)	*Lullabye for a Jazz Baby*
Swanson, Howard (1909–1978)	*Piano Sonata I*
Fax, Mark (1911–1974)	*Three Pieces for Piano*

VIII

JAZZ FORMS, STYLES, TECHNIQUES, AND PERFORMANCE

Forms, styles and techniques are important ingredients for the correct performance of any music. In jazz performance, creativity is supported by compositional, improvisatory and technical skills as well as historical and technical styles being coordinated within a certain framework or construction. Although the history of art music entails similar technical, emotional and formal influences, the ultimate goals and effects of abstract music and jazz differ in that jazz discourages pedantry or strict conformity to set rules.

Form

Form in jazz is not always clearly defined. Nevertheless, it is a most substantial element around which improvisers weave their jazz. Partially defined by its number of measures such as from the 8, 12, 16 or 32 bar schemes, the idea of form in jazz is melded together with the definitions and descriptions of blues, ballads and theme and variation.

Many agree that a number of forms count toward the whole picture of form in jazz composition. In *Jazz: Its Evolution and Essence*, Andre Hodeir talks about "thought" as a "determining ingredient in the process of creative performance" and emphasizes the influence of theme and variation upon jazz improvisation. In *Early Jazz*, Gunther Schuller stresses the "African formal elements of the repeated refrain concept," while Dan Morgenstern, in *An Outline History of Jazz*, points out the forms whose characters retain communicative traits and lend themselves to "almost infinite variation" such as the blues.

The earliest forms consisted of those pieces influenced by traditional calls, hollers, spirituals, blues, work songs and hybrid art music compositions of vocal and instrumental types. Later forms were influenced by marches, preludes, ballads, ternary and binary structures, rhapsodic or fantasy-like pieces, quadrilles, fugues and toccatas. The contemporary era has already witnessed more extended varieties from jazz ballet, operas and symphonies to liturgical masses.

While early jazz sprang from African outgrowths which were directly influenced by the oral tradition, still other aspects of jazz were inherited from European art music. Numerical systems for measures of entire pieces and phrases were borrowed from European standards consisting of eight, twelve or sixteen bars, or symmetry in general. European contributions of harmony also served as the structural basis of more sophisticated forms and of melodic concepts. Dependence upon textual outlines evolved also from Africa such as the call and response, improvisation and other formal elements.

This section has introduced some definitions and general characteristics of form, some related forms pertinent to the historical progression of jazz and the idea of form in "creative thought" performances of jazz. In the following sections, some ancestral forms and musical "offshoots" will be discussed in more detail based on the characteristic styles seen in the works directly preceding and succeeding the origin of the term "jazz."

Ragtime

Emerging from minstrel bands, ragtime was popularized in the late 1800's. It was born earlier than the first published composition by the Black composer, Thomas Turpin, whose *Harlem Rag* was succeeded by many others like Scott Joplin, Jelly Roll Morton, Louis Chauvin, James Scott, Anthony Jackson, Luckey Roberts, James P. Johnson, Bob Caldwell and Fats Waller.

Although having been influenced by singers, bands, banjo and other instruments, the pianist became a preferred substitute for familiar minstrel ensembles at clubs and cabarets. Primarily because of economics, this caused the piano to ultimately dominate ragtime at one time. Yet it was clear that the piano style became unique only after its associations with the "missing" instruments which it imitated.

At one time, ragtime could have been synonymous with the music called jazz. Rudi Blesh stated that "Negro ragtime was essentially an instance of racial improvisation" while H. E. Krehbiel, in the preface of his *Afro-American Folksongs*, felt that rag was a debased form of the spiritual. Some others referred to rag as "clogging," "shuffling" or "swinging," all terms of which partly defined certain aspects of minstrelsy as well as jazz. Besides the elements of improvisation, ragtime was also composed music, much of which was written and performed by outstanding Black musicians.

Ragtime was both classically and popularly oriented. Some composers of the form termed it "classical" music. Not only was it influenced by the styles of the nineteenth century concepts of the quadrilles, marches and other solo pieces, but also by the coon songs, shouts, clogs, jigs, ballads, banjo pieces, country dances and so-called "barrelhouse rhythms" of the Blacks. Ragtime was often a multi-sectional composition, representative of many piano solo pieces of the nineteenth century, usually written in 2/4.

Ragtime was technically difficult, and consisted of eighth note or sixteenth note figurations above a walking, "um pah" bass, whose main beats and frames were quite march-like. Its rhythm was frequently that of the "cake-walk" (♪♩♪). Generally, the melody was syncopated or dotted and was ornamented above a bass which jumped about from register to register. Sometimes the bass made use of double octaves or single tones in sounding the root on the first and third beats, and alternated with the other chord tones on the second and fourth beats. Another feature of the bass line was the inclusion of the tenth with the root and third or fifth of the chord being played simultaneously with one hand. Still other examples, as in the music of Joplin and James Johnson, resembled "etudes" or studies similar to art music examples of the nineteenth century, particularly the A and E Minor *Etudes* of Frederick Chopin, as compared in Examples 22 and 23:

The "walking" characteristic found in ragtime involved a manner of accenting the offbeat of the bass pattern, especially when played in tenths. This was referred to as "stride" piano. It involved mainly diatonic movement in the left hand, and often was accompanied by foot stamping. In his *Ragtime Instruction Book*, Joplin instructed that rags were not to be played at a fast tempo. Discussions of tempo by other composers instructed one to play either fast or slow. Since "stride" implied a walking gait, the term

Ex. 22. Ragtime techniques.

Etudes in A and E Minor, Opus 25, Nos. 4 and 5, Chopin.

Ex. 23. Walking basses

necessarily depended upon whoever did the "walking" and therefore left a problem as to approximate tempos. However, stride did resemble a proud, show-off manner of performance, thus perhaps implying a maestoso movement, as illustrated in Example 23. (Also see Billy Taylor's *Jazz Piano*).

In addition to being played by small band ensembles or piano, ragtime music was also sung, particularly as in minstrel and vaudeville ballads. *Ragtime Songbooks* listed a vocal version of Scott Joplin's *Maple Leaf Rag* in comic lyrics, shown in Example 24, which makes use of the same theme as in the piano version of Example 31.

Ex. 24. *Maple Leaf Rag*, vocal version, Joplin. © Copyright, Edward B. Marks Music Corporation. Used by permission.

Blues

Perhaps the blues has influenced jazz more than any other form. So great has been this association that the very soul of jazz has been primarily defined around it, sometimes under the guise of "soul music". When W. C. Handy published his *Memphis Blues* and his *Saint Louis Blues*, the blues gained unexpected publicity which highlighted and promoted it to a position above that which had not been seen for decades in the minstrel shows. There is no question as to the validity of contributions from both the older, rural type (solo, ballad, or free form, "sung speech") and the urban type (classic form of 12 bars with instrumental "breaks" improvised).

Virtually a vocal form, the blues was born years before the birth of Handy, and was derived from the same emotional and environmental experiences as those which produced the work songs, spirituals, calls and hollers. Its popularity, however, did not occur until around 1915, somewhat overshadowing the craze for ragtime. The blues has never yet released its effect of melodic, harmonic and emotional concepts from the entities of jazz styles.

Generally secular, the words were important to the blues. Into the blues went both the religious and secular moods of Blacks. For as a man felt, he played and composed. Ecstatic emotions of the church gleaned from the belief in a Deliverer were coupled with the bewilderment of a lost love. Topical developments ranged from the time of day to the position of an individual in society. And politics, segregation, housing, WPA and the depression were pitted against the accompaniment of musical prayers exhibited in up-tempo "blue jazz" processions for funerals.

It is interesting to note that recorded evidence strongly resembling both gospel and jazz fused with blues elements have been collected from various church services by Lomax, Spivacke and others. Their performances, instrumentations and emotions bordered on the secular forms. Some of these examples were entitled *Wasn't That a Mighty Storm, Certainly, Lord, Oh, The Lamb of God, The Lord Done Sanctified Me* and *Do Lord, Remember Me*. The fact could not be ignored that some of the blues and jazz sessions were about as "sanctified" in spirit as were these religious songs, and that the religious songs, when slow, were just as "bluesy" as the blues.

Exceptions to the contrary, standard blues form usually consisted of twelve measures, having three lines of poetry whose first and second lines were identical. An illustration of both the "classic" structure and the poetic form are shown in Example 25, a frame common in urban blues.

Ex. 25. 12-bar blues with melodic outline and poetic scheme (classic form).

Woke up dis mawning, found m' baby gone,
Woke up dis mawning, found m' baby gone,
If she went to stay, I won't be here too long.

A great variety of blues forms consisted of two-part, three-part, or small through-composed forms. Some blues contained as many as 32 measures, or as few as eight. Ballads, spiritual and strophic forms were also used. This variety was common practice in country or rural blues.

The blues made use of "blue notes," so named to denote sad or mournful qualities and were chromatic-like or semi-tone waverings between major and minor thirds, or simply the lowering of the third and seventh of a scale. Mainly derived from African scales and vocal approximations of tones, this was a natural characteristic inherent in the language and the ornamented melodic lines.

Blues melodies served as the focal point of interest, but also suggested the harmonic punctuations of the accompaniment. Most often of a homophonic or chordal texture, the form made use of tonal chord progressions in support of generally small melodic intervals, occasionally interspersed with larger skips of sevenths, fourths, fifths and octaves. The commonest progressions were I, IV, I, V, I or later, 17, IV7, V7, IV7, 17. As in the case of many Afro-American songs, the blues showed a strong preference for thirds, particularly in the cadential or ending patterns. Some of the musical characteristics discussed here are shown in Example 26.

Ex. 26. Blues progressions, harmonic, melodic, cadential.

a. simple chords
b. complex chords
c. melodic idioms
d. cadential patterns

The new "rhythm and blues" pointed out the importance of the musical element of movement with emotion, a closer harmonic base to jazz complexities and more instrumental qualities. Next to the text, all blues forms revealed the nature of spontaneous rhythm from a spoken language. Not altogether as simple as its verse, however, blues rhythms were composed in long notes such as whole, halves, quarters and eighths, which in actual performance, were intended to be improvised into shorter ornamental note values. Triplets, mixtures of rests in elongated or syncopated fashion, sixteenths and thirty-second notes were also sparingly used, except in ornamentation. Although most blues appeared in duple meter and also retained the same meter throughout, rare cases of frequently changing meters within the short tunes were used. The following chart shows some of the rhythmic practices of blues which were ultimately used and rejuvenated by jazz performers and composers.

Ex. 27. Chart of blues rhythms.

Boogie-Woogie

According to Big Bill Broonzy (*Big Bill Blues* by Bruynoghe), "boogie" was originally a dance which was popular even during his uncle's generation of the early 1800's. Around 1930, ragtime was supplanted by the boogie-woogie as still another piano style. A rowdy, fun-type composition, the boogie seemed unrelated to the heartfelt emotions of the blues or the whines of calls and hollers, and rather lent itself to a complete abandonment of the weariness of foregoing centuries and encouraged an optimistic anticipation of newer things to come.

Partly derived from guitar principles as well as other instrumental timbres, boogie was sometimes used in vocal ballads as accompaniment figures or as a spontaneous technique to excite one to dance the "huckle-buck" or the "jitterbug." Beside the ballad-type structure, there were original, through-composed compositions and some in ternary form. Boogie-woogie forms further consisted of "ostinato" principles which were repeated short bass figurations of eight eighth notes per measure.

The "jumping" or "bouncing" quality of boogie rhythms was conceived by simply dotting the bass notes, as in ragtime, or by using jagged rhythms in the melody as well. Even when the score did not indicate the dotted effects, it was expected in the actual performance. Written in duple time, boogie concentrated its efforts upon an ornamental melody above swiftly moving progressions of tonic, sub-dominant and tonic (I, IV, I, V, I or I, IV, V7, I), usually with an addition of seventh tones.

Technically, boogie basses were not too unlike some octaves, tremolos and arpeggios used in Beethoven or Mozart sonatas. It was also similar to ragtime techniques. Yet the rotating sound of the boogie was far more comprehensible and manageable than either the bass of ragtime or the sonatas of the Classical composers. The most common of boogie patterns are shown in Example 28; they were either alternated within sections, or one pattern was continued throughout the composition.

Ex. 28. Boogie patterns.

Gospel

Gospel music, a vocal form used mainly for church worship but also found in night clubs and concert halls, originated before its popularity in the 1920's. Perhaps more often a technique than an original form, gospels were nevertheless products interwoven with the forms of the blues, spirituals and the sanctified shout. Gospels differed from spirituals in that they did not bear the simplicity of style of the older songs. They were not used as protest or survival songs and were directed toward revelation, evangelical teachings, revivalism and good will. They stressed the "coming of the Lord" and were not sung with ambiguity or allegory. A happy spirit and one's soulful worth were intentionally stressed—a fact generally also true of older jubilees.

Indubitably, the most important characteristic of gospel music was the word communication. Deriving its messages from late Biblical (New Testament) or original sources, either narrative or ornamental techniques of the blues and folk songs were common. The use of word interpolations between lines such as "ummm," "Lord," "oh," "yes" and other phrases was typical. Unquestionably, words determined the ultimate style of the melodic line and their meaning would direct the corresponding rise and fall of the pitches. Directly related to the words, the element of emotion was next in importance to these songs which sought to save the soul.

Tambourines, guitars, trombones, clarinets, organs and pianos were generally most frequently used as accompanying media when the compositions were not performed in "a cappella" fashion. Clapping, an African concept of drumming, also accompanied the voices. Harmonically, gospels were tonal, and were not much influenced by atonal harmonies of the 1900's. By 1960, however, gospel/jazz chords employed almost constant seventh and ninth chords, somewhat paralleling the compositional trends of other contemporary music, from strophic to ballad types.

Rhythmically, jazz penetrated gospel in syncopated techniques, accents and complex polyphony. The use of obligatos melded into the polyrhythmic patterns. Basically, however, gospel was homophonic. Some of the most characteristic techniques have included dotted notes and frequent instrumental "breaks." Whether or not gospel was simply the name for church or liturgical jazz, the subject became one of conflict mainly because of its rhythmic factors which inspired close similarity to rhythms of shouts as well as other dances. The interpolation of many improvisations became standard means by which triplet figures or sixteenths and eighths against the quarter caused the dance-like spirit as shown in Example 29.

Ex. 29. Gospel techniques (rhythmic and melodic).

a. Original hymn tune
b. Gospel improvisation

Rock

Rock and Roll was a later outgrowth of jazz. Designed primarily for dance, its popularity became real during the early 1950's. Greatly influenced by the boogie-woogie and blues, it settled into the style and presentation of gospel music. Like gospel, the most important aspect of rock was the message and the emotion of high-pitched sounds and loud dynamics. Based on secular subjects, rock expanded and capitalized upon interpolation, fragments and additions to lines of poetry such as in gospel. Entire structures could be based upon expansions of words such as "Oh Yeah," "Babeeee," "Uh" and "Uh Huh," sung in either a fluid melismatic style or in a hollering production.

The harmony of rock emphasized the tonic and subdominant chords, and generally terminated with the plagal cadence of IV to I, or it could follow the standard classical pattern of I, IV, V, I. In general, these harmonic trends were the same as in gospels.

Before the popularity of Aretha Franklin and Jimi Hendrix, rock was stylistically simpler, its use of harmony less sophisticated. Originally for dance, it has now grown to include music for listening, and the sounds of the electronic and space age have furthermore rendered the form more interesting. Once commonly performed as a vocal group or soloist with a small rhythm section of drums, piano and guitar, the media has now expanded into using more woodwinds and brass, strings (as in the case of John Creach) and film (videos).

The form of rock was built around ballads or tin pan alley. Like the gospels, it also resembled the blues in its waverings of pitch with short sections, or within strophic or free-style forms. The use of instruments, in addition to accompanying the voice, also expanded the form with short introductions or by engaging in "breaks" or interludes during the progress of the songs.

Gospels, rock, blues, boogie, and ragtime, although complete entities, have nevertheless formed a union of relative kinship to formulate the principles of great variety and similarity. The term rock implied "hardness," durability and "swing." Even the church sang of "Rock-a My Soul," "solid rock" and "Let the Church Roll On!" No one can deny the latter force of swing as seen in "Take Me to the Water."

Styles and Techniques

Style, a characteristic way of writing or performing music, was interrelated with technique, a mastery of the overall skills practiced in various types of jazz performance and composition. Thus, style and technique involved a method of procedure as well as a manipulation of idioms. In addition to forms, the history of jazz also represented evolutionary styles and techniques of respective composers as well as a tradition of performance bound by the emotions of each. Since musical developments in the past have sometimes resulted from revolt against the emotions, styles and techniques of the preceding generation, the philosophy and practice of jazz musicians were no exceptions to this rule.

Many of the jazz idioms were difficult and varied enough to indicate concepts of subjective performance. Some of the most common of these styles could apply to more than one kind of music, and their terms implied as much emotion as form. For example, "sweet," "hot," "funky" and "cool" were descriptive words meaning pleasantness, improvisation and earthy activity, and the relaxed, subdued dynamics or emotions, respectively. These were aspects of style which could be determined by actually playing in a certain way and had to be considered in the following not only as forms, but as "up-tempo" and happy emotions.

"Dixieland" was developed between the 1890's and the 1900's, and may or may not have been chiefly the result of White achievement. Directly related to ragtime, it influenced most styles within the era of ragtime and blues, until it was replaced by the Chicago type around 1920. Based on individualism and melodic concepts, it resembled counterpoint of the Baroque period in its overall effects, but was a tonal example of band ensemble in jazz action. Besides its melodic make-up, timbre was important to the sound of dixieland, whose early instrumentation consisted of a lead clarinet, a melodic cornet or trumpet and the trombone, tuba, banjo and drum. In Chicago, the piano and saxophone were added, and the guitar replaced the banjo. Particularly in dixieland, the clarinet served as one of the melody instruments whose rule it was to play eighth notes around the harmonies of the other instruments. The structure eventually sponsored ensemble playing against solo improvisations, but the outlines of the works were written out for the players to follow.

"Hot jazz" consisted of an exciting, energetic style of freedom to interpolate, to manipulate and to improvise. Made famous in the early 1920's, Louis Armstrong and others practiced the art. Hot jazz simplified harmonies, made use of "scat singing" or nonsense syllables, vibrato, piercing tones, high-pitched cadences and interrelated vocal aspects with those of instrumental ones. Although bands were directly involved with the style, the "hotness" of the era also penetrated piano and vocal styles, as well as categories of instruments dominated by the trumpet.

"Swing" was a term which defined motion for the set undertaking of big bands made popular during the 1930's. Its organization was larger than previous band ensembles, and it emphasized sections rather than single instruments; however, some solos were planned against a section. Generally, swing included brasses, woodwinds and percussion, the latter section of which consisted of the drums with piano, string bass and other varieties such as the vibraharp. Primarily designed for dances, swing was meant for the accompaniment of the two-step and other popular dances of the "charleston" days, and was usually composed in steady, duple time.

"Bebop" was another intense emotion of popular form which was developed during the 1940's and extended into the 1950's. With the efforts of Charlie Parker and Dizzy Gillespie, followed by Thelonius Monk, Charlie Christian, Bud Powell and others, there began an emphasis upon improvisation, technique and faster tempos. Bop was characterized by the use of nonsensical language such as "Hey Boppa Rebop," being sung to the accompaniment of instruments, but used as either rhythm or expressions of joy. Accompanying accessories to the music were the unusual clothes worn. Sunglasses, berets and short beards were common to the "hip," "knowledgeable" and "sharp" kind of music that was bop.

Bop was instrumental in returning to the melodic emphasis of instruments, instead of continuing the sectional and large ensembles of swing and was also more technical. It was also important to the preparation of more complex harmonies such as elevenths, thirteenths and dissonances in general. The ultimate aims directed themselves toward more difficult "classical" concepts of higher forms so to impress and inspire a listening audience to dwell on things intellectual, as well as the speed.

After 1940, jazz became more polished, developed, difficult, and of greater variety than its predecessors. Greater independence of form and technique were established while retaining some basic characteristics of its origins. Whereas simpler rules had governed many of the older forms, varieties of devices such as contrary motion, polyphony and obligatos were now employed. Other features were extensions of melodic ranges and unisons. Instrumental styles promoted expanded registers; broken octaves transferred to melodic elements, with more grace notes, more solo emphasis, closer chord clusters, block chords and unique endings. Independence of parts and of inner voices were developed which were compelled to last longer than any time before, and with breathless urgency, jazz grew into a most complicated art form.

Performance

Performance involved a reconstructing of the music and an enlivening of the printed intentions of the composer. Therefore, all of the skills of jazz from ornamentation, basic progressions and even to the methods of decorum had to be perfected in order to begin, to sustain the interest of listeners and to terminate in a proper jazz style.

The best performer was one who was aware of the materials which a composer had at his disposal such as melody, harmony, etc. He was aware of their function, texture, balance and emotion. He concerned himself with improvisational skills, the reading of scores and a knowledge of composition.

Each successive era created greater demands on performance. Consequently, the best performers met the challenge by a ready knowledge of score reading, improvising written and unwritten music and developing instrumental or vocal skills as demanded by the musical materials. Amazingly, some Black performers developed fantastic skills without much formal study. Others, however, found that both the music and the competition were soon so strong that it was wiser to depend less on talent alone. Many of these performers became scholars of composition and have distinguished themselves as composers.

Of all the aspects of jazz, its rhythm was the most exciting and perhaps the most difficult of all of the elements to perform. One therefore had to be keenly aware and responsive to rhythmic alterations of dotting, augmenting and diminishing. It was the responsibility of the performer to practice all of the perfections in rhythm such as polymeters and polyrhythms. At first in duple time, jazz later included other meters, and by the era of cool and progressive, used multimeters or polymeters in rapid exchange.

Improvisation was the next most difficult feat to develop, since this required a knowledge of chords, scales, melodic direction and imagination. Symbols and other developments in art music from the Classical period to that of Charles Ives and Igor Stravinsky of the modern period influenced labels in jazz. Some others were defined differently. The varieties of chords, although derived from the same bass outlines and inversions, were depicted in many of the progressions shown in Example 30.

Ex. 30. Jazz techniques in performance.

Code: M = major; m = minor; O – diminished; O = half-diminished; + = augmented

IX

COMPOSERS OF JAZZ AND ITS ALLIED FORMS

Jazz and its allied forms refer to secular and religious genders which are closely connected in somewhat parallel background developments. Composers of such genre who are contained within this chapter are represented by only a few in number. Complete documents of the earliest oral-tradition slave composers were not recorded in written history since many were found in plantation performances, minstrel shows, dance halls, outings and churches. Much of their music was performed but not necessarily written.

Composers of Jazz

Composers in early jazz and minstrelsy numbered quite a few. In part, they were Richard Milburn, William Turk, Sammy Ewell, (One-Leg) Willie Joseph, Jack The Bear, William Tyers, Blind Boone, Richard McLean, Plunk Henry and others. Some were born in the late 1800's or early 1900's. These were Thomas Turpin, Bob Caldwell, Stephen (Beetle) Henderson, (Piano) Price Davis, Tony Jackson, Sammy Davis, Jelly Roll Morton, Scott Joplin, Scott Hayden, Luckey Roberts, Arthur Marshall, James Scott and Louis Chauvin and Artie Matthews. Their successors were Willie (the Lion)

Bunk Johnson and Huddie Leadbetter. William P. Gottlieb, Photographer.

Smith, Eubie Blake, James P. Johnson, Bunk Johnson, Ma Rainey, Bessie Smith, Huddie Ledbetter, Alberta Hunter, Ivie Anderson, and Helen Humes, Victoria Spivey, Fats Waller, James Sylvester, Clarence Williams, and Fletcher Henderson.

SCOTT JOPLIN (1868–1917)

Scott Joplin, around whose dates ragtime flourished, was the most outstanding composer, conductor and rag pianist of the late 1800's. Born in Texarkana, Texas, he lived in Sedalia, Missouri, before traveling to Saint Louis, Chicago and New York. As the teacher of Scott Hayden and Arthur Marshall, he was largely self-taught, but had some lessons in piano, harmony and sight-reading from a local musician. It is doubtful that he studied with Chauvin (1880–1908), except in a reciprocal association, as some sources seem to indicate. Chauvin and Joplin definitely collaborated in Saint Louis, where they both served as pianists at cafes, clubs and other places. Joplin also conducted the St. Louis World's Fair Orchestra in 1893, and was generally rated above the other local composers.

Recently, a revival of ragtime was made possible through the discoveries of his works, one of which was the opera *Treemonisha*, which enjoyed a premier performance in Atlanta, Georgia (with T. J. Anderson as the orchestrator). The staging was quickly followed by a program at the Wolftrap Center in Washington, D.C., and rags in movies.

Scott Joplin. Courtesy of Fisk University Library.

Sometimes called the "Apostle of rag" or "Rag King," Joplin produced more than fifty rags and light classics, many of which were published, and some of which were given to the Fisk University Library to be microfilmed and catalogued in the Special Collections Room. Like Tom Turpin, Luckey Roberts, Blind Boone, Eubie Blake and others, he felt that some of the ragtime music was classical and of European style. But his music was not as readily accepted in art music as were Gershwin's *Three Preludes*, Debussy's *Golliwog's Cakewalk* or examples by other White composers whose positions in society allowed them easy accessibility into professional musical circles. Some of Joplin's pieces resembled country dances, waltzes and pieces common to art music. Yet the consistent syncopations, dotted notes and "buck and wing" dance styles offered somewhat less variety than many of those by the above European composers. Nevertheless some of his compositions employed the same concepts as classical etudes or studies (Example 24), and as seen in his *Ragtime Instruction Book*, were equally difficult to perform. In his efforts to command respectability for his music, he objected to some of the "scat singing" and dirty word contexts of some rags.

One of the most famous of his piano rags was the *Maple Leaf Rag* in Ab major (Example 31, first sixteen bars). Structured into five sections with an emphasis upon the sub-dominant key in the fourth section, the work makes use of 2/4 meter, sixteenth note figurations of the right hand with sporadic chords being superimposed over a bass line of four eighth notes comprised of octaves and chords in alternation.

Ex. 31. *Maple Leaf Rag*, Joplin, Copyright Edward B. Marks Music Corporation. Used by permission.

Some of Joplin's works were: *Sunflower Rag, School of Ragtime, Maple Leaf Rag, Palm Leaf Rag, Euphonic Sounds, Pineapple Rag, Sugar Cane Rag,*

Country Club Rag, Wall Street Rag, Pleasant Moments, Solace, Frolic of the Bars, Kismet Rag, Entertainer Rag, Original Rag, Treemonisha, Magnetic Rag, Hilarity Rag, Frogs Leg Rag, A Picture of Her Face (waltz), *Please Say You Will, Mississippi Rag, The Great Crush Collision March, Combination March, Harmony Waltz, Swipsy Cakewalk, Sunflower Slow Drag, Peacherine Rag, The Easy Winners, Augustan Club Waltzes, I'm Thinking of My Pickanniny Days, A Breeze From Alabama, Cleopha Two-Step, March Majestic, Ragtime Dance, Elite Syncopations, The Entertainer, A Guest of Honor, The Strenuous Life, Weeping Willow, Something Doing, Little Black Boy, The Cascades, Heliotrope Bouquet* and *Stoptime Rag.*

THOMAS M. TURPIN (1873–1922)

A significant pioneer who both influenced and inspired others to optimistic careers was Thomas M. Turpin. Born in Atlanta, Georgia, after the Civil War, he later moved to Saint Louis, Missouri, where he indulged in politics as well as music. Turpin was important because he was not only a competent composer, but was the first to publish a ragtime composition, *Harlem Rag*, which began the promotion and craze of the early jazz form. Published in 1897, it was succeeded by his *Bowery Buck, Ragtime Nightmare, St. Louis Rag, Buffalo, Siwash-Indiana Rag, Pan-Am Rag*, and *When Sambo Goes to France.*

WILLIAM CHRISTOPHER HANDY (1873–1958)

William C. Handy was born shortly after Scott Joplin, but earned his fame as "Father of the Blues" when he became the first publisher of written blues. Born in Florence, Alabama, he later settled in Memphis, Tennessee, where he was a band director, composer and performer. Even though Handy was a teacher, his education was mostly gained in the public schools. He nevertheless became one of the giants in the field of popular music, and his talents were recognized for his arrangements of music from jazz to Black spirituals.

During his career, Handy became a member of NAACC, led the Mahara Minstrels, made various recordings, ran a publishing house in New York (where he died), and was also able to find time for writing not only the music scores themselves, but books about music in general. He wrote his own autobiography called *Father of the Blues* and various articles. He compiled a list of musicians and their works and generally educated the public about the achievements of Blacks. His fame, however, came mainly from his conducting of the band which he led on tour until he became blind and ceased to perform. He was also an accomplished cornet player. A statue of Handy with his cornet is located in the Handy Park at Memphis, Tennessee.

W. C. Handy. Courtesy of Duncan Schiedt, Photographer.

Handy used African and American characteristics in his music, as reflected in blues features and harmonic outlines. He emphasized the lowered third and seventh, and frequently slurred between the major and minor modes. In addition to the blues, he wrote marches, pieces for the orchestra, piano, voice, chorus and various arrangements for many media.

Among his compositions are: *Memphis Blues, Saint Louis Blues, Beale Street Blues, John Henry Blues, Harlem Blues, The Temple of Music* for chorus, *They That Sow in Tears* for chorus, *Opportunity, Pasadena, When the Black Man Has a Nation of His Own, Who Was the Husband of Aunt Jemima? Mr. Crump, Joe Turner Blues, Careless Love, Hail to the Spirit of Freedom, The Big Stick Blues March, Blue-Destiny Symphony, Afro-American Hymn, Oh, Didn't He Ramble? Black Patti* (of Siseretta Jones), *East St. Louis, Friendless Blues, Basement Blues,*

Goin' to See My Sarah, Golden Brown Blues, Hawaiian Guitar (Blues Album), *Hist de Window, Noah, Nigrita, Mozambique, The Bridegroom Has Done Come, Give Me Jesus, Yellow Dog Blues, Hesitating Blues, John Henry*; the musicals *Opportunity* and *Gettysburg Address*; the collections *Treasury of the Blues, Negro Spirituals* and *Book of Negro Spirituals*, and the book *Negro Music and Musicians*.

FERDINAND (JELLY ROLL) MORTON (1885–1941)

Ferdinand Morton, born Ferdinand La Menthe, was an arranger, composer, conductor, singer and pianist. He was primarily a rag pianist. A native of New Orleans, he died in Los Angeles after having lived in New York and Washington, D.C. While the popularity of rag lasted until about 1915, Morton's life extended beyond this, thereby frustrating his last efforts to prolong the waning span of the rag style while attempting to shift to elements of jazz and blues. Although a talented person who evolved from the classics to jazz, his style was perhaps too classical too soon to be appreciated by the new jazz audiences. For the major changes in concept and style toward classicism *per se* were only accepted after his death.

A member of ASCAP in 1939, Morton was educated in New Orleans through private lessons. He was greatly influenced by Tony Jackson, another rag composer. He practiced the French, African and Spanish dances as well as the technical exercises and feats common to the formal study of

Ferdinand (Jelly Roll) Morton. The Amistad Research Center, Tulane University; New Orleans, Louisiana.

music. In addition, Langston Hughes pointed out in his *Famous Negro Music Makers*, that Morton must also have been influenced by the guitar literature which he played from time to time. His band, J. R. Morton's "Red Hot Peppers" and his own composing-performing talents kept him busy in the cabarets, clubs, theatres and recording sessions until his later years. He accompanied and played solos in New York, New Orleans and other cities, after which time he traveled to Washington and California. Much of his venturous styles in music were recorded by the Library of Congress. This recording was labeled *The Saga*.

Among Morton's many works were *The Tiger Rag, The King Porter Stomp, Milnebury Joys, Wolvering Blues, Wild Man Blues, Kansas City Stomp, Mournful Serenade, Shreveport Stomp, Ponchartrain Blues, Jelly Roll Blues, Whinin' Boy Blue, The Pearls, Shoe Shiners' Drag* (London Blues), *The Crave, Buddy Bolden's Blues, Perfect Rag, Fro-i-more Rag, Mama'nita, Grandpa's Spells* and *Original Jelly Roll.*

JAMES P. JOHNSON (1891–1955)

James P. Johnson, pianist-composer of rags and early jazz ballads, was born in New Brunswick, New Jersey. He was hailed as the "Grandfather of Harlem Piano" or "hot piano" and as one who established many of the techniques which distinguished him from the "chaff." Johnson was not only competent in jazz where his reputation was made, but in classical music as well, and he was naturally responsible for influencing the techniques of other musicians. Having been taught by his mother and Bruto Giannini, he in turn taught Thomas Waller, influenced Edward Ellington and generally flourished as an accompanist to Bessie Smith, Ethel Waters, Mamie Smith, Laura Smith and others.

Johnson also made many piano rolls for the player piano. In his style of the "stride" piano, which he originated, he employed techniques of a heavy left hand in alternation of single roots and accented, offbeat chords in an exciting accompaniment to a syncopated melody. He toured Europe with the *Plantation Days* cast, formed his own band at the Clef Club during the 1920's and played at summer resorts, theatres, and night clubs.

Johnson was educated through private study and the New York public schools. In 1926, he became a member of ASCAP. Among his collaborators were Mike Riley, Nelson Cogane and Cecil Mack. His own works included: *Symphonic Harlem, Symphony in Brown, African Drums, Piano Concerto in Ab, Mississippi Moon, Yamacraw* (a Negro *Rhapsody*), *Symphonic Suite on St. Louis Blues, City of Steel, De Organizer* (folk opera), *Kitchen Opera* (operetta), *The Husband* (operetta), *Manhattan Street Scene* (ballet), *Sefronia's Dream* (ballet), *Old Fashioned Love, Don't Cry, Baby, Charleston, If I Could Be With You One Hour Tonight, Stop It, Joe, Mama and Papa Blues, Hey, Hey, Running Wild, Porter's Love Song to A Chambermaid, Snowy Morning Blues, Eccentricity Waltz, Carolina Shout, Keep Off the Grass, Yours All Yours, I was So Weak, Love Was So Strong, Aincha Got Music, Stop That Dog, There Goes My Headache, Rhythm Drums, Caprice Rag, Daintiness Rag, Riff,* and *Sugar Hill.*

CLARENCE WILLIAMS (1898–1965)

Clarence Williams, a pianist-composer, arranger, publisher and orchestra leader, was born in New Orleans and traveled to New York at the age of 19. Williams worked in New Orleans in the Main District before joining other jazz groups. Williams did sing, too, but it is reported that his artistry as an accompanist for other singers was greater. He accompanied Ethel Waters, Bessie Smith, Clara Smith, Rev. J. C. Burnette, Peg Leg Howell, Willie Jackson, and George Williams. In addition to performing on stage and in recording sessions, Williams became a pioneer pianist in the small band ensembles and a solo pianist in his own right.

Among his works were *Baby, Won't You Please Come Home, Sugar Blues, I Ain't Gonna Give Nobody None of My Jelly Roll, You Can Have It, I Don't Want It, If You Don't Believe I Love You, Gulf Coast Blues, Squeeze Me, Sister Kate*, and *Royal Garden Blues*.

FLETCHER HENDERSON (1898–1952)

Fletcher Henderson, a native of Cuthbert, Georgia, earned a degree in chemistry from Atlanta University, but also became an accomplished director of orchestras, an accompanist for the Black Swan Troubadours, a song demonstrator and a band director and pianist. A member of the Harlem Symphony, Henderson performed at many of the famous clubs, theaters and cabarets. He accompanied vocal recitals by Bessie Smith, Clara Smith, Ma Rainey, Ida Cox and Ethel Waters. Henderson's fame, however, came from his innovations in the jazz bands where he led his own ensemble into the "swinging" hot jazz types of New Orleans-style dixieland.

Formal orchestration was his main strength, and according to some sources, he was responsible for setting aside breaks for improvisation within a written composition. He also used the instruments with an individuality uncommon to the mass ensembles before him, wherein sections for instrumental blocks were placed one against the other in alternation. New Yorkers were treated to years of good music through his arrangements and original compositions. He played in the Benny Goodman Orchestra for a few years. In his own band, Fletcher worked with some of the other jazz greats such as Louis Armstrong. Since Henderson produced more arranged works than original works, there was some confusion over which of those attributed to him were really original. Among his own works, however, were *Body and Soul, Down Home Blues* and *King Porter Stomp*.

EDWARD KENNEDY (DUKE) ELLINGTON (1899–1974)

Edward Ellington, a composer-pianist, arranger and band leader, was born in Washington, D.C. A fantastic giant of the jazz world, he bridged the era from Jelly Roll Morton to Ornette Coleman. By conducting several tours throughout Europe, the United States and other countries, he steadily became a proud legend for this nation.

A member of ASCAP since 1953, he was educated in the Washington public schools, and also studied piano with Henry Grant. Two Black composers whom he favored were Will M. Cook and Will Vodery. Having influenced others, he continued his efforts through the tradition of jazz, commanding the respect of many and never remaining in one musical position. Wilberforce University, Morgan State College, Fisk University and Milton College were among those who awarded honorary degrees to Ellington, and his seventieth birthday celebration was held at the White House.

Ellington's compositional styles ranged from ballad type songs with lyrics to the big-band arrangements for which he was best known. His innovations even led him into large classical art forms such as the liturgical mass. In addition to his original compositions, he arranged works by Grieg

Edward (Duke) Ellington receives an honorary degree from Morgan State College. Courtesy of Maurice Strider.

and Tchaikovsky for jazz orchestras and also wrote pieces for voice, piano, band and other media. His collaborators included the late Toby Hardwick, among others.

Ellington's works include *Bird of Paradise, Black and Tan Fantasy, Don't You Know I Care (Don't You Care to Know), Black, Brown and Beige, Deep South Suite, New World A-Comin', Sepia Panorama, A Drum Is a Woman, Harlem, Suite Thursday, Liberian Suite, Shakespearean Suite, My People, Night Creatures, Non-Violent Integration, Blind Man's Bluff, Sophisticated Lady, Mood Indigo, Creole Love Call, Crescendo in Blue, Christmas Surprise, The Mooche, Prelude to a Kiss, Satin Doll, The Blues, Mass*, Tchaikovsky-Ellington's *Nutcracker Suite*, Grieg-Ellington's *Peer Gynt Suite*; film scores to *Anatomy of a Murder, Jump For Joy, Beggar's Holiday*; and *Paris Blues.*

DANIEL LOUIS (SATCHMO) ARMSTRONG (1900–1971)

Louis Armstrong was a composer-performer of the "hot" jazz tradition. A trumpeter born in New Orleans, Louisiana, he was afforded opportunities at an early age to study various instruments at a Waifs' Home in New Orleans, and to continue his experiences first as an apprentice and later as the top attraction of such famous bands as King Oliver's Creole Band, Fletcher Henderson's Band, Kid Ory's Band and his own groups, the Hot Five and the Sunset Cafe Stompers.

With celebrated artists such as Ma Rainey and Bessie Smith, Dave Brubeck, Duke Ellington and Fats Waller, Armstrong did several recordings, concerts and festival performances. Along with his world tours from Russia to Australia have been his famous concerts in America at the Metropolitan Opera House, Carnegie Hall, the Apollo, and Connie's Inn, to name only a few. Among the several movies and Broadway shows in which

Louis Armstrong. Hogan Jazz Archives, Tulane University, New Orleans, La.

Armstrong appeared were *Hello Dolly* with Barbra Streisand, *Pennies from Heaven* with Bing Crosby and *Connie's Hot Chocolates*.

Although more famous for his technical flair and the clear, penetrating sound of his instrument, Armstrong also was instrumental in providing extended compositional skills, ranges and idioms for the trumpet which were uncommon at one time. A leader in a real sense of the oral tradition of Blacks, he often sang to demonstrate this speech communication, and followed it with an imitation on the trumpet. As illustrated in his performances, he made frequent use of ornamentations, improvisation, short trills, some triplets and mainly simplicity of style. However, the spirit of his style influenced perhaps more jazz artists than almost any other pioneer in that field.

Among his arrangements and original works were some 50 recordings including *Everybody Loves My Baby, How Come You Do Me Like You Do, Big Butter and Egg Man From the West; 50 Hot Choruses for Cornet, Weather Bird Rag, Sister Kate, Dippermouth Blues, Potato Head Rag; Some Day; Don't Jive Me; Cornet Chop Suey*; and *Yes I'm in the Barrel*.

THOMAS (FATS) WALLER (1904–1943)

Thomas Waller, a pianist-composer, singer and vaudeville participant, was born in New York and died in Kansas City. An accomplished pianist, he engaged in solo playing, accompanying and recording. He worked as piano accompanist with Florence Mills, Bessie Smith, and also played the organ. Waller was perhaps the first to play jazz publicly on the Hammond and pipe organs. Virtually a legend in the world of jazz, he possessed a good technical facility, and he proved his ability by his frequent performances in both Europe and America. In spite of the short-comings in his personal life and a premature death, he nevertheless left a musical legacy to jazz.

Waller wrote in a mixed style which resembled rag, boogie-woogie and traditional jazz. Some of his music, like that of Joplin and Eubie Blake, was semi-classical and classical. In many of his pieces, the blues penetrated his style, particularly in his vocal music. His mixtures of compositional devices saw *Rig Dem Bells* as being representative of boogies; his vocal pieces were most often ballads, and his *Handful of Keys* was semiclassical. Example 32 outlines some of the features common to Waller's music. *The Genius of Fats Waller* (Big 3) contains piano solo arrangements of similar works.

Ex. 32. Waller idioms (introduction, bass and rhythmic excerpts).

Among Waller's works were: *Squeeze Me, My Father, in Your Hands, Honeysuckle Rose, Blue Turning Gray Over You, Zonky, I've Got a Feeling I'm Falling, Keep Shifflin', Ain't Misbehavin', Hot Chocolates, Doin' What I Please, If It Ain't Love, Aincha Glad, Early to Bed* (musical), *Minor Drag, Ring Dem Bells, Viper's Drag, London Suite* and *Handful of Keys*.

WILLIAM (COUNT) BASIE (1906–1984)

William Basie, composer-pianist and conductor, was born in Red Bank, New Jersey. His mother was his first teacher and he also studied with "Fats" Waller. Having served as accompanist in vaudeville productions, he played both piano and organ, and later organized his own orchestra which rivaled contemporary bands, including Ellington's.

Basie once joined with the Bennie Moten Orchestra in Kansas. He also appeared on radio, made records and sparkled at numerous hotels, theatres, clubs, jazz festivals and concerts. In 1958, his reputation gained him a place in the down beat Hall of Fame.

Basie, one among nine persons from North America honored in the 1981 *Encyclopedia Britannica* Awards, was a mainstay in the continuing history of jazz. He exhibited his wares as conductor-performer-arranger at the Kennedy Center, Washington, D.C., in the 1980 Pablo Jazz Festival. Also associated with James J. Johnson, "Fats" Waller and pianists of the "stride" piano style of the 1920's and 1930's, his orchestral techniques were more typical of his own interests: uptempos and contrasts from slower march tempos and other techniques borrowed from the era. The "screaming" sensation used by trumpeters (ala Armstrong) and the equality of writing independent bass and treble melodies were attributed to his pioneer efforts.

Among Basie's works are: *One O'Clock Jump, Every Tub, Good Morning, Blues, John's Idea, Jumping at the Woodside, Basie Boogie, Blues and Sentimental, Gone With the Wind, Two O'Clock Jump, Swingin' the Blues, I Ain't Mad at You, Futile Frustration, Good Bait, Riff Interlude, Miss Thing, Don't You Miss Your Baby?, Panassie Stomp, Shorty George, Out the Window, Hollywood Jump, Nobody Knows, Swingin' at the Daisy Chain* and *I Left My Baby.*

ART TATUM (1910–1956)

Art Tatum, born in Toledo, Ohio, was a legendary pianist of the swing era. He has been described with superlatives from "outstanding" and "virtuoso" to "far ahead" and "incredible." Because of his strengths in performance, both printed and spoken sources such as Leonard Feather, Billy Taylor, Mark Gridley, Joseph Howard, Gunther Schuller and Edward Jablonski praised his stupendous technique, his flawlessly manipulated scales executed in unbelievable tempos, his avant-garde harmonic concepts, and spontaneity in improvisation.

Hailed as a champion of stride piano, and as a role model to be emulated time and again by many pianists, he was himself, according to Edward Jablonski's *Encyclopedia of American Music,* perhaps influenced by the slightly older "Fats" Waller. Yet Tatum must undoubtedly have also been stimulated by such earlier pianists as James Price Johnson, "father of Harlem piano," as well as by others, in that he demonstrated such commanding exhibitions of various styles from ragtime and blues to stride and swing. Billy Taylor, who heard Tatum perform many times, and who learned his styles by watching him play up close and by accepting impromptu coaching, noted in his *Jazz Piano,* that Tatum not only inspired major pianists, but other jazz artists as well. Without much formal education, Tatum managed to develop a huge reputation for fantastic pianism which was the envy of jazz and classical musicians alike.

Record jacket notes by John Brown, seen on *The Art Tatum Legacy,* suggested that Tatum could not read music; but this would be doubtful

Art Tatum. William Gottlieb, Photographer.

since other reports stated that Tatum did indulge in some violin and piano study at an early age. What was true, however, was the fact that poor eyesight from his semi-blind condition certainly must have hindered his reading abilities. That notwithstanding, he was able to build a fabulous career—as piano soloist (beginning on radio in Toledo, where Ronnie Schiff's preface to *Jazz, Blues, Boogie & Swing for Piano* said that Fletcher Henderson and Paul Whiteman heard him), as accompanist to vocalist Adelaide Hall, as ensemble player in his own trio and as a superb recording artist.

Sheer talent and keen energy are shown in his performances of quasi-fantasy forms containing sectional with ornamental runs and speed changes which interrupt the flow of the tune with rhythmic connotations resembling Chopin, by barely fitting into a time scheme, and requiring equally as much practice for anyone other than Tatum. Gunther Schuller, in *Early Jazz*, specified Tatum's sound as possessing an "open-toned, natural quality of African speech and song. . . . " Excellent analyses and assertions have also been made by Mark Gridley and Joe Howard. No matter how his talent and demonstrations may be described by various writers, and no matter whether or not he, Hines, Waller or Teddy Wilson was the best or the most important pianist of the swing era—Tatum's skill was indubitably awesome.

Among his improvisatory arrangements were both classical and popular music such as Dvorak's *Humoresque* (transcribed by Lou Stein for *Jazz and Keyboard Workshop*), *Aunt Hagar's Blues* (based on Handy's *Aunt Hagar's Children* and recorded by Capitol), *Tea for Two, I've Got a Right to Sing the Blues, Sweet Emaline, My Gal Back Home in Indiana, I Can't Give You Anything But Love, Baby, Sunny Side of the Street, If I Could Be With You, etc.* Two original pieces that were included in *Jazz, Blues Boogie & Swing for Piano* (MCA/Mills) were *Carnegie Hall Bounce* and *Gang O' Nuttin'*. His prolificacy in numerous recordings was seen in *Art Tatum: At the Piano*, vols. 1 & 2 (Crescendo), *The Art Tatum Legacy* (Olympic), and *The Genius of Art Tatum*, vol. 1–5.

MARY LOU WILLIAMS (1910–1981)

Mary Lou Williams, composer-pianist, and arranger, was born in Pittsburgh, Pennsylvania. Called the "Queen of Jazz," she studied with Ray Lev and showed further development in England and France while touring and residing there. After moving to New York, Williams began a brilliant career around the vaudeville circuits, serving as pianist with the Andy Kirk Band in 1929, and as arranger for the Ellington, Kirk, Crosby, Goodman, Dorsey and Armstrong Bands from the 1930's through 1940's. In 1977, she joined the faculty at Duke University.

As a performer, she possessed a more technically demanding style than many of the pianists before and during her time. Having also performed as solo recitalist, she has given concerts at Town Hall, the New York Philharmonic Hall and at Newport. Her styles spanned jazz from the newer stages of the 1940's to the progressive 1970's.

Among her compositions are: *Camel Hop, Roll 'Em, Blue Skies* (arrangements), *Zodiac Suite, Cloudy, What's Your Story, Morning Glory?, Ghost of Love, In the Land of Oo Bla Dee, Little Joe from Chicago, Pretty Eyed Baby, Juniper Tree* and *Jazz Opera*.

THEODORE (TEDDY) WILSON (1912–1986)

Teddy Wilson was born in Austin, Texas (according to pertinent records), and later moved to Detroit. Documents support accounts of his having studied for short periods at Tuskegee Institute and Talladega College in Alabama. Because of his background, he also held several teaching positions—at the Metropolitan Music School (where ASCAP noted that he taught jazz piano to Arthur Cunningham); at the Juilliard School of Music from 1945–52; and at his own private studio, etc. He worked on staff jobs at New York City radio and television in the thirties, gave many workshops such as those presented at the Museum of Natural History in 1975, and gave workshops with Hank Jones and John Lewis.

The career of Wilson was equally exciting as that of Tatum, his contemporary. He served as concert artist at radio and television stations on such programs as the Mike Douglas Show, the Tonight Show, etc. He also played at the Brussels World's Fair, and at innumerable clubs and taverns, etc. While establishing his individual work, rendering him as one of the great pianists of his time, Wilson also formed his own band. Furthermore, he served as pianist for Benny Goodmans' Trio—this being at a time when such a move was unthinkable in America (even though it is also true that Goodman hired such artists as Count Basie, Lionel Hampton, Fletcher Henderson, and Charlie Christian for some of his Sextet recordings). Wilson also played with important personalities from Louis Armstrong and Benny Carter to Lionel Hampton and Billie Holiday.

No matter that Art Tatum developed such a huge reputation as a great swing pianist, many writers such as Humphrey van Loo and Arie Ligthart defended Theodore Wilson as "the most important pianist of the swing era" (*Teddy Wilson Talks Jazz*). Labels depicting Wilson's talent consisted of "the most innovative" of the swing era, the most "famous for his left hand," the "excitement of his tenths," and "flowery" contrasted by "horn-like" characteristics. His performances gave the impression of straight-forward, clarified structures, but nevertheless with the freedom of improvisatory expression and articulation. Billy Taylor claimed that Wilson "swung like no one I had ever heard before."

In addition to performance, Wilson exhibited talent in composition, and did respectable orchestrations to fit the mold of his ensembles of a sextet, a trio, etc. Beyond that, he wrote original piano solos and arranged countless tunes by other writers, some of which appeared in *The Genius of Teddy Wilson: Piano Solos*, now published by the Big 3 Music Corporation. Examples found therein (such as *Charmaine, Black Eyed Susan*, etc.) showed his tonal music interspersed with interesting varieties of techniques for both hands. Melodic lines of the right hand contained single notes being alternated with octaves, as in ragtime, or with thirds, fuller chords, etc., sometimes being set in rhythmic schemes from triplets and sixteenths to quintuplets and to stride in walking tenths in support of a fancy, syncopated melody, or it consisted of voicings with vocal tendencies in support of a spiritual or more lyrical right hand. However conceived, the writing remained interesting, though more predictable than Tatum's.

Some of his compositions for solo piano published in the thirties and forties were *Piano Patterns* (*Miller Music, 1939*, reprinted/The Big 3), *Five Original Piano Solos* (*Leeds, 1942*), *Piano Creations* (*Robbins Music, 1944*), and *Teddy Wilson Piano Rhythms* (*Leo Feist, 1937*). His recorded music can be found in the *Smithsonian Collection of Classic Jazz* (*Statement & Improvisation* for small ensemble, vocal arrangements, etc.), *Jazz Piano Greats* (Folkways or Educational Records), *Teddy Wilson* (Everest), *Helen Sings, Teddy Swings* (Catalyst), *Billie's Blues* (Columbia), *Teddy Wilson: Striding After Fats* (Black Lion), and *Jazz Odyssey: The Sound of Harlem* (Columbia—with his orchestra).

JOHN (DIZZY) GILLESPIE (1917–)

John Gillespie, a composer-arranger, trumpeter and "bop" innovator from Cheraw, South Carolina, was instrumental in helping to establish the manner of improvising and planning within the more modern aspects of jazz. Having studied music as a child, Dizzy won a music scholarship to

John (Dizzy) Gillespie: William Gottlieb, Photographer.

North Carolina, traveled later to Philadelphia and New York, where he began to perform. At first a participant of the swing bands, playing with Earl Hines Band, the Coleman Hawkins Band, and Duke Ellington's Band, he soon formed his own smaller bands.

Gillespie's formal training was more extensive than that of Charlie Parker, who influenced his style. He studied privately, a luxury which Parker could unfortunately not manage because of his neurotic behavior. Nevertheless, under Parker's influence, he was able to abandon some of the traditional methods and formulate a new way of expressing jazz. With his melody extending over longer lines, in contrast to vocally short phrases of blues and ballads, his studied style became more and more instrumental. Yet many of these works incorporated characteristics of the blues. Gillespie was also influenced by collaboration with Ornette Coleman, the younger musician who followed in the modern concept of instrumentation and change. Dizzy employed independency of instruments within the given orchestration and utilized differences in timbre, intervals and general effects. No one doubted that the shape and position of his damaged trumpet had more than a little to do with these concepts; he yet commanded and gained the respect of his own country and others. In 1990, he was honored with a Kennedy Center Award.

Among his works and arrangements are: *Groovin' High, Jessica's Day, Passport, Leap Frog, Salt Peanuts, My Melancholy Baby, Mohawk, Ow, A Night in Tunisia, Algo Bueno, Dizzy Atmosphere, Anthropology, Behop, Blues and Boogie, Hot House, I Can't Get Started, One Bass Hit, Oo Bop Sha Bam, Two Bass Hits,* and others.

CHARLIE (BIRD) PARKER (1920–1955)

Charlie Parker, composer, arranger and saxophone player, was also an innovator of the difficult and abstract bop style. Jazz, which once placed

Charlie Parker and Miles Davis: William Gottlieb, Photographer.

emphasis upon the melody with short, fragmentary lines, now resorted to long, instrumental tendencies, "breathy" measures and melodic lines several measures long. Those, coupled with new harmonic advancements and more freedom of texture, were used to make jazz newer in concept and design.

Although Parker left high school at an early age and joined the band at Clara Monroe's Uptown House and those of Earl Hines and Billy Eckstine, he was at first very musically inept. But he made his way by trial and error, luck and the desire to succeed. With ample help from his fellow musicians, he managed to develop his talents and to grow in spite of his frequent bouts with drugs. Even though Parker acknowledged no formal knowledge of any rules of music, his insight and his talent combined to make his saxophone speak a language of its own. According to Lillian Erlich, he listened to and enjoyed Bartok and Stravinsky, particularly the *Firebird Suite*, and he also spoke fondly of Bach and other classical musicians.

Atonal qualities with large intervals placed his compositions into the category of the unusual. The free exchange of popular and art music acted in complementary fashion to one another, and jazz ceased to be just "dance music." Although some of the music retained its characteristic beat for movements typical of the dances, most of these latest developments were also designed for listening and playing.

Among his compositions were: *Now's the Time, Yardbird Suite, Relaxing at Camarillo, Confirmation, Donna Lee, Scrapple From the Apple, Billie's Bounce, Cheryl, Embraceable You, Lover Man, My Little Suede Shoes, Dexterity, Quasimodo, Thriving on a Riff, Anleu-cha, Count-Down, Little Willie Leaps, This Love of Mine, Just Friends, Cherokee, Ornithology* and others.

THELONIUS MONK (1920?–1982)

Thelonius Monk, a pianist-composer born in Rocky Mount, North Carolina, and who lived in New York, was a jazz innovator directly associated with Dizzy Gillespie and Charlie Parker. Monk was also influenced by the styles of Earl Hines, James P. Johnson, Teddy Wilson, Fats Waller, and Willie (the Lion) Smith. A fusion of the new with the older styles, his compositional devices were characterized by the "blurps and bleeps" of the keyboard's outer extremities of sound and touch, block chords and dissonances, and a feeling of atonalism, abstractness and novelty.

Monk grew to this stage somewhat gradually, as his style was originally traditional. His own experimentations began approximately the same time as Parker's. By the 1950's, his style was molded into newer concepts and were demonstrated at the Apollo, at festivals and on recordings.

At first not accepted, his jazz results were really no more irregular than those of Charles Ives in art music. There were those who felt that jazz, like its followers, should not be restricted and should not be allowed to voice the harmony of dissent in other than a traditional sound. Yet the new music continued to be influenced by its environment as well as ideas from art music. The more sophisticated intellectualism of musical features also encouraged the jazz players to conform to their own individual capacities.

Called the most important figure after Ellington's era, Monk has been featured in *Time* magazine, *Current Biography*, and *down beat*. Of his music, there is yet a feeling for the blues, having been versed in the "hotness" of jazz. There is the difficulty of bop, and the harmonies of the progressive era merge to provide an ultimate outcome. His compositions denote improvisation, freedom of time, with the appearance of form, variation and other simple or multi-sectional forms.

Among his works are: *Round About Midnight, Crisscross, Misterioso, Off Minor, Evidence, Ruby, In Walked Bud, Blue Monk, I Mean You, Hackensack, Epistrophy, My Dear, Fifty-second Street Theme*, and *Well You Needn't.*

WILLIAM (BILLY) TAYLOR (1921–)

William Taylor, a composer, author, conductor, pianist, educator and business executive, was born in Greenville, North Carolina. He later moved to Washington, D.C. and eventually to New York City. Educated at Virginia State College as a student of Undine Moore, he later served as pianist with the Ben Webster Quartet and the Cozy Cole Quintet (in *Seven Lively Hits*, broadway musical). He toured with Redman in Europe and has otherwise remained in demand for concerts at major institutions and halls throughout Europe and the Americas. A recipient of honorary degrees, and of an earned doctorate from the University of Massachusetts, he has been hailed as one of the greatest jazz composer-performers also because of the fine work which he has exhibited with his own trios, duos and other ensembles.

William (Billy) Taylor.

Taylor has performed as the music director of the David Frost Television Show. He has taught at the Manhattan School of Music and other institutions, and has lectured about jazz in a jazzmobile. He was perhaps the first to be sponsored on an NBC broadcast called *The Subject of Jazz*. He has arranged scores for several personalities, including Ethel Smith and Dizzy Gillespie, and has served as vice-president of the Musicians Clinic in New York City. In addition, Taylor has been an appointee to the New York State Commission on the Cultural Resources and an advisor on jazz at the Lincoln Center, among other commendations.

Having begun with the "bop" tradition, Taylor, a knowledgeable and scholarly musician, contributes to jazz in emotion, style and competence and experiments with other styles and techniques common to the twentieth century. Mostly of the tonal variety, his compositions emphasize melody, independency of melody against clearly defined harmony and ornamental improvisation of the highest caliber. Featuring intricately difficult cross-rhythms and technically unique lines in contrary motion, he also employs chord clusters sparingly, occasional dissonances and contrapuntal implications. His style, however, is ever-developing.

Lecturer and author of *Jazz Piano: A Jazz History* (1982), Taylor used a jazz mobile to promote the study and acceptance of jazz and performed numerous concerts throughout the world. A first-rate educator and performer, he also produced and performed with his trio on an excellent filmstrip, *Listening to Jazz* (Singer/EAV Productions), defining and demonstrating various aspects of jazz and blues. As jazz lecturer, he spoke at many institutions on jazz performance and the business of music (at the University of D. C., Howard University, the D. C. public schools, New York institutions and elsewhere in the Northeast).

As much involved in civic affairs as in music, he was council member of the National Endowment, the Harlem Cultural Committee, and other important groups. For his intense community concern, as well as his significance to the field of music, he has been given many awards and recognitions. He was honored by the Mayor of Washington, D.C., with a "Billy Taylor Day," and received the New York Mayor's Award of Honor for Art and Culture.

Taylor also continued to excel in composition. He wrote the ballet music for the musical, *Your Arm's Too Short to Box With God* for the media of jazz piano and orchestra, and also wrote *Suite for Jazz Piano and Orchestra* which *Jet* reported "was commissioned especially to be played at the Mormon Tabernacle." Also conducted by Leon Thompson at a New World Symphony concert held at Carnegie Hall for Black History Week, it was described by *down beat* as having "contrapuntal" idioms and Taylor's playing, as having "dexterity." In 1977, Taylor premiered Frederick Tillis's *Concerto* for piano and jazz orchestra at the University of Massachusetts and received rave reviews from the media. He was invited to give a lecture demonstration at the International Piano Festival, University of Maryland, in 1981, where he exhibited a very high level of proficiency in performance and improvisation.

Taylor has written 12 books on jazz, some 300 songs and manuals of instruction. He has also composed: *Basic Bebop Instruction, Dixieland Piano Solos, Mambo Piano Solos, Ragtime Piano Solos, Midnight Piano, Cuban Cutie, Ever So Easy, Dido, Just the Thought of You, You Tempt Me, It's a Grand Night for Swinging, A Bientot, Capricious, Rosetta* (arr.), *Sweet Lorraine* (arr.), *Tune for Tex, Biddy's Beat, Feeling Frisky, Theodora,* and others.

Some of his compositions originally printed by Hansen in 1953 were republished in *Jazz Giants* (*Bits of Bedlam, Cool and Caressing,* and *A Live One*). Also published in *Modern Jazz Piano Solos* were the same ones as well as *Muffle-Guffle*; in *Bebop* were *Good Grove* and *Cuban Caper* (Hansen copyright) and others. Several of his recordings appeared on Prestige, Paramount and other labels. His *Duane* and *I Wish I Knew How It Would Feel To Be Free* were recorded by Arcana (Novello Nelson album), and pieces *Rejoice* and *Spiritual Impromptu* (w/Manny) for piano and jazz orchestra.

JOSEPH J. KENNEDY, JR. (1923–)

Joseph Kennedy, Jr., composer, violinist, composer and arranger was born in Pittsburgh, Pennsylvania, but moved later to Richmond, Virginia. Educated at Carnegie Mellon University, Virginia State College and Duquesne University (where he received the Master's Degree), his first teachers were family members. He has since been influenced by the late Jimmie Lunceford. His association with Ahmad Jamal in composing, arranging, conducting and performing on recordings and at other concerts has added to his practical experiences. He has performed at Carnegie Music Hall, the Arts Festival in Birmingham, Michigan, and the Jazz Festivals at Hampton Institute.

As an active art musician, Kennedy performs with the Richmond Symphony Orchestra and conducts various ensembles, having served as guest conductor at the Mid-West National Band and Orchestra Clinic in 1968. Also in 1965, he conducted the Cleveland Summer Symphony in a premiere of his own work, the *Suite for Trio and Orchestra.* As an educator, he teaches at John Marshall High and Virginia Commonwealth.

Although Kennedy has composed traditional jazz compositions and art music, he has done other works during the contemporary period which border on third stream music. This is particularly true of his *Dialogue for Flute, Cello and Piano,* which he composed for Trio Pro Viva. His reputation, however, has been established as a jazz composer of a modern style similar to the "bop" tradition, merging with techniques from the early progressives. His harmony is related to that of Bud Powell who moderately restricts the music to contemporary practices within a tonal frame. Steeped in the emotion of the blues and other forms, Kennedy also employs ornamentations and frequent altered sevenths, dissonances and free-flowing rhythms. His clear comprehensible forms vary from ballad styles and three-part forms to that of the free fantasy. Two excerpts of his writing are shown in Example 33.

Ex. 33. *Serious Moods* and *Somewhat Eccentric* (first measures), Kennedy. Used by permission of Hema Music Corporation.

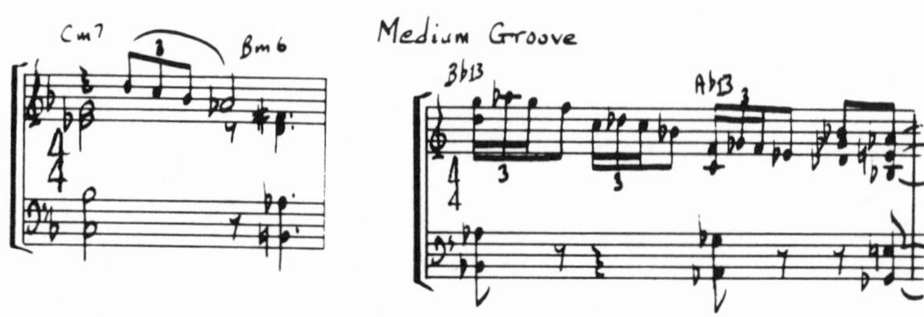

Joseph Kennedy.

Among Kennedy's other works are: *A Lazy Atmosphere, Tempo for Two, Surrealism, You Can Be Sure, The Fantastic Vehicle, Illusions Opticas, Nothing to Fret About, Disenchantment, Hynoptic, Serious Moods, Charming Attitudes, Somewhat Eccentric, Suite for Trio and Orchestra, Dialogue for Flue, Cello and Piano,* and others.

EARL (BUD) POWELL (1924–1966)

Leonard Feather described Earl Powell as "the first and foremost of the bop pianists . . . ;" Mark Gridley claimed that Powell was "the most imitated of all bop pianists;" and Billy Taylor referred to him as the "quintessential bebop pianist" who "was one of the first pianists to equal the intensity achieved by Gillespie and Parker. . . . " Although somewhat thwarted by his illnesses, he nevertheless managed to develop a successful enough career to become an internationally known artist of worth.

Powell demonstrated both creativity in compositional and pianistic skills. Scores show that he was a wizard at improvising interesting varieties of rhythmic configurations full of interruptive triplets alternating with eighths, or groups of sixteenths versus groups with two sixteenths and a triplet, various ornaments, long melodic phrases as well as close and expanded harmonies of sevenths, ninths, etc. Far more attention seemed to be given to the right hand, however, complete with ornaments, dissonances and scalar patterns of various types (except when a piece was conceived in vocal terms as in "*I'll Keep Loving You,*" etc.). A fuller discussion of comparative compositional concepts of bebop pianist can be found in Billy Taylor's *Jazz Piano.*

In *The Amazing Bud Powell: Jazz Piano, volumes 1 & 2* (transcriptions by Hank Edmonds, as heard on the Blue Note record; published by Patricia Music), are his arrangements and originals *Monopoly, Sub City nos. 1 & 2, Dry Soul, John's Abbey, Marmalade, Buster Rides Again,* and *Time Waits*; in *Bud*

Powell (Bob Himmelberger and Jerry Kovarsky, w/Stuart Isacoff arrangements; published by Consolidated), are found his *Celia, Night in Tunisia* arrangement of a Gillespie-Paparelli piece, *Strictly Confidential* (w/Kenny Dorham), *I'll Keep Loving You, Tempus Fugit,* and *Hallucinations.* The latter examples were taken from *The Genius of Bud Powell,* a Verve recording. Several other solo and ensemble records were produced by Blue Note, Verve, Roost, Savoy, and others.

DOROTHY DONEGAN (1924–)

Dorothy Donegan, dynamic pianist who was born in Chicago, Illinois, studied, according to Leonard Feathers, at the Chicago Conservatory, at Chicago Musical College and at the University of Southern California. A musician equally capable of playing Chopin *Sonatas,* she has worked in various places from churches to clubs, to television (where channel 32 has shown her performing boogie-woogie in a stand-up position), to broadway plays and movies (such as *Sensations*).

Program notes on a 1988 CD earlier released on Black and Blue label, *Makin' Whoopee,* stated that she recorded for Bluebird and Continental records as early as the mid–forties, but that because she preferred not to tour with bands, and instead chose to play solo or trio ensemble performances (mainly at the "Round Table" lounge in her native Chicago), the excellence of her talent was not as exposed as were those of her male counterparts. Her technical proficiency and superb brilliance of delivery are immediately evident from the first few notes of this solo album (without a rhythm section), employing styles from rag seen in the Goodman-Sampson *Lullaby in Rhythm,* to the most modern of jazz harmonies. Fantastic thirds, left–hand stride accompaniments and marvelous scalar and arpeggiated patterns seen in *Am I Blue* and *Those Foolish Things* outweigh occasional tendencies to impose startlingly unexpected vocals not at all on the same high level of her pianism (a thing which Glenn Gould used to do).

Her originals, *Goodbye Blues, Tonky Honk,* and *I Just Want to Sing* take us back to an earlier era with fascinatingly difficult right–hand syncopations and left–hand basses from rag and stride to thirds equal to those of "Fats" Waller's *Smashing Thirds*; her arrangement of Lennon-McCartney's *Yesterday,* can only be described as glorious and majestic with its range from pop to gutsy gospel-blues effects; *Makin' Whoopee II* uses right–hand sixths versus improvisatory melodic notes in interesting renditions of the Donaldson-Kahn piece; and other skills of boogie, lush full chords and tremolos coupled with a few contrapuntal bits here and there all appear in the music.

WILLIE (BILL) HARRIS (1925–1988)

Willie Harris, born in Nashville, North Carolina, and formerly residing in Washington, D.C., was one of the few composer-performers for guitar in jazz. Once a teacher at Federal City College, he began the study of the guitar after venturing into trumpet techniques and a variety of other professions before concentrating on music. Educated by his mother on the piano, as well as by members of the Washington Junior College and Sophocles Papas, he studied both classical and popular guitar and generally made a name for himself on the east coast. Harris has composed and performed for numerous concerts, festivals, institutions, and clubs and has made recordings. Especially important was his work with the Clovers.

Although primarily of the established key concept, his music showed traditional techniques interspersed with contemporary harmonies. However, the bulk of his music was centered around the "bop" era and the modern styles of "funk." His work included chromatics, up-tempos, a slight obscurity of keys (not atonalism), parallelisms and improvisational features (written and unwritten and occasionally coupled with his blues singing). His varieties of natural guitar sounds were both fascinating and pleasing. An excerpt from his *Ethyl* is shown in Example 34.

Ex. 34. *Ethyl*, Harris. Used by permission of composer.

Among Harris' original and arranged works are: *Ethyl, Blue Angel, K. C. Shuffle, Possessed, Dreaming, Ivanhoe, Your Majesty, The Harris Touch, Jazz Chords, Jazz Introductions, Jazz Endings, Octave Study, Runs and Chords, Intaglio, Elizabeth's Card, Baker's Dozen, Peg O' My Heart, Blue Moon, Satin Doll, Flying Home, Don't Blame Me*; and others.

OSCAR EMMANUEL PETERSON (1925–)

Proclaimed the number one jazz and pop pianist in 1968, Oscar Peterson is considered the present-day combination of Art Tatum and James P. Johnson. An internationally renowned pianist-composer and singer, he has gained fame as a giant of pianism, controlled technique, and of organized complexities of mind-storming lessons in jazz. A native of Montreal, Canada, he began his education in music with an introduction to the trumpet at age five. According to the preface of his *Jazz for the Young Pianist*, he later switched to piano, continuing private lessons with the classical pianist, Paul deMarkey, until graduation from high school.

As a teenager, he won first prize on the "Ken Soble Amateur Show" and was given his own weekly radio show over the CBC network. He soon abandoned the job for a more active performance schedule both as concert pianist and as a part of the Johnny Holmes Orchestra. After his new schedule had barely begun, he was signed by RCA to make his first recordings.

Peterson was introduced to the American concert stage around 1950, making his appearance at Carnegie Hall with such established jazz personalities as Ella Fitzgerald. So successful was the concert and so complimentary the reviews, Peterson seemed destined for raves and applause for his perfectly superb mastery of complex harmonic and melodic skills, virtuosic technique, and artistry. Followers of excellence began to study with the *maestro*, forcing him to open a school which he unfortunately had to abandon because of frequent concert schedules. He continued to give seminars and workshop sessions while on tour, as well as to work sporadically at the School of Jazz in Lenox, Massachusetts.

Peterson has excelled at the Newport Jazz Fest, at the Stratford Shakespeare Festival, and at countless halls and auditoriums in the United States and abroad. Touring with Ella Fitzgerald, with his trio, or with other ensembles as sideman, he steadily built a reputation for himself as one of the finest of pianists in this era, drawing crows and responses such as "incredible," "dazzling," and "indescribably fantastic." For his sense of musicianship, compositional accomplishments, and contributions to the field of jazz, he has earned the prestigious down beat Award, the Metronome Award, several awards from England, Japan, Germany, France, Belgium, and from elsewhere, as well as the 1953 Critics Poll.

Jet reported that he was commissioned to write, play, and conduct for the royal wedding of Britain's Prince Charles and Lady Diana Spencer. For the affair, he composed *A Royal Wedding*, a jazz suite in two movements, written for a forty-piece orchestra (Pablo Records). Still other honors have appeared in newspaper reviews such as the 1975 *Washington Post* caption, "Peterson: In Command of the Keyboard," and in the contents of the article written by Hollie West which declared that "In jazz people talk about Oscar Peterson's technique the way their classical peers ponder a Horowitz or a Serkin. And for many of the same reasons." Indubitably, only superlatives such as stupendous, magnificent, dazzling, ultimate, or monumental fit the massiveness of his talent.

Peterson has also given the world some exciting jazz compositions, some of which are contained in *Jazz Piano Solos*, published by Tomi Music, Toronto (also Hansen): *Hallelujah, Hymn to Freedom, Smedley's Blues, Roundalay, The Smudge, The Strut,* and arrangements of standards. Still other samples of his originals and arrangements are found on records made with his Oscar Peterson Trio, with Ella and Dizzy, made alone (Tracks, etc.) as piano solist, etc. on Pablo label. His *Canadiana Suite* appears on *Oscar Peterson with Swinging Brass* (Verve); his *Blues Etude* and *Chicago Blues* appear on *The Trio* with Joe Pass, N. Pedersen (Pablo Records); his *Wheatland* is on *Great Connection* (MPS Records); and *Noreen's Nocturne* and *Sandy's Blues* appear on *In a Mellow Mood* (BASF Records). His *Beginning Jazz for the Young Pianist* contains easy exercises and minuets, and some of his latest originals appear on *Oscar Peterson Trio: Live at the Blue Note, Sushi, Peace for South Africa* and *Blues for Big Scotia* (Tomi Music, Telarc cassette, 1990).

The composers of jazz were responsible for maintaining many aspects of Africanism in American music and for influencing all musical forms while developing a newer art form. They also paved the way for the later developments and elevations in contemporary jazz itself. These musicians exhausted the stylistic elements of the Baroque and Romantic periods in their diligent penetration of all music, and have made significant gains in the Modern Period.

Gospel Composers

Some of the earliest writers of gospel music are contained in this section—from those who improvised strophic hymns to those who composed originals. It is critical to view origins of this music with vestiges of plantation spirituals and blues, etc., as well as with the preliminary work in hymnology of Richard Allen, the Philadelphia-born methodist minister, who published *Collection of Spiritual Songs* highlighted by the Smithsonian Institution in 1987, and the work of John Lea, the ex-slave who was born in Africa in 1773, and whose hymnal, *Collection of Hymns* (containing both his own songs and those of others), was identified by Dr. Henry Louis Gates, Jr. at Yale University (*New York Times*, Feb. 21, 1985). A continuation of these composers are found in chapter XII.

CHARLES ALBERT TINDLEY (1851–1933)

Reverend Charles Albert Tindley, from Philadelphia, was a forerunner of Thomas Dorsey. Hailed in tribute by the Smithsonian Institute in 1982, he was spotlighted as pastor of the Methodist Episcopal Church, where he gained prestige as an influential speaker and baritone singer, and as an important link in the gospel music development.

His works were reviewed in a *Washington Post* article by Ralph Jones (whose book about Tindley was published by Abingdon Press), as "creations . . . " which "embellished the sermons he delivered," and as "messages of hope." Smithsonian claimed that Tindley's compositions influenced all of the early gospel music composers from Dorsey and Campbell, to Martin and Brewster. Among his titles were *A Better Home, After a While, A Stranger Cut the Rope, Consolation, I Have Found at Last a Savior, From Youth to Old Age, I'll Overcome Someday, It May be the Best for Me, Leave It There, Nothing Between, Stand by Me, The Storm is Passing Over, etc.*

LUCIE E. CAMPBELL (1885–1963)

Lucie Campbell, a native of Duck Hill, Mississippi, who was raised in Memphis, gained recognition as an educator and as a major force in the musical development of the National Baptist Convention. As musical director of the New Congress of the National Baptist denomination, she helped set the standards for the music of the National Sunday School and the educational curriculum of the church; she also committed herself to promoting better criterion for the community by playing piano and directing choirs.

From about the time that jazz was publicized in the media in 1919 to the 1950's, she began writing hymns which were published by the Sunday School Publishing Board (*Gospel Pearls* and other songbooks). She also wrote various hymns, a portion of which were listed at the Library of Congress: *Even a Child Can Open the Gate* (w/Williams, collab.); *Footprints of Jesus; He Understands, He'll Say Well Done* (w/Williams); *I Need Thee, Precious Lord; In the Upper Room With Jesus* (w/E. Isaac); *Jesus Gave Me Water* (w/C. R. Williams); *Just As I Am* (w/Williams); *Just To Behold His Face* (w/Williams); *Looking to Jesus* (w/Williams); *The Lord's Prayer; My Lord and I; Not Yours But You; A Sinner Like Me* (w/Williams); *They That Wait Upon the Lord* (w/Williams); *This is the Day the Lord Hath Made (arr.); Touch Me Lord Jesus* (w/Williams); *Then I Get Home* (w/Williams, for solo voice & SATB). The Angelic Gospel Singer, Mahalia Jackson, and others have recorded many of her songs.

THOMAS ANDREW DORSEY (1899–)

Thomas Dorsey, gospel musician, pianist, composer, and band leader, was born near Atlanta, Georgia. He was educated in the Atlanta public schools and at Chicago Musical College. Erstwhile exponent of the blues and musical accompanist for Ma Rainey, he epitomized the very essence and origin of that music which John W. Work III described in his article entitled "Changing Patterns in Negro Folk Songs" (*Journal of American Folklore*, April-June 1949) as having a "strong appeal for the young people" when first formed in the churches and as invoking "consternation" and "bitter opposition" among the older members, particularly when the "rhythmic piano" was added to the music. Further described as music in which the "written note is a negligible factor in the instrumentalists' performance scheme" and as being "improvisation," it was described as an "aggregation of idioms." Also perceived as having a "melismatic flavor characterizing the singing style of the Negro . . . which may very well be derived from . . . earlier 'Dr. Watts' short and long meters" (fast and very slow tempos of the Primitive Baptist Church), gospel music has long since survived the arguments.

John Work III apparently was a frequent observer of many denominations using gospel music. With an interest in folklore and as one of the more eloquent among the intellectuals, he clearly described what he felt grew from the spirituals into a gospel song form, a hymnal-type gem, sometimes accompanied by guitar (as observed in the Sanctified churches), sometimes by a saxophone, trombone, or violin, and "concomitant with the appearance of this intensive instrumental rhythm . . . the religious dance." Describing several song forms in gospel music which he heard being originated, he explained that the sixteen or thirty-two measure songs were generally those referred to as the "Dorsey song." "These songs," he wrote, were "copyrighted and . . . issued in printed form," gradually approaching "big business proportions."

Thomas Dorsey. Moorland-Spingarn Research Center, Howard University.

Thomas Dorsey was cited as National Music Award winner in 1976 for "virtually creating the modern gospel style, reshaping the older Black religious tradition into a 20th century expression." Starting as a dance band pianist, he joined the Pilgrim Baptist Church in Chicago in 1921 and began writing hymns. Later in the 1920's he was engaged by the pioneer blues singer, Ma Rainey (1886–1939), to form a band and tour with her, which he did as Georgia Tom, exponent of the blues. Credited with writing "some 400" gospel songs and with founding the National Convention of Gospel Singers, among other credits, he was hailed as the "Patriach and Father of Gospel Music" by gospel music historian, Clayton Laverne Hannah (*Gospelrama News*, December 1980). Dorsey, a contemporary of W. Herbert Brewster, was reported by Ralph Jones to be influenced by Rev. Charles Albert Tindley (1851–1933).

Some thirty-seven of his compositions are published in *Great Gospel Songs* by the Aberbach Group, New York, and include his most famous *Take My Hand, Precious Lord, Peace in the Valley*, and others. Most gospel performers have recorded and programmed his songs. Earlier performances of Dorsey with Tampa Red are found on the *Smithsonian Jazz Collection*.

ALEX BRADFORD (1926–)

A native of Bessemer, Alabama, Bradford was listed in the *Eileen Southern Dictionary* as a gospel singer who graduated from the Snow Hill Normal and Industrial Institute, and who, like Dorsey, also performed in secular shows before ultimately attaining fame in church music. A review of the gospel music and lyrics found in the musical, *Your Arms Too Short to Box with God*, was done in the *Free Voice News* (March 5, 1976), by Ron Heermans. Seen at D. C.'s Ford Theater, Alex Bradford was a principal performer, whose "vocal exercises and contrived business," Heermans felt "channeled . . . the audience into frenzied submission." Of the same show, Hollie West (*Washington Post*) wrote that Bradford was "an engaging singer" whose voice "ranges from the dark, throaty tones of a field holler to the ringing, falsetto notes of a sanctified cry. Little Richard probably borrowed his famous falsetto technique from Bradford."

The Library of Congress lists him as composer of over fifty songs, some of which are: *After It's All Over; At the End* (w/R. Martin); *God is Good to Me; He Lifted Me* (Venice Music); *He Will Deliver Our Souls from Sin* (w/R. Martin); *He'll Be There; He's My Friend Until the End* (Martin/Morris Music); *He's a Wonder; Holy Ghost 'I Dare You' I Feel the Spirit; I Heard Him When He*

Called My Name (Martin Studio); *In Him I've Found Perfect Peace; Is My Name on the Roll?; Just the Name Jesus; Let God Abide; Life's Candlelight* (Venice Music); *Low is the Way; My Crown; Turn Away From Sin,* etc. Recordings of his music are seen in *Save the Children* (*I'm Too Close to Heaven to Turn Around*; Motown); *We Remember Clara Ward* (*Come in the Room*/BMI; Scepter); *The Best of Alex Bradford* (*Lord, Lord, Lord; Holy Ghost; Too Close to Heaven*; and *I Can't Tarry*), etc. His *Too Close to Heaven* reportedly sold more than a million copies.

JAMES CLEVELAND (1931–1991)

Reverend James Cleveland, clergyman and singer, was born in Chicago. Before becoming pastor of the Cornerstone Baptist Church, he attended Roosevelt University. His talents and outstanding achievements have been reported in *Ebony, Jet,* encyclopedias and other media as "multi-talented," "praiseworthy" and "one-man landslide." *Ebony* rated him in a poll as "King" of Gospel, and *Jet* polls have rated his *I'll Do His Will, Jesus is the Best Thing That Ever Happened to Me,* and *God Has Smiled on Me,* among the top 10 gospel soul brothers several times. Various workshops, recordings, scores, and his commanding voice all attest to the fact that he was indeed a giant among many talents.

Among his Savoy Music scores seen in the Roberta Martin collections are: *God Has Smiled on Me; God Is Enough; He Will Come in a Hurry* (Crossroads Music); *I Can't Stop Loving God; I Stood on the Banks of the Jordan; I Told Jesus to Change My Name* (Screen Gems/Columbia Music); *I've Come a Long Ways'; Jesus Is the Best Thing That Ever Happened to Me; Joy of My Salvation; Life Can Be Beautiful; Lord Help Me To Hold Out; Love Lifted Me* (Crossroads); *My God Can Do Anything; Nobody Knows; Nothing But God; No Cross—No Crown; One More River* (Morris/Martin Music); *Peace Be Still; Save Me Lord; Thank You Jesus for My Journey; There's a Bright Side Somewhere* (Crossroads); and *Walk in Jerusalem.* Recordings of his originals and arrangements are on the following: *Afro-American Music and Its Roots* (Silver Burdett); *James Cleveland and the Angelic Choir; James Cleveland with the Southern California Community Choir; James Cleveland and the Harold Smith Majestics; Reverend James Cleveland & the Cleveland Singers; The Gospel Soul of Sam Cooke w/The Soul Stirrers,* vol. 1; *The Third Annual Black College Gospel Festival; The Roberta Martin Singers* (mainly Savoy labels), etc.

Other gospel music writers of this era include some who do many styles, from rock to jazz, and cannot be easily categorized, as well as the following:

Inez Andrews, composer of *Lord, Don't Move the Mountains* (ABC Records);

Alma Irene Bazel Androzzo (1912–), born in Harriman, Tennessee, graduate of Pittsburg, Pennsylvania High School (Don White files), composer of *Bless His Name* (w/K. Morris), *Deliver Me From Evil* (w/K. Morris), *Doing Good Deeds* (w. & m.), *He's Such a Great Savior, I Am Willing Lord to Walk With Thee* (w. & m.), *I Carry My Burdens to the Lord & Leave Them There* (for solo/SATE), *I Will Walk With Jesus* (w. & m.), *If I Can Help Somebody* (Boosey & Hawkes) and *I Have Something to Give.*;

Shirley Caesar, born in Durham, North Carolina, composer of *Give Me Strength* (Flomar Music), *God Is Not Dead* (arr.), *He Heard My Cry, He Never Sleeps, Increase My Faith, It Will Be Glory, I've Been Saved, The Last Days, Life's Mountain Railway, Message to the Nation, No Never Alone* (arr.), *Oh Lord I Want You to Help Me, Sweeping Through the City, Take Up Your Cross* (arr.), *To Be Like*

Jesus, You Must Live Right (arr.), recorded by HBX—*Be Careful of the Stones You Throw, Best of Shirley Caesar* (HGS), *Get Up My Brother, I'll Go, The Invitation, The King and Queen of Gospel, Message to the Nation, More Church in the Home, World's Greatest Gospel Singers*, etc.;

Dorothy Love Coates (born Dorothy McGriff), composer of *Won't Let Go, Take a Little Time to Pray, Everyday Will Be Sunday, They Won't Believe*, etc.;

Rev. Cleavant Dericks, among whose approximately 100 songs are *When God Dips His Love in My Heart* (R. Martin Music);

Clarence Fountain, educated at the Talladega School for the Blind, writer of *Alone and Motherless* (w. & m., Flomar Music), w/John Bowden—*Beams of Heaven, Hold Me in the Hallow of Your Hand, Jesus Is a Friend, Jesus, Love Divine, Just a Closer Walk With Thee, Running for My Life, Something's Got a Hold of Me, Steal Away* (arr.), *When the War is Over* (in score *Soul!*, Flomar Music), recordings of whose pieces are on *Blessed Assurance* (Jewel Records), *Soul Gospel* (Jewel), *Clarence Fountain—In the Gospel* (Light), *Live and In Person, At His Best, Soul, Spirit & Song*, etc.;

Bessie Griffin (1922–1989), composer of *Run to the Mountain* (Our Children's Music/BMI), recorded on Scepter, Nashboro and Hob Records;

Mahalia Jackson (1911–1972), born in New Orleans, singer, composer of *Sign of the Judgment* (ms./Library of Congress), arranger of *Walk in Jerusalem, The Upper Room, He Calmed the Sea, Move On Up a Little Higher, Nobody Knows the Trouble I've Seen* (M. Jackson Pub. Co./BMI), recording artist of Columbia labels *Bless This House, Come on Children, Everytime I Feel the Spirit, Great Gettin' Up Morning, Great Songs of Love and Faith, I Believe, Mahalia Jackson, Mahalia Jackson's Greatest Hits, Make a Joyful Noise Unto the Lord, Newport, Power and the Glory, Sweet Little Jesus Boy*, etc.;

Dr. C. J. Johnson (ca. 1915–), from Atlanta, Georgia, pastor of several missionary Baptist churches, known in 1964 as Georgia's Top Evangelist (record notes/*The Old Time Song Service*, Savoy), composer of *You Better Run to the City of Refuge, One Morning Soon, There's A Dark Cloud Rising, The Storm Is Passing Over, In a Time Like This, I Heard the Voice of Jesus Say, Oh Lord I Want You to Move, I'm Just Feeling My Way Through This World, You Don't Know What the Lord Told Me, Sitting Down in the Kingdom*, etc.;

Roberta Martin (1912–), nationally known lyricist, publisher, arranger, and composer of *Anytime, God is Still on the Throne, If You Pray, Only God, Try Jesus, They That Wait*, arranger of *Everybody Won't Get There* (w/J. Powell), *I Heard the Voice of Jesus Say, Count Me, Every Day Every Hour* (w/A. Bradford), *Will You, Shall I?, There's Not a Friend Like Jesus*, and others from her series of books and the *New National Baptist Special*, etc.—some of which are recorded on Savoy label (*Roberta Martin Singers* et al.); Sallie Martin, composer of *Let Us Give Our Best in Service, Wonderful is His Name, They Found No Fault in Him, Yes, God is Real* (Bowles Music, Savoy Records);

Kenneth Morris (1917–), at least seventy of whose songs are listed at the Library of Congress such as *Amazing Grace* (arr.), *Bless His Name* (w/ Androzzo), *Blessed and Brought Up by the Lord* (w. & m.), *Christ is All, Come Home, Come Ye Disconsolate* (arr.), *Crucified* (w/S. Lewis), *Day by Day* (w/Androzzo), *Dig a Little Deeper in God's Love, Ease My Troublin' Mind, Everytime I Feel the Spirit, I'm Waiting on the Lord* (w. & m.), *It's a Highway, a Slow Way, A Hard Way Up to Heaven* (w. & m. w/J. Cleveland), *It's Worth It* (w. & m.), *Glory, Glory Hallelujah* (arr.), *God's Got His Eyes on You* (arr.), *He Will Give Me Rest* (w. & m.), *I Can Put My Trust in Jesus, I Can't Turn Around* for solo, choir, chorus, quartette, etc.;

Rev. Cleophus Robinson, originally from Canton, Mississippi, cited favorably by *Ebony* and *down beat* polls, and who, according to *Jet*, claimed authorship of "more than 250 songs," recorded about 70 singles and 45 albums of sermons and songs, including reported million-record sellers *Pray for Me, How Sweet It Is To Be Loved by God*, and *There is Only One Bridge*, composer of *He Did It All, Traveling Shoes, He's Alright, Shout, Shout, God's Love* seen on Peacock recording of *The Best of Rev. Cleophus Robinson* (Lion Publishers), etc.;

Harold Smith, born in Detroit, Michigan, composer of *In These Last Days, The Lord Will Carry You Through, He's the One* (seen on *The Harold Smith Majestics* Savoy record), and others on *I Just Want to Testify, Oh How Wonderful It Is* (Martin/Morris Music);

Willie Mae Ford Smith, evangelist, born in Rolling Fort, Mississippi, and raised in Memphis, appeared at the Newport Jazz Festival and at Radio City Music Hall, composer of *If You Just Keep Still, Salvation Is Free*, and various arrangements;

Gloria Spencer, award winning composer of work seen on recording *For Once in My Life* (Creed), *Thy Will O Lord* and *Glad To Be in His Service* (Excellorec Records), and others on Soulville Records;

Rosetta Tharpe (1921–1973), born in Cotton Plant, Arkansas, arranger and recording artist;

Albertine Walker, composer of *Jesus Heard My Earnest Plea* (w. & m., Morris Music Studio), *Lord, I Want to Thank You* (w. & m.), one-time "queen of gospel" in *Jet* report, and recording artist on *Share! The Caravans* (Birthright Records);

Clara Ward (1924–1973), born in Philadelphia, singer, composer of *Glory, Glory to the King* (w. & m.), *Great Is the Lord* (w. & m.), *How I Got Over* (w. & m.), *I Am Climbing Up High Mountains Trying to Get Home* (w. & m.), *I Feel the Holy Spirit* (w. & m.), *I Know It Was the Lord* (w. & m.), *I'll Anchor in the Harbor of the Lord, I'm Going Home* (w. & m.), *King Jesus Is All I Need*, recording artist with Clara Ward Singers on Niktom/Atlantic and Savoy labels;

Marion Williams (1927–   ), from Miami, erstwhile singer with Clara Ward, formed own group, has appeared in national and international settings, reviewed in Feather's *Jazz Encyclopedia, Washington Post*, composer of *Heaven Belongs to You, These Old Burdens*, etc., arrange of *Milky White Way*, and recording artist on Savoy records *Trials and Tribulation, Dr. C. J. Johnson & His Family Present The Old Time Song Service, Heavenly Stars* (Cotillion), etc.;

Pearl Williams-Jones. Stevie Zweig Photographers.

Pearl Williams-Jones (1931–1991), born in Washington, D.C., acclaimed as "first rank" pianist-singer concert artist, author, honor graduate of Howard University, with further study at Columbia, was choir director at her father's Bibleway Holiness Church, professor of music and director of gospel studies at the University of D.C., recipient of honorary degrees on the basis of her educational advancement of gospel studies in the college curriculum, arranger of songs *Take Me To the Water, Jesu Joy of Man's Desiring*, etc.;

And others such as Rev. C. F. Franklin (Aretha's father), and those seen in chapter XII.

Blues, Rock, and Pop Composers

Although many of the following creators are being separated from those of gospel, most have their origins in church music. Certain piano blues creators are discussed among the jazz composers; rap is offered in later general discussions of cognate forms of jazz; and still others may be found in auxiliary sections because of the ever-prevailing tendencies of modern fusions, which render the process of separation or labeling an impossible task. Among the participants are also rhythm and blues composers. Again, because the list is so long, just a few are highlighted in this book (also see chapter XII).

Blues

Pioneer blues makers were: early blues singers Gertrude Melissa Nix Pridgett (Ma) Rainey (1886–1939), from Columbus, Georgia, who recorded on Riverside; Arthur Blake (Blind Blake) from Jacksonville, Florida, heard on Folkways' *Jazz Volume 10*; William Lee Conley (Big Bill) Broonzy (1893–1958), from Scott, Mississippi, composer of, according to Charters, over 300 songs, some of which were *Just a Dream (On My Mind), Keys to the Highway, Looking Up At Down; Louis Louise Blues*, and others seen in Yannick Bruynoghe's book, *Big Bill Blues* (Oak), and in Woody Mann's score, *Six Black Blues Guitarists* (Oak), and whose talent can be heard on Folkways recordings *Big Bill Broonzy, Big Bill Broonzy Sings Country Blues*, and *Jazz Volume 10*; Bessie Smith (1894–1937), from Chattanooga, Tennessee, composer of *Back Water Blues, Preachin' the Blues, Long Old Road, Shipwreck Blues*, and recording legend of Columbia records' *The Bessie Smith Story* and others; Alberta Hunter (1897–1984), born in Memphis, and raised in Chicago, toured abroad with broadway companies, composer of *Downhearted Blues*; Blind Lemon Jefferson (1897–1930), singer and guitarist born near Couchman, Texas, who produced about 80 recordings, one of which was *Blind Lemon Jefferson* (Milestone); Robert Johnson (1898–1937), singer and guitarist, born in Mississippi, whose work *Hellhound on My Trail* appears on Martin Williams' *Classic Jazz* (Smithsonian); Blind Willie Johnson (1902–1949), from Beaumont, Texas; Eddie (Son) House (1902–), from Lyons, Mississippi, composer of *Grinnin' in Your Face* and *That's A Plenty*; and others such as Rev. Gary Davis, whose work is seen on *Ragtime Guitar*; Helen Humes (1913–), born in Louisville, Kentucky, composer of *Be Ba Ba Le Ba Boogie, Married Man Blues* and *Drive Me Crazy*, whose work is seen on Storyville's *Helen Humes*; legends such as Muddy Waters, Sonny McGhee, and W. C. Handy, discussed in earlier pages, as well as the following listed separately below. Bear in mind, too, that artists such as Sam Cooke, Lou Rawls and others did gospel, blues, or rock, depending upon the special circumstances at career intervals, or that performers like Ray Charles might even show up on jazz albums (such as *The Definitive Jazz Scene, vol. 2*, Impulse records).

RILEY (B.B.) KING (1925–)

"B. B." King, a native of Ita Bena, Mississippi (Indianola, according to Lawrence Reed), is the King of the blues. In an interview by Jeffrey Frank of the *Washington Post*, King stated that he grew up in Kilmichael and in the Delta, before moving on to Memphis. A particular, down-home, but classy musician, whose mellow voice and gutsey guitar compliment each other in dexterity and sound, King drives his material straight to the heart of the matter with love themes, up-tempo songs full of sassiness, or certain commentaries upon the nature of life. An international figure whom all of the blues performers attempt to imitate, he is a model of perfection.

An award winning achiever, he has rated tops in the *Ebony* polls for years, has been the subject of various media from the *Yale Alumni News* to the *Afro-American*, and has been awarded honorary degrees from Yale University, from Tougaloo College, etc., both for his tremendous performing ability as well as for the huge number of hit recordings, some of which have stayed on Billboard charts for 15 weeks. He received over 25 other honors such as the Medal of Arts, the Grammy, etc. In addition to playing all over the world, he loomed large at the old Howard Theater, the Appollo, Blues Alley, Anton's, and at major jazz festivals and in major cities throughout the U.S.

Some from his long list of compositions include *BB Songbook, Just a Little Love, My Mood, Sweet Little Angel, I Want You So Bad, Friends, Get Off My Back Woman, Let's Get Down To Business, Why I Sing the Blues* (recorded on *BB King: Live and Well*, Bluesway label), *Mother Fuyer, Loving You Turns Me On*, etc. Among his numerous records are *BB King: King Size* (ABC), *The King B, The Best of B. B. King, B. B. King's Greatest Hits, Blues Is King*, etc.

Rock, Rhythm 'n' Blues

ANTOINE (FATS) DOMINO (1928–)

"Fats" Domino was born in New Orleans, Louisiana. Beginning as a jazz pianist, he encountered an accident which caused him to switch from rock and roll (before it was renamed "rhythm and blues") and to add singing to piano accompaniments, thus becoming one of the first to formulate the bases for this popular dance and song music. At times, he worked with groups, which he formed, and toured throughout the States, emerging upon stages in dance halls, clubs and theaters.

Compositions which he composed were *Fats Domino's Album* (Internationale), *Favorite Songs of Fats Domino* (Commodore Music), *Ain't That a Shame* (w/D. Bartholomew), *All By Myself* (w. & m.), *Bo Weevil* (Reeve Music), *I'm in Love Again* (Ibid.), *Poor Me* (Commodore), *I'm Still Waiting, It's You I Love, I Still Love You, Whole Lotta Lovin", Be My Guest, Walking To New Orleans* (w/ W. Young), and originals *Fat Man, Love Me, Don't Leave Me This Way*, and *I Can't Go On*. Listing only a few of his various records, were *Here Comes Fats, Fats On Fire, Getaway With Fats, Stompin' Fats Domino, Fats Is Back, Fats Domino: Blueberry Hill* (on which are his originals *Please Don't Leave Me, Let the Four Winds Blow* (w/D. Bartholomew), *Whole Lot of Loving* (w/D. Bartholomew), etc.), *Urban Blues, vol. 2 With Fats Domino* (Legendary), etc.

JAMES BROWN (1928?–)

James Brown, singer, dancer and band leader, was born in Macon, Georgia near Augusta, that same city in which (Little) Richard Penniman was born. Variously listed as having been born in 1934 by the Library of Congress, and in 1933 by several other sources, Baker's *Biographical Dictionary of Musicians* lists his birthdate as 1928. Leaving high school in the mid-fifties because of economic reasons, he worked at various jobs before forming the James Brown Trio which cut a record at a Macon, Georgia radio station that launched his career. Later appearances at the Appollo, Madison Square Garden, in movies, and at festivals propelled him toward stardom, eventually earning him the title of "Mr. Godfather of Soul." Clearly the top rhythm and blues performer for years, his vocal antics as well as his dancing ability (which must have influenced Michael Jackson) and energetic stagings kept him on a high level of achievement for years. Like Domino, Brown was designated one of the pioneers of rock.

His titles, from *The Best of James Brown* score, are *Shout and Shimmy* (w. & m.), *Papa's Got a Brand New Bag* (w.& m.), *Cold Sweat 1 & 2* (w/A. Ellis), *Don't Be a Drop Out* (w/N. Jones), *Ain't That a Groove 1 & 2* (w/Nat Jones), *I Got You (I Feel Good), Bring It Up, Tell Me What You're Gonna Do, I'll Never, Never Let You Go, Gonna Try, I'll Go Crazy, Fine Old Foxy Self, I Don't Mind, No, No, No, No, Please, Please, Please* (w/J. Terry), *Try Me, Money Won't Change You* (w/N. Jones), *Good Good Lovin'* (w/A. Shubert), etc. Certain records are *Good Foot* (Polydor), *Revolution of the Mind (Polydor), James Brown: Soul Brother No. 1* (King), *It's A Man's World* (King), *Payback* (People), etc.

RAY CHARLES (1932?–)

Born in Albany, Georgia, Ray Charles (Robinson), internationally known pianist, singer, arranger, and composer, studied at the state school for the blind in Orlando, Florida, after having lost his sight at an early age. Also orphaned during his teens, he joined bands and played in various cities (sometimes staying in homes of such families as the Felders of Tampa), until his career blossomed into an incredibly unbelievable successful adventure. An award winner and exponent of blues and rock, he has also performed country-western, jazz and gospel, starred in movies and commercials, and generally held high standards in his renditions.

For his distinctive accomplishments, he was awarded the National Music Award in 1976 for his "uncommon musical ability"; he has won at least 10 Grammy Awards in the rhythm and blues category; and, in 1986, the coveted Kennedy Center Award. He has been favorably reviewed in various media such as the *down beat* magazine, *Ebony*, several encyclopedias and the *Washington Post*, wherein Bill Bennett wrote about Charles' Carter Barron appearance: "God is in his heaven and Ray Charles is in his groove, and all is right with the world."

Although noted for his rustic vocal tones, he nevertheless has done several original piano pieces containing blues and jazz and boogie such as *A Bit of Soul, Blue Fun, Blue Genius, Blues Waltz, Charlesville, Cosmic Ray, Dawn Ray, The Genius After Hours, Hornful Soul, Joy Ride, Rockhouse, X-Ray Blues and Sweet Sixteen Bars* (*Ray Charles Instrumental Folio*, pub. Progressive Music). He had also done the *Ray Charles Song Folio* released by the same company. Other original songs consist of *Rockhouse* (Hill/Range), *Hallelujah, I Love Her So, Love on My Mind, What'd I Say, Ain't That Love, This Little Girl of Mine, Mary Ann, Don't You Know, I Got A Woman, From the Heart, Chitlins With Candied Yams* (Tangerine Music/BMI), etc. Among some of his prolific array of recordings are *A Man and His Soul* (ABC), *The Soul Years* (Atlantic), *Ray Charles: Rock and Roll* (Ibid.), *Ray Charles* (Everest and Pickwick), *Take Ten With Ray Charles* (Grand Prix), *Ray Charles, Vol. Two: Modern Sounds in Country and Western Music*, and others on Impulse, etc.

Postscript I: Other Composers

Other composers, including artists whose performing or auxiliary production skills overshadow their compositional pursuits, are:

Pearl Bailey (1918–1990), movie star and night-club singer, originally from Newport News, graduate of Georgetown University, copyrighted *Jingle Bells Cha Cha Cha, I'm Gonna Keep on Doin', Don't Be Afraid of Love*, and *A Five Pound Box of Money*;

Oscar Brown, Jr. (1926–), who, the *Afro-American News* reported, has 450 songs to his credit, some of which are listed at the Library of Congress in *Songs of Oscar Brown* (E. B. Marks, contains "jazz, blues and soul"), words to *Joy* (a "musical-come-together," E. B. Marks), and *Brown Baby* (Belwin Mills);

Nathaniel (King) Cole (1917–1965), a native of Montgomery, Alabama, award-winning singer-pianist of both jazz and popular music, appeared in movies, on television, radio, night clubs, etc., whose flair for jazz composition is seen mainly in his piano trio ensemble work, composer of *Straighten Up and Fly Right, Because of Rain* (w/R. Poll & B. Harrington), *Early Morning Blues* for piano, *Calypso Blues* (Crestview Music), *I Get Sentimental Over Nothing, King Cole Piano Capers* (trans./Paparelli), *Robin Crusoe* (w/R. Wells & H. Leeds), *Easter Sunday Morning, Nat King Cole Album of Recorded Hits* (w/H. Arlen, etc.), *Nat King Cole Piano Solos* (trans./Feldman, Leeds Music), *I'm a Shy Guy, That Ain't Right, It's Better to Be by Yourself, Just for Old Time's Sake, With You on My Mind, To Whom It May Concern*, and others documented in his many recordings;

Sammy Davis (1925–1990), from New York City, singer, drummer, dancer, movie and television star, etc., composed songs;

Robert Felder (1930–), composer-arranger, educator, band leader; born in Tampa, Florida and educated at Fisk University (B.A.) and Catholic University (M.A.); erstwhile director of one of the marching units of the United States Air Force Band which toured Africa, Europe, and America during the 1950's; worked in Florida and D.C. public schools before beginning the instrumental program at the University of D.C.; rock conductor-arranger of Blue Notes Band; composer of songs *Our Glorious UDC, Firebirds Fight Song* (both recorded by the UDC Striders Marching Band, 1982), *Bird's Word, Buck's Hill, Tri-X, Bobby in Bassoonville* (recorded on Charlie Bird's *Jazz at the Showboat*, vol. 1, Offbeat Records); and arranger of several unpublished tunes for marching band, stage band, and other ensembles.

Ella Fitzgerald (1918–), the singing legend from Newport News, recording artist, band director and composer of pieces outlined in ASCAP, on recordings, and in the Library of Congress such as *A Tisket, A-Tasket, You Showed Me the Way, Spinnin' the Web, I Found My Yellow Basket, Chew, Chew, Chew, Please Tell the Truth, Oh! But I Do, Just One of Those Nights, Oh Boy I'm in the Groove* (w. & m.), and *Rough Ridin'* (w/H. Jones and W. Tennyson), and others documented on recordings;

Erroll Garner (1923?–1977), pianist-composer from Pittsburgh, who created *Misty*, countless arrangements, and *In The Beginning* (on *Early Erroll* album, Jazz-tone);

Billie Holiday. William P. Gottlieb, Photographer.

Billie (Lady Day) Holiday, born Eleanor McKay (Fagan?) (1915–1959), singer and recordings artist from Baltimore, Maryland, winner of 1976 National Award, composer of *Billie's Blues, Fine and Mellow, Long Gone Blues, Somebody's on My Mind, Tell Me More and More, Don't Explain* (w/Herzog), *God Bless the Child, Strange Fruit*; seen in E. B. Marks edition, *The Best of Billie Holiday*, and 55 original hits seen on *Billie Holiday* (Adam VIII), whose voice is heard on several LPs such as *Billie's Blues* (Harmony), *The Sound of Harlem* (Columbia), *Billie Holiday and Al Hibbler* (Sunset), and on the *Smithsonian Collection of Classic Jazz*, etc.;

Calvin Jones (1929–), a jazz trombonist, string bassist, conductor, educator, composer-arranger; born in Chicago, Illinois and educated at Tennessee A&I University and Howard University (B.S. and M.A.); worked in Louisiana and D.C. public schools before initiating the jazz studies program at the University of D.C.; erstwhile director and arranger of the 75th

Army Band, former member of the Ray Charles Band, Howard Theater Band, and participant in various Broadway shows at Washington, D.C. theaters; composer of recorded works *Blues, Passion, The Hump,* for big band; *Brown Sugar, Conception, Dues, Whip Lady, Inside Out, Carefree, Beef Stew, Easy Cookin', Over the Hump, Ten Speed, Minor Blues, Blues for Two,* etc. for Septet; *Holiday Suite, Contact, Blues Alamode,* for octet; and several arrangements for big band, septet, octet, quintet, and trio such as *St. Thomas.*

(Little) Richard Penniman (1932–), singer-songwriter born in Macon, Georgia, pioneer of rock, graduate of Oakwood College, Huntsville, Alabama, became minister but returned to rock singing career after trying gospel, appeared on several television shows in 1990–91, composer of *Tutti Frutti* (w/D. La Bostrie & Joe Lubin, Venice Music), *Long Tall Sally* (w/E. Johnson & R. Blackwell), *Lucille* (w/A. Collins), *Slippin' and Slidin'* (w/E. Bocage, A. Collins & J. Smith), songs in *Little Richard's Original Hits* (Los Angeles, West Coast Pub.), record star with Jimi Hendrix on ALA label, also recorded on Camden record label, etc.;

Nina Simone, born Eunice Kathleen Waymon (1935–), in Tryon, North Carolina, studied at Juilliard and the Curtis Institute, began job at nightclub as pianist, recorded and concertized, composed, according to David Ewen, "more than fifty of her own songs," including *Wild Is the Wind.*

In 1976, Marva Cooper and the author compiled a list of other Black composers in various areas of music, both popular and art music. Taken from books by Samuel Charters (*Negro Musicians in New Orleans*), Paul Oliver (*Ma Rainey and the Classic Blues Singers*), Leonard Feather (*Encyclopedia of Jazz*), W. C. Handy (publishing catalog and Father of the Blues), recordings, and musical compositions, as well as news media, several hundred names were assembled—far too many to be discussed in detail in an introductory book of this sort. At least 250 names, for example, were found in jazz alone. Some of the selected ones are given below in only partial order as representative of the lists. All those listed below composed several works, lists of which may be found at the Library of Congress, and some of which are being reissued. In no way do these lists imply, however, the worth of the composer, or a musical placement higher or lower than the above examples, as these compilations contain some of the most dynamic and talented personalities not only in American music, but in world music. Nor can these be considered complete, as current history precludes this.

In Gospel: W. Herbert Brewster, Delois Barrett Campbell, Virginia Davis, Theodore Frye, Antonio Haskell, Claude Joseph Johnson, Sallie Martin, Rev. Cleophus Robinson, Myrna Summers, Jesse Whitaker, and groups such as The Dixie Hummingbirds, The Mighty Clouds of Joy, The Ward Singers, The Caravans, Deep Sea Fishermen, The Soul Stirrers, Harold Smith Majestics, Pilgrim Jubilee Singers, Gospelaires, the Long Sisters, and others (continued in chapter XII).

In Blues, Rock, Soul, Rhythm 'n' Blues: Lavern Baker, Brook Benton, Chuck Berry, Ruth Brown, Solomon Burke, Chester (Howlin' Wolf) Burnett, Jerry Butler, Dave Clark, Sam Cooke, Ida Cox, Jimmie Cox, Arthur (Big Boy) Crudup, Ernest Willie Dixon, Earnest (Chubby Checker) Evans, Marvin Gaye, Berry Gordy, Al Green, Isaac Hayes, Gil Scott-Heron, John Lee Hooker, Eddie James (Son) House, Alberta Hunter, Bullmoose Jackson, Etta James, Blind Willie Johnson, Albert King, Huddie (Leadbelly) Leadbetter, Curtis Mayfield, Rose Marie McCoy, Elias (Bo Diddley) Mc-

Daniel, Brownie McGhee, Memphis Minnie, (Little) Richard Penniman, Wilson Pickett, Lloyd Price, Lou Rawls, Otis Redding, Jimmy Reed, Smokey Robinson, Memphis Slim, Victoria Spivey, Sonny Terry, T-Bone Walker, Muddy Waters, Barry White, Chuck Willis, and groups Nickolas Ashford and Valerie Simpson, The Blenders, The Cardinals, The Clovers, The Drifters, The Flamingos, The Four Tops, The Harptones, The Immortals, The Impressions, The Miracles, The Moonglows, The Nutmegs, The Opals, The Orioles, The Penquins, The Platters, The Pretenders, The Solitaires, The Supremes, The Swallows, Ike and Tina Turner, The Valentines, The Willows, and others (continued in chapter XII).

In Ragtime, Piano Blues, Boogie Woogie, and Early Jazz: Albert Ammons, Lovie Austin, Blind Blake, Blind Boone, Charles (Cow Cow) Davenport, Rev. Gary Davis, (Champion) Jack Dupree, Lemuel Fowler, Fred Griffin, Harry P. Guy, Toshua (Tosh) Hammed, Robert Hampton, Scott Hayden, Eddie Heywood, Irene Higginbotham, Jack (Jay C.) Higginbotham, Claude Hopkins, Anthony (Tony) Jackson, Pete (K. H.) Johnson, Richard Myknee Jones, Joe Jordan, William Osborne (Billy) Kyle, Meade Lux Lewis, Arthur Marshall, Artie Matthews, Jay (Hootie) McShann, Blind Willie McTell (Blind Sammie, Georgia Bill, Hot Shot Willie, Barrelhouse Sammie, pseudonymns), Eurreal Wilford Montgomery (Little Brother), Fred Norman, Rufus Perryman (Speckled Red), Samuel Blythe (Sammy) Price, Leon Rene, Hazel Scott, James Sylvester Scott, Benjamin Shook, Clarence (Pinetop) Smith, William Henry Joseph Berthol Bertholoff (Willie The Lion) Smith, Otis Spann, Fred Stone, Roosevelt Sykes (Roosevelt Sykes Bey), Hudson Whitaker (Tampa Red), and Jimmy Yancey.

In Popular: Pearl Bailey, Harry Belafonte, Perry Bradford, Tiny Bradshaw, Harry Brooks, Harvey Oliver Brooks, J. E. Brown, Cabell (Cab) Calloway, Elliot Carpenter, Nathaniel Adams (King) Cole, Charles Cooke, Sidney Easton, William Clarence (Billy) Eckstine, Roberta Flack, Porter Grainger, Donald Heywood, W. Alexander (Alex) Hill, John Leubrie Hill, Clarence Marvin Jones, Irving Jones, Clinton Kemp, Tom Lemonier, Thomas Morris, Odetta (Felious Gordon), Spencer Odom, W. Benton Overstreet, Ernest Peace, Dave Peyton, Maceo Pinkard, Arthur Porter, Wilbur Sweatman, Wendell Talbert, Blanche Keturah Thomas, Charles Warfield, Bert Williams, and Billy Williams. Calloway, Cole, etc. also performed jazz.

In Jazz: Al Jarreau, Nina Simone, Julian Edwin (Cannonball) Adderley, Nathaniel (Nat) Adderley, Brother Ahh (Robert Northern), Monty Alexander, Rashied Ali, Henry Allen, Eugene Ammons, Lillian Hardin Armstrong, Dorothy Jeanne Ashby, Roy Ayers, Albert Ayler, Ernest Harold Bailey (Benny), Kenneth (Kenny) Barron, Edgar Battle, George Benson, William Thomas Keter Betts, Leon (Barney) Bigard, Walter Bishop, Arthur Blakey, Peter Bocage, Earl Bostic, Anthony Braxton, Clifford Brown, Oscar Brown, Raymond (Ray) Brown, Raphael (Ray) Bryant, Milton (Milt) Buckner, Kenneth Earl (Kenny) Burrell, Donald Byrd, Bennett Lester Carter (Benny), Donald Cherry, Charlie Christian, Kenneth Clarke, Stanley Clarke, Billy Cobham, Cozy Cole, Alice Coltrane, Jean Lawrence Cook, Stanley Cowell, Benny (Hank) Crawford, William (Sonny) Criss, Eddie (Lockjaw) Davis, Nathan Tate Davis, William Strethen (Wild Bill) Davis, Jack DeJohnette, William Ballard (Bill) Doggett, Eric Allan Dolphy, Lou Donaldson, McKinley Howard (Kenny) Dorham, Kenneth Sidney (Kenny)

Drew, David Roy (Little Jazz) Eldridge, Mercer Kennedy Ellington, Arthur S. Farmer (Art), Ella Fitzgerald, Sonny Fortune, Ernest (Ernie) Freeman, Curtis Fuller, Walter Fuller, Erroll Garner, Benny Golson, Paul Gonsalves, Dexter Gordon, Foreststorn (Chico) Hamilton, Lionel Hampton, Herbert Jeffrey (Herbie) Hancock, Eddie Harris, Hampton Hawes, Coleman Hawkins (Bean), Erskine Hawkins, James Heath, Richard Andrew (Rick) Henderson, Wayne Henderson, Earl Fatha Hines, John Cornelius (Johnny) Hodges, Shirley Horn, Richard Holmes, Robert Holmes, Frederick (Freddie) Hubbard, Robert (Bobby) Hutcherson, Milton (Milt or Bags) Jackson, Jean Baptiste Illinois Jacquet, Ahmad Jamal, James Louis (J. J.) Johnson, Woodrow Wilson (Buddy) Johnson, Jonathan Jones, Thaddeus Joseph (Thad) Jones, Clifford L. Jordan, Louis Jordan, John Kirby, Rahsaan (Roland) Kirk, Earl Klugh, Oliver Lake, Yusef Lateef, Hubert and Ronnie Laws, Bill Lee, George (Zeno) Lewis, Ramsey Lewis, Melba D. Liston, Taj Mahal, Henry Lee (Hank) Marr, Leslie Coleman McCann, Brother Jack McDuff, Howard McGhee, Jimmy McGriff, John (Jackie) McLean, Lloyd McNeill, Charles Barron (Charlie) Mingus, Henry (Hank) Mobley, John Lewis, John Leslie (Wes) Montgomery, James Moody, Phil Moore Jr. (George Philip Moore), Consuelo Lee Morehead, Lee Morgan, Benny Moten, James Mundy, Joseph (King) Oliver, Melvin (Sy) Oliver, Edward (Kid) Ory, Oran Page (Hot Lips), Oscar Pettiford, Armand John Piron, Earl (Bud) Powell, Dewey Redman, Donald (Don) Redman, Sam Rivers, Freddie Roach, Theodore Walter (Sonny) Rollins, Willie Ruff, Patrice Rushen, Luis Russell, Shirley Scott, Woody Shaw, Archie Shepp, Wayne Shorter, Horace Silver, Jimmy Smith, Leo Smith, Lonnie Smith, Warren Smith Jr., Sonny Stitt, William (Billy) Strayhorn, Art Tatum, Cecil Taylor, Clark Terry, Tobert (Bobby) Timmons, Stanley Turrentine, McCoy Tyner, Phil Upchurch, Mal Waldron, Grover Washington, William (Chick) Webb, Benjamin Webster, Frank Wess, Randolph (Randy) Weston, Anthony (Tony) Williams, Charles Melvin (Cootie) Williams, Gerald Wilson, Teddy Wilson, Bill Withers, Samuel Wooding, and Lester Young (continued in chapter XII).

X

ART MUSIC: ITS DEFINITION, TRENDS, AND TRADITIONAL COMPOSERS

Simultaneous with developments in American jazz, composers wrote brilliantly in the area of art music. Originally designed for the society's elite, art music, or classical music, created a hierarchy and a stratification between high and low economic classes of society. Because the majority of African Americans were of the lowest economic strata, art music traditionally excluded them. Yet their talents and efforts directed many to be successful in this classical art form.

Definition

Based on an imitation of the "classicism" found in early Greece and Rome, art music, whose foundations partially originated in Africa, became an intellectual, academic and traditional fine art. It stressed the abstract and readily aesthetic response to an appreciation of higher values. Also used to denote the musical period of the late eighteenth century, the word "classical" evolved around the time of Franz Joseph Haydn (1732–1809), Wolfgang Mozart (1756–1791), early Ludwig van Beethoven (1770–1827) and George Bridgetower (1779–1860), a Black contemporary.

Art music was a highly involved system which demanded of its listeners as much concentration and knowledge of its historical and theoretical aspects as it did from its composers and performers. Unlike African communal participation, the response of listeners was passive rather than active, while the performer was spotlighted in the role of reenacting or recreating the work of a composer. It also concentrated upon the realization of history through "correct" or exactly prescribed performance within the given styles or periods. Unlike popular music whose beginning was less formal in its restricted habits of performance and composition, the history of art music was once collected and formed most directly by the Catholic Church. Therefore, most of western music history depended upon a church which attempted to codify a large body of compositions by purging the trite and the secular from the religious (popular versus art music).

Later art music further set itself apart from the popular music by use of certain rigidities in maintaining specific timbres for some of its forms. The orchestra was divided into strings, woodwinds, brasses and percussions, with strings predominating. Symphonies made use of these orchestrations as opposed to the chamber quality of winds and percussion common to popular orchestras. Voices were likewise divided into soprano, alto, tenor and bass; subdivisions within these voices were coloratura, lyric or mezzo soprano, contralto, contratenor and baritone. Even though instruments assumed characteristic styles common to their own technical capacities in a given era, all instruments before the modern period imitated the "singing" style of the voice. Composers were aware of the ranges and characteristics of style common to instruments and voices, and wrote accordingly.

Even though the history of this music was based on many African contributions and the universality of music in general, this fact was generally omitted in the documents important to the study of art music in modern Europe and America. Consequently, art music in America became unrightfully associated with the educated, the privileged and the White European. Unnecessarily placed on a pedestal above the minds and reaches of most Blacks, it assumed a separation of races. This created a separation of certain music from a certain class of people, and was yet another reason why Blacks have been omitted from the modern history of music. It also explained why such a piece as Debussy's *Golliwog's Cakewalk* was catalogued within art music while Scott Joplin's *Maple Leaf Rag* was placed in jazz.

Forms

Black composers in America used forms already established in art music. The structures of its music were, in part, based on popular European music derived from dances, vocal and instrumental forms. Some absolute (abstract) or descriptive forms were conceived from original or traditional pieces such as motets, canons, gigues, bourrées, gavottes, preludes, intermezzos, etudes and symphonic poems. Some of the most common forms which contained several movements were: the sonata, a piece written for one to three instruments; opera, a music-drama for vocalists, dancers and orchestra; ballet, a piece for dancers and orchestra; the mass, a liturgical piece in celebration of the Last Supper; and the fugue, an imitative piece based upon a theme which is highly developed, and greatly resembling the antiphonal quality of a call and response.

American Forebears in Retrospect

Composers of North America have a far richer and more lengthy historical background than many have imagined. Beginning with the earliest days of colonialism when anonymous figures of color were omitted from historical documents or were alluded to only in parenthetical context such as in Thomas Jefferson's writings, there were evidences that talented musicians excelled in the art of making music and in equalling the accomplishments of others throughout the world.

While some composers were treated as curiosities, others were recognized ever so slightly, thereby causing wide gaps in the documentations of many. On the other hand, some musical creativity and gifts were so monumental that history could not entirely ignore their lucent manifestations or their loud exclamations of excellence.

Composers before 1865 were of both slave and free status. Much information about the American slave background has been recorded, but not enough about the free Blacks. However, the authoritative John Hope Franklin's *From Slavery to Freedom* includes a chapter, "Quasi-Free Negroes," which states that "There had been some free Negroes during the entire colonial period; but for the most part they were inconsiderable in number and inconsequential in influence. . . . But in the South, the existence of a large group of free Negroes proved to be a source of constant embarrassment to the slaveholders, for it tended to undermine the very foundation on which slavery was built." Although the Southerners carried on "a campaign of vilification against the free Negroes" in order to "keep them in their place," and even though the free Blacks were described as "an incubus upon the land" and must have experienced great difficulty in attempting to maintain a decent and trouble-free existence while practicing an artistic profession, this horrible condition could not entirely suppress the quality of the musical compositions being formulated, nor the possibilities of European educations when they could be afforded by the family or granted by another.

Participation in the world of art music in America during the early eighteenth and nineteenth centuries was far more widespread, then, than the slave apparently knew and certainly far more than the outdated curricula would have had twentieth century contemporaries believe. However, because America was a growing frontier country at that time and not yet a renowned learning center, most musicians preferred traveling to Europe, particularly Paris, although this meant a disruption of historical information and a further displacement of important records. Had America been more developed, or had America not been so steeped in the myth about the African mind, or had the economic importance of slavery not been so real to the European pioneers, the more enlightened of the Black Americans might not have felt so compelled to interrupt their living here for a sojourn in Europe. Even now, the prestige and compelling urgency to seek a European education is founded more upon the myths and opportunities of yesteryear than upon the realities of today.

Those who helped set the tone for the advancement in musical composition by Blacks also plotted the plans for developments in all American music. In part, the earliest of the documented names were found in James Trotter's *Music and Some Highly Musical People* and in Maud Cuney Hare's *Negro Musicians and Their Music.*

It is important to note that James Trotter, in his *Music and Some Highly Musical People*, published scores in the appendix for the following: Basil Barés (b. 1846?), *La Capricieuse Waltz*; William Brady (d. 1854), *Anthem for Christmas*, SATB; W. F. Craig, *Rays of Hope March*; Edmund Dédé (1829–1903), *Le Serment del' Arabe*, dramatic chant; John T. Douglass (b. 1847?), *The Pilgrim*, overture; Justin Holland (b. 1819), *Andante* for guitar; Lucien Lambert (b. 1828), *Au Clair de la Lune* for piano; Sidney Lambert (b. 1823), *Les Clochettes*, fantaisie-mazurka; F. E. Lewis, *Scenes of Youth*, descriptive-fantasia for piano; Jacob Sawyer, *Welcome to the Era March* (Perry, 1877); Samuel Snaer (b. 1834), *Mass for Three Voices*, excerpts of *Gloria, Agnus Dei*; H. F. Williams (b. 1813?), *Lauriett, Ballad* and *Parisian Waltzes*. He also included others.

In addition to the above, Maud Cuney Hare, in her *Negro Musicians and Their Music*, listed Fierville Repanti; J. M. Doublet; E. V. McCarty; Cleveland Luca (c. ?–1872), *National Anthem for Liberia*; John T. Douglass as composer of pieces for orchestra and piano; William Brady, quadrilles, polkas, waltzes; William Starr, quick steps and marches; DeKoven Thompson (1879–1934) *Love Comes But Once, A Heart Disclosed*, and *If I Forget*; Arthur Cochran (b. 1878) *Communion Office in F Major*; Francois Clarens and Edmund Jenkins, *African War Dance* for orchestra, *Sonata in A Minor* for cello, *Rhapsody No. 2.* for orchestra, and *Spring Fantasy*. Hare also listed at least twelve song titles of Lucien Lambert (b. 1828) who was born in New Orleans, was a graduate of the Paris Conservatory, gained fame as a pianist-composer, and who eventually moved from Paris to Brazil. Son of Richard with whom he first studied, brother of Sidney, and father of Lucien Lambert (ca. 1858–1945) discussed in the European section, he was the composer of *Au Clair de la Lune, La Bresiliana, L'Americaine, Cloches et Clochettes, Pluie de Corails, La Rose et le Bengali,* and *Ah! Vous disais-je Maman.*

Various written sources by Eileen Southern, John Gray, Samuel Floyd, the editors of *Philadelphia Public Ledger, Baker's Dictionary, the New Grove,* as well as guest writers in *The Black Perspective in Music* listed more complete dates for some of the Trotter findings as follows: Basil Barés (1846–1902), Walter F. Craig (1854–192?), John T. Douglas (1847–1886), Lucien Lambert (ca. 1828–1878), Justin Holland (1819–1886), and H. F. Williams (1813–1903). For some Hare introductions, ending dates were: Eugene V. McCarty (1821–1881), Cleveland Luca (1838–1872), and Edmund Jenkins (1894–1926).

Henry F. Williams. From James Trotter's *Music and Some Highly Musical People.*

The Library of Congress has preserved a few copies of Justin Holland's compositions: *Carnival of Venice Fantaisie* for guitar, 1866; *Choice Melodies for the Guitar,* 1867; *Gems for the Guitar,* 1856? and *Winter Evenings,* six pieces of waltzes, polkas, variations, fandangos, and marches. Holland was said by Hare to have composed more than thirty-five pieces for solo guitar, including Holland's *Comprehensive Method for the Guitar,* published by Peters in 1874.

One of the most colorful orchestra leaders and composers presented by Hare and others was Frank Johnson (c. 1809–1844) from Philadelphia. The most comprehensive sketch on Johnson was written in 1974 by Arthur LaBrew at Southern University, who fixed Johnson's dates as 1792–1844. Set forth in a monograph booklet, LaBrew reviewed Johnson as violinist, trumpeter, and composer, and as contemporary with such as A. J. R. Connor. Some of the scores contained in the LaBrew research were *Voice Quadrilles* arranged for the piano; *Hark the Merry Trumpet*; and *General Cadwaladers March.* Others at the Library of Congress were: *Captain J. G. Watmough's Kent Bugle Slow March* for Piano (before 1820); *A Choice Collection of New Cotillions* for piano; *Colonel S. B. Grant's Parade March* for flute and piano (c. 1839); *Favorite March in the Cateract of the Ganges,* originally for band, arranged for piano; *General Cadwaladers March* (1820?); *Johnson's March* for piano with flute or voice; *Oh Turn Away those Mournful Eyes; Victoria Gallop,* saloon music (1839); *Voice Quadrilles* arranged for piano with chorus; and *Philadelphia Gray's Quick Step,* arrangement based on themes of Bellini's opera *I Puritani.*

Frederick E. Lewis. From James Trotter's *Music and Some Highly Musical People.*

Justin Holland. From Trotter's *Music and Some Highly Musical People.*

Neo-Romantic Composers of the Modern Period

The modern period of art music consisted of various styles built upon formulas of past eras as well as the more dissonant techniques of the modern century. It also reflected a continuation of German romanticism. Without question, the latter period served as the model for the majority of the earliest composers discussed in this chapter, with its emphasis upon praise of beauty and nature, love of humanistic approaches and especially nationalism.

HENRY (HARRY) T. BURLEIGH (1866–1949)

Harry T. Burleigh, a baritone-composer, arranger, and teacher was born Henry T. Burleigh in Erie, Pennsylvania, and lived to the age of eighty-three before he died in Stamford, Connecticut. His life began at Reconstruction and lasted well into the second stage of Black musical developments. His own style reflected both of these ages in that he forged ahead in the popular minstrel shows while maintaining representative works in the field of art music within the modern period.

H. T. Burleigh. Courtesy of Moorland-Spingarn Research Center, Howard University.

He studied with Max Spicker, John White, Rubin Goldmark, Christian Fritsch and others. At National Conservatory, Burleigh also came under the influence of Anton Dvorak, the Czech composer who inspired America to use indigenous material such as the Black and Indiana folk songs, rather than to continue within the inspirations and forms of the European tradition.

A capable baritone as well as a good composer, Burleigh found the time to sing spirituals and other songs for Dvorak, who in turn, promoted the use of spirituals by including thematic or similar emotional material in his *New World Symphony*. Another for whom Burleigh sang was Darius Milhaud, the French composer who came to America during the early 1900's and diligently attended jazz clubs and other places where Black music was performed. Milhaud showed this influence in some of his works such as *La Création du Monde*.

In addition to his work at the Conservatory, Burleigh gained a reputation for his fine musicianship at the Temple Emmanuel (Jewish) and the Saint George's Church in New York (where he became a soloist). Of his voice, some reviews of the day noted:

> Honor to Negro Spirituals and to Harry T. Burleigh. His voice, robust and clear, rang out in joyous strains of the hymn . . . front rank of the musicians of our time—*International Negro Press*, June 1936.

Having won many awards for both his composition and his singing, among which was the Spingarn Medal given by the National Association of Colored People, he also earned other prizes and gave concert tours. He was the musical spokesman for Black achievements.

Burleigh wrote innumerable songs, arranged many spirituals and popular songs, and edited a few volumes of spirituals and ballads. One book so edited contained twenty-one songs by H. C. Work, Stephen Foster and others. They were also representative of his own style of writing. Burleigh's style consisted of tonal Romantic types of simple harmonies and techniques. Among his works were: *Young Warrior; The Soldier, Oh Brothers Lift Your Voices; Love's Garden; Five Songs* (text Lawrence Hope); *Ethiopia Saluting the Colors; The Grey Wolf; Saracen Songs; One Year; Little Mother of Mine; Carry Me Back to the Pine Woods; A Corn Song; Just Because; If Life Be a Dream; I Love My Jean; From the Southland; The Glory of the Day was in Her Face; Keep a Good Grip on de Hoe; Mammy's Li'l Baby; Her Eyes; Twin Pools; Balm in Gilead; Ain't Going to Study War No Mo'; Behold that Star; By an' By; Couldn't Hear Nobody Pray; De Blin' Man Stood on de Road an' Cried; De Gospel Train; Deep River; You May Bury Me in de Eas'*; and *A Jubilee*.

HARRY LAWRENCE FREEMAN (1869–1954)

Harry L. Freeman, a little known and little publicized composer, was born in Cleveland, Ohio, and was buried in New York after a career of art music and popular involvement. Primarily interested in drama and music together, he was credited with the organization of the Freeman School of Music in 1911, the Freeman School of Grand Opera in 1923, and was the founder of the Negro Opera Company in 1920. Because it was uncommon for Black opera singers to join unions or any organizations for Whites, and because of the stereotype that Blacks "could sing music but not necessarily opera," his work was highly significant.

A winner of the Harmon Award in 1930, and conductor of many

concerts and the pageant at Chicago during the World's Fair in 1934, Freeman was cited as being the first Black composer in the United States to conduct a symphony orchestra in a rendition of his own work (*O Sing a New Song*) which he directed in Minnesota in 1907. He was also cited as being the first Black to write fourteen grand style operas. Freeman studied theory with J. H. Beck, piano with E. Shonert and Carlos Sobrino. From 1902 to 1904 he taught at Wilberforce, and from 1910 to 1913 at the Salem School in North Carolina.

Among his works were: *O Sing a New Song* (orchestra); *The Martyr; Valdo; African Krall; Octoroon; The Tryst; The Prophecy; Athalia; The Plantation; Vendetta; American Romance* (jazz opera); *Voodoo; Leah Kleschma; Uzziah; Zululand* (tetralogy: first part, 2150 pages); *The Slave* (ballet for orchestral and choral ensemble); *If Thou Didst Love; Whiter*; and others.

N. CLARK SMITH (1877–1935)

Major N. Clark Smith was born in Fort Leavenworth, Kansas. A legendary band director-composer made famous at Tuskegee Institute, Alabama, his record of excellence is yet told with admiration by Lexine House Weeks and other Tuskegee residents familiar with his work. Educated in the public schools of Leavenworth, and later in Kansas City, he also graduated from the Chicago Music College.

One newspaper announced his death with headlines of "Major N. Clark Smith, Noted Bandmaster Taken by Death" and "Made Famous at Tuskegee." Mourned as one whose "reputation as a musician and composer was nationwide" (*Chicago Defender*, October 12, 1935), Smith had established an international reputation with his tours to the Hawaiian Islands, Australia, and New Zealand with the N. B. Curtis Minstrels in 1899, and in tours with the Tuskegee band. Smith returned to Kansas as musical director of Lincoln High and later to Chicago as musical director at Wendell Phillips until his 1934 resignation.

The *Defender* also described Smith as "A university graduate and composer of hundreds of songs, choral works and an African symphony" who "won many honors, including the Wanamaker prize in 1930 with his folk song suite dealing with the life of the stevedores in the West Indies," seen in *The Orange Dance, The Pineapple Lament,* and *Banana Walk* movements, for example. He was further described as "one of America's most colorful characters" (*Kansas Plaindealer*, October 11, 1936).

Maud Cuney Hare mentioned Smith on a list of prizewinners as a second place winner for his *Negro Folk Song Prelude*. The Library of Congress has catalogued the following as some of his musical samples: *Favorite Folk-Melodies* (1914, unpublished); *A Group of New Plantation Songs* (Clayton Summy, 1906); *Negro Choral Symphony* (Lyon & Healy, 1933); *Century of Progress*, edition for piano, soli, SATB (1930); *Negro Folk Suite* (incomplete, includes only I. *The Orange Dance*—British Guinea, and II. *Pineapple Lament*—Martinique and III. *Banana Walk*—St. Helena Island, piano, Lyon & Healy, 1925); *New Plantation Melodies* (1909, unpublished); *Plantation Folk Songs*, TTBB, for high school and other levels; and *The Tuskegee March*—two step song. Smith also composed *The Tuskegee Song* to words of Paul Laurence Dunbar, a stately piece in G with secondary dominants and stirring, marchlike sturdiness within a thirty-two bar, three verse frame.

CLARENCE CAMERON WHITE (1880–1960)

Clarence Cameron White, violinist, composer and educator, was born in Clarksville, Tennessee. Educated at Oberlin College, White studied violin with Zacharwitsch, won two Rosenwald Fellowships and was awarded honorary degrees from Atlanta University and Wilberforce. He also was awarded the David Bispham Award for his opera *Ouanga* and a Harmon Foundation Medal. After having served as a teacher in public schools and music studios in Boston, he served as chairman of the music department at West Virginia State College in 1924, as director of music at the Hampton Institute, and taught at the Washington Conservatory.

C. C. White. Courtesy of Moorland-Spingarn Research Center, Howard University.

As guest artist with Samuel Coleridge-Taylor, the Black European composer, White toured the United States and London for three years. He concertized extensively, organized programs for the National Recreational Association and wrote articles (one of which was a study of Bridgetower, another Black European). He was a member of ASCAP, which he joined in 1924. His genuine interest in his profession coupled with his intense desire to devote more time to performance and the writing of music, forced him to resign from the chairmanship of Hampton Institute after only three years. Eventually, he settled in New York where he died.

A talented composer of the neo-Romantic style, he also employed the use of modern techniques. White wrote various compositions for vocal and instrumental media and during his lifetime, he was hailed as "America's foremost composer of opera."

Among his works were: *Two Pieces, Opus 60 for Piano; Bandanna Sketches* (Slave songs); *Five Songs; Improvisation; Levee Dance; Camp Song; Fleurette; Ouanga* (music drama in 3 acts); *Plantation Song; Dance Caprice; The Question; Tuxedo; Nobody Knows de Trouble I've Seen* (and numerous other spiritual arrangements); *Piece for Strings and Timpani; A Night in Sans Souci* (ballet); *Violin Concerto No. 2 in E minor; Symphony in D minor*; and *From the Cotton Fields*.

ROBERT NATHANIEL DETT (1882–1943)

Robert Nathaniel Dett, pianist, composer, arranger, and educator, was born in Drummondsville, Ontario, and died at Battle Creek, Michigan. Dett was educated at the Oliver Willis Halstead Conservatory in Lockport, New York; at Oberlin College (where he received the B.M. and Mus. D. degrees); at Columbia University; the University of Pennsylvania; Harvard University; the Eastman School of Music (where he received the M.M. degree) and at the Niagara Falls Collegiate Institute. Two honorary Doctorates were given to him by Howard University and Oberlin Conservatory. Highly trained, Dett joined ASCAP in 1925 and continued to create a legend for himself in his own time.

His many professional positions included church pianist in Niagara Falls between 1898 and 1903; director of music at Lane College between 1908 and 1911, at Lincoln Institute from 1911 to 1913, at Bennett College in 1937 and finally at Hampton Institute in Virginia where he was a teacher of Dorothy Maynor, soprano. He was credited with founding the American Art Society. He served as a conductor of many choral ensembles and wrote articles and edited many collections. In addition, Dr. Dett was the deserving recipient of various awards, among which were the Harmon Foundation Award, Francis Boott Music Prize at Harvard, Bowdoin Literary Prize, and the Palm and Ribbon Royal Belgian Band Award.

Although some people still did not consider his music worthwhile, Dett was nevertheless a composer of reputable qualifications and talent whose works generated his success. From contemporary newspaper articles at that time, captions revealed Dett's professionalism and respect, and cast light

Robert Nathaniel Dett. Courtesy of Hampton Institute Library.

upon the subject of his competence and acceptance into the world of art music. In part, the news media stated:

> Dr. R. Nathaniel Dett in Rochester Attracts Attention *Afro-American*, 1934

> We are a great people with strange dreams and a wonderful heritage lost somewhere in the years between. . . . (Dett) *Afro-Dispatch*, 1934

> Oratorio by Dett Played by Symphony (*The Ordering of Moses*).
> *Kansas City Call*, 1937

As a matter of one man's opinion . . . one of the most thrilling . . . (said of Dett's Choir performance by Douglas Gordon)

Dett was a totally competent and praiseworthy composer of his day. His general style of writing was quite organized and refined, as well as both established and experimental. For his works he received honors for producing *The Ordering of Moses*, the first large oratorio to be based on motifs of Black folk music. This production was a Cincinnati Broadcast with Eugene Goosens conducting 350 voices. He was also chosen by the Rochester Exposition to furnish music for a drama then in progress (*Pathways of Progress*) which he prepared in three weeks and which was termed a "splendid effect." His final virtues of choral conducting and management were beyond reproach. Vivian McBrier, for her doctoral dissertation at Catholic University, has further reviewed the works and worth of the man in an extensive study.

Although Dett composed for several media, he did equally well in both vocal and instrumental styles. In addition, he composed and arranged compositions for vocal combinations, and for media such as piano and other instruments. Dett's style was virtually Romantic, but rhythmically and harmonically exciting in his frequent and refreshing use of technically demanding material. His controlled balance of voices and complete knowledge of instrumentation attested to his virtuosity. Chromaticisms or other techniques were used in various ternary, operatic or symphonic forms of art music. Some of his music also bordered on popular varieties, particularly such as the familiar *Juba Dance* (from In the Bottoms) with its ragtime-like bass and dancing, dotted melodies. Yet the calmness and technical style of the second section resembled the traditional song form styles of the 1900's. An excerpt of the latter work is shown in Example 35:

Ex. 35. *Juba Dance*, Dett. Copyright 1913 by Summy-Birchard Company, Evanston, Illinois. Copyright renewed. All Rights Reserved. Used by permission.

Among Dett's other works were: *Noon Siesta; To a Closed Casement; A Bayou Garden; Legend of the Atoll; America the Beautiful;* (1918); *Drink to me Only with Thine Eyes; the Daybreak Charioteer; Parade of the Jasmine Banners; Oh Hear the Lambs A-Cryin; Pompons and Fans; Now Rest Beneath Night's Shadows; The Ordering of Moses* (Biblical folk scene of soli, chorus, and orchestra available from Talladega; includes Dawson and Work.); *Go Not Far from Me; Sit Down, Servant, Sit Down; O Lord, the Hardwon Miles; Magnolia* (piano suite); *Enchantment* (piano suite); *In The Bottoms* (piano suite); *Don't be Weary Traveler*

(motet, Francis Boot Prize); *The Chariot Jubilee* (for tenor solo, chorus and orchestra); *An American Sampler* (orchestra); *Ramah* (violin); *I'm so Glad Trouble Don't Last Always; Sinners Won't you Hear; Deep River; I'll Never Turn Back No More; Listen to the Lambs* (women's voices); *Who Made Thee?; Walk Ye in God's Love; Religious Folk Songs of the Negro* (edited); *Dett Collection of Spirituals* (4 volumes); and other works.

CARL ROSSINI DITON (1886–1969)

Carl Diton, a native Philadelphian, was a graduate of the Institute for Colored Youth (1898–1902), Central High School (1902–05), and the University of Pennsylvania. He did further study in Germany.

As a pianist, Diton concertized extensively and was marked by some as the first Black pianist to tour the United States. Maud Hare described him as a prizewinning composer whose music was "advancing the cause of good music in the race and in the United States." Reviewed in *Who's Who in Colored America*, the *Negro Yearbook*, Evelyn White's *Bibliography of Published Choral Music by Black Composers*, and Penman Lovingood's *Famous Modern Negro Musicians*, he was depicted as a distinguished and talented musician and a member of Omega, NANM, and the Fisk University Club of Philadelphia.

Diton worked at Paine College, Augusta, Georgia, and at Talladega, Alabama, until 1918. Thereafter returning to Philadelphia, he continued his work by conducting, teaching, and composing. He also was organist of St. Thomas Church in Philadelphia for some time.

His compositions, in part, were *Entreaty* (in Rogie Clark's *Negro Art Songs*, E. B. Marks, 1946); *Thirty-six South Carolina Spirituals* (Schirmer, 1928); *And He Never Spoke a Mumbelin' Word* (Schirmer, 1921); *At the Beautiful Gate* (Schirmer, 1921); *Deep River* (Schirmer, 1915); *The Hymn of Nebraska; Pilgrim's Song; Poor Mourner's Got A Home; Roll, Jordan;* and others.

CAMILLE NICKERSON (1887–1982)

Camille Nickerson, noted pianist-singer and educator, was born in New Orleans, Louisiana. She resided in Washington, D.C. Having begun an early study of music with her father, William Nickerson, she attended the Oberlin Conservatory where she received the Bachelor of Music and Master of Music degrees. She later did post-graduate work at the Juilliard School of Music and at Teachers College, Columbia University.

Camille Nickerson.

As an educator, Camille Nickerson began teaching at the William Nickerson School of Music in New Orleans. In 1926, however, she moved to Howard University School of Music in Washington, D.C., where she was eventually elevated to the rank of professor. By 1930, her talents as a composer and research scholar won her many honors and awards, among which was a Rosenwald Fellowship for Study in the field of Creole Folk Music of Louisiana. Through her diligence in this area, an impressive legacy of early folk music from Latin influences was documented in her writings, depicting themes of romance; she also wrote compositional arrangements of Creole songs for choral ensembles and solo voice, many of the latter of which she herself performed in innumerable concerts at halls, institutions and festivals throughout the United States and Europe.

Her compositions show tonal examples of both homophonic and slight polyphonic trends. Highly sensitive in lyrical and harmonic concepts, the beauty of the music is highlighted within simplicity and delicacy of form and style, yet very concretely woven to support the unusual Creole poetry, rhythms of the habernera, or simple lines of melodic emphasis.

Among her compositions are: *Mazelle Zizi; Christmas Everywhere; The Women of the USA; Five Creole Songs (Chère Moi, Lemme Toi; Lizétte, To Quitté la Plaine; Dansé Conni Conné; Fais Dodo and Micheu Banjo); When Love Is Done; Aurore Pradere; Suzanne, Belle Femme*; and *Spring Song*.

FLORENCE PRICE (1888–1953)

Florence Price. Courtesy of Moorland-Spingarn Research Center, Howard University.

Florence Price, composer, pianist, organist and educator, was born in Little Rock, Arkansas, and died in Chicago, Illinois. She was educated at the New England Conservatory, by Cutter, Chadwick, and Converse; at the American Conservatory; at Chicago Musical College; at Chicago Teachers College; at Central YWCA College; at the Lewis Institute; and at Chicago University. Price also was influenced by her teachers Henry Dunkan, Charles Denner, A. Anderson and others. Her teaching career was spent at Shorter College, Clark University. Her memberships included the NAACC and the ASCAP organizations, and among her awards was the coveted Wanamaker Prize.

Florence Price wrote many compositions and arrangements for various media. Her works were performed by herself, Margaret Bonds and others. Her style was Romantic, and consisted of some technically difficult devices as well as smaller designs intended for intermediate levels.

Among her works were the following: *Symphony in E minor* (Wannamaker Prize); *Symphonic Tone Poem; Piano Concerto; Violin Concerto; Quintet for Piano and Strings; Concert Overture* (based on Black spirituals); *The Wind and the Sea; Three Little Negro Dances; Lincoln Walks at Midnight; Rhapsody for Piano and Orchestra; Negro Folksongs in Counterpoint; a String Quartet; Moods for Flute, Clarinet, and Piano; Organ Sonata; Passacaglia and Fugue for Organ; My Soul's Been Anchored in de Lord*; etc. Althea Waites record of her piano music is by Cambria.

FRANCIS HALL JOHNSON (1888–1970)

Hall Johnson, a composer, author, conductor, and arranger, was a resident of New York City at the time of his unfortunate death in his apartment on April 30, 1970. Born in Athens, Georgia, he was the recipient of many awards and other honors. On an April Sunday, a Musical Tribute to Hall Johnson was given at which many local and national musicians and other dignitaries performed in his honor. At the occasion, Major John Lindsay presented Dr. Johnson with New York City's "highest and most coveted award," The Handel Award; the John Motley Chorus sang his cantata, the *Son of Man, Music in Negro Idiom*; and the Carl Fisher Music Company was among others who presented him with honors.

During his lifetime, Johnson received an honorary Mus. D. degree from the Philadelphia Music Academy as well as countless other awards. Having studied with Percy Goetschius and others, his education was received at Allen University, Atlanta University, Knox Institute, the University of Pennsylvania and the New York Institute of Musical Art. Johnson also specialized in languages such as French and German, but his primary emphasis was music. A member of ASCAP, his specialties became the violin, voice and composition.

He concertized on radio, television and films and also recorded many songs. He played the violin with the Vernon Castle Orchestra, served as arranger and musical director for the Broadway production *Green Pastures*, and as writer of the music for the Broadway stage score *Run Little Chilin.* In his many tours, he performed with the Festival for Negro Choruses of Los Angeles which he organized in 1936. He formed the Hall Johnson Choir in 1925, and toured the United States and Europe for the State Department in 1951.

Like those before and after him, Johnson developed a greatness from within which spoke of the heritage of the Black spirituals. Having been influenced by those older folk who constantly sang the songs around him, he developed an early sensitivity for the musical heritage and gained a reputation for his writing as well as the performance of his songs.

His style, mainly Romantic and homophonic, ranged from the somber and the religious to the forthright gay styles and pleasantries of life. His spirituals showed a command of the keyboard and vocal line, as well as of ornamentation. Generally, his lines of such songs also used unadorned vocal lines and simplicity of form, although technical and emotional aspects ranged high. His other works also reflected his command of instrumental characteristics and their inherent possibilities. His most exciting developments, however, stemmed from the enthusiasm which he used in his efforts to develop and promote the spirituals.

Among his works were: *Book of Negro Spirituals; Honor, Honor; Oh What a Beautiful City; Steal Away; His Name So Sweet; The Green Pastures* (a collection of 25 spirituals from the play); *Take My Mother Home* (based on a narrative from St. John); *I Cannot Stay Here By Myself* (a slave's lament); *Tradition* (arr.); *Run Little Chilun* (stage score); *Son of Man* (cantata); *Fi-Yer* (Fire), and many others for various media.

PENMAN LOVINGOOD, SR. (1895–)

Penman Lovingood, composer, author, and singer, was born in Marshall, Texas. According the ASCAP, he was educated at the Samuel Huston College (which Don White points out as really his high school education), at Temple University, and a Compton College. He studied with William Happich at the Symphony Club in Philadelphia and also with J. Rosamond Johnson in New York.

Penman Lovingood. From Lovingood Collection.

In 1925, he made his singing debut at Town Hall in New York and also had his orchestral works performed at that recital. A prizewinner, besides, he was listed by Maud Cuney Hare as a secondary prizewinner of the Wanamaker Award in 1930. Lovingood was also awarded the Bronze and Silver Medals in voice and composition by the Griffith Foundation of Newark, New Jersey; an award from ASCAP for the performance of *Menelik*, his opera in three acts (manuscript in Library of Congress); and in 1963, he was given membership into ASCAP.

In addition to authoring *Famous Negro Musicians* (published by Press Forum, New York, in 1921), Lovingood wrote songs and instrumental works such as *Menelik of Abyssinia; Saturday's Child; Christus Natus Est* (carol); *Lament of the Passionate Pilgrims* (SATB); *The Romance of Noah* (cantata); *Supreme Deliverer* (Cantata); *San Juan Overture; Vitania Suite* for orchestra; Prelude in E^b for piano and orchestra; *Mass in B^b*; *Twelve Spirituals*; and others published by his own company, Compton, California.

EVA JESSYE (1895–)

Eva Jessye, a world renowned choral conductor, composer, and arranger of spirituals and other songs, was born in Coffeyville, Kansas. She received her first musical training at Western University in Kansas and later attended Langston University in Oklahoma, graduating in 1916. In addition, she was awarded an honorary Master of Arts degree from Wilberforce and an honorary doctorate from Allen University.

Jessye taught for a number of years in Taft, Haskell, and Muskogee, Oklahoma, and thereafter traveled to New York. She also worked at Morgan State, Claflin College, Maryland State College, and the Junior Black Academy in Texas. At other institutions such as Glassboro State College, she became composer-in-residence and organizer of the Eva Jessye Choirs. She was selected to direct "Paradise Lost and Regained" and was awarded the State Medal of Achievement upon the occasion of Pittsburgh State University's Diamond Anniversary as well as composer-in-residence status. She also organized an Eva Jessye Choir at the University of Michigan to whom she donated her music collection of books, records, and manuscripts, and from whom (according to Abdul Raoul) she received a Doctor of Determination degree.

Eva Jessye. Courtesy of Bernice Hammond, Association for the Preservation and Presentation of the Arts.

In 1935, George Gershwin chose her to direct the Eva Jessye Choir in his *Porgy and Bess* and to appear as a substitute "strawberry woman." She was chosen to become music director of the King Vidor film *Hallelujah* and she also served as choir director and composer of the song for the celebration of American and Soviet Friendship Orders of the Day in 1944, which was performed in several large cities of the United States. In addition, she conducted the choir for the Martin Luther King March on Washington in 1963.

The Eva Jessye Choir performed at the Capitol Theatre on Broadway, at the first folk festival held in Windsor, Canada, and in many other cities throughout the United States and abroad, including Berlin, Paris, London and Vienna. She was perhaps the first to interpret Virgil Thompson's *Four Saints in Three Acts* (opera); she also gained fame by conducting the Eva Jessye Choir on the radio for many years.

Other honors have been bestowed upon Eva Jessye. She has appeared with conductors Eugene Ormandy, Stokowski, Mitropoulos, Steinberg, Smallens, Coppola, William Grant Still, and others; the Association for the Preservation and Presentation of the Arts, Inc., honored her in Washington, D.C. at their forty-third anniversary Awards Dinner in 1982; she was selected as an Outstanding Woman of Kansas; and she was the subject of many articles and books such as *Who's Who in Colored America, ASCAP*, and *Negro Yearbook*. In her book *Negro Musicians and Their Music*, Maud Cuney Hare described her as "the only Negro woman conductor on radio . . . [whose] . . . groups . . . give programs of Negro music which are well planned as to both historical and musical merit." Ebony cited her as the "first Black woman to receive international distinction as a choral director."

Mainly an arranger of spirituals, Jessye has produced tonal structures of various compositional and vocal techniques. Of her *Paradise Lost and Regained*, Joan Reinthaler wrote after the Washington, D.C. premiere at the Washington Cathedral that "Dr. Jessye has perceived the unexpected affinity between Milton's elegant and purple poetry and the personalized romanticism of the spiritual idiom" and that Jessye had "forged a niche all her own." Written for SATB, soloists, dancers, organ, piano, and percussion, the folk oratorio consisted of a suite of spirituals.

Her published compositions are: *Simon the Fisherman* (Summy-Birchard); *My Spirituals* (sixteen in number, Robbins-Engel); *By Heck* (Henry) and *When the Saints Go Marching In* (E. B. Marks). Other works representative of her style are *Chronicle of Job* folk drama; *Life of Christ in Negro Spirituals; The Spirit of the Lord Done Fell on Me; Who Is That Yondah?; I Belong to That Band; John Saw De Holy Numbah*; and others.

WILLIAM GRANT STILL (1895–1978)

William Grant Still, a legendary giant of American composers, was born in Woodville, Mississippi. Partially reared in Arkansas, Still relocated to Los Angeles, California, where he continued to pursue his love for music daily. Fondly hailed as "Dean of Negro Composers", he should rather have been named "Dean of American Composers" because of his place in time, and the value of his contributions.

Still was educated in Arkansas, at Wilberforce University, Oberlin Conservatory, and the New England Conservatory. A winner of many awards, Still excelled in composition which brought him the Guggenheim and Rosenwald Fellowships. In 1955, Still became the first Black to conduct a major symphony orchestra in the deep South when he directed the New Orleans Philharmonic in two of his own works. In addition to the New Orleans Philharmonic, he has conducted the Los Angeles Philharmonic at the Hollywood Bowl.

Other honors have been awarded the composer-conductor in the form of commissions from the Columbia Broadcasting System, the New York World's Fair, Paul Whiteman, the League of Composers and the Cleveland Orchestra. The Cincinnati Symphony Orchestra awarded him a prize in 1944 for the writing of an overture in celebration of its jubilee season. He also won the Harmon Award in 1928; a trophy from Local 767 of the Musicians' Union was also given, and honorary degrees have been awarded

William Grant Still.

him from Wilberforce University (M.M.), Howard University (Mus. D.) and from Bates College (Doctor of Letters).

Still began the study of music under the encouragement of his mother. However, she warned him of the difficulty of many fine musicians who were not invited to the best of homes (as was the case of the early jazz and minstrel composers) but did not prevent his musical career. He was instructed on the violin at an early age, and his compositional traits showed a reflection of this training. Still also came under the strong influence of his teacher, Edgar Varèse.

Having composed in virtually all major forms and media from popular to classical, his thorough knowledge of orchestration, keyboard and vocal capacities are well known. Reviews, newspapers and other printed media related his accomplishments:

> One of our greatest American composers. He has made a real contribution to music. —Stokowski, 1945

> This American composer shows remarkable qualifications which place him as one of the very greatest living composers of the New World; a sense of immediate observation; the taste for a rigorous and brilliant orchestration; spontaneity and sincerity characterize his compositions. —*Micro Magazine*, 1955

> This is real music, music of a composer of exotic talent and temperament, who has a keen sense of beauty and sensuousness which is controlled by taste . . . and unquestionable gift and warm feeling, now sad, now gay, characteristic and sincere in expression . . . increasing mastery on the part of the composer . . .
>
> —*New York Times*

In his piano suite, *Bells*, the movements *Phantom Chapel* and *Fairy Knoll* were derived from an impressionistic period of obscured harmonies. Measures 27–30 (*Phantom*) and 67–70 (*Fairy*) are given: Still's *Afro-American Symphony* earned the respect, inspiration and interest of younger composers. Based on themes derived from the blues, spirituals, jazz elements and familiar devices to the populace, Still integrated two worlds of music through quality writing and adaptation. This work became popular around 1933 and has been performed many times. His *Little Song That Wanted to be a Symphony* has been compared to Prokofieff's *Peter and the Wolf* in design. He also composed operas, choral works and various other smaller forms.

Ex. 36. *Phantom Chapel* and *Fairy Knoll*, Still. © Copyright 1944 by MCA Music, A Division of MCA, Inc., 445 Park Avenue, New York, New York 10022. Used by permission. All rights reserved.

Fairy Knoll © Copyright 1944 by MCA Music. All rights reserved. Used by permission.

Some of Still's works show fragmentary phrases and tremolo devices as in measures five and seven (piano introduction) of his *Plain-Chant for America*, a piece for baritone solo with piano accompaniment. Perhaps the highlight of the piece is its message of measures 99–104, Ex. 44.

Ex. 37. *Plain-Chant for America*, Still. Copyright by William G. Still. Used by permission.

Much of Still's music uses romantic sounds. Yet his avant-garde tendencies and uninhibited use of jazz and blues within his structures, his early examples of modern harmonies (especially as seen in the piano works), as well as the time in which he began these innovations, position him in a transitional state between the neo-romantic and modern styles. Fortunately, the releases of his other symphonies by the Still Music Company better clarify and confirm his status and output as a musical genius.

Among the extraordinarily extensive list of Still's works are: *In Memoriam: The Negro Soldiers Who Died for Democracy; Songs of a New Race; From the Black Belt; Lenox Avenue* (ballet); *Troubled Island* (opera, lyrics by Langston Hughes); *Mota; La Guiablesse* (ballet); *Sahjdi; And They Hanged Him on a Tree; Songs of Separation; Suite for Violin; From the Delta; Highway 1, USA* (words by Verna Arvey); *Miss Sally's Party* (ballet); *In Memory of Jan Sibelius; Little Song that Wanted to be a Symphony; Afro-American Symphony; Every Time I Feel the Spirit; Poem for Orchestra; Three Visions* (piano); *Seven Traceries* (piano); *Bells* (two pieces for piano: *Phantom Chapel* and *Fairy Knoll*); *Danzas de Panama* (string quartet); *Miniatures; Vignettes; Folk Suites Nos. 1, 2, 3; Winter's Approach* (voice and piano); *From the Lost Continent* (chorus); *Plain Chant for America* (voice and orchestra); *From the Delta* (band); *Darker American* (orchestra); *Suite* (violin, *African Dancer*, etc.); *Those Who Wait; Here's One; A Deserted Plantation; Five Animal Sketches* (piano); and other spirituals and original compositions.

FREDERICK DOUGLASS HALL (1898–)

Frederick Hall, educator, arranger, composer, author, lecturer, and organist, was born in Atlanta, Georgia, where he attended public schools for his basic education. Graduating later from Morehouse College, Pittsburgh Musical Institute, the Chicago Musical Institute, and Columbia University Teachers College, he received the doctorate in 1952 from the Royal College of Music.

Hall worked as chairman of the music departments at Jackson College from 1921–1926, at Clark College, at Brown College, at Dillard and at Alabama State University. In addition, he taught church music at the Gammon Theological Seminary and lectured on socialized music at the School of Social Work at Atlanta University. He also founded the Association of Music Teachers in Negro Schools.

As author, Hall has written several published articles for the Cardiff *Musical Quarterly* (1934), the *Gold Coast Journal* (1935), the *Eisteddfod Review* (Wales, 1934), and others. A book in manuscript was entitled *Music in the Life of the American Negro*. Reviewed in several books himself, he had been included in Eugene Claghorn's *Biographical Dictionary*, Evelyn White's *Selected Bibliography*, the *Negro Yearbook* (with a birthdate of 1896), *Who's Who of Colored America*, *The Black Perspective*, Rogie Clark's *Negro Art Songs* (in which his birth is recorded as 1896), and other books, and has been represented as a distinguished educator, musician, and scholar.

Among his compositions are *Adi Dako and His Songs*, an anthology for solo voice; *Afro-American Worksongs* (Cycle); *Songs of the Southland* (Rodeheaver, 1955); *Swing Low, Sweet Chariot* (Rodeheaver); *Dawn* (solo in Rogie Clark's *Negro Art Songs*, E. B. Marks, 1946); *Deliverance* Oratorio for chorus (Rodeheaver, 1963); *Mandy Lou* for solo voice (Rogie Clark's *Negro Art Songs*); *Yonder Come Day* (Summy-Birchard); and other spirituals and folk songs published by Rodeheaver in 1939. Some of the remaining titles are *Pearly Gates* (spiritual fantasy); *Heritage* (folk song fantasy); *Morning* (voice and piano); *Dry Bones; Get Up Chillun'; Hand Me Down; Jackson Fair* (college songs); instrumental works are, in part, *Angels Done Changed My Name* (two-piano arrangement); *Sinner, Please Don't Let This Harvest Pass* (two pianos); *Suite for Piano*.

EDWARD H. BOATNER (1898–1981)

Edward Boatner, composer, conductor, singer, arranger, and educator, was born in New Orleans, Louisiana. ASCAP records show he was educated at the Chicago College of Music and did compositional and other musical studies with Louis Saar, Felix Deyo, Effie Grant, Otley Cranston, Charles Cease, Arthur Wilson, Arthur Frank, and others. According to Maud Hare, he was also educated at Western University at Quindaro, Kansas, studied privately with teachers at the New England Conservatory, and was a scholarship student at Boston Conservatory for one year. Boatner held several positions, including that of Dean of Music at Wiley College and at Houston College.

An internationally known arranger whose music was recorded for RCA by Paul Robeson, Marian Anderson, and others, his works enjoyed performances by several concert artists. White's *Selected Bibliography of Published Choral Music By Black Composers* mentioned his pioneer research and development in Afro-American studies, his music directorship for the National Baptist Convention (1926–32), and some of his other writings.

Maud Cuney Hare stated that Edward Boatner (whose birthdate she gave as 1918–   ) produced *Trampin'* which became the first publication of William Maxwell, formerly of the Ricordi and Company (second publication, Galaxy, 1954). His other works were entitled *Gospel Train, I Want*

Jesus to Walk With Me (Galaxy, 1949), *Oh, What A Beautiful City, Soon-a Will Be Done* recorded by Anderson, *On My Journey* (France—recorded by Robeson and Marian Anderson), and others.

WILLIAM LEVI DAWSON (1899–1990)

William Levi Dawson, a composer, conductor, trombonist and educator, was born in Anniston, Alabama, near Tuskegee Institute, Alabama. Once the organizer and chairman of the Department of Music at the famed Tuskegee Institute, Dawson ran away from home at an early age in order to attend the School. Thereafter, he made his way to the Horner Institute of Fine Arts in Missouri, the American Conservatory of Music in Chicago (where he received the Master's degree), and eventually became the first trombonist of the Chicago Civic Symphony Orchestra where he remained for several seasons.

Dawson served as director of innumerable choirs and orchestral ensembles while lecturing and traveling extensively in the United States and abroad. He was so effective a conductor of the Tuskegee Choir that he was invited to perform at Radio City, Carnegie Hall and the White House. In addition, his conducting ability placed him in demand as guest conductor at many festivals, contests and institutions. He conducted the Fisk University Choir in a performance of Coleridge-Taylor's *Hiawatha*, the Fredonia New York State Choir and Orchestra in a performance of his *Symphony*, and the Talladega Choir in Dett's *Ordering of Moses*.

William Dawson.

Among many honors were a 1940 CBS Commission to write music for the American School of the Air orchestra; the honorary Doctor of Music degree awarded by Tuskegee Institute in 1956 and the 1956 appointment by the State Department to conduct choirs abroad; the 1958 appointment to conduct the Fisk University Choir and the 1963 Alumni Award from the University of Missouri. Awards included the prestigious induction into the Alabama Arts Hall of Fame and honorary recognition by the American Choral Directors Association for his "pioneering leadership, inspiration and service to the Choral Arts" in 1975; the honorary degree Doctor of Laws conferred by Lincoln University in 1978; citation from the University of Michigan School of Music for "distinguished contributions . . . to the presentation and understanding of the Afro-American folk-song and to American music in general. . . . "; honorary plaque from Georgia State University and its Department of Music "for his outstanding musical contributions as a composer and conductor" (concomitant with this was an honorary citizenship of the City of Atlanta by Mayor Maynard Jackson); the Alabama Fine Arts Award given by the Alabama Coalition for the Arts and Humanities at Alabama State University in 1980; the Marshall Bartholomew Award given in 1981 by the Board of Directors of the Intercollegiate Musical Council for the male chorus contribution as practiced by Bartholomew; the Doctor of Music degree awarded by Ithaca College in 1982; and the Heinecke Award, the highest accolade given by the Society of European Stage Authors and Composers, in 1983.

Upon several occasions, Dawson was also invited to guest conduct his *Negro Folk Symphony*, but he was mainly called to direct choirs in programs devoted to his vocal compositions. At Ithaca, half of the program at the time of his degree conferral was devoted to his vocal music. In Washington, D.C., the D.C. Youth Orchestra frequently programmed his *Symphony*; it was also performed by the Crescent Youth Symphony Orchestra of Greenville, South Carolina, the Huntsville Symphony Orchestra in Alabama, Detroit Symphony Orchestra, University High School at Newark (where he also conducted his own work), and others.

Dawson's reputation developed early in his career. His *Symphony*, in the early 1930s was praised by the *Philadelphia Public Ledger*, the *Philadelphia Inquirer*, the *Evening Bulletin*, and the *Washington Daily News* among others. The latter newspaper wrote that of the four symphonic works which Stokowski programmed, "It was no wonder Stokowski put his 'Negro Symphony' last on the program, and no wonder the audience heralded the end of each movement with spontaneous applause and stood to cheer the young composer at the finish." About his conducting of his works and compositional skills, the *Evening Star* of June 4, 1946 captioned an article as "Sheer Beauty marks Local Concert by Tuskegee Choir" in which there were references to the "affectionate naturalness" and "richly toned" characteristics of the group, and to the composer as a "gifted . . . and expert leader. . . . " The legendary choir inspired George Weida Spohn, professor of English at St. Olaf College, to write a six-verse poem in their honor.

Neil Kjos billed the composer as one who has "fashioned the most widely performed selection of distinguished American choral music of our time" and as one " known and revered the world over." The president of Ithaca College, James Whalen, hailed Dawson as one whose music speaks to the souls "of all races." Accolades from abroad spoke of the religiously intense emotion and beauty of the spirituals as he taught them, and noted that in a farewell address to Dawson, Maestro Gorostidi, director of the Orfeon Donostiarra of San Sebastian, cited him as "A great musician. . . . modest," as one who had won the hearts and admiration and gratitude of the Spanish people, and as a "giant of choral music."

Since his own early recordings made with the Tuskegee Choir at Westminister Records (WGM-8154), Leopold Stokowski and the American Symphony Orchestra have recorded his *Negro Folk Symphony* on the Decca label (also available on Lyons Ed. Records); Eugene Simpson has conducted the Virginia State Choir in a recording of his music in the *William Dawson Songbook; Out in the Fields*, now available with wind or orchestral accompaniment, was recorded by Desto for soprano and orchestra (on *Music by Black Composers*) while still another version was recorded by the Alabama State University Choir on Prestige; and Samuel Bonds has conducted the Woodson High School Boys Choir of Washington, D.C., in a recording of *Care-O* and *Slumber Song*.

Others of his newest works published by Kjos: *Slumber Song* (1974); *Rugged Yank*, "a song for a man"—baritone or tenor voice, or for male chorus, and *Dorabella* (1981). The songs are both humorous and clever in the sense of compositional ingenuity and surprises in choices of counterthemes or underlying motivic suggestions, as in *Rugged Yank*. Equally unique are the comments upon married life, as in *Dorabella*, the music and poem of which were composed in honor of his friend, Bruce Montgomery. Dawson also conducted upon request of the University of Pennsylvania Glee Club Graduate Club which sponsored the event. Both songs also perpetuated the interesting rhythmic idioms and folk roots of the African-American, as seen in Example 36 (measures 10–31) and Example 37 (measures 28–29).

Ex. 38 *The Rugged Yank*, Dawson.

Ex. 39 *Dorabella*, Dawson.

One wonders why Dawson withdrew from the extended forms of art music and later concentrated solely on the vocal medium of folk spirituals. He had composed for small chamber ensembles, piano, trombone and other media. His bulk of compositions, however, showed many arrangements in the vocal idiom. Within the folk idiom were seen both contrapuntal and homophonic techniques.

A winner of the Wanamaker Contest in 1930 and 1931 for his song and orchestral compositions, and a winner of the Chicago Daily News prize for the Contest of Band Directors in 1929, Dawson still suffered setbacks in his profession. For example, at the time of high praise during the popularity of his *Symphony*, he was called upon to defend his style of writing, to which he responded that he had not tried to imitate any other composer. His *Symphony* was a reflection of the experiences which had fashioned the wisdom of his very soul. Its essence revealed his knowledge and love of Self, and of his roots, and showed his dedicated belief in the preservation of this unique American music. No one asked Milhaud and Ravel or anyone else to defend their music, as it was expected of them to compose art music in any style they chose. However, Dawson's composition was so beautifully constructed and well presented that his critics could not contain themselves.

Another adverse circumstance to his case was the fact that Dawson was instructed to sit in the balcony of the Horner Institute auditorium while his own pieces were being performed upon the date of his graduation from the School. Even though the pieces won first prize, he was nevertheless not allowed to walk on the stage in order to receive the applause or acknowledgement. Despite this, however, William Dawson's ability, hard work and excellence of achievement brought eventual respect and acceptance of his talent finally realized by the awards and subsequent honors bestowed upon him. There was no question but that William Dawson knew his work as both conductor and composer, for he performed accordingly each time he came before the public.

One of the highlights of his career was undoubtedly the completion and performance of his *Negro Folk Symphony*, which was presented in Philadelphia with Leopold Stokowski as conductor. *The Folk Symphony* was written during the early 1930's and consisted of three movements. Also of the Romantic style, its homophonic texture was off-set by other features of call and response, overlapping, and motivic themes. His keen sense of balance in both the vocal and orchestral works were exciting and well written. In the *Symphony*, the organization was built around the Black spirituals, folk songs and African influences.

FIRST MOVEMENT:	(Introduction) *The Bond of Africa*, based on folk song *Oh my Lit'l Soul Gwine-a Shine* and African themes
SECOND MOVEMENT:	*Hope in the Night*, reflecting a slave's lament; sorrow and despair; children's dance, scherzo; abandonment of care.
THIRD MOVEMENT:	*O le' Me Shine* *Hallelujah, Been Down to the Sea* *O le' Me Shine*

Dawson's style of writing encompassed many technical devices common to art music as well as to Black folk songs. Generally of the Romantic style, using tonal centers, various overlapping and syncopated and irregularly accented rhythms were typical of his music. His *I Wan' to Be Ready* for mixed voices was published in 1967, a composition consisting of four to seven voice parts. With the additional use of pedal points and other suspended tones, Dawson used polytonalities which added to the pleasure of the work. The beginning measures are seen in Example 38.

Among Dawson's best works are *Ansioso (Anxiety) For Piano; Scherzo* (for orchestra); *Jump Back, Honey, Jump Back; The Rugged Yank; Negro Folk Symphony No. 1; Out in the Fields; Untitled Composition* (Moorland Room, Howard University); *Trio for Piano; Soon Ah Will Be Done Wid de Trouble of de World*, mixed male voices; *Good News*, mixed male voices; *Oh What a Beautiful City*,

Ex. 40 *I Wan' to Be Ready*, Dawson. Copyright 1967 by William L. Dawson. Tuskegee Institute, Alabama. International Copyright Secured. Printed in the U.S.A. All rights reserved. Neil Kjos Music Co., Park Ridge, Ill., sole Distributor.

mixed voices; *There is a Balm in Gilead,* mixed male, female voices; *Deep River; Steal Away,* mixed male; *Hail Mary,* mixed male voices; *Swing Low, Sweet Chariot,* mixed male, female voices; *Mary Had a Baby*; *Ezekiel Saw de Wheel; Zion's Walls; Behold the Star; Lover's Plighted; A Negro Work Song* for orchestra; and other songs, both arranged and original.

WILLIS LAURENCE JAMES (1900–1966)

Willis Laurence James, composer, violinist, singer, and musicologist, was born in Montgomery, Alabama. A graduate of Morehouse College and Chicago Musical College, he was also a recipient of Rosenwald, Carnegie, and other foundation grants.

James worked at Morehouse in Atlanta, Georgia; Leland College and Baker in Louisiana; at Alabama State Teachers College; Fort Valley State; and Spelman. He also performed on NBC and CBS network programs such as the Firestone Hour, Bell Telephone Hour, and Contented Hour.

James is listed in *Who's Who of Colored America* and the Eugene Claghorn *Dictionary and the Negro Yearbook,* among others. He was also recently reviewed by the Black Caucus *Newsletter,* wherein he was reported to be a consultant to the Institute of Jazz Studies and member of the advisory board for the Tanglewood Roundtable, as well as a lecturer at Tanglewood for three years.

As composer of many arrangements and original works for choir, he composed *Hail Alabama* for Alabama State, as well as others listed in the Library of Congress: *Cabin Boy Call,* Schirmer, 1942; *Captin', Look-a Yonder* (TTBB, Remick, 1953); *Negro Bell Carol* (C. Fischer); and *Reign King Jesus* (Remick).

Perhaps the most comprehensive sketch by far is that done by Rebecca Cureau, educator from the Department of Music at Southern University at Baton Rouge, and submitted for publication in the 1983 edition of the *Dictionary of Georgia Biography* by the University of Georgia Press. In it, she pointed out his "distinction as a talented violinist and singer" at Morehouse, his work with jazz and swing bands, including his composing of Leland's *Alma Mater* as well as Alabama State's *Fight Song* and his long affiliation with Spelman as the conductor and musicologist. Cureau also delved into his work as folklorist and preserver of his cultural heritage, prepared his *Stars in de Elements: A Study of Negro Folk Music,* for possible publication in 1984 (the University of Georgia Press). The 1948 manuscript contained other arrangements of Willis James's folk song collection and was also referred to by Wendell Whalum for his arrangements of *Male Glee Club Songs*.

JESTER HAIRSTON (1901–)

Born in North Carolina, Jester Hairston, a world-famous composer, lecturer, arranger, conductor, singer, author, and actor, moved his residence to Los Angeles, California. Educated at Tufts University, where he majored in music, Hairston did additional work at the Juilliard Institute of Music in New York. In 1964, the University of the Pacific in Stockton, California, awarded him an honorary Doctor of Music; the University of Massachusetts, in 1972, awarded him the Doctor of Fine Arts; and also in 1972, Tufts awarded him the Doctor of Music.

During his extensive career, he has directed choirs for Hall Johnson and trained choirs for radio and Broadway musicals; he has composed music for films and television programs (including *Duel in the Sun, Portrait of Jenny, Friendly Persuasion*). He traveled to Hollywood with the Hall Johnson Choir in 1936 and performed in *Green Pastures*, and for fifteen years, directed a Federal Theatre Project. A director of his own choir, he also has conducted countless workshops for colleges, high schools, and conventions such as the Music Educators.

Jester Hairston.

Hairston acted in "That's My Mama" and other television programs, and in movies such as *Lady Sings the Blues* and *Amen*. He served the U.S. State Department as "Ambassador of Good Will," worked with choirs in Uganda, Tanzania, Zambia, Kenya, and Madagascar in Africa, and in Yugoslavia, Finland, and Norway. In 1971, he conducted a special choir of music teachers in Mexico and in Anaheim, California, among others.

His music has been sung and recorded by the Schola Cantorum Singers at Da Anza College; his music has also been performed at the 1974 Symposium on Black Composers, Houston; in Los Angeles and other cities—by the touring Airman of Note and the Singing Sergeants; the Jubilee Singers of Fisk; the Bronx Borough-Wide Chorus of New York; AAMOA's Black Music Symposia (held in Minneapolis in 1975); and by many other groups for many other years.

The National Black Music Caucus *Newsletter* (Fall 1982) reported that for his long years of achievement and outstanding contributions to music, Hairston was honored in 1982 by the African Sisters Committee of the Los Angeles Mayor's office. Members of the MENC and NBMC assisted the Committee.

A first-rate interpreter of spirituals, their performance and history, Hairston has written interesting tonal settings of both spirituals and songs. His *You Better Mind* is rhythmically reflective of Beethoven's theme from the Fifth Symphony, but with differences in chords; his *Negro Folk Song* displays the leader-choral response common to Black music, and the simplicity of style and serenity of many emphasize their age and heritage. Rhythmically interesting and exciting in richness of sounds, the works are mainly for SATB or male ensembles. Among his compositions which are published by Bourne, are *Amen; Angels Rolled De Stone Away; Band of Angels; Crucifixion; Dat Ol' House is Ha'nted; Deep River; Dis Ol' Hammer; Dis Train; Don't Be Weary, Traveler; Elijah Rock; God's Gonna Buil' Up Zion's Wall; Go Down in de Lonesome Valley; Goin' Down Dat Lonesome Road; Goodbye Song; Gossip, Gossip; Great God A'Mighty; Hand Me Down; Hold My Mule While I Dance Josey; Hold On; Home in Dat Rock; I Can Tell the World; I Want Jesus; I'm*

A-Travelin Man; Joshua Fit de Battle of Jerico; Let the Church Roll On; Long John Done Gone; No Ne Li Domi; Sakura Sakura (Song of the Cherry Blossom); *Scandalized My Name; Swing a Lady Gum-Pum; Tataleo* (West African Folk Song); and others.

JOHN WESLEY WORK III (1901–1967)

John Wesley Work III, a composer, theorist, vocalist, educator and humanitarian, was born in Tullahoma, Tennessee. A true scholar and friend of all people, Work inspired those who met him to imitate his intense love of life, of worthwhile endeavors and of music. A proud, honest and conscientious teacher of legendary significance, he instilled a willingness to work and a need to achieve.

Educated at the Fisk School (when Fisk was a high school) and at Fisk University, he also studied at the Institute of Musical Art, at Columbia University (where he received the Master's degree) and at Yale University. His professional career was spent in compiling music history through the study of folk songs and in writing scores as well as articles about music.

Work remained at Fisk from 1926–1966, variously serving as theorist-composer, and as director of the famed Jubilee Singers and the Fisk Men's Glee Club. In addition, he served for five years as chairman of the Fisk University Department of Music. Upon his retirement from Fisk in 1966, he could count 39 years of dedicated service. On one occasion, Work was awarded an honorary doctorate by Fisk University, who loved him as he loved the University. His tireless energies brought many rewards and honors for the University and his diligency in striving for perfection of his ideas and thoughts on Black music or music in general was of flawless quality.

His writing began when he was in high school at which time he composed *Mandy Lou*. He received a prize from the Fellowship of American Composers in 1946 for still another work, *The Singers*. Considered by some to be his most significant composition, it was based on a poem by Henry Wadsworth Longfellow and was originally scored for chorus, baritone and orchestra.

After a trip to Haiti in 1945, Work returned home to write a piece based upon the music of that country, *Yenvalou*, which was once performed in 1959 by the total Symphony at Saratoga, N.Y. Work subsequently wrote another version which was scored for two pianos and was performed at Fisk in 1947. Another of his works, *Golgotha*, was also presented by the Fisk University Choir during the 1949 Festival, a work based on a poem by Arna Bontemps.

John Work's forte was his choral and vocal solo works, and he excelled in both conducting and writing. Yet his other works contained music of worth, and as compiled and discussed by Simona Atkins and Dorris Williams, totalled well over 100 compositions. His works were written for piano, chamber ensembles, chorus and other media, but the bulk was choral in nature.

While his basic writing appeared in the Romantic vein, some of the elements used were contrapuntal, closely interwoven chords of altered varieties, and jazz. While the instrumental pieces showed a characteristic instrumental idiom, they were more often based on a vocal linear concept, or singable lines.

John W. Work III. Courtesy of Fisk University.

Some works incorporated a gospel-like spirit of a recitative while others moved in syncopation. One of the most interesting features was the rhythmic excitement found in many of the works, both spiritual and otherwise, which typified African rhythms. The fast-slow note scheme and the syncopated effects were used frequently as in ♪ ♩ or ♩ ♩ ♩ and ♪ ♩ ♪ while other rhythms were strict, straightforward and hymn-like in appearance and sound, such as in the first movement theme of the piano suite, *Scuppernong*.

Ex. 41 *Scuppernong*, Work. Copyright 1951, Templeton Publishing Co., Inc. International Copyright Secured. All Rights Reserved. Sole Selling Agent: Shawnee Press, Inc., Delaware Gap, Pa. 18327.

Not all of John Work's music was strictly romantic and homophonic. Some melodic overlapping, as well as open harmonies and mild dissonances were also used. *Soliloquy*, one of his vocal art songs, displayed a more modern background of harmony and style. So did *Night in La Vallée*.

Ex. 42 *Soliloquy*, Work. Copyright 1946 by Galaxy Music Corporation. Copyright renewed by Edith M. Work. Used by permission.

Recently, his works were presented to the Fisk Library, the Special Collections. Among the approximately 113 compositions were: *Appalachia for Piano; Canzonet for Humming Chorus; American Negro Songs and Spirituals* (collection of 221 religious and secular examples); *Nocturne* (3 pieces for violin and piano); *Variations on an Original Theme* (piano); *Family Album* (5 piano pieces); *Golgotha is a Mountain* for 4 soloists and mixed voices, poem by Arna Bontemps); *Taliafero* (concert overture for Symphony orchestra); *Danse Africaine* (mixed voices, piano, drum, triangle; poem by Langston Hughes); *Do Not I Love Thee, O My Lord; Dusk at Sea* (art song); *Give me Jesus; Give me your Hand; All I Want; This Little Light O' Mine; Three Glimpses of Night; To a Mona Lisa; This Ol' Hammer!; T'was on One Sunday Morning; Unto the Hills I Lift Mine Eyes; You May Bury Me in the East; When Your Lamb Burns Down; Wasn't that a Might Day?; Little Black Train; Lord of All Being; Mandy Lou; Soliloquy* (solo voice and piano); *Sassafras* (piano); *Sing, O Heavens; Sinner Man, You Need Jesus; Issac Watts Contemplates the Cross; Night in La Vallée* (2 pianos) and others.

UNDINE SMITH MOORE (1904–1989)

Undine Moore, a composer, arranger, pianist, organist, lecturer and educator, was born in Jarratt, Virginia, before assuming her permanent residence in Petersburg, Virginia. Educated at Fisk University where she graduated with honors as the highest ranking student in her class, she also studied at the Juilliard School of Music, Columbia University and the Eastman School of Music. Among her various teachers was Howard Murphy with whom she studied theory.

For her exceptional work as a teacher of students (which included Camilla Williams and Billy Taylor), Virginia State College awarded Mrs. Moore an honorary doctorate upon her retirement as co-director of the Black Music Center. Undine Moore was a visiting lecturer at several colleges, including Carleton College in Northfield, Minnesota. In demand as guest lecturer on music by Black composers, her lectures and workshops have been given at such institutions as Howard University, Fisk University and Indiana University. Her professional experiences have also included those of supervisor of music in Goldsboro, North Carolina, and theorist and lecturer at Virginia State's Department of Music.

Undine Moore.

Undine Moore's commissioned compositions have been heard at innumerable concerts such as the Fisk University Spring Festival of Music and the Fisk Jubilee Day celebration, Indiana University's Festival of Black Music, and at Town Hall in New York City, where her former students sponsored a tribute of her original works in concert. Although her compositions are generally of a clear, concise, tonal style, two of her most recent works, the *Afro-American Suite* (commissioned by Trio Pro Viva) and the *Three Pieces for Flute and Piano*, have gradually expanded into more dissonant concepts of modern harmonies such as block chords or clusters and twelve-tone assimilations, as seen in *Before I'd Be a Slave* for piano. Of homophonic and polyphonic textures, her structures are well formed and full of emotional sensitivity and change.

Among her other high honors have been her works as the subject of several graduate dissertations, the Undine Moore Day proclaimed in Petersburg, Virginia, by the Mayor, citations from several associations and institutions as a leading contributor to the field of music such as the 1980 Black Music Caucus Achievement Award, and a second honorary doctorate of music from Indiana University, following the first by Virginia State University. Moreover, Moore was also given a grand tribute by the nomination of her cantata, *Scenes From the Life of a Martyr: To the Memory of Martin Luther King*, for a Pulitzer Prize.

The music of Undine Moore is heard frequently by congregations in such churches as the Peoples Congregational in Washington, D.C., by many institutions, at festivals and conventions, and by many concertgoers. Special recordings of her works were made by Region 5 of the D. C. public schools, the Evelyn White Chorale (Howard University) which released her *Lord We Give Thanks* and by the Virginia State University Choir, which included many of her compositions in the *Undine Smith Moore Songbook*. Directed by Carl Harris, *Songbook* was produced in 1971 and was made available through the VSU Department of Music. Delta Fine Arts Center of Winston Salem, North Carolina, also recorded a fine production.

One of the highlights of her work is seen in the cleverness of the climactic chromatic harmonic progression found at the ending section of *Daniel, Daniel, Servant of the Lord.* Although written in F#, the chords move upward through five chromatic chords which hesitate on the four-three resolution at the C# chord, but nevertheless create the illusion of a modulation. The resolution, however, having paused with a piercing leading tone in suspended motion, leads still farther up as it resolves to a single F# in the tenor solo voice and proceeds toward the final cadence.

Two other pieces, *Glory to God* (anthem) and *I Would Be True*, represent some of her most recent work since 1973. The opening of *Glory to God* (Example 41) depicts rhythmic influence of Africa as well as the gospelized response of the Black church as the intricacy of movements among voices

Ex. 43. *Glory to God*, Moore, measures 1–6. © Copyright 1979. Augsburg Publishing House. All rights reserved. Reprinted by permission.

Ex. 44. *I Would Be True*, Moore. Copyright © 1979 Augsburg Publishing House. All rights reserved. Reprinted by permission.

glorifies the God of mankind. *I Would Be True*, Example 42, reveals a portion of her piano style as it syncopates against the voices in parallel chord frames within a polymetric scheme.

Moore has written well over seventy-five works for various media such as voice, piano, chorus, organ, flute, and clarinet. Significantly, in 1979, Augsburg released her new scores for chorus as follows: *Choral Prayers in Folk Style; Come Along in Jesus' Name; Glory to God in the Highest; Believe This is Jesus; I Would Be True; I'm Going Home; Long Fare You Well; Lord Have Mercy; O That Bleeding Lamb; We Shall Walk Through the Valley of Peace;* and *Walk Thro' The Streets of the City*. Within the 1970s, she also wrote *Alleluia; Arise, My Love, My Fair One; Benediction; A Little Spring Soliloquy; Glory to God* (TTBB); *Here Comes Another One to Be Baptized; I Want to Die While You Love Me; Lyric for True Love* for soprano and piano; *Mama, Is Massa Goin' to Sell Us Tomorrow?; O Holy Lord; Organ Variations on "Nettleton": Set Me as a Seal on Thy Heart; Take Me to the Water; Tambourines to Glory; A Time for Remembering; To Be Baptized; The Voice of My Beloved; Watch and Pray;* and others.

Additional works are: *Afro-American Suite for Flute, Cello and Piano; Lord, We Give Thanks to Thee for These Thy Servants; Mother to Son; Hail Warrior; Daniel, Daniel, Servant of the Lord; Let Us Make Man in Our Image; Striving After God; The Lamb; Bound for Canaan's Land; Just Come from the Fountain; A Christmas;* and others, such as *Soweto* for violin, cello and piano.

NORMAN LAVELLE MERRIFIELD (1906–)

Norman L. Merrifield, composer, pianist, and educator, was born in Louisville, Kentucky. After moving to Indianapolis as a child, he began his foundation studies with Ellen T. Meriwether in piano and at the Arsenal Technical High School. Thereafter, he graduated from Northwestern in 1927 with the Bachelor of Music, and again in 1932 with the Master of Music. Receiving a study grant, he continued his work at Trinity College in London, England, in 1946. He was awarded a Special Study Fellowship to Northwestern University in 1964, and he also furthered his education with supplementary work at Indiana, Jordon College of Music, Michigan State University, and Ball State University.

Merrifield has worked in several positions—at Fisk University (1927–28), Austin High School in Knoxville, Tennessee (as chairman until 1931), at Alabama State Teacher's College, at Florida A&M College in Tallahassee (Dean of Music, 1932–34), at Crispus Attucks High School in Indianapolis (chairman, 1934–42), and at Hampton Institute as choir director and instructor of music. He served as band leader for seven Army Bands, organized and directed the 92nd Division Artillery Band, the Fort Riley Cavalry Band, and the 1349 Engineer Band. In 1968, he became coordinator of the Douglass South of Flanner House while continuing his compositional activities. A member of NEA and MENC, Merrifield has also been a member of ASCAP since 1961. His biographical data was also included in *Who's Who of Colored America*.

Some of his compositions are *Ah Done Done* (TTBB, Handy, 1941); *Motherless Child; Now Look Away; Remember, O Lord* (SATB, 1964) and *Show Me Thy Way, O Lord* (SATB, 1962, published by Boston Music with above); *Tryin' to Get Ready* (SATB, Richmond Press, Indiana); *And He Never Said A Mumblin' Word* (Richmond); *Symphony* (unpublished); numerous other vocal and instrumental works and literary publications, among only a few of which are found in *Music Educators Journal, The School Musician,* the *Choral Journal* (1965) and *Sports Afield* (1965).

GILBERT ALLEN (1907–   )

A native of Indianapolis, Indiana, Gilbert Allen graduated from the University of California at Los Angeles where he received a Bachelor of Arts degree in philosophy and a minor in music. Thereafter, he studied piano and composition at the Juilliard School of Music for three years followed by extensive work in English, education, and journalism at the Universities of Virginia, Indiana, and Virginia State College, and later, more music study at the University of Southern California. Allen taught at Samuel Huston College (now Huston-Tillotson) in Austin, Texas, at the Hayden High School in Franklin, Virginia, and at Wiley College where he served as chairman of music.

Gaining his reputation as conductor, composer, and arranger, Gilbert Allen toured extensively with the Gilbert Allen Singers who performed on the Los Angeles Philharmonic Orchestra Concert Series and the George Gershwin Memorial Concerts with Paul Whiteman, conductor (the latter, sponsored by the U.S. Treasury Department); and on the Federal Music Project Series of Los Angeles, held at UCLA's Royce Hall. The Gilbert Allen Singers also performed with the Los Angeles Symphony Orchestra with James Sample as conductor and Igor Stravinsky, guest conductor; they appeared in concert with the world famous baritone, Paul Robeson, in the special CBS program called "Ballad for Americans," which was held in Los Angeles Philharmonic and Shrine Auditoriums; they broadcasted regularly on "What's on My Mind," the CBS program from Hollywood which was sponsored by Planters Peanut Company.

Gilbert Allen.

The Wiley College Choir, which Allen directed, broadcasted regularly on ABC Radio's "Outstanding American College Choirs" Series, sponsored by the UNCF; and both the Wiley College and Samuel Huston Choirs toured Mexico, sponsored by the U.S. Foreign Service Department and Samuel Marti Attractions, performing in Mexico City's Instituto Nacional de Bellas Artes. The Wiley College Choir also was sponsored by the U.S. Foreign Service Department and the National Department of Education of Mexico in a televised performance in "Musica U.S.A." Undoubtedly, the most famous of Allen's choirs was the Wings Over Jordan Choir, which he conducted over the CBS radio network for ten years. Internationally known, the choir performed with the San Antonio Symphony Orchestra with Max Rieter, conductor, performed with the Carnegie Pops Concert Orchestra in New York City, and performed at Symphony Hall in Boston. The choir also recorded on the RCA Victor label.

In his busy years, Allen was able to indulge in other fields such as publishing a book of poetry called *Prelude*; serving as erstwhile secretary to Roland Hayes, the world famous tenor; writing articles for the *Journal & Guide, Suffolk Herald* newspapers and others. His article on the "Mc-Phailen Story" was excerpted in *Ebony* in 1952 under "People Over 100 Years Old."

During his Mexican tours, Allen was captioned as "Director del Coro, está considerado como uno de los más prometedores directores de coro de la nueva generación" (Director of the Choir, is considered as one of the most promising choral directors of the new generation). He was approved as a teacher of music by the Virginia State Board of Education to teach high school; he was also approved by the Texas State Board of Education, being awarded a Certificate for Life which meant that students in grades 9 through 12 could receive high school credit for studying privately in his studio. Allen also was a much sought after organist. In each city in which he lived, he worked as organist at churches such as Avalon Christian, Eighth and Town AME, and AME Zion Methodist in Los Angeles; Salem Methodist in New York; Ebenezer United Methodist in Marshall, Texas; and at several others in Shreveport, Louisiana, and Portsmouth and Suffolk, Virginia.

Some of his music reveals the use of tonalism, as well as "blue note" effects imitated over tonic to sub-dominant and dominant seventh chords; keen sensitivity is shown in his alteration of voice parts and simplicity of style, as seen in *I Jes' Can't Stay Here By Myself*. Among his many works are six choral pieces published by Row/Fischer: *Amen; O, Religion is a Fortune; Scandalize My Name; I Jes' Can't Stay Here By Myself; I Got Shoes; Sweet Little Jesus Boy;* three intermediate piano pieces published by Summy-Birchard: *Spiritual, Jazz Impromptu, Lament* (the latter was listed and recorded by the National Federation of Music Clubs in Chicago for intermediates); and several compositions in manuscript such as the concerto for piano and choir entitled *Impromptu in Eb* which was performed at Texas State Teachers Association and an unpublished opera, *Steal Away*.

JOHN DUNCAN (Ca. 1911–1975)

John Duncan, music educator, composer, arranger, author, and academic administrator, was born in Lee County, Alabama, around 1911 (his obituary recorded no date of birth; other sources listed 1911 and 1913). Educated in the public schools of Monessen, Pennsylvania, he earned both the Bachelor of Music and Master of Music degrees in composition and orchestration from Temple University. He also did further work at New York University, studying composition and orchestration with Philip James and musicology with Curt Sachs and Gustave Reese. In 1974, Alabama State University, where he had worked for 34 years, honored him with the degree, Doctor of Humane Letters.

An important figure in the compositional world of thought and action, his music was gaining in recognition during the early 1970s. In 1972, Xavier University Theater gave the world premiere of his *Gideon and Eliza*, an opera which he felt could be easily produced. Written in two acts and six scenes, it lasted about fifty minutes and told a story about a slave couple's experiences with the auction block. Favorable reviewed by Frank Gagnard of the New Orleans *Times-Picayune* newspaper, it included voodoo dancing, church revivalism, jazz, and Afro-Caribbean elements. Gagnard wrote that Duncan (who composed his own libretto) "resorts to narrative shorthand to get all the story in, and eclectric though consistently pop-conservative musical style to speed the story forward. He is melodically inventive as he ranges from Italianate lyricism to slightly more austere modernism. . . . "

In 1973, both Phi Mu Alpha Sinfonia Fraternity of Alabama State University and the concert choir of Mississippi College sponsored Duncan's music. Mississippi featured his *Burial of Moses* (cantata) in a world premiere. Alabama presented an entire program of his music, including *Joshua March; Three Atavisms* for brass, percussion, and a voice; *Ormalu* for brass quintet; *Evocation* and *Dance* clarinet and piano; *Bamboula* for solo trombone, alto sax, brass quintet, and timpani; and *The Tenor and the Prima Donna* for trumpet, baritone, and percussion ensemble.

His music became the subject of doctoral dissertations at the University of Southern Mississippi by Edwin Romain, pianist, and Martha Blanding Spence, who used the "*Bluz* (Blues) *Set*" for soprano and piano. Robert

Gray, one of the Eastman School of Music candidates for the DMA degree, used nine pages from Duncan's *Divertimento for Trombone and String Quartet,* the latter having been a commissioned work for Dave Shuman.

The Doctor of Humane Letters award recorded that his works were performed at "leading colleges and universities throughout the nation," notably among which were: *Three Proclamations for Trombone and String Quartet,* at the Fourth Annual Symposium of Contemporary Music for Brass at Georgia State University; *An Easter Canticle* performed by a chorus, soloists, fifteen wind instruments, and selected members of the Salt Lake City Choir; *Concerto for Trombone and Orchestra,* performed by the New York City Symphony Orchestra; and *Three Obscurants* for tenor, oboe, and string quartet at the University of Alabama; *Divertimento* for trombone and string quartet in Town Hall, New York; *Six Chamber Songs* for voice, flute, and string quartet at Bennington College; *Atavistic,* string quartet by the Claremont Quartet in Winston-Salem; and *Gideon and Eliza,* an opera in two acts by Xavier University Opera Theater.

In addition, Duncan also wrote articles on music and was much sought after as a music reviewer of books, and as contributor to music journals and research. Unlike the majority of his contemporaries, he did not consider the spiritual as the most important of the Black folk forms worthy of inspiring the composers. He was upset that from thirteen pounds of musical scores ranging from symphonies to chamber music and operas which he sent to a publisher, only the spiritual arrangement "I'm Tired Chile" was chosen for publication. His position was that the public should push for upgrading standards of publishing and the choice of such.

In July 1975, Duncan wrote that his application for a plaque to mark the Montgomery, Alabama, birthplace of Nat "King" Cole had been approved by the Historical Landmarks Committee, that he had just been appointed by the National Federation of Music Clubs to serve on the Bicentennial Committee for the State of Alabama, and that he was completing the orchestration for a new opera for the Xavier University Opera Theater. Entitled *The Hellish Banditti,* he composed both the music and libretto, basing the episodes on the exploits of Jean Lafitte, the pirate, set in and around New Orleans during the War of 1812.

Among his total works of approximately ten large orchestral works, two ballets, four band compositions, three string quartets, two operas, three piano works, three large choral works (some of which may be viewed at the Fleischer Collection in the Free Library in Philadelphia) are also *Rural Americana* (suite for orchestra); *Black Bards* (commissioned by Trio Pro Viva for recording); *Rococo Theme* for alto sax and band; *Waiting* (SSAA, flute, harp); *Diversion No. 1* (flute, horn, string orchestra); and numerous others.

MARGARET BONDS (1913–1972)

Margaret Bonds, composer, author, conductor and pianist, was born in Chicago. She was educated at Northwestern University, where she received the B. M. and M. M. degrees, and the Juilliard School of Music. She also studied with Roy Harris, Emerson Harper, Robert Starer, William Dawson and Florence Price, and received awards from the National Association of Negro Musicians, the Alpha Kappa Alpha Sorority, the Julius Rosenwald Foundation, Roy Harris and the Wanamaker Foundation.

An accomplished pianist, Margaret Bonds appeared innumerable times in concerts, engaged in the accompanying of many vocal artists (such

Margaret Bonds. Courtesy of Charlotte Hollomon, whom Bonds accompanied.

as Charlotte Hollomon and Abbie Mitchell), and also used her skills to good advantage in the performance of her own compositions for piano. In the *International Library of Negro Life and History*, she is pictured as guest soloist with the Women's Symphony Orchestra in 1934, where she performed Florence Price's *Concerto in F Minor*.

As a composer, Miss Bonds was well known for her countless arrangements of spirituals, her piano works and other orchestral and vocal compositions, both dramatic and abstract. Because she taught at the American Theater Wing, served as musical director of the Stage for Youth, the East Side Settlement Hose, and the White Barn Theater, she was well experienced in work for the stage. Such compositions as her *Shakespeare in Harlem* and *USA* are representative of her dramatic works. With her instinct for culture, she directed her efforts in promoting topics and techniques of the Black American. Such collaborators as Countee Cullen, Langston Hughes and others were instrumental in the strengthening of such works as her *The Negro Speaks of Rivers*. Both her productivity and the ideas used in her works have been far-reaching and commendable.

Much of Bonds' established compositions were representative of the Romantic style. Others used idioms of the modern era. Having tested her ideas in various media without restricting herself to vocal music alone, she demonstrated certain natural writing she herself described as being a mixture of Marion Cook, H. T. Burleigh and Tchaikovsky. Her works show "jazzy" chords, both altered and augmented. The featured sevenths in clusters and widely spaced intervals and a jumping, rag-time bass, imitation and syncopations all reflect her style. In her *Ballad of a Brown King*, the combination of drama and music show a skill characteristic of a sound musician. In her spiritual arrangement of *I Got a Home in that Rock*, another style of writing is shown where syncopation and jazz chords border on ragtime.

Among Bonds' compositions are: *The Negro Speaks of Rivers; Three Dream Portraits; Peter and the Bells; Mass in D; Troubled Water; Empty Interlude; Peachtree Street; Spring Will Be So Sad; Fields of Wonder; Dry Bones; Lord I Just Can't Keep from Crying; I'll Reach to Heaven; Sit Down Servant; Suite for Piano; Music for Voice and Piano; He's Got the Whole World in His Hands.*

WALTER F. ANDERSON (1915–)

Walter Anderson, composer, organist, pianist, and administrator, was born in Zanesville, Ohio. Educated at Oberlin College (B. M.) and Capital University (where he studied with William Bailey), he also earned the Fellow's Degree from the American Guild of Organists (AAGO and FAGO). In addition, he was awarded an honorary Doctor of Musical Arts in 1979 by the Cleveland Institute of Music.

Recently the Special Assistant to the Deputy Chairman for Public Partnership at the National Endowment for the Arts, Anderson's career as educator at Kentucky State (1939–42) and at Western Reserve (1944–46) moved swiftly. He then was selected to become head of the prestigious music department of Antioch College in Yellow Springs, Ohio (from 1946–1968) and project director of the music programs of the National Endowment for the Arts (from 1967–1978). He also maintained a position as director of the Karamu House in Cleveland and director of Wilberforce's Concert Artists Series; he started the talent contest for the Metropolitan Opera in Cleveland and, in 1983, served as advisor and organizer of the

First National Symposium on the Performing and Fine Arts for Historically Black Colleges and Universities.

As organist and pianist, Anderson toured widely throughout the United States, often also as accompanist for Catherine Van Buren, soprano (1939–42). For his musical achievements, he won a Bartol Scholarship. Reviewed by Camille Taylor in the *Black Music Caucus Newsletter*, he was also listed in the *Negro Yearbook*, the *Negro Alamanac*, the Claghorn *Dictionary*, and *Who's Who of Colored America*, among others.

As a composer of note, Anderson composed a Cantata in 1950, based on President Roosevelt's D-Day prayer. Entitled the D-Day *Symphony*, the piece was performed from a CBS-TV Network score. In 1946, the Cleveland Symphony Orchestra performed his *Symphonic Variations* (Lord, Lord, Lord). He also composed *Settings of Spanish Christmas Carols* (SATB, Schirmer, 1958?); *Concerto for Harmonica and Orchestra; String Quartet* (performed by the Cleveland Alumni String Quartet); *Carols From Different Countries* (for Folk Music Councils; Augsburg Press, o.o.p.); and booklets of *African Folk Tunes* released by the Cooperative Recreation Service.

LEONARD DE PAUR (1915–)

Born in Summit, New Jersey, Leonard de Paur, composer, conductor, and administrator, has become a legend in his own time, One whose work resounded brilliantly over the years throughout the world, his accomplishments have stood as a guiding beam for those who wish to follow in his footsteps.

Educated at the Juilliard School of Music, at Columbia University, and at L'Universite Laval, de Paur also studied privately with Henry Cowell, Hall Johnson, Sergei Radamsky, and did special study with Pierre Monteux. For his outstanding work in the field of music, he has been awarded the Doctor of Music degree from Lewis and Clark College and from Morehouse College.

Between 1947 and 1968, de Paur created and conducted more than 2,300 concert performances in foreign tours to South America, the Caribbean, Japan, France, Germany, and fifteen African nations. Managed by one of the more prestigious agents, Columbia Artists Management, he was skillfully scheduled and carefully routed into dignified settings of lectures, concerts, or conducting throughout the world. He was guest conductor of the Cincinnati Symphony Orchestra, the Orchestra of America, the Miami Beach Symphony, the Minnesota Symphony (Hennepin Choirs), and the Buffalo Philharmonic. Additional, he was also guest conductor of several Broadway plays including *Purlie* and *Hallelujah Baby*. With *Purlie*, he conducted a national tour.

Currently the director of Community Relations at the Lincoln Center for the Performing Arts, de Paur has been cited especially for his fine career as the founder-director of the de Paur Infantry Chorus which he trained and directed on some of the above named tours and for which he was the arranger-composer. A multitalented musician, his accomplishments also consisted of founding and touring with the de Paur Opera Gala and the de Paur Gala Chorus and of researching, recording, and collecting folk music. De Paur also was the director of the Choral Programming for the J. C. Penney Bicentennial Musical Celebration, 1976.

From 1971 to 1973, de Paur was hired as conductor of the Symphony of the New World and of Opera South, both based in New York. He was also invited to guest-conduct and lecture at many institutions, among which were Howard University, the University of Rochester, Talladega College, Olympia College, the University of California, New York State Historical Association, and at several Music Educators Regional Conferences.

As an educator and conductor, de Paur has been associated with summer workshops at Kent State University (Blossom Festival), the University of Colorado, the University of Washington State, and the Lewis and Clark College. He has furthermore served as consultant for G. Schirmer Music (repertoire, 1981), for Group W. Network (Black Pride), for EPCOT Center of Walt Disney World, for the New York City Board of Education (CHIP program), for the Westport Music Program, as well as for the intercultural program on Cultural Development for the Republic of Tunisia.

The distinguished de Paur has been selected for many awards and other honors: the Mayor's Award of Honor for Arts and Culture, the University of Pennsylvania Glee Club Award of Merit, and the two honorary doctorates list but a few of the most recent of these. In the military, he carried the rank of Captain USA when he served in the World War II Infantry, Air Corps as Special Staff. As co-chairman of the American Committee on the First World Festival of Negro Art (held in Dakar, Senegal) and as associate director of the Lincoln Center International Choral Festival (1970–1975), he also added to his list of prestigious positions and varied experiences. His accomplishments have been praised in many magazines and newspapers such as *Time, Newsweek, Musical America, Who's Who, Colliers, Pathfinder, Essence,* and others.

A member of ASCAP, the Society of Black Composers, and other organizations, he also was musical director for many television and radio shows such as at PBS-METV for Opera South productions, arranger-conductor for the Hallmark "Hall of Fame" (nominated for an Emmy), music director for the Bell Telephone Hour, Chicago Symphony Series. He also arranged and conducted various commercial announcements for radio and television (J. Walter Thompson Company and Ted Bates and Company) and was arranger-conductor for more than 100 radio programs on major networks, as well as choral arranger and conductor for Twentieth Century Fox, Paramount, and MGM. In addition, he has produced ten albums from Infantry Chorus repertoire (Columbia Records); two albums from repertoire for Philips-Mercury records; researched, arranged, and directed a five-album anthology of Afro-American folk music (RCA Records) and various other recordings ranging from opera to children's educational material. He conducted for United Artists Records (featuring Brock Peters and Odetta) and arranged and conducted single albums with Leontyne Price and Shirley Verrett (RCA Records). Besides the above, he worked as writer-commentator on "Music Makers" for WQXR, as arranger for ten Broadway musicals, and as musical director of the Federal Theatre Project, Negro Theater, thereby combining several careers worth several lifetimes.

As a composer-arranger, he published his Choral Series (Lawson-Gould/Schirmer), and others by Michael Brent, the American Book Company (Choral Art Series), Elsa-Childs and Clara Music (Belafonte Enterprises). Among some of the original and arranged compositions for TTBB, SATB, etc. are: *All Round de Glory Manger; Ay, Ay, Ay; Cer'n'y Lord; City Called Heaven; First Nowell; God Rest Ye Merry Gentlemen; In Bright Mansions*

Above; Jerry; Lo, How A Rose E'er Blooming; Marry a Woman Uglier Than You; Nobody Knows de Trouble I See; Oh, Po' Little Jesus; Rio Que Pasa Llorando; Swing Low, Sweet Chariot; Tol' My Cap'n; Water Boy; and *Ye Ke Omo Mi.*

KENNETH BROWN BILLUPS (1918–1985)

Kenneth Billups, educator, arranger, composer, and conductor, was born in St. Louis, Missouri, where he attended Sumner High School. He earned his Bachelor of Arts degree from Lincoln University and the Master of Music degree from Northwestern.

Billups served as chairman of the Department of Music at Sumner High, as choir director of Douglas High and Webster, as well as the director for the NYA Concert Choir, of the Wings Over Jordan Choir, and of several church and school choirs. In addition, he organized the first interracial choir in St. Louis, the Cosmopolitan Choir, and the Jewish Community Centers Association Choir, the Kol Rinal. He has taught also at many summer school sessions of several universities including Lincoln University, Texas Southern, and Northwestern and has also served as critic teacher at Washington University in St. Louis.

A member of the National Association of Negro Musicians, several singing association, Phi Mu Alpha, Phi Delta Kappa, and other groups, he has been a winner of several awards, among which were the Emancipation Award from the *St. Louis American* newspaper in 1945, the Achievement Award from the National Association of Colored Women (1947), the St. Louis Citizens Award (1959), and Man of the Year Award from Frontiers International (1959–60). He also served on several advisory boards such as for the Missouri Council on the Arts.

Billups's works are tonal examples. Although other compositions have been written, his frequent use of spirituals has become associated with his style of writing. Among the compositions are *Cert'ly Lord* (Belwin Octavo, 1950); *Everytime I Feel the Spirit* (Scholin Choral Pub.); *I Want Jesus to Walk With Me; I Stood on the River of Jordan* (Scholin); *My Soul is a Witness* (Choral Press, 1950); *New Born Again* (Belwin Octavo, 1951); *Cain and Abel* (Galaxy); *Stand the Storm* (Sam Fox); *Swing Low, Sweet Chariot* (Schirmer); *Weep Little Mary* (Shattinger); and other works, both arranged and original.

ROGIE CLARK (Ca. 1922–1980?)

Rogie Clark was born in Atlanta, Georgia. The year of his birth has been confirmed by Clark himself as 1922. Various other sources had previously recorded it as 1913, 1914, 1915 (the Library of Congress), and as 1917 (ASCAP Dictionary). A graduate of Clark College (Bachelor of Arts) and of Columbia University (Master of Arts), he also studied at Chicago Musical College, Juilliard School of Music, and at Tanglewood in Massachusetts.

Clark has held positions at Fort Valley State College as music director; at the New School for Social Research, New York, as lecturer; and at the 110th Street Community Center of New York. He has also worked as instructor of music at the New Lincoln School in New York, as chairman of the Department of Music at Jackson State College, and as music instructor of the Toledo Board of Education. Clark was also hired in Detroit as music instructor, Warren Board of Education and as Black Studies Professor at Wayne State University, Public School Black Focus, the Detroit Public Library, and at Shaw and Marygrove Colleges.

His other experiences have included weekly radio programs, Broadway productions, directorships of a weekly television program at WLBT, and other productions. He additionally conducted the Harlem Folkloric Choir, several workshops, festivals, and other professional duties such as writing the script for a film project held at the New School for Social Research. A member of ASCAP, the National Opera Association, the Detroit Musicians Association, the African-American Society, the American Music Centers, and other associations, he founded the International Council for Negro Folklore.

A prize winning talent whose work has commanded a faculty fellowship from the Ford Foundation, the John Hay Whitney Foundation, Tanglewood, the National Endowment for the Arts, and from the National Association of Negro Musicians (Award for Merit, 1973), he proved his merit by writing *The Black Bard* (A Study of Negro Folk Music), a play entitled *Where the Myrtle Tree Grows*, and poems entitled *Lamentations From A Long Hot Summer*; by producing a film called *My Haiti*; and by publishing several articles in the *Journal of American Folklore Survey, Musical America, International Musician, Music Journal, Negro Digest*, the *Journal of Human Relations, Phylon Magazine, Negro History Bulletin*, the *Nats Bulletin* and the *Detroit Free Press*. Listed in the ASCAP *Dictionary*, Ray Lawless's *Folksingers and Folksongs in America*, and the *Contemporary Opera*, Clark is known for presenting vocal concerts and for generally advancing the role of the composer in American music.

Among his original compositions are *Pippa's Song, Song of the Pop Bottles*, and *Flower Woman* (from opera *Ti Yette*, found in Ollie McFarland's *Afro-America Sings*, Detroit Public Schools, Hal Leonard Music); arrangements and adaptations of the following also appear in the book: *Before Dinner, The Uncertainties of Life, Lullaby, Otube Oma*, and *Little David* (SAB), *One Sunday Morning, Take This Hammer, Bounce Around, Shake Hands, Mary; Pack She Back to She Ma* (West Indian song), and *Water Come a Me Eye*. The Library of Congress also lists *Copper Sun* (Bryn Mawr, 1957), *Go Down Moses, Mango Walk* (Jamaican rumba, SATB, Boosey & Hawkes, 1956), *Mister Banjo* (Creole folk song, SATB, Neil Kjos, 1955), *Ride On, King Jesus* (Neil Kjos, 1951), *Tinga Layo* (Donkey Song from Martinique, Boosey & Hawkes, 1956).

One of the most important anthologies, *Negro Art Songs*, published by E. B. Marks in 1946, was compiled by Rogie Clark from a group of "Negro folk songs" for voice and piano, originally published by T. Presser, 1957. Contained in the book were compositions by Clark (*Copper Sun, Northboun', Impression: Le reveillon*, and *Soon-a Will Be Done)* along with works by other composers: J. W. Work II, Edward Margetson, Frederick Douglas Hall, Carl Diton, Cecil Cohen, R. Nathaniel Dett, J. Rosamond Johnson, Mark Fax, and Florence B. Price.

Others of his songs are *Six Afro-American Carols* (SATB, E. B. Marks), *Six African Songs* for baritone SATB (E. B. Marks, 1975), *Gwine Up* (Music Products, Chicago), *Sing Ye Glad Praises* (Fischer, J. J.), *Song of Judea* (Shawnee), *Wade in the Water* (E. B. Marks) and others in manuscript such as a ballet, *The Lonely Island*; the operas, *Ti Yette* and *The Stranger; Three Preludes: Negrillo, Tarantella* and *Chimera* for piano; *Figurine* for cello and piano; *Fantasia* for clarinet and piano; *Divertimento* for string (quartet; *Fete Creole* (1973); *Elegia*, and *Cantate Bachinegras* for orchestra (1974); *John Henry Fantasy* for band, *Etude* for violin (1974); and others.

MITCHELL SOUTHALL (1922–1989)

Mitchell Southall, a composer, arranger, conductor and educator, was born in Rochester, New York. He moved to Itta Bena, Mississippi, and served as theorist-conductor at Mississippi Valley State College, and also taught at Langston University, Lane College, Southern University, Miles College, etc.

Dr. Southall was educated at Langston University, the University of Iowa and at the Oklahoma College of Liberal Arts. His experiences have won him several listings in *Who's Who In Music* as well as other awards given him by universities and associations. He has appeared as both classical pianist and guest conductor at many concerts, choral festivals and on radio and television broadcasts; he has also conducted and performed jazz at night clubs and institutions, for which he has been praised by *down beat* magazine.

His compositions have enjoyed equal success in performance, having been used at festivals and other concerts throughout the United States. Of a tonal style, these works range from homophonic to slight overlapping in harmonic and melodic interplay. His arrangements of spirituals such as *Sometimes I Feel Like a Motherless Child* are consistent with modern rhythmic features including syncopation and slight deviations from the traditional framework. Yet the ever-changing metric pulses flow easily with the familiar melodies, altered chords and concrete form.

His works also include: *Romance* for Piano; *Elf Dance; Impromptu; In Silent Night* for mixed chorus; *Piano Concerto*; numerous spiritual arrangements for choral ensemble; *Lady Be Good* for male voices; *Intermezzo*; and *De Lawd God A'Mighty's On His Throne.*

PHILLIPPA DUKE SCHUYLER (1931?–1967)

Phillippa Schuyler, child prodigy, author, journalist, and pianist, was born in New York. She met a tragic death at a young age in a helicopter crash in Vietnam, where she was concertizing, working as a correspondent for the Manchester, New Hampshire *Union Leader*, doing research for another book, and assisting with the airlift of children from a war area.

Schuyler began private music study at an early age, quickly showing her talents in piano and compositional techniques by the age of four. Writing for various media from piano to orchestra, she made her debut, according to the *Washington Post* obituary, at the age of six at the 1939 New York World's Fair, playing her own works. According to ASCAP, her debut was cited as an appearance with the New York Philharmonic when she was fourteen years old (her age varies in newspaper reports perhaps because it was popular, according to former child prodigy Shirley Temple, for mothers and movie firms to date a child's age at least one year later than the child was actually born). After that time, she appeared in concerts all over the United States, in Mexico, the West Indies, and in Africa. For the Queen Mother Elizabeth of Belgium, she gave command performances. The State Department sponsored her in more than fifty performances which took her to the independence celebrations for Leopoldville, Ghana, Madagascar, and to command performances in Ethiopia for Haile Selassie.

Phillippa Schuyler. From Moorland-Spingarn/Van Vechten Collection.

Labeled "a gifted performer" by *Who's Who in Colored America* and a "genius" by many others, Schuyler was said to have penned her fifty-first composition at age eight. She also produced notable works for contests, several of which she won: *Rumpelstiltskin* (written at thirteen, awarded the

Wayne University and Grinnell Foundation prizes and published by Ricordi Americana S.A. in Buenos Aires in 1955); *Sleepy Hollow Sketches* (composed at age fourteen). She was cited by numerous organizations for her tremendous demonstrations—by Wayne University, the New York World's Fair, Haiti, the New York Philharmonic, the National Piano Teachers' Guild, the Music Education League, the Detroit Symphony Orchestra (for *Manhattan Nocturne*), and by the Omega Psi Phi Fraternity at the 1959 Conclave held in Town Hall. The *Negro Yearbook* of 1947 noted that she won the Philharmonic Society's Notebook Contest prize eight times and that she was then barred from the contest because of her brilliance; she also won the National Guild prize eight consecutive times with marks of "superior." Yet it seems amazing to some that America did not honor her more; the "why" is left to clear speculation of times, places, and practices of this century. It is also left to the fact that she had not completed her growth before such as untimely death.

An attractive musician, Phillippa Schuyler was featured in many popular magazines such as *Ebony, Newsweek, Crisis*, and *Seventeen* and she was also listed in the *Negro Yearbook* and the *Negro Almanac*. She authored books entitled *Who Killed the Congo?* and *Christ in Africa*.

Schuyler's compositions have been programmed by the New York Philharmonic, Boston Pops, New Haven, and other orchestras. Among her piano works were *Eight Little Pieces; Six Little Pieces; White Nile Suite* (musical saga depicting Arab history in Egypt and Jordan). Although some were published, they are unavailable for purchase at this time. Howard University's Moorland Room and the Library of Congress have listed pieces by Schuyler, but they have been reported as missing. Although other copies may be found, perhaps the most complete body of information and extant scores have been codified and studied by Kathryn Talalay at the Shomburg Library in New York (article appeared in the *Black Perspective in Music*, Spring 1982).

WENDELL WHALUM (1931–1987)

Wendell Whalum, author, educator, organist, choral conductor, administrator, clinician, and composer-arranger, was born in Memphis, Tennessee. A 1952 graduate of Morehouse College of Atlanta, Georgia (B.A.), he also received the M.A. degree from Columbia University in 1953 and the Ph.D. degree from the University of Iowa in 1968. In 1968, the University of Haiti awarded the Music Doctorate to him for his skill in conducting, his reputation as a folklorist, his thorough scholarship, and his choral distinctions both in the United States and abroad.

Except for temporary, honorary, or summer appointments, Whalum has worked continuously at his alma mater, Morehouse, since 1953, where he was appointed chairman of the music department from 1965 to 1974 and again from 1977 to the present time. Whalum also taught as Professor of Music at Atlanta University during the summers from 1967 to 1977, as a Fellow of Atlanta University's Center of African and Afro-American Studies. He has taught at Spelman; South Dakota State University; Emory University (Department of Religion); the University of Chicago; Dade Junior College of Miami; the University of the West Indies in Kingston, Jamaica; the Church Choir Festival in Lagos, Nigeria; Central Michigan University; Tufts University; Howard University; the First New World Festival in Brazil; and in other South American countries and at other institutions. Primarily disseminating data on aspects of Afro-American music, he also conducted choral workshops at still other events such as the annual conferences of National Association of Negro Musicians, church conferences, and at various festivals throughout the United States. He has also served as musical director of Allen Temple Methodist Episcopal Church (1956–1977).

An expert in the field of choral conducting, he was honored with numerous opportunities to conduct at prestigious events. In 1966, he organized the Atlanta University Center Community Chorus and conducted it upon many occasions including the 1976 concert for the Dorie Miller Award Festival in Chicago's Auditorium-Theatre when Benjamin Mays was being honored; the 1978 groundbreaking ceremony for the new Atlanta Life Insurance Company building; and for the Friendship Force's reception for visitors from Belgium held in Atlanta's Memorial Arts Center. He led the Spelman-Morehouse Christmas Concert at Avery Fischer Hall at New York's Lincoln Center in 1978; he gave a concert with Coretta Scott King at the White House in 1978, and directed the choir for the special program honoring President Carter in 1979 at the MLK Peace Prize acceptance event. He prepared the chorus for the Atlanta Symphony presentation of Beethoven's *Fidelio* in 1971, for Gershwin's opera *Porgy and Bess* and for other special programs, and in 1974, he also prepared choruses for the Atlanta Symphony presentation of Beethoven's *finale to Symphony No. 9*.

But it was as leader of the Morehouse Glee Club (to which he was appointed in 1953) that he developed a reputation of competence and for which he has been given many honors. The Glee Club toured both in America and abroad, singing at such events as the Second International Choral Festival at Lincoln Center in 1969; a performance with the National Symphony Orchestra with Warner Lawson conducting in 1968 (in honor of Martin Luther King); the Atlanta Symphony presentation of Stravinsky's *Oedipus Rex* in 1972; the Atlanta Mayor Maynard Jackson's Inauguration in 1974; the Atlanta Symphony's presentation of Schoenberg's *Gurre Lieder* in 1975; and at the opening session of the United Nations and World Tribute meeting at the Georgia World Congress Center which featured the United Nations Special Committee Against Apartheid. The State Department sponsored the Glee Club in a tour of West Africa in 1972, where it performed for heads of states.

An influential educator of the Atlanta community, Whalum, a member of Phi Beta Kappa, Phi Mu Alpha Sinfonia, American Guild of Organists, Alpha Phi Alpha Fraternity, also joined other important committees and organizations. He served as a patron of the John W. Work III Memorial Foundation; as board member of the Scott Joplin Foundation, the John A. Middleton Education Foundation, the National Association of Negro Musicians, the Atlanta Community Arts Center Governing Board, the Black Music Center of Indiana University, the Board of Sponsors of the Atlanta Symphony Orchestra and the Advisory Council of WRFG-FM Radio.

In addition to the honorary doctorate from Haiti, Whalum was appointed Fuller E. Callaway Professor of Music at Morehouse College in 1974. He was awarded a Merrill Grant for travel and study in Europe in 1958, the Danforth Teacher Grant (University of Iowa in 1961); the United Negro College Fund Faculty Grant in 1963, the Powers Grant for travel in West Africa in 1971, the Bronze Award from WETV of Atlanta in 1978, and at least two White House invitations (for the Horowitz Fiftieth Anniversary Recital in 1978 and the Black Musicians Association Dinner in 1979).

Whalum has composed and arranged well-conceived, tonal compositions published by Lawson-Gould. Among those arranged for SATB are the hymn tune *Amazin' Grace*, West Indian folk tune *De Morning Come*, and spirituals *Mary Was the Queen of Galilee* and *Give Me Jesus*; arranged for TTBB are *Roberta Lee* (old Negro love song from the Willis Laurence James Collection), and the spirituals *You'd Better Run* and *Somebody's Callin' My Name*. Roger Dean Publishers of Macombe, Illinois published his TTBB arrangement of *Mary Had A Baby* and an original, *The Lily of the Valley*, as well as the spiritual arrangement for solo voice, *Been in the Storm*. Other solo spirituals in manuscript are *God is a God, Sweet Home*, and *Sweet Jesus*. His arrangement of *Gonna Study War No More* is found in the *Songbook* of the Fourth Lincoln Center International Choral Festival (1974) and his *Oh Freedom*, in the J. C. Penney Bicentennial Music Publication. His scholarship has also been exhibited in articles such as the introduction of Willis Patterson's *Anthology of Art Songs*, Southern Baptist Association *Journals*, and various chapters of books, position papers, and other references.

Other TTBB arrangements have been made of Bach's *All Breathing Life*, Williams' *Zacchaeus, Come Down* (shape note hymn), *Done Made My Vow* and of the Olatunji-Whalum Nigerian Christmas song, *Betelehemu*.

EUGENE THAMON SIMPSON (1932–)

Eugene Simpson, song recitalist, pianist, lecturer, choral conductor, educator, and arranger, was born in North Wilkesboro, North Carolina. Educated at the Palmer Memorial Institute in Sedalia, North Carolina (high school diploma, 1947), at Howard University in Washington, D.C. (Bachelor of Music degree, 1951), at Yale University (both the Bachelor and Master of Music degrees, 1953, 1954), and at Columbia University (where he received the Ed.D. degree in voice in 1956), he also did further study at Columbia in the area of College Teaching and Administration (1966–68). His teachers of voice were Frederick Wilkerson (in Washington, New York, Germany between 1948 and 1949), Ugo De Caro and Donna Paola Novikova (1960–67). In composition and other areas, Simpson studied with Mark Fax, Ellsworth Grumman, Leland Thompson, Allen Forte, Thomas Richner, and Robert Pace.

Eugene T. Simpson.

As educator, Simpson held positions at Fort Valley State College, Georgia, in 1955, in the New York public high schools from 1956 to 1968, and as private voice teacher and coach at Carnegie Hall from 1964 to 1968. Thereafter, he assumed the position of associate professor of music and chairman of the voice area at Virginia State College, then transferring to Bowie State as chairman of the Department of Music, and to the Johns Hopkins University (as assistant to the provost and as Academic Administration Fellow of the American Council on Education). Since that time, Simpson became chairman of the Music Department at the Glassboro State College in New Jersey.

His affiliations include the Music Educators National Conference, the American Choral Directors Association, the American Guild of Television and Radio Artists, National Association of Teachers of Singing, Phi Delta Kappa, Pi Kappa Lambda, Phi Mu Alpha Sinfonians, and others. In addition, throughout his professional career, he found time to perform as vocal soloist in both academic and commercial situations; accompany soloists on the piano-forte; to deliver numerous workshops and clinics; to guest conduct at many institutions, conventions and clinics, and choral festivals; and to serve on the adjudication panels for auditioning potential Yale students. Even as pianist, he has performed extensively and has made his debut in Fischer Hall, New York, in 1956.

Hailed by Yale in its Spring/Summer Alumni *Newsletter*, 1974, as a prideful alumnus, the article stated that "Though a piano major at Yale, he has sung with the New York City Opera, BSO at Tanglewood under Leinsdorf and on records, RCA Victor."

As concert singer, he gave recitals under the stage name of Eugene Thamon, appearing at churches, St. Martin's Little Theater, the Brooklyn Museum, Steinway Hall, Town Hall, and the Berkshire Music Festival. In addition to the above, he did operatic performances with the Harlem Opera Company. He also sang in commercial backgrounds for all major labels and with many major stars—on radio and television commercials including Texaco, Blue Bonnet Margarine, Tube Rose Snuff, Three Musketeers Candy, Axion, and others. Major television appearances were seen on the Ed Sullivan Show, Camera Three, Lamp Unto My Feet, Project Twenty, and Get Set Go.

Dedicated and industrious in the practice of his profession, Simpson has collaborated with such eminent conductors as Leonard de Paur, David Labowitz, Richard Woitach, Claude Frank, and Erich Leinsdorf, and as either singer or conductor, he has made at least thirty recordings, among which are *Danse Calinda* with Leonard de Paur, *Swing Low, Sweet Chariot* with Leontyne Price, *Born to Sing the Blues* with Brook Benton, *I Love You Because* with Al Martino, *18 Yellow Roses* with Bobby Darin, *St. Martin De Porres Mass* with Mary Lou Williams (in which he sang solo parts), and *The Wonderful World of Folk* with Harry Belafonte (in which he sang solo parts).

It was at Virginia State University in 1970 that he produced and conducted the Virginia State Choir in a three-record set of spirituals arranged by composers Hall Johnson and William Dawson (entitled *Song Books* 1 and 2, available at Virginia State Department of Music). In the area of conducting, he also has been invited to quite a few honorary positions: choral assistant of the All-City Chorus of New York under Peter Wilhousky (1962); contributing conductor at the Third International University Choral Festival at Kennedy Center in Washington, D.C. (1972); contributing conductor at the International Choral Festival in Rome, Italy (1973); and observer-conductor at the Fourth International University Choral Festival at Lincoln Center in New York (1974).

Contributing to the advancement of folk music, Simpson wrote an article in 1970 on the Hall Johnson Legacy (Choral Journal). As composer-arranger, he has completed several arrangements of spirituals (some published by Bourne, starting in 1974) in a Black Heritage Series similar to the idea of his recordings at Virginia State. Four in the first series are: *Hold On!* (Murbo, 1973); *Nobody Knows De Trouble I've Seen* (SATB and TTBB); *Sinnuh, Please Don't Let Dis Harves' Pass*; and *Steal Away, True Religion, Too Late Sinnuh*, and *Sister Mary Had-A But One Child* (Bourne, 1976–81). The unique harmonies of the latter makes it one of the more successful scoring for SATB available in that it makes use of contemporary meter practices (contains 3/4, 5/4, 4/4 in frequent alternation), and does not necessarily feel the need for root positions of the traditional phrase endings, although tonality prevails within modulatory frameworks and altered chords of the sevenths. Contrasting with the other arrangements which are as comfortable as most in tonal construction and anticipated vocal lines, the interest here lies in slight alteration of traditional openings and rhythmic movement against familiar lines.

SALONE THEODORE CLARY (1939–)

Salone Clary, arranger, choral conductor, educator, and composer, was born in Portsmouth, Virginia. Beginning his earliest studies with his own mother at age six, he expanded his interest in instrumental music by taking up band and learning techniques for the trumpet, French horn, alto horn, baritone horn, trombone, clarinet, and flute. Continuing his education at Norfolk State College, he received the Bachelor of Science degree in 1963. In 1973, he graduated from Virginia State College, Petersburg, where he was awarded the Master of Science degree in Music Education, with emphasis on performance. At Virginia State, he gave two recitals on the piano in partial fulfillment of the degree requirements.

Maintaining an interest in all media, he then "banded together" with former students and friends of Noah Francis Ryder and founded the Noah Ryder Chorale, a group which gained a local reputation which increased after the Chorale appeared on the locally produced Pride television in Norfolk, 1973. Not entirely abandoning the instruments, he directed several bands and choral groups in the area while teaching at Norfolk State University and while serving as organist-director of music at the Shiloh Church. The latter choir also became well known in its area and gave concerts both in Norfolk and in Ohio, as well as in Lynchburg, Raleigh, and White Plains. He later became a teacher at the Duke Ellington School of Music in Washington, D.C.

Several honors have been awarded Clary. In 1972 and 1973, he was selected as accompanist for the All-City Junior High School and Elementary Choruses in Norfolk; in 1972, Alpha Lambda Chapter of the National Sorority of Phi Delta Kappa presented him with a citation in "recognition of the years of valuable services rendered to the citizens of your community, state, and nation"; in 1968, he gained membership in the American Society of Composers, Authors, and Publishers.

Clary's compositions are mainly tonal examples with clear simplicity of design. Of the four spirituals which Warner Brothers published in 1968 (*I Want to Live With God, The Blind Man Stood on the Road and Cried, When You Hear Those Bells*—an original in the style of a spiritual, and *Where Shall I Go?*), the first, *I Want to Live With God*, sold by 1976 over 25,000 copies. Through national and international sales, it received congratulatory responses from Governor Mills Godwin and President Lyndon B. Johnson. The uniqueness of the piece is that, although tonal, it is written in an interesting fugal style which adds to the stateliness and dignity of the arranged spiritual form. Other compositions are *Let's Have a Union, I'll Tell the World* (Walton, 1976), and various others in manuscript.

Modern Composers

Black composers of modern music are participants in techniques involving establishments of the Impressionistic era and the early 1900's. Characteristics of Debussy and Ravel as well as Charles Ives, Erik Satie, Poulenc and jazz set the stage for parallelism, block chords, polytonality, polyrhythms, longer melodic lines versus sporadic melodies, extended chords and ultra-chromatic harmonies, as well as the use of atonalism or the abandonment of a tonal center. Composers now use pentatonic or other modal harmonies intertwined with elements of the Baroque and earlier periods in order to denote a "new" sound and approach.

The modern period of the twentieth century denotes the machine and space ages, and is typified by the intervallic, instrumental approach rather than the vocal. The music is considered more impersonal and void of exaggerated emotional characteristics, and is an attempt to express the freedom of all emotions with restraint and perfect moderation. Continued in Ch. XIII, composers of this section are the largest of this style.

HOWARD SWANSON (1909–1978)

Howard Swanson, a composer who was born in Atlanta, Georgia, and reared in Cleveland, became a resident of New York. He attended the Cleveland Institute of Music, and later won the Rosenwald Fellowship which sent him to Europe for study with Nadia Boulanger of Paris. Swanson also studied with Elwell and was influenced by the Romantic and Modern styles.

Swanson achieved fame through his songs, some of which were performed by Marian Anderson. His *Short Symphony*, written in 1948, was judged the best work of the season by the New York Music Critics Circle in 1952, and the same piece was performed in 1950 with Mitropoulos as conductor of the New York Philharmonic Orchestra. His art songs *I've Known Rivers* and *Joy* were widely used as effective concert pieces.

Swanson's style of writing varies from the Romantic to the Modern. His compositions also depict well planned melodies of long or short durations, sound balance between melody and accompaniment of piano versus vocal solo, or violins versus orchestra background. While the art song *Joy* uses mainly consonances and virtuosic techniques for both voice and piano, the orchestral piece, *Night Music*, employs more dissonance and polyphony of the modern period. Both, however, "court" atonal sounds.

His piano *Sonata's* contrapuntal and contemporary aspects weave together a pattern unlike any other in demand and scope and unlike any other in the uniqueness of its style. Composed in three movements and making use of polytonal devices as well as melodic, rhythmic, and harmonic complexities, a part of its essence is seen in Examples 45 and 46 (closing of first movement and opening of the third). Although tonal, its syncopation obscures the keys.

Among his works written are numerous vocal and instrumental examples: *Short Symphony; Symphonies 1 & 3; Night Music* (for small orchestra, woodwinds, horn, and strings); *Suite for Cello and Piano; Sound Piece for Brass Quintet; The Cuckoo* (piano scherzo); *Music for Strings; Seven Songs for Voice and Piano recorded/Helen Thigpen; Piano Sonata; Death Song; Cahoots; Fifteen Songs; Four Preludes; Concerto for Orchestra; I Will Lie Down in Autumn, Pierrot,*

Ex. 45. *Sonata for Piano, No. 1*, Swanson, first movement ending. © Copyright 1950, Weintraub Music Company. Used by permission.

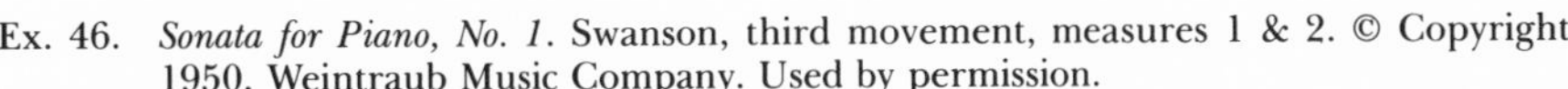
Ex. 46. *Sonata for Piano, No. 1*. Swanson, third movement, measures 1 & 2. © Copyright 1950, Weintraub Music Company. Used by permission.

etc. Papers and manuscripts of his are placed at the Amistad Research Center in Atlanta, Georgia.

MARK FAX (1911–1974)

Mark Fax was a composer, educator and director of the Department of Music at Howard University. Born in Baltimore, Maryland and educated at Syracuse University and the Eastman School, he taught at Paine College before joining the Howard faculty. Until his death, Fax was also organist-director of the Asbury Methodist Church of Washington, D.C.

Mark Fax. Courtesy of Dorothy Fax.

Fax used both Romantic and Modern styles of writing, as well as contemporary techniques which leaned toward atonality. his works were well organized, well balanced and challenging to perform. Intervals of seconds, fourths, fifths, or the use of altered chords and chromatics were pitted against clear, concise lines of sixteenth notes or sustained, smooth melodies. Many of the rhythmic, harmonic and intervallic patters were so intricately constructed that the impression of atonalism was predominantly felt. Yet a mixture of both tonal and atonal features were used in his works, with unusual skips in the upper and lower registers, trills and difficult rhythms, and slight traces of jazz influence. This style is reflected in *Toccata* from *Three Pieces for Piano*, the first measures of which are seen in Example 47:

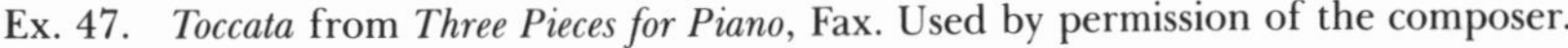
Ex. 47. *Toccata* from *Three Pieces for Piano*, Fax. Used by permission of the composer.

Fax's compositions are for orchestral, chamber, vocal and other media, and include art songs, arrangements, opera, piano and organ pieces. Some of these works are *Three Organ Pieces, Three Piano Pieces, Longing, May Day Song*, and *Only Dreams*.

NOAH RYDER (1914–1964)

Noah Ryder, composer, educator and conductor, was born in Nashville, Tennessee. Earning the B. S. degrees from Hampton Institute and the University of Michigan, respectively, he was influenced by R. N. Dett, C. C. White and Ernest Hays.

In 1935, he began his career as choir director of Dillard High School in Goldsboro, North Carolina. Subsequently, he became head of the music department at Winston-Salem Teachers College and in 1941, director of the Hampton Institute Choir. Resuming his teaching career after military service, he was appointed conductor of the choir and director of the music department at the Norfolk Division of Virginia State College (now Norfolk State), and simultaneously, leader of the H. t. Burleigh Glee Club, and minister of music at the Bank Street Church among other choral groups. He was also a member of ASCAP, AGO, AFM and MENC.

Ryder composed for various media, the most famous of which were his vocal songs. Arranged for solo voice and chorus, he wrote spirituals and art songs which used both traditional harmonies and modern techniques. His style of writing showed an advanced mastery of his art as well as a genuine feel for the media for which he composed.

Noah Ryder. Courtesy of Georgia Ryder.

His piano work, *Idyll,* was written in 6/4 meter and incorporated an effect of a barless measure in its phrasing of "three". Arranged in legato intervals of fifths, the melodic implication was fresh in its similar motion. Ryder's *Rhapsodie* was reflective of both Rachmaninoff and Bartok. By using extremities of the keyboard, pedal points effecting obscure harmonies, and frequent metric changes from 4/4 to 2/4 he developed interesting effects. The use of three measure phrases rather than the traditional four, the triplet figures in quarters (♩ ♩ ♩ 3), and continuous parallelism were equally interesting features of his music.

Among Ryder's varied compositions were: *Idyll* (piano) *Rhapsodie* (piano); *Serenade* (piano); *Sea Suite* (male voices); *Haul Away, Mateys, We're Almost Home* (Navy War Writer's Prize); *Balm in Gilead; By an' By; Done Paid My Vow; Let Us Break Bread Together; Gonna Journey Away; Great Day; Gwine Up; Hear the Lambs A'crying; I Got a Mother in Heaven; I Heard the Preaching of the Elders; I Will Never Betray My Lord; Nobody Knows; O Lemme Shine; Run to Jesus* (vocal), published by C. Fischer, J. Fischer, Schirmer, Handy, Spratt and Lorenz.

THOMAS KERR (1915–1988)

Thomas Kerr, a native of Baltimore, Maryland, moved to Adelphi, Maryland. Having received three degrees as a scholarship and fellowship student at the Eastman School of Music, he also studied at Howard University School of Music where he retired as Professor Emeritus of the piano department.

Kerr has been awarded prizes in composition from the Composers and Authors of America Contest in 1941 to the Rosenwald Fellowship. Recitals of his organ works have been performed in the United States and Europe, at the Washington Cathedral, the Shrine of Immaculate Conception, Mormon Tabernacle and the Martin Luther King broadcast on Voice of America in 1971. Others of his works have been performed at various institutions and on recordings. His honors have also included his numerous piano appearances with the National Symphony Orchestra, at the National Gallery, Phillip's Gallery and at many universities throughout the United States.

Kerr wrote in both tonal and atonal styles of the twentieth century. His ability to use clusters or blocks of sounds as well as simple homophony or mild polyphony is evident. His rhythmic patterns were exciting, and he was able to deal with short or long melodies with equal charm, using themes from original or folk sources.

"The Compleat Musician," an article by Hortense Reid Kerr (*D.C. Music Educator's Newsletter* (Winter 1983) listed Kerr's compositional arrangements

Thomas Kerr. Courtesy of Norma McCray.

for Carol Brice, Lawrence Winters, Todd Duncan, and Jessye Norman and also revealed that the performances of his organ works had been played "in more than twenty cathedrals and churches in Europe," in addition to American churches and halls.

Kerr performed a Chopin recital at the Howard University Chapel in 1982, and enjoyed several performances of his music such as the one on the WGMS station for two years, 1975–76, devoted to what Kerr described as his "twiddlings and tweedlings." He had a preference for the style seen in his *Caprice on Two Dance Themes* (the last page of which was lost almost immediately after a Roach performance in 1967). This style represented his most advanced altered chord constructions, tone clusters as well as the difficult rhythmic and technical aspects of his more adventuresome composition.

Other performances of his works were *Prayer for the Soul of Martin Luther King* by the D.C. Youth Chorale in a 1975 Kennedy Center appearance (a program sponsored by the Oratorio Society of Washington for purposes of honoring Washington composers Kerr, Evett, Weck and Woolen); *I Will Extol Thee* by the Evelyn White Chorale at the National Gallery, 1976; *Suite Sebastienne* with movements entitled *Theme Cantus, Frolicking Flutes—Homage to Vierne, Fugato and Toccata for Full Organ; Trio, Allegro Barbaro—Procession of the Gargoyles* and *Reverie*, programmed at a Howard University graduation recital, 1976; his *Riding to Town* was placed in Willis Patterson's *Anthology of Art Songs; Easter Monday Swagger* was recorded by Natalie Hinderas on Desto Records; and examples of his *Spirituals*, a suite, were published by E. B. Marks in *Chapel Echoes*, v. X, consisting of *You Better Mind, Swing Low, Walk Together Children*, and *It's Me, Oh Lord. Arietta* for organ was published in *American Organ Music*, v. 2 by Summy Birchard.

Among his compositions are: *Caprice for Piano; Organic Metamorphoses on an Afro-American Melody; Filets of Soul for Woodwind Quartet; Anguished American Easter; Easter Monday Swagger (Scherzino); Arietta; Seven Dancetudes for Piano; Fanfares for Christmas* (chorus); *Three Dunbar Songs; Centennial Anthem* for large chorus, brass and organ; *Prayer for the Peace of the Soul of Martin Luther King* (chorus); Wayfaring Stranger, and others.

ULYSSES SIMPSON KAY (1917–)

Ulysses Kay, currently a composer and music consultant for Broadcast Music Inc., in New York, was born in Tucson, Arizona. Graduated from the University of Arizona, Kay also attended the Eastman School of Music in Rochester (M.A.), the Berkshire Music Center and Yale University. His teacher of composition was Paul Hindemith.

A recipient of many awards and honors, Kay was granted a Ditson Fellowship for creative work at Columbia University; the Julius Rosenwald Fellowship; a Prix de Rome for residence at the American Academy in Rome for the seasons 1949–1950 and 1951–1952; a Fulbright Scholarship to Italy in 1950–1951; a grant from the American Academy of arts and Letters; and a grant from the National Institute of Arts and Letters. Other prizes have been awarded for several of his works, including *Suite for Orchestra, A Short Overture* and *Of New Horizons*. Moreover, Kay was awarded a Guggenheim Fellowship and honorary doctorates from Lincoln College and Bucknell University.

A well established composer of note, Kay has composed in styles rang-

Ulysses Kay.

ing from popular to art music. Commissions have come from the Cornell University A Cappella Choir; the Greater Boston Youth Symphony; Illinois Wesleyan Collegiate Choir; Interracial Fellowship Chorus of New York; the Koussevitzky Music Foundation and others.

Kay has been to the Soviet Union as a member of the first group of American composers sent on a cultural exchange mission by the State Department. His distinguished career has also involved composing scores for films and television. In addition, Kay has lectured at Boston University, the University of California at Los Angeles, and currently serves as Professor of Music at the Herbert H. Lehman College of the City University of New York.

Of his music, Howard Klein of the New York Times has said: "Mr. Kay calls himself a traditionalist—an evasive term. But his music is tonal and very direct. It comes out of romantic and expressionist chromatic styles of this century . . . " Also described as rhapsodic, melodic, classical and modern, Kay's works invite analysis relating it to many periods. He is very representative of the contemporary era.

Even though a good many of Kay's works are of the neo-Baroque tradition in contrapuntal features and forms, much of that which has gone before reflects the classical period in form. His latest works such as *Parables* show a decided change in the intervallic concept of the contemporary period. Seconds, fourths, sevenths, etc., always characterized his music, as did rhythms typical of the contemporary period. Kay is significant for linking the Modern Period with the Space Age in his forward use of contemporary techniques, much as did Beethoven who bridged the Classical and Romantic periods. Kay is one who produces quality works, and his courageous approach of maintaining a traditional principle amidst irregular, or contemporary methods, is unique.

One of the examples of his works is the *Four Inventions* for piano. An advanced compositional technique of fugal or imitative features, it uses twelve tone principles fused with tonalism, and generally obscures the key while functioning within a harmonic structure. Written in four movements: Andante moderator, Scherzando, Larghetto, and Allegro, the movements are scored without a key signature but do not always remain in C Major. The first movement ends on G minor; the second on A minor (without a third); the third on Ab major; and the fourth in C major. Slightly vocal, the piece, particularly in the first movement, sounds atonal despite its movement within G minor chord progressions. This results from a rhythm which places chord tones an eighth note apart from other chord tones, while the melody accents the dissonance. Nevertheless, the first movement does use all the notes of the G minor chord both in the first and last measures, thus confirming a tonal center:

Ex. 48. *Four Inventions*, Kay. © Copyright, 1964, Duchess Music Corporation, 445 Park Avenue, New York, New York 10022. Used by permission. All rights reserved.

The second movement (Ex. 49), given in 5/8, outlines irregular phrasing at the beginning. In its unique expression, inverted mordents, incomplete scale passages and short phrases are typical. It terminates in extreme registers, and makes use of wide intervals within the melodic lines:

Ex. 49. Second Movement.

The third movement makes use of accidentals which are written in, and jazz harmonies of elongated sevenths, ninths or polychords. Typical rhythmic changes alternate between 4/8 and 6/8 in its somewhat sectional character. Melodies shift from bass to treble in the exchange of the main subject. Dynamic extremes and the use of three clefs are also used. The main subject is seen in Example 50.

Ex. 50. Third Movement, main subject.

The last movement, a two-part invention, is the most difficult of the four. Even though written in 4/4, its accented staccatos and breaks slurred meticulously throughout make it a challenge to perform. Scales in contrary motion, unexpected metric changes, and variations in dynamics bring the work to a close:

Ex. 51. Fourth Movement.

While the above examples exhibit his piano technique, Kay is equally noted for his quality of style in orchestral and other music. Although his long list of works include music for virtually all media, the great majority of compositions are written for the orchestra and for chorus. His *Umbrian Scene* has been performed by the Louisville Symphony Orchestra. The *Serenade for Orchestra* has been performed by the Chicago Symphony Orchestra. And his opera, *Juggler of Our Lady*, was recently included in the repertoire of Opera South, of Jackson, Mississippi. With keen sensitivity to taste in orchestral colors and combinations of sounds in general, Kay uses the extremes in high and low pitches with unusual dissonance.

Ancient Saga, a design for modern dance, was written in 1947. Scored for piano, three violins, violas, cello and contrabass, it includes parallelism, polymeters, many key and tempo changes and interesting rhythmic patterns. Measures 173–176, excerpted in Example 52, point out some of these features:

Ex. 52. *Ancient Saga*, Kay. © Copyright Carl Fisher, 445 Park Avenue, New York, New York 10022. Used by permission of Carl Fischer, Inc. 1983. All rights reserved.

Kay was one whose compositions were featured at the Colloquia and Competition held at the Kennedy Center, Washington, D.C., in 1980 (*Partita in A* for violin and *Four Inventions*, also in excerpt in *International Library* V.8) and at many other performances such as were held at the regional symposiums on Black music, 1976–82. In addition, his *Markings* (1966, Duchess Music) for orchestra was recorded on the Columbia Black Composers Series, 1976, while *Choral Triptych* (Associated, 1967) was recorded by Cambridge Records; still other works were recorded on Turnabout/34546 (the interesting *Six Dances* for instruments); on Folkways (*Brass Quartet*); CRI (*What's in a Name?* and *How Stands the Glass Around* for SATB; *Round Dance and Polka* and *Sinfonia* for instruments); with others on CRI, Desto and Louisville recordings.

Selected by Antal Dorati, conductor of National Symphony, as one whose composition would be commissioned for the U.S. Bicentennial, Dorati said that the criterion for selection was "purely musical" (*Washington Post*). His opera, *Juggler of Our Lady*, was programmed by Opera/South; the New York Philharmonic performed his *Three-Pieces After Blake* in 1977; his musical style was discussed in a paper delivered by Lucius Wyatt in San Antonio at the Southwest Chapter meeting of the American Musicological Society; *Short Wind* and others were released by Peters; he wrote for *Portrait of Aaron Douglas, A Thing of Beauty* with Ossie Davis as narrator (Fisk University for perusal); he was listed in the *Compositores de América* published by the Pan American Union in Washington, D.C., and in virtually every important book on music in America.

His newest style reflects atonalism and one of his most brilliant assets: that of logical and innovative design. One of the latest published by MCA, *Nocturne for Piano*, shows creative command of structural organization, for it reads like a painting, ever-changing and ever-revealing at each scrutiny.

The following outline seems to depict the quality of thought behind his compositions and offers a general overview of a clever use of four elements of music, revealing a cyclic return to the opening, in an effective mirrored reflection.

Part	Meas.	Melodic	Harmonic	Rhythmic	Formal
I	1		Atonal, Expanded Chords. Opening Tone Center: d	4/4	A Section Introduction
	10	Theme in r.h.; small & large skips	Homophonic	4/4 (3/4)	A Theme
	38			3/8	Bridge B Section
II	44			4/4	New & Old Material in
	50		Contrapuntal	5/4	diminution, augmentation & inversion
III	65		Homophonic	3/4 (2/4)	A Section Introduction
	70	Theme in l.h.; sm., lge. skips		4/4	A Theme
	85			4/4	A Theme accomp. & head
	90				A Theme with Arpegg.
	98				Bridge (intro. material)
	102		Closing Tone Center: d		Coda (intro. abridged to 8 meas. in reverse order)

Among his works are: *A Short Overture; Aulos; Concerto for Orchestra; Fantasy Variations; Markings; Overture; Of New Horizons; Portrait Suite; Orchestra; Symphony; Trigon; Umbrian Suite; Choral Triptych; Inscriptions from Whitman* (cantata for voice and orchestra); *Stephen Crane Set* (94 pieces for SATB and 13 players); *Three Pieces After Blake* (soprano and orchestra); *Six Dances; A Lincoln Letter; A New Song; How Stands the Glass Around?* (vocal); *Come Away, Come Away Death; Flowers in the Valley; Four Hymn-Anthems; Grace to You and Peace; Song of Jeremiah; Tears, Flow No More; What's in a Name?; Brass Quartet; Four Inventions* (piano); String Quartet Nos. 2, 3; *Trumpet Fan-Fares* (4 trumpets); *Ten Essays for Piano; Two Short Pieces for Piano* (4 hands); *The Boor* (opera); *The Juggler of Our Lady* (opera); and many others.

HOWARD A. ROBERTS (1924–)

Howard A. Roberts was born in Burlington, New Jersey, and moved with his family to Cleveland, Ohio, around the age of five years. Educated at Baldwin-Wallace College and Western Reserve University, he attended the Cleveland Institute of Music for the Bachelor and Master of Music degrees earned in 1950 and 1951, respectively. Among his teachers were Marcel Dick, Mordecai Bauman, and Maggie Teyte of London; Pierre Bernac of Paris; and Marinka Gurewich of New York.

Roberts has worked as educator and choral conductor, arranger and singer as well as composer. He has held positions at North Carolina Central University, Morgan State College in Baltimore, Maryland (1959–61), and also at institutions in Cambria Heights, New York. He has performed in numerous Broadway musicals as singer, in instrumental ensembles with Lionel Hampton and others as trumpeter, and as choral conductor with his own Howard Roberts Chorale which he founded in 1969. Roberts also performed as singer in Broadway shows *Porgy and Bess* and *Shinebone Alley*, as tenor soloist with the Robert Shaw Chorale, the American Concert Choir; and he has served as musical director for Harry Belafonte, the Alvin Ailey Dance Company, Broadway shows *Raisin, Guys and Dolls* (revival), the *Wiz*, and *Comin' Uptown*. His accomplishments are documented in such sources

Ex. 53. *Let My People Go*, Roberts. © Copyright 1970 Lawson-Gould. All rights reserved. Used by permission.

as Evelyn White's *Selected Bibliography*, in Eileen Southern's *Dictionary*, and in the ASCAP *Directory* (of which he became a member in 1965).

Let My People Go, recorded on Columbia label by the Howard Roberts Chorale and published in 1970, a tonally conceived spiritual adaptation, shows his unique rhythmic calculations and unusual instrumentation of high, middle, and low drums along with slight interpolations of alternations of meters not found in the traditional songs. Arranged for SATB, the piece is suggested for *a cappella* with optional percussion preference, but its use of the drums reflects an African heritage with prideful concern (see Example 53).

Among his compositions are popular, jazz, and art music: for SATB, published by Lawson/Gould in 1970: *I Want Jesus to Walk With Me, Let My People Go, Motherless Child, Soon I Will Be Down, Steal Away,* and *Talk About a Child.* Other compositions are *Sinner Man* (recorded by Alabama State University on *From This We've Come*, Prestige Records/760603), *Rock-O My Soul, God Almighty;* Songs: *Look Over Yonder, Be My Woman, Gal, Shake That Little Foot, Always Left Them Laughing, False Love, Hoe Down Blues;* Scores: (Broadway shows): *Trumpets of the Lord, Every Night When the Sun Goes Down, A Nation is Born, TV Cindy, Young, Gifted and Black;* Ballets: *Revelations, Blood Memories, Long Remembrance* (cantata); *Burst of Fists*; Film: *Lord Shango.*

JULIA PERRY (c. 1924–1979)

Julia Perry was born, according to Grove's *Dictionary*, in Lexington, Kentucky, although some other sources such as the ASCAP *Directory* and Eugene Claghorn's *Dictionary*, claim Akron, Ohio, as her birthplace. Akron was the site where she lived for some time, and where she composed *Homunculus, C. F. for Ten Percussionists.* Her date of birth has been given as 1924 and 1927 by different sources. Grove's listed her dates as 1924–1979; Raoul Abdul gave a birth date as 1927.

According to a short sketch registered at Southern Publishers and CRI Records, she was educated at Westminster Choir College in Princeton, New Jersey, where she received her Master of Music degree in composition. She did further study in Italy and France, and also did guest conducting there. As her earliest studies were in piano, violin, and voice, she taught herself to play other orchestral instruments.

Perry was reviewed in the MENC/Black Caucus *Newsletter*, in *Musical America*, January 1953; in *Hi Fidelity*, June 1975. She was listed in *Who's Who in Colored America* and the 1947 *Negro Yearbook*, the *Selected Bibliography of Published Choral Works by Black Composers* by Evelyn White, the *Eagon Catalog of Published Concert Music*, but perhaps the Southern *Dictionary* contained the fullest factual outlay of her career.

A prizewinner, she was twice a Guggenheim recipient and winner of the American Academy and National Institute of Arts and Letters Award (1964). For her *Violin Sonata* she was awarded the Boulanger Grand Prix. Her pieces have been performed throughout the nation and in Europe. Also, while in Europe, she was chosen to conduct concerts sponsored by the U.S. Information Service.

Perry makes use of tonality and slightly contemporary features. Of her *Homunculus, C. F. for Ten Percussionists*, she wrote that her father was a physician and the clinical surroundings of his office inspired the piece and evoked memories of the medieval laboratory "where Wagner, youthful apprentice to Faust, made a successful alchemy experiment, fashioning and bring to life a creature he called homunculus. Having selected percussion instruments for my formulae, then maneuvering and distilling them by means of the Chord of the Fifteenth (C. F.), this musical test tube baby was brought to life. The Chord of the Fifteenth was created from a succession of superimposed thirds with 'E' as the fundamental tone."

Writing music in both the old and the new styles of post-romantic and modern eras, Perry is said to be at her best in church music. She makes use of neo-Baroque techniques in her *Stabat Mater* for voice and strings (piano/vocal score, movement no. 5, measures 1–4) and in the string/vocal score, measures 1–3, movement no. 4 seen in Examples 54 & 55.

Ex. 54. *Stabat Mater*, Perry. Piano/vocal score, movement no. 5, m. 1–4. Copyright 1954 by Southern Music Publishing Co., Inc. Copyright renewed. International copyright secured. All rights reserved including the right of public performance for profit. Used by permission.

Ex. 55. *Stabat Mater*, Perry. String/vocal score, movement no. 4, m. 1–3. Copyright 1954 by Southern Music Publishing Co., Inc. Copyright renewed. International copyright secured. All rights reserved including the right of public performance for profit. Used by permission.

Among her works are SATB pieces published by Galaxy: *Be Merciful Unto Me, O God; Our Thanks To Thee,* anthem with contralto; *Song of Our Savior; Ye Who Seek the Truth* with tenor solo; for solo voice, medium, published by Galaxy: *By The Sea; Free at Last; How Beautiful Are the Feet; I'm A Poor Li'l Orphan in This Worl'*; instrumental pieces published by Peer-Southern: *Short Piece* for Orchestra (recorded/CRI); *Homunculus, C. F. for Ten Percussionists* and harp (recorded/CRI); *Stabat Mater* (recorded/CRI); *Pastoral for Flute and Strings; The Cask of Amontillado* (opera); others: *Carillon Heigh-Ho* for SATB (C. Fischer); *Lord, What Shall I Do?* for voice (McLaughlin/Reilly); and others.

ROBERT LEE OWENS (1925–)

Robert Owens was born in Denison, Texas. A composer, coach, pianist, and actor, he first established a reputation as a pianist with his performance of a piano concerto with the Berkeley Young People's Symphony at the age of fifteen. He began studies with his mother, Alpharetta Helm. After her death in 1937, he continued lessons with Genvieve Longrus of Berkeley. Receiving a number of scholarships while in Berkeley High School, Owens moved to San Francisco to work for the Civil Service Commission instead of engrossing himself fully in his musical career; later he joined the Army Air Corps as a cadet and served in Alabama and Stuttgart, Arkansas.

After the brief interruption of his studies, he traveled to Paris, France, in order to study with Alfred Cortot at the Ecole Normale de Musique. After a 1952 debut in Copenhagen, he continued his work with Grete Hinterhofer at the Vienna Academy of Music in 1953 and gave concerts in Denmark and Austria by 1957.

Robert Owens.

Returning to the United States, Owens taught music at Albany State College in Georgia, at which time he also began to compose more seriously. Returning to Berkeley in 1958, he traveled to Harlem in New York and then to Europe in 1959, visiting Germany and playing his compositions. He then decided to take up permanent residence in Munich.

Owens has visited the United States sporadically, once returning to the University of Michigan School of Music where his vocal compositions were sponsored in a program by the faculty and students with Owens himself as accompanist. His works have enjoyed many other performances in the States and abroad and have generally been favorably described.

Two of Owen's songs from his *Mortal Storm* are represented in Willis Patterson's *Anthology of Art Songs by Black American Composers* (E. B. Marks). Entitled *Faithful One* and *Genius Child,* they employ tonal harmonies with enough sevenths and modulations to momentarily obscure the home key or intended modulation. Full chords, parallelism, and repetitions are handled skillfully underneath simple vocal lines with intricately interesting rhythms. His *Kalifornische Sonata for Klavier,* Opus 6, and *Carnival* (Klaviersuite), Opus 7, employ jazz rhythms, slightly contemporary features of harmony (although tonal), and unique background content.

Among his works published by Edition Sikorski of Hamburg, Germany, are *Border Line* (Liederzyklus für Bariton und Klavier), *Desire* (Liederzyklus für Tenor und Klavier),*Heart on the Wall* (5 Lieder für Sopran und Klavier), *Four Motivations* für Gesand und Klavier, *Silver Rain* (Liedezyklus für Tenor und Klavier), *Stanzas for Music* (4 Lieder für Tenor und Klavier), *Three Songs* for a high voice and piano; and others.

CHARLES COLEMAN (1926–1991)

Charles Coleman, organist-composer of Detroit, Michigan, was educated at Wayne State University, where he received both the Bachelor of Music and Master of Music degrees in 1952 and 1955, respectively, graduating with honors (A.A.G.O.). Among his teachers were Mildred Clumas, August Mackelberghe, Robert Cato (St. Paul's Cathedral), and Virgil Fox (Riverside Church in New York). In addition, he studied organ and piano with Van Dessel, conducting with Walter Poole.

Having worked in the Detroit system, Coleman was noted for his untiring efforts to create in the worlds of performance, composition, and education. A member of the American Guild of Organists, he gave numerous concerts at Wayne State, at the NANM Convention in Chicago (1955), and at the American Guild of Organists (1955). He gave a church organ recital in Windsor, Ontario, Canada (1960) and four television performances for the Detroit Council of Churches (1961). He was also invited to accompany on the organ such works as *Elijah*, which was held at the Ford Auditorium. For many years, Coleman worked as organist-director at Tabernacle Baptist Church in Detroit; he founded the Northwestern School of Music in Detroit and once held positions at Calvary Baptist, St. Cyprian Episcopal, St. Mark's Presbyterian, and Greater Macedonia Baptist Churches.

Among his compositions are the following choral works published by Word Publishers: *Blest Be the Tie, Be Thou Faithful Unto Death, Let Us Break Bread Together, Live-a Umble, Let All Those That Seek Thee Rejoice, Before the Throne of God, O Perfect Love,* and *Alleluia* (which along with *Break Bread* is shown in Ollie McFarland's *Afro-America Sings*, Detroit Public Schools, Hall Leonard Music). Others which he has composed are *Sonata in F* for organ, *Sonatine* for piano, *Fantasia* for flute, *Suite* for two violins, *John Kennedy* (SATB), and others.

EDWARD M. MCLIN (1928–)

A native of Chicago, Edward McLin received his educational foundation in the Chicago public schools. Beginning his musical career in the high school band with the study of the trumpet and French horn, he was awarded a musical scholarship to Kentucky State College. By 1950, he had earned the Bachelor of Music degree from Chicago Musical College and by 1951, his Master of Music degree from the same institution. Among other career activities, he was staff arranger for Hansen Publications, Inc. between 1966 and 1968.

Although the Library of Congress has listed only a few of his works (*Chorales* for strings, *For Four B^b Trumpets, Matinee and March* for band, *Sourwood Mountain* for band, all published by Pro Art in 1959, 1960, 1958, 1956, and 1963, respectively), Don White has compiled an unpublished list which numbers well over 100 published original and arranged pieces (some by pseudonym). Among some published by Hansen are *Drummin' Drummin' Drummin', Grand Hotel Jazz March, I Wanna Be Like You* (Jungle Book), *Mission Impossible Them, Spanish Flez—Lonely Bull, Sunny*, and others for "Quickstep Band"; several books for half-time shows; music for elementary concert band (published by Pro Art) such as *Chop Sticks* (Red Band Series), *Circus March Medley, Go Down Moses*; for intermediate band: *Calypso Carnival, Haitian Holiday*; for stage band: *Beatnik Bounce Bongos, Brasses and Reeds* (Pro

Art); *Theme for a Rock and Roller* (Pro Art); *From These Halls* for SSA (Pro Art); and others.

BETTY JACKSON KING (1928–)

Betty Jackson King, before moving to Wildwood, New Jersey, was a resident of New York, Chicago, and New Orleans. A native of Chicago, she was educated at Wilson Junior College and Roosevelt University (where she received the Bachelor of Music in piano and the Master of Music in composition); she also attended Oakland University in Rochester, Michigan, Glassboro College, Peabody Institute, Westminster Choir College, and Bank Street College.

Her extensive teaching experience was gained at Jacksonian Community Center in Chicago, the University of Chicago Laboratory School, Roosevelt University, Dillard University, and at Wildwood High School. In addition, her reputation as a choral director has been made at Chicago with the Grace Notes, Pre-Professional Choral Ensemble, the Congregational Church of Park Manor, and in New Orleans with the Dillard University Choir, in New York with the Riverside Church School Choirs and other ensembles.

For her professional contributions to choral music, she was nominated for a Ford Foundation Grant on Choral Music by Black Composers. She has served as guest conductor of many festivals such as the Choral Festival of Black American Music at the Alabama Center for Higher Education and she has served as choral lecturer and clinician for many associations.

Among her honors have been a scholarship to Roosevelt University, a prize for a composition contest from the Coleridge-Taylor Club, and awards from the Outstanding Secondary Educators of America, the Outstanding Leaders in Elementary and Secondary Education and a citation from the National Association of Negro Musicians for outstanding contributions to the field of music. A member of NANM, she was voted to its presidency in 1976. She also joined the First Water, an organization developed in 1975 for the purpose of "promoting the finest classical works by Black artists of African descent."

Her works have been widely performed at National Association of Negro Musicians Conventions, by the All-City Chorus in a 1977 televised presentation for the Chicago Board of Education, by Consortium Choirs at the Alabama Center for Higher Education Festival, and at the Metropolitan Museum of Art.

Although King uses tonalism, her employment of fourths, fifths, and octaves along with skillful repetition, imitation, and echoes within familiar spirituals are effective and compact. Published by Pro Art, Somerset, Kjos, Hope, and E. B. Marks, her works range in intensity and insight. An excerpt of *Sinner, Please Don't Let This Harvest Pass* utilizes African lyrics within the spiritual setting for SSAATB, as seen in Example 56.

Representative of her style are also the arranged spirituals: *I Couldn't Hear Nobody Pray; Come Down, Angels; Two Christmas Spirituals; This Little Light of Mine; I Want God's Heaven To Be Mine*. Some of her original works are: *Saul of Tarsus* (oratorio written for master's thesis); *My Servant Job, Simon of Cyrene* (Easter cantata), *The Kids in School With Me* (a ballet), *A Requiem; The Nuptial Suite* (organ); *Life Cycle* (solo instrument and piano); *A Vocalise* for soprano, cello, and piano; and numerous vocal solos, choral works, piano works, instrumental pieces for orchestral instruments, and other spirituals.

Ex. 56. *Sinner, Please Don't Let This Harvest Pass*, King. Copyright, 1978, Pro Art Publications, Inc. All rights reserved. Used by permission.

LENA JOHNSON MCLIN (1928–)

Lena McLin, the active composer, arranger, educator, conductor, administrator, and lecturer was born in Atlanta, Georgia. She received her Bachelor of Arts from Spelman College in 1951, her Master of Arts from the American Conservatory in 1954, and also furthered her education at Roosevelt University and Chicago State College.

McLin has worked as teacher and director of the music department at Kenwood High School in Chicago, Illinois, for many years. She also founded the McLin Ensemble for operatic productions and became the director of the Chancel Choir at Southfield United Methodist Church. A member of the Board of Education, the National Association of Negro Musicians, Music Educators National Association, and of several other groups, she has been selected for honors for her superb work in the field of music. In 1973, she was awarded the Virginia Union University Award for "Outstanding Composer." Other awards included the Chicago Best Teacher of the Year Award, 1972–73, and the Critics Association Award for Outstanding Composer, 1971.

McLin became known as a composer through her church music and for her interest and development of rock music for the sake of aesthetic art. She also produced *The Origin of the Spiritual*, a 25-minute film discussing pertinent points about aspects of the form. McLin is prolificity personified. Her ability to "turn a tune" in a timely fashion resulted in a large bulk of compositions published by Neil Kjos. She writes with unbelievable ease and speed in mainly tonal keys. Her works consist of anthems and spirituals for chorus, or of secular choral pieces with rock-based instrumentations such as accompaniments of piano, flute, cello, electric bass guitar and electric piano, or other combinations with either piano or organ accompaniments. Some of the works contrast choral and solo sections with the accompaniments. Still others are written for solo voice, piano solo, etc.

Running the gamut of styles from art music to rock, McLin has excelled in prolificity of church music. She has a gift for both recapturing the oldtime revivalism (as seen in measures 9–14 of *Glory, Glory, Hallelujah,* Example 57) and for satisfying the mildly contemporary spirit of an artistic and sacred type (as in the piano introduction of the anthem, *All the Earth Sing Unto the Lord,* (Example 58).

Ex. 57. *Glory, Glory, Hallelujah,* L. McLin. Edition no. 5430. © Copyright 1966. Neil Kjos Music Company. Reprinted by permission, 1983.

Ex. 58. *All the Earth Sing Unto the Lord.* L. McLin. Edition no. 5459. © Copyright 1967. Reprinted by permission, 1983.

For Odell Hobbs, Choir Director, Virginia Union University

All the Earth Sing Unto the Lord

(SATB a cappella)

Text based on Psalm 96

Lena J. McLin

In part, her published compositions are *All the Earth Sing Unto the Lord; Cert'nly Lord, Cert'nly Lord; Done Made My Vow to the Lord; Down By the River; Eucharist of the Soul* (Liturgical Mass); For Jesus Christ is Born; Free at Last (Portrait of Martin Luther King); *Friendship; Glory, Glory, Hallelujah; Gwendolyn Brooks* (A Musical Portrait); *If They Ask You Why He Came; I'm So Glad Trouble Don't Last Always; In This World; Let the People Sing Praises Unto the Lord; The Little Baby; Lit'le Lamb, Lit'le Lamb; My God is so High; New Born King; Sanctus and Benedictus; The Torch Has Been Passed; What Will You Put Under Your Christmas Tree?; Winter, Spring, Summer, Autumn; Writ'en Down

My Name; Psalm 100; Psalm 121; Psalm 124; Psalm 117; Lift Up Your Heads; Out of the Depths; Oh Be Joyful All Ye Lands; A Creed; Nehemiah Chapter 6; I Am Doing a Great Work; For Mine Eyes Hath Seen Thy Salvation; Give Unto the Lord; Keep Silence Before Him; Judas; Abiding Faith; God Made Us All; for piano: *A Summer Day, Fun in C Minor, Impressions* nos. 4, 5, 6, and 7 (the latter including strings, oboe, horn and piano); for organ: *Impressions* nos. 2 and 3; *Hallelujah Hallucination.*

KERMIT MOORE (1929–)

Kermit Moore, cellist, conductor, educator, and composer, was born in Akron, Ohio. Educated in the Ohio public schools, Moore later studied at Cleveland Institute of Music (B. M., 1951), at New York University (M. A.), at Paris Conservatory (receiving the artist's diploma in 1956), and also at the Juilliard School of Music. Among his teachers were Paul Bazelaire, Nadia Boulanger, and Georges Enesco in Paris, Felix Salmond in New York, and Marcel Dick.

Moore was awarded several honors, among which were the Edgar Stillman Kelly Award from the State of Ohio, the Lili Boulanger Award in 1953, and a special medal from Queen Elizabeth in 1958. He was also given a Knight Publications grant, a plaque and award from the Dean Dixon Society of New York, as well as several commissions and opportunities for prestigious guest conducting and cello performances.

A member of ASCAP and co-founder of both the Society of Black Composers and of the Symphony of the New World, he has taught at the University of Hartford, has served as project director of the Symphony of the New World, and has worked as conductor of symphony orchestras, as well as the teacher of artist pupils in New York. According to the notes on his record, *Kermit Moore* (on which he recorded his *Music for Cello with Raymond Jackson*), "has conducted in New York's Philharmonic Hall and had the honor of conducting the New York Festival Orchestra in the General Assembly Hall of the United Nations." He has conducted the Symphony of the New World and many ensembles such as the string quartet reviewed in *down beat* in the early 1970s. He has conducted many orchestras in performances of his own works. Of his conducting, the *National Music Journal*

Kermit Moore. Photo by George Jackson Foster.

wrote of his "authoritative" capabilities and of his selection of a "demanding, difficult program and managing to enthrall the appreciative audience." The *New York Post* reviewed Moore's directing as having "authority and conviction."

Moore has concertized as cellist throughout the United States, Europe, Far East, and Africa, performing with the Orchestra de la Suisse Romande, the Concertgebouw of Amsterdam, the National Radio Symphony of Paris, the Belgian National Orchestra, and others. In the United States, he has played in Lincoln Center and Carnegie Hall. He was described as "a most musical cellist" by Alvin Fossner, (*Jersey Journal*, Jersey City, December 7, 1965), and as "one of the music realm's most gifted who should be seen and heard more" (*Music Journal*, April, 1975). Other accolades were from Peter Davis of the *New York Times* who wrote that "Moore vaulted every technical hurdle of his formidable recital with disarming ease and he instinctively found a precise stylistic voice for each composer. He is a virtuoso cellist, a sensitive musician and something of a hero."

The *San Francisco Chronicle* reviewed Moore's cello recital as being "impressive on many counts. . . . Moore showed a fine understanding for musical line and style. His tone is all honey and warmth, glowing in the soft intensity of its focus." Still other captions read, "A Great Cellist" and "Moore has three rare assets; a flawless technique, a warm, singing tone, and a questioning, original approach to music" (Janos Gereben, *San Francisco Post*, March 7, 1980). Still other adjectives and quotes describing his performances include "remarkably gifted" (Paul Tinel, *Le Soir* of Brussels); "accomplished virtuoso" (*Journal de Geneve*); "magnificent . . . astonishing expression and finest of comprehension. He adds to this an elasticity of nuance and an accuracy of style" (*Koelnische Rundschau* of Cologne, Germany); "entirely successful in holding our interest musically" (*Monthly Music* Magazine of Seoul, Korea). Raoul Abdul, author of *Blacks in Classical Music* wrote a timely summation: "Moore is a musician of the highest order and a superb cello player."

Moore's cello playing is recorded not only on his own *Kermit Moore* album released by Performance/Cespico Records, as well as on Musical Heritage (*Lyrical Suite* for mezzo and instruments), Orion and CRI labels, but also on virtually every recording by major jazz artists (such as Oliver Nelson's *A Dream Deferred*; Yusef Lateef's *Part of the Search, Gentle Giant* and two others, a record by Sonny Stitt, three albums by Ron Carter; and others). A review of discs by Daniel Buckley of Tucson's *Newsreal Magazine* stated that "he is also probably the most often recorded single cellist alive today (check the personnel on literally hundreds of jazz albums featuring a string section, and the name Kermit Moore is often encountered)."

Equally commendable is the man's worth as a composer. His style of serialism or twelve-tone rows in such works as *Music for Viola, Piano and Percussion* and *Music for Flute and Piano* reflects his record as an achiever and honor graduate and his inquisitiveness as a researcher. Yet his keen knowledge of jazz and the intellectualism in all performances merge to define his readiness and preparedness for his very professional output.

His compositions, available from Rudmor Publishing Company in New York, include solo works for cello and flute (a sonata), a timpani concerto, and two string quartets. Some are entitled *Many Thousand Gone* for chorus, flute and percussion; *Concerto* for timpani and orchestra; *Music for Viola, Piano and Percussion; Music for Flute and Piano; Songs* for soprano and piano;

Four Arias adapted for soprano and orchestra; *Music for Cello and Piano* (Cespico Records); and a recently completed *Cello Concerto*.

EUGENE WILSON WHITE HANCOCK (1929–)

Eugene Hancock was born in St. Louis, Missouri. Having received his Bachelor of Music from the University of Detroit in 1951, he was awarded the Master of Music degree from the University of Michigan in 1956. He also attended the School of Sacred Music, Union Theological Seminary, where he received the Doctorate in Sacred Music in 1967.

Rated as a very fine organist in addition to being an educator and composer, Hancock became a member of the American Guild of Organists and proceeded to teach and perform in various cities. He held positions at St. Phillip Lutheran Church in Detroit from 1944 to 1948, at St. Titus Lutheran Church (1946–51), at the Cathedral Church of St. John the Divine in New York (as assistant organist and choirmaster from 1963–66), and at New Calvary Baptist Church in Detroit beginning in 1967. He served on the Detroit Board of Education in the Vocal Music Department from 1960 until he moved again to New York in order to teach at the Manhattan Community College (from 1970 to the present) and to assume an organ position at St. Phillip Episcopal Church.

Eugene W. W. Hancock.

Included in Evelyn White's *Bibliography of Published Choral Music by Black Composers*, and reviewed by William B. Garcia in the *Black Perspective in Music*, Hancock is held in high esteem. The Evelyn White Chorale has performed his works in Washington, D.C., as has Clarence Whiteman, who played his *I'm Troubled* at the National Cathedral in 1970. Hancock is also a member of NANM, AGO, and ASCAP, among other associations.

The Library of Congress lists his *An Organ Book of Spirituals* as being published by Lorenz Publishers in 1966 and his *Thirteen Spirituals for Equal Voices*, unison and two parts with organ or a cappella, as being published by H. W. Gray in 1973; *Palm Sunday Anthem* for SATB, junior choir, and organ and *A Babe is Born* for SATB or TTBB, by H. W. Gray in 1971 and 1975 respectively; and *Come Here, Lord* by J. Fischer in 1973.

In addition, his *Absalom* and *Nunc Dimittis* are published in Willis Patterson's *Anthology*. Several unpublished works exist such as *Mass in Honor of Saint Domenic* for congregation, two voices, and oboe; *Short Mass* for SATB; *Magnificat* for soprano; *Toccata, Adagio and Fugue* for nine percussion instruments and piano; and others. Some of his most recent works are *O Taste and See* (H. W. Gray, 1980) and *There's a Star in the East* (*The Candlelight Carol Book*, McAfee Music Publishers, 1982).

CLARENCE JOSEPH RIVERS (1931–)

According to Evelyn White's *Bibliography of Selected Published Choral Music by Black Composers*, Father Clarence Rivers was born in Selma, Alabama. A priest of the Catholic Archdiocese of Cincinnati, Ohio, he has served as composer, arranger, conductor, and lecturer. According to William Burres Garcia, whose article on church music by Black composers was printed in the *Black Perspective in Music*, Rivers has been a pioneer in incorporating spirituals, gospels, jazz, and other folk elements into Catholic church music.

Among his compositions listed at the Library of Congress are one published by World Library of Sacred Music, 1964—*American Mass* (for voices and organ with chord symbols for guitar, second edition by Papale, 1968); *The Brotherhood of Man*—Mass dedicated to the Apostles' Creed (also other arrangements by William Foster McDaniel, etc.); *Prayer of St. Francis, 1970*; and *That We May Live* for unison voices, piano with narration, the latter compositions of which were published by the company which Rivers founded, Stimuli Music.

FREDERICK ALFRED FOX (1931–)

Fred Fox, composer, conductor, and educator, was born in Detroit, Michigan. Educated at Wayne State University, he received his Bachelor of Music in 1953 and moved to the University of Michigan at Ann Arbor for additional study from 1953 to 1954. From Indiana University, he earned both the Master of Music degree in 1957 and the Doctor of Music degree in composition in 1959.

An NEA grantee in 1976 and 1979, and erstwhile composer-in-residence for the Minneapolis Public Schools, the Young Composers Project (1962–63), he became professor of composition and director of the New Music Ensemble at Indiana University in 1974; in 1976, he worked at the Music Department of California State College in Hayward, California (according to Galaxy Corporation) while continuing a high level of productivity within his professional commitments and compositions.

His compositions have enjoyed performances throughout the United States. The New York City Queens Borough Wide Chorus, directed by Anne Marie Hudley, clinician, featured his *I'm Ganna Sing* (Galaxy) and his music has also been heard at the National Association of Negro Musician Conventions, in concerts at institutions and in several prestigious halls. Among those works listed at the Library of Congress are *Variations* for beginning string orchestra (Ann Arbor Microfilms-CMP); *A Heritage of Spirituals*, arranged by Fox, J. W. Work III and James Miller, Galaxy, 1975; *Alleluia* (Ann Arbor, Univer-Microfilms, 1968); *The Descent* (Seesaw Music, 1972); *Essay for French Horn and Wind Ensemble; Fanfare and March* for band (Ann Arbor Microfilms); *Psalm 47* (CMP, Ann Arbor Microfilms); Sequence for *French Horn and Piano* (Ann Arbor, University Microfilms, 1967); *Serenade* for solo oboe and chamber orchestra (Ann Arbor, University Microfilms, 1968); and *Ternion* for oboe and orchestra (New York, Seesaw Music, 1972). ASCAP listings also include *A Stone, A Leaf, An Unfound Door* (for soprano, clarinet, percussion, and small chorus); *BEC-1* for winds and percussion; BEC-10 for chamber orchestra; *Variables—1* for violin and piano; *Variables—3* for flute, clarinet, horn, violin, cello, and piano; *Time Excursions* for soprano, speaker, flute, clarinet, violin, viola, cello, piano, and two percussion; and several others.

LESLIE ADAMS (1932–)

Born Harringson Leslie Adams in Cleveland, Ohio, Leslie Adams, pianist-composer, organist, conductor, and writer, attended the Cleveland Public Schools for his earliest music education. He later enrolled in the Oberlin Conservatory of Music in 1955, acquiring a Bachelor of Music Education degree with emphases in composition, voice, and piano; he then was awarded the Master of Arts degree in composition and choral music from the California State University at Long Beach in 1967. His Doctor of Philosophy degree in music education was earned at Ohio State University in 1973. His teachers have included Herbert Elwell, Joseph Wood, Robert Starer, Vittorio Giannini, Leon Dallin, Edward Mattila, Eugene O'Brien, and Marcel Dick.

Positions which Adams held from 1957 to 1962 consisted of piano accompanist for the American Ballet Center, the Robert Joffrey Ballet, the June Taylor Dancers, the Ballet Theatre, the Newark Ballet Academy, the Karl Shook Dancers, and the Ruthanna Boris Ballet; vocal music teacher at Soehl Junior High School in Linden, New Jersey; and choir director at Stillman College, Tuscaloosa, Alabama, in 1964, at the University of Kansas, Lawrence, in 1969, and at various churches. In addition, his jobs included musical directorships at Karamu House in Cleveland, Ohio, in 1965, of the New Mexico School for the Performing Arts during the summers of 1967 and 1968, of the Kaleidoscope Players National Touring Company in 1968, as well as other teaching positions at Florida A&M University, Tallahassee.

His honorary positions have included composer-in-residence at Karamu House and at the Cleveland Music School Settlement. He was awarded the Rockefeller Foundation Bellagio Study Artists Grant to its Saratoga Springs, New York Center and others. Other awards have been presented by the Department of Music at California State University, the National Association of Negro Women, Inc. for his *Pastorale for Violin and Piano*, the National Education Defense Act Fellowship of Ohio State University, the University of Kansas for research and writing of his works performed at the Contemporary American Music Symposia at the University of Kansas, the National Annual Choral Competition Award for his *Psalm 21* for mixed chorus, and the Ohio Chamber Orchestration Commission for its Tenth Anniversary.

Leslie Adams.

Leslie Adams is listed in the *World Edition of International Profiles, Blacks in the Performing Arts: 1850–1976, Contemporary American Composers: A Biographical Dictionary*, and other books. A member of many organizations, he was appointed to the Advisory Council of the Musical Arts Association of the Cleveland Orchestra in 1981 and to the adjudicating panel for BMI awards, and to other important panels and associations involving the future of music and musicians.

As a composer, his reputation is steadily growing throughout the United States and abroad. His works for various media have enjoyed performance by vocalist Barbara Conrad, the Evelyn White Chorale, the William Appling Singers, organist Leonard Raver of the Juilliard School, cellist Donald White, violinist Paul Zukofsky, the Cleveland Philharmonic Orchestra with William Slocum, conductor, and by the Buffalo Philharmonic Orchestra with Julius Rudel, conductor.

Reviewed favorably, some of his works have been described as being written "in the contemporary idiom, expressing strong thematic and rhythmic vitality tailored to the virtuosity and skill of today's performer." Among enthusiastic responses have been "very fine work, well constructed and well orchestrated" (Eugene Ormandy); "The Ode to Life was marked by pronounced echoes of twentieth century America . . . in which Adams sings of lives marked by exuberance" (*Springfield News*, January 20, 1980), and "The third movement of the Cello Sonata seemed a fascinating cross between jazz and classical, and I couldn't tell where one left off and the other began."

When the Evelyn White Chorale was reviewed, the November 2, 1982 issue of the *Washington Post* carried an article by Lon Tuck which read: "The most exciting moment came in the Washington premiere of a fairly short work called *Hosanna to the Son of David* by Leslie Adams."

Lon Tuck described techniques in the *Hosanna* as having "ascending patterns of wide intervals, never suggesting a clear tonic key," as having "sudden contrasts of strutting athletic leaps with short fragments of melting lyricism."

Clearly a competent compositionalist, Adams using tonality skillfully enough to suggest atonalism in sections of the piece as evidenced in sequences found in the beginning section, or in the key changes found in the sectional structure dictated also by frequent meter changes. Some of the most interesting parts of *Hosanna* are found in measures 51 to 54 in which syncopations are alternated among voice groupings of parallel fourths versus fifths. (Example 59).

Ex. 59. *Hosanna*, Adams. © Copyright 1976 by Walton Music Corporation. Used by permission.

Still another example, *Madrigal* for mixed chorus, shows his clear, strong style in measures 26–28, in which both the rhythmic sense and excitement of counterpoint are held in high array against the text (Example 60).

Ex. 60. *Madrigal*, Adams. © Copyright 1976 by Son-Key, Inc. Used by permission.

A composer with an already reputable status, Adams shows works in quantities of published and unpublished states. Of the published are vocal songs *Madrigal* for the SATB (The New Music Company of Aurora, Col., 1979); *For You There is No Song* (in Willis Patterson's *Anthology of Art Songs by Black American Composers*, E. B. Marks, 1978); *Hosanna to the Son of David* (Walton Music); *Sonata for French Horn and Piano; Largo* (Associated Music); *Dunbar Songs* for voice and orchestra or voice and piano (Edizioni Nuova Musica); *Love Song* for SATB and piano (Lawson-Gould); *There Was an Old Man* for SATB and piano (Lawson-Gould, 1982); *Tall Tales* for SATB (Lawson-Gould). Other works, unpublished but frequently performed, are *Symphony No. 1, Ode to Life and A Kiss in Xanadu* for orchestra; *Cello Sonata, Violin Sonata, Trombone Quartet, Piano Preludes*, and others. Adams is represented in New York by Elaine Schuman-LeMoyne of Flushing, New York.

Postscript II: Other Composers

There are other composers who carry the same message and philosophy of identity, change and musical freedom, together with a knowledge of the world about them. Their talents are equally varied, imaginative, artistic and perceptive, and their accomplishments point out the great varieties of musical talents found during this era. Many have been cited at symposiums in Indiana, Atlanta, Washington, Boston, and in Minneapolis by AAMOA, in New York by the Black Society of Composers, and in writings by Vada Butcher, Eileen Southern, John Rogers, and others. It is not possible to report full sketches of each of these composers who lived or who is living in the United States and abroad. However, the following composers warrant mentioning in that some of their accomplishments are as great as some of the above aggregation of persons.

Emma Azalia Hackley (1867–1922), born in Murfreesboro, Tennessee; educated in Detroit; an educator, concert singer, choral director, humanitarian, and composer of piece published by Handy Brothers, and in whose name the Hackley Collection of Detroit's Public Library was established by the National Association of Negro Musicians in 1943.

John Wesley Work II (1873–1926), born in Tennessee; a graduate of Fisk and Harvard; educator at Fisk for forty years; compiler and editor of songs found in *Folk Songs of the American Negro*, composer of the *Fisk Song* and arranger of other folk songs published by Theodore Presser, father of John Work III.

Maud Cuney Hare (1874–1936), author-composer of *Six Creole Folksongs* with translations, published by C. Fischer in 1921 (seen at Library of Congress).

Wellington Adams (1879–?), born in Washington, D.C.; Wanamaker prizewinner and composer of published and unpublished works found in Library of Congress: *Drifting* (1947); *Bwano Tumbo* (Welcome March and 2-Step) arranged for piano duet (Shapiro Publishing, 1910); *Lil Black Child* lullaby, (Handy Bros. c. 1937, Rodman Wanamaker prize series—song and piano accompaniment); and *What A Friend We Have in Jesus*, arranged for chorus or quartet with obligato and female trio (1947). The Indiana University Calendar listed his birthplace as Zanesville, Ohio; Hare simply noted that he was "from Washington, D.C.," and Handy noted that he was included in *Modern Music and Musicians* Encyclopedia, V. 1, the Philharmonic Edition on Great Composers.

Bessie Viola Johnson (b. 1880?), born in Burlington, Iowa; composer of songs.

Eugene Mikell (1880–), born in Charleston and educated at Tuskegee, at State College in Orangeburg, South Carolina; composer of *Father to Thy Dear Name* anthem, songs and marches, some of which were published by C. Fischer.

Frederick J. Work (1880?–1942), born in Nashville, Tennessee; brother of John Work II; collector of folk songs, compiled in the *New Jubilee Songs* (published by Fisk, 1901) and *Songs of the American Negro* (1907); also the composer of *String Quartet in F*.

Melville Charlton (1880–1973?), born in New York; educated at the National Conservatory of Music and the College of the City of New York; organist-composer of *Poeme Erotique* for piano (Schirmer); and others.

Frank S. Butler (1883–) born in Philadelphia; graduate of the Institute of Musical Art, etc.; concert pianist-composer of *Blossoms* (published by Ascher), of *Master School of Professional Piano Playing* (an instruction book which was used by many schools, according to *Who's Who of Colored America*, as a shortcut method of teaching beginners), and *Somewhere Jesus is Calling* (at the Library of Congress).

Luke Upshure (1885–), born in New York; a composer of several compositions in manuscript as well as poetry.

Nora Holt (c. 1885–1974), born in Kansas City, Kansas; primarily worked as a journalist; composer of *Rhapsody on Negro Themes* for her master's degree in composition, others in manuscript for piano, voice, string quartet, chamber, and symphonic groups.

Eugene Aldama Jackson (1886–); composer of spirituals, published by H. W. Gray.

Roland Hayes (1887–1976), born in Curryville, Georgia; internationally renowned tenor and arranger of spirituals, some examples of which are reprinted in Ollie McFarland's *Afro-America Sings*, Detroit Public Schools and which are recorded by himself and others (RCA, etc.).

Estelle Ancrum Forster (1887–), born in Wilmington, North Carolina; composer of piano compositions and a musical play, published by Theodore Presser.

William Astor Morgan (Jean Stor, pseudonym) (1890–?), born in New York; composer of works seen at the Library of Congress, in W. C. Handy's *Unsung America Sings* (listed under Jean Stor and entitled *George Washington Carver* with words by Razaf; Lincoln's *Gettysburg Address*; and co-authored with Handy, *The Curator* and *Monroe Trotter*); under Morgan, the Library of Congress listed *Adagio In Memory of Our Friend Franklin D. Roosevelt* for orchestra (manuscript, 1945), *Be Still and Know, Depression* (allegorical folk play), *God Be Praised, God Is Our Refuge, Four and Twenty, Going to Hold Out, Heaven-Bound, The Kingdoms of our Lord*, the *Lord's Prayer, The Love Sting* (operetta), *One Hundred Thirty-Seventh Psalm, The Resurrection* (contata with spirituals as themes), *These Are They, The Water of Life*, and others. Handy's publishing catalog listed Jean Stor as the composer of spirituals, anthems, and songs for vocal solo. Besides some of the above, also catalogued were *Sit Down, Hold the Wind, I Want Jesus to Walk With Me, My Way is Cloudy, Pale Horse and Rider*, and *This is a Sin Trying World* (collection of eight spirituals).

Purnell F. Hall (1890–), composer of *Life* (Purnell Music, 1946); *I Am Traveling* gospel hymn; *Christian Traveler's Triumphant Praise* (Handy Brothers); *Let Us All Bow Together*; and others listed at the Library of Congress.

George Morrison, Sr. (1891–), born in Fayette, Missouri; educated at the University of Colorado School of Music (1908–11), Columbia Conservatory of Music in Chicago; composed five violin solos, spirituals for piano and violin (Handy Brothers Music Company).

Tougee Dubose (1893?–1971), born in Talledega, Alabama; teacher at Southern University for many years; composer of *Intermezzo* for piano, and others.

Cecil Cohen (1894–1967), born in Chicago; pianist-teacher at Howard University for many years; educated at the Institute of Musical Art, Juilliard, and Columbia; composer of several songs published in Rogie Clark's *Anthology, Negro Art Songs* (two of which are listed at the Library of Congress—*Four Winds* and *Epitaph for a Poet*) and *Death of an Old Seaman* (in Willis Patterson's *Anthology of Art Songs by Black American Composers*, Belwin/ E. B. Marks, 1977).

Ulysses Elam (1896–?), born in Virginia; composer of *Jesus Hung and Died* for SATB (Lawson-Gould); and erstwhile associate of Leonard de Paur's Chorus.

Ellen Virginia Carrington Thomas (1897–), born in Wilmington, Delaware; composer of *All Organ Medleys* (Wagner Music, 1970); *The Chimes of Bethlehem* (Ethel Smith Music, 1951); *Christmas Eve* (Mills Music, 1951); *Easy Church Music for All Faiths* (Ethel Smith, 1951); *The Day of Birth* (Christmas Service: Mills Music, 1954); and *Negro Folk Song* (mentioned by Hare).

William Lawrence (1897?–1981), born in Charleston, South Carolina; served as Roland Hayes' accompanist; composer of *Three Spirituals* for string quartet, *Rhapsodie Africaine—Bambara*, and several choral and other works listed at the Library of Congress for primary and intermediate grades along with spirituals and hymns for praise.

Maude Wanzer Layne (1899–), born in Charleston, West Virginia; educated at Chicago Musical College (M.M.) and earned the doctorate from New York Musical College in 1937; further study was done at the American Conservatory of Music in Fontainebleu, France (1925). Educator, music supervisor in Charleston, West Virginia schools and composer of several musical pageants and songs; authored pamphlets about the ethnic music of her race.

J. Harold Brown (1902–), born in Shellman, Georgia; educated at Fisk; organist-composer of *Six Spirituals* (Birchard, 1934) and other works.

Sonoma Carolyn Talley (1902), born in Jacksonville, Florida; graduate of Fisk, the Institute of Musical Art; composer of *Collection of Folk Songs*, 1924.

Jules Bledsoe (1902–1943), born in Waco, Texas; baritone-composer of *African Suite* for orchestra and several songs.

Wynn Leo Boyd (1902–), born in Gaithersburg, Maryland; educated at the Ithaca Piano School; opened piano tuning studio for blind veterans, founded own firm for rebuilding pianos; composer of *Make a Joyful Noise Unto God* anthem; *Dance of the Dolls, Kindergarten March, Rondo; American Art Songs* on poetry by Dunbar, *23rd Psalm* (Golden Eagle Press and ASCAP).

William H. Butler (1903–), born in New York; musician, publisher, educated at Chicago Musical College with further study at the Royal Academy of Music (1935) and at Juilliard School of Music (1945); conductor, arranger of musicals such as Lew Leslie's *Blackbirds* and *Rhapsody in Black*, Ed Sullivan's *Harlem Calvacade*, Bill Robinson's *Hot From Harlem* and others; listed in *Who's Who of Colored America*.

Walter Henri Dyett (1904–), born in St. Joseph, Missouri; educated at the University of California (1920) with further study at Columbia School of Music in Chicago, the American Conservatory of Music, the University of Chicago (M.B.), Chicago Musical College (M.M., 1942) and others; violinist, conductor and educator who worked at DuSable High in Chicago (chairman), with Army Bands, and as arranger for concert orchestras and dance bands.

Willie Belle Stevenson (1904–), musician author, pianist, organist and composer of spirituals, songs, Egyptian-type music and poems; born in Lexington, Kentucky; studied with Percy Grainger, won Grainger Scholarship; educated at Chicago Musical College; worked in Paris, Kentucky at Western High, former supervisor of music; prizewinner of various contests for poems; honorary member of International League of Nations of Literature, National Songwriters Guild; director of choirs and studio teacher of vocal and instrumental music.

Oscar Anderson Fuller (1904–1989), born in Marshall, Texas; educated at Bishop College, New England Conservatory, and the University of Iowa; director of music departments at A&T, Prairie View and Lincoln University in Jefferson City, Missouri; composer of an oratorio, *Creation* (dissertation for his doctorate) and other works.

Altona Trent Johns (1904–1977), born in Asheville, North Carolina; educated at Atlanta University, Teacher's College at Columbia University, educator, pianist-composer who taught at Virginia State University for many years; composer of *Barcarolle* (spiritual arrangement, intermediate, published by Handy), *Play Songs of the Deep South* (published by Associated, with directions for children's dances), and *Finger Fun With Songs to be Sung* (Handy Publishers) co-authored with Vivian Flagg McBrier, author of *R. N. Dett.*

James Elmo Dorsey (1905–), born in San Antonio, Texas; graduate of Tuskegee, Lincoln, and the University of Pennsylvania; composer of *An American Vignette*—a choral symphony written in 1949 and *Two Negro Spirituals* published by G. Schirmer in 1947 (listed at the Library of Congress with the above piece) and several other published works such as *Eight Songs* for voice and piano, *Rondo and Allegro, Theme and Variations* for string and quartet.

Shirley Graham (1907–), wife of W. E. B. DuBois, graduate of Oberlin, Howard Institute of Musical Art, Syracuse and further study in Paris; composer of *Tom-Tom*, an opera, and books published by Johnson Publications.

Edgar Battle (1907–) composer, author, conductor, arranger, producer, publisher, and trumpeter; born in Atlanta, Georgia; educated at the Georgia Conservatory and through private study, he soon led his own orchestra and also became the music director for the War Department, USO, before moving to New York. A member of the National Association of Negro Musicians, ASCAP, and other organizations, Battle has had several piano compositions published and recorded, among which are: *Swingphony* (based on a Blind Tom theme), published by Cosmopolitan Music, 1973; *Bahia Banda*, Gem Music; *Baiaso*, Cosmopolitan Music, 1973; *Bebop Lullaby*, Cosmopolitan, 1948 (score); *Black Beauty*, Gem Music, 1955; *Design for Bouncin'*, Gem Music, 1955; *Goofin' and Spoofin'*, Gem Music (w/Slock); *House Rent Music for a Harlem House Hop*, ms. 1965; vocal/piano: *Ballad Beautiful*, 1965, ms. Library of Congress; *Continental Suite*, Cosmopolitan, 1974; *The Edgar Battle Song Production Book*, ms. 1973; for ensemble: *Symphony No. 7*, Bb,

Cosmopolitan, 1972, *Symphony Alla Jazz*; and numerous other titles found at the Library of Congress which were published between 1947 and 1955; albums: *Ballads Beautiful, Harlem House Hop* and others.

Eugene James Broadnax (1907), lived in New York; composer of *I Heard the Voice of Jesus Say* (Galaxy) and others at Library of Congress: *Alas, That Spring Should Vanish With the Rose*, 1953; *African Dances; Barn Dance; Western Suite; Sudan; Trucks; Flute Song; Limited; Clouds; I Have Taken the Woman of Beauty; Brazil.*

James Miller (1907–), born in Pittsburgh, Pennsylvania; composer, arranger of *Heritage of Spirituals* (including works by J. W. Work and Fred Fox, published by Galaxy, 1975), *I Am Seeking For a City, Please Don't Drive Me Away, So Fades the Lovely Blooming Flow'r, I Wanna Be Ready* and *Daniel, Didn't My Lord Deliver Daniel?* (the latter two of which were recorded on *From This We've Come* by Prestige Records for Alabama State University Choir).

Marie Busch (1908–), composer of *Setting of Nine Dunbar Poems* (one of which is listed at the Library of Congress—*Why Fades a Dream* as published by Boston Music Company in 1954).

Clarence Jacobs (1909–), graduate of Howard, Juilliard and Queens College; composer of several works published by Joli-Tinker and recorded by Leonard de Paur's Infantry Chorus.

J. Orville B. Mosley (1909–), graduate of Chicago Musical College, 1939, the University of Michigan, 1941, and the Army Music School in 1943; worked at Natchez College, Southern University, Tougaloo College, and Morgan State College and in Los Angeles; composer of many compositions assembled by Don White, such as *Piano* Variations; nine vocal pieces for solo voice; several chamber pieces for strings and other orchestral instruments; orchestral music including *Suite for String Orchestra and Tone Poem*; numerous choral pieces from anthems and patriotic songs to Black folk songs, some entitled *Come Ye Blessed, Lord Have Mercy Upon Us*, and *Hallelujah*; various band pieces such as the Official March-Song, *The Tuskegee Air Field* (published); and the "considerable commercial music" referred to by Don White in his files. A 1929 graduate of Morehouse College, he also composed the *Morehouse College Hymn* (published) as well as a *Book of College Songs* and other collections of note.

Lillian Evanti (1909–), born in Washington, D.C.; singer-composer of *Beloved Mother, Dedication, God's Promise, High Flight, Himno Pan-American, Slow Me Down Lawd, Thank You Again and Again* (Handy examples at the Library of Congress).

Herbert Franklin Mells (1909–1956), whose list of spirituals and anthems at the Library of Congress number about twenty-seven, and include *Awake to Righteousness* (Handy), *Burden'd Chile, Drinking of the Wine, Here is One, I Heard the Preaching of the Elders*, and at least one piano piece, *Lost Tresses*.

Ruth Helen Gillum (1909?–), pianist, educator, arranger, born in St. Louis; educated at the University of Kansas (M.B. and M.M.) and the New England Conservatory of Music, Boston University, and Prairie View College; worked as staff pianist for radio station WREN in Lawrence, Kansas (1930–33), at Philander Smith College and at North Carolina College at Durham (1944–), author of the *Influence of the Negro Folk Song in American Music* (1943 thesis) and composer of piano works and arranged spirituals.

Edward Emanuel Barefield (1909–), born in Scandia, Iowa; clarinetist, arranger, educator, educated at the Northshore Conservatory of Music, studied with Joe Burns, Joe Allard, Rudolph Schramm, Schillinger Foundation, and at New York University; arranger at Charles Colin's Studio; played with Fletcher Henderson, Ella Fitzgerald, and other major figures; founded Eddie Barefield Orchestra.

Julian C. Work (1910–), composer-arranger, brother of John W. Work III and son of John W. Work II; born in Nashville, Tennessee; a graduate of Fisk; arranger for vaudeville, radio, and television by 1931, and staff arranger of CBS; the composer of band pieces *Autumn Walk* (1958), *Driftwood Patterns* (1961), *Moses* (1956) and other Biblical portraits such as *Shadrach, Meshack and Abednego*, and *Stand the Storm* (1963), all by Shawnee Press.

Virginia Carrington DeWitty (1911–), born in Wetumka, Oklahoma; graduate of Tillotson College, American Conservatory (1963) and director of music at several churches; composer of several pieces for church such as *Magnify the Lord, The Greatest of These is Love, The Will of the Lord*, and *One Church, One Faith, One Lord* (published athems) and gospel songs *Use Me O Lord, All That I Need Is In Jesus, Who Shall Separate Us*.

Zenobia Perry (1914–), educator, lecturer, composer; born in Boley, Oklahoma and retired in Wilberforce, Ohio; studied with William Dawson at Tuskegee Institute (Bachelor of Music Education degree) and with Darius Milhaud at Wyoming University and at Aspen; also received the Master of Music Education at Northern Colorado State at Greeley; taught at AM&N College (now Arkansas State) and Central State University from whence she recently retired. Featured in the *Women in American Music* by Block & Neuls-Bates, she composed over forty piano works (the most popular of which was *Reflections*), three string quartets, works for soprano (her *Threnody* for soprano was sung by Janice Peri at Carnegie Hall and *From the Hidden Words of Baha'u'llah* has proved to be well received), and works for orchestra (*Four Hymns for Three Players* for two sets of percussion, flute and piano, narrator, and orchestra was commissioned by the San Francisco Orchestra and written atonally). The Sinfonia Prize was given her *Threnody* in 1977.

Samuel Lowe (1918–), born in Birmingham, Alabama; educated at Tennessee State University, jazz trumpeter, composer-arranger, whose works at the Library of Congress are entitled *Double Shot* (w/Julian Dash), published by Arnell Music, 1954; *My Baby*, published by Jay & Cee Music, 1953; *Function at the Junction* (Jay & Cee); and others.

Joseph Hayes (1920–), native of Marietta, Ohio; graduate of Boston University (1950) and Oberlin Conservatory; composer of *Praeludium* for organ (1953); *Sunday—3:00 p.m.*, a symphony for viewing, written for SATB, orchestra, and dancers; *Song of the Colours* and *Time Capsule* for chorus; *Quartet Miniature* for strings; *Quintet* for violin, bassoon, and piano; *Lullaby* for SATB (seen in Ollie McFarland's *Afro-America Sings*, Detroit Public Schools, Hall Leonard Music, 1979); *Haven't You Heard* (Nordyke Publishing Company.)

William B. Cooper (1920–), a native of Philadelphia, Pennsylvania; compositions published by Dangerfield Publishing Company: *Bread of Heaven, Pastoral, Toccatina, Beatitudes, Mass for Choir and Congregation, Port Royal Te Deum* for solo, quartet, SATB, dancers; *Spring Carnival* for piano

(Southern); *Suite* for brasses (Hansen); and *Lord, Keep Us Steadfast in Thy Word* (performed by Clarence Whiteman at the National Cathedral in Washington, D.C. in 1970); others for percussion and organ, *Psalm One Hundred Fifty, Psalms and Canticles* (choral service based on spirituals for SATB, 1973); and others.

Edward (Eddie) Balentine Bonnemere (1921–), graduate of New York University, educator in New York public schools as well as conductor of the Brooklyn-Borough Choirs and specialist in Latin music (featured on Roost Records); winner of grant from the National Endowment of the Arts; composer of *Missa Laetare* (Mass of Joy), *O Happy the People* (Contemporary Setting of Matins and Vespers, both this and above published by Fortress Press); *Umoja* (Amity Press); *Originals* for piano (Le Bon Music, 1961), and others.

Laurence Hayes (1921–), from Sedalia, Missouri; graduate of Dillard, Fisk, and Teachers College at Columbia University; and educator in public high schools in Charlotte, North Carolina and at the Alabama State University; composer of published works *Piano Suite in Four Movements, Three Short Pieces* for clarinet and piano, *L'envoi* (song), *To the Moon* (SATB) and *Urban Echoes* for cornet and piano and unpublished works and arrangements.

Matthew Kennedy (1921–), born in Americus, Georgia; graduate of Fisk and Juilliard, with further study at Peabody, Nashville, Tennessee; teacher-pianist at Fisk, director of Fisk Jubilee Singers; arranger of *Two Spirituals* published by Abingdon Press (*Ev'ry Time I Feel the Spirit* and *Steal Away*); and other unpublished arrangements.

Rachel Eubanks (1922–), born in San Jose, California; education at Columbia, Eastman; chairman of the Department of Music at Albany State College (1947) and at Wilberforce University; composer of *Prelude* for piano (Music Mart, Oakland, California) and numerous unpublished works.

Ella Jenkins (1924–), composer, singer and author of educational game and songs for children; born in St. Louis, Missouri; educated at Du Sable High, Wilson Junior College (A.A.), Roosevelt College, San Francisco State College (B.A. in Sociology); composer of *You'll Sing A Song and I'll Sing A Song; Play Your Instruments and Make a Pretty Sound; My Street Begins at My House; If I Were an Animal; Did You Feed My Cow; I Like The Way That They Stack Hay; Tah-Boo*; and others.

Roy Howard Lindsey (1926–), born in Chicago; a graduate of Los Angeles City College; composer of *Slave of Jesus* (Choral Press, 1950) seen at the Library of Congress; compositions published by Tatlin Music include *Nocturne* (SATB), *Portrait of a Piano, Sonatina No. 1, Bells of the Cathedral, Christmas is Here, Kiss Me My Love, Praise Ye The Lord, Sing To The Lord* (SATB), *Tell, Nocturne*.

Don Lee White (1930–), born in Los Angeles, California; educated at California State University; composer-arranger of *Jesus Keep Me Near the Cross*, choral prelude for organ (Davike); *Magnificat* for organ (Davike, 1976); *Masque* for SATB, tonettes, autoharp, tympany, and dance; and (Music in Orbit) and *Glorious Things of Thee* (Haydn-White, Davike, 1972); and others.

Carrie Beatrice Holloway (1930–), born in Meridian, Mississippi; educated at Tennessee State (B.S., 1957), further study at University of

Colorado; composer-lyricist of children's songs *Look To Jesus* (1973), *Love for Mankind* (1974), *Love Me Always, This Is My Home, Mother-Dear, Mountain Tide, Jacob's Ladder* (Collins Publishing, Denver, Colorado).

Shirley Cartman (1931–), born in Chicago; educated at University of Illinois (B.S.), further study at the University of Indiana, American University; appeared with Louis Jordan, Earl Hines, billed as Sheila Carr; presently teacher at Prince Georges Community College; author of published children's books, lyricist and songwriter of disco, religious, ballads, country and western, and author of *Begin Your Songwriting Career* (Car-Mitch Associates).

Roy Hicks (1931–1990), born in McGregor, Texas; worked at Tuskegee Institute, graduate of Paul Quinn, Prairie View, and North Texas State; composer/arranger of *I Couldn't Hear Nobody Pray* and *Ready* (Hope-Somerset, 1973).

Roland Carter (1932–), native of Chattanooga, Tennessee; educator, choral director; arranger of *Give Me Jesus, I Want to Die Easy* (E. B. Marks).

Jacqueline Butler Hairston (1932–), born in Charlotte, North Carolina, now an educator at Merritt College in Oakland, California; educated at Juilliard, Howard University, Teacher's College; composer-arranger of *Nowhere to Lay His Head* for SATB (E. B. Marks); *Creation* (found on *Black Man, Sidney Poitier Reads*, RCA Victor label, Unart Music), *Reminiscing, A Change Has Got To Come* (performed by London Philharmonic), and others recorded by Andre Kostelanetz and Barbara Carroll.

Bertha Desverney, born in Dallas, Texas; graduate of Prairie View State College and composer of *Hallelujah and Amen!, On the Plains, Hallelujah* for solo voice and several published and unpublished works mainly for SATB or solo voice (one of which was listed by the Library of Congress—*De Ole Sheep Done Know De Road*).

Andrades Lindsay, born in New York; composer of *Concert Fugue* for piano.

Eugene Alexander Burkes, composer of *Sonata*.

Earl LaRue, arranger of *Poor Me* (Hope Publishing Company, 1974).

Gloster B. Current, musician, author and longtime NAACP Director of Branches; also retired pastor of West Chester United Methodist Church, Bronx, New York; led own band as college student; composer of songs.

Drucilla Atwell, composer of *Wade in de Water*.

Carlette C. Thomas, composer of *I Got Me Flowers*.

Ethel Ramos Harris, born in Rhode Island; educated at Hans Schneider Piano School, New England Conservatory, Boston University, Carnegie Institute, Tanglewood; singer-composer of *I've Been in the Storm So Long, Stan' Steady, Paquita Mia, Yolanda, The Girl Friend's Hymn, There'll Be a Jubilee,* and *When I Reach the Other Side* (SATB with piano and drum), published by Volkwein Brothers in Pittsburgh.

Gerald Tyler from St. Louis, composer of *Syrian Lullaby, Dirge for a Soldier, Heart o' Fancy, Ships That Pass in the Night, Little Red Riding Hood* (petite descriptive suite for piano, at Library of Congress, published by Shattinger, 1920) and, according to Hare, one of three musicians chosen to write the Centennial Drama Music in commemoration of the 100th Anniversary of Missouri's admission into the Union.

J. Bruce, composer of *All I Want*, a spiritual (it is unclear whether the

James Bruce, composer of several songs listed at the Library of Congress, published by Nordyke, etc. is the same person referred to by Hare).

W. Arthur Calhoun, composer of *Down in the Valley A-waiting My Jesus* (Handy), *Steal Away to Jesus, Let Us Cheer the Weary Traveler, Give Me Jesus, Stand on the Rock a Little Longer, I've Heard of a City Called Heaven.*

William Andrew Rhodes, born in Greensboro, North Carolina; graduate of New England Conservatory, composer of *Three Songs, Choral Piece, Prayer of the Crusaders* and spirituals arranged.

Composers And Performers

Black composers of art music showed talent, drive, skill and patience in their efforts, and a courage keenly related to the truth and freedom sought in the subsequent contemporary era. They proved and conquered! They proved that they could indeed compose in any style chosen. The question of "stereotype" or the myth that Blacks could not be intellectual was weakened to the extent that all America could more readily relate to the idea of freedom in musical professionalism. This fact was true despite the laxity in the promotion of this music.

The fact that not all Blacks could compose jazz was realized. Not all Blacks wanted to do so! It was also a reality that many Blacks within art music used jazz techniques within the art music forms long before the third stream music was popularized in the 1960's. Whether or not these composers developed jazz or art music, however, is not as important as the fact of their contribution to American music, and their efforts to remove obstacles encountered by all Black musicians. For these composers were not so much involved in the definition of "true" Black music as they were in the struggle and right to pursue self-expression. They were as concerned with their identity as any musician, but were also involved in working within the established definitions of music.

Throughout this chapter, composers have been stressed as writers of music, rather than as performers who specialized in recreating the musical score in public demonstration. Yet many composers of art music played instruments or sang quite well, and thus participated in various concerts along with persons designated expressly as performers rather than composers. A select number of such achievers from older generations, including the composers, consisted of orchestral instrumentalists such as Frank Johnson, F. E. Lewis, H. F. Williams, Clarence C. White, and John Douglass; as keyboardists such as William Lawrence, Hazel Harrison, Melville Charlton, Tougee DuBose, and Margaret Bonds; of singers such as Elizabeth Taylor Greenfield (ca. 1819–1876), documented in a detailed monograph entitled *The Black Swan* by Arthur LaBrew as a Mississipian slave who, after manumission, traveled with her mistress to Philadelphia, was found to possess a three-octave vocal range, and was sponsored in numerous concerts; and of such singers as Marian Anderson (contralto), Roland Hayes (tenor), Camille Nickerson (soprano), and Paul Robeson (baritone).

A select sample from later generations consists of rare singers Leontyne Price, Robert McFerrin, Dorothy Maynor, George Shirley, William Brown, Shirley Verrett, Grace Bumbry, Mattiwilda Dobbs, Jessye Norman, Carmen Balthrop, and numerous others as outlined in a book by Patricia Turner, *Afro-American Singers*, an index to discographies; such pianists as Frances Walker, George Walker, Natalie Hinderas, Armenta Adams, Raymond

Jackson, Michael Caldwell, Andre Watts, Nina Kennedy, and Leon Bates; wind players Harold Jones, Langston Fitzgerald, and Hubert Laws (equally sought after in classical and jazz); as harpist, Ann Hobson; and string players Ron Carter (jazz & classical), Joe Kennedy (jazz & classical), Kermit Moore (equally productive in classical and jazz), Sanford Allen, and Ron Lipscomb.

Conductors of orchestras ranged from the earlier Frank Johnson to William Grant Still, Everett Lee, Dean Dixon, James de Priest, James Frazier, and Michael Morgan. Far more numerous leaders of choral music included the likes of R. Nathaniel Dett, William Dawson, Eva Jessye, Hall Johnson, Warner Lawson, John Motley, John Work, and Evelyn White. Yet these are but a sample of the artists who produced over the years of time.

PART THREE

FREEDOM NOW

(1950's–1990's)

XI

CONTEMPORARY PERIOD: THE BLACK REVOLUTION

Many voices of the twentieth century coordinated a cultural, artistic and proud revolution during the era of the new Civil Rights struggle. Frustration from centuries of injustice and denial culminated in new campaigns for civil rights during the mid-1950's and the early 1960's. These activities began in the southern regions of the Country, moved to the north and throughout the Nation. Leaders from Martin Luther King and Malcolm X to Stokely Carmichael, Frantz Fanon and C. L. R. James urged demonstrations and confrontations which ultimately resulted in some changes in public and educational accommodations as well as some liberties of mind and morals. Civil rights struggles occurred before Reconstruction, and occurred thereafter, but never had they commanded the right to exist in so loud a voice as in the silence of the marches. The struggle for dignity arid respect focused their attentions on the conscience of all America.

Then came a revolution of arts and ideas which served as a guide to worthwhile achievements and progress. Pan-Africanism had greatly spurred the challenge for the right to pursue happiness and freedom. There was much pride felt by Blacks in America in the recent independence won by African states. The colorful leaders of Africa and their new image caused Blacks to closely relate to those inhabitants of the Mother Country with renewed respect and brotherhood. A bitterness welled inside the hearts of those Afro-Americans who had not won in America an independence easily seen elsewhere. The loss of dignity and self-esteem and the loss of language and cultural norms were seen as an affront to human justice, and as a punishment for being Black. African-Americans were determined to follow their African brothers.

They were furthermore determined to overcome the barrier which spoke so stoicly of the "status quo" in America, and sang a blues which reiterated their frustration: *I'm Tired of Bein' Jim Crowed*. They also fervently sang an old spiritual in march time, *Many Thousand Gone*, paraphrased to suit the new occasion of *We Shall Overcome*. This song showed the unity of spirit and mind which vowed not to become destined to the sad status of semi-slavery in 1960 as seen in 1619. This time, the Constitution had guaranteed the rights for which they struggled; this time, Black soldiers in Korea and Vietnam had defended American freedom. And this time, they were aware of the heritage which produced advancements of civilizations, both old and new.

The Breakthrough

The direct confrontations with society ultimately led to the breakdown of some of the barriers of segregation during the 1960's. Simultaneous with these developments came the lessening of obstacles in the field of music. Perhaps this was the result of early pioneers of long ago; it could also have been the early acceptance of the vocalists, or the belated realization that Blacks could indulge in more areas than the art of singing.

Nevertheless, unions generally changed their rules to admit a few tokens, and performers and composers were gradually admitted into more levels of professional advancement than before. Significantly, a few players became members of symphony orchestras. The New World Symphony Orchestra was composed and organized for minorities. More opera stars were allowed to compete in higher levels of achievement, and conductors were slowly being accepted.

Still, these composers were hampered by both publishers who did not advertise extensively and recording industries who did not promote their works, but this era did indeed represent some promise of a greater degree of freedom in all aspects of African-American lifestyles.

XII

CONTEMPORARY JAZZ AND ITS AGNATES

Jazz of the contemporary era includes elements of "soul" blues and funky elements which penetrate gospel, rhythm and blues or rock and folk, as well as derivatives of its main styles of bop, "cool," "avant-garde" and "third stream." Jazz is yet influenced by European concepts but attempts to reemphasize the African elements of music. During the present era of further experimentation with form, manner of performance and compositional materials, new media from plastic, electrical timbres, and video to those traditional are used, and there is a continual change based upon experiments culminating in the late fifties and early sixties which began in the 1940's.

In New York, "cool" jazz merged in the 1950's, overshadowing the popularity of "bop" and resembling the "progressive" punctuations in California. Practiced by Lester Young, Miles Davis and others, the styles were similar and emphasized the easy-going, the subdued and the relaxed. Cool jazz employed clear sounds, muted sounds, calmness, and yet a skillful technique and control. Also called "chamber jazz" because of its smaller instrumentation, subdued sound and intellectual possibilities, melodic lines became extended in length and technical content of instrumental character. It also sponsored the addition of the flute, french horn, oboe, and English horn. Not particularly emotional, intense or over-active, "cool" utilized modern dissonances with traditional, close harmonic progressions, hazy sounds, obscurity of meters and abstractions akin to those of art music.

In quick reaction to "cool" came "hard bop," "soul" and "funky" styles of jazz which recaptured some of the earthy roots originally planted by the blues and older, influential forms, and in affiliation with rock, its offspring. Polyrhythms, blocks or clusters and intricate accents continued along with the improvisational and other syncopated effects in order to direct jazz back to its original course. The complexities of styles already introduced within bop continued as exciting interrelated activities of small ensembles, soloists, and singers. Many of these latter types were also employed and originated by John Coltrane, Art Tatum, Bud Powell and Cannonball Adderley.

"Avant-garde" employs the freedom of self, an array of various improvisations, scales, arpeggios, leaps, and primarily melodic emphasis. With its influence of African, Asian and American elements, it also features modal as well as traditional western scale patterns. Yet the overall effect of the music is that of atonalism. Practiced and mainly promoted by Ornette Coleman and others, avant-garde boasts arbitrary and intricate procedures which have reaped quantities of both criticism and praise. The free interplay in collective ensemble may imply disorder to some, but to others, the freedom of expression in improvisation denotes the heart of jazz and a reflection of the era.

Third stream jazz, realized in the 1950's, involves the fusion of classical music and jazz in an ingenious compositional form which renders one almost inseparable from the other. Although jazz musicians had been previously influenced by art music, the similarity of technical devices and overall dignity of each form was never organized into structures as they exist today. The abstractions of both cool jazz and art music merges with the most sophisticated kinds of jazz to develop both tonal and atonal examples of third stream music. Like avant-garde and bop, third stream can either reflect its association with the blues or can relate to the simple homophony of a hymn. While cool and avant-garde may use instinct and spontaneity in performance, third stream is generally pre-constructed and generally outlines the period of improvisation as opposed to structured form.

Composers

The composers of the most recent jazz trends have joined in massive efforts to define, penetrate and reveal the nature and function of jazz. Their philosophies have become as important as their techniques for composition and are typical of the struggle for freedom and identity within the society. Spectacular timbres and emotions are decidedly representative of the era which these composers are attempting to portray. Representative persons of each style common to jazz are discussed in the order of their successive eras.

JOHN LEWIS (1920–)

John Lewis, composer, arranger, music director and pianist, was born in LaGrange, Illinois, and settled in New York. With Milt Jackson, he formed the Modern Jazz Quartet and became known for quality music. A teacher at the Manhattan School of Music, Lewis was educated at the University of Mexico in both anthropology and music, and at the Manhattan School.

Influenced by Dizzy Gillespie, Charlie Parker and others, his own style also reflects those masters of the past: Bach, Haydn, Mozart, and Beethoven. This is apparent in his fugues, rondos and episodes which he fuses with third stream jazz fundamentals in various classical situations. Having once worked with Gillespie as arranger and pianist, their exchange of ideas merged with his own concepts.

Specializing in chamber jazz groups, Lewis has recorded with the Modern Jazz Quartet and with Asmussen, the European jazz violinist. His music reflects the "progressive" features, the "cool" tendency and the aloofness and sensitivity of "bop." His music also represents organization, keen development and direction, for his thorough training lends to the music a sophistication which it might not otherwise have had to distinguish it from any other composition of traditional jazz. Certain of his compositions are written as though improvised, while other demonstrate substantial and clear organization. Much of his inspiration comes from the blues to which he reportedly feels a kinship. His penetrating style promotes a creative rhythmic certainty and a feel for jazz.

Among his compositions are: *Smoke Gets in Your Eyes; Delaunay's Dilemma; Two Bass Hit; Emanon; Stay on it; Sait-on Jamais; Exposure* (film score); *Odds Against Tomorrow* (film score); *Django* (guitar); *Jazz Quartet; Vendome; Versaillers; Concorde; The Queen's Fancy; Move; Budo; Rogue; Love Me; Three Little Feelings; Bluesology; Festival Sketch; Two Degrees East; Three Degrees West; The Golden Striker*; and others.

MILES DAVIS (1926–1991)

Miles Davis, composer-trumpeter and arranger, was born in Illinois. He later moved to St. Louis, and eventually to New York, where he studied at the Juilliard School of Music. Highly influenced by Charlie Parker, Miles studied with Parker while attending Juilliard and expanded greatly during their association.

Miles organized a band for recording in 1948, headed several quintets and sextets, and performed both in the United States and abroad. He worked with Gil Evans, pianist; Max Roach, composer-drummer; Bud Powell; and John Coltrane. Since the later forties, his growth and performance abilities in concerts, recordings and films have created a popular following.

Miles developed several styles before he settled into a lyrical, sustained and introspective manner of composition. The long, extended lines of ornamental quality or the short, fragmented melodies flow over polychordal, sometimes atonal harmonies, orchestrated in either ballad style or in free, fantasy-like compositions. His rhythms move but are not considered swift. Intervals range from chromatics to wide varieties of skips and non-chordal tones, and the overall technique, though serene, is difficult to produce. He also experiments with various schemes for blues.

Among Davis' works are: *Deception; Sipping at the Bells; Olés; Dewey Square; The Theme; So What; Blue n' Boogie; Walkin'; Little Leaps; Sid's Ahead; Weirdo; Budo; Move; Venus de Milo*; and others, also seen in videos.

JOHN COLTRANE (1926–1967)

John Coltrane, a composer-saxophonist, was a jazz artist of many styles from traditional jazz to hard bop, and was also influential in establishing procedures and experiments toward avant-garde. Coltrane worked in New York and on several concert tours with Miles Davis and Thelonius Monk, whose intensive styles also helped mold Coltrane's own manner of playing and composing. In addition, Coltrane's principles of approach and familiarity with the saxophone were reflective of Coleman Hawkins. Some aspects can be heard in his recordings: *A Love Supreme; Duke Ellington w/ Coltrane* and *Coltrane w/Johnny Hartman.*

John Coltrane. Bob Thiele, Photographer.

A leading figure during his short lifetime, his works consisted of wide ranges of pleasant instrumental sounds to those of harsh qualities. His approach was ultimately from a lyrical standpoint, and melodically interpolated around harmony. With a highly ornamental melody as his predominant characteristic, complete dissonant tones would be employed with the harmony. Even though Coltrane used tonal actions in some compositions, many of his late works were atonal in quality, particularly because of the urgent, breathless and ornamental extensions of cadences.

Coltrane used western scales as well as modal characteristics of Asian and African scales. As one deeply interested in the identity of self, he used other characteristics of African derivatives. Improvisation, complex rhythms and the overlapping of rhythmic patterns were fused with the mixtures of scales and emotions. Partly under the influence of hard bop traditions of blues and other roots, his style also contained many elements of sharp intensity. Other explorations, however, were almost devoid of this fiery tradition of self and soul. Besides the blues form which he extended into different formal patterns of measures and meters, Coltrane used traditional ballads and free forms.

Much of his exploratory features were not conducive to relaxation but this became increasingly true of many contemporary jazz forms. Because of the many intricate sounds and rhythms created, one was forced to listen and sort the material presented in quite different ways than in the case of swing or other earlier music. For example, a simple fragment improvised innumerable ways, or the large amount of notes within a single phrase in either tonal or atonal patterns were presented along with extensions of vocal and instrumental timbres to include screams, grunts, and squeaks. There were rapidly repeated tones in complex multi-rhythmic frames, or "sputterings" of tones chromatically or diatonically styled as if unrelated to each other. The functions of harmony were contrary to the usual procedure, and the use of block chords and altered chords suggested by his lines were not always captured or readily comprehended by the listener. However, his music was exciting, difficult and demanding but representative of the times in which he lived.

Among his works arranged and composed were: *My Favorite Things; A Love Supreme; Suite; Transition; Chasin' the Trane; Take the Coltrane; How High the Moon; Impressions; Ascension; Crescent; Double Clutching; Summertime; But Not for Me; Shifting Down*; and others.

ORNETTE COLEMAN (1930–)

Ornette Coleman, composer and saxophone player, is credited with much of the freedom of expression which contributed to contemporary jazz. Of the "avant-garde" school, his experiments have matured into a focus of the newest musical form. Born in Forth Worth, Texas, Coleman traveled extensively, and settled in New York. Having performed with numerous bands, he formed his own group on his return to Fort Worth. From carnivals in Fort Worth to tours and concerts elsewhere, he has gained in both experience and professionalism. At first mainly self-taught through instruction manuals, Coleman was influenced by John Lewis to attend the School of Jazz at Lenox, Massachusetts. Before that, he was influenced by Charlie Parker, Lester Young and James Jordan.

Some of Coleman's music is highly improvised, melodically conceived, and atonal. *His Circle with a Hole in the Middle*, recorded on his *Art of the Improvisers* album, is representative of his latest style. He is quoted by Ostermann in the National Observer of June 7, 1965, as having described the aspects of his avant-garde music: "I don't know how it's going to sound before I play it any more than anybody else does." With conventional or plastic timbres that imitate the human voice, he makes his way across a continent of emotions and techniques of scales and arpeggios. Chromatics and complex rhythms are typical of the music.

Among his compositions are: *Lonely Woman; Antiques; Broadway Blues; Round Trip; Sadness; Free Jazz; Complete Communion; Mapa; Ramblin'; Cross Breeding; Snowflakes and Sunshine; Dawn; Turn-Around; Congeniality; Focus on Sanity; Peace; Sphinx; Chippie; Something Else; Circle with a Hole in the Middle*; and others.

OLIVER NELSON (1933–1975)

Oliver Nelson, a Pulitzer Prize winner, conductor, arranger, composer and saxophone player, was born in Saint Louis and lived in Los Angeles until his death. Having once lived in New York, Oliver Nelson made the rounds as a performer in all types of combos from those of the Temptations, Jimmy Rushing, Ray Charles and Sonny Rollins to Cannonball Adderley.

Educated privately, at an early age Nelson developed an interest in conducting after hearing Duke Ellington, Ravel and Hindemith. He was also influenced by others with whom he had worked, such as Count Basie and Quincy Jones. Yet his more advanced education prepared him for both traditional jazz as well as for his own independence with the concepts of third stream and classical music.

Educated further at Washington University with Elliot Carter, Robert Wykes and George Tremblay, Nelson had many credits to his name: *More Blues* and *The Abstract Truth* won the 1965 Edison Award in Amsterdam; *The Kennedy Dream* won the Deutsche Grammophone Award for 1967; and *The American Wind Symphony* presented a "Tribute to Oliver Nelson" by performing some of his classical and jazz pieces. During his productive life, Nelson served as lecturer at universities (including Washington University where his compositions, *Piece for Orchestra*, was premiered in 1969), won the 12th International Jazz Critics Poll which was held by *down beat* magazine, and was well reviewed in an outstanding tribute by *Ebony*.

His talents kept him in demand both as a lecturer and performer, conductor and composer. He also found the time to arrange for recordings which number about 20. Nelson also arranged for Nancy Wilson, Brook Benton, Jimmy Smith, and others. In addition, he wrote a text book on the improvisation of jazz, and was capable of writing works in styles which dictated compositions within any type of music and for various media, without restriction and without reservations, from blues and gospels to orchestral pieces.

The music employs tonalities of traditional and contemporary types, meters in duple and triple time, and call and answer patterns of melody versus chords. Even though lyrical, the compositions nevertheless employ independence of line and harmonic patterns, and move in improvised and planted structures. Equally and keenly aware of instrumental and vocal characteristics, the music represents qualitative content and substance.

Examples of his piano works are seen in his jazz album *Blues and the Abstract Truth* wherein both secular and religious emotions are apparent. Most interesting are *The Meetin'; In Time; Lem and Aide*; and *Shufflin'*, whose beginning measures are shown in Example 61.

Ex. 61. *Shufflin'*, Nelson. © Copyright Edward B. Marks Music Corporation. Used by permission.

Among some of his compositions are: *Hobo Flats; African Sunset; Hoe Down; Miss Fine; Emancipation Blues; Kilimanjar; More Blues; Abstract Truth* (recording); *Blues and the Abstract Truth* (eleven original piano solos); *The Kennedy Dream; Walk on the Wild Side; Who's Afraid of Virginia Woolf?; Ironside* (background score for television show); *Patterns for Saxophone* (textbook on jazz); *Goin' Out of My Head* (w/West Montgomery); *It Takes a Thief* (original background music); and others.

QUINCY JONES (1933–)

Quincy Jones is a composer, conductor, trumpeter and pianist with some very notable achievements. A native of Chicago, Illinois, he was reared in Bremerton, Washington. He attended Seattle University and later traveled to Boston where he held a scholarship at the Berkeley School of Music. He also traveled to Paris in order to study with Nadia Boulanger and to Rio de Janeiro for study with Villa-Lobos. Many of his musical techniques were also developed as a result of associations with Ray Charles (from whom

Quincy Jones.

Jones gleaned many of his feelings for jazz at an early age) and with Clark Terry and others.

Quincy Jones has performed in Europe and American with various ensembles, from groups of his own to those of Dizzy Gillespie and Lionel Hampton. He became vice-president of Mercury Records soon after he returned from a European tour, but he then decided to continue in composition due to a demand for his work. Head of A&M Record Company, and once the musical director for the *Bill Cosby Show*, Jones has arranged recordings and other hits for many, including Sammy Davis, Count Basie, Bill Eckstine, Sarah Vaughan, Andy Williams, Frank Sinatra, Peggy Lee and others. His film scores have rated Academy Award nominations.

One of the most prestigious and talented in the field, he has served as mentor, arranger and sponsor of several young artists such as the Brothers Johnson (also composers), and has co-produced and written material for Michael Jackson. Also a conductor of note, he has organized youths into singing choruses to accompany budding stars whose careers he inspired; he directed the group of professionals who sang the Lionel Richie–Michael Jackson tune, *We Are the World*, to help rid the world of hunger, and he has led jazz orchestras in places from Fisk University to recording studios.

Among the many honors bestowed upon him, Jones has received Grammy (at least 19), DownBeat, and Image Awards, the latter for *Back on the Block*—the "best album" in jazz for 1990. *Afro-American News* captioned his local D.C. appearance with "today's renaissance man of modern music," whose music goes from "Bebop to Pop to Hip Hop." Cover stories about him have appeared in *Emerge, Ebony*, and many newspapers, with captions such as "Filmdom's most sought-after movie scorer . . . ," "360 Degrees of

Music," "Man Behind the Music," "On a Brand New Block," etc. One of the grandest recent tributes was the movie *Listen Up*, which highlighted his incredible career and contributions to music.

The compositional style of Jones is an imaginative, astutely interesting mixture of form, unique orchestrations and balance of parts. He employs both an academic approach and a looseness of manner with his materials, which now range from the gospel fusion arrangements of Hawkins's *Oh Happy Day (Walking in Space)* to idiomatic characteristics of rap. Everything he pens seems to sound in gold terms!

Among his works are: *The Four Winds*; Music for the films: *The Pawnbroker; Walk, Don't Run; The Lost Man; In Cold Blood; The Mirage; The Slender Thread; The Boy and the Tree; Sanford and Son*; and *The Bill Cosby Show*; and innumerable recordings: *Walking in Space; Smackwater Jack; Gula Matari and the Black Requiem*, with Ray Charles collaborator, *Mellow Madness (A&M)*, *Come Back Charleston Blue* (w/Al Cleveland), *Body Heat* (A&M), score for *Ironside, In the Heat of the Night, The Anderson Tapes, Hikky-Burr* (Bill Cosby Show), *Roots*, etc.

There are numerous other musicians in jazz and its agnates who are also representative of the Freedom Era.

RONALD LEVIN CARTER (1937–)

Born in Royal Oak Township, Michigan, Ronald Carter, composer-performer on bass, cello, violin, clarinet, trombone, and tuba, has achieved a success within a career which has prospered since his childhood. Beginning the study of the cello at age ten, he continued his music while attending Cass Tech in Detroit. In 1955, he won a scholarship to the Eastman School of Music as a bass player and, in 1962, earned his Master of Music degree from Manhattan School of Music.

Ron Carter. Photo by Phil Bray. Courtesy of Fantasy, Inc.

Even though he was, according to the biography released by CTI Records of New York, "the first Black musician to appear with several . . . classical orchestras," he switched to the field of jazz and continued an accelerated advancement toward recognition for his proficiency and astuteness in technical skill and musicality. Composers such as Noel Da Costa and William S. Fischer sometimes wrote demanding music especially for him, knowing that the excellence of their writing would be honored by an equally excellent player. About his performance on a new album, Steve Wilson commented that "The real action begins with Carter's oddly appealing bass line. He anchors the piece with taste and imagination. . . . He has a knack for using the harmonics of a tune very imaginatively. His lines reflect the melody, but never degenerate into simple paraphrasing." Among some of the countless concerts in which he has performed, were those with Miles Davis, Eric Dolphy, Wes Montgomery, Jaki Byard, Randy Weston, Bobby Timmons, and others, traveling throughout America, Europe, and Japan.

In demand as an educator, he has taught at the University of Buffalo and at Washington State University and has produced records. In addition, Carter has also excelled in composition. His *Building a Jazz Bass Line*, which eventually became a series of three books, was assembled for his own teaching purposes (published by his own Ron Carter Music Company in New York). The set was based on tonal realizations and presented systematic technical exercises for developing skills in jumps, walking basses, ornamentations, and originality of touch. Within the various bass patterns were a few of his original melodies given alongside corresponding bass lines, such as *A Little Waltz, Einbahnstrasse, First Trip,* and *R. J.*, recorded by Miles Davis.

A star achiever, he has received recognition not only for his excellence as a performer, but also as a composer. According to Leonard Feather, Carter won the *down beat* New Star Award for bass; according to the Howard Ethnic Center listing, he won the jazz poll in *Swing Journal* (Japanese) in 1969, 1970, and 1971 and was also chosen as adjudicator at the International Jazz Festival held in Vienna, 1966.

Among his compositions and recordings are the popular *Spanish Blue* for flute, piano, bass, guitar, electric piano, and percussion (CTI label); *Pastels* (Milestone label, includes originals *Woolaphant, Ballad, One Bass Rag, Pastels,* and *12 + 12*); *Blues Farm, Rufus, A Feeling, Light Blue, 117 Special, El Noche Sol, Sabado Sombrero, Arkansas*; and many others. Other recordings on which he performs include those made with Horace Silver, Miles Davis, and the above collaborators.

HERBERT JEFFREY (HERBIE) HANCOCK (1940–)

"Herbie" Hancock, pianist, band leader, composer, arranger, publisher, and movie personality, was born in Chicago, Illinois. Beginning piano study at the age of seven, he later attended Grinnel College (bachelor's degree), Roosevelt University, the Manhattan School of Music, and the New School of Social Research.

An award-winning celebrity of note, he was given an honorary doctorate, according to *Jet*, from Grinnel College. In the third annual *Ebony* poll, he placed above all others as "Most Innovative Artist" of 1976. His compositions have held top placements in *Jet* polls and *down beat* citations; he was featured in a 1975 November/December *Contemporary Keyboard* article by Len Lyons; and at a New York Jazz Festival, a "retrospective" was devoted to his career. Hancock has also added to his list of achievements the hosting of Showtime's *Coast to Coast*, the teaching of seminars at UCLA, Salzburg, and other festivals, and the development of educational video, etc.

Herbert (Herbie) Hancock. Courtesy of AGM/Hanson & Schwam Management.

Hancock has enjoyed one of the most versatile careers of performing, writing and conducting. Beginning in the 1960's, he played piano in several bands—his own, and in others with Donald Byrd, Phil Woods, Oliver Nelson, Miles Davis, Wes Montgomery, Quincy Jones, Kenny Burrell, Wayne Shorter, etc. He composed, conducted and performed music for Charles Bronson's movie *Death Wish*, and composed music for the movie based on *The Spook Who Sat By the Door*, directed by a fellow African American, Ivan Dixon.

He has been credited with expanding "the color concept of the band" by using the "bass trombone, bass clarinet and the C flute in addition to the basic instrumentation of his sextet" (notes by Herb Wong, KJAZ, San Francisco). A short controversy once began about the fact that Hancock would not stay with the elements of jazz alone, claiming that he "sold out." Newspaper interviews revealed that Hancock admired rock artists, but he appreciated and learned from the classics as well as popular music. He felt that his role was to bridge the gap between jazz and pop music. His multitalented facets prevailed, and today, Hancock is considered one of the most important jazz players and, according to many media reports and reviews, one of "the most sought-after studio musicians in the business." In a 1990 television production of the life of Dale Turner, he accompanied the principal star, sax artist Dexter Gordon (1923–1990), as a competent and exciting pianist and band leader at Parisian clubs. And he has performed all over the world on major stages such as Washington, D.C.'s Kennedy Center, the Blue Note, etc. Beginning with classical piano studies, he played well enough at the age of eleven to perform a *D Major Mozart Concerto* with the Chicago Symphony, thus making his pianism well-grounded in the basics of both "worlds" of art music and jazz.

In the area of composition, Hancock has also excelled, as depicted in the facts that he has done several important productions: commercial jingles for Chevrolet, Pillsbury, Virginia Slims, etc., as well as numerous albums, band scores and movie soundtracks. An innovative talent, he has added other sounds to his array of available media to the acoustic piano—synthesizers, the wah-wah, and other electronic transmitters. Examples of his writing are found in *Jazz Giants—Herbie Hancock*, piano (*Headhunter*/sketch score, *Herbie Hancock's Greatest Hits*/piano, *Manchild*/sketch, *Thrust*/sketch scores from Hansen House); in Ramon Ricker's *Pentatonic Scales for Jazz Improvisations* (Jamey Aebersold); in Hancock Music (pub.)scores *I Have a Dream, The Prisoner, He Who Loves in Fear, Promise of the Sun, Chameleon* (w/Jackson, Maupin & Mason), *Butterfly*, and others. His *Watermelon Man* (on *Head Hunters* with his *Sly* and *Vein Melter*—popularized by Mongo Santamaria, and featured on Burdett's *Music and Its Roots*), has appeared on top polls, and on albums by others (such as Erroll Garner's *Up in Erroll's Room*, and *Albert Live* (Utopia/CyL 2); his keyboard support and solos, and original pieces *Madness and Riot* are found on Miles Davis's *Nefertiti* (Columbia); he played on Davis's *Miles in the Sky*; he is prominently featured on CTI's *Freddie Hubbard, George Benson, Joe Farrell, Milt Jackson*, and *Hubbard/Turrentine* records; both his performance and writing may also be observed on his own albums: Sundown Record's *Flood*; Columbia label's *Man Child; Head Hunter; Watermelon Man; Secrets; Toys* from *Speak Like a Child*; Blue Note label's *Maiden Voyage* (inc. originals *Dolphin Dance & Maiden Voyage*), *Thrust, Chameleon, The Prisoner* (includes *I Have a Dream, The Prisoner, He Who Lives in Fear, Promise of the Sun*), *Herbie Hancock, Takin' Off, My Point of View, Inventions and Dimensions, Empyrean Isles, Best of Herbie Hancock*, and others too numerous to list here (38 of which are in the *Contemporary Keyboard* article).

ANDREW NATHANIEL WHITE (1942–)

Andrew White, arranger, composer, oboist, electric bassist, and alto and tenor saxophone player, has been praised as performer, educator, publisher of his music, and transcriber. A native Washingtonian, he was educated in the Nashville public schools and at Howard University where he earned a Bachelor of Music degree in music theory in 1964. His teachers at various institutions and cities were John Reed, Brenton Banks, Don Cassel from Nashville, and Richard White, Ralph Gomberg, Louis Speyer, Stephey Adelstein, and Etienne Baudo from other cities in the United States. In Europe, he studied with Marcel Tabuteau, Leon Goosens, and Terrance McDonnah. In addition, his conducting experience was gained in performance and consultations with Lukas Foss, Henri Pousseur, Carlos Alsina, Mel Powell, Vincent Persichetti, Erich Leinsdorf, Eugene Ormandy, Gunther Schuller, and others.

Hollie West of the *Washington Post* termed White as "virtuosic," while

Joel Dreyfuss wrote, "No wonder that an apocryphal tale is told about the European and Japanese jazz critic who descended upon Washington on a packaged tour and bewildered their guides by demanding to see Andrew White" (*Post*, September 30, 1975). An astute thinker and brilliant businessman as well as performer, White has accumulated other honors such as fellowships and grants from WGMS Berkshire Music Center (1963), the John Hay Whitney Fellowships, Rockefeller Foundation, Tanglewood Fellowship, and the National Endowment Fund. Furthering his study of new music and of oboe performance, he studied at the Conservatoire Nationale Superieur de Musique de Paris, among other institutions. Gathering experience from two worlds of music, White claims to be equally at home with classical, jazz, rock, or other music.

White is known for the difficult transcriptions of John Coltrane's music—no small feat in producing over two-hundred jazz solos over a period of several years (catalogued and priced and sold from his South Dakota avenue residence in D.C.). White has also produced and sold over fourteen records of his own music. A player of many genres, he has toured with Stevie Wonder, Weather Report, McCoy Tyner, Otis Redding, and others and retained a position of principal oboist with the American Ballet Theater Orchestra for two years.

At the Library of Congress are listed his *Concertina* for three oboes, two English horns, and two tenor saxes. Others from his recordings are *Bb Rhythm; Theme Grand; Who Got De Funk?; Smiling Jane; Polly, Polly, Wherefore are Thou?; Beau Soleil Noir, Amis Pourquoi Pas?* (vocal); *Chanson Triste; Dear Nobody; Tribute to John Coltrane*; and others such as *My Little Shy Sparrows* for oboe and piano. A few of his recordings are entitled *Live at the Foolery*, vols. 1–5 (1974–75).

Other Composers of Jazz and Agnate Forms

The following section is a continuation of the above section as well as of earlier Jazz Composers, chapter IX. It includes data about composers of jazz, gospel, rock, pop forms and new developments which are only just now being formulated. By no means complete, it nonetheless contains some of the most visible of the artist-composers of each genre.

Jazz

Jazz of the Space-Age generation is a corollary of forms and styles from jazz/rock and jazz/funk to "fusion music," seen in composers such as:

Rashied Ali (1935?–   ), Philadelphian band leader, drummer, and composer of *As-Salaam-Alikum*, and *Akela* (on Survival album *New Directions*, Ali Music), who performed with Archie Shepp, and John Coltrane;

Roy Ayers (1940–   ), born in Los Angeles, California, lead and background vocals, vibes player, arranger and composer of *Domelo* (w/E. Birdsong), *Baby I Need Your Love, Higher, The Memory of You* (w/Birdsong and W. Allen), *Come Out and Play* (Ibid.), *Better Days, Searching, One Sweet Love to Remember* (w/Allen), *Vibrations, Moving Grooving*, and *Baby You Give Me A Feeling* (w/Birdsong), who has released recordings such as *Roy Ayers Ubiquity Vibrations*, Polydor);

Albert Ayler (1936–1970), from Cleveland, Ohio, saxophone player, composer-arranger whose work is seen on Impulse's *Last Album, Vibrations* (Arista), *My Name is Albert Ayler* (Fantasy), *Spiritual Unity* (ESP), etc.;

Kenny Barron (1943–   ), Philadelphian, pianist-theorist at Rutgers University, composer of *Ten Years Hence, A Flower*, and *Peruvian Blue*, whose work is seen on records *Peruvian Blue* (Muse), *Sunset to Dawn, Bad Benson,* and on albums with Albert Heath, Freddie Hubbard, Jimmy Health, etc.;

Anthony Braxton (1945–), from Chicago, alto sax and contrabass clarinet player, composer of BWC-12/N-48K (Stages 1–3), NR-12-C (33M), RFO-M (I/F(32), JMK-80, CFN-7 (as recorded on his *Saxophone Improvisations/Series* (Inner City label), whose work is also featured on *Together Alone* (Denmark), *New York, Fall 1974, Creative Orchestra Music 1976* (Arista) and numerous others;

George Benson (1943–), born in Pittsburgh, Pennsylvania, award-winning guitarist, singer, with own band after having played with Miles Davis, etc., composer of *My Latin Brother, The Changing World* (w/Art Gore), on CTI's *Bad Benson, The Cooker, Benny's Back, Bossa Rocka, Big Fat Lady, Benson's Rider* and *The Borgia Stick* (on Columbia's *George Benson Cookbook*), whose work is included in Don Sebesky's *Contemporary Arranger* (Music America Magazine, Colorado), and in albums *Breezin', Beyond the Blue Horizon, White Rabbit, Body Talk,* and others on CTI, Warner Bros. and Columbia labels;

Marion Brown, player of alto sax, zomari, percussion, African instruments, and composer of *Afternoon of a Georgia Faun* and *Djinji's Corner,* recorded on *Afternoon of a Georgia Faun* (ECM records);

Don Cherry (1936–), from Oklahoma City, player of trumpet, conch shell, bells, and singer-composer of *Mahakali, Karmapa Chenno, California, Buddha's Blues, Eagle Eye, Journey of Milarepa* and *Universal Mother* w/ Sherab-Barry Bryant, Eternal River and Cotillion Music, *Complete Communion, Symphony for Improvisors, Where Is Brooklyn* (Blue Note), *Relativity Suite* (JCOA), *Organic Music,* and who also recorded with Ornette Coleman, etc.;

Stanley Clarke (1951), Philadelphian, award-winning bassist cited by *Ebony, down beat, Jet,* composer of *Dayride, Jungle Waterfall, Excerpt from the First Movement of Heavy Metal* and *Interplay* (on Corea's *Return to Forever*), and *Journey to Love* (Nemperor);

Stanley Cowell (1931–), born in Toledo, Ohio, graduate of Oberlin College and University of Michigan (with study also in Austria), internationally known acoustic and electric pianist-composer of *Departure, Sweet Song, The Shuttle, Blues for the Viet Cong, Wedding March, Photon in a Paper World, Travellin' Man* (on *Blues for the Viet Cong,* for ensemble, Arista), and *Abscretions, Equipoise, Prayer for Peace, Illusion Suite* (found on *Musa: Ancestral Streams,* solo piano, Strata-East records, Stanco Publishing);

William (Billy) Cobham, Jr., player of percussion and synthesizer, and composer of *Panhandler, Light at the End of the Tunnel, A Funky Thide of Sings* (also album name, Chippewa Music, Atlantic), and of works on *Shabazz* (Atlantic) such as *Turian Matador, Red Baron* and *Tenth Pinn,* who also released *Spectrum, Crosswinds, Total Eclipse,* and who has performed with such composer-performers as Ron Carter, etc.;

Nathan Davis (1937–), from Kansas City, flutist-composer of *Happy Girl* (original songs from recording, pub./Musikuerlag), and *A Guide to Jazz Solo Flute Playing* (improvisations and exercises, etc.);

Jack DeJohnette, player of drums, piano and organ, and band leader-composer of *Pictures 1–6* as seen on his ECM album;

George Duke (1946–), born in San Rafael, California, graduate of San Francisco Conservatory of Music and San Francisco State University, teacher of jazz and improvisation courses at Merritt Junior College and

San Francisco Conservatory, described by Lee Underwood (*down beat,* 3/10/77) as "multi-keyboardist," trombonist, singer-composer, of *Dawn, For Love, Foosh, Floop De Loop, Malibu, Fools, The Aura* (Mycenae Music, recorded on *The Aura Will Prevail,* MPS records), and *Seeing You, Back to Where We Never Left, What the . . . , Tryin' & Cryin', I C'n Hear That, After the Love, Tzina* (Mycenae Music, MPS label);

Robin Kenyatta, flutist-composer of *Girl from Martinique, Blues for Your Mama, Thank You Jesus* and *We'll Be So Happy* (Yatta-Song Publishing, on *Girl From Martinique,* ECM records);

Andrew Hill (1937–), born in Port Au Prince, Haiti, moved to U.S., highlight in *down beat (3/10/77)* by interviewer Chuck Berg as "Innovative Enigma" and erstwhile composer-in-residence at Colgate "where his various compositions for string quartet and orchestra were performed," pianist-composer of *Black Fire, One For One, Laverne,* and of others on albums *Live at Montreaux, Spiral, Divine Revelation, Invitation,* etc.;

Rahsaan Roland Kirk (1936–1977), player of tenor sax, lyricon, manzello, and bagpipes, etc., composer of *Primitive Ohio and Chili Dogs, Freaks for the Festival, Portrait of Those Beautiful Ladies* (on *The Case of the 3 Sided Dream in Audio Color,* Atlantic), and composer-arranger of *Serenade to a Cuckoo, Steppin' Into Beauty, Bright Moments, Lyriconon,* etc., on *Kirkatron* album, Warner Bros.;

Earl Klugh, acoustic guitarist and composer of *Dr. Macumba, Cago Frio, Catherine, Jolanta, Summer Song,* and *This Time* (on *Finger Paintings* Blue Note album, United Artists Music);

Yusef Lateef (1921–), born William Evans in Chattanooga, Tennessee, award-winning player of saxophone, flute, oboe and instruments such as orgol, rebob, earthboard, etc., conductor, who played with Charles Mingus, Babatundi Olatunji, Cannonball Adderley, Hot Lips Page, Roy Eldridge, Lucky Millinder, and his own combo, featured in *down beat* reviews, *Ebony* polls (as jazz flutist), and who composed *Trio No. 1 for Flute, Violin and Piano* (recorded by Trio Pro Viva on *Black Images,* Teaneck, N.J., Alnur Music, holograph at Library of Congress), *Renunciation* (poem for orchestra), *String Quintet no. 1, Saxophone Quintet, Trio for Flute, Piano and Violin, Flute Book of the Blues* and others such as *Oatsy Doatsy, Soul's Bakery, Strange Lullaby, Big Bass Drum* (on Atlantic's *Part of the Search*), *Soul Blues* (on *The Roots of Modern Jazz,* Olympic), and whose other work can be seen on albums *Yusef Lateef* (Everest), *Ten Years Hence* (Atlantic), etc.;

Hubert Laws (1939–), from Houston, Texas, graduate of Juilliard School of Music, award-winning flutist, saxophonist, who joined with Ron Carter, Mongo Santamaria, Jazz Crusaders, Oliver Nelson (*Dream Deferred*), with classical organizations such as the New York Metropolitan Opera and New York Philharmonic Orchestras, to play equally well in various styles, whose music is included in Don Sebesky's *Contemporary Arranger* (Alfred), composer of *Flute Improvisation* (Hulaws Pub.), *Mean Lene* (on *In the Beginning,* CTI), and co-arranged with Bob James (same album) *Come Ye Disconsolate,* whose other work can be seen on albums *Ronnie Laws and Pressure,* Atlantic's *The Laws of Jazz, Fire Into Music,* CTI's *Chicago Theme, Morning Star, Carnegie Hall, Afro-Classic,* etc.;

Taj Mahal (1942–), performer on banjo, mandolin, guitar, acoustic and electric piano, "smoky vocals," and composer of *When I Feel the Sea Beneath My Soul, Dear Ladies, Further on Down the Road* (lyrics, w/music by

Wynton Marsalis. Courtesy of AMG International.

him and others), and *Music Keeps Me Together* (also name of album, Columbia), who has recorded various styles of music from reggae to blues;

Wynton Marsalis (1961–), born in New Orleans, studied at Tanglewood and Juilliard School of Music, brother of Branford (who himself was associated with the music in Spike Lee's *Mo' Better Blues*), award-winning trumpet virtuoso of both classical and jazz performances, who played with Art Blakey as well as with symphony orchestras, and his own combo, who was featured in *College Musician Winter, 1986*, in an interview by Chris Doering entitled "Renaissance Jazz Man," composer of three originals on *Standard Time, Vol.3* (which is done with his father as pianist on this his tenth album and reviewed favorably in the *Post* by Mike Joyce), *Knozz-Moe-King, Delfeayo's Dilemma, Skain's Domain* (*Blues Alley*, CBS), and works such as *In the Afterglow* and *Soon All Will Know* (on *Standard Time*), whose classical performances can also be heard in recordings of Handel, etc.;

Robert (Bobby) McFerrin, son of operatic star of same name, 1989 Grammy award-winning singer-composer of *Don't Worry, Be Happy* (*Simple Pleasures* album), who also composed pieces on *Medicine Music* (EMI), who also performs on the older *Bobby McFerrin* (Elektra);

Charles Mingus (1922–1979), born in Nogales, Arizona, moved to Los Angeles, then to New York, author of *Beneath the Underdog*, internationally known, award-winning bassist (International Jazz Poll, *DownBeat*, et al.), band leader who studied with M. Rheinschaugen (principal bassist with the New York Philharmonic), played with Stan Getz, Billy Taylor, Art Tatum and, according to Janet Coleman's and Al Young's *Mingus/Mingus: Two Memoirs*, with "everyone from Kid Ory to Lionel Hampton to Charlie Parker," often reviewed and debated in the *Washington Post* (especially when his innovations and experimentations were new to the public); composer of *Hora Decubitus* (on M. Williams' *Smithsonian Collection of Classic Jazz*), *Alice's Wonderland, Blue Cee, Boogie Stop Shuffle, Celia, The Clown, Dizzy Moods, Don't Come Back, Don't Let It Happen, Here Freedom, Haitian Fight Song, Jive Five Floor Four* (and numerous others listed at the Library of Congress), of works on Columbia's *Better Git It In Your Soul* (includes *Far Wells, Mill Valley, Jelly Roll, Self-Portrait in Three Colors*, etc.), and other albums such as *Town Hall Concert, Charlie Mingus, Changes One, Changes Two, Mingus Moves*, and others on Fantasy, Atlantic, Impulse, Limelight, etc., whose largest and latest atonal work of 18 sections, *Epitaph*, was funded by the National Endowment for the Arts and the Ford Foundation so that, wrote his widow in the *Post*, "preparation of the 500-page score for performance—following three years of cataloging—required 30 computer operators and musicians who worked for half a year with two computer programs, countless hours on the part of conductor Gunther Schuller and musicologist Andrew Homzy and a week of full-day rehearsals with 30 musicians" (performed at Wolf Trap and Tanglewood and recorded fully a decade after the composer's death);

Sun Ra, composer of such music as *Strange Dreams—Strange Worlds—Black Myth and It's After the End of the World, Black Forest Myth, Watutsi, Egyptian March, Myth Versus Reality* and *Duos* (on *It's After the End of the World*, BASF label);

Theodore Walter (Sonny) Rollins (1930–), born in New York City, Guggenheim Fellow, internationally renown saxophone player who performed with Art Blakey, Bud Powell, Max Roach, and his own group (which performed locally at Howard University in 1975, and at George Washington University's Lisner Auditorium in 1990, etc.), called one of "two most prominent figures of the post-Parker era . . . " by Larry Rohter (*Book World* review, 7/27/75), included in Feather's *Encyclopedia*, some *Afro-American* and *Washington Post* reviews (Hollie West's "Return of a Recluse" in July 1973 and "At the Eye of a Jazz Storm", 1/30/75, etc.), in Jamey Aebersold's "Learn to Play" series, who has composed works such as *Airegin* (H. Laws' *In the Beginning*, CTI), *Pent-Up House* (on the Martin Williams's *Smithsonian Collection of Classic Jazz*), St. Thomas, Freedom Suite, Doxy, Oleo, whose other work can be seen on Atlantic's *The Modern Jazz Quartet at Music Inn*, and on numerous Atlantic, RCA, Milestone, Blue Note, Prestige, etc. labels;

Sonny Rollins. Courtesy of United Negro College Fund.

Archie Shepp (1937–), saxophonist, born in Fort Lauderdale, Florida, moved to Philadelphia at early age, graduate of Goddard and Vermont Colleges, teacher of English in New York, musical artist in residence and performer with his quintet or such as Cecil Taylor at many symposiums, etc., subject of reviews in *Washington Post* by Hollie West, in writings by Leroi Jones, *down beat*, et al., author of plays *June Bug Graduates Tonight, Revolution*, composer of *Rufus* (early), *Attica Blues, Steam* (w & m), *Blues for Brother Jackson, Ballad for a Child* (Impulse), and other tunes seen on albums such as *Live at the Donalschingen Festival* (Saba), *Doodlin'* (Inner City), Impulse's *Four For Trane, Fire Music, The Girl From Ipanema, On This Night, There's a Trumpet in My Soul, A Sea of Faces* (Black Saint), etc.;

Cecil Taylor (1933–), native of New York City, pianist, educator (who joined the faculty at Glassboro State, gave workshops at institutions such as the Smithsonian in 1973, etc.), 1973 Guggenheim recipient as well as winner of International Critic's polls (such as record of the year in 1975, etc.), profiled in Leroi Jones' *Black Music*, in *down beat, Post*, and other media, also included on Martin Williams' *Smithsonian Collection of Classic Jazz* in a rendition of *Enter Evening*, and whose other work occurs on Blue Note's *Unit Structure* and *Conquitador*, Fantasy's *At the Cafe Montmartre*, and others on JCOA, Contemporary, etc.;

Stanley Turrentine (1934–), from Pittsburgh, Pennsylvania, tenor sax-composer of *Papa T, If You Don't Believe, Joao* (Columbia's *Nightwings*), *River's Invitation* (Blue Note's *Three Decades of Jazz*), *A Subtle One* (Jimmy Smith's *Midnight Special*), *T's Dream, Tommy's Tune* (Fantasy's *Have You Ever Seen the Rain*), as well as others on over 25 recordings;

McCoy Tyner (1938–), native of Philadelphia, Pennsylvania, and considered "one of the best pianists in the world today," (as reviewed by Geoffrey Himes of the *Post*), also plays the dulcimer in concerts, winner of International Critics polls (such as record of the year in 1975, etc.), who was featured in *down beat* (Lee Underwood's "Savant of the Astral Latitudes", 9/11/75), and in Leroi Jones' *Black Music*, who has played with John Coltrane, Art Blakey et al., and who composed *Sama Layuca, Above the Rainbow, La Cubana, Desert Cry, Paradox* (as seen on Milestone's *Sama Layuca*, Aisha Music), *Blues Back* (on Art Blakey's *A Jazz Message*), and whose various styles also include his arrangement of Cole Porter's *You'd Be So Nice To Come Home To* (on Impulse's *The Definitive Jazz Scene, vol. 2*), and others on Milestone's *Fly With the Wind* (w/William Fischer conducting), Blue Note's *The Real McCoy, Tender Moments, Time for Tyner, Expansions*, all selections on Milestone's *Sahara*, etc., and several persons whose names appear in Postscript III, who also have music to their credits.

McCoy Tyner. Photo by Phil Bray. Courtesy of Fantasy, Inc.

Gospel

Within the gospel scene are composers, arrangers, piano and vocal soloists, groups and conductors, and background accompanists. Not only are gospel associates found within the church community and the concert stage as entertainers, but the genre has reached the schools and has merged with the curricula of several colleges and universities. It now enjoys an international reputation.

Although many spiritually-inspired presenters still exist, gospel performance suffers when present day videos show charlatans, who know nothing of the true meaning, tastelessly pit secular dance movements against gospel-based sounds and incorrectly label it as "gospel music". The sincerity and dignity needed in religious exhibition thereby surcease, as it is easy enough to detect whether the intensity of the vocal improvisation is spontaneous fluidity or planned practice, and whether one is mesmerized by the Spirit or by the camera.

Some gospel creators are: Andraé Crouch, internationally known singer, recording artist, and composer of words and music for pieces found in the Lexicon (pub.) choral album *Just Andraé* such as *Bless His Holy Name, Come On Back My Child, God Loves the Country People, If Heaven Never Was Promised to Me, In Remembrance, It's Not Just a Story, Lord You've Been Good To Me, Lullaby of the Deceived, That's What It's All About, What Does Jesus Mean To You?* (w/W. Thedford), *You Ain't Livin'*, recorded on Light Records, as well as on Lexicon's *Soulfully: Andraé Crouch*, containing 9 originals of words and music;

Robert Fryson (1944–), singer, director, and composer of *Give Your Life to Jesus* (anthem, w/Jim Taylor, Cotillion Music, recorded on the *Third Annual Black College Gospel Festival*, TSOP label), *Jesus Is All You Need* and *A Symphony Unto God* (recorded on *Washington E.D. Chapter Choir of the Gospel Workshop of America*, Savoy), and *To the Glory of God* (on James Cleveland's *To the Glory of God*, Savoy);

Edwin Hawkins (1943–), singer, director, composer of *Every Man Wants to be Free*, which won a Grammy in 1970 for "Best Soul Gospel Performance of 1970," contained with others for which he wrote words and music in the *Edwin Hawkins Choral Collection* (w/arrangements by Frank Metis, Kamma Rippa Music, & E. Hawkins Music/Cimino), composer of the 1969 Grammy award winning *Oh Happy Day* (an arrangement of which is on Quincy Jones' *Walkin' in Space* recording), *He's Mine All Mine, Come Go With Me To My Father's House* (on *Third Annual National Black College Gospel Festival* recording, TSOP records/CBS), and composer of all compositions and arrangements found on his recording *Edwin Hawkins and the Edwin Hawkins Singers* such as *By and By, He's Wonderful, Just Tell Jesus, Isaiah 53, Come On Children (Let's Sing About the Goodness of the Lord), Keys to the Kingdom, I Must Confess, Up On The Mountain, He Won't Leave You*, and some of whose work is also found on the record *The Edwin Hawkins Singers: Peace is Blowing in the Wind* (Buddah Records; Birthright Music);

Richard Smallwood (1948–), pianist, director, singer, and composer of unpublished works such as *Won't You Come By Here, Reach Out for Someone Who's Lost His Own, Don't Give Up (Just Keep Holding)* and *I Wish You Joy*, founder of Smallwood Singers with whom he has toured internationally;

Myrna Summers, director, arranger, composer, and soloist with the Interdenominational Singers, composer of *Tell It Like It Is, Communion with*

God, Prayed and I Prayed, Where Is Love, Witness, Said He Would, Try, arranger of *More Love to Thee* and *I Am Thine* (recorded on *Tell It Like It Is*, Cotillion) and *God Gave Me a Song* (on *Heavenly Stars*, Cotillion Music and records);

Micki Grant, composer of *Don't Bother Me, I Can't Cope*, and many others such as seen in the subsequent Postscript III; Roderick J. Bell (1961–), born in Houston, Texas, composer of pieces recorded on St. Thomas More Church Choir, etc., Archdiocese of Washington, D.C.

Rock and Rap

To "rap" is to talk, to sermonize, to communicate, to admonish, to flirt, and to project leader versus group messages important to certain recipients. On first impulse, one is tempted to specify "rap music" as the live and recorded rock used in its background; for the main focus of rap itself seems more poetry than music because the audience is saturated with bombardments of verbiage. But past practices of classical composers have certainly used spoken parts in their works, from narrations to "sprechstimme," so the fact that the creators wish to call rap "music" could be seen as their highlighting bit parts of musical liasons. As in rock, choreography (African "break" dancing, "go-go," modern and gymnastics) and vocal accompanying are common to the performances; DJs or disc controllers also contribute to the background effects used in rapping.

M. C. Hammer.

Because rap is being defined as it is being formulated, its appraisal is fragmentary. As promoted by television videos, the aims of rap are seemingly more related to the philosophical and political goals of Jamaican reggae (outgrowth of mento poetry), and the "rapso" of Jamaica's Brother Resistance; yet it also resembles the Caribbean "dub" poetry known in Barbados and Trinidad. On the other hand, rappers M. C. Hammer and others point to James Browns' rock as the root of their rap.

All rappers are not necessarily music composers, for music has often been borrowed or bought as background to accompany the wordy, uptempo renditions. Among some of the more palatable presenters are M. C. Hammer, Moove Society, Salt & Pepa, D. C. Scopio, Chubb Rock, New Edition, and Fresh Prince. On the other hand, certain other lyrics by other groups have been denounced because of debased lyrics (a fact also true of some unsavory vocal ragtime a century ago, as well as of some blues and rock, etc.). Some "rapping" elements have been used in "cross-over" music by Quincy Jones, and in gospel music of the Winans, P.I. D., Michael Peace, Stephen Wiley, etc. (reviewed in *USA Today* on August 7, 1990 by James Jones as "urban/contemporary" gospel).

The following composers are representations of the most contemporary 'space age' rock creators. Especially beginning in the 1990's, albums very often appeared in video versions as well as on discs without visual representations. For earlier generations, see chapter on Composers of Jazz and Its Allied Forms.

Rock and Pop

ARETHA FRANKLIN (1942–)

Aretha Franklin, singer, pianist, arranger and composer, was born in Memphis, Tennessee. Having moved to Detroit with her father, Rev. C. L. Franklin (also a gospel singer), she gleaned much information about her music and her heritage through work with church choirs. According to Billy James' notes on Columbia labels, Aretha joined her father's gospel group and toured with them at an early age, thereby commanding the attention of Mahalia Jackson and others. Since that time, she has played many major halls and concert stages, including Appollo, Radio City Music Hall, and others.

Aretha Franklin. Courtesy of Arista Records.

Possessing an exquisitely priceless voice which was designated, in the 1980's, as one of Michigan's "historic treasures," her styles, progressions, and accolades are multifarious. She has been proclaimed for several different years the "favorite female soul vocalist," "America's best-selling female singer," the "Queen of Soul," and a Grammy award winner for "the best soul gospel performance" (especially for her *Amazing Grace*, which stayed on *Jet's* "Top Ten" poll for weeks), and stylistically, she has been listed in "pop" categories. In 1976, *Ebony* also listed her with others under "favorite rhythm and blues" instrumentalists (!), thus adding to the confusion of categorical placement and medium of performance. In 1990, she received the Grammy Legend Award for "ongoing creative contributions and influences in the recording fields," adding to her already large collection of Grammies. *Jet* magazine (July 7, 1986) reported that her platinum album *Who's Zooming' Who*, which contained the Grammy Award-winning tune *Freeway of Love*, had been on the charts for nearly a year.

Atlantic records has released many of her discs, among which are *Aretha's Greatest Hits, Aretha: Live at Fillmore West, Young, Gifted and Black, Aretha, Until You Come Back to Me, Sparkie* (composed and produced by Curtis Mayfield), and *Amazing Grace*. She has also recorded with others on the albums *Heavenly Stars, Memphis Sound, The Total Black Experience in Sound*, and Silver Burdett's *Afro-American Music and Its Roots*. It is as though her unique vocal talent and her numerous brilliant recordings were not enough, for she has expanded her skills to the playing of piano, occasionally in accompaniment to her own singing, to television and movie performances (in both singing and acting performances), and to the art of composition as well. To her credit are such songs as *Call Me, Sister From Texas, Think* (also on Lonnie Smith's *Think!*, Blue Note records), *Dr. Feelgood* (w/Ted White), and *Spirit in the Dark* (Pundit Music).

STEVELAND JUDKINS MORRIS (STEVIE WONDER) (1950–)

Stevie Wonder, the epitome of rock and exponent of the new political communicative type rock, was born Steveland Judkins Morris in Saginaw, Michigan. He moved to Detroit at an early age and proceeded to dominate the business and compositional world. Awarded an honorary doctorate by Fisk University in 1980, Wonder was hailed by President Leonard as a "musical giant" and was acclaimed for " . . . singing the book of life, being a symbol of courage in adversity, for sharing the continual first finale of your fulfillment, and for being the sunshine of all our lives."

Stevie Wonder. Photo by Phil Bray. Courtesy of Motown Records.

The amazing Wonder, reflecting the talents of Ray Charles, B. B. King, and others, represents the emerging generation of innovative composers who grew from simple forms, goals, and purposes to a political counterpart of the reggae, and to an Africanized communication. Musical media and the spoken word stand for more than dance music or childhood dreams; he uses this to deliver the important messages—of love, or happy aspirations, of soul, and of a strong belief in Self. An exponent of the varied definition of soul, rock, or just music, Wonder blends the blues-felt heart of a B. B. King coupled with that of a gutsy Ray Charles style into a contemporary fusion of rock, gospel, ballad, blues, or any other available idioms which might happen to appear.

A gifted musician and businessman, he has produced some of his music through electronic backgrounds, doubled with acoustic media into such mixtures that sound larger than a one-man rendition of a piece, and has completed large quantities of compositions from his *Talking Book* to the ballad *You Are the Sunshine of My Life*. Correlating published scores by Jobete Music with records by Motown, Wonder produced works which won as many as fourteen Grammys. Captions of "Toto and Stevie Wonder Lead Grammy Nominees," a full-blown superstar "Back on Top" appeared in the *Washington Post*. Featured several times in such books and news media as the *Post, Ebony, Current Biography,* and *Jet,* he has become recognized for his excellence in music, and in generating hit songs and records such as *For Once in my Life; My Cherie Amour; I Call it Pretty Music; Fingertips; Tell Me Something Good; Signed, Sealed and Delivered; Where I'm Coming From* (1970); and albums *Fulfillingness; First Finale; Talking Book* (1972, 1974); twelve gold records; and others. In addition to politicizing on behalf of the Martin Luther King Holiday, for which he composed *Happy Birthday*, he also wrote a lovely wedding song, *Ribbon in the Sky*, and the film score for *Jungle Fever*.

Wonder's contributions to the development of rock—the new media, the use of electronics, the duplications of vocal backgrounds, African drumming, and other features—may change the definition of rock and may merge the gist of a simple part into the complex of the whole (world of music).

MICHAEL JACKSON (1958–)

Michael Jackson, internationally renown, award-winning singer, dancer, recording artist and songwriter, was born in Gary, Indiana and moved to Detroit. Beginning his career as a young member of The Jackson Five family enterprise, he worked with Motown to make the group a household name. He left the group to do solo productions of his own and eventually propelled his trade into big business achievements, thus highlighting him as one of the most celebrated of talented performer-composers in any field.

Michael, as he is fondly called, heaped up many awards and honors such as Images, Grammies, and command performances for the Queen of England and the President of the United States. His super-refined, artistic dance moves, some of which resembled footwork by James Brown, was praised by top dance personalities of pop and classical worlds alike, and were copied by innumerable fans, especially the famous "moon walk" involving a backward slide in time to the exciting rhythms. His childlike, easy-going vocal sound captivated audiences everywhere, and coerced many a young, aspiring talent to pattern his way after the giant figure. He was featured in countless magazines and newspapers throughout the world, especially after his world tour of 1987. The brother of Janet and Germaine (also gifted achievers in their own right), he worked with Diana Ross as the singing scarecrow in the movie *The Wiz*, starred in videos (some of which were produced and refined by the super-giant of jazz composition, Quincy Jones), and his various hit recordings stayed on top rock charts for weeks at a time. His fame (notwithstanding the recent 1991 "topping" of charts by Janet), became a legendary fact of history.

Michael Jackson. Courtesy of Epic Records.

He composed many songs viewed on videos and heard on recordings such as *Thriller* (*Wanna Be Startin' Somethin', The Girl is Mine* w/Paul McCartney, *Billy Jean*, and *Beat It*), *Bad, Heartbreak Hotel,* and *Don't Stop 'Til You Get Enough* (his first song). Jackson co-authored *We Are the World* with Lionel Richie, the song used by numerous performers in joint rendition, to combat hunger mainly in Ethiopia. Michael also wrote an autobiographical delineation of his experiences entitled *Moon Walk*. Jackson now performs under the auspices of Sony.

Various other artist-composers and arrangers exist in the personalities of:

Anita Baker, born in Detroit, Image award winner of 1990's "best female recording artist," singer and co-composer of *Sweet Love* (Jobete Music), and some of whose album titles are *The Song-stress, Giving You The Best That I Got, Rapture* (which, according to Tracy Hopkins of *Afro American News*, sold five million copies), *Compositions, Talk To Me*, etc.;

Natalie Cole (1950–), born in Los Angeles, composer of *Peaceful Living* and *Your Eyes* (Cole-arama Music, recorded on Capitol's *Natalie Cole*);

Marvin Yancy and Chuck Jackson, collaborators in compositions on *Natalie Cole: This Heat, Still In Love, I've Got Love on My Mind, Unpredictable You, Be Mine Tonight, I Can't Breakaway* (Chappell Music);

Roberta Flack (1939–), Grammy award singer, pianist and Howard University graduate, a native of Black Mountain, North Carolina (near Asheville), whose several recordings and concert appearances followed her discovery by Les McCann at Mr. Henry's club in Washington, D.C., and whose recordings and arrangements include popular and gospel tinges, as seen in "Go Up Moses" (in *Quiet Fire* album), "I Told Jesus" (on *Heavenly Stars*, Cotillion), and in Atlantic releases *Killing Me Softly, First Take, Chapter Two, The First Time Ever I Saw Your Face*, and *Roberta Flack and Donny Hathaway*;

John (Johnny) R. Mathis. Courtesy of AGM/Hanson & Schwam. David Vance, Photographer.

John Royce (Johnny) Mathis (1935–), internationally recognized singer, born in San Francisco, California, attended George Washington High School and San Francisco State College (in physical education and English rather than in music), who first studied music with Clem Mathis, his father, and later with Connie Cox, gained experience in the church choir, in school glee clubs, at community events, and night clubs before signing with Columbia records in the mid-1950's (thereby giving up the opportunity to join the USA Olympic Team), who has been invited to sing for British Royalty and the American White House, has won 60 gold and platinum records for outstanding sales, whose album *Johnny's Greatest Hits* stayed on the Billboard top album chart for 490 consecutive weeks, who made appearances in film such as *Lizzie* and *A Certain Smile*, who attained legendary status as a television and stage star singing such romantic ballads as *Chances Are, I's Not For Me To Say*, and *The Twelth of Never* in a "velvety-smooth voice," has released approximately 100 albums, and who composed such originals as the six released on his ninety-first album (*Once in a While*);

Prince Rogers Nelson, rock singer whose styles are fused with gospel and other influences, guitarist and star of such movies as *Purple Rain*, recording and video star of several albums, and composer of songs and movie soundtracks;

Sly Stewart (1942–), a Californian who studied at Vallejo Junior College, arranger, composer of music performed by his group the Family Stone, as seen on albums *Dance to The Music* (Epic), *Higher, Ride the Rhythm*, and whose song *The Swim* (which he wrote at age 18) sold a million copies;

Luther Vandross (1951–), born in New York, 1990 Image Award winner for best male recording artist ("The Best of Love") singer, arranger, producer, and co-composer (w/Marcus Miller) of titles found on the Epic record *The Night I Fell in Love: Till My Baby Comes Home, The Night I Fell in*

Love, It's Over Now, composer of *My Sensitivity (Gets in the Way), Other Side of the World* and *Wait For Love* (both w/Nat Adderley, Jr.), and of titles found on CBS record *Any Love,* variously composed with Marcus Miller, Nat Adderley, Jr., H. Eaves and Gamson-Carroll, Jr.: *Are You Gonna Love Me, For You To Love, The Second Time Around, I Wonder, She Won't Talk To Me, I Know You Want To, Come Back, Any Love, The Power of Love,* etc.

Lionel Richie (1949–), singer-songwriter, born in Tuskegee, Alabama, started his career with the Commodores, toured Europe with the Jackson Five in 1971, eventually recorded with Motown, gaining three gold albums, composer of songs heard on albums and seen in videos, *Lady* (for Kenny Rogers), *Endless Love* (for Diana Ross), *We Are the World* (collaborative), *All Night,* etc.

Postscript III: Other Composers

Other composers whose sketches are absent occur in varying categories, but often overlap styles to fit the molds of jazz, rock or pop. Additionally, as in earlier eras, practically all "cross" lines onto any genre germane to the point of personal election. The following lists therefore simply point out some of the predominant fashioners.

In Gospel: Composer-arrangers Milton Bronson, Joan Hillsman, William Hubbard, Kenneth Louis, Leon Roberts, James Tatum, Henry A. Thomas, and Donald Vails. Gospel is so popular in the D.C. area, expanding until at least 30 "top gospel choirs" (listed in the December, 1990 issues of the *Afro American News*) became prominent, including the D.C. Mass Choir, the Gospel Music Workshop of American, the Howard University Gospel Choir, the Imani Temple Gospel Choir, and the Richard Smallwood Singers. Several other contemporary groups are Florida Mass Choir, Mississippi Mass Choir, The Staples Singers, the Winans, Bennu Ausar Aurkestra, Take Six, After Seven, Roberts Revival Singer, the Wesley Boyd Workshop, and Bernice Reagon's Sweet Honey in the Rock.

In Rock, Rap, Pop, Disco: Also Nat Adderley, Jr., Joan Armatrading, Thom Bell, Frankie Beverly, Bobby Brown, Lamont Dozier, Caesar Frazier, Kenny Gamble, Johnny Gill, Brian Holland, Eddie Holland, Leon Huff, Charles (Chuck) Jackson, Germaine Jackson, Janet Jackson, A. J. Johnson, Eddie Kendricks, Carole King, Gladys Knight, Billy Ocean, Jeffrey Osborne, Bill Pettaway, Najee, Donna Summer, Maurice White, Deniece Williams and groups Earth, Wind & Fire, The Jackson (Five), Gladys Knight and the Pips, The Pointer Sisters, and Sly Steward & the Family Stone.

In Jazz: Dorothy Ashby, Albert Ayler, Gary Bartz, Jaki Byard, Michael Cochrane, Alice Coltrane, Norman Connors, Ethel Ennis, William Fischer, Curtis Fuller, Roland Hanna, Julius Hemphill, Eddie Henderson, Andrew Hill, Freddie Hubbard, Phyllis Hyman, Al Jarreau, Robin Kenyatta, Oliver Lake, Ronnie Laws, Bill Lee (music score for his son's movie, *Mo' Better Blues,* and compiler of *1002 Jumbo, The All-American Jazz Album* "fake book"), Mundell Lowe, Branford Marsalis, Marion Meadows, Alphonse Mouzon, Idris Muhammad, Pharoah Sanders, Archie Shepp, Wayne Shorter, Horace Silver, Lonnie Liston Smith, Marcus Roberts, Patrice Rushen, Warren Smith, Henry Threadgill, Charles Tolliver, Allen Toussaint, Mal Waldron, Kim Waters, Frank Wess, Michael White, Nancy Wilson, Modern Jazz Quartet, Rashied Ali Quartet, Jazz Crusaders, Descendants of Mike and Phoebe, etc.

XIII

CONTEMPORARY FORMS, TRENDS, AND COMPOSERS OF NEW MUSIC

The forms and styles of the contemporary scene are both traditional and new, and are influenced by both African and western contributions. Art forms range from familiar symphonic forms, chamber music and opera to interludes and hybrids. Popular forms are represented in structures from musicals to rock. Both types experiment with electronic and computer music, filtered to meet the challenges of a tomorrow.

Rock operas, jazz sonatas or symphonies, jazz preludes, jazz masses or blues sonatas are as common as traditional forms and are placed in well organized structures. In addition, forms of electronic and new music in general are composed with titles of tapes, vacuum cleaners, violins or other permutations such as the Moog synthesizer.

The primary function of art music is still designed for listening, while jazz and other popular forms have somewhat followed suit, being intended for both active and passive participation. Folk forms and jazz forms are still found mainly in the night clubs, etc., but this music is also performed on concert stages. Rock is still used mainly for dancing and is generally restricted to simple forms and techniques, as are most folk and popular songs.

As forms have changed, so have their concepts. Where composers once established a separation of popular and art music forms through practice of one type, many composers of today openly practice all types and more readily accept all music which they write as art, *per se*. Although many categories of rock, blues and folk are unfortunately written mainly by amateurs who have a lack of either talent or achievement, well-written jazz and rock music, on the other hand, is constantly practiced and promoted by professional and talented musicians. The use of jazz in art music, initiated by Still and others has now reached an equal level with art music, and in some cases, is almost indistinguishable one from the other, as to applied and compositional techniques.

Compositional Trends

Timbres and orchestrations for all music also show more freedom of choice and change. Partly influenced by jazz instrumentation, guitars, banjos, saxophones and other nontraditional instruments have joined the orchestras for art music, while the flute, violin, oboe and French horn are seen more frequently in jazz. More orchestral instruments also perform in rock, while African instruments also account for many new ideas of timbre. Whereas the latter instruments have performed in popular music before the contemporary era, such practices are becoming more standard than uncommon. Spectacular instrumentation now includes a single player with two or more instruments performing simultaneously, or electric extensions of traditional instruments such as the trumpet, flute, and guitar.

Techniques of contemporary music range from the European major-minor schemes to the African and Asian modal scales. Block chords continue from the modern period of the twentieth century, and polyrhythms and other cross rhythms are standard as well as sporadic and fragmented examples. In addition, dissonances of seconds and sevenths combine with the traditional sounds to present Space Age concepts of music.

Twelve tone music, as practiced by Anton Webern and Arnold Schoenberg, is now a more accustomed sound both in classical music and avant-garde jazz, particularly since the experimental pioneering of electronic sounds. Its lack of emphasis upon a key center promotes the aspect of atonalism and specializes in tone rows, retrogrades, inversions and higher mathematical symbols. This music has also encouraged composers to write music involving extremes in sound and to include half spoken-half sung vocal techniques (Sprechstimme).

Melody, irregularly phrased, may be constructed of three or five measures rather than the traditional two or four. Melodies with irregular meters may also employ a single number placed on the grand staff to denote its triple or duple time.

Many contemporary techniques such as polyrhythm, polymeters and asymmetrical phrases are similar to those discussed in African music. Some aspects of irregular instrumentation, improvisation and asymmetrical form are related, as well as the fusion of scales and chords. Stylistically, atonal music employs many of the African features along with newly contrived methods of composition. While homophonic music does exist today, the new emphasis is mostly on individual polyphonic lines in ensemble and dissonances.

One of the more contemporary concepts of harmony involves the principle of intervallic relationships wherein the distance form one note to another becomes increasingly important. Even though many altered chords result in this process (as harmony results from polyphony) the method of procedure differs from the norm. Within these practices are found tone clusters of close intervals from two to three or more. Its linear style emphasizes the horizontal movement of tones, while the vertical approach places sounds against simultaneous movements. Other features are the displaced tones, or those placed in other registers within the line of melodic tones and chord patterns. These are being used as terminations, beginnings, interpolations or as resolutions of tones or chords from their traditional use. Some of the principal aspects of the new music are seen in Example 62 including symbols of traditional and chance music.

Although definite barriers are outlined in this book in order to classify situations and styles into some organized scheme, it must be stressed that periods and philosophies overlap, making it virtually impossible to place a composer completely within a period or style of writing. This is true particularly in reference to contemporary composers, or in the case of those discussed in the Modern Era who are yet in a state of change. For composers are people who learn and turn with each new discovery or innovation. Therefore, modern techniques coincide in part with those of the contemporary era.

The new always retains a part of the old. In this respect, composers already discussed such as Ulysses Kay, Billy Taylor, of Joseph Kennedy could very well be discussed within the contemporary according to some devices in their recent works, and according to their present status in this era.

Ex. 62. Contemporary symbols and techniques of music.

1. Computer symbols: $\frac{I \times I \times I = I}{I \times I \times I}$; $\frac{n(n-1)}{r}$; $\frac{6 \times 5 \times 4 \times 3 \times 2}{3 \times 3 \times 1 \times 1}$

2. Miscellaneous symbols: meters; ties and prolongations; accents and arpeggios.

3. Forms: traditional and new measures.

2 + 2 = 4	2 + 1 = 3
4 + 4 = 8	3 + 3 = 6
8 + 8 = 16	3 + 5 = 8

4. Rhythms.

5. Melodies: asymmetrical; displaced registers.

6. Harmonies: atonal cluster, polytonality, intervals.

7. Scales: pentatonic, twelve tone, diminished; symbols of twelve tone row.

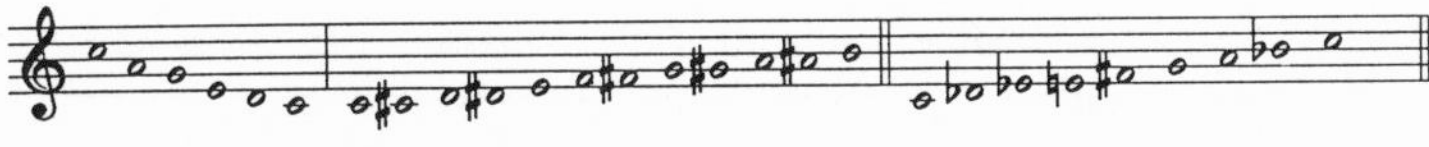

R = Retrograde
I = Inversion
RI = Retrograde Inversion

Composers

The contemporary period is difficult to place as to time or composers. Because periods often overlap in technique and style, and so many diverse practices move in simultaneous procession, no definitive date can be exact. The Modern period of the early 1900's overlaps with the contemporary. However, the 1960's did show more marked differences and freedom in style and ways of composing than did previous years. The period was also a resulting fact of the freedom movement in the present decade. Therefore, this section is devoted to this most recent period.

Contemporary composers are difficult to place or categorize. As to specific practices, today's composers use all available media, styles, emotions and musical types. The tools are no longer the orchestral instruments and voices divided into the elements of music. The structured form may be implied, or may be entirely extemporaneous. It may also be entirely composed note by note. The rhythm may be regular or irregular, strict or obscured. It may even be unsingable. The media may range from car horns to the strings of the piano.

Composers of today are keenly aware of purpose, intent, and character in music. They are also scholars, humanists and seekers of identity. They practice within a freedom of thought never before allowed in the direct eclecticism and acceptance of the merger. Many write third stream music or rock equally as well as they write jazz without the inclusion of art music. The recent trend of jazz being taught in colleges and other institutions has permitted this, as well as the knowledge that jazz has become difficult and "respectable."

Black composers feel the strong need and compulsion for the expression of Self, of a heritage and a national acceptance. By also using the musical tools contributed by a people within this country, both the realization of nationalism and inheritance from another country are fixed. Likewise, the inclusion of blues, spirituals, and jazz as inspirations for compositions further implants nationalism into their music. The direct penetration of African scales and rhythms are some of the most exciting aspects of the music, and are continued in the fusion with European features.

Few composers omit the techniques of twelve tone music, or at least the principles of atonalism. Many are also inspired by electronic devices. Even the noise elements of instruments are part of the equipment for the new music whose sound reflect immediate substances of the present, of life, reality and change.

GEORGE THEOPHILUS WALKER (1922–)

George Walker, a composer-pianist of repute, was born in Washington, D.C. Currently a professor of music at Rutgers, he was educated at Oberlin College (Mus.B.); Curtis Institute of Music in Philadelphia (Artist Diploma); American Academy in Fontainebleau, France; the Eastman School of Music in Rochester, New York (Artist Diploma and Doctorate); and has further studied in Paris with Nadia Boulanger in composition and with Curzon and Casadesus in piano at Fontainebleau. He has also studied with Rudolf Serkin, Rosario Scalero, Piatigorsky, Primrose, and Menotti.

Walker has taught extensively in various capacities. He has served at the Curtis Institute of Music as an assistant to Rudolf Serkin, and has taught at Dillard University in New Orleans, at the Dalcroze School of Music in New York, at Smith College, the New School of Social Research, and at Rutgers University, where he is chairman of the department of music.

For his work as pianist and composer, his honors have included scholarships and fellowships from Oberlin, Eastman, John Hay Whitney, The MacDowell, the Bennington Composers Conference, the American Symphony League and the American Music Center, as well as the Guggenheim and Rockefeller Foundations. In 1945, Walker was a winner of the Philadelphia Youth Auditions where he appeared as soloist with the Philadelphia

Orchestra with Eugene Ormandy as conductor. In 1945, he was awarded a Town Hall debut by Efrem Zimbalist. In 1958, he was again awarded a Town Hall recital by Mrs. Efrem Zimbalist.

As a concert pianist, he has made numerous tours of the United States, Europe, Canada, and the West Indies. The Bok Award for concerts in Europe as a piano soloist was awarded in 1963. As a composer, he has merited an equal number of honors. The Rhea Sosland Chamber Music Contest brought him an award for his *String Quartet* in 1967; the Harvey Gaul Prize for the *Sonata for Two Pianos* in 1964; and a citation from Eastman for contributions to the field of music.

George Walker.

The recipient of Distinguished Professorship at the University of Delaware in 1975, Walker continued at Rutgers University in administration, education, and composition. He accepted an award from the American Academy and Institute of Arts and Letters (1982) and an Honorary Doctorate of Fine Arts from Lafayette College.

Virtually each major symposium has programmed his music, such as the Colloquia and Competition of 1980 held at the Kennedy Center, Washington, D.C. and elsewhere in the U.S. Additionally, special programs featured his music such as that given in tribute in 1982 by Boris Slutsky, who performed his *Spektra and Spatials* in the Terrace Theater of Kennedy Center. At the 1982 International Piano Festival at the University of Maryland, pianist Frances Walker, his sibling, gave a lecture demonstration of his piano works. In other concerts between a ten-year span, pianists who performed his works at the Kennedy Center in Washington, D.C. were Delphin and Romain, duo-pianists, and soloists Raymond Jackson, Robert Jordan, Leon Bates, and Allison Deane.

Among his commissions have been those from the New York Philharmonic for the *Concerto for Cello and Orchestra*; from the Harlem Boys Choir for *Cantata for Boys Choir*, soloists and chamber orchestra; and others from the Fromm Music Foundation and the Eastman School of Music. Major performances by the New York Philharmonic featured his *In Praise of Folly* (Concert Overture), while others by Eastman Philharmonia, Boston, and Atlanta Symphonies included his *Eastman Overture, Lyric for Strings*, and *Address for Orchestra*, respectively. Additionally, his *Music for Brass* was commissioned by Hans Kindler.

Walker has distinguished himself as a gigantic composer. Although his talent is revealed in compositions for various media, it is the piano compositions which have enjoyed immense popularity during this decade. His talent for both performance and writing are seen in the music from the difficult *First Sonata* to *Prelude and Caprice* with its tonal, yet contemporary setting which projects technical and harmonic (theoretical) challenges also typical of his style. His unique handling of tonalities often gives an illusion of atonality

Very significantly, his *Bauble* was commissioned for use at the 1982 International Piano Festival by the University of Maryland. The last measures of the well-constructed, avant-garde piece are seen in Example 63 as a sample of his atonal writing.

A few of his newest works, available from General Music, are *Lament* and *Red, Red Rose* (included in Willis Patterson's *Anthology*, E. B. Marks, 1977); *Sonata for Two Pianos* (which, as researched in William Moore's 1975 dissertation *The Cyclical Principle as Used in the Construction of Piano Sonatas*, is Walker's arrangement of *Sonata No. 2*); Sonata No. 3 (1975); *In the Bleak*

Ex. 63. *Bauble*, Walker. © 1981. Copyright by General Music Publishing Company, Inc. Used by permission.

Mid-Winter; Lyric for Strings (recorded on the Columbia Black Composers Series, 1976); *Spirituals for Orchestra* (1974); *Dialogues for Cello and Orchestra* (1976); *Passacaglia for Orchestra; Prelude and Caprice for Piano; Serenade for Chamber Orchestra; Music for Diverse Instruments; Three Spirituals* for voice and piano (1975); *Mass* for chorus and orchestra (1975); and *Five Fancys* for clarinet and piano (1974). Other works are recorded by CRI (songs) and Mercury Records (*Eastman Overture*).

He composes for voices, orchestral instruments, piano, and various combinations. Highly difficult, complex and technically demanding, his music is both tonal and atonal and deals with contemporary idioms in sound and form. Linear independency is shown in lyrical idioms. Orchestrations of sound may occur in blended homophony or percussive blocks of atonal notes. Irregular intervals and extremities of complex rhythms and registers mark his style of composition.

Additional works are: *So We'll Go A-roving; The Bereaved Maid; Lament; I Went to Heaven; Gloria in Memoriam* (for women's voices); *Two Poems; Piano Sonatas Nos. 1–4; Sonata for Violin and Piano; Stars* for mixed chorus; *Sonata for Cello and Piano; Spatials* (for piano); *Fifteen Songs; Concerto for Trombone and Orchestra; String Quartet; Ten Works for Chorus; Perimeters for Clarinet and Piano; Three Lyrics* for chorus; *Guido's Hand* for piano; and others.

HALE SMITH (1925–)

Hale Smith was born in Cleveland, Ohio, and has now become a resident of Freeport, Long Island, New York. An energetic free-lance composer, arranger, lecturer and performer, Smith was educated at the Cleveland Institute of Music where he studied with Ward Lewis and received the B.M. and M.M. degrees. He also studied composition with Marcel Dick and others. Smith has lectured extensively; served as associate professor at the University of Connecticut; as an Adjunct Associate Professor of music at the Post College of Long Island University; and as editor of Sam Fox Co.

A solid and confident composer whose works command a proper respect and attention for their sound content and their technical applications, he has been hailed by the late Arthur Loesser and Herbert Elwell as a "huge, rich and significant talent." For his work, honors and awards have earned him frequent public performances, citations and commissions. His *Contours for Orchestra* was commissioned by Broadcast Music, Inc., as part of its twentieth anniversary celebrations. He was a winner of the Broadcast Music Student Composers Award in 1953. His works have been performed by the Society of Black Composers, the Louisville Orchestra, the Cleveland Orchestra, the Symphony of the New World, the Cincinnati Orchestra, pianist Ward Davenny, the Tougaloo College Choir and others.

Hale Smith.

A composer in virtually all types of modern jazz and art music, Smith has composed third stream music, popular and art music, and has engaged in projects from publishing to arranging and performing. In the field of jazz, Smith has arranged for Chico Hamilton, Oliver Nelson, Quincy Jones, Eric Dolphy, Ahmad Jamal, and others. His original compositions have included music for television dramas, documentary films, recordings and for numerous dramatic and concert occasions. He is also active in various organizations. In the American Composers Alliance, he serves on the Board of Governors and has recently been elected to the Board of Directors of Composers Recordings, Inc.

Smith has been the subject of discussion in many dissertations, one of which was Malcolm Breda's *Hale Smith: A Biographical and Analytical Study of the Man and His Music* (The University of Mississippi, 1975). The Breda study was also used to expand the new *Grove's Dictionary*. Among other publications, he has been reviewed or listed in books by Hansonia Caldwell, Maurice Hinson, Evelyn White, Eugene Claghorn, and many others including Eileen Southern's *Biographical Dictionary* and Edward Jablonski's *Encyclopedia of American Music*.

A partial account of his most exciting accomplishments included an Achievement Award given by the Black Music Caucus of Music Educators National Association at the 1982 Convention in San Antonio, Texas, for his "outstanding work in composition." Significantly, he also was awarded several commissions from artists and institutions. His works, *Sochas, Epicedial Variations; Anticipations, Introspections and Reflections* (Merion/T. Presser, 1979), and *Evocation*, were chosen to be among those performed at the Kennedy Center Symposia at both the 1980 Colloquia and Competition, and at those sponsored by AAMOA throughout the United States.

Smith's *Contours* for orchestra was reviewed by Irving Lowens (*Washington Post*, 1975) as a "curtain-raiser"; his *Comes Tomorrow*, a jazz cantata which was performed at Howard University by the Tougaloo Choir, was described by Joseph McLellan (*Washington Post* critic) as having "stood out from the rest of the program" and as being a "style . . . flavored with a variety of jazz rhythms and harmonies, introduced chiefly in a torchy soprano solo, a male duet with chorus and an interlude for drums."

Some of his newest compositions were centers of attention within the last ten years. *Ritual and Incantations* (1974) was recorded on the Columbia Records Black Composers Series in 1976; *Valley Wind* for soprano and *In Memoriam Beryl Rubinstein* were recorded on CRI Records (*Schwann* catalog, 1976); *Evocation* was placed in the *International Library*, Volume 9, as standard piano repertoire; *Velvet Shoes* for voice was printed in Willis Patterson's *Anthology of Art Songs* (E. B. Marks, 1976); his *Allison* was recorded by Ahmad Jamal on Cadet Records; and *Three Brevities* for flute, cello, and piano was recorded by Antoinette Handy-Miller on *Contemporary Black Images* (T & T Associates of Raleigh, N.C.).

Belwin has become the principal supplier of the music once published by E. B. Marks (*Faces of Jazz* for piano; *Music for Harp and Orchestra*); *Evocation* for piano and *Contours* for orchestra were placed with C. F. Peters, and one of his arrangements for Nina Simone's *To Be Young, Gifted and Black* was placed with Sam Fox. Among the newest titles are *Innerflexions* for piano and orchestra, 1977; *Toussaint L'Overture 1803* for chorus and piano, 1977; *Variations* for sextet, 1975; *Introductions, Cadenzas and Interludes* for octet, 1974; and *Symphonic Spirituals* (performed recently by Simon Estes and other mixed media).

Smith composes chamber music as well as solo and ensemble vocal music. Although his music is contemporary, his techniques range from traditional chords to the most difficult twelve tone varieties, altered chords, clusters and polyphony. His music possesses dynamic sounds and shows improvisatory characteristics, cadenzas of virtuosic flare, trills and other compositional techniques.

Melodically, Smith employs repetitions of tones. In such cases, both the rhythm and harmony become main factors of interest. He also uses traditional skips of thirds, diatonic tones, octaves and fifths in exclusive skill. *Two Kids* for SATB, featured at a recent Choral Convention, uses difficult intervals in small and large atonal relationships. Always tastefully and logically written, his works show both a vocal and instrumental sensitivity.

His rhythms are both complex and simple. However, even when seemingly simple, many are ingenious and challenging. Meters are clear in the use of either common time or more complex ones. Some of the cadences use long rhythmic terminations, while others end on short notes; sometimes the general movement of rhythms are fairly uniform.

Harmonically, all techniques of homophony and polyphony are employed in the music. Certain examples of his music are also conceived from the intervallic approach, as in *Three Brevities* for solo flute. His *Faces of Jazz* for piano shows an uncluttered style of merging jazz harmonies and classical techniques. Partly based on blues, fugues, and tin pan, the piece uses consonances, dissonances, ostinato basses, lyricism, and complex rhythms to support the body of emotions and techniques therein. His *Evocation* for piano and the *In Memoriam—Beryl Rubinstein* for chorus show still another style from simple homophony to improvisation. Other works show blocks of sound, full harmonies and an advanced style of writing for all media. His *Two Kids* shows a use of 2nds and other dissonances in atonal harmony.

The Three Brevities for solo flute is an unaccompanied example employing the dodecaphonic trends and atonal features of contemporary music. Written in three movements, it outlines exciting melodic and rhythmic characteristics:

Ex. 64. *Three Brevities*, Smith. © Copyright Edward B. Marks Corporation. Used by permission.

The *Music for Harp and Orchestra* outlines a most complex organization of rhythms and harmonies. Swiftly passing chords indicated by full orchestral sounds in blocks, clusters, and various intervals are placed against long melodic lines of atonal quality. A portion of the work is illustrated in Example 65 and is scored for violins 1 and 2, violas, celli, basses, alto flute, piccolo, oboe, clarinet, horns, bassoons and harp.

Among Hale Smith's works are: scores for Lorca's *Yerma* and *Blood Wedding; In Memoriam—Beryl Rubinstein* (chorus); *Epicedial Variations; Sonata for Cello and Piano; Two Love Songs of John Donne* (soprano and nine instruments); *Three Brevities for Flute; Contours for Orchestra*; score for *Bold New Approach; Somersault* (band); *Take A Chance* (band); *Evocation* (piano); *Or-*

Ex. 65. *Music for Harp and Orchestra*, Smith. © Copyright Edward B. Marks Music Corporation. Used by permission.

chestral Set; Music for Harp and Orchestra; Three Songs for Voice; Trinial Dance (elementary band); *By Yearning and By Beautiful* (string orchestra); *Faces of Jazz* (piano pieces); *Comes Tomorrow* (jazz cantata); *Mirrors* for 2 pianos (Meriod), and others.

ARTHUR CUNNINGHAM (1928–)

Arthur Cunningham, composer, author, conductor, pianist and bass player, was born in Piermont, New York, but now resides in Nyack, New York. Educated in the Metropolitan Music School, Fisk University, the Juilliard School of Music and Columbia Teachers College, he has studied with John Work, Peter Menin, Normal Lloyd, Henry Brandt, Peter Wilhousky, Margaret Hillis, and others. A precocious beginner at the age of six, Cunningham began the study of piano. He wrote and performed piano pieces at the age of seven and eventually graduated to various other instruments at a later time.

Brilliantly alive in both philosophy and professionalism, Cunningham is a firm believer in special aims and standards for the serious music student. He describes his attitudes as representing "a new departure in professional education in the field of music, and addresses itself to those who seek a more thorough training. . . . a high degree of excellence and a sophistication of artistic expression designed to contribute to the profession and to the country as a whole." In realistic terms, his music has shown that his talent can indeed be used to encourage the production of a new breed of musical participants in whom sound training in technique and style can be instilled. Cunningham sums up the educational curriculum as one which must stress the aspects of music as well as related businesses or commercialism. He feels, "To know music is not enough, one must also know life". As a member of ASCAP and ACA, Cunningham writes various source materials and articles and gives lectures and seminars about music.

Cunningham is rich in both experience and awards. In Special Services, he wrote for the army band and toured with a trio as a string bass player. As a student at the Metropolitan Music School, he appeared frequently on radio station WNYC in the performance of his works. He has played double bass with the Suburban Symphony, Rockland County, and has served with the Rockland County Summer Theater as musical director. He has written *Ostrich Feathers* and *Violetta* for the stage. In addition, he has written innumerable compositions for piano, chorus, solo voices, orchestra and various other instrumental combinations. He has written ballets, opera, string quartets, chamber music, and approximately 400 popular songs, as well as ballads, rock and jazz compositions. Among his advanced works for shows, revues, television and art music concerts are those for such musicals as *Patsy Parch, Susan's Dream* and *Ostrich Feathers*, (a rock musical) and *His Natural Grace* (a one-act mini-rock opera).

His honors and awards are seen in performances of his works, commissions and grants. His own works have been performed on programs with those of Howard Swanson. His commissions have come from Fisk University, the Suburban Symphony, the Rockland County Composers and the New World Symphony, as well as Earle Madison. The *Eclatette for Cello* was requested for the 1970 Tschaikowsky Competition in Moscow, Russia; the *Ostrich Feathers* was premiered at the Martinique Theatre, New York City, in 1964; *Concentrics* was premiered at Philharmonic Hall in 1969 (by

Arthur Cunningham.

the New World Symphony); and his works have enjoyed many other performances.

Cunningham considers virtually every style of writing and every form, both sacred and secular. His music is freedom expressed in sound, thinly veiled with a demand that offers no freedom of relaxation in spirit or performance. His music employs a meticulous care as to directions for dynamics, control, rhythms, and techniques. With dynamics sometimes appearing on each phrase of two to three or more notes, they sometimes appear in each measure. The use of grace notes, slides, trills and various meters are also typical of his music. He, like Baker, is apt to use closely aligned meters of 5/4, 2/4, 4/4, 9/8, 5/8, or 3/4. In addition, he uses no meters at all whenever there is a desire for complete freedom of movement.

Both diatonic and irregular melodies are typical. Always melodic, despite his rhythmic interest, each musical element seems equally important to the overall effect. Short and long phrases are frequently arranged against repetitions of a beginning or ending of a melody, augmented or diminished around the fragments of the original. The fragments, in turn, are used to "break" the linear or harmonic motions, or are interpolated as the main melody shifts registers. These fragments also introduce and conclude phrases or sections.

Cunningham has written in both tonal and atonal forms, making use of both traditional western scales and of modal and serial techniques. One example of his work, *Thisby*, a lament for flute and cello (or by cello alone) was adapted from the characters Thisby and Pyramus from his own *A Mid-Summer Nights Dream.* Composed in 1968, it moves in linear patterns interspersed with arpeggi from the cello line. The opening measures of the first movement show no meter:

Ex. 66. *Lament from Thisby*, Cunningham. Used by permission of the composer-publisher.

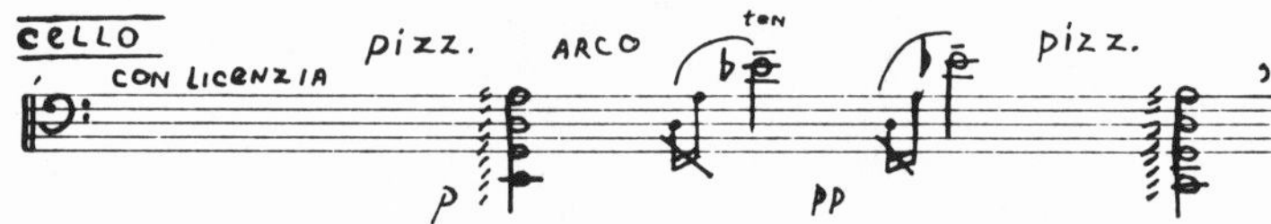

After the brief introduction, the cello begins in fifths in accompaniment to the chromatic melody of the flute:

Ex. 67.

The flute, in the middle of the composition (section A or "Essay"), again makes use of the barless measures with attractive trills, grace notes and sixteenths:

Ex. 68.

Although the entire piece emphasizes the atonal, the beginning and the ending of the piece outline the C major triad. A unique element of the ending is the indefinite pitch markings in the slurred, downward slide effect common to jazz:

Ex. 69. Excerpts from *Thisby*, Cunningham. Used by permission of composer-publisher.

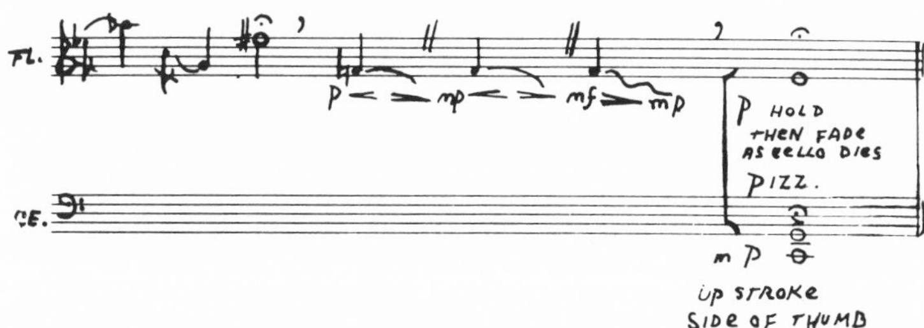

Some of Cunningham's finest compositional and pianistic techniques occur in a piece for piano, *Engrams*, an atonal structure whose multi-sections vary between slow and fast portions of different thematic materials and moods (now published by T. Presser), indicated in Example 70.

Ex. 70. *Engrams*, Cunningham. Used by permission of composer-publisher.

His compositions were included in the symposiums given by Afro-American Opportunities Association during a week-long session of orchestral and chamber music performances. The Fisk Jubilee Singers frequently sang his compositions throughout the United States during their frequent tours (especially his *We Gonna Make It*); and his *Harlem Suite* (including *Sunday In the Evenin', World Goin' Down, Harlem Is My Home; Hinkty Woman, Sunday Stone*, and *Studies for Singing the Blues*, T. Presser) was sung by the Martin Luther King, Jr. Male Glee Club of New York at the 1982 Choral Festival, led by founder-conductor, A. Patterson. Natalie Hinderas, pianist, recorded his *Engrams* and frequently programmed it on concert tours during the 1970s. Several grants and commissions from the National Endowment of the Arts and other sources were awarded him. In 1980, other honors came when his *Walton Statement*, played by John Clayton on string bass, was heard in the Colloquia and Competition at the Kennedy Center, as were others in Afro-American Opportunities Association's symposia of the 1970s.

Cunningham has continued to use many modes of expression. His style yet reflects the jazz influence seen in *Lullaby For a Jazz Baby* for trumpet (recorded on Desto's *The Black Composer in America*); atonalism, as recorded in Natalie Hinderas's fine performance of *Engrams* for piano (Desto Records); rock and gospels as composed in his *Munday Man* for voices, T. Presser.

Among Cunningham's other works are the following: *Two Haitian Play Dances; Four Shadows* (piano); *Sugarhill* (piano); *Engrams* (60 piano pieces); *Amen; Hymn of Our Lord; In the Year Seventeen* (choral); *Ring Out Wild Bells* (choral); *Fruitful Trees More Fruitful Are* (choral); *Organ Prelude and Hymn* (choral); *When I Was One and Twenty* (choral); *He Met Her at the Dolphin* (choral); *Fifty Stars* (female voices); *Into My Heart* (female); *From Where I Stand* (choral); *The Gingerbread Man* (male); *Then The Cricket Sings* (choral); *Song of Songs* (soprano); *Turning of the Babies in the Bed* (baritone); *Jabberwocky* (soprano); *Midsummer Nights Dream* (soprano with instruments); *Forty Pieces* (jazz orchestra); *Adagio for Oboe and Strings; Jazz Pieces* (band); *Ballet* (string quartet, jazz); *Concentrics* (orchestra); *Dim Du Mim* (English horn, orchestra); *Lullabye for a Jazz Baby* (orchestra); *Eclatette for Cello; Dialogue for Piano and Chamber Orchestra; Perimeters for Flute*, clarinet, vibraharp, and double bass); *Louey Louey* (mini-rock opera); *Violette; Ostrich Feathers; Trio for Flute, Viola and Bassoon*; and many others.

THOMAS J. ANDERSON (1928–)

Thomas J. Anderson, composer-in-residence with the Atlanta Symphony Orchestra for the 1969–70 season, and a composer retired from Tufts University in Massachusetts, was born in Coatesville, Pennsylvania. Educated at West Virginia State College, Pennsylvania State University, the Cincinnati Conservatory and the State University of Iowa, where he earned the Ph.D., he has also taught at West Virginia State, Langston University, Prairie View and Tennessee A&I University.

A member of ACA, he has held fellowships at the MacDowell Colony in Peterborough, New Hampshire, from 1960–68 and was given commissions by the Oklahoma City Junior Symphony Orchestra, and West Virginia State College. He won the Fromm Foundation Award in 1964, and the Copley Foundation Award in 1964. One of America's foremost composers, he engaged in writing articles, delivering lectures and working as the Chairman of Music at Tufts University (until 1980). In 1976, Tufts honored him with the position of Fletcher Professor of Music.

His 1983 award of an honorary doctorate from the College of the Holy Cross in Worcester, Massachusetts, capped a long list of other honors which included prestigious commissions from Fisk University to write a work in 1966 in celebration of its 100th anniversary (*Personals*, based on an Arna Bontemps text); the National Endowment for the Arts for the Bicentennial of the U.S. (*Horizons*, 1976); Thor Johnson for the National Symphony Orchestra (*Chamber Symphony*); Robert Shaw (*Intervals*); Berkshire Music Center and the Fromm Music Foundation (*Transitions*); Thomas Ayres for the University of Iowa performance of *Swing Set*; Symphony of the New World for Betty Allen's performance at Lincoln Center, New York; Richard Hunt for Chicago performance of *Re-Creation*, 1978; Thomas Everett for Brown University premiere, 1978 (*Minstrel Man*); American Wind Symphony for *Fanfare* (1976); Richard Hunt for *Vocalise* (980); and recently in 1979 and 1980 respectively, commissions from the United Methodist Church for *Spirituals* and from Indiana University and the National Endowment for the Arts for *Soldier Boy, Soldier*, his first opera (although his list of works already included the operetta form).

T. J. Anderson. Photograph by Richard Wood. Used by permission.

Still other honors received since his rise included a Fellowship to the MacDowell Colony in Peterborough, New Hampshire, 1983; a Fellowship to the Yaddo Foundation in Saratoga, New York, 1977; honorary membership into Phi Beta Kappa, 1977; Distinguished Achievement Award from the National Association of Negro Musicians, 1979; Leadership Award from the National Black Caucus of Music Educators National Conference, 1980; the Arts Award from the NAACP, 1980; the Alumni Fellow Award from Pennsylvania State University, 1982; numerous lectures such as the U.S. Department of State at universities and conservatories in Brazil, 1976 and at the University of Zurich, 1978; the consultations for the Honorary National Arts Award Panel, Educational Testing Service; Southern Illinois University Press; Meet the Composer Advisory Board in New York and a host of others too numerous to list here.

Anderson's talent and professionalism have been discussed by Stanley Sadie for the new *Grove Dictionary*; David Ewen and Edward Jablonski in *Dictionaries of American Composers*; Christine Oliver in her dissertation (Florida State University), and in other works by Eileen Southern, Roger Johnson, Leonard Feather, and many other scholars. Anderson has published several articles and contributed to journals and has proved to be one of the best sources for pinpointing his own style and role in music. His jazz background developed when he was growing up in Washington, D.C. (he traveled as a professional while a teenager) and played a part in his compositional writing. This can be seen in the inclusion and profound knowledge of gospel, orchestral riffs accompanying a jazz quartet, and other idioms written into *Spirituals*; it can also be seen in the improvisations and cultural experiences emblazoned into his opera, *Soldier Boy, Soldier*. In general, his writing techniques run the gamut of collective experiences gleaned both from his own living and intellectual experiences as well as those lessons imparted by such teachers as Darius Milhaud (from his article

"So You Want to Write an Opera?" printed in the Tufts *Criterion*, Winter 1983). Several adjectives readily define his music as having his own constructed synthetic scales, or as using modes, as being intriguingly intellectual, yet strongly relative to the essence of realism and roots.

His composition, *Spirituals* for orchestra, recently premiered at the Union United Methodist Church in Boston and was reported by the *National Leader* (February 10, 1983) as "a historical event." The piece was described by Anderson as containing an "integration of jazz, classical and traditional Black musical modes," as being written for orchestra, choir, children's chorus, soloist, and narrator of Robert Hayden's poetry. Such spirituals as *Keep Me From Sinking Down* were heard in the work.

Alfred Thompson's dissertation, *Musical Style and Compositional Techniques in Selected Works of T. J. Anderson* (1978), sponsored by Indiana University and a grant from Phi Mu Alpha Sinfonia Foundation, described his music as embracing many influences "from ethnic and popular music to post-Webern and avant-garde regiments." He furthermore used a description of "experimental phenomena and as embracing freedom as well as order."

Other significant activities have taken place in his musical career. In 1976, *Schwann* listed CRI as having recorded his *Chamber Symphony*; Nonesuch, his *Variations on a Theme* by M. B. Tolson; and Columbia Records Black Composers Series as having included his *Squares* for orchestra. Also honored by performances of his music on regional symposiums on Black music, and the Colloquia and Competition held at the Kennedy Center in 1980, Anderson has further expanded his reputation and proficiency at compositional complexities and microtones by conducing and annotating the *Classic Rags and Ragtime Songs* (Smithsonian, 1974) and by the recent releases of three pieces published by Bote and Bock, entitled *Watermelon Man* and *Street Song* (both for piano) and *Minstrel Man* (scored for hi-hat cymbals, bass drum and bass trombone) as seen in Example 71.

Ex. 71. *Minstrel Man*, Anderson. © Copyright 1978. Bote and Bock. All rights reserved. Used by permission.

In 1982, he composed *Call and Response* for piano which may be played together in a cycle with *Watermelon Man* and *Street Song* under a new title of *Urban Recollections*.

A scholar as well as a leader, his relationship with the Smithsonian Association and his special expertise in the field of orchestration produced a recording entitled *Classic Rags and Ragtime Songs*, in which the music of Black composers Eubie Blake, James Scott, Luckey Roberts, James Reese Europe, and Arthur Marshall were presented alongside the music of Scott Joplin (namely the *Real Slow Drag* from his opera *Treemonisha*, which Anderson orchestrated for the premiere performance in Atlanta, Georgia, and *Pineapple Rag* for tenor, chorus and piano; Smithsonian N-001, 1974).

Among his other most recently listed works were delightful titles such as the piece for "small hands," *Play Me Something* for piano, 1979, which should endear younger or less advanced players to the music of T. J. Anderson. Others (published by ACA) were: *Introduction and Allegro* for orchestra; *New Dances* for orchestra; *Trio Concertante* for winds and band; *Connections*, a fantasy for string quintet, 1967; *Variations on a Theme by M. B. Tolson* for voices, winds, and piano, 1969; *Intervals for Orchestra*, 1972; *Transitions* for chamber ensemble; 1971; *This House* for male glee club and four chromatic pitch pipes, 1971; *Block Songs* for voice, children's toys, 1972; *Swing Set* for clarinet and piano, 1972; *Beyond Silence* for tenor, winds strings, and piano, 1973; *Five Easy Pieces* for violin, piano, and jew's harp, 1974 (also in Roger Johnson's *Anthology of New Music*, Macmillan, 1977 and 1980); *In Memoriam Malcolm X* for voice and orchestra, 1974; *Horizons '76* for soprano and orchestra, 1975; *The Shell Fairy*, a two-act operetta, 1977; *Variations on a Theme by Alban Berg* for viola and piano, 1977; *Re-Creation* for speakers, dancer, winds, strings, piano, and drums, 1978; *Spirituals* for choirs, orchestra, jazz quartet, solo, and narrator, 1979; *Vocalise* for violin and harp, 1980; *Soldier Boy, Soldier*, two-act opera, 1982; *Inaugural Piece* for three trumpets and four trombones; *Jonestown* for children's choir and piano, 1982; *Call and Response* for solo piano, 1982; and *Thomas Jefferson's Minstrels* for solo baritone, male glee club, and jazz band, 1982. Others by Bote and Bock Publishers: *Street Song* and *Watermelon Man* for piano, 1977; and *Minstrel Man* for trombone and percussion (one player), 1978. *Fanfare* for trumpet and four mini-bands was published by C. F. Peters, 1976; *Messages, a Creole Fantas* for orchestra was published by Carl Fisher in 1979.

Anderson has described his own style as one whose "works show the adaptations of pluralistic values which range reflects the influence of primitive music jazz, post-Webern, and avant-garde styles. I feel that it is the duty of the composer to make audible the inaudible and thus link some part of mankind. The compositions do not represent any style or school of composition but seek a continuous arrangement of sound in a given time and place context. Its only meaning grows out of my experience with humanity and therefore manifests a genetic state of flux."

Anderson also describes the style and tendencies of compositional technique in the following manner: "The projection and receding of instrumental colors at different levels of densities tend to produce sound platforms within dynamic possibilities. The works are organized around motific sets or small patterns of notes which function in many types of musical environment associations. Emphasis is on the use of effects which relate directly to the musical ideas. Melodies tend to be predominantly disjunct and show a preference for symmetrical rhythm. These ideas are expanded by use of numerical proportionalism, multirhythmic values and metric modulation. Compositions, in general, favor a plastic single movement structure in which there exist a series of cause and effect relationships. The mood within sections tends to run a wide gamut of densities, ranges of sound elements, developmental manipulations, and the free distribution of independent units. Harmony functions from a linear context and tends to be identified with free atonalism."

In many cases, the titles do not reveal the forms of his pieces, giving a semi-unorthodox air to his art. For example, *Six Etudes and and Fancy* is a piece for woodwind quintet and *Squares* is an essay or orchestral piece. These terms are used rather than "symphony" or "woodwind quintet". On the other hand, Anderson appears, in some respects, within the art music tradition rather than of third stream or jazz. In no way, however, does this make him a conservative composer, for his style is influenced by many of the same elements and techniques of which jazz is composed, and his works are undoubtedly contemporary.

Melodically, Anderson is sensitive to the medium at hand and the emotion desired. He uses both diatonic and wide skips, within short fragmentary phrases or an extraordinarily long one. He may also write two lines in intervals of the second or other dissonances, interspersing the lines with major or minor resolutions. His free choice of materials of composition

Ex. 72. Rhythms of Anderson.

Ex. 73. *Personals*, Anderson. © 1967, T. J. Anderson, Jr. All rights reserved including the right of public performance for profit. Reprinted by permission of American Composers Alliance.

are not restrictive in his stress on either chromaticism or diatonicism, tonality or atonality.

Rhythmically, sixteenth notes move to dotted eighths in schematic successions or from fast to very slow (such as from an eighth or sixteenth to a tied whole note). At times, there are rows of eighths in succession being interrupted by a rest, dot or tie to effect syncopation. Meters and polymeters from 4/2 to 12/8 and 4/4 are used distinctly with dynamic extremes. One meter sign found in *Chamber Symphony* simply shows the symbol of "four" being placed above a quarter note: (4). Other rhythmic notations are seen in Example 72.

Harmonically, Anderson uses homophony, but appears more linear in style as he emphasizes the instrumental independencies of each instrument, giving special and individual attention to the typical needs and extensions of all. Low and high register instruments are written to explore the realms of possibilities.

An example of some demands required by the chorus part of *Personals*, in addition to singing, are such dramatics as spoken lines in discordant fashion shaped into the score above the narrator and orchestral part at measures 177–81, Example 73.

Sometimes the melodic and harmonic aspects become inseparable in either a polyphonic setting or in an interchange of one melody being extended from voice part to voice part, as in measures 183–187 of the same composition:

Ex. 74. *Personals*, Anderson. © 1967, T. J. Anderson, Jr. All rights reserved including the right of public performance for profit. Reprinted by permission of American Composers Alliance.

Whenever Anderson uses homophony, the fullness of sounds as reflected in the cadential progression of the harpsichord part of his *Five*

Bagatelles is typical of the possibilities. Composed for oboe, violin and harpsichord, the piece contains five movements based on dance rhythms and folk forms such as the fourth movement, entitled *Blues*. Excerpted below, the piece uses no key signature and stresses no tonal center, as its characteristic dissonances are set at its opening by minor seconds. Another composition, *Five Portraitures* for two pianos, exhibits a barless movement, entitled *Contemplation*, which has difficult rhythms and atonal harmonies (Examples 75 and 76).

Ex. 75. "Blues" from *Five Bagatelles* (Measures 1 & 2), Anderson. © 1966, T. J. Anderson. All rights reserved. Reprinted by permission of American Composers Alliance.

Ex. 76. *Contemplation from Five Portraitures*, Anderson. © T. J. Anderson, Jr. All rights reserved including the right of public performance for profit. Reprinted by permission of American Composers Alliance.

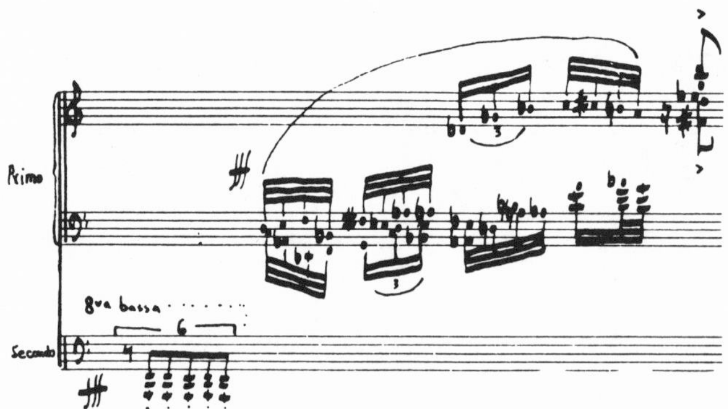

He has written piano duos and solos, chamber ensembles, chorus and orchestral pieces, many of which have been widely performed. His most important works are *Five Portraitures of Two People* for piano duo; *Squares* for orchestra; *Connections*, a fantasy for string quintet; *Rotations for band; Chamber Symphony; New Dances* for orchestra; *Classical Symphony; Six Pieces for Clarinet* and *Chamber Orchestra; Five Bagatelles for Oboe, Violin, and Harpsichord; Symphony in Three Movements; Five Etudes and a Fancy* for woodwind quintet; *Personals*, a cantata; *Rotations* for band; *In Memoriam Zack Walker*; and many others.

NOEL G. DA COSTA (1930–)

Noel Da Costa, composer-violinist, was born in Lagos, Nigeria. He was taken to the West Indies at three years of age and later to America at the age of eleven. Da Costa now resides in New York City and works as a free-lance violinist while composing, recording, concertizing and teaching at Rutgers University. Formerly a violinist in the accompanying orchestra for *Promises, Promises,* Da Costa was educated at Queens College and Columbia University. He has also been the deserving recipient of a Fulbright Scholarship to Italy where he studied with Dallapiccolo during the 1958–60 season.

A member of the Black Society of Composers, he has taught at Hampton Institute, Hunter College and Queens College. In addition, part of his time has involved concerts at Colleges and other institutions in and around New York and in the South.

Da Costa has been active in conducing Opera Ebony, the Triad Chorale, and other ensembles in several New York concerts featuring works of Black composers and of others. Now an educator at Mason Gross, he was recently a recipient of a grant from the New York Council for the Arts; his work as violinist, producer, and composer-educator continues in the professional tradition.

Noel Da Costa.

As presented in several books by Eileen Southern, Eugene Claghorn, and others, Da Costa has expanded his lists of works and his reputation is growing. His *Ceremony of Spirtuals* for choir, solo jazz sax, and soloist was described favorably when performed by the New World Symphony with Sam Rivers as saxophonist and Barbara Grant, vocalist. Held at Carnegie Hall for the 1982 Black History Week, it was well reviewed by *down beat.* He achieved excellence also in *Counterpoint* for chorus, solo quintet, and piano which was performed by the Triad Chorale's Tenth Anniversary Celebration, October 1982. The settings of Eva Jessye's *Spirit of the Lord* and Eubie Blake's *Memories of You* were sung by the Triad Chorale; *Two Songs for Julie Ju* was published in Willis Patterson's *Anthology of Art Songs*; Stanley Hall played his *In Space* for string bass at the Colloquia and Competition of 1980, Kennedy Center, Washington, D.C., while Ronald Lipscomb played his *Five Verses with Vamps* for cello. In still other concerts in the Washington, D.C. area, the Evelyn White Chorale frequently programmed his *Little Lamb* and Frances Walker, pianist, included his music in a program reviewed by the *Post News.* Da Costa was also an honoree among those composers sponsored at the AAMOA symposia throughout the United States.

His newest pieces included *Babu's Juju* (children's opera) and others from Atsoc Music. The National Association of Negro Musicians also listed as new works his *Beyond the Years* for voice and organ, *Chili-lo* prelude for organ, *Through the Valley,* and *I Have a Dream.*

His *Five Verses with Vamps* was performed by Ronald Lipscomb, cellist, and Charles Burkhart, pianist, at the Queens College Concert in 1969. Although most of his works have been composed for art music ensembles and soloists, he has recently been commissioned to write semi-jazz and rock pieces which have also been performed.

Da Costa's music moves toward all the possibilities of harmonic, melodic and rhythmic features of the contemporary era. However, definite linear qualities predominate, with intervallic tendencies planned where chords might otherwise be. Dramatic leaps compete with diatonic and chromatic devices, and twelve tone rows and their retrogrades dot the pages in daring parallels, contrary motions, discordant agreement, improvisations and other interpolations resembling architecture. Highly critical and conscientious in his projects, he proceeds scholarly toward each composition as though it were the study of life itself.

Among his works are: *Five Verses with Vamps* for cello and piano; *The Confession Stone* for soprano and ten instruments; *Extempore Blue; The Singing Tortoise* (a play for children scored for soprano, baritone, narrator and chorus, and accompanied by flute, percussion, temple blocks and bongos); and *Cikan Cimalo* for electric guitars, fender bass and percussion; *Silver-Blue* (flute); *Three Short Pieces* and others.

FREDERICK C. TILLIS (1930–)

Frederick C. Tillis, composer-performer, arranger and conductor, was born in Galveston, Texas. Having taught in Frankfort, Kentucky, where he was head of the Department of Music and professor of composition, he now serves at the University of Massachusetts. Having been educated at Wiley College and the University of Iowa, where he received the M.A. and Ph.D. degrees in composition, Tillis is a talented composer of technical strength and praiseworthy ingenuity. Widely performed and well received, his music should soon become standard repertoire in western music.

Tillis was appointed director of the 3560th Air Force Band in 1954, for which he wrote and arranged music. He has served as a teacher at Wiley College and Grambling College, and has often been invited to participate in forums and lectures as well as to conduct various ensembles. Upon such occasions, he served as guest composer at the 1967 Symposium of Contemporary Music at Illinois Wesleyan University, where his chamber works were performed, and also the Festival of Contemporary music at Spelman College in 1968, where his *Design for Orchestra No. 2* was performed by the Atlanta Symphony Orchestra with Robert Shaw as conductor. Assuming new positions at the University of Massachusetts in Amherst, he increased his experience and reputation—in administration, first as special assistant to the provost on the arts and succeeded by his present directorship of fine arts; in music, as professor of music; and in composition, as the writer of at least sixty-five compositions by 1983.

At first a jazz saxophonist active in many American traditions and performances, he has expanded his compositional trends within art music as well. Deliberately writing in a style based upon elements that are natural outgrowths of his ethnic and cultural background since 1966, "his rhythmic and some structural influences in his works reach back to Africa and include some elements of jazz. Melodic and harmonic textures reflect elements of various musics of the world, including Oriental and Western cultures."

For his works, Tillis has been honored with awards from the United Negro College Fund Fellowship and the Danforth and Rockfeller Foundations. A member of the Board of Directors for Concerts in Black and White (Boston, 1980), he has served as national chairman of the Theory Compositions section of the Music Teachers National Association. His biographical sketches have been included in works by Eileen Southern and Alice Tishler, and he has also been included in the *International Who's Who in Music* (8th Edition, 1977). Several commissions and performances were supported by Harvard University, the University of Massachusetts, Regis

Frederick Tillis.

College, the Atlanta Symphony Orchestra, Westminister College, Howard University, and others both in the States and abroad.

Featured on the AAMOA and Kennedy Center symposia held in various regions of the United States, his *Cappricio* for viola, rendered by Marcus Thompson, violist, was roundly applauded at the Kennedy Center Colloquia and Competition, January 1980. His *Brass Quintet* (published by Southern) was recorded by the New York Brass Quintet (1976 *Schwann* listing, Ser. 12066) and *Ring Shout Concerto for Percussion and Orchestra* became available through the American Composers Alliance, New York.

Tillis utilizes various source materials for content. Twelve tone composition, free composition, frequently with lyrical pantonal melodies and terse harmonic textures, as well as features from periods other than contemporary. In addition, jazz rhythms typify certain of his movements. He explore most effectively the extreme ends of instrumental resources. In addition to scoring for band, orchestra, chorus, solo voices, and chamber ensembles, he also makes use of non-conventional methods of using instruments such as the "fixed" strings of the piano (a la Cage).

Mixtures of major, minor and other chromatic and diatonic practices are employed on both traditional and non-traditional forms. In addition to regular chordal and scalewise procedures, leaps, octaves, pluckings, slaps or drumming effects, impressionistic extensions of sound and dissonances characterize his music. From the guitar-effect of the piano to the aesthetic beauty of a major chord being plucked in approximate tones against the reverberation of a glissando in motion, the unpredictable, but interesting style of Tillis resounds.

Among some of the newest pieces are: *Music for an Experimental Lab Ensemble Nos. 1, 2, 3; Poems for Piano* (1970); *One Dozen Rocks* for jazz orchestra (1971); *Three Movements for Orchestra; Three Songs; Music for Violin, Cello and Piano; Metamorphosis on a "Scheme"; Blue Stone Differencia; Music for Recorders* (1972); *Seasons* for women's chorus; *Seton Concerto for Trumpet* with jazz orchestra; *Reflections* for medium voice and piano; *The Blue Express* for jazz orchestra; *Pastorale for Wind Ensemble; Navarac* for jazz orchestra; *Niger Symphony for Chamber Orchestra* (1975); *Five Spirituals for Mixed Chorus and Brass Choir* (1976); *Secrets of the African Baobob* for jazz wind ensemble (1976); *Five Poems* for piano (1979); *Concerto for Piano and Jazz Orchestra; Three Songs* for voice and piano (Southern Pub. Com); *Phantasy* for viola and piano; *Capriccio* for viola and piano; *Spiritual Fantasies*, no. 1 for piccolo trumpet, no. 2 for string bass and piano, no. 3 for piano, four hands; *Autumn Concerto* for trumpet and jazz orchestra, (1979); *Five Spirituals* for chorus; and *Jazz Concerto* for piano (ACA); *Passacaglia for Brass Quintet; Quartet for Flute, Clarinet, Bassoon and Cello; The End of All Flesh, baritone and piano; A Prayer in Faith; Psalms, baritone and piano; Capriccio for Viola and Piano; Concert Piece for Clarinet and Piano; Overture to a Dance, band; Militant Mood for Brass Sextet; String Trio; Phantasy for Viola and Piano; Passacaglia for Organ in Baroque Style; Brass Quintet; Quintet for Four Woodwinds and Percussion; Three Movements for Piano; Motions for Trombone and Piano; Music for Alto Flute, Cello and Piano; Sequences and Burlesque, for string; Two Songs for Soprano and Piano; Freedom—Memorial for Dr. Martin Luther King, Jr., for chorus; Music for Tape Recorder No. 1; Three Plus One, for guitar, clarinet and tape; Alleluia for chorus*; and others.

Many of his compositions were recorded by Mark Custom Records/ MC1849; *Freedom* for mixed chorus, published by Southern, was recorded by Serenus; *Niger Symphony* and *Music for Violin, Cello and Piano* were also released by General and Serenus; *Quintet for Four Woodwinds and Percussion* and *Music for Alto Flute, Cello and Piano* were published by Southern. Other publications included *Jazz Theory and Improvisation* (Manual/Textbook published by Charles Hansen.)

DAVID BAKER (1931–)

David Baker, composer, conductor, author, educator and cellist, was born in Indianapolis, Indiana. He presently resides in Indiana where he teaches at Indiana University and heads the Jazz Department. He was educated at Indiana University where he received the Bachelor's and Master's degrees in music education. He has also studied with several musicians such as John Lewis, J. J. Johnson, Gunter Schuller, Murray Grodner, George Russell, Russell Brown, Thomas Beversdorf and others.

Baker has taught at Lincoln University in Missouri, the Indianapolis Public Schools and Indiana Central College. In addition, his professional experiences have included numerous tours, concerts, lectures and workshops in various countries. He has traveled extensively with Quincy Jones, and has played with other jazz groups such as Stan Kenton, Maynard Ferguson, Lionel Hampton, and the Wes Montgomery Sextet. His performances have not been restricted to jazz, for Baker has also performed with the Indiana University Philharmonic; the Indiana University Opera Orchestra, the Indiana University Wind and Brass Ensembles; the Butler

David Baker.

University Orchestra, Band and Brass Ensembles; and the Indiana Central College String Quartet.

A musical giant of great talent, Baker is competent on several instruments: piano, tuba, trombone, and bass. He has performed as soloist with the Boston Symphony and the Evansville Philharmonic. As conductor, he was invited to lead the Indianapolis Symphony & Civic Orchestras, and the Indiana University Concert Symphony Orchestra. In addition, his own groups of octet, quintet, or "ensembles" have performed extensively in concerts and on recordings.

Honors for Baker have come from the Indianapolis Jazz Club, Inc., which made him a lifetime member. He holds membership in Gamma Tau Chapter of Phi Mu Alpha Sinfonia, the Indiana Philharmonic Gold Award, and from Lenox School of Jazz and Indiana University. He has also been awarded the *down beat* New Star Award, and the Outstanding Musician Award from the National Association of Negro Musicians.

Baker's works, over 100 in number, consist of mass media types from religious to secular themes, third stream music, art music, and jazz. His works also range from orchestral ensembles to piano solos and other combinations. Baker has also authored source books on jazz improvisation and contemporary music.

His style of writing, based upon time and change in the Space Age, elect versatility and order, measured against improvisation and plan. Polymeters, tempo markings of "fast", "slow", "nonchalant", "medium blues", or "lazily", along with traditional European markings are used.

Though rhythmically interesting, Baker uses melody well. The *Cello Sonata*, for example, begins with a beautiful theme which moves in triplets toward polymetric values of meticulous intricacy. He makes use of altered tonic chords and of ninths, elevenths as well as atonalism. The opening bars of the *Sonata* are excerpted:

Ex. 77. *Sonata for Cello and Piano*, Baker. Used by permission of the composer. Now published by Associated Music.

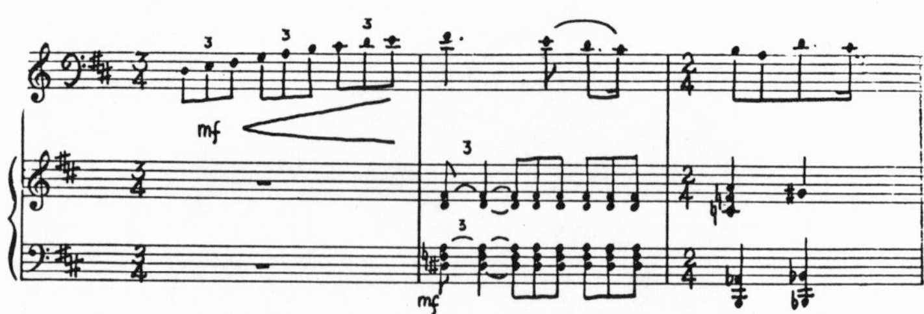

In addition to the sequences, parallelism, polytonality, polymeters, and double stops, there are lyrical melodies and large intervallic jumps and altered tones for the cellist, with challenging technical problems. The overall harmonies are traditional, as well as atonal. Some chords are composed in fourths and clusters rather than in the customary thirds. The termination of the piece consists of a D major chord, while the piano support uses polychordal features, thereby distorting the emphasis of the D major texture, as seen in the last cadence of the first movement:

Ex. 78.

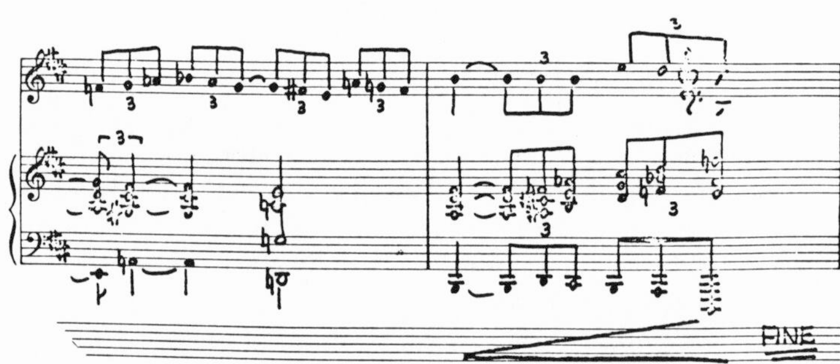

Another composition, a *Piano Sonata* dedicated to Natalie Hinderas, concert pianist, is composed of three movements entitled *Black Art, A Song After Paul Lawrence Dunbar*, and *Coltrane* (reference to jazz musician). The traditional form of the sonata becomes real to the trained listener in that the first movement follows the conventional "sonata-allegro" form while the titles captivate and invite attention with elements of blues, jazz and classicism. The use of octaves, chromatics, glissandos, imitation, and the outer extremities of the keyboard together with dynamic contrasts are used in challenging concensus of atonalism, polymeters and cross rhythms. The opening bars and measures 19–20 of the first movement are shown in Example 79 (now published by Alfred).

The second movement is based on the same material as *A Song*, from his cycle of *Five Songs for Soprano and Piano*. Inspired by the Black poetry of Paul Lawrence Dunbar, the vocal melody is simulated in the right hand of the piano version in an ultra-lyrical style. Both versions are shown in Example 80.

Co-author of *The Composer Speaks* (Scarecrow Press, 1977), he was honored by a commission from J. C. Penny to write *Soul of '76* for stage band and jazz-blues-rock ensembles in celebration of J. C. Penney's Bicentennial

Ex. 79. *Piano Sonata*, Baker. Used by permission of the composer.

Ex. 80. *A Song* (vocal art song), Baker. Used by permission of the composer.

Piano Sonata Movement.

Musical Celebrations. He was one of six composers chosen for the 1976 event. He was honored by the New York Philharmonic with performances of *Kosbro*, January 1976 and *Cello Concert* in 1977; his *Early in the Morning* and *A Good Assassination Should be Quiet* were published in Willis Patterson's *Anthology*. In addition, the *Sonata* for cello and piano (1973) was recorded on the Columbia Records Black Composers Series and was also excerpted for Silver Burdett's recording, *Afro-American Music and Its Roots*. Likewise, the *Sonatina for Tuba and String Quartet* was recorded by Golden Crest Records (Schwann, 1976); *Sonata* for piano and string quartet, by AAMOA; and *Honestly* (Russ-Hix Music) by Milestone Records on the *George Russell* album (1975).

Baker, an awardee of the National Music Awards, 1976, was cited in the area of blues and jazz as a musician-composer and educator. He was announced as a Master Musician for the Bennington College Jazz Laboratory (*down beat*, April 22, 1976) and his compositions continued to receive widespread performances—at the AAMOA symposia, at a Fisk University Festival of the 1970s (*Now That He Is Safely Dead* and *Dream Boogie*, by the Jubilee Singers), and others.

Composer of over one hundred works, his pieces were advertised regularly in the *down beat* magazines. From the 1970s and 1980s were his *Jazz Improvisation*, "a comprehensive method for all players"; *Advanced Composition* "with a ninety minute rhythm section play-a-long cassette" described as "truly a challenge"; *Jazz Styles and Analysis*, as a "must for all trombonists," and others (James Abersold or Maher publications). Baker also edited many of the transcribed works listed in the *down beat/Maher* advertisements.

Among the numerous works of Baker are the following: *Dream Boogie*, for chorus; *Black America—to the Memory of Martin Luther King Jr.; Black Thursday* (jazz ensemble); *But I am a Worm* (mixed voices); *Catalyst (jazz ensemble); Deliver My Soul (voices, dancers and jazz ensemble); A dollar Short and a Day Late (jazz ensemble); The Dude (cello and piano); Hymn and Deviation (brass, quartet); I Am Poured Out Like Water (male voices and strings); Jazz Mass (voices and jazz septet); Catholic Mass for Peace (chorus and jazz ensemble); Le Chat Qui Pêche (jazz ensemble); Concerto (violin and jazz ensemble); John Coltrane in Memoriam (jazz ensemble); Lutheran Mass (Introit soprano and piano); Masque of the Red Death (unfinished ballet); Passion (jazz ensemble); Quartet No. 1 (strings); Sonata (violin and piano); Sonata (cello and piano); Splooch (jazz ensemble); That's the Way, Lord Nelson (trumpet, saxophone and double bass); Verism (jazz ensemble); Thou Dost Lay Me in the Dust of Death (voices and strings); Abyss (soprano and piano); Afro-Cuban Suite (band); The Screamin' Meemies (jazz ensemble); Le Roi (jazz ensemble); Soul on Ice (jazz ensemble); Al-ki-hol (jazz ensemble); All the Ends of the Earth Shall Remember (mixed voices and string orchestra); Ballads (saxophone, horn and violin and cello); Beatitudes (chorus, narrator, dances and orchestra); Romanza and March (three trombones)*; many others. Baker has also written publications of *Jazz Improvisation; Developing Improvisational Technique, based on the Lydian Concept; Developing Improvisational Facility with II-V Progression; Developing Improvisational Facility with the Turnback* and others are in progress.

COLERIDE-TAYLOR PERKINSON (1932–)

Coleridge-Taylor Perkinson, composer, conductor and educator, was born in New York. He was educated at New York University and the Manhattan School of Music (where he received the Bachelor and Master of Music degrees). He also did further work at the Berkshire Music Center in choral conducting, and in orchestral conducting at the Mozarteum, the Netherlands Radio Union and the Hilversum. His wide experience in compositional studies has included Vittorio Giannini, Charles Mills and Earl Kim as his teachers.

As an educator, Perkinson has served as music director of the Professional Children's School and as a faculty member of Manhattan School of Music and Brooklyn College. He has also held the positions of assistant conductor of the Dessoff Choirs and conductor of the Brooklyn Community Symphony Orchestra.

Coleridge-Taylor Perkinson continued to conduct, arrange, compose, teach, and lecture during the last decade. He participated in several events held in Washington, D.C., as lecturer at the Howard University session on the business of music, at a "Meet the Composer" session of the 1980 Colloquia and Competition as well as at subsequent panel forums sponsored by the Committee on Cultural Diversity in Performing Arts at Kennedy Center.

His well-conceived compositions achieved recognition and were well received at the Kennedy Center, especially his *Scherzo* as performed by Cecil Lytle at the Colloquia and Competition Concert in 1980 and by Raymond Jackson at both the Kennedy Center and Peoples Congregational Church in 1982. His music was heard at the various regional symposia sponsored by AAMOA, New York's Music Educators Choral Clinic, and in both art music and jazz settings. His *Toccata* for piano has enjoyed several performances by this author.

Coleridge-Taylor Perkinson.

In New York, Perkinson directed the popular *Lena Horne* musical of 1982, conducted the musical, *Ceremonies in Dark Old Men* given by the Negro Ensemble, and additionally, conducted the New World Symphony and other orchestras and arranged for various types of music including film scoring and jazz arrangements.

His *Sub-Structure* was recorded by Strata-East and his *Child's Grace* and *Melancholy* were published in Willis Patterson's *Anthology of Art Songs*. He also wrote *Toccata* for piano, stage scores for *Great MacDaddy* and *Lusitanian Bogey Attitudes* for tenor and piano, film scores for *A Warm December* and *Buck and the Preacher* (in which Sidney Poitier and Harry Belafonte starred).

A composer of many styles, his technical and demanding traits are partially seen in the measures 213–215 of *Fredome-Freedom*, one of his most popular works for chorus and piano (Example 81).

As evidenced by the various titles and commissions which he has received from the Arthur Mitchell Dance Company, the Lou Rawls Special, the Barbara McNair Television Show, the Martin Luther King Film Production, the Jayjen Productions and U.S.I.A., Perkinson has undertaken many challenges in composition. His skill has also been exhibited on recordings with Donald Byrd, Max Roach and others. Of his most outstanding works are those for ballet, chorus and orchestral ensembles, films, theatre, vocal and piano music.

His style ranges from the conventional to the unconventional, with both tonal and atonal examples of writing being portrayed to fair advantage. A typical feature is to use extremities of sound or of widely placed

Ex. 81. *Fredome-Freedom,* Perkinson. © Copyright 1970 Tosci. Permission granted by the publisher, Belwin-Mills.

accompaniments against closely woven voices. Also characteristic are blocks of sound (as in various representations within the *Fredome-Freedom* work for chorus and piano), polymeters and sectionalism. Perkinson also uses approximations of pitches, glissandos, syncopations and other technically difficult idioms of tonal and polytonal varieties.

Among his compositions are: *String Quartet* No. 1—*Calvary; Variations and Fugue* on *The Ash Grove* for violin and piano; *Sonatina for Percussion; Piano Sonata; Psalm Twenty Three; Fredome-Freedom; Songs to Spring; Thirteen Love Songs in Jazz Settings; Concerto for Viola and Orchestra; Grass Poem* for piano, strings and percussion; *Ode to Otis; Man Better Man* (w/Erroll Hill); and others.

CARMAN MOORE (1936–)

Carman Moore, composer, author, lecturer, music critic, and conductor, was born in Lorain, Ohio, near Cleveland. Reared in Elyria, Ohio, he gained his basic education in nearby public schools before gaining entry into college in 1954.

Currently a teacher at his own private studio in New York City, he also lectures at Manhattan College, Yale University and other institutions, writes articles on music subjects for the *Village Voice* newspaper and served as president of the Society of Black Composers. Once a student at Oberlin Conservatory, Moore graduated from Ohio State University and attended the Juilliard School of Music where he earned the Master's degree. He was a student of Hall Overton, Vincent Persichetti and Luciano Berio.

An esteemed composer of over forty pieces, and one who possesses talent for literary as well as compositional writing, he has worked as a music critic not only for the familiar *Village Voice*, but for *Vogue, Saturday Review, New York Times, Collier's Encyclopedia,* and others. In addition to the previous listings, he has worked at Manhattan College, Brooklyn College, and at the Harlem Educational Project, among other institutions.

Moore has received commissions from the New York Philharmonic for *Wildfires* and *Field Songs* which *Hi Fidelity* (May 1975) reviewed as a "blend of modern jazz improvisation, tone clusters . . . polyrhythmic and polytonal clashes . . . and motifs which reflect Moore's own Afro-American heritage. . . . " while *Musical America* (1975) typed the premier of the work as a "fascinating blend of modern jazz improvisation. . . . " The second movement was recorded by Silver Burdett in an album entitled *Afro-American Music and Its Roots*, and offered with an accompanying booklet for children's directed listening.

Moore, whose works were represented in Washington during the International Festival of Contemporary Music in 1968, is an award-winning composer of chamber music, theatrical and vocal works. Commissions have come from the New York City Ballet, the Anna Sokolow Dance Company and from other festivals and institutions who recognize his musical talents.

Moore termed his *Gospel Fuse* as "really a church service" and as "a 22-minute atomic age gospel cantata." Premiered by the San Francisco Symphony Orchestra the night before his *Wildfires* was premiered by the New York Philharmonic, he set a record for himself and the compendium of his works. *Gospel Fuse*, reviewed in *Newsweek* (February 3, 1975), stated that "Moore heard the San Francisco Symphony, under the fiery leadership of Seiji Ozawa, rip through his *Gospel Fuse*, an ambitious uneasy blending of dissonant symphonics and Black gospel singing. With the applause still ringing in his ears, he jetted back to New York to hear Pierre Boulez and the New York Philharmonic give a steely, arresting performance the following night of his *Wildfires* and *Field Songs*, a work of equal complexity." Consisting of the orchestra itself used as a "congregation," a soprano sax as "the Preacher" and a quartet of "women gospel singers," it was conceived in a two-movement form entitled *The Dream* and *Love Sermons*, whose original libretto is comprised of original sermonettes of driving verve which have special meaning to the Pan-African world and the twentieth century.

Carman Moore.

Other commissions given Moore were for *Catwalk* and *Saratoga Festival Overture* by the New York Ballet, first performed by the Buffalo Philharmonic Orchestra and the Interplayers with Moore as conductor; *The Great American Nebula*, a cantata for choir, band, strings, synthesizer, gospel singer, and narrator, for the Elyria, Ohio Bicentennial, 1976; *For Movements for a Five-Toed Dragon* for the American Symphony, written for Chinese instruments, jazz quintet, and orchestra, 1976; and others. A grant winner, he has accepted awards from the Guggenheim Foundation, from Creative American Music Center, and others.

Youth in a Merciful House is recorded on Folkways 33902 and Desto; *Wildfires*, excerpted to accompany the children's booklet, is recorded by Silver Burdett, 1976; others are *Crossfires* for piano and taped piano; *Flight Piece* for flute and piano (Music in Our Time Series); *Piano Sonata* (premiered at the Juilliard School of Music by David del Tredici and recorded by Phillips); *Sonata for Cello and Piano in Two Parts, Drum Major; African Tears* for mixed media of actors, dancer, eleven instruments, and choir (1971); *Oh Lord, Thou Hast Searched Me; How Long, Oh Lord* (motet); *Behold the Lamb of God* for voice; *The Illuminated Working Man* for African xylophone, Moog synthesizer, four cellos, exotic flutes, saxophones, guitar, electric bass, dance; the Guggenheim funded *Museum Piece* and *Music for Film* (1975), and others published by Sweet Jam Music, New York. His compositional talent is expanded to include rock music. He wrote the words to more than a dozen rock songs, including *Rock 'n Roll Outlaws*, on the *Foghat* album.

JOHN CARTER (1937–   )

John Carter, a talented pianist-composer, was born in St. Louis, Missouri. Traveling to New York where he established significant advancements in his writing and performance opportunities, he later moved to Washington in 1968, upon acceptance of the honor of composer-in-residence with the Washington National Symphony Orchestra. He received his education at Oberlin University, and received grants from the Rockefeller Foundation, the American Music Center and the ASCAP organization.

Once a teacher at the new Federal City College in Washington, D.C., Carter became recognized as an early entrant into the mainstream of American composers when his works were performed by concert artists such as Betty Allen, Martina Arroyo, Leontyne Price, George Shirley, Adele Addison, William Warfield and Julius Katchen. In addition to the *Requiem Seditiosam* which both he and Katchen have performed, his orchestral ver-

John Carter.

sion has enjoyed a performance by the Washington Symphony with Howard Mitchell as conductor. The same piece had already received its premiere at the Philharmonic Hall at the Lincoln Center in New York City. In 1967, an entire program devoted to Carter's works was given at the New York Public Library-Museum of Performing Arts at Lincoln Center, which included his *Cantata*, a published work. The reviews were favorable.

The New York Times' Raymond Ericson wrote of his *Saetas Profanas* as being as "fine as anything . . . an effective vocalise." Of the same work, the Hagerstown, Maryland, *Evening News* and the Delta County *Independent* of Colorado termed it "A tremendous offering" and as having "excited everyone." Other reviews have found his works "impelling," "breathtaking *tours de force*," "beautiful, delicate and dramatic," and "Sensitive lyricism and deeply poetic." Carter also received complimentary reviews of his own piano playing. As a pianist he won competitions in many cities throughout the United States.

Composed of both traditional and contemporary elements, his compositions have been written with an emphasis upon melodic and harmonic imitation, thematic interchange and motive relationships which bridge polytonalities and tonal structures rather than atonal examples effected by the times. At intervals, his full chords, chromatics, extended intervals, clustered tones, dissonances and consonances together obscure the major or minor feeling only temporarily. Chords built in fourths, fifths, and other unusual combinations prevail in alternation with the traditional. Melodic, rhythmic and harmonic repetitions are used as effective descriptions of the subject.

His sensitivity in writing provides a just presentation of the instruments in his list of works, a freshness of style and a beckoning of the lively aspects at his disposal. Both emotional and serious in content, Carter has borrowed from the blues (especially for the *Valses*), the spirituals and from the era in which he lives in order to mold his compositions.

His *Cantata* for voice and piano shows his style of simplicity of ideas with a complex foundation of techniques discussed above. Containing five parts or movements, it consists of a prelude, rondo, recitative, air and toccata, and shows a developing style mixed with either no meter at all, or with polymeters ranging from 8/8 to 5/4. Carefully marked with dynamic extremes and directions for performance, the piece makes use of barless measures, improvisational effects producing a flow of interesting rhythms from the simple to the complex. The work, excerpted in Example 82, gives a feeling of direction and character:

Ex. 82. *Cantata* by John Carter. Prelude and Rondo movements, first measure of each. © Copyright 1964 by Southern Music Publishing Co., Inc. International copyright secured. All rights reserved including the right of public performance for profit. Used by permission.

Immediately after the death of his mother, he resigned from Federal City College (now UDC) and mysteriously disappeared, leaving no clue to his whereabouts. Before that time of the mid-70's, Carter had written the following works: *Cantata; Epigrams* (ballet); *Requiem Seditiosam; In Memoriam, Medgar Evers* for orchestra; *Valses Pour Les Danseurs Noirs* (Waltzes for Black Dancers and piano); *Saetas Profanas; Japanese Poems; Emblemes* for violin; *Piano Concerto* and others.

OLLY WILSON (1937–)

Olly Wilson, composer, bass-violist, was born in St. Louis, Missouri. He attended Washington University in St. Louis, received the Master of Music degree from the University of Illinois and the doctorate from the University of Iowa. As a pupil of Robert Wykes, Robert Kelley and Phillip Bezanson, he studied composition and electronic work at the Studio for Experimental Music at the University of Illinois. After teaching at Florida A & M, he began work at the University of California in Berkeley.

Wilson has performed on the bass with several orchestras, including the St. Louis Philharmonic Orchestra, the St. Louis Summer Players and the Cedar Rapids Symphony Orchestra. As a teacher, he has instructed at Florida A & M University, West Virginia University and the University of California at Berkeley. A recipient of the 1968 Dartmouth Arts Council Prize, he was also awarded the prize at the first International Competition for Electronic Compositions for his work *Cetus*. In 1973, Wilson studied African music on a Guggenheim grant.

Olly Wilson.

Orchestras such as the Dallas Symphony Orchestra, the Minneapolis Symphony Orchestra and the Atlanta Symphony have performed his works. A composer of chamber works, vocal works, orchestral and electronic works, his compositions have also received numerous hearings. Some of his pieces were rendered at the Music Educators' National Conference Black Music Workshop in Chicago in 1970, and at the 1967 Contemporary Music Festival in Oberlin, Ohio.

His music and academic achievements have also brought him such honors as commissions from the Oakland Symphony Orchestra in both 1973 and 1980, the San Francisco Chamber Music Society in 1976, the Boston Symphony Orchestra in 1981, the National Endowment for the Arts in 1976, and Pitzer College. In addition to the above performances of his works, the Dallas, Baltimore, St. Louis, Denver, Minneapolis, Detroit, and Atlanta Symphony Orchestras also engaged him for performances of his works. Other prizes have come from the Guggenheim Fellowship in 1977–78 (in addition to the one awarded for his African study trip to West Africa in 1971–72); and from the American Academy of Arts and Letters and the National Institute of Arts and Letters in 1974 for "outstanding achievement in music composition."

He was also offered the position of visiting artist at the American Academy in Rome during part of 1978, and was placed as semifinalist in the Friedheim Award for orchestral composition. Clearly a scholar, he has published several artices on African and Afro-American music (*Perspectives of New Music*, IX. No. 1, Fall/Winter, 1970; *The Black Perspective in Music*, I, No. 1, Spring, 1973 and 1974); on Schoenberg and on contemporary music in general (*American Organist*). Wilson's career is further outlined by Raoul Abdul, David Baker, Dominique de Lerma, Edward Jablonski, Eileen Southern, and by Christine E. Oliver (*Selected Orchestral Works of T. J. An-*

derson, Arthur Cunningham, Talib Hakim and Olly Wilson, unpublished doctoral dissertation, Florida State University, 1978).

His music has enjoyed a great many fine performances during the last decade and mirrors his knowledge of jazz, which he practiced at an early age as pianist and bassist. His *Piece for Piano and Tape* was presented at the 1980 Kennedy Center Colloquia and Competition and other works were included in the popular AAMOA regional symposiums held throughout the United States from 1980 to 1982. His art song, *Wry Fragments*, was compiled into the Willis Patterson *Anthology*; the Columbia Black Composers Series of 1975 contained his *Akwan* for piano, amplified string, and orchestra; *Cetus*, the electronic award winner, was recorded on Turnabout; the Oberlin choir recorded his *In Memorium Martin Luther King* on Century Records in 1969 with Robert Fountain, conductor ; *Piece for Four* was recorded by Robert Willoughby and others on CRI, 1971; *Echoes* by Phillip Tehfeldt, clarinetist, and *Sometimes* by tenor William Brown on CRI (each 1977); and *Piano Piece* by Natalie Hinderas on Desto/DC 7102–03, in 1970.

The listings of his works are one for orchestra, premiered by the Boston Symphony Orchestra (with Ozawa conducting) in 1984; *Black Martyrs*, 1972; *Spirit Song* for soprano solo, double chorus, and orchestra, 1973; *Echoes* for solo clarinet and electronic tape, 1974–75; *Sometimes* for tenor and electronic tape, 1976; *Trio* for piano, violin and cello, 1977; *Reflections* for orchestra, 1978; *Expansions* for organ, 1979; *Lumina* for orchestra, 1981; and others.

Wilson is familiar with traditional forms. His music, however, speaks of the present. In his use of complex rhythms, atonal harmonies, intervallic concepts and cacophonous undertakings, he dwells on penetrating settings of contemporary moods.

Among his works are *Prelude and Line Study* for woodwind quartet; *Trio for Flute, Cello and Piano; Two Dutch Poems; Structure for Orchestra; String Quartet; Wry Fragments, Tenor and Percussion Ensemble; Violin Sonata; Gloria for a cappella chorus; Dance Suite; Soliloquy* for bass viol; *And Death Shall Have No Dominion* for tenor and percussion ensemble; *Sextet; Three Movements for Orchestra; Chanson Innocent* for contralto and two bassoons; *Dance Music II; Piece for Four; Biography* (Leroi Jones); *Cetus; In Memoriam Martin Luther King, Jr.*, for chorus and electronic sounds; *Piano Piece* for piano and electronic sounds; *Orchestral Piece* and others.

TALIB HAKIM (STEPHEN CHAMBERS) (1940–1988)

Talib Hakim, a composer born in Asheville, North Carolina, moved to New Haven, after having been educated at the Manhattan School of Music, at the New York College of Music and the New School for Social Research, and after studying privately with Robert Starer, William Sydeman, Hall Overton, David Reck, Morton Feldman, Chou Wen-Chung, Charles Whittenberg and Ornette Coleman.

His works have enjoyed various performances throughout the United States, but mostly in New York City. From 1965 to the present time, his works have been presented on *Music in Our Time* over the YMHA radio station at the ASCAP Composers' Showcase in 1965 in a joint concert with the Ornette Coleman Trio-Quartet and the Philadelphia Woodwind Quintet in 1967, to mention a few. A composer worth noting, his music stands out as innovative and avant-garde.

Chambers served as lecturer and panelist on various occasions, such as the Music Workshop in Harlem in 1968, and at Hofstra University in 1968. He also served as conductor-panelist at other programs and conferences. Other honors have been received from ASCAP. He was a co-founder and first vice-president of the Society of Black Composers, a group of New York composers. Chambers wrote a book of first poems, released by Fro-Arts, and generally maintained a level of continuous involvement in the field of fine music.

Of his music, he had this to say: "I write Black contemporary music in all musical idioms and forms". Chambers used elements from rock to art music in contemporary techniques to create a spontaniety of style and imagination. Basically a believer in the fact that music must bear likeness to the lifestyles of Blacks and their environment, his music bears slight similarities to a jazz format. Although various linear characteristics punctuate his works, the main emphasis is intervallic construction with total "sound image."

Sponsored at the Kennedy Center "Meet the Composer" forum held in conjunction with the Colloquia and Competition in 1980, and featured with other composers at the Concordia College Festival of Black Music, he also achieved the following: his *Sound-Gone* was recorded by Natalie Hinderas on Desto as were his *Visions of Ishwara* for orchestra by Columbia Records, his *Placements* by Folkways and his *Shapes for Orchestra* by Desto on *Black Composer in America*. Still other honors consisted of the performance of his music on the regional symposia in the United States. His educational duties were correlated with his teach-composing and arranging of music, as well as his performing jazz and other art styles of the twentieth century.

Among his compositions are the following: *Elements* for violin, viola, flute, clarinet, cello, piano, glass and bamboo, winds and chimes; *Quote-Unquote* for bass-baritone, oboe, trumpet, 2 percussion; *Sound-gone* for piano; *Roots and Other Things; Moments; Contours; Shapes for Chamber Orchestra; Titles*, for woodwind quartet; *Portraits* for alto flute, bass clarinet, 3 percussion and piano; *Three Play Short Five* for double bass, percussion, bass clarinet; *Four* for clarinet, trumpet, trombone and piano; *Encounter; Six Players and a Voice; Duo* for flute and clarinet; *Song-Short; Sketches* for brass quintet; *Sound-Images* for 3 percussion, string bass, 3 brass, 6 female voices; *Inner-Sections*; and others.

Selected Composers from "Now": The Space Age Generation

ROGER D DICKERSON (1934–)

Roger Dickerson, composer, lecturer, and educator, was born in New Orleans. A product of Dillard College (Bachelor of Arts degree) who attended as a scholarship student and graduate with cum laude status in 1955, he also studied at Indiana University where he received the Master of Music degree in music composition in 1957, and at the Akademie für Musik und Darstellende Kunst in Vienna, Austria. Among his teachers were Miriam Panalle, pianist, who gave him foundation enough to establish himself as a jazz pianist and early accompanist of such musicians as Joe Turner and Guitar Slim while yet a student at Dillard. His teachers at the Akademie were Karl Schiske and Alfred Uhl.

Dickerson has become known as a capable educator, author, conductor, consultant, and performing musician both in the United States and abroad. Hired as Adjunct Professor at Southern University and Xavier University since 1979, he also became Program Associate/Consult in Humanities (Institute for Services to Education in Washington, D.C.) and music editor for three books on humanities produced by I.S.E., and was invited to many lectures, workshops, and conducting engagements throughout the United States. He has also made a number of appearances on radio and television, both as critic and lecturer and as interviewer discussing his work. At least twenty-one such documentaries and interviews have been listed which were produced in New Orleans, Washington, D.C., Tennessee, and many other states, the most famous of which was the discussion of his *New Orleans Concerto* for piano and orchestra profiled in a 60-minute film and aired on national television in February of 1978. Produced by filmmaker Jim Hinton of New York, it also featured Leon Bates as pianist preparing for a premier performance of the work.

An excellent performer, he has played in the French Quarter of New Orleans and traveled with various groups on tour. He has also given many stage appearances on lyceum programs throughout the United States, worked in several recording sessions, and while stationed in Heidelberg, Germany, also performed in and wrote and arranged for the USAEUR Headquarters Band. Rhodes Spedale (*Musicmakers*, June 1982) described his pianism as having "more than a trace of Errol Garner in his stylings and with a modicum of Oscar Peterson."

Roger D. Dickerson.

Twice a Fulbright Fellow who expanded his music composition experiences in Austria from 1959 to 1962, he was given fellowships from the John Hay Whitney Foundation in 1964, the National Endowment in 1979, and the Marcus-Christian Award from the University of New Orleans in 1979. He was also honored with annual ASCAP Awards from 1978 to 1982; the first Louis Armstrong Award by N.O.R.D. of New Orleans in 1981 (as well as one given by the Armstrong Cultural Foundation in 1977); special citation for creative work from the City Council of New Orleans; National Distinguished Achievement Award in the Arts given by the Links' 21st National Assembly in Chicago, 1978; the Key to the City of Austin, 1978; Bicentennial Certificate awarded by the New Orleans Bicentennial Commission, 1977; Citation of Achievement and Key to the City of New Orleans, 1977; Outstanding Musicianship Trophy awarded by the Masons of New Orleans, 1977; and a plaque from Jarvis Christian College in 1976. Dickerson was also honored with other composers who had their compositions played at the Kennedy Center during the 1980–82 Symposia and at the AAMOA Symposia held throughout the United States.

Honors notwithstanding, it was as a composer that he perhaps received the most publicity and praise. A very significant and moving force during this part of the century, he has stood for excellence and exceptional energy in composition. His composition have been performed in many settings. In 1964, the New Orleans Philharmonic Symphony Orchestra performed his *Concert Overture for Orchestra* with Werner Torkanowsky as conductor; his song for soprano and piano, *The Negro Speaks of Rivers*, was featured on NET's "Black Journal" in a 1969 Black Culture special; the New Orleans Symphony, which commissioned Dickerson to write a work in tribute to the late Louis Armstrong, premiered the composition (*A Musical Service for Louis*—a requiem) on March 7, 1972, and thereafter programmed it in Texas, Alabama, and St. Louis; and the Symphony of the New World performed the requiem in 1973 with Leonard de Paur as conductor. His piano *Sonatina* was used in the Kennedy Center Symposia of 1982; the New Orleans Orchestra also played his *Orpheus and his Slide Trombone*, a twenty-three-minute work for narrator, trombone quartet, and orchestra with actor Roscoe Browne as narrator; and the New Orleans Bicentennial Commission and the New Orleans Chapter of Links, Inc. offered one of his largest commissions for the completion of the *New Orleans Concerto* for piano and orchestra.

Reviews of various presentations offer insight into the receptivity and revelations of the music. Joel Simpson wrote very favorably about his *Musical Service for Louis* (*Gambit Newspaper*, May 30–June 5, 1981), which he termed "Symphony in Black" because of the predominance of grief, inner meditations, and characteristic "interiority." Simpson felt that Dickerson intertwined the instrumental techniques with the emotions being portrayed and that separate melodic lines in juxtaposition to each other expressed two different aspects of that somberness—read "as a parable of a mind's struggle with grief." Rhodes Spedale (*Musicmakers*, June 1982) examined both the man and his music and determined that the essence of his music was in the "personal expression which" helps define his music, that "he encompasses and exemplifies the best of many possible worlds" and that "His compositions . . . are starkly realistic with abstract overtones abounding in fascinating musical ideas." Lon Tuck of the *Washington Post* (Feb. 28, 1982) discussed the numerous performances with Dickerson's music has enjoyed and furthermore characterized it as combining materials of classical music with jazz, and the *Piano Concerto* as having "fresh and engaging variation on the lean and kinetic three-movement . . . 20th-century concerto format" and as having "originality, both dramatic and lyric." Ken Scarbrough pointed out the aspects of humility, piety, and the human spirit reflected in the music (*Scholastic*, Vol. 122, No. 8, April 1981).

Dickerson himself feels that his work was an expression of inner devotion and freedom and that "The only real value we can place on music is the degree to which it expresses the soul of man." Cathy Trione quotes Dickerson as emphasizing improvisation in his music by "moving about in the oral tradition with freedom . . . " Dickerson also apparently felt that the return to his New Orleans roots consummated the merging of both his jazz and classical heritages.

Roscoe Browne called Dickerson one with "passionate intellect"; Hollie West of the *Washington Post* used "outstanding" and "a new kind of composer" to describe the "authentic step toward integrating jazz and classical elements"; *Saturday Review* commented that " . . . Dickerson typifies a new strain. . . . "; and *Times Picayune* noted that his "honesty is rugged. Though the composer uses elements of popular music—spiritual-based blues, swing and jazz—at various places in the score, his technique is sophisticated and his textures thick. . . . " Other adjectives such as "confidently written," "positive impact," "uncommon gifts" appear in articles of other writers.

A member of ASCAP since 1965, he has shown prolificity in the development of various works, some of which are as published by Southern Music, New York: *Sonatina for Piano*, 1980 (chosen piece for piano competition); *Ten Concert Pieces* for beginning string players, 1977; and *A Musical Service for Louis* (requiem), 1973; others under contract for publication or rental by Southern: *New Orleans Concerto—rental; Orpheus an' His Slide Trombone*—rental; *Concert Overture* for orchestral—rental; *Quintet for Wind Instruments; String Quartet; Essay for Band; and Movement for Bb Trumpet and Piano*. Another work is *Chorale Prelude* on "Das Neugeborne Kindelein," 1956 for organ. A recording of his *Dickerson Strut* appears on Kon-Ti records with trumpeter Teddy Riley. A film documenting both his life and works is available: A Discussion Guide for the *New Orleans Concerto* Film, from the Institute for Services to education, Washington, D.C., 1978.

WILLIAM S. FISCHER (1935–)

Born in Shelby, Mississippi, William Fischer was reared in Jackson and New Orleans. He has excelled in the art of composition on various levels of commercial and artistic realms of communication. A jazz clarinetist as well as educator, arranger, and composer, he is a well-qualified graduate of Xavier University in New Orleans (where he earned the Bachelor of Science degree) and of Colorado College (Master of Arts degree). He has also done further study at the Academy of Music in Vienna, Austria.

Brilliantly exhibiting talents of two worlds while also serving as educator and conductor, Fischer has been awarded many grants for his dedication and outstanding achievements. For his European study, he was awarded the Fulbright and the Akademischer Austauskienst and Austrian Government grants; he was also granted awards from the Rockefeller Foundation, the Edgar Stern Family Fund, the National Endowment, and the Council on the Arts. In addition, Fischer has been invited as guest conductor in several cities, including Washington, D.C. where he conducted the Youth Symphony Orchestra in a rendition of his *Experience in E*.

As educator, Fisher has worked in several positions, beginning with his own alma mater, Xavier University, where he was associate professor (1962–66), thereafter followed by lecturer status and both Newport College and Cardiff College (1966), and in New York public schools (since 1967). In addition, he had become his own publisher (Ready Productions), served as music director of Atlantic Records (1968–1970), and as composer-arranger for many productions such as for Novella Nelson who recorded on Arcana Records. His *Omen* (Arcana) contains *Omen, Part Two Circle Suite*, and *The Trancelike State of Creating Music*.

Jacqueline Trescott, a *Washington Post* critic, described Fischer's music as being "devoted to the American idiom in music" and as being "jazz-influenced." Certain of his compositions showing various styles and combinations of media are *A Quiet Movement* for orchestra (1967, recorded on Desto DC 7107); *Introduction and Song, Baptismal* for two horns, two violas, cello, and piano; the opera, *Jesse Or the Rejection* (both in the Library of Congress and available through Ready Productions); *The Gospel Spirit* (available by Cimino, distributors—for voice); *Circles; Time I* for saxophone, viola, cello, percussion, and tape; *Batucada Fantastica* for two tape recorders and two percussionists; *Gift of Lesbos* for cello, piano, and tape recorder; and numerous others listed by the Howard Ethnic Center, including operatic forms, orchestral music, electronic music, solo and ensemble instrumental music and vocal music forms.

JOHN ELWOOD PRICE (1935–)

John Price, composer, arranger, coach, educator, director, lecturer, was born in Tulsa, Oklahoma. After beginning his first formal study of piano with his own parents, Price attended the Tulsa public schools. Concentrating on piano and composition, he received his Bachelor of Music from Lincoln University, Jefferson City, Missouri, in 1953, and later earned the Master of Music degree in composition from the University of Tulsa in 1963. He also studied at Washington University in St. Louis, Missouri, from 1967 to 1968. Among his teachers were Bala Rozsa, Robert Wykes, Paul

Pisk, Harold Blumenfeld, O. A. Fuller, Gwendolyn Belcher, Horace Mitchell, and David Baker.

From 1964 to 1974, Price served as chairman of the Department of Music and Fine Arts at Florida Memorial College in Miami; he taught at Eastern Illinois University from 1974 to 1981, at which time he became composer-in-residence at Tuskegee Institute, Alabama, as a Portia Washington Fellow. He has held other posts such as staff composer and pianist-vocal coach for the Karamu Theater in Ohio; military service status (1959–61); minister of music at Vernon A.M.E. Church in Tulsa and music director for "Jamaica" (the AMS Players of Atlanta with which he toured Europe in 1963).

Price has been awarded several honors, among which were the Ford Foundation Study Grant (1967), the Phelps-Stokes Research and Scholar Exchange Grant, the Eastern Illinois University Research Council Grant (1975), and the Illinois Arts Council Completion Grant (1969). He has been honoredwith listings in the *Composers of the America*, v. 19 (published by OAS); *Contemporary American Composers*, edited by Hugh-William Jacobi (1975); *Black American Composers* by Alice Tischler; and the Greenwood *Dictionary of Black Music* by Eileen Southern. Still other prizes were the status of composer-in-residence at Florida Memorial College (1969–74); the Golden Apple Award from Florida Memorial College in 1972; the Outstanding Educator Award of 1971; the Distinguished Faculty Award from Eastern Illinois University in 1979; and commissions from Boston Avenue Methodist Church of Tulsa for "Litany for Seven Memories," scored for dancers, speakers, and soloists; and others.

John Price.

His compositions have been praised and well graded for their brilliance and originality of style and content. They have been widely performed by the Contemporary Chamber Ensemble at Rutgers; by the Oakland Youth Symphony of Oakland, California; by the Society of Black Composers at Carnegie Hall; and by William Warfield at Indiana University and the Auburn City Commission. His music has also been performed at Eastern Illinois, Tuskegee Institute, and a various centers throughout the United States. Entire programs have been devoted to his music at Tuskegee, at Auburn, Alabama, and at other locations. His music was among those works selected for the NANM and Black Colloquium Competitions.

In March 1982, Tuskegee Institute announced that Price wrote three pieces commemorating the one-hundredth anniversary of Tuskegee Institute: *Booker T. Washington: Address Delivered at the Dedication of the Robert Gould Shaw Monument in Boston, May 31, 1897, For the Union Dead*, and *We Wear the Mask*. In them, he showed an affinity for the deep historical heritage of a people marked by dignity and strength. According to a Howard University Ethnic Center report, Price also composed and arranged music for *Tomorrow is a Day*, a color film in commemoration of the 150th anniversity of the state of Illinois. Still another announcement noted his lectures on Black Culture which were videotaped as a prime resource for use in elementary and secondary schools in Tuskegee, Alabama.

His style encompasses techniques from the mildly contemporary tonal pieces seen in *Spirituals* arranged for intermediate piano (published by Belwin in 1979) to the most difficult rhythms and harmonies and physical demands of his *Piano Sonata*. The use of atonalism seen in measures 21 and 22 of his *Quartet* for violin, viola, horn, and bassoon (Example 83) shows only a small part of the intricacies involved in his works.

Ex. 83. *Quartet*, Price. Used by permission of composer.

Others among his approximately 563 representations are mainly in manuscript. In part, they are: *Invention I* for piano (published by *The Lamp*, 1969); *Two Typed Lines* for voice and piano (Lamp, 1966); *Spirituals for the Young Pianist*, Set I (Belwin); *Impulse and Deviation I* for cello; *Blues and Circle Dance I* for viola; *Five Folk Songs* for piano; *A Ptah Hymn; Movie I* for percussion ensemble; *Movie II* for organ and percussion; *Sea Calm* for voice and piano; *Scherzo I* for clarinet and orchestra; *Song on a Poem by Blake* for soprano and piano; *Duet* for french horn and trombone; *Set I* for voice and piano; *Hymn and Deviation* for brass quartet; *Thirteen Pieces* for harpsichord; *Carol VII* for tenor and flute; *Concerto* for violoncello; *Beach Verse I* for flute, oboe, clarinet, and bongos; *The Damnation of Dr. Faustus* for tenor solo, SATB, and orchestra; *Rags for People and Friends; Barely Time to Study Jesus* for SATB and percussion; *Booker T. Washington: Address Delivered at the Dedication of the Robert Gould Shaw Monument in Boston, May 31, 1897* (1982); *For the Union Dead* for SATB and band and others. Publishers: The Lamp (Florida Memorial College, Miami, Florida 33055; Belwin-Mills, Melville, N.Y. 11747; Slave Ship Press, c/o John Price, 309 Gregory Place, Tuskegee Institute, Tuskegee, Alabama 36088 or Route 2 Box 153, Charleston, Illinois 61920).

JAMES FURMAN (1937–1989)

James Furman was born in Louisville, Kentucky, where he received his early education. A graduate of the University of Louisville with the Bachelor of Music Education in 1958 and the Master of Music degree in 1965 (emphases upon theory and composition), he also studied for his doctorate at Brandeis, completing his residency for the Ph.D. by 1964. In 1966, he attended summer school at Harvard University for work in choral music and early literature.

Furthering his career through the teaching of music, he worked in the Louisville public schools in 1959, in Mamaroneck, New York public schools, and at Brandeis University where he served as assistant choral director of the chorus and chamber chorus. He also worked in the World Touring Army Show "Rolling Along of 1961" as musical director-arranger-pianist, based in Fort Devens, Massachusetts. Settling at Western Connecticut State College in 1965, Furman conducted both the chorus and the orchestra, among other teaching duties. Also devoted to church music, he served as choirmaster and organist at the Church of our Merciful Savior in Louisville, Kentucky, at the Congregational Church in Weston, Massachusetts, at the Fort Devens Chapel No. 6. Massachusetts and at the Jewish Scientist Church in New York City.

As conductor, he directed both the chorus and orchestra in a documentary film on the life of Charles Ives for the British Broadcasting Company; he conducted the American Symphony Orchestra at the Danbury, Connecticut Fairground on July 4, 1974; and he conducted avant-garde music on a 1970 Desto recording. At Harvard, he directed the chorus and chamber chorus during the summer of 1966; for the 1967 American Guild of Organists, he conducted at the Choir Festival and he conducted his *I Have a Dream* in the premier performance by the Greenwich Connecticut Choral Society, which was released by Recorded Publications Company of Camden, New Jersey. Other conductors which have recorded his music include Nathan Carter (*Come, Thou Long Expected Jesus* is sung by the Morgan State University Choir for the Classics Record Library, Book of the Month Club). Furman himself, in addition to conducting, has given recitals in piano and voice.

Recognition came to Furman through performances of his music and through commissions and grants. He won the Omicron Delta Kappa Award as the top ranking music student of the 1958 graduating class of the University of Louisville. He won first place in the Louisville Philharmonic Society's Young Artists' Contest and appeared with the Louisville Symphony Orchestra in 1953 as soloist. He also received a Brandeis University Fellowship from 1962 to 1964. The Brookline Library Music Committee awarded him first place in the Composition Competition in 1964 and the National Federation of Music clubs awarded him a Merit for distinguished service to music in 1966 (announced in the 1967 Parade of American Music).

As a member of ASCAP, the Society of Black Composers, Phi Mu Alpha, the American Federation of Teachers, and other associations, Furman was made aware of issues and philosophies of the day, particularly concerning the rights and regulations of composers living in an American society. He was versed in areas of many musical concentrations, recognized by publishers and the public, and was sought after enough to lecture at various universities and to be included in several dissertations, books, and articles on the subject of his music. He was listed in books by Dominique de Lerma, Alice Tischler, Ruth Anderson, Vada Butcher, Max Garrison, and other biographical dictionaries.

Furman's works have been performed frequently at Western Connecticut State College by both the chorus and orchestra, in New York, Washington, and at other locations. Of his *Declaration of Independence* for narrator and orchestra, the *News-Times Review* of Danbury, Connecticut wrote that "Musical history was made in the Ives Concert Hall . . . with the world premiere of James Furman's *Declaration of Independence*. . . . " and "The evening was electric with excitement." The article stated that "The music always fitted the words with drum rolls and cymbal brushing . . . effective . . . inspiring"; of his *I Have a Dream*, Max Garrison of Danbury's *New-Times* wrote that the work "is one of the most inspired contemporary writings it has been my pleasure to hear in some time," and that Furman had "most successfully combined jungle rhythms, hymns, blue grass sounds and marvellous gospel rhythms with symphonic orchestral and choral writing." He furthermore wrote that the "12-tone effects were interestingly woven into beautiful melody . . . " and that Furman is a "current, living composer of high merit. . . . "

Other characteristics of his style are seen in *Salve Regina*, with its straightforward, religiously inspired, deep simplicity punctuated with interesting triplets, wide vocal skips against undaunted sevenths which carry spirits of both serenity and strength. Others range from tonal to mildly contemporary examples of harmony. One of the more frequently performed compositions for mixed chorus is *Hehlelooyuh—a Joyful Expression*, whose measures 1–4 are show in Ex. 84 below.

Ex. 84. *Hehlehlooyuh*, Furman. Copyright © 1978 by Hinshaw Music, Inc., P.O. Box 470, Chapel Hill, N.C. 27514. Used by permission. February 2, 1983.

To my mother, Ollie Furman

Hehlehlooyuh

(A Joyful Expression)

for Mixed Voices, S. A. T. B., a Cappella

JAMES FURMAN

Light and Spirited, ♩= c. 168*

S. A.

Heh - leh-loo-yuh, heh-leh-loo - yuh, heh - leh-loo - yuh, heh - leh-loo - yuh,

T. B.

Among his other compositions are: *Come, Thou Long Expected Jesus* for SATB (advertised by Music 70 Publishers as being "an unusual sacred work with a wonderful text by the theologian Charles Wesley. Although the piece is reverent and supplicant, it is not submissive, but powerful and forthright in its structure and texture."); *The Quiet Life* for SATB, also advertised by Music 70 as being "Two short, beautifully wrought compositions, sensitive and evocative, with texts by Alexander Pope. Although these contemporary settings employ 20th century procedures, they are readily accessible and not difficult to perform."; *Four Little Foxes* choral suite (Oxford University Press); *Go Tell It on the Mountain* and *Some Glorious Day* gospel anthem (published by Sam Fox, 1971); other gospel anthems, unpublished: *I Keep Journeyin'; Hold On*, SATB with piano, electronic organ; theater music: *Hey Mr. Jefferson*; and the *Virgin Voter; Vocalise Romantique* for voice and piano; *Variants*, Trio for violin, cello, and prepared piano; the *Threefold Birth* for SATB, boys' voices, and organ; *Suite* for solo clarinet; *Songs of Juvenilia* for voice and piano; *Sonata* for solo violin; *Roulade* for solo flute; *Let Us Break Bread Together*; and *Incantation* for clarinet and strings.

ROBERT A. HARRIS (1938–)

A native of Detroit, Michigan, Robert Harris was educated at Chadsey High School, at Wayne State University (where he earned the Bachelor of Science degree in music education and voice as well as the Master of Arts degree in composition). In 1971, he was awarded his Ph.D. in composition and theory from Michigan State University, after having also completed advanced work at both Wayne State and the Eastman School of Music.

Harris worked at the Music Settlement House from 1960 to 1963 and taught vocal music to elementary and secondary students of the Detroit public schools from 1960 to 1964. From 1964 to 1970, he was hired by his alma mater, Wayne State University, to teach theory and to conduct the

Women's Chorale. He was then hired in 1970 by Michigan State University, still another alma mater, to conduct the University Chorale, the State Singers, and to teach music theory. In addition, Harris was employed to teach studio voice at Eastern Michigan in Ypsilanti, Michigan, and to direct a choral ensemble of the University of Choral Workshop.

As both conductor and baritone soloist, he had done large works by several composers from Bach to Hindemith. He has conducted John Work's *The Singers*, William Walton's *Missa Brevis*, Vaughan Williams' *Benedicite, Magnificat* and *Mass in G Minor*. As baritone, he has sung in Bach's *St. John Passion*, Beethoven's *Christ on the Mount of Olives*, Brahms' *German Requiem*, Howard Hanson's *Drum Taps*, and others. He has also devoted much time to the directorships of music and conducting for church choirs in both Detroit and East Lansing.

Harris's music has been widely performed and well rewarded. Three commissions were awarded him in 1969 by Wayne State University Women's Glee Club for *Three Children's Prayers* and by the Chancel Choir of Grosse Point Memorial Church, Michigan, for *O Come, Let Us Sing Unto the Lord*, and in 1972, by Wayne State's Choral Union for *A Collect for Peace*, written for SATB and brass. For study and participation at the Aspen Choral Institute in Colorado, he received a Rockefeller Grant. Doris McGinty, chairman of the Department of Music at Howard University, has described his music as "toward the dissonant linear style heard in *Glory to God*."

Among his vocal works, written from the 1950s to the 1970s, are: *Three Children's Prayers* for women's voices; *May the Grace of Christ, Our Savior* (motet for SATB); *O Perfect Love* (motet, SATB); *Psalm 47* (women's voices and flute, clarinet, violin, viola, cello); *Intreat Me Not to Leave Thee* (motet, SATB); *Te Deum* (TTBB and two trumpets, horn, trombone, and tuba); *Missa Brevis* for SATB; *For the Beauty of the Earth* (anthem for SATB and organ); *Rejoice, Ye Pure in Heart* (motet, SATB); *Glory to God* (motet, SATB); *Kyrie and Gloria* (SATB); *The Lord's Prayer* (SATB and organ); *A Study* for flute and clarinet; *Fantasia* for flute; *Sonatine for Two Violins; Five Bagatelles for Three Woodwinds* (flute, clarinet, bassoon); *String Quartet*; and *Psalms* for soprano, horn, and piano. Some of those written in the 1970s are: *Incidental Music for Caligula* by Albert Camus; *A Wedding Intercession* (medium high voice and piano or organ); *Moods* for orchestra; *Contrasts for Four Winds and Strings; A Canticle of Immortality* (soprano, baritone with chamber choir, chorus, and orchestra); *A Collect for Peace* for SATB, two trumpets, two horn, two trombones, and tuba; *Thirty-three Contemporary Responses for the Church Service* for SATB and organ.

HOWARD C. HARRIS, JR. (1940–)

Howard Harris, Jr., conductor, arranger, trumpeter, producer, author, educator, and native of New Orleans, Louisiana, was graduated from Southern University (B.S.) and Louisiana State University (where he earned the Master of Music degree). He also pursued additional training at North Texas State University in jazz studies, at Washington University, at Southern University (Jazz Institute), as well as composition with William S. Fischer of New York. In 1974, he was awarded a National Endowment Grant to survey studio techniques and to study trumpet privately with Bobby Bryant of Hollywood.

As an educator, he taught at Delaware State College, the Southern University Laboratory School, and Dawson High School before beginning at Texas Southern in 1971. As band director, co-director of jazz ensembles, trumpet teacher, and arranger, he also served as founder-director of the Peoples' Workshop for Visual and Performing Arts at Texas Southern. Additionally, he has served as clinician in the area of improvisation and composition; affiliate producer with the Royal Shield Recording Studio, and as conductor, arranger, and A&R person for the Whitfield Recording Productions, both of Baton Rouge; host of radio station KTSU's "Roots to Fruits," an anthology of Black ethnic and jazz-oriented music; director of the Summer Jazz Workshop of Houston; composer-arranger-producer of various projects such as the Houston Police Department Jingle; and assistant choir director at the St. Benedict Catholic Church.

Howard C. Harris, Jr.

An able writer, Harris was contributing editor for *Jazz Spotlight News* of New York and co-author with Joseph Schmoll of *Music in the Humanities* (Burgess; Minn., 1983). He also authored *The Complete Book of Improvisation/ Composition and Funk Techniques* (four complete books published by DeMos Music Publishers, Houston, 1981). A member of ASCAP since 1973, he also gained memberships in MENC, Pi Kappa Lambda, honorary status in Phi Mu Alpha Sinfonia. He has also served on the Advisory Committee for radio station KTSU in Houston.

His music has been performed frequently by symphony orchestras, individual artists, and school ensembles. *Folk Psalm* was played by the Baltimore, New Orleans, and Fort Worth Symphony Orchestras; *An American Music Tree* was premiered by the Houston Orchestra; and others of his stage band works have enjoyed exposures at numerous collegiate jazz festivals as rendered by the TSU Jazz Ensemble (at the Kennedy Center in Washington, D.C., the McCormick Center in Chicago, and at the Mobile, Longhorn, New Orleans, and Notre Dame jazz festivals). His song, *Hell of a Fix*, written for Marion Jarvis and recorded on Roxbury Records, became number 25 in *Billboard* during autumn 1974. His newest work, *Music from Northup*, a collection of fifteen songs from the musical play, *Solomon Northup*, was commissioned by a Louisiana Arts Council in collaboration with Le Theatre des Bon Temps and was scheduled for a June 1983 premier performance in Louisiana.

Among his works published by Southern Music Company of San Antonio are *Black Roots* and *Passion Is* for stage band (1972, 1983) and *Folk Psalm* for orchestra (1973). Others are *A Jazz Memorabilia* for jazz orchestra and voice; *Blues of the New World* for jazz ensemble; *Pro Viva* for flute, piano, cello, congas; and *An American Music Tree* for symphony orchestra. Harris also publishes through DeMos Music for Houston, Texas.

WENDELL MORRIS LOGAN (1940–)

Wendell Logan, educator, composer, and performer, was born in Thomson, Georgia. He received his Master's degree at Southern Illinois University at Carbondale, Illinois, and his Ph.D. at State University of Iowa. Logan has taught at Ball State University, at Florida A&M University, and at Oberlin College, where he currently chairs the Jazz Studies Department.

A frontrunning exponent of both jazz and art music styles, his accomplishments have warranted recognition of many kinds. He is listed in the works of Eugene Claghorn, Eileen Southern, and others.

The composer of several works for choir, chamber ensembles, songs for voice and for jazz ensembles, his *Songs of Our Time* is recorded on Golden Crest (S-4087); his art songs *If There Be Sorrow* and *Marrow of My Bone* are published in Willis Patterson's *Anthology of Art Songs*; and his *Morty's Blues* and *Your Father's Mustache* are recorded by Western Illinois University's Jazz Band (limited distribution in 1973–74). One of his latest works is *Proportions for Nine Instruments*.

DOROTHY RUDD MOORE (1940–)

Dorothy Rudd Moore, born in New Castle, Delaware, where she received her basic education, distinguished herself as both a noted composer and soprano. A 1963 magna cum laude graduate of Howard University, she was awarded an undergraduate degree in music theory and composition. Having begun her studies with Mark Fax and Thomas Kerr, she continued with Nadia Boulanger at the Conservatoire de Musique in Fontainebleau, France, an honor made possible by a Lucy Moten Fellowship. Returning to the United States, she resumed the study of composition with Chou Wen Chung at Columbia University in New York City.

Moore held positions at the Harlem School of the Arts in 1965, at New York University in 1969, and at the Bronx Community College in 1971. In addition, she has also taught piano and vocal students in private studios for several years.

As a soprano and member of the Lola Hayes Studio in New York, Moore has been widely acclaimed. In 1975, the *National Music Journal* wrote that her "voice is mellow and clear, her diction is flawless and her presence angelic"; in 1980, the *Evening Journal* of Wilmington, Delaware, described her voice as having "a penetrating quality that soared well beyond the small confines of the hall" and as having "stylistic taste and know-how" when traversing a wide range of music.

But her compositions have perhaps earned the most attention. Highlighted many times in important halls of New York City such as Carnegie, Town Hall, Tully Hall, and Philharmonic, they have been performed throughout the United States by such eminent performers as Hilda Harris,

Dorothy Rudd Moore.

Willis Patterson, the Reston Trio, Raymond Jackson, and the Symphony of the New World.

The *Evening Journal* wrote that "The most compelling part of the recital came in Mrs. Moore's own music—Sonnets on Love . . . " (a 20 minute song cycle); on October 14, 1977, the *Ann Arbor News* wrote that "Moore welded eight different poems by seven different authors into a song cycle . . . which was . . . highly sophisticated" and "most ambitious single song of the evening"; on September 1, 1977, Robert Kimball reviewed the Black Composer Fete which included her "Weary Blues" and recorded that this "drew the concert's biggest ovation"; in a September 2, 1977 *New York Times* article, Donal Henahan discussed the song cycle as "one of the ups" of the evening; and her *In Celebration* was reviewed in the *New York Times* by Peter Davis (June 13, 1977) as having "struck appropriate notes of upbeat affirmation." Her *Moods for Cello and Viola* was described in the *New York Herald Tribune* by Eric Salzman as an "excellent short, intense, chromatic little piece," while the *New York Times* described the piece in 1965 as "an unscheduled treat" when used as an encore by Kermit Moore and Selwart Clarke. The *New York Times* and *The Jersey Journal*, respectively, listed her song cycle, *From the Dark Tower*, as "cultivated in a vibrant romantic idiom" with "the vocal line, expressively and strongly contoured . . . supported by tonally pungent harmonies, luminously scored . . . luscious" and as "beautifully expressive and idiomatically written for voice and orchestra . . . eminently worthy of the superlative. . . . "

Moore has been the recipient of an American Music Center Grant and was co-founder of the Society of Black Composers. The *New York Times* has termed her "a gifted and creative mind at work." Among her works are tonal and atonal ones available a the American Composers Alliance: *Reflections for Symphonic Wind Ensemble* (1962); *Songs* for soprano and oboe—cycle; *Symphony No. 1* (one movement); *Baroque Suite* for unaccompanied cello; *Three Pieces* for violin and piano; *Modes* for string quartet; *Moods for Viola and Cello*—duo; *Lament for Nine Instruments; Trio No. 1 for Violin, Cello, and Piano; From the Dark Tower* for mezzo soprano, cello and piano cycle (also scored for mezzo and orchestra); *Dirge and Deliverance* for cello and piano; *Weary Blues* for baritone, cello, and piano (published in Willis Patterson's *Anthology of Art Songs*, E. B. Marks/Belwin); *Dream and Variations* for piano; *Night Fantasy* for clarinet and piano; *Sonnets on Love, Rosebuds and Death* for soprano, violin, and piano cycle; *In Celebration* for chorus, soprano, baritone, and piano; and *A Little Whimsey* for piano (1982). Among her work in progress is an opera entitled *Frederick Douglass. Dirge and Deliverance* appears on Kermit Moore's recording entitled *Kermit Moore*, cellist (Cespico Records, New York).

JERALDINE SAUNDERS HERBISON (1941–)

Jeraldine Herbison, educator, violinist, and composer, was born in Richmond, Virginia. Educated in the Richmond public schools, Virginia State College (B.S., 1963), she did further study in literature, analysis, composition, and performance at Virginia State College in 1969 and at the University of Michigan at Interlochen—the latter institution of which awarded her full scholarships in 1973 and 1979. Some of her composition teachers included Tom Clark, George Wilson, and Undine Moore.

Herbison has taught at public schools in Prince George County, Maryland, and in Goochland and the Isle of Wright Counties, Virginia. At present, she is an educator, orchestra, and choral director at Hampton and Newport News, Virginia and is a member of MENC, ASTA, NSOA, AF of M, and the Tidewater Composers Guild.

Her compositions were presented at the Kennedy Center Symposia in the early 1980s. Her *Intermezzo for Cello and Piano* and *Fantasy in Three Moods* for cello and piano had already received attention in the news media from *Richmond Times Dispatch*, the *Norfolk Star, The Daily Press*, and *Times-Herald Newspaper*. Her music had already been performed on Channel 5 television in Washington, Channel 10 in Norfolk, on WGH-FM radio and at such institutions as Virginia Union University, Old Dominion University, the College of William and Mary, Hampton Institute, University of Michigan, Christopher Newport College, and Virginia State College. In addition, certain of her works were presented at New York University at the First National Congress of Women in Music, in the National Music Camp Brochure of Performances (1979), and elsewhere.

Jeraldine Saunders Herbison. Reprinted from the *Times-Herald*, Newport News (Barnes photo).

Her works total approximately twenty in number, including the following unpublished titles: *Suite 1* in C for string (1960, rev. 1977); *Suite No. 3* for strings, flute, and oboe (1963, rev. 1971); *Variations* for string orchestra, 1974; *Promenade* for chamber orchestra, 1982; *Introspection* (quartet for flute, violin, cello, and piano), 1973; *I Heard the Trailing Garments of the Night* (ibid, 1975); *String Quartet No. 1978; Fantasy in Three Moods* for cello and piano, 1972; *Intermezzo* for cello and piano, 1969, rev. 1975; *Six Duos* for violin and cello; *Metamorphosis* for 2 violins, cello, guitar, and piano, 1978; *Trio* for guitar, violin and flute, 1979; *Sonata No. 2* for cello and piano, 1980; *Sonata No. 1* for unaccompanied cello, 1977–78; *Five Sketches* for mezzo-soprano, tenor and piano, 1977–78; *Four Sonnets* for soprano and piano, 1981–82; *Spring* for SSA and piano.

ADOLPHUS CUNNINGHAM HAILSTORK (1941–)

Born in Rochester, New York, Adolphus Hailstork, composer, conductor, and theorist, attended Albany High School (1956–59), received his Bachelor of Music degree in theory from Howard University in 1963 (graduating magna cum laude), the Bachelor and Master of Music degrees in composition from the Manhattan School of Music (1965 and 1966, respectively) and his Ph.D. degree in composition from Michigan State University (1971). He studied conducting with Warner Lawson, Hugh Ross, Nicholas Flagello, and composition with Flagello, Ludmila Ulohla, H. Owen Reed, Vittorio Giannini, David Diamond, and Nadia Boulanger (at the American Institute in Fontainebleau, France). He did additional study at the Electronic Music Institute in New Hampshire and a SUNY (Buffalo, New York).

He served as a student assistant director of the Howard University Choir. From 1966 to 1968, he was stationed in Germany as a captain in the United States Army. Later, he was employed by Michigan State University, by the Federal-funded Triple T inner city project as a teaching fellow, by Youngstown State University, and by Norfolk State University (1976 to the present).

Hailstork's music has been recognized by several organizations with commissions and other awards. In 1976, his *Celebration* was among those commissioned for national distribution by the J. C. Penney Bicentennial Musical Celebration Committee; his *Mourn Not the Dead* was selected as co-winner of the 1970–71 Ernest Bloch Award for choral composition; his

Bellevue, an orchestral prelude, was commissioned by Southern Baptists Convention in 1974; his *Spiritual* was commissioned in 1976 by the Edward Tarr Brass Ensemble in Europe; his *American Landscape No. 1* was commissioned by the Boardman, Ohio High School Band in 1976 (premiered in 1977); and his *Psalm 72* was commissioned in 1981 by the Westerly, Rhode Island Community Chorus for a tour of Great Britain.

As a lecturer, pianist, conductor, and theorist-composer, Hailstork has also received many other honors. He was the subject of articles in two books—*Music*, by Jasper Patton and *Fifteen Black Composers* by Alice Tischler. Other honors were the election to the national honor society for music by both Howard University and Michigan State University, the Lucy Moten Travel Fellowship from Howard to study in France, performances of his master's thesis by the Baltimore Symphony (1966) and the Atlanta Symphony (1968) (composition entitled *Statement, Variations and Fugue*).

Adolphus Hailstork.

His *Celebration* was performed by at least five orchestras and was televised nationally by Indiana University in 1976; his *Spiritual*, in addition to being performed on tour in Europe, was also performed at the Lincoln Center in 1979 by the Juilliard School of Music Chorus; and his *Epitaph: For a Man Who Dreamed* was performed in 1980 and 1981 by the Baltimore and Detroit Symphony Orchestras. *Out of the Depths* was selected by the College Band Directors National Association as the winner of the 1977 Belwin-Mills Max Winkler Award.

Several of his works show clear, uncluttered scores with deceptive marks of seeming simplicity of style. Upon closer scrutiny, the music reveals line against line in contemporary intervals of 4ths, etc., thirds in succession being accompanied by more thirds, seconds or melodic figures in contrary motion or imitation. Other features are the use of extended chords such as elevenths, which are arranged in widely spaced positions suggesting intervallic conception as well, repetitions which are written with just enough variation to provide contrast and invite interest, dotted note patterns with ties cleverly placed to thwart easy manipulation, and accents added to create effective syncopation. Other rhythmic examples make use of eight notes being followed by triplets and sixteenths in rolling succession, coupled still with frequently changing meters.

The overall effect of some of his music seems logical and well conceived, whether tonal or atonal. He writes for various media as though he thoroughly understands each individual characteristic of the medium at hand. A small sample of his writing can be seen in the *Spiritual for Brass Octet* (measures 46–57), Example 85.

Among his list of compositions are at least seven published ones: *Celebration for Orchestra* (published by J. C. Penney and distributed in 1975, also recorded by Columbia for the Black Composers Series); *Sonatina for Flute and Piano* (Fema Publications, Illinois); *Bagatelles for Brass* (Fema); *Duo for Tuba and Piano* (Fema); *Cease Sorrows Now* for SATB (E. B. Marks); *A Charm at Parting* and *I Loved You*, two songs in Willis Patterson's *Anthology of Art Music by Black Composers* (E. B. Marks).

In manuscript, Hailstork has penned: *Ignis Fatuus* for piano; *Concerto for Violin, Horn and Orchestra*; arrangement of *Celebration* for band; *Five Friends* for piano; *Guest Suite* for piano duet; *Oracle* for SATB and tenor solo; *If We Must Die* for baritone and piano; *American Landscape No. 2* for violin and cello; *Canto Carcelera* for flute and guitar; *Who Gazes at the Stars* for organ; *Piano Sonata; Set Me as a Seal* for SATB; *A Romeo and Juliet Fantasy*

Ex. 85. *Spiritual for Brass Octet*, Hailstork. Used by permission of composer. From the Howard University Ethnic Center Collection.

for violin, cello, and piano; *Suite* for violin and piano; *Elegy* for cello and piano; *Easter Music* for cello and piano; *The Cloths and Heaven* for SATB; orchestral works: *Statement, Variations and Fugue; Capriccio for a Departed Brother; From the Dark Side of the Sun*; and over fifty others for SATB, band, piano, voice, guitar, organ, violin, flute, SATB with organ and brass, trumpet, string orchestra, and a chamber ensemble of ten players, and many others.

WARRICK CARTER (1942–)

An arranger, composer, educator, administrator, author, and performer, Warrick Carter was described as an "expert of History of Jazz and Jazz Materials for Teacher Education" by the reviewer of the Jazz Workshop held at Jackson State University, Jackson, Mississippi. Carter was born in Charlottesville, Virginia. After having graduated from Burley High, he attended Tennessee State University, obtaining the Bachelor of Science degree in 1964 and Michigan State University where he earned the Master of Music in music education and the Doctor of Philosophy degree. In addition, he studied privately at the Blair Academy of Music for the purpose of advancing his knowledge of percussion.

His work experience includes instructorships in Chattanooga, Tennessee public schools, at Grinnell's Music Store in Flint, Michigan, and the University of Maryland, Eastern Shore (1966–68), as well as the Governors State University at Park Forest South, Illinois (1972 to the present). Additionally, Carter was the director of Music Education for Urban Schools Symposium at Michigan State University (summers of 1970 and 1971). He has also acted as adjudicator and consultant for various clinics. Recently, he was appointed Chairman of the Division of Fine and Performing Arts at the Governors State University.

Warrick Carter.

During the 1965 and 1968–70 seasons, he was a member of Lansing Symphony Orchestra while continuing his work in composition, producing arrangements and original compositions which were frequently performed by musicians at Tennessee State, the University of Maryland, George Peabody Teachers College, Michigan State, and University of Wisconsin, Southern University, Thornton Junior College, and others, including the Governors State University. In 1968, he made an arrangement for Mercer Ellington. As drummer, he has performed extensively both nationally and internationally at army bases and jazz festivals.

Also listed in the *Dictionary of International Biography, Outstanding Personalities of the South*, and other sources, Carter has likewise been honored with Best Drummer awards from the Collegiate Jazz Festival held at Notre Dame in 1970, a Graduate Fellow award from Michigan State University's Center for Urban Affairs, the Faculty Member of the Year Award from the University of Maryland, Eastern Shore, and others.

His list of works (available from the composer at the Governors State University) includes for jazz ensemble (five reeds, four trumpets, four trombones, and rhythm section): *First Love, ICC, Little People, Memo, Clay* (from 1963–1979); for jazz combo: *Two Tunes* for quartet, *Questions, Music to be Sounded* for octet and electronic tape; for percussion ensemble: *Eight Quartets for Percussion, Poco A Poco* (quintet), *Rondo*; and others for brass and percussion, marching band, and other arrangements. For orchestra, he has written *Concerto for Bassoon and Nose Whistle* (1966) and *Life Part I* (1963). As a published author and recording artist, he has contributed a number of articles on jazz education.

MAURICE MCCALL (1943–)

Maurice McCall, composer, educator, and administrator, was born in Norfolk, Virginia. After completing his basic education in the Norfolk public schools, he attended Carnegie Institute for his degrees, Bachelor and Master of Arts, and later earned the Doctor of Musical Arts from the College Conservatory of Music at the University of Cincinnati.

McCall taught at Hampton Institute from 1967 to 1970. He then worked at the University of Cincinnati's radio station, WGUC, as Director of Minority Affairs (1973–74), as Assistant to the Dean (1974–76), as College Registrar at Clermont General and Technical College of the University of Cincinnati in Batavia, Ohio (1976–80), as College Registrar and Admission Officer in 1981, and as the University Registrar at Virginia State University in Petersburg, Virginia, since 1981. In addition, his volunteer and paid musical experiences have included directorships of the Hanarobi Contemporary Gospel Ensemble at the University of Cincinnati, research and lecturing in music (such as at the Music Symposium at Morgan University in conjunction with the Baltimore Symphony Orchestra, seminars given at St. Joseph's College and the University of Louisville, and the publication of a thirteen-part radio series on the music history of Afro-Americans).

His works have been performed at the Black Symposiums held in various parts of the United States, in Baltimore, Maryland, and in Cincinnati, Ohio. McCall has given a terse summation of his style as being "melodically oriented contrapuntal homophony." His writing as seen in the two examples of Willis Patterson's *Anthology* shows competence, interesting varieties of materials from rhythmic to melodic elements, and the use of contemporary features of a clear, solid type which invite curiosity, and ready acceptance. In the vocalise, *Chanson Triste*, a waltz tempo fits easily with the changing rhythms which follow and interrelate with the seeming duple contrasts of some measures (being set up by the triplet to eighth note figures). The sparse harmonies perfectly complement the vocal line which flows above in both easy and difficult leaps, but ever singable lines. The rhythms of *Sweet Sorrow* first set up in the vocal line are echoed succinctly in the accompaniment, which always changes its music to fit whatever the poetry and the melodic line suggest. Well written and exciting in its use of running notes against the slower quarters (resembling counterpoint) or its use of chord patterns in loud punctuation, the piece, ending softly and serenely with bitonal implications, terminates in sharp contrast with its forte opening.

Maurice McCall.

Among his works are those for youth string performance: *Petite Suite; Sinfonia Brevis; Little Trio* for two violins and double bass; those termed "recomposed traditional spirituals" for SATB: *Were You There?; Done Made My Vow; Run to Jesus*; those for SATB and instruments: *Ola*, a survey of the Black man's history and journey to North America, with text and music by the composer; *Were You There?* with soprano solo, oboe, SATB, and organ, and *Dark Symphony* for soli, SATB, and orchestra without flutes or violins; *Two Spirituals* (*I Will Arise* and *Swing Low*) for solo voice, oboe, and strings; two songs (*One Woman* and *Whom*) for voice and piano; and *In Parting*, a song cycle for voice and piano; for instruments: *Wedding Music* (suite of four pieces for string quartet); *Study No. 1* for solo piano; and *Olde Musick* for recorder, cello, and harpsichord. The works are available from the composer at Virginia State College, Petersburg, Virginia. *Brother Jack* for six pianos and *Which Way* for two pianos are published in Cleveland Page's *The Laboratory Piano Course*, Book I (Dodd, Mead & Company, 1974).

RONALD ROXBURY (1946–198?)

Yet another promising young composer is Ronald Roxbury, born near Salisbury, Maryland. A graduate of the Peabody Institute, he studied composition with Earle Brown and Stefan Grove and received the Master's degree. He has achieved some success as both singer and composer. He sang in *Mass* by Bernstein, *Lazarus* by Eric Salzman, and as a member of the Philip Glass Ensemble, premiered the Wilson/Glass *Einstein on the Beach* and performed the role on a European tour. Roxbury also taught at Tanglewood and served as intern for music critic study for the *Washington Star*.

His own works have been performed at various halls in Baltimore, New York, Washington, and in Brazil, including concerts by the Evelyn White Chorale at the National Gallery, Carnegie Hall, and at various institutions. Of the choral works, *Ave Maria* and *As Dew in Aprille* have been published by Walton Music. In part, they are (unpublished) for piano: *Combination Cyclops, Three Transcendental Etudes, Sonata* (1968), *Hommage for Rick Myers, Pictures of an Exhibitionist, Preludes*; for organ: *Chordorgelbüchlein* (Magnus Opum); for guitar: *Haiku and Joe*; for violin: *Pygmies*; for voice: *Chants des Oiseaux* for high voice, *Insect Fear*, vocalise for counter-tenor and piano; for chamber: *Maelcum Soul/Designs* for three flutes; *Journey to Y-ha'nth-lei* for organ and eight male performers, *Ecstacies for Mi-Go/Several Bags of the Abominable Snowman* (for fourteen guitars and nine cellos with piccolo solo), *Briyga-ha* for two pianos and seven hands, *Requiem for Bill Null, Afternoon of an Evening*—a movable feats II, *Apotheosis and Dirge* in Eb—a movable feats IV, *A Dream Come True*—a movable feats V, *Le Sofa des Solfèges* for female voice and guitar; and others with equally unique names and combinations of media.

EDWARD BLAND (1946–)

Edward Bland, according to his own comments and those of Jeannie Pool (found on the record jacket of his original compositions released in 1986 by Cambria), started in the music business as a jazz musician. Educated at the University of Chicago in philosophy and musicology, he "composed, arranged and produced more than forty albums and numerous singles in six different markets: rock, pop, soul, country, jazz and muzak," ten of which made the *Billboard* charts. Some of his work also consisted of his being head of A&R, Executive Producer and Producer for Vanguard Record; composer, music supervisor and orchestrator for Cannes' Film Festivals, movies; and Presidential Commissioner on the White House Record Library Commission from 1979–1981. In 1984, he moved to Los Angeles and continued as composer and orchestrator for the films *A Soldier's Story* and *A Raisin in the Sun*, and honored several important commissions for such organizations as the New American Orchestra of Los Angeles. Persons for whom he has composed or arranged also included George Benson, Dizzy Gillespie, Lionel Hampton, Country Joe and the Fish, Al Hirt, Richie Havens and King Harvest. As an educator, he lectured at Loyola Marymount University in Los Angeles, presented clinics at colleges around the country, and delivered over one-hundred and forty concerts in New York Museums.

Ed Bland.

Bland switched to a fusion of art music with other genre, supposedly after being impressed with Stravinsky's *Rite of Spring*, which he said brought his career as a jazz musician to "an abrupt halt." His compositional style is described as being "an organic process, flowing from the very essence of the musical ideas, and not dictated by formula or theoretical dogma," with the structure being derived from the musical substance of the work. His recorded compositions on *The Music of Ed Bland* include single movement pieces entitled *Sketches Set 1* (a fine work with exciting rhythms played on the timpani), *The Brass Quintet, Piece for Chamber Orchestra, For Violin* (unaccompanied), and *For Clarinet* (unaccompanied); the Library of Congress also lists others such as *Sketches Set(s) 4 & 5*, and *Passacaglia*, etc.; and Althea Waites has recorded samples of his work.

PRIMOUS FOUNTAIN III (1949–)

This extraordinary young composer was born in St. Petersburg, Florida, and moved to Chicago, Illinois, for his basic education. He attended DePaul University, Chicago in 1968, among other schools, and was then awarded commissions and BMI and Guggenheim grants for the continuation of his compositional advancement.

His name appears in Eileen Southern's *Biographical Dictionary* (Greenwood, 1982), magazines, newsletters, and other media. He was reviewed several times in the 1970s by *Jet*, and was described as "one of the John Simon Guggenheim Memorial Foundation's youngest fellows at the age of 24." He was cited in the article for *Manifestation*, which was performed by the Chicago Civic Orchestra in 1970, and *Ritual Dance of the Amaks*, a three-movement work commissioned by Harvard University. In still another issue, Fountain was captioned under "New York Beat" with Arthur Mitchell who "opened his latest month-long season at the Uris Theatre with a brand-new dance spectacular he choreographed, *Manifestations*, to the original score by Chicagoan Primous Fountain III." The work was also described as a "sensual and flawless piece" which dramatized the Biblical fall from grace of Adam and Eve.

His compositions have been performed at many concerts and symposia around the nation, being sponsored by the Afro-American Opportunities Association, the Kennedy Center, and others. His *Meditation on a Theme* and *Ricia* for piano were both presented on different programs at the "Meet the Black Composer" panel and the National Black Music Colloquium and Competition held at the Kennedy Center in 1980.

Although his output is impressive, it is not yet what it will be at musical maturity. However, the accolades for their present scope and substance already predict a brilliance in futurity.

A very fine article written by Lucius Wyatt for the *Black Music Newsletter* (from Fisk, edited by S. Floyd) revealed that "Primous Fountain III is being hailed by conductors, performers, and reviewers alike as the most promising young American composer." Among the other orchestras which he listed as having performed Fountain's works are the Minnesota Orchestra, the Buffalo Philharmonic, and the San Francisco Symphony. Wyatt wrote that the music of Fountain "synthesizes both traditional and twentieth-century practices to produce a new sound," and that "it may well be that to the list of great composers, the striking name, Primous Fountain III, will be added."

Fountain's works include *Meditation on a Theme* and *Ricia* for piano; *Ricia for Trio* for violin, cello, and piano; *Evolution Quaestionis* for orchestra; *Manifestation; Huh*; and others. Originally published by Hinshaw Music of Chapel Hill, North Carolina, the music is now held in limbo by the Reynolds, Gruber, Herrick, Flesch and Kasdorf Firm in Madison, Wisconsin.

LESLIE BURRS (1952–)

Leslie Burrs, flutist, educator, composer, and administrator, was born in Philadelphia, Pennsylvania. A 1975 graduate of the Philadelphia College of the Performing Arts, he surfaced as the founder of the Creative Artists' Workshop which fosters "interest in lesser-known and minority musicians and composers," and which maintains a summer camp for high school students in music. He was Jazz-Artist-in-Residence with the York, Pennsylvania School District during the 1981–82 season and was also a member of the Music Advisory Panel of the Pennsylvania Council on the Arts.

Leslie Burrs.

A gifted flutist, Burrs has been featured as guest soloist with jazz saxophonist Grover Washington, Jr. in concerts at the Quaker City Jazz Festival, the Academy of Music, Temple University Music Festival and has performed as special guest soloist on Washington's *Live at the Bijou* album. Burrs was guest soloist with the Duke Ellington Orchestra, performing on tour some of his original compositions. As the Pennsylvania School District's Artist-in-Residence, he performed with the students, produced an album of the results, and also gave children's concerts entitled "The Magic of Music" at the Philadelphia Free Library, the Philadelphia Civic Center, and the University of Pennsylvania Museum.

As a member of the Affiliated Artists Group, he was engaged in tours throughout the nation, rendering praiseworthy exhibitions of classical and jazz music, such as the 1983 production given at the National Symposium on the Performing and Fine Arts for Historically Black Colleges and Universities, held at the Johnson Foundation, Racine, Wisconsin. For his work, he became one of ten nominees for a Pennsylvania Governor's Award for Excellence in the Arts in 1982.

Burrs has used jazz and classical idioms to compose *Precarious, She Stands in Quiet Darkness, Elegance*, and *A Woman's Song* (unpublished), and continues his growth toward a bright future.

Postscript IV: Other Composers

George Russell (1923–), internationally renowned theorist, performer, conductor and composer of the *Lydian Chromatic Concept* (James Abersold Concept Publishing Company); *Concerto for Self-Accompanied Guitar* (Jazz Composer Orchestra Association); *Cubana Be-Cubana Bop* (Robbins, 1949); *Electronic Organ Sonata* (Jazz Composers Orchestra Association); *Electronic Sonata for Souls Loved by Nature* (bid); *Ezzthetic* (Russ-Hix Music); *Listen to the Silence* (Jazz Composers Orchestra Association); *Outer View* (Russ-Hix, music and record); and others.

Ruth Norman (1927–), pianist-composer; born in Chicago, Illinois; reared in Omaha, Nebraska, resident of Washington, D.C.; educated at Nebraska University, Eastman School of Music (M.M.); composer of unpublished compositions *St. Francis of Assisi, I Shall Lift Up Mine Eyes Unto the Hills, The Lord Is Thy Keeper*, and *Lord, Make Me An Instrument of Thy Peace* for SATB, and several instrumental pieces.

Reginald Parker (1929–1970), graduate of Howard University and Manhattan School of Music; taught at Norfolk State; composer of *Make a Joyful Noise and O God of My Salvation* (D'Laniger).

Robert Banks (1930–), born in Newark, New Jersey; educated at Newark State Teachers College, Juilliard, and Montclair State Teachers College; composer of *Praise Chorale*, a gospel style cantata (Belwin).

James Tatum (1931–), pianist, composer-arranger; born in Mineola, Texas; educated at Prairie View A&M (B.A.) and the University of Michigan (M.U.S.), also received a scholarship to Berkeley School of Music in Boston; composer-educator in Detroit, Michigan; composer of *Contem-*

porary Jazz Mass, eleven movements (C. Collins Publishing Company or available at James Tatum Trio Plus, Inc., Detroit Michigan); *Spiritualotta Jazz Suite, Proud Heritage, Hallelujah, Unknown Destiny*, and others.

Ralph Simpson (1933–), born in Birmingham, Alabama; graduate of Parker High School, Alabama State College (B.S.), Columbia University (M.A.), and Michigan State University (Ph.D.); worked at Dillard University, as a professor of music at Tennessee State University; awarded honors such as the Omega Psi Phi Achievement Award, the key to the city of San Diego, California from Mayor Curran for excellence in performance at the San Diego Community College in 1968; composer of *Two Settings on Negro Spirituals* for organ (1962), *Presentiment* for piano (1959), *Overture 1776* for orchestra and arrangements of spirituals, including *Swing Low, Sweet Chariot*, and *Jacob's Ladder; Lied* for trumpet and piano and *Impromptu* for piano included in *Anthology* compiled by Samuel Floyd (1983).

Phil Medley, composer-arranger, lecturer, currently scoring for films; first American songwriter of a hit song made popular by the Beatles rock group, and whose compositions at the Library of Congress number about ten (some also published in *The Motown Era* by Jobete Music); former student of Undine Moore.

Robert Holmes (1934–), conductor, arranger, pianist, cellist, singer, and composer; born in Greenville, Mississippi; educated at Tennessee A&I University, the University of Iowa, and Brandeis University, awarded the master's degree by Tennessee State; worked at Felix High in West Memphis, Arkansas, with the 6th U.S. Army Band in San Francisco, and worked both in the Nashville school system and at Fisk University (composer-in-residence); served as pianist and arranger for Joe Tex, Herb Alperts Band, Les Brown Sextet, and others; has also played cello and French horn with orchestras; composer of rock, classical, and jazz pieces and gospel music (Cremona Music, Nashville, Tennessee; ASCAP affiliation).

Percy Gregory (1934–1991), born in Washington, D.C.; pianist, choral director at University of D.C.; educated at Howard University and University of Maryland; composer of unpublished works: *Lift Ev'ry Voice* for SATB, *Five Miniatures* for piano, *Joy is Not Great* for soprano, *Sonatina* for Oboe and Piano, *Choral Tryptich* and *In A Lowly Bed* for SATB.

William Howard Moore (1934–), born in Sparta, Tennessee; pianist, choral director, arranger, educator, and chairman of music at the University of the District of Columbia; educated at Fisk, Juilliard, Indiana, and Columbia University (Doctorate); studied composition with John W. Work III, Edward Boatner, Hall Overton, Vincent Persichetti, and Ed Levy; composer of *The Status Seekers* (ballet), *The Birth of Christ* (cantata for baritone), *A Blind Man's Prayer* for soprano, *Brown Baby, Taste and See* (SATB), *Sweet Little Jesus Boy* for solo voice, *Drinking Gourd, Let Us Break Bread Together* (SATB), *Xango* (SATB and drums), incidental music for *Man, Better Man* and *Orwell's Farm* and *Five Settings* for soprano and piano (poems from Llanto Azul)—all unpublished. The latter work has been performed in the U.S. and Spain with William Moore as pianist and Shirley Moore, soprano.

James Anderson De Priest (1936–), born in Philadelphia, Pennsylvania; nephew of Marian Anderson and one-time associate conductor of the National Symphony Orchestra; listed in Eugene Claghorn and Leonard Feathers Dictionaries. Feathers notes his performance on drums, tympany and piano; composer of ballet score premiered at the Philadelphia Academy of Music.

James Frazier (1940–1985), young composer who received rave reviews in Soviet press about his conducting abilities; perhaps first Black to conduct the Philadelphia Orchestra (*Jet*) and composer of *Twelfth Street*, a soul musical integrating "rhythm and blues and gospel music into the structure of a symphony".

Kalvert Nelson (1951–), studied in Tulsa, Oklahoma and Indiana University; recorded on CRI with Professor Eaton and wrote several compositions which have lately been in review; now located in Austria.

John Childs.

Alvin Singleton (1940–), born in New York, now in Austria; the composer of several compositions; graduate of Columbia, Juilliard, and Yale University.

John Childs (1932–), composer of *Andalusian and Flamenco Music* (1973), *Poem-Waltz*, Opus 10 (listed in the Howard University Center); work reviewed in Washington *Post* when performed on Frances Walker piano concert.

Ambrose C. Jackson (1940–), composer, conductor, trumpeter, ethnomusicologist born in Washington, D.C.; educated at Catholic University and Ecole des Hautes Etudes en Sciences Sociales in Paris, France (Docteur de Troisième Cycle diploma, 1979); work with the U.S. Army Band led to participation in various ensembles from jazz to orchestra (1962–79); as trumpeter-conductor, he performed his own music frequently in U.S., Europe, and Africa; taught at Howard University and the Potomac School in McLean, Virginia; composed *Brass Quartet No. 1* (Gerard Billaudot Publishers, Paris, France, 1978) and several other chamber music pieces as well as musical score for a film (*Ronde Enfantine*, 1977) and jazz music.

William Foster McDaniel (1940–), priest of Catholic Archidiocese of Cincinnati; educated at Capital University and Boston University (Evelyn White's *Bibliography*); compositions seen at the Library of Congress, published by Stimuli: *Mass*, 1972; *Chamber Concerto; Fantaso* for violin and piano; *Prelude and Sonata* for piano; *Woodwind Quartet*.

Charles Brown (1940–), singer-composer, arranger; born in Marianna, Arkansas and educated at Morehouse and the University of Michigan (B.M., M.M.); listed in Willis Patterson's *Anthology* as the composer of *The Barrier* and *Song Without Words, Three Inventions* for oboe and bassoon, and choral pieces both original and arranged.

Robert Morris (1941–), composer, educator, arranger, and graduate of Indiana University; born in Chicago, Illinois; award winner; composer-arranger of *Every Time I Feel the Spirit, I'll Never Turn Back No More*, music for *Duke Ellington Show in 1963* (choral music); member of the First Water, an association of Black composers, artists, and literary figures.

Charles Lloyd, Jr. (1948–), born in Toledo, Ohio and a graduate of Norfolk College and the University of Michigan (voice and piano); composer of art song listed in Willis Patterson's *Anthology* entitled *Compensation* as well as *Sonata* for piano, pieces for other instruments, and several vocal arrangements.

Uzee Brown (1950–), born in Cowpens, South Carolina; educated at Morehouse (B.A.) and Bowling Green in Ohio, received M.M. and D.M.A. from the University of Michigan; presently on faculty at Morehouse; arranger of *I'm Buildin' Me a Home* (TTBB), *Mary Had a Baby* (SATB)

Lorenz Publishing 1983; also composer of *Ebony Perspectives* (a song cycle for tenor and nine instruments).

Philip McIntyre (1951–1991), organist, choir director, born in Portsmouth, Virginia, educated at Catholic University and Westminster Choir College, also studied organ with Daniel Roth of St. Sulpice in Paris, taught in public schools of the District of Columbia and at the University of D.C., and served as church musician for Ebenezer Baptist in Richmond, Virginia, at Lincoln Congregational Temple and Metropolitan AME Church in Washington, and Grace Presbyterian Church of Baltimore, and who has concertized nationally; composed a volume of spirituals for voice and piano (H. T. Fitzsimons), and other anthems such as *That's How Good God Is.*

Gregory Holmes (ca. 1960–); music composer for the Maryland Center for Public Broadcasting in Owing Mills, Maryland; songwriter and underscorer for commercials and programs, as reported by *Jet* in 1981.

Robert Tyler, listed in the Howard University Ethnic Center; Cortez Reese (–1910), Evelyn LaRue Pittman, Elmer Davis, Clarence Jones (1889), Leon Roberts and others.

Garrett Morris, composer of *If I Had-a My way, Set Down,* and *Tell God All of My Troubles* (Lawson-Gould).

William F. Lee, composer of *Earth Genesis*; (Hansen, 1971), *Festival* for piano (Souther, San Antonio), *Mosaics* for brass quintet (Miami, Hansen, 1969), *Regimentation* for brass quintet (Fox).

Julius Williams, composer of work announced by the Black Caucus *Newsletter*; educator at Hartford's Hartt School, graduate of Wesleyan University.

Roy D. Merriwether, composer of *Black Snow* which was reviewed in the Fisk *Black Music Newsletter.*

Ollie McFarland, Detroit public schools educator; composer of *Lullaby* for voice and piano, *Fireworks, Who Has Seen America?*, and *Alphabet Travelogue* found in *Afro-America Sings.*

PART FOUR

THE PAN-AFRICAN AXIS—RESTORATION AND REVIVISCENCE

PAN-AFRICANS ABROAD

XIV

PROLUSIONS THREE: RESEARCH, RACE, AND PAN-AFRICANISM

Prolusion I: Research and Reason

Research is defined as "searching exhaustively." It consists of discovering, discarding, documenting, compiling, completing, comparing, investigating, investing, experimenting, recording, reporting, and searching it all again. In Pan-African research of composers, the names alone can demand more arduous work than one can imagine even before the music is ever reached. Identifying names, however, determines the exact concept upon which Pan-Africanism is based.

The business of "naming names" and making proper lists in preparation for researching Pan-African is no small feat and is incomplete even once the work is "completed." As in any historical project involving the past, present, and future, ongoing events and achievements continually affect the written word. In naming, both research and reason must be of one accord.

One of the first Americans to compile Pan-African names for music was Walter Whittlesey, director of the Music Division al the Library of Congress during the early 1900s. Beginning in 1901, he terminated the project in 1927, nine years before the Maud Cuney Hare publication. Recently unearthed by Wayne Shirley of the Music Division, the huge amount of information which he had collected consisted of a correspondence folder, six boxes of index cards of mostly handwitten notes, names, and data. Only a few dates were registered alongside the composers.

His correspondence revealed that Whittlesey wrote to publishing houses, musicians, the Smithsonian Institution, state historical societies, and citizens both here and abroad. His requests were for "foreign and American negro composers of music—vocal and instrumental—and their work." The collection represented approximately 308 composers mainly from Europe and the Americas. Although lengthy, this list was by no means complete as it had omitted three whom James Trotter had included (Repanti, Starr, and O'Fake). Yet his working list stood as the most extensive one registered among the lists of W. C. Handy (1938), Hare (1936), J. A. Rogers, and Alain Locke. The Hare list, however, uniquely represented about thirteen centuries of Pan-Africans throughout the Diaspora.

Hopefully, the element of error in determining names for this volume has been eliminated through the confirmations of educators, letters, embassies, news media, photographs, and the service and support of many interested persons. Many names became available from many sources which could not be checked because inquiries went unanswered or because leads grew cold. For example, among the names sent by one of the publishing companies was Guido Haazen, arranger of *Missa Luba*, a mass based on Congolese music. Although neither the Embassy of the Congo nor the Belgium Embassy of D.C. could identify him as to race, both the accompanying notes to the *Mass* and Father Joseph LaPauw of the Missionhurst

Monastery stated that Haazen was a Belgian missionary who traveled to the Congo from Belgium in 1953. Haazen, who has now returned to the Procure des Missions Franciscaines in Belgium, does, however, underline the importance of the role which the Catholic Church has played throughout the history of European and African music.

Hopefully, too, mistakes have been avoided by systematically eliminating those composers whose implications of race or background ancestry could not be fully supported by the sparse facts at hand. Perhaps each current writer has been confronted with research lists which included both well-known and less familiar persons such as Beethoven or Pergolesi, who were being tested as a review of history and of the manner in which previous historians wrote about race. Such lists challenged one to either delete or retain, or to at least consider the issues suggested by descriptions or other data. This points to only one of the many problems involved in writings of this sort and to the fact that much weight must be placed upon rituals of restraint, rejections, research, and reasoning which might correctly identify Pan-Africans abroad.

Prolusion II: Race and Rumors

Race is both an illusive and elusive thing to define. When W. E. B. DuBois wrote that the number one problem of the twentieth century would be that of "race," he might not have thought of that problem in terms of classifying Pan-African composers into anthropological types to fit a subject such as Pan-African music. In North America, Europeans had sought to simplify the matter by cataloguing Black Americans into categories of octoroon, African, mulatto, or Creole, as partly evidenced on chattel records listing tax properties at the National Archives and as seen in various other written accounts. Yet none of these labels suffice when seeking flawlessness in a system of races where no one race is exempt from mixtures of people.

The matter of race in the Third World countries of Central and South America further complicate the classifications when national countries are substituted for race rather than the specific statement of ancestry. Therefore, Mexican or Brazilian or Puerto Rican means nothing in terms of ancestral clarity, for less emphasis is placed upon the differences between the races than in North America. This is only one statement of the monumental obstacles involved in pinpointing those eligible for inclusion in this book.

Writers might rather prefer dispensing with the matter of race as a forgotten factor, but race is the essence of Pan-Africanism. In addition, several outstanding rumors have abounded on the issue of race which involve popular figures of the Americas. Maud Cuney Hare typed the Brazilian composer Antonio Carlos Gomez (1839–1896) as an "outstanding racial figure" while also relating that *Musical America* of February, 1924, referred to Gomez as "mulatto." This composer of *Il Guarany* and *O Escravo* (The Slave) was placed in Grove's and Baker's *Biographical Dictionaries of Music* as "Brazilian . . . of Portuguese parents." A recent commentary in the *Black Perspective in Music* (Southern, editor) stated that Gomez, "although often cited as a black musician, appears to have had no African ancestry." Therefore, Gomez, like Louis Gottschalk of New Orleans whose music was also based upon African elements of the American society and whose Creole label was equally unclear, was shrouded in mystery. Definitions for Creole, the subject of a book by George Cable in 1884, showed a

French origin and various mixtures which could well feed rumors about such persons as Gottschalk.

Likewise, the Cuban composer Alejandro Garcia-Caturla (1906–1940), a contemporary and friend of Amadeo Roldan, was discussed by Alain Locke and others as "Afro-Cuban." However, Alejo Carpentier, quoted in volume 3 of *Composers of the Americas*, vehemently denied that Caturla had a "drop" of African blood, despite the facts that he was "attracted" to the people and the music, and that he "defied the bourgeois prejudices of his wealthy caste and married a negro woman." Even Beethoven was described as "brown" by Czerny (Thayer, p. 227).

In light of the above pros and cons, and despite John Hope Franklin's reminder that slavery began in Mexico and the "outer" Americas before it began in North America, no clear-cut confirmations can be brought to bear upon these rumors, all of which should be discounted for now. This is particularly so since there seems to be no definite or more powerful statement to support any strong lineage. Nevertheless, Caturla and Gomez should be important as carriers of African elements used in their music such as Caturla's *Bito-Manue, Mulata y Yambambo, Bembe—Movement Afro-Cubaia*, and *Comparsa*.

Some very excellent sources offered insights on the subject of Blacks in the Americas, especially in Brazil. One of the best by Gerard Béhague, *Music in Latin America*, followed the pioneer works of the Pan American Union, Nicolas Slonimsky, Gilbert Chase, Luis de Azevedo, Renato Almeida, Mario Andrade, and Albert Luper, among others. The studies combined have presented problems and solutions to Creole, Carib, Maroon, Mestizo, and Zambo, as well as unique information about the noteworthy and plenteous Black Brazilian musicians of Bahia, Pernambuco, Minas Gerais, and Rio de Janeiro. They have also emphasized the existence of churches, schools, and fraternities for mulattos such as the Escola de Santa Cruz, the Brotherhood of Senhora das Merces dos Homens Crioulos, the Brotherhood of Vila Rica de São José dos Homens Pardos, and the Church of St. Joseph.

A few examples of "mulatto" musicians were recorded in Europe, but others may have been omitted because of short-sightedness, or apathy, or because less emphasis was placed on race in Europe than in America. Distinctions of class and caste might have been more important—especially in certain parts of Europe such as Italy and France, rather than England. In this case, then, the omission of a racial label might well have hindered the further identification of certain competent citizens of the musical arenas.

Problems of categorizing people also exist even in Africa. Although the release of Eileen Southern's *Dictionary* will assist with African and American identifications, racial classifications in Africa remain as difficult to judge as anywhere else in the world, especially when one is confronted with the Arabs to the north versus the "Coloreds, Bastards, and Blacks" to the south, or with "Egyptian" versus "Ethiopian." Consequently, apartheid practices, geographic proximity of the Middle East, and the slave remnants from Western countries have perpetuated an anthropological complexity understandable to no one and feasible to only a few. Therefore, whenever the subject of African music is connected in any way with the Egyptian contributions to Western culture or to the heritage of the Blacks, certain critics object—despite the facts recorded in "Abyssinian" contributions to

Western civilization, despite the earliest dark inhabitants noted by Herodotus, the Greek historian, of the fifth century, and despite the ancient descriptions of the elements, situations, and personalities seen in one of our oldest written historical sources—the Bible. For example, interrelationships between Moses and the Cushite, Solomon and the subjects of his Songs, the Ethiopian connections between Coptic and Christian affiliations of liturgy and lineage, the ancient European occupations of North African territories such as Tunisia, as well as the ancient Greco-Roman and Arabian slave practices—all guaranteed the descendants many colorful and revealing changes in physical types throughout successive generations.

Many Black Americans such as Thurgood Marshall, Langston Hughes, Charles Chestnutt, Walter White, the Morials of New Orleans, and the "Blue bloods" of Virginia resemble people from the Third World countries, from Egypt to South Africa, from Morocco to Nigeria, and from Mexico to South America. Yet castes and cultures of the African worlds have become too separated. Still, skin color alone does not solve the problem of who should be considered a part of the Pan-African complex.

Pan-Africanism—about the brotherhood of man first before the factor of race—may be the corrective force. In this era so earmarked for Pan-African unity, continental correlations could cut across the lines of race and assemble people together for a new time and new change. The justifications, then, for including in this book any African offspring or any Third World composer from any part of any continent lies somewhere between the color of a person's skin and that person's preferred brotherhood, heritage, or cultural association.

Prolusion III: Pan-Africanism

The theory of Pan-Africanism, developed by such luminaries as C. L. R. James, Franz Fanon, and others, is defined as a Diaspora—Blacks in worldwide kinship and significance whose roots can be traced to an African ancestry. Pan-African composers who are discussed in this book consist of such persons who were born in the United States of America, and abroad.

The following sections include Pan-African music and composers identified according to definitions presented in Prolusion I. Pioneer composers introduced at the commencement of several sections are primarily documented by Maud Cuney Hare, James Trotter, and by standard music dictionaries, both foreign and domestic. Discussed here in new review caused by a revival of interest in both the Hare and Trotter books as well as in some of the forebears, they serve as retrospective reminders of the historical use of African elements in the music. Later composers who follow are presented in the same chronological outline and reflect the legacies of those progenitors of musical ideas who went before them, thereby projecting images of both the influential and the influenced.

XV

PAN-AFRICAN COMPOSERS: LATIN AMERICA, THE ISLANDS, AND EUROPE

Introduction

A study of the music from the outer Americas must be prefaced by discussions of similarities in speech, climate, coastal territory, and mutual lifestyles to territories of North America, particularly in the Georgia Sea Islands and in the Charleston area of South Carolina where some of the clearest connections can be made. It is interesting to note that facts of historical and linguistic kinds directly melded into both worlds, and that the common geographic ocean which connected the two societies, lent credence to the commonality of idioms and cultural practices. The striking sameness of the Boone Hall and Magnolia plantations once maintained by slave labor, and the rice marshes of Charleston competed with Annenberg Sugar Mill Plantation and companion farmlands of the Caribbean as background accompaniments to the music which was made in those places. Charleston, home of the "shag" (official State dance accompanied by rhythm and blues), was important to the analogous use of African elements in formulating the "Charleston" dance—the dance itself perhaps being inspired by the "James P. Johnson's and Richard McPherson's Charleston" song from the 1923 musical *Runnin' Wild*.

Likewise, a study of composers from the outer Americas must be prefaced by a word about the music found in certain locations. Caribbean music from Guyana, Jamaica, Puerto Rico, St. Thomas, and similar islands have had a great impact upon that of North America, as proven by various scholars such as John Storm Roberts, Erroll Hill, Ricardo Alegria, John Sealey, Hector Vega Druet, and Vada Butcher. Some older Caribbean forms most directly related to Africa have been documented well. Just to name a few, there is calypso from Trinidad, the bomba and plena dances and songs from Puerto Rico, the méringue from Haiti (a salon dance identical to the habanera of Cuba), the habanera or criolla from Cuba (related to the African bamboula), the calinda or fandango-like dance from Santo Domingo, the (religious) comfa music and kwa-kwa (or queh-queh—dance-songs for weddings, complete with kwa-kwa sticks to accompany) from Guyana, Shango religious music, the baquiné or wake music in keeping traditions for the deceased, shanties (for house moving, etc.), blowing tunes (melodies, according to John Sealey's *Music in the Caribbean*, sung "in tongues" with "deep throaty sounds called groaning," and like the hocket of Baptist spirituals), and so on. Newer forms such as reggae, ska, soca, etc. have also had a close connection with North American music, but have themselves, in turn, been influenced as much by mainland music. But perhaps one of the most important affiliations of the past was that of the calypso connection, discussed in the next section.

The Influence of Calypso

Almost concurrent with the proclamations about the new jazz music in various media, came the transportation of calypso to the mainland by Trinidadian Frederick Wilmoth Hendricks (1896?–1973). Although the origin is unknown, writers such as Hector Vega-Druet, John Sealey, J. D. Elder, John S. Roberts, P. A. Braithwaite and others documented that the history of calypso travelled along the routes of slave eras as did the other folk songs. Mainly a vocal ballad-type music, calypso involved topical story-songs or commentaries whose associations mingled with acts from social entertainment with accompanying instruments (such as kwa-kwa sticks, guitar, African drums—replaced by the more recent steel drums) to protest attestations with fighting sticks and associated physical routines. Variously spelled as "careso," caliyso, etc., its history was directly related to words such as kaiso, kaliso, kaito, kaico or kaicho, cariso, rouso, wouso and kalenda, and showing a heritage of innumerable derivatives from Africa to the Islands, and song literature from Hendricks's *Johnny Take My Wife, Gin and Coconut Water*, and *Stone Cold Dead in the Market*, to Lord Valentino's *Shot Gun Wedding* to Lord Coffee's *Thelma's Pork* to Calypso Rose's *Come Leh We Jam*.

According to Errol Hill's research published in the *Ethnomusicology* Journal (September, 1967), the earliest use of the word "calypso" appeared in Trinidad in 1900 when a song containing seven two-line stanzas of creole and English lyrics was published in the *Port of Spain Gazette*. He furthermore stated that theories of origin ranged from names of sailing vessels, to names of persons such as the lady from Curaçao and the slave, Cecile Calipso, who was listed on an 1821 deed from the Laurel Hill Estate. However, he concurs with those who traced calypso backwards to Atilla the Hun, and an African origin.

Primarily sustained in Trinidad by such composer-performers as Lord Coffee, Mighty Terror, Emperor Selassie, Lord Cristo, Calypso Rose, Mighty Sparrow, Lord Kitchener, and others, concepts appeared throughout the Caribbean in terms of masquerade or carnival music, road marches and festivals. Supposedly partly related to paseo rhythm (a modern rumba), it has evolved into the modern "soca" (or the "soul calypso" coined by Lord Shorty). Most of these songs appeared in strophic form.

It is interesting to note an improvisatory nature and word collection with similarities to jazz. While calypso is a simpler form of music than jazz, the use of bands jamming in "jammette" tents, the catchy, impromptu creations with ever-changing possibilities dependant upon the whims of the chantwell or lead singer, and the longer historical and cultural associations with the slave history of its people, lend credence to the fact that calypso is at least one of the older forms which influenced the history of early jazz.

Other Forms

It is revealing to observe that small musical forms familiar to our ears were richer in historical significance and longevity than imagined. Derivatives in Guyana, for example, such as "comfa" (or "cumfa") implied religious services lasting over several days, with feasts, dancing, unusual utterances to gods and ancestors, secret codes, as well as elaborate preparations and languages for receiving the benefits of such worship. In this ritual to which one has to be invited or allowed to enter upon special request (or suffer embarrassing or adverse consequences), one notes a relationship to Protestant dances of North America, and a kinship with the shango-type spirits of other areas throughout the Pan-African world of yesteryear.

The calypso, discussed above, meant not only the entire masquerade scene of pan tents, pan drums, road marches, royalty associations and appropriate costumes, etc., but a long history of languages of first the French, and then the English. The word also entailed history beginning in the early 1800's, rather than in the 1900's when Hendricks first brought the modern-day versions to North America, and factors complete with political overtones, slave revolts and stick battle music. As in the cumfa forms, it also was derived from things African.

Still other musical forms amassed in the Caribbean consisted of shanties, shangos (orisha, etc.), blowing tunes (speaking in tongues), whaling songs, kalindas, jonkanoo and masquerade forms, parang, and others mentioned in the introduction, some of which were related to Spanish-speaking slaves. In general, present-day vestiges of African forms were found in the Caribbean in such structures as the following: cumfa and queh-queh (kwa-kwa) were encountered only in Guyana; calypso was more popular in Trinidad than elsewhere; only in San Juan were the bomba and plena danced and delivered; and in St. Thomas, no African-derived form was left in the culture of the people. There, the quadrille was a popular dance from the past, but was not African-derived. Unfortunately, not enough has been done with the indigenous Indian forms.

Puerto Rican dancers of the bomba and the plena.

Instruments

Although European-derived instruments were certainly observed by slaves of the Islands, it was still a fact of life that the majority of early music-making devices were those made by hand. Throughout the Carib-

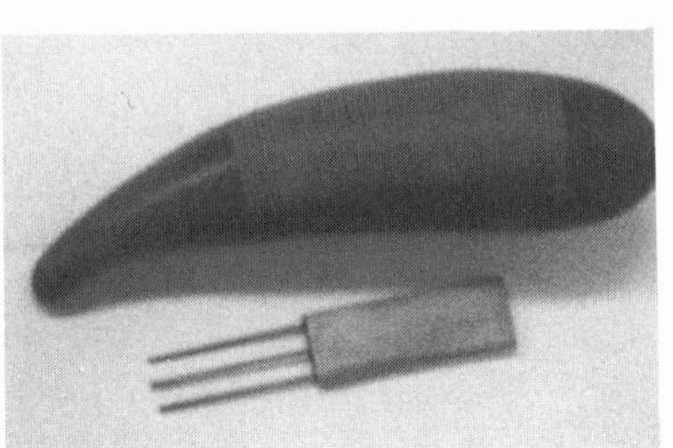

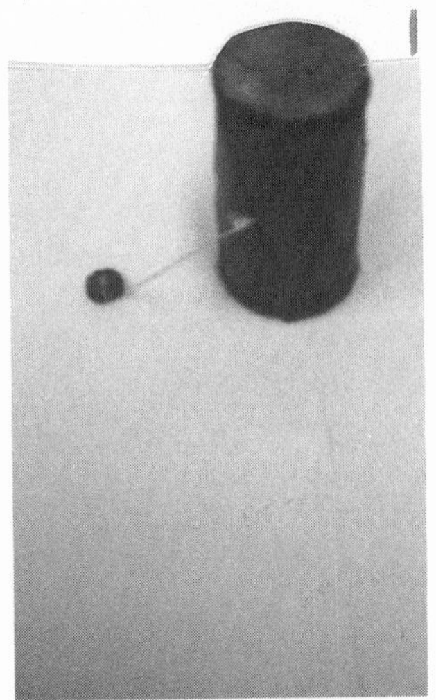

Caribbean Instruments: a. Maracas; b. Guiro (scrape or scratch instrument); c. hand drum; d. steel pan.

bean today, western instruments live alongside the homemade ones as before, and the drums, maracas, gourds and sticks are just as popular as always. The guitar is a standard accompanying for the calypso forms, while the newer steel drums, developed by Trinidadians during this century, serve the population with either pop music for masquerades, or classical pieces for concerts.

Composers of Latin America and the Islands

Pan-African composers abroad have a direct link to African American music in that many of their works reflect influences and traceable transformations of Africanism. In addition, this modern era points to pentrating signs of Black American music in a reciprocal affiliation with that of Europe and the Americas and as depicted in the origins and progressive chronologies of jazz and ragtime. Therefore, the Americas, the Islands, and Europe serve as worldwide rings in the connective chain.

This chapter will deal with Pan-Africans of Europe and the outer Americas. In this case, Pan-African composers of the Third World will include those from Central and South America and the islands with the closest proximity to North America—the Bahamas, other Caribbean islands, and the West Indies, thereby leaving the continent of Africa as the final chapter. Discussed in two separate but related parts, the following geographic partitions, nevertheless, point to an omnipresent influence and cultural heritage of Africa as seen throughout the foreign segments of the Pan-African world.

There has been a recent revival of interest in two books by Maud Cuney Hare and James Trotter. Similar excitement accompanied the release of the Black Music Series by Columbia Records during the late 1970s. Contained in the set are musical compositions by the classical contemporaries of Mozart, Haydn, Beethoven, and Bridgetower: Joseph Bologne Chevalier de Saint Georges and José Maurício Nunes Garcia, who begin the chain of Latin American and island composers to follow.

JOSEPH BOULOGNE CHEVALIER DE SAINT GEORGES (1739–1799)

Chevalier de Saint Georges was born in Basse-Terre, Guadeloupe, West Indies, to a French father (M. de Boulogne) and a West Indian mother. Taken abroad by his father to be educated in Paris, France, as violinist, composer, actor, and fencing master, he excelled as a pupil of Jean Marie Le Clair, Francois Joseph Gossec, and others. The *Oxford Companion*, J. A. Rogers, the *Nouvelle Biographie Universelle*, and Maud Hare registered a birthday of 1745. However, the most recent studies by Dominique de Lerma for Columbia records and the *Black Perspective* make a convincing case of the earlier date of 1739. Hare also noted that St. Georges was added to his name in honor of a very fine ship which was docked at Guadeloupe. Dominique de Lerma stated that his father's surname, Boulogno, might not have been used.

Acclaimed in both the music and social worlds, his fencing engagements were as much announced in the media as were his musical tours. As a composer of the classical era, he was hailed as one of the first "French composers of sting quartets." As a violinist, his merits were commended by many important musicians of Europe. In fact, his accomplishments were excellent enough to ensure him the job of director of the Concert des Amateurs upon the retirement of his teacher, Gossec. Rogers pointed out, however, that one of the musical companies which he directed had to be disbanded by Marie Antoinette because of prejudices. He was intensely interested in drama and his acting in some of his original plays received several reviews.

Joseph Chevalier de St. Georges. From Maud C. Hare's *Negro Musicians and Their Music*. (Associated/Da Capo).

As a personable and informed citizen, his varied experiences and relationships included friendships with the Duke Montesson of New Orleans and his wife, with Marie Antoinette and the French court. A person who sought further excitement in the military until he was unfairly jailed for one year, his taste for the army and politics was well known.

In addition to the Hare document, his life and work have also been recorded by J. A. Rogers, Jean de Beauvoir, John Duncan, and Henry Angelo and in various biographical dictionaries of both domestic and foreign publication. Yet it was the tangible evidence of a real kind that made the difference in association and acceptance through the study of score and sound together. Clearly, the publisher, editor, Columbia Record Company, conductor, and the finest performers had outdone themselves by producing a recording of his *Symphonie Concertante* and *Symphony No. 1*.

Among the compositions at the Library of Congress were *Concerto* for violin (edited by D. de Lerma for Peer-Southern and Columbia Records); *Trio Sonata* (score at Indiana University Center); *Deux Symphonies Concertantes* for violins (Paris: Chez M. Bailleux); *Six Quartets* for two violins, viola, and bass (Chez M. Sieber, Paris); *Six Sonatas* for violin (Chez Pleyel, 1800?); *Sonata III* for two violins (B. Schott's Sonne). Others were *L'Âmant Anonyme* for voices and orchestra (ms. in Paris Conservatory); *Symphonie*, Opus 11, No. 1 (also recorded by Columbia and published by Peer-Southern); *String Quartet* (excerpt in Hare's *Negro Musicians*); *Sonata in Bb* for violin (Indiana Center); *Scena Ernestine* for soprano and orchestra (Columbia recording); *Le Marchand de Marrons; La Fille Garcon; La Chasse Tarantella*; and possibly *Adagio in F* for piano (recorded by Raymond Jackson and Natalie Hinderas).

JOSÉ MAURÍCIO NUNES GARCIA (1767–1830)

Not until his *Requiem Mass* was published by Schirmer in 1976 (edited by Dominque de Lerma and recorded on Columbia Records with Nathan Carter conducting Morgan State University Choir, and with Paul Freeman conducting the London Symphony Orchestra), did North Americans take note of what the Brazilians had known all along: that Padre José Maurício Nunes Garcia was a first-rate composer of the classical period. In his time, his work as choirmaster, organist, and teacher was highly praised and was considered with great admiration and respect by the Europeans who visited as well as by the Brazilians themselves.

Because, as Albert Luper pointed out in *The Music of Brazil* (Pan American Union, 1934), the "cultivation of fine-art music in Brazil was carried on almost entirely by the Church," José Maurício was a front-runner in the music of Brazil. Born in Rio de Janeiro, Brazil and educated at the Escola de Santa Cruz, this composer of "mixed Indian and Negro blood" composed more than the "about two hundred works" suggested by Luper. Cleofe Person de Mattos, in *Cataloga Temático das Obras do Padre José Maurício Nunes Garcia*, compiled in 1970 a list of mainly sacred compositions numbering over twice that number, including such titles as *Massas* (nineteen), *Credos* (nine), *Graduais* (twenty-seven), *Laudamus* (three), *Ofertorios* (three), *Qui Sedes e Quoniam* (three), *Sequencias* (five), *Vesperas* (four), *Motetos* (twelve), *Te Deum* (seven), *Beneditos* (two), and others, both sacred and secular.

José Maurício Nunes Garcia. Courtesy of Brazilian Embassy.

Although the Albert Luper account is very informative, the Luis Correa de Azevedo books are more comprehensive and numerous (*A Música Brasileira e Seus Fundamentos*, Pan American Union, 1948; *150 Anos de Música no Brazil*, Livraria José Olympio Press, 1956, Rio de Janeiro; and others listed in his *Bibliografia Musical Brasileira*, Departamento Municipal de Cultura, 1946). He describes José Maurício as being the "son of humble Negro parents whose ancestors had been slaves" and writes that Segismundo Neukomon, a student of Haydn, considered him "the foremost improviser of the world."

Garard Béhague wrote in his *Music of Brazil* that "there is no evidence that he studied music at the Fazenda Santa Cruz established by the Jesuits in the surroundings of Rio de Janeiro as has often been reported. He apparently did have some training in solfege under a local teacher, Salvador José . . . and he received formal instruction in philosophy, languages, rhetoric and theology." Yet he admitted that the intellectual brilliance of the priest was meritorious and noted his appointment as chapel master of the Rio de Janeiro Cathedral as the "most significant musical position in the city," thereby supporting the genuine worth and genius of the composer, whether or not he considered Escola de Santa Cruz a myth.

Important are several titles written by Mario de Andrade such as *A Modinha de José Maurício*, 1930. Very helpful also are the program notes by Dominique de Lerma which thoroughly review Cleofe Person de Mattos's *Catálogo Temático das Obras do Padre José Maurício Nunes Garcia.* It was the work of Cleofe Person de Mattos, according to Correa de Azevedo, who first produced the proof of José Maurício's correct date of birth by publishing a photocopy of the baptismal certificate in the *Cultura Política*, and V. N. 52, 9/1945. Still another good resource is the Gilbert Chase *Guide to Latin American Music* (Library of Congress compilation with no date) which includes both commentary and bibliographic information. Also of importance is the Associacao Brasileira do Produtores de Discos, MEC/Funart/INM, which recorded certain of his works such as *Missa Pastoril para a Noite de Natal.*

José Silvestre de los Dolores White. From James Trotter's *Music and Some Highly Musical People.*

CLAUDIA JOSÉ DOMINGO BRINDIS DE SALA (1800–1912)

The reputation of Brindis de Sala from Havana, Cuba—chevalier, band conductor, and violinist—outlived the whereabouts of his compositions, bound copies of which, according to Hare, he presented to the Queen of Spain when serving as court violinist. Educated at the academy under the tutelage of Ignatius Calvo, he was awarded a degree upon passing examinations given by Corporation of Havana; he also did further study at the Paris Conservatory and in Germany.

As a pioneer in the field of music, de Sala stood as a symbol for present-day violinists because of his numerous concerts in Europe, the islands, and Latin America and because of the numbers of honors bestowed upon him by royalty. Also listed in the *Oxford Dictionary of Music,* which described him as "another Negro violinist," he, like many others of the contemporary Americas, chose Europe as the road to success.

JOSÉ SILVESTRE DE LOS DOLORES WHITE (1839?–1920)

Perhaps the most comprehensive sketch of José White was done by James Trotter in 1881. But the study of José White, a native of Matanzas, Cuba, was partially revived by Paul Glass in his collaboration with Paul Freeman for the purpose of the Columbia recording (c. 1976) when he "unearthed" the *Violin Concerto* which led to further excitement in the aggregation of names and works. White, also acclaimed as a brilliant violinist-composer, gained an education at the Paris Conservatory, accumulated several prizes, and delivered numerous concerts in Europe, in the Islands, and the Americas, including North America.

According to Hare, his compositions include *Quatuor* for strings, fantasies, violin studies, and others published by Schirmer. At the Library of Congress are his *La Bella, Cubana* (habanera for two violins and piano, c. 1910), *Jeunesse* (habanera for two or four violins with piano, c. 1897), and *La Jota Argonese* (*caprice* for violin and piano, Opus 5, edited by Paul Glass, 1975).

OCCIDE JEANTY (1860–1936)

Occide Jeanty was born in Port-au-Prince, Haiti. Sent to Paris by his government to continue his studies, he returned to Haiti as musical director of the Republic. Composer of many marches for military band, he was the creator of *Haitian March 1804* and the *Vautours de 6 Decembre.* Both Nicolas Slonimsky (in *Music of Latin America,* Crowell, 1945) and the Pan American Union listed his achievements.

Ludovic Lamothe. From his *Valses, Dances Espagnoles, Scenes de Carnaval.*

LUDOVIC LAMOTHE (1882–1953)

Ludovic Lamothe, born in Port-au-Prince, Haiti, began his musical studies at an early age and followed in the footsteps of Jeanty when he traveled to Paris in 1910 in order to study at the conservatory. Called the "Black Chopin," he was a composer of many waltzes and compositions, some of which were entitled *Nibo* for piano, *La Dangereuse* for piano; others of his works were recorded, according to Slonimsky, on RCA Victor label (*Fleurs d'Haiti*) and also printed in New York. When interviewed by Slonimsky around 1944, Lamothe was then Chief of Music in the Republic of Haiti. He was also discussed in Pan American Union books and in the Eileen

Southern *Dictionary*. The Library of Congress houses an album of his piano works.

JUSTIE ELIE (1883–1931)

Justin Elie was born in Cap Haitien; his death came in New York. Hailed in the Pan American Union's *Compositores de América* as the composer of *La Suite Babylon, La Kiskaya; Suite Aborigene* and *Danses Tropicales* based on Haitian and Cuban themes, he was also discussed in Nicolas Slonimsky's *Music of Latin America* as one who also studied at the Paris Conservatory. Upon his return to Haiti, he was obsessed with the voodoo rituals and wrote pieces in the manner of the rites. Slonimsky noted that his pieces for piano, violin, and voice have been published in the United States.

EDWARD HENRY MARGETSON (1891–1962)

Edward Margetson was born in St. Kitts, British West Indies. After graduating from grammar school in St. Kitts with the Cambridge University Senior Local Certificate, he attended Columbia University as a composition student of Seth Bingham.

Margetson became a teacher of music in 1922, a director of the choir at the Church of Crucifixion in New York, a position which he took in 1916, according to *Who's Who in Colored America*, also serving as organist as well. In 1931, he was the organizer of the Schubert Society of New York as well as its director. In addition, he was an associate of the American Guild of Organists.

He was a recipient of the Victor Bajer Fellowship in 1925, and in 1927, a second prize winner of the Harmon Foundation for Distinguished Achievement Among Negroes. Reviewed in Hare's *Negro Musicians*, the *Negro Yearbook*, in Evelyn White's *Selected Bibliography*, in several newsletters, journals, and in writing by William Burres Garcia, he was also seen in the *Black Perspective* and the Grove's *Dictionary*.

His compositions at the Library of Congress include *Hark, Hark My Soul* for children's voices and SATB; *I Think, Oh My Love* (in Rogie Clark's *Negro Art Songs*); *I Think When I Read That Sweet Story*, SATB and soprano with organ; *O Lord, Support Us* for SATB; *A Sailor's Song* (in Rogie Clark's *Negro Art Songs*, E. B. Marks); *Still, Still With Thee* for SATB, all published by the Boston Music Company except the Rogie Clark anthology. Another example held in the Sarah Sweetwine Collection at Eastern Michigan and published by Boosey/Belwin is *Tommy Lad*.

Maud Cuney Hare also lists additional compositions: *Echoes From the Caribbees*, a group of songs for solo voice with piano; *When You No More* and *Far From My Heavenly Home*, a madrigal and motet; the Evelyn White Chorale also programs his *Fair Daffodils We Weep*; the *Who's Who of Colored America* lists *Ronda Caprice* for full orchestra, *Ballade Valse Serenade* for cello, and "pieces for violin, piano, organ, etc."; and Don White adds these titles of *Break Forth Into Joy; Hosanna; Blessed Is He That Comes; Jesus Lives; Alleluia; Morning Hymn of Praise; Strong Song of God; Immortal Love; Through the Day Thy Love*; while Evelyn White adds *Come Ye Disconsolate; O Taste and See; Search Me, O Lord; Sing Unto the Lord*; and *Why Weep Ye By the Tide*.

JUAN FRANCISCO GARCIA (1892–)

Juan Francisco Garcia, according to the Pan American Series, *Compositores de América*, volume 2, was born in Santiago de los Caballeros, Dominican Republic. As a student at the Academia Municipal, he studied solfeggio and trumpet as well as other instruments, including the piano.

Significantly, Garcia stressed the folk songs of the Dominican Republic, where he was long "considered to be the foremost composer." Also a teacher, he wrote many articles. In *Panorama de la Música Dominicana*, he wrote of composers Luis Emilio Mena, Pedro Echavarría Lazala, Pablo R. Campos, Juan Bautista Espiñola, Jacinto Leopoldo Sanchez, Gabriel del Castillo, Aristides Rojas, José Feliu Hijo, Emilio Arte, Gabriel del Orbe, Manuel de Jesus Lovelace, and of himself. He also wrote that he was director of the Bandas Municipales de Santiago de los Caballeros y de Puerto Plata, and other orchestras. In 1944, he was appointed director of the Conservatory of Cuidad Trujillo.

Juan Francisco Garcia. From *Compositores de América*, v. 2. Used by permission of Pan American Union.

For his compositions (one tonal example is given in *Compositores de América*, volume 2, from his *Sinfonía No. 1*), he received first prize in the National Exposition's Creole Dance Contest (1927); the Pro Arte National Medal was awarded by the Society Ateneo Amantes de la Luz Santiago de los Caballeros (1942) as first prize in the Symphony Contest held by the radio-television station "La Voz Dominicana" (1954). No publisher was listed for his works. Some orchestral ones were *Scherzo y Trio*, 1940; *Sinfonía No. 2*, 1941; *Triade Sinfónica*, 1953; *Simastral*, 1947; *Loor a Trujillo*. Works for piano included *Catorce Caprichos Criollos* (fourteen pieces); *Doce Valses* (12 pieces); *Rondos, Ocho Danzas Criollas* (eight Creole Dances). Works for voice and piano; *Cuatro Cantos Escolares; Una Gira a la Otra Banda*; and others (volume 2 of *Compositores de América* listed forty-seven works between 1935 and 1949, all unpublished).

Nicolas Slonimsky, in *Music of Latin America* (Crowell, 1945), noted that Garcia was largely "self-taught" but nevertheless "acquired a solid technique of composition which enabled him to write in symphonic forms," and which evidently enabled him to win prizes for *Second Symphony* at the Dominican national contest for the best in 1944. Slonimsky also wrote that a collection of Garcia's piano pieces, *Ritmos Quisqueyanos*, was published in New York in 1927.

ASSIS REPUBLICANO (1897–)

In his *Music of Latin America* (T. Crowell, 1945), Nicolas Slonimsky identified the Brazilian Assis Republicano as a "Negro composer" who studied with Francisco Braga and began to compose at an early age. He was said to have composed mainly for voice, producing "four operas, *O Bandeirante* (The Pioneer), *Natividade de Jesus* (Birth of Jesus), *Amazonas*, and *O Ermitão de Gloria* (The Hermit of Glory); a *Symphony of Multitudes* for orchestra, chorus, and band; *Improviso* for cello and orchestra; and a song *Magdala*. Slonimsky noted that the *Improviso* was in the Fleisher Collection, Philadelphia, Pennsylvania.

ESTEBAN PENA MORELL (c. 1897–1938)

Esteban Morell was identified by Nicolas Slonimsky as "a Negro musician" who was born in Santo Domingo about 1894. Juan García, who did not mention the race of anyone discussed in *Panorama de la Música Dominicana*—a common "oversight" by people of the Islands—placed different dates—1897–1938) and cited him as a "notable musico dominicano" of international renown who received his first instruction from Alfredo Soler.

In 1911, Morell performed some of his first compositions for the municipal band. Returning to his native city, he continued his studies and also began collecting folklore on which he based some of his musical works such as *Folklo-Música Dominicana, Anacaona, Sinfonía Barbara, Embrujo-Antillano, Alma Criolla,* and many others. Upon Morell's death in Barcelona, Spain, Juan García wrote that many friends came from Europe and North America to mourn his passing.

JOSÉ DOLORES CERÓN (1897–)

José Cerón was born in the capital of the Dominican Republic. Identified as "a Negro musician" by Nicolas Slonimsky in his *Music of Latin America,* he was also discussed in Juan Garcia's *Panorama of Dominican Music.* After first beginning a medical education, Cerón studied with José de Jesús Ravelo and Pena Morel and eventually used his knowledge to compose both popular music as well as symphonic compositions.

As director of the orchestra, he composed valses, danzas, criollas, and dancetas. As director of the Primer Banda del Regimiento in 1930, he found the time to compose a large group of works including poemas sinfónicos *Enriquillo y las Vírgenes de Galindo.* He wrote for the Orquesta Sinfónica Nacional and other works including *Sinfonía, Tres Preludios.*

MAUDE CUMMINGS TAYLOR (1897–)

Maude Taylor, composer, teacher, and organist, was born in Bermuda. Educated at Chicago Extension University in 1925, she later attended Columbia University, Matlock College in England, the American Conservatory in Fontainebleau, France, and the Conservatory in Mozarteum, Salzburg. Teaching privately and also administering the music of Cornerstone Baptist Church in Brooklyn for forty-one years, she still found time to compose such works as *The Day Is Nearly Done, He Hath Put a New Song in My Mouth,* and *They Shall Run and Not Be Weary* (anthem). In 1964, she became a member of ASCAP.

AMADEO ROLDÁN (1900–1939)

Amadeo Roldán was born in Paris, France, of Cuban parents. He studied at the Royal Conservatory of Madrid and was awarded a prize for his violin playing by age fifteen. His teachers were Pablo Hernandez, Agustín Soller, Antonio Fernandez Brodas, and Conrado del Campo.

The *Compositores de América* series, volume 1, traced his return to Cuba where he became concertmaster of the Philharmonic Orchestra of Havana, played with the Chamber Music Society as violist, and founded the Havana String Quartet in 1927. He was appointed assistant conductor of the Philharmonic Orchestra in 1925 and conductor in 1932. Roldán also taught at the Philharmonic Conservatory and at the Conservatorio Municipal de Music (by 1935) as professor of harmony and composition.

Significant also for devoting himself to "the conscientious study of African influences on Cuban music," the *Compositores* series gives him credit for being the "first to write symphonic works using Cuban themes and rhythms of African origins." Also listed in Joseph Machlis's *Introduction to Contemporary Music* as "a mulatto, [who] had a vivid feeling for Afro-Cuban rhythms," he is also mentioned by Alain Locke, Eileen Southern, Dominque de Lerma, Barnes and Noble, Maude Cuney Hare, and others. His *Preludio Cubano* shows the use, in Example 87, of African rhythms of the bamboula dance rhythms (measures 1–4) and the rhythmic complexity of thirds in the left hand and cross rhythms (measures 55–56).

His list of works at the Library of Congress are *Canciones Populares Cubanas* for cello and piano; *Motivos de Son,* a photocopy of Nos. 5 and 6 of the eight songs with percussion, written for voice and piano; and *Preludio Cubana* for piano (Peer-Southern published all above except *Motivos de Son* which was published by New Music of San Francisco). Listed in the volume 1 series are ballets: *La Rebambaramba* and *El Milagro de Anaquillé*; orchestral works: Obertura Sobre Temas Cubanos; Tres Pequeños Poemas; suites: *La Rembambaramba; A Changó; Tres Toques; Rítmicas* I, I, I, and I for flute, oboe, clarinet, trumpet, bassoon, and piano; *Rítmicas* V and VI, for Cuban and percussion instruments; *Poema Negro* for string quartet; works for voice: *Danza Negra; Mulato; Trozo* for piano and others. The music of Roldán is also recorded on Mainstream.

Ex. 86. *Preludio Cubana,* Amadeo Roldán, mm. 1–4 and mm. 55–56. © Copyright 1967 by Southern Music Publishing Co., Inc. International copyright secured. All rights reserved including the right of public performance for profit. Used by permission.

ROQUE CORDERO (1917–)

Roque Cordero was born in Panama City, Republic of Panama, where he received his early education under Maximo Arrates Boza, Pedro Rebolledo, Herbert de Castro, and Myron Schaeffer. In the United States, he studied at the University of Minnesota and in 1947 graduated magna cum laude from Hamline University. His teachers of composition were Ernst Krenek among others, and of conducing, Dimitri Mitropoulos, Stanley Chapple, and Leon Barzin.

Cordero has distinguished himself as professor of composition at the National Institute of Music in Panama from 1950 to 1966, as director of the National Institute of Music from 1953 to 1964, as conductor of the National Orchestra of Panama from 1964 to 1966, and as assistant director of the Latin American Music Center and professor of composition at Indiana University from 1966 to 1969. In addition, he has served as music consultant for Peer-Southern International Corporation since 1969 and as professor of composition at Illinois State University since 1972. He became a member of Kennedy Center's National Committee on Cultural Diversity in the Performing Arts in 1980 and a member of the Creative Artists Division of the Illinois Arts Council for 1981 and 1982.

In 1949, he won the Guggenheim Fellowship and in 1974, a Koussevitzky International Recording Award for his *Concerto for Violin* (recorded by Columbia Records on the Black Composers Series and performed by Sanford Allen, with Paul Freeman, conductor of the London Symphony Orchestra, 1977). His *First Symphony* received honorable mention in the Reichhold Music Contest in 1947, Detroit, Michigan; *Rapsodia Campesina* was awarded first prize in the Ricardo Miro Contest held in Panama in 1953; *Second Symphony* won the Caro de Boesi prize in the second Inter-American Music Festival, Caracas, 1957; *String Quartet No. 3* received the Chamber Music Award in the Inter-American Music Contest in Costa Rica in 1977; and in 1975, he was given a fellowship grant from the National Endowment for the Arts to compose *Cantata For Peace*. In August of 1974, the Panamanian Government issued him the Gold Medal, National Honor, and in June of 1982, the Grand Cross of the Order of Vasco Núñez de Balboa, delivered by the President of Panama.

Many artists, groups, and orchestras of American and Europe have performed Cordero's music. Commissions have been received from Dimitri Mitropoulos for *Introduction and Allegro Burlesco*; the Civic Orchestra of Minneapolis for *Five Short Messages*, the Coolidge Foundation for *String Quartet No. 1*; the Koussevitzky Music Foundation for *Concerto for Violin and Orchestra*; Adolfo Odnopossof for *Sonata* for cello and piano; the Third Caracas Festival for *Symphony With One Theme and Five Variations* (No. 3); Hamline University for *Two Short Choral Pieces*; Alabama University for *String Quartet No. 2*; Catholic University of Chile for *Concertino for Viola and Strings*; the Second Music Festival of Guanabara for *Música Veinte*; the National Institute of Culture and Sports of Panama for the film score *An Mar Tule*; Illinois State University for *Momentum Jubilo, Six Mobiles for Orchestra, Music for Five Brass, Soliloquios No. 5* for string bass; and the Kennedy Center for the *Double Concerto Without Orchestra* for violin and piano.

Roque Cordero.

Cordero has been guest conductor for the Bogota Symphony Orchestra of Colombia, for the Philharmonic Orchestra of Chile, and for the Municipal Theater Orchestra of Rio de Janeiro. He also conducted at the first International Festival of Buenos Aires. In addition, he has lectured extensively in America and Europe, has served as adjudicator for the International Composition Competition in San Salvador in 1957, in Caracas in 1966, in Tuscaloosa, Alabama, and Rio de Janeiro in 1969, New Orleans in 1970, and New York and San Juan, Puerto Rico in 1980.

His latest works employ contemporary techniques of highly intricate rhythmic and harmonic complexities such as constantly changing meters seen in Example 86, measures 122–129 of *Sonata Breve* for piano, rhythmic groupings of seven or eight notes in rapid succession, and the bamboula rhythm as seen on the first beat of measures 151–152, Example 87.

Cordero's works have been performed in many locations throughout the Americas—at symposiums held in Washington, D.C., and Houston, Texas, and at festivals in Panama. Highlighted in festivals, numerous halls, and institutions, his compositions listed in the Pan-American Union series, *Compositores de América* between 1939 and 1956 total at least thirty, while examples at the Library of Congress, between 1960 and 1970 show twenty-seven. Primarily published by Peer-Southern, his works in part are for orchestra: *Oberaturo Panameña No. 2; Primera Sinfonía; Ocho Miniaturas*; for solo and orchestra: *Concertos* for piano and violin; for string orchestra: *Movimiento Sinfónico; Adagio Trágico; Danza en Forma de Fuga*; for chamber groups: *Tres Mensajes Breves* for viola and piano; *Sonata* for cello and piano;

Ex. 87a. *Sonata Breve*, Roque Cordero, m.m. 122–129. © Copyright 197 by Peer International Corporation. International copyright secured. All rights reserved including the right of public performance for profit. Used by permission.

Ex. 87b. *Sonata Breve*, Roque Cordero, m.m. 151–153. © Copyright 1970 by Peer International Corporation. International copyright secured. All rights reserved including the right of public performance for profit. Used by permission.

Dos Piezas Cortas for violin and piano; *Sonatina* for violin, cello, flute, and clarinet; *Sonatina Rítmica; Sonata Breve* (1970); *Five New Preludes* for piano (1983 manuscript); *Dúo 1954* for 2 pianos (1965); *Tres Piececillas para Alina* 1978; *Variations and Theme for Five* woodwind quintet (1976); *Solioquios* Nos. 1, 2, 3, and 4 for solo flute, alto sax, clarinet, percussion, respectively, the latter of which is in manuscript (1975–1981); *Poetic Nocturne of the Min River* for four flutes, two alto flutes, bass clarinet, and two percussions (1981 manuscript); and for voice: *Two Short Chorale Pieces (Dos Pequeñas Piezas Corales)*; and others.

Postscript V: Other Composers

This section has surely not completely delivered all of the composers of the Islands and of the Americas. For in many cases, because photographs were unavailable for study of those long since passed, and since the geographic locations are not accessible at this time, the answers to identification and contribution remain incomplete. Likewise, because some of the composers could not be located, the list must necessarily remain a challenge for scholars to pursue.

Among some of the incomplete biographies are those from Brazil and adjacent Americas. Grove's *Dictionary of Music* lists 1551 as a date when Africans were used to welcome visitors to Peru and reports that "Probably the earliest picture of negro musicians (there) is to be found in a miscellany of local curiosities collected in northern Peru between 1782 and 1785 by Baltasar Jaime Martinez Compannon (1737–97) and sent between 1788 and 1790 to Madrid, where the collection survives." Other documents pinpoint development in Bahia, Brazil (the major slave trade center in South America) as early as the 1600's. Names that have been passed down through the centuries include:

Galindo Salinda from Lima, Peru, an improviser of witty topical verses, although not formally trained.

Brazilians discovered in Minas Gerais by Francisco Curt Lange, (also discussed by Gerard Béhague) as well as representatives of the other Americas include:

José Joaquim Emerico Lobo de Mesquita (c. 1740's–1805), composer of *Regina Caeli, Masses in Eb and F, Salve Regina,* and other works now available in modern notation; chapel master of several churches in Rio de Janeiro and Vila Rica.

Ignacio Parreira Neves (1730–c. 1792), composer of *Credo* and *Oratioio*; also a singer and member of the Brotherhood Nossa Senhora.

Francisco Gomes de Rocha (b. 1808–), composer of *Spiritus Domini*; successor to Mequita at Vila Rica for the Terceira Ordem do Carmo.

Manuel de Almeida Botelho, born in Recife in 1721; composer of *Mass*, and *Lauda Jersualem*; also traveled to Lisbon.

Luis Alvares Pinto (1719–1789), born in Recife, Brazil; composer of missas, matinas, movenas, and sonatas; and organist at St. Cecelia; also traveled to Lisbon.

Antonio Manso de Mota (b. 1732–), composer of operas and chapel master at São Paulo in 1768.

Frederico Espinosa (1820–1872), composer of polkas, mazurkas, marches, and valses.

Xisto Bahia, an "untrained" folk musician of the nineteenth century known for his singing and composing of modinhas (Brazilian ballads) and discussed by Albert Luper.

Zenon Rolon (1856–1902), born in Argentina; pianist, conductor, and composer of symphonies, operas, zuelas, salon, military, and sacred works; author of political literature.

Alton Augustus Adams (1889?–1987), born in St. Thomas, Virgin Islands; composer of band compositions: *Virgin Island March* (Mercury Music), *Governor's Own Military March* (Carl Fisher) and *Spirit of the U.S.N. March* (Candy-Bettoney) introduced in Maud Cuney Hare's *Negro Musicians and Their Music* (1936).

Othelo Bayard, writer of *Haiti Cherie*.

Frederick Wilmoth "Wilmouth Houdini" Hendricks (1896?–1973) or (1901–19730—ASCAP), the Trinidadian born in Port of Spain who delivered calypso to the United States, including *Johnny Take My Wife, Gin and Coconut Water, The Calypso Way, Don't Do That To Me*, and *Stone Cold Dead in the Market*.

Carlos Hayre, an eminent contemporary Black Peruvian musicologist-composer of *Cimarrones* as seen on a film released by the Cinema Guild.

José Gonzaga Sobrinho, guitarist-composer of *O Preliminar* (*Exercicios para Violão, Guitarra Método*, published by Bandeirante Editora Musical, 1973), from São Paulo, Brazil.

Jack Jeffers (1928–), from Montserrat, British West Indies, who was listed in the Howard Ethnic Center as the composer of *Theme and Variations, Elegis for Brass Quintet, March for Woodwind Quintets*, and on records. According to record jacket notes of *Black Music: The Written Tradition* (on which he plays tuba), Jeffers is conductor of the New York Classics big band, and teaches at the State University of New York at Old Westbury.

James Ingram Fox.

Blas Emilio Atehortua (1933–), born in Medellin, Colombia; composer of works listed in the tenth volume of Pan American Union's *Compositores de América*.

Emile and Emanuel "Picho" Volel, song writers and singers originally from Port-au-Prince, Haiti (Marc Records).

Jimmy Cliff and Bob Marley (1945–1981), Jamaican reggae composers (Island Records).

Ernest Ranglin, from Jamaica, guitarist-composer of *ska*.

Olive Lewin, member of the Escuela de Música de Jamaica and organizer of the internationally known folk singers of popular songs; a graduate of Real Conservatory of London.

Danny Gloucester Hill of Jamaica, composer of songs recorded on Dynamic Sound Records.

Kenneth "Lord Laro" Lara (1940–), a Trinidadian now living in Jamaica, whose songs are recorded on Federal Records and others.

Additional music creators throughout the Caribbean are: Reggae stars Akabu, Aswad, Peter Broggs, Bob Andy's Dub Rock, Judge Dread, Clancy Eccles, Alton Hortense Ellis, Gregory Isaacs, Shaba Ranks, and Yellowman;

Alton Augustus Adams of St. Thomas, West Indies (above);

James (Jamsie) Brewster, calypso musician from St. Croix;

Lemuel Christian, Director of Christian Musical Class, of Roseau, Dominica, and composer of *Isle of Beauty*, the national anthem;

Augustus Hinds (Bill Rogers).

Composers from Guyana: P. A. Braithwaite, author, compiler of *Folk Songs of Guyana* with Serena Braithwaite, composer of *Mashrarane Flounce*;

Rev. Mortimer Aloysius Cossou, trained at Queen's College and Howard University, who was minister at St. Catherine in Christianburg from 1914 to 1920 and also served later at St. Clements and All Saints Scots Church in New Amsterdam, Guyana, and who, in 1937, composed a coronation song, *Come Raise Your Voices*;

James Ingram Fox (1916–), pianist, author, conductor, relocated to New York City, was educated at New York College of Music and Columbia University, served as director of music and choir at Wiley College, as visiting lecturer at Western Michigan University, Chicago University, Brooklyn College, etc., and, according to *Outstanding Guyanese in America*, published two symphonies, an opera (*Dan Fodio*), a piano concerto, and songs, and also composed works for string orchestra, string quartet, 2 piano sonatas, a violin sonata, 4 suites for piano and violin, several choral works and sixty songs, etc.;

Augustus Hinds (Bill Rogers), who, according to record jacket notes, was called "shanto originator," "first Guyanese put on disc by RCA (1939)," "first to put Cumfa Dance on stage and the first to attempt to take Trinidad Carnival to Guyana . . . ," singer-composer of *The King's Abdication*;

Eddie Hooper, born in Guyana, moved to America, composer of words and music to songs in *Down in Guyana* (*Little Farmer, Sweet Sugar Cane, My Small Canoe, New Amsterdam, Kimbia, Bourda Market, Bartica*, and *Down in Guyana*);

Francis Percival Loncke (1900–1966), violinist, tenor, choirmaster, and organist at RC Cathedral, educated at Charlestown Convent, conducted Princesville Orchestra, composed *My Guiana*;

Patricia Adora Theresa Loncke (1945–1983), pianist who was first taught by violinist-teacher Francis Percival Loncke, her father, was educated at Queenstown RC School, University of the West Indies in Mona, Jamaica, and at Jamaica School of Music, composer of two songs for soprano, a vocal duet, several piano solos such as *L'Ombre Des Palmiers* (No. 2 from *Tropiques*);

Vesta Hyacinth Einifred Lowe (1909–19 ?), singer, educator, and folk song collector (*Guiana Sings*), who was educated at Teachers Training College (now C Potter Teachers College), at Tuskegee Institute, and who did further study at University of Pennsylvania State College, Cornell University and the University of Nebraska, moved to Brooklyn, New York, composer of *Four Folksongs for Guyana Independence (Nation, Bartica Grove, Teacha Gal, & Reuben)*;

George W. Noel.

George W. Noel, guitarist-singer, composer of *Sing! Guyana's Children* (*To Serve my Country, We Joinin' Di G.N.S., Farmerman, I Love my Country*, etc., pub./Min. of Cul.);

Phillip Edward Theodore Pilgrim (1917–1944), pianist-composer of music for A. J. Seymour's *The Legend of Kaieteur* (1944), large work for three pianos (originally intended for orchestra), 100 voices, soli, of six songs title *Come, O Come, Nod, Pan, Cradle Song, Dawn* and *Stephen and Herod*, who was educated at Queen's College and the Royal Academy of Music in London;

William R. A. Pilgrim (1920–), brother of Phillip, pianist, conductor of recorded version of his brother's *Legend*, and of choirs in England and Jamaica as well as in Guyana, composer of *Salute to Guyana* and *The Birds* (vocal); and arranger of Phillip Pilgrim's *Legend* for steel orchestra and two pianos;

Robert Cyril Gladstone Potter (1899–1981), author, educator and musician, was educated at Queen's College, Mico Training College in Jamaica, taught in Roman Catholic, Moravian, Wesleyan, Anglican and Presbyterian Schools, Kingston Trade Centre, Queen's College, etc., became principal of Georgetown Teacher's College, Deputy Director of Education, composer of *National Anthem of Guyana, Way Down Demerara, A Christmas Carol, Song of Hope*, and *My Guyana, Eldorado*;

Valerie Rodway, composer of *O Beautiful Guyana* and *Guyana The Free* (found in *Ten National Songs of Guyana*, Ministry of Culture), *Frolic, Sir Graeme* (East Coat Train) for piano;

Hugh Sam, pianist, now located in New York, composer of *Stabroek Fantasy* and *Steel Band Tramp* for piano, *Fantasia on Three Guianese Folk Songs* (*Sitira Gal, Timber Man and Itanimi* for piano);

Other Guyanese-born composers, found in interviews with composers, especially William Pilgrim, and in articles by Ras Michael, E. M. T. Moore, Norman E. Cameron, and Olivia Ah-young: P. M. De Weever, J. F. Rose, Caroline Moore, S. E. Blades, Kinsell Joseph, G. W. Newsom, H. N. Chapman Edward, Foster Francis, A. Briggs, Clem Nichols, Harry Mayers, J. De Cambra, J. L. V. Casimir, and arranger Morris Watson, Olivia Ahyoung (now of Tallahassee, Florida), Hilton Hemerding, Mildred Lowe (sister of Vesta), Lynette Dolphin, Horace Taitt, Cecile Nobrega, Walter Franker, Rev. Hawley Bryant, Wordsworth McAndrew, Keith Waite and Marc Matthews (both now in London), Bucky Brandt, Jo-Jo Felix and Eddie Grant (now in Barbados), Ian Hall (1940–), etc.;

In Jamaica: Olive Lewin, folk-song collector and arranger (*Brown Gal in de Ring, Hol' Yuh Han'*, etc.), Danny (Gloucester) Hill, Jimmy Cliff, Monty Alexander, and Kenneth Lara listed above; arranger Marjorie Whylie (*Traditional Songs of the Caribbean* as recorded by Organization of American States), reggae artists Bob Marley, Peter Tosh, Erald (Englishman) Briscoe (based in Washington, D.C.), Ras Michael, Marcia Griffiths (composer of *The Electric Slide*), *Burning Spear*, and others; according to Olivia Ahyoung's article, "Tradition and Change in Music in Guyana and the West Indies" (*Kyk-Over-Al*, No. 31, June, 1985), Jamaica has been the "leader" in the field of indigenous pop styles in that more of its composers get better exposure than other Caribbeans, and in that its reggae (developed from Rastafarian poetry and the earlier rhythms and styles of mento) has gained outside popularity; folk composers Bob Marley ("sufferah" music), Peter Tosh, Mickey Smith (dub poetry) and Mataburuka have been instrumental in this dissemination;

In Trinidad: J. D. Elder (1913–), author, choir director, folk–song collector, arranger, studied at London University; calypso artist-composers such as Mighty Sparrow (neé Slinger Francisco, composer of *Welcome to Trinidad Calypso*), Mighty Chalkdust (Hollis Liverpool), Mighty Terror (Fitzgerald Henry), Lord Kitchener (Aldwyn Roberts), Lord Superior (Andrew Marcano), Lord Pretender (Alric Farrell), Attila the Hun (Raymond Quevedo), Lord Invader (Rupert Grand), Growling Tiger (recorded *Knockdown Calypsos*, Rounder Records), The Destroyer, Crazy (*Dust Bin Cover Calypso*), Shadow (*Sugar Plum Calypso*), Merchant (*Norman, Is That You?*, Soca music), Calypso Rose (*The Soca Jam Calypso, Her Majesty Calypso*), Johnny King (*Wet Me Down Calypso*, hit in 1988), Len 'Boogsie Sharpe (*Woman is Boss*, calypso hit in 1988), Tambu (neé Chris Herbert), composer of *This Part Is It* (1988 hit), and Uprising (group); composers listed on Hollis Liverpool's *Portrait Calendar of Calypsonians of Trinidad and Tobago:* "Chieftain" Walter Douglas (1895–1982), composer of *The Murder of Olga, The Woodblock Scandal, Why Mi Neighbour Vex Wid Me, The Camel Walk and Dog Catching*; "Chinese" Patrick Jones (d. 1965), Julian (Mighty Unknown) Pierre (1914–1979), writer of *A.T.S. Girl, Prick for Judges, Emerline and the Tram Line, Ah Vex*; Erroll (The Growler) Duke (d. ca. 1950), composer of *The Farmer and the Breadfruit Tree, Old Lady You Mashing Mi Toe, Excursion to Grenada, Britain Will Never Surrender, Don't Hide Him Behind the Door, Bore a Hole in My Constitution and Stick You Grind*; Lady Iere, composer of *A Warning to Mothers, The Follyfication of the United Nations*; Randolph Thomas (1909–1974), composer of *Mariann*, and who teamed with Lady Iere; and Frederick Wilmoth Hendricks discussed above;

In Venezuela: classical guitarist Jorge Guillen (1959–), born in Caracas, taught at Escuela Superior de Música, J. A. Lamas, and Proyecto Alfa in Venezuela before joining the faculty at the University of D.C., received a Certificate of Musical Studies from Centro Superior de Estudios Musicales, studied with Rodrigo Riera at Universidad Centro Occidental "Lizandro Alvarado" Barquisimeto where he was awarded the Diploma in Guitar Technique and Repertoire, studied with José Rafael Cisneros at Escuela Superior de Música "José Angel Lamas," did further studies with

Regis Ferruza at the International Conservatory of Music in Washington, D.C., and with Romulo Lazarde, appeared on radio and TV throughout Venezuela and the U.S., recorded *Reminiscencias Latinas, El Sonido de la Tranguiladad*, etc., and composed *Canela (Venezuelan Waltz), Ebonita, Suite, Graficos, Prelude*, etc.;

In Brazil: folk artist-composer Martinho da Vila, recorded on RCA in renditions of *O Pequeno Burguês*, etc.; Gilberto Gil, recorded on WEA/Tropical Storm in *Realce* (Highlight et al.); and Djavan, on Sound Wave Record's *Flor de Lis* and others.

Still other musical ancestors must exist whose identities have not yet been revealed. Albert Luper mentioned that the Escola de Santa Cruz graduated many Black musicians. Gerard Béhague offered names of several orders and churches which accommodated such musicians. Others like Francis Williams from Jamaica, composer of *Welcome, Welcome Brother Debtor* (Hare), have also not been completely researched. The summary analysis, then, is that some have been identified, but the job is yet unfinished.

Jorge Guillen.

Composers in Europe: Forebears, Followers, and Figurations

The European influence in American music has been well documented in the history of art music and has been pointed out in the compositions of Black composers found in both volumes of this book. The harmonic persuasions of the European system were also noted in jazz progressions as well as in certain of the structural considerations. In turn, the eclectic adaptations of Claude Debussy and Darius Milhaud, among others, also brought to light the interrelationships of Pan-African music to that of other continents.

If history has served us correctly, native Black European composers who stood as forebears totaled far fewer than in America. Those obscured names still may be uncovered. However, the ancient Blacks referred to in Frank Snowden's *Blacks in Antiquity* remain anonymous, or we might otherwise be able to pinpoint more musical professions or talents. Nevertheless, some few accounts which have been preserved by Thayer, Hare, Trotter, Sayers, and dictionaries of music have pointed to two of the most outstanding individuals whose accomplishments easily burst into the historical limelight: George Bridgetower of the classical period and Samuel Coleridge-Taylor of the Romantic period.

GEORGE AUGUSTUS POLGREEN BRIDGETOWER (1779?–1860)

A student of Josef Haydn, George Bridgetower developed as a child prodigy, performing violin concerts in Europe when he was only ten years old. Recorded in several sources such as the Grove's *Dictionary* as being born in Biala, Poland, he might have, according to Gratton Flood, been born in the English colonies. Accompanied by an African father (called the "Abyssinian Prince") who had married a European, Bridgetower traveled throughout Europe, giving concerts for the Prince of Wales, King George III, and for prestigious patrons of the arts at the Haydn-Salomon Concerts.

In his *Beethoven* (Macmillan, 1970), H. C. Robbins quoted a *Mercure de France* review (Paris, 1789) which stated that the "young Negro from the colonies . . . " was in concert. Landon also wrote that Bridgetower was the son of August, Prince Nicolaus I Esterhaz's personal page. Landon's latter source was Joseph Carl Rosenbaum's *Diary*.

George Bridgetower. From Maud C. Hare's *Negro Musicians and Their Music* (Associated/Da Capo).

A contemporary of two writers with a Black heritage, Aleksandr Sergeevich Pushkin (1799–1837) from Russia and Alexander Dumas (1802–1870) from France, his fame grew even more after his performance of

Beethoven's "Kreutzer" *Sonata* for violin. Less significant as a composer, Bridgetower left a small legacy of works to the world, some of which have amazingly been preserved in the British Museum (*Violin Concerto* and *Henry*, a ballad also found at the Indiana University Center). Others were said to be forty-one piano studies (*Diatonica Armonica*) and two books of minuets for violin, mandolin, German flute, and harpsichord.

LUCIEN LEON GUILLAUME LAMBERT (1858–1945)

Lucien Lambert, son of Charles-Lucien Lambert, was born in Paris (*Encyclopedia de la Musique*). Listed in the Slonimsky, Baker, and Grove dictionaries of music as "French composer and pianist" taught by his father, Lambert was, however, not listed in the *Encyclopedia Britannica* (along with Herbert Lambert, the clavichord maker) and was not identified with America or New Orleans. Maud Cuney Hare and James Trotter spoke of the Lambert family of New Orleans whose father was Richard Lambert (c. 1840) and whose sons and daughters were musical. Among them was Lucien Lambert (1828–?) who travelled to Paris because of prejudice and eventually to Brazil, taking up a trade in clavichord building (evidently the father of this younger Lucien).

The Library of Congress has miraculously preserved some copies of the music of Lucien Lambert (1858–1945) such as the *Legende Roumain* in a piano reduction of orchestral parts. Among the others listed in the catalog are *Andante et Fantaine Tzigane* for piano and orchestra (Heugel & Cie, c. 1892); *Overture de Broceliande*, an opera in four acts (Heugel & Cie; full score); *Esquisses Creoles* for orchestra on themes by Gottschalk, transcribed for four hands and orchestra (Macken & Noel, c. 1898); *La Flamenca*, a drama musical in four acts (Choudens, c. 1903); *Le Marseillaise*, a lyrical work in one act for singer and piano (Choudens c. 1900); *La Penticosa*, a lyric drama in two acts (in manuscript, c. 1980); *La Roussalka* ballet-pantomime in two acts (Choudens Music, c. 1911—vocal score and piano accompaniment); *Sire Olaf* dramatic legende in three acts (J. Mamalle/Maho, vocal score with piano); *Le Spahi*, a lyric poem in four acts for singer and piano (*Prix du Concours Musical de la Ville de Paris*, 1896).

SAMUEL COLERIDGE-TAYLOR (1875–1912)

The Anglo-African composer, Samuel Coleridge-Taylor, was born in Holborn, England, to an English mother and an African father. Educated at the Royal Academy of Music in London, he excelled in composition and violin performance. One of the most colorful figures born during the Romantic-Impressionistic era, he became an internationally known musician of repute who was rated among England's top composers of his day.

In *Heritage of Samuel Coleridge-Taylor*, his daughter, Avril Gwendolyn, wrote that Samuel's father was named Daniel Peter Hughes-Taylor. Hughes-Taylor attended King's College in London from 1873 to 1876, was listed in the Medical Directory from 1877 to 1882 and thereafter on the rolls of R.C.S. up to 1904. She stated that he left London because of prejudice and mistreatment and died prematurely in Sierra Leone. In any case, Coleridge-Taylor, his son, was destined to reprogram his future in a European setting.

He was also a favorite of the American people who invited him to conduct choirs in performances of his music and who named choral societies in his honor, in Washington, D.C. for example. Carl Stoeckel (1858–1925), first head of the Yale School of Music and Ellen Battell Stoeckel founded glee clubs at Norfolk, Connecticut (the Norfolk Glee Club and the Litchfield County Choral Union) which performed in Stoeckel's Music Shed, and sponsored Samuel Coleridge-Taylor at the suggestion of H. T. Burleigh, baritone. In turn, Burleigh, Lola Johnson, soprano, and Felix Fowler Weir, violinist, toured with Coleridge-Taylor during his American visit.

Samuel Coleridge-Taylor. Photograph by Cavendish Morton. From Jessie Coleridge-Taylor Collection.

An imposing figure, Coleridge-Taylor commanded the respect of many persons of grand stature. In her *Memory Sketch*, also entitled *Personal Reminiscences of My Husband*, Jessie Coleridge-Taylor recalled that President Theodore Roosevelt had invited Coleridge-Taylor to the White House during one of his American tours.

Coleridge-Taylor was inspired by composers such as Anton Dvorak and H. T. Burleigh to write music based upon folk elements. An astute being, he chose African themes such as the bamboula on which he based a spirited piano composition with the same name (Ex. 88). He used spiritual themes such as *Deep River* and *Steal Away* to arrange other pieces for piano contained in the same *Twenty-Four Negro Melodies*, Opus 59. His ethereal and virtuosic *Concerto for Violin* used the spiritual *Many Thousand Gone* in a setting which bordered upon religiosity of the highest order. In addition, he composed several pieces for orchestra, for cello, and marvelous art songs for voice such as *Songs for Sun and Shade* and *Life and Death*. He also structured such cantatas as *Hiawatha's Wedding Feast* in which he used American Indian themes as roots for the work from whence the aria, *Onaway, Awake, Beloved*, is taken (Example 89):

Ex. 88. Samuel Coleridge-Taylor. *Bamboula*, Op. 59. O. Ditson, 1905.

Ex. 89. *Onaway, Awake, Beloved*, Coleridge-Taylor. © Copyright 1898, Schirmer.

His style was consistent with the harmonic and other practices of the nineteenth century and at times resembled the music of Johannes Brahms (as, for example, in comparing a Brahms *Intermezzo* with the piano composition *Nourmahal's Song*). Because he was a violinist, one might be inclined to consider his music for violin as his finest pieces, particularly after hearing the flamboyance of the *Concerto*. On the other hand, his cello *Variations* and the orchestral works such as *Ballade* and *Danse Nègre* all received glowing commentaries. And yet, his complete understanding of melody must undoubtedly have been influenced by his knowledge of the violin—a factor which could well have led any singer to type him as a vocalist rather than as a violinist.

Various of his works bearing different opus numbers sometimes made use of the same themes. For example, Opus 58 used the same introduction for both the *African Idyl* for piano and for the violin piece, as well as the same African theme. His skill in designing and arranging for other instruments was seen similarly in descriptive compositions. His works received much praise during his lifetime and were discussed in numerous dictionaries, both in the United States and in his native Europe.

Avril Coleridge-Taylor noted that the list which she compiled of his works was more comprehensive than that done by J. H. Smither Jackson for Berwick Sayer's book on Samuel Coleridge-Taylor in 1915. Among some of them were works for piano, voice, and other instruments found at the Library of Congress as well as some taken from the books in question. These included the following for piano: *Twenty-Four Negro Melodies*, Opus 59 (Ditson, 1905, also recorded by Francis Walker, pianist, on Orion label); *African Dances, Romances,* and *Valses; Scenes From an Imaginary Ballet*, Opus 74; *Nourmahal's Song and Dance*, Opus 41; *Bamboula*, from Opus 59 (now reprinted by Hinshaw Music, ed./Hinson, 1981); *They Will Not Lend Me A Child* from Opus 59 (in International Library, v. 8); *Moorish Tone-Pictures; Three Humoresques; African Suite; Incidental Music to Herod*, Opus 47; *Cameos; Forest Scenes*, Opus 66; *Three-Fours* (Valse Suite); *Two Impromptus*; and others published by Augener; for organ: *Ethiopia Saluting the Colors* (Othello); *The Willow Song* (arr./Brown; in Cramer's *Library of Organ Music by British Composers*—Augener); *Melody, Arietta* and *Elegy* (in Books 12, 16, & 15 of the *Village Organist* published by Novello); for cello: *A Gypsy Dance*, Opus 20, No. 2 (Augener); *Variations*; for violin: *Concerto*, Opus 80; *Two Romantic Pieces*, Opus 9; *Legend; Hiawathan Sketches*, Opus 16; *Gypsy Suite; Valse-Caprice; A Negro Love-Song; Dance Nègre; African Dances; Romance Ballade*; all published by Augener; for orchestra: *Danse Nègre, Ballade* in A minor; *Ethiopia Saluting the Colours*, Opus 51; published by Augener. Augener also released numerous vocal art songs, three-part songs for female voices, four-part songs, *The Gitanos* (Cantata for female voices), *Morning and Evening Service* (Te Deum, Benedictus, Jubilate, Magnificant & Nunc Dimittis) for TTBB; other anthems, arrangements, and originals, such as *The Death of Minnehaha*, and others. In addition, Novello published *The Blind Girl of Castilcuille*, a cantata. Publishers Ditson, Schirmer and Boosey (*Songs for Sun and Shade*) also produced music on the behalf of Samuel Coleridge-Taylor.

Postscript VI: Other Composers

As evidenced by the numbers of spirituals arranged and used in compositional form both directly after Coleridge-Taylor's death and during this contemporary era, many composers must have been both impressed and influenced by his contributions. The practice pioneered by Samuel Coleridge-Taylor and others assured that the African folk traditions would last throughout the centuries in a reflection of the old and new.

Figures for present-day native Black European composers are not easily available as to race and profession. Several of the Blacks who reside in Europe were born in the Islands, in America, and in Africa. American composers such as Robert Owens who studied and continued living there and the displaced jazz composers such as Dexter Gordon are not counted in the number of natives. Neither, unfortunately, is Ignatius Sancho (1729–1780), who lived in England for all but two years of his life.

More recent song makers in Britain are: Tracy Chapman, college graduate, guitarist, singer, and composer of *All You Had Is Your Soul* and *Fast Car* which are now recorded; the London-based reggae stars "Aswad," noted for *Don't Turn Around, Beauty's Only Skin Deep*, etc; Maxi Priest, known for his gold album, *Bonafide* (*Close to You, Hit*, etc.); and jazz artist-composer Courtney Pine, saxophonist, who combines reggae with jazz and other music.

XVI

PAN-AFRICAN COMPOSERS: AFRICA

New Africa: A Cyclic Return

The fact of African independence was instrumental in setting the stage for the call to freedom, and for the Second Black Renaissance of today. Suddenly, luminaries from George Bridgetower and Samuel Coleridge-Taylor to Alexandre Dumas became increasingly important. From this came a swift and decided turn toward the sincere study of Black culture, from mores to music.

As America had borrowed from African music, it now used those aspects which it needed, and with full knowledge of the reasons why. The traditional African aspect of the music penetrated forms from jazz to art music.

America hastened to learn about the music of Africa. Many scholars followed the advice of African writers who urged that Africa itself had to become the center of learning. They traveled to Africa in order to partake of the traditional activities and resources which were present. Musicians in jazz and art music also studied African features intensely and encouraged the rapid acceptance and use of music. Western musicians once again reaffirmed the base from whence a part of western music was derived.

Many people pursued a theory of Pan Africanism in relating music of all Blacks to that of Africa. It was important not only for the relationship of Black cultures, but for music in all such cultures. For some, the closer the link with older precepts the better the understanding and knowledge of musical origin became. Since many aspects of music were universal, Africa became speculative in the derivation of all music.

American institutions sought out musicologists and composers from Africa so that further interchange could begin in the study of African music. Teams of American composers were greatly interested in the music of traditional African composers. Among those whom they sought were Halim El-Dabh from Egypt, Fela Sowande from Nigeria and J. Kwabena Nketia from Ghana. All well trained and gifted musicians in both composition and historical research and performance, these musicians became the modern "griots" of the contemporary world who could relate to the musical tradition in Africa.

In addition to their being steeped in the practices and knowledge of African music, these composers were themselves ironically influenced by, and keenly aware of, western traditions in music. They had, like the Black American, composed in an African and a western style, and had sought to determine the truth of their own styles. Consequently, that which had begun in Africa and moved to the west had now returned to influence once again. The primary source, Africa, had been replenished by generations of mutations, and had become new Africa, while America benefited as the keeper of the tradition.

Pedagogy, Predecessors, Placements, and Projections

In this part of the twentieth century, Africa continues to take a leading role in expressing and teaching ideas for growth. Bridges of understanding are being built through publications, demonstrations, and cultural exhibits, and other exchanges such as faculty-student appointments, as seen in the cases of El Dabh, Sowande, Kebede, and Nketia at institutions and/or important advisory boards. Music and other information are found in centers and museums and bookshops such as the Library of Congress, the Smithsonian Museums, and African-Art museums in Chicago and Washington, D.C. Important study programs and seminars are being conducted in both African and American institutions, such as the African-American Forum Study Programs and the Department of State Cultural Performances. Without question, Africa has joined hand in hand with the West to help promote and preserve African culture and to promote worldwide Pan-Africanism in music.

Today, Africa has assumed the role of pedagogue, has taught our music a new freedom, and has injected a new life. She has influenced our definitions—of the drum, of compositional organization, and of purpose. She has affected our rhythms—with new meters, new time concepts, idioms, and polymetrics. She has altered our instrumentations—with unusual combinations, with the drum effects, with different techniques and new names; and she has influenced our melodies—with melisma and ever-changing improvisation. Africa has changed our course with the ancient message of communication and response.

Likewise, the role of African composers seems always to have been multifarious, multinational, and masterful. Lending a knowledge about rhythms and cultural practices common to Africa, they have assisted with the twentieth century transition into the Pan-African concept of kinship and collective communion. Akin Euba has written of mainly two kinds of composers in Africa—the traditional one whose music remains functional in scope and purpose and the newer, more prepared composer whose works are now being offered as listening music. Ashenafi Kebede, who divided the composers into traditional and "third-stream" (art music with Euro-American elements), pointed out that African musicologists have "crossed over" and have begun to write compositions as one of the many outbursts of freedom and aspiration spurred on by the new initiatives in promoting and teaching the music to other continents. He also noted that the definitions and tasks of such musicologists were multifarious and multifunctional, that they have promoted the study of African music by simultaneously compiling, organizing, and composing African music.

J. K. Nketia, in *The Music of Africa*, described the musical traditions and defined the roles of various socio-cultural musicians from specialists to Royal types, as well as the performers, their recruitments and training. He enumerated intricacies of musical societies such as for hunters' associations, cult associations, and others. Nketia also included discussions about the Arab versus indigenous influences, features of melody, polyphony, and harmonies merged therein.

All of these kinds of African composers are discussed in the forthcoming section. They are but a few of the musician-composers found in Africa who continue the work of spreading the wealth of information about many aspects of African music, who practice the art of composition as an abstract form, and who bridge a small gap of information between themselves and those composers presented in other sets. Importantly, it must be reiterated that there is no attempt to place the work of one composer above that of another, but rather an account given for purposes of worldwide identification within the Diaspora, for purposes of summation and of correlating historical collaboration with chronology.

Forerunner and Griots

Early griots must have been among the first, ancient African forebears. They must have taught the music of Africa through demonstration and oral traditions. They might have been among those to whom Frank Snowden's *Blacks in Antiquity* referred as those anonymous, but visible figures found on ancient European pottery. Partly obscured by marks of time, placements, and position, these bards remain unknown.

In her *Negro Musicians and Their Music*, Maud Cuney Hare also points out "world musicians of color" who were visible in various parts of the continents of Asia. If they, like some of the slaves transported to other territories during colonialism and before, were actually born in Africa before that transportation took place, then they should also be considered as African musical predecessors.

At a later time, a composer with an African name became a stellar example of early Blacks involved in art music. Although neither a teacher of African functional music nor one who actually experienced life on African soil in the most technical sense, this individual must be classified as an African predecessor because of his place of birth. Seemingly, the first known African native with a musical education, and heading the long line of African composers in succession, was the African—Ignatius Sancho.

Ignatius Sancho. From Maud C. Hare's *Negro Musicians and Their Music* (Associated/Da Capo).

IGNATIUS SANCHO (1729–1780)

Ignatius Sancho, only technically an African, was reportedly born aboard a slave ship positioned just off the coast of Guinea and destined for the Spanish West Indies. An orphan by age two, Sancho was taken from the West Indies and given to three cantankerous English maidens. Befriended and educated by the Duke of Montague, Sancho subsequently became the butler for the Duchess after the death of the Duke. But as for Africa, he never really knew his home. Only by virtue of his birth was he the one known African who succeeded centuries ago in building a reputation within a world of art music.

The composer of *Twelve Country Dances* for harpsichord, published by S & A Thompson of London, 1779 (an excerpt of which is stored at the Library of Congress), he was also the author of some plays and a *Theory of Music* book. Since inclusion in the Maud Cuney Hare document, Sancho has been the subject of a recent book by Josephine R. B. Wright, published in 1983 by Garland Publishing Company which gave his dates as 1729–1780, and which contains several of his pieces such as The Complaint, The Sweetest Bard, Minuets, 12 Country Dances, Strawberries & Cream.

Composers in Changing Traditions I: African Traditionalism

Composers in this section represent those who deal mainly with traditional song forms and related artistic devices. As described by Nketia and others, they promote the study of African music through writing, lecturing, and performing such demonstrative structures. The following render but a small sample of such traditionalists.

J. O. AJIBOLA (1898–)

Chief J. O. Ajibola, barrister-at-law, minister, educator, linguist, songwriter and compiler of African music, emerged as a classic case of the enthusiast whose interest in music grew from the hobby status to a higher desire to promote and produce the music of Nigeria. Born in Ago-Iwoye, a town in the Ogun State of Nigeria, he was trained as a teacher at Wesley College in Ibadan, graduating in 1918. After teaching in a primary school of Ibadan for one year, he was a tutor at Wesley College from 1920 to 1932. In 1932, he was appointed Senior Tutor at the Ijebu-Ode Grammar School, and finally, Senior Tutor at the Abeokuta Grammar School.

It was at Abeokuta that he first developed an interest in African music and began copying original African music into modern notation, while also developing pieces of his own. He accepted a scholarship to study linguistics for two years at the School of Oriental and African Studies at the University of London (where he met J. K. Nketia). Simultaneously, he decided to study law and to eventually become a barrister. Returning to Nigeria to work as solicitor and advocate for six years before being appointed President Customary Court in 1958, he became chairman of the Local Government Service Board in 1976.

J. O. Ajibola.

It was in London in 1946 that Ajibola, before traveling back to live in Ibadan, Nigeria, published his first edition of *Orin Yoruba*, the collection of forty songs written in melodic notation and published by Oxford. His second edition, now published by the University of Ife Press, Ile-Ife, Nigeria, based its origin upon the first edition and expanded into seventy-two songs with two, three, and four parts with piano accompaniments, English translations, and Yoruba phonetics as well.

A valuable resource for presenting the music of Africa to the world, all of the songs in *Orin Yoruba* represented the styles of sounds and rhythms common to the traditional world of Nigerian music. Composed by Ajibola are twenty songs (twelve sacred and eight secular); included also are songs by Rev. J. J. Ransome Kuti, Dr. A. T. O. Olude, Prince S. A. Adeosun, S. A. Sogunro-Pitan, and Rev. Canon I. O. Ransome-Kuti; eight songs by Chief J. A. Ayorinde; and forty-one by others unknown. Each sacred song is designed to fit the particular scriptural text accompanying it.

Ajibola also became a promoter of African music in London by demonstrating Yoruba music, complete with instruments, singing, and lectures. For this reason and the fact of the *Orin Yoruba* publication, he is important to musicology and to introductory pedagogy. His work in linguistics rather directly made the translations apropos. His *Owe Yoruba*, the five-hundred proverbs translated into English and accompanied by vocabulary and phonetic explanations, showed the non-syllabic words on all the three tonal levels of the Yoruba language. This made the word communication being correlated with the musical tones much clearer (see Example 1, Chapter II).

In addition to his books on music, Ajibola has also published books and writtern manuscripts about religion, law, nutrition, and economics. He has also written unpublished compositions and four *Biblical Plays.*

BENNY KALANZI (19 ?–)

Benny Kalanzi was significant among African composers as being one of the very few known Ugandans introduced to the West in the 1970s. According to advertising information sent by the late Leon Thompson from the Office of Educational Activities of the New York Philharmonic, Benny Kalanzi was born in Villa Maria, Uganda, East Africa. He graduated in 1955 from Eukalasa College, receiving the University of Cambridge Overseas Certificate, and then did further study at Katigondo Major Seminary from 1956 to 1961 where he was trained in philosophy and theology as well as in music. Upon traveling to Europe in 1962, he studied German and French at the University of Fribourg in Switzerland, piano at the Conservatory of Fribourg and Zurich, and musicology at the University of Cologne, West Germany.

Having worked with choirs at Eukalasa College and at Katigondo Major Seminary, Kalanzi set about the task of preserving and promoting the study of Bantu music, dedicating himself to the performance and teaching of this music at various African, European, and American institutions. He worked briefly at Radio Deutsche Welle in Cologne as program-director and specialist on African music, also conducting and transcribing ancient and contemporary music and performing folk songs from his native Africa.

He conducted seminars at Hunter College in 1972, gave lecture-demonstrations at Columbia University for the Institute of African Studies, at Cornell University, Harvard University, Sarah Lawrence College, and at public schools in New York City, Tarrytown, and New Rochelle. In presenting the music, he would play at least six different African instruments: the bowl-lyre, African harp, bamboo flute, xylophone, shaker, fiddle, and some percussion instruments.

As a composer, he preferred to emphasize Bantu song forms. He wrote *Abange Mutyaneo* (Song of Welcome), composed in traditional style for bowl-lyre and maracas; *Mbuzi Yange* (Shepherd's Song) for drum; *Okulimba Kub* (Never Tell Lies) for harp and maracas; *Guno Muka* (Carousing Song) as modern African rhythms; *Sematire* (Famine Song) for hand-clapping and dancing; *Kawa* (Coffee Is Delicious); *Kachachali-Samatemba* (Potato Song); *Omusango GW Ennyama* (Song about Food) for harp and shaker; and *Wuyo Nanka* (Wedding Song) for bowl-lyre and maracas.

MICHAEL BABATUNDE OLATUNJI (1927–)

Born in Nigeria, Michael Olatunji, master drummer and lecturer, was graduated in 1954 from Morehouse College in Atlanta, Georgia. He also began studies for his Ph.D. degree in Public Administration at New York University.

Michael Olatunji. Used by permission of Bagwell and Miles.

Like Miriam Makeba, his contributions as folk collector, lecturer, and disseminator of things African distinguish him as an invaluable performer-teacher. As co-author of *Musical Instruments of Africa* with Betty Warner Dietz (John Day, 1965), he helped compile vocabulary, photographs, and explanations, and together with the recording done by Colin Turnbull, submitted the product to the elementary curriculum for use in various schools. Because of the African designations and clear explanations, however, the information would be just as informational for the beginning student on any level of related studies. In addition to his collection of instruments, Olatunji is now compiling traditional songs and arrangements for future publication.

Observed in several concerts held at New York halls in the 1950s, at the Fayetteville State University in the 1960s, and elsewhere, his interpretations as both drummer-singer inspired the dancers throughout their traditional and modern designs and brought character to the special traditionalism of recreational, festive, or occasional music. On March 25, 1983, the Morehouse College Male Glee Club featured his Nigerian Christmas Song, *Betelehemu*, co-arranged with Wendell Whalum, then the director. Sung in Yoruba, the piece was scored for master drum and other drums, voices and hand claps in exciting, polyrhythmic accompaniment. Others of his arrangements may be found in such recordings as *Drums of Passion, Olatunji,* and other from Columbia and Roulette labels.

The June 1970 issue of *BMI* magazine announced that Michael Olatunji, "performer and specialist in African music" would do a five-week survey of "Traditional Musical Practices in Africa, South of the Sahara." Reviewed by Roberta Brandes Gratz in the *New York Post* (July 26, 1969) and reported in *BMI* magazine (October 1969), Olatunji was cited for his Olatunji Center, a school opened on Harlem's 125th Street in 1967 which offered ten African languages, dance, drums, and crafts; for his "overwhelming" appearances at Radio City Music Hall as solo drummer with the resident symphony orchestra; for his lectures at churches and school; and for his leadership of the Union of Nigeria and Cameroon Students in North America. The successive years have been a continuance of his work in promoting the study of African music, although his major contributions were in oral traditionalism in performance rather than in written composition.

FRANCES BEBEY (1929–)

Francis Bebey, guitarist, singer-composer, and lyricist, was born in Douala, Cameroon. Trained at the Sorbonne in musicology and French literature, he is significant in that he has performed and written about African songs in an effort to promote an international understanding. A self-taught guitarist, he has performed numerous recitals in Europe, Africa, and America, appearing at Wigmore Hall in London, the Martin Luther King Library in Washington, D.C., at the yearly International Music Festival in Bratislava, Czechoslovakia, at the yearly International Guitar Festival in France, and at other sites throughout those continents.

Francis Bebey.

Bebey has written several articles and books, perhaps the most famous of which is *African Music: A People's Art,* published by Lawrence Hill. In music, he has restricted his work to small song forms in promoting the culture of Africa. His guitar compositions are: *The Chant of Ibadan: Black Tears, Black Woman, Christ Was Born in Bomba,* and others, all of which were recorded on *Compositions for Solo Guitar* by Ocora in France; *Concert Pour Un Vieux Masque* (recorded on Philips, France) and *Guitare D'Une Autre Rime* (EMI, France). Others among his compositions are *The Ashanti Doll Is Sleeping, Tingrela, The Meaning of Africa, Fali Orison, Breaths, E Titi Bu* (Duala language), and *Idira.*

MIRIAM ZENZI MAKEBA (1932–)

Miriam Makeba, according to *Time* magazine (February 1, 1960) was born with the full name of "Zensi Mariam Makeba Ogwashu ogu vama yi keti le nenxgoma sittu xa saku aga ba ukutsha sithathe izitsha sizi khalu sivuke ngomso sizi chole ezo zinge knayo zinga bikho nfalo singamalamu singa mangamla nagithi." A native of Johannesburg, South Africa, she was born of the Xhosa tribe, and educated at Kilmerton Training Institute in Pretoria, South Africa.

She was featured in U.S. tours as a Harry Belafonte protégé during the 1950s. She performed at many of the most prestigious institutions, halls, and recording studios from Yale University to Manhattan's Village Vanguard and Angel. A Grammy Award winner, she became a member of ASCAP in 1951. Her remarkable talent was displayed in Europe before arriving in America; she also performed for Haile Selassie and the OAU

Conference in Ethiopia in 1963 as well as for President Kennedy at his Madison Square Garden birthday party. In addition, she had many recording sessions before returning to Africa in 1990.

Primarily a singer, Makeba may be considered a folk song collector and teacher through her exceptional delivery of the music from the Xhosa and Zulu tribes and her invaluable explanations of the various folksongs given on her recordings and at live concerts. Additionally, she also helped to transcribe some of the oral-tradition folksongs onto pages of her *World of African Song* (Quadrangle Press, 1971), some of which also appeared on the recording bearing her name (RCA/LMP2267). In exile for many years, she returned to South Africa in 1990.

Typical of her own originals found in both sources above are *The Click Song, Umhome Nomeva, Saduva*, and *Iya Guduza*. Her list of works at the Library of Congress include *Aba Ngoma, I Ye Ya* (1966), *Isilwani* (1966), *Liwa Wechi* (1961), and three arranged with S. T. Brown: *Magwaladnini, Drums of Africa*, and *Amampando* (Breathing Song, 1963). ASCAP lists also her *Pole Mze, Boot Dance*, and *Mangwene Mpulele*.

Composers in Changing Traditions II: "Third Stream"

Composers found in this part are those who, in addition to work in traditional music, also compose art music or music for listening. Described by Kebede as "third stream" composers, these musicians are highly trained in the field of music and have contributed greatly to the field of Pan-African education. In part, they are as follows:

EPHRAIM AMU (1899–)

The Black pioneer of systematic West African research was Ephraim Amu who, when he returned from England as a stranger to his indigenous music, decided to devote his lifetime to the study, transcription and teaching of African music. Born in the Volta Region of Peki-Avetile, Ghana, he was educated at Peki, then the Training College of Basel Mission Seminary, Abelifi (Presbyterian Trinity, Akwapen-Akropong). Further training was done in London at the Royal College of Music. Among his honors was the honorary doctorate from the University of Ghana.

Ephraim Amu.

His teaching experience began in 1930 at the Bremen Mission (Evangelical Presbyterian Middle School, Peki-Blengo). He also taught at the Presbyterian Training College, Achimota College, the College of Art, Science and Technology at Kumasi, and served as Music Researcher at Kumasi Technology, and the University of Ghana at Accra.

According to a 1987 interview by Kofi Agawu (*Black Perspective in Music*, Spring 1987), Amu continued to compose at his home in Peki-Avetile, after having retired from the University of Ghana as a Senior Research Fellow. In his spare time, he conducted his church choir in the singing of African music and carved Ghanaian musical instruments.

As a composer, teacher and performer, he has been instrumental in influencing other leading musicologists and African musicians to follow his example to study and preserve African music. Following the publication of his book, *Twenty-five African Songs*, serious scholars became interested in his concept of cultural preservation and research.

Amu shows a preference for the vocal medium, although he has composed for both western and African instruments. He also prefers the Twi language. In some of his music, African scales and harmonies prevail while western styles of major and minor tonalities with dynamics and other marks of interpretation appear. A piece entitled *Traditional Atentenbenj Prelude*, a duet for two wind players, contains clusters of ornaments common to early Baroque and polyphonic textures. The rhythms are characteristically African as shown:

Ex. 90. *Atentenbenj Prelude*, Amu. Used by permission of African Institute, University of Ghana at Legon.

Another of his pieces, *Wo Nsam Mewo* is written for male voices in tonal hymn style, excerpted in Example 91.

Ex. 91. *Wo Nsam Mewo*, Amu. Used by permission of African Institute, University of Ghana at Legon.

Among Amu's works are: *Adawura Bome; Three Solo Songs; Two Pieces for Bamboo Flute and Piano; Twenty Piped Pieces; Ten Vocal Pieces; Wo Nsam Mewo; Enee Ye Anigyeda*; over 100 songs, and one book entitled *Twenty Five African Songs* (1932), now out of print.

FELA SOWANDE (1905–1987)

Fela Sowande was born in Nigeria, and was once a teacher at Howard University. He was educated at the C. M. S. Grammar School and King's College in Lagos. Later, Sowande traveled to London where he studied as a Fellow of the Trinity College of Music (B. Mus.) and at the Royal College of Organists. He was taught by Oldroyd, Cunningham, Rubbra and others.

His experiences have included popular and art music. He led a dance band in London where he also became a recording artist for Decca Records. He served as musical director to the Colonial Film Unit, provided background music for several educational films, and was organist and choirmaster to the West London Mission. He founded the Kingsway Musical Society and directed the Yoruba Life Series in preserving indigenous music and folklore.

Sowande also received various awards and honors. Among these have been the Rockefeller Foundation Grant, the Ford Foundation Grant and others. He also served as guest conductor of the BBC Symphony Orchestra, as guest conductor of the New York Philharmonic, and the BBC Northern

Orchestra. In Africa, he was a visiting Fellow and Member of the Advisory Council at the Hansberry College of African Studies, and the University of Ibadan in Nigeria, and was also Professor of Musicology at the University of Ibadan.

Other honors have included commissions for his works from the Nigerian Government for Independence Celebrations; the Nigerian Federal Ministry of Information for a special arrangement of the Nigerian National Anthem; and the Traditional Chieftaincy Award by the Lagos State, Federation of Nigeria, in recognition of research into Yoruba folklore.

An eminent organist, composer, and educator, Sowande persisted in his expressions, expansions, and dissemination of knowledge not only about African music but also in the use of African-American spirituals. A participant with Halim El-Dabh in the African-American Folk Festival held in Washington, D.C. in 1982 (the Diaspora), he captured the interest of many performers who regularly programmed his music both locally and nationally.

The music of Sowande is based on both western and African techniques. Many of his actual themes are traditionally Nigerian such as the *Obangiji* which greatly resembles the Black spiritual, *Nobody Knows*. Significantly, Sowande has also used Black American spirituals as source materials. Sowande's concept of derivative materials is more representative of Pan Africanism than are the other African composers in that his subjects reflect both African and other universal themes of Black folk. His compositional substance generally outlines the Romantic and early Modern tradition. Some aspects of his music are emphasized in the rhythms seen in Example 92.

Ex. 92. Rhythms of Sowande.

Among Sowande's organ compositions are: *Kyrie* (based on a theme of Juti); *Yoruba Lament* (Nigerian theme); *Obangiji* (Nigerian theme); *Go Down Moses* (spiritual); *Joshua Fit de Battle; Jesu Olugabala; K'a Mura; Gloria* (based on a theme of Juti); *Oyigiyigi; and Prayer* (Nigerian theme). His vocal works include *Three Songs of Contemplation* for tenor; *Because of You for tenor; Sit Down Servant; The Gramercy of Sleep* (male choir); *Words* (males); *Sometimes I Feel Like a Motherless Child; My Way's Cloudy; De Ol' Ark's a Moverin'; Same Train; Steal Away; Roll de Chariot; All I Do; Goin' to Sit Down; Couldn't Hear Nobody Pray; Heav'n Bells are Ringin'; De Angels are Watchin'; Nobody Knows de Trouble I See; Wheel, Oh Wheel; Stan' Still Jordan*; and *Wid a Sword in Ma Han*. Sowande has also written *African Suite for Strings* (African themes) and *A Folk Symphony* (Nigerian themes) for full orchestra.

Many of his organ works may be found in Broadcast Foundation Recording, N. 543, Columbia Records (*African Suite*) and on Nigerian Art and Artists: Music Program 1. His publishers are Chappell (for *African Suite* for strings; *Go Down Moses; Joshua Fit the Battle; Kyrie*—Kuti Theme; and *Obangimi* for organ; Leeds (for *Folk Symphony*, orchestra); PRS (for *Nigerian Miniatures*—an orchestral suite); Franco Colombo (for *Gloria*—Kuti Theme; *Oyigiyigi* and *Prayer*—Nigerian Themes for organ; and *Sit Down Servant, Gramercy of Sleep, All I Do, Goin' to Set Down* and other spirituals for voices—TTBB or SATB); and Novello (out of print?): *Jesu Olugbala* and others for organ. Some of his scores are located at the University of Ibadan in Nigeria.

There are still more composers living in Africa who are not represented here. Notable among those missing are composers from Liberia, Morocco, Sierra Leone, Zaire, Ivory Coast, Kenya, etc. Unfortunately, because of countless wars, various "hot spots" do not induce as easy a study of African third stream music as one would like, and some African contributions have remained as in the "dark continent" days of old. Happily, certain musicians have been recruited to teach in America, such as J. K. Nketia.

J. KWABENA NKETIA (1921–)

J. Kwabena Nketia, the leading musicologist-composer of Ghana, served as the director of the African Institute at the University of Ghana. Nketia was educated at the Teacher Training College, Akropong Akuapem; the School of Oriental and African Studies at the University of London; Trinity College of Music, London (B.A.); at Columbia University; the Juilliard School of Music and Northwestern University. Once a student of Amu, he was greatly influenced by that pioneer of Ghanaian research.

J. Kwabena Nketia.

His scholarships and honors include citations from the Ghana government, Rockefeller Foundation and Ford Foundation scholarships as well as the Cowell Award. An active and capable teacher, performer and musicologist, he once directed the musical ensemble which accompanied the Ghana Dance Troupe, while frequently lecturing at American Universities and other institutions abroad. His teaching experience also includes the Presbyterian Training School where he has also served as principal and a Research Fellow and eventual Professor at the University of Ghana. Currently, he is an Andrew Mellon professor at the University of Pittsburgh.

Nketia's style of composing ranges from the African to western types. His scales are either modal or are major and minor. His pieces are generally traditional in chord structure and are primarily consonant. His intervals are generally traditional elements of African and western music; (i.e., seconds, thirds, fourths, fifths, and octaves). The rhythm is the exciting aspect of his writing in which the smoothly constructed melodies flow unhampered within irregularly organized measures. One of his best compositions, the *Suite for Flute and Piano*, consisting of seven movements in all, contains many of the elements discussed. The first and second movement themes are excerpted in Example 93 and are not as easy to perform as they appear.

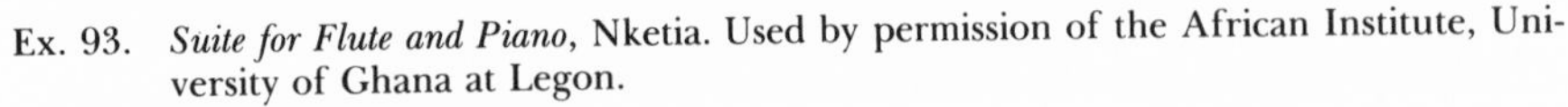

Ex. 93. *Suite for Flute and Piano*, Nketia. Used by permission of the African Institute, University of Ghana at Legon.

In addition to his lectures and composing, Nketia has written over 100 articles and books on music. Some of his publications are: *African Music in Ghana; The Poetry of Drums; Drum Proverbs; The Development of Instrumental African Music in Ghana; Drums, Dance and Song; Traditional Music of the Ga People; The Hocket Technique in African Music; Folk Songs of Ghana; Drumming in Akan Communities of Ghana; The Artist in Contemporary Africa; The Challenge of Tradition* and many others.

His *Suite for Flute and Piano* (seven movements) and two piano pieces entitled *Volta Fantasy* and *Contemplation* were performed at Brockport College (State University of New York) Keyboard Festival in 1979. He was elected as a Member of Honor of the International Music Council (UNESCO) in 1979—the association from which he received the UNESCO-IMC Music Prize at the General Assembly of the International Music Council held in Budapest in 1981.

Among Nketia's musical works are: *Four Akan Songs; Suite No. 1 for Flute and Piano; Four Flute Pieces; Canzona for Flute, Oboe, and Piano; Chamber Music in the African Idiom* (violin and piano w/Partos); *Eight Piano Pieces*; and other works.

HALIM EL-DABH (1921–)

Halim El-Dabh was born and educated in Cairo, Egypt. He studied at Sulez Conservatory in Cairo from 1941–44. Graduating in agriculture, he later devoted full time to his music and by 1950 traveled to the United States, then attended New Mexico University, the New England Conservatory and Brandeis University. A Guggenheim recipient, he studied with Irving Fine, Francis Cooke, and Aaron Copland. His teaching experience includes Howard University and Kent State University.

Halim El-Dabh, Egyptian.

Halim El-Dabh has continued an active schedule of teaching, delivering workshops, and performing throughout the United States, as well as composing in various contemporary styles for unique combinations. In the December 1974 issue of *The Theatre Paper*, Robert Labaree produced a long article entitled "Music for the Ear: Looking for a Socially Committed Music" in which he featured the works of El-Dabh. He quoted El-Dabh: "The African never thought about putting his art work on the wall. He is involved in the making of it. Aesthetics have been forced on him. His aesthetics are not looking at it, his aesthetics are doing it." Labaree cited him as a potent member of society who, as a non-Westerner, has entered into Western musical culture by way of the classical milieu and has composed functional pieces such as the five musical-dramatic works composed especially for performance by high school students, three symphonies, one concerto for Egyptian drum and orchestra, numerous piano pieces, vocal and choral music, pieces for drum, electronic music, chamber music, and ballets. And because El-Dabh's roots rest in the oral improvisational tradition of his country, Labaree noted, he was influenced by the sounds which he transmitted into his own music—a similarity which Labaree termed the "ear" of orientation.

"Halim El-Dabh . . . may be said to be the only Egyptian composer who is conveying basic Eastern ideals through Western media and instruments," according to James Su-Brown of the *Christian Science Monitor* (March 2, 1957). Program notes from a 1981 performance at Washington, D.C., quoted *Time* magazine as describing his dance opera, *Clytemnestra*, as being "marvelously integrated with the dance action" of Martha Graham's choreography seen as the premiere performance in New York. The *New York*

Times termed his music as an "inseparable element in theatrical collaboration." Hailed as a milestone by those who viewed the work, it was followed by symphonic music for the ballet *Lucifer*, performed by Rudolf Nureyev and Margot Fonteyn to Martha Graham choreography in a 1975 premiere.

In 1981, El-Dabh was sponsored in a multipartite symposium-concert-lecture by the Arab-American Cultural Foundation. With demonstrations and lectures being held in various parts of the city, the activities were highlighted by the original compositions for voice and winds, *Drink of Eternity*, performed at Georgetown's Gaston Hall, and the performance of his *Concerto for Durbakka* with the Washington National Symphony Orchestra. The latter, first premiered in 1959 by the American Symphony Orchestra with Leopold Stokowski as conductor, was revised by El-Dabh for the Washington concert held in Kennedy Center on May 17, 1981. The symposiums also showed his skill as wind player and string player, thereby exhibiting some of the varieties of sound and African reference which he has at his command with a European-based art music tradition.

Two of the important features of his music are improvisation, in which repeated materials never quite appear exactly the same no matter how much the duplications of materials, and the rhythmic base on which some of the compositions are based, such as in the *Samai* seen in Example 94.

Ex. 94. *Samai* (from *Mekta' in the Art of Kita'*, Bks. I/II), El-Dabh. Copyright © C. F. Peters Corporation, 373 Park Avenue South, New York, New York 10017. International copyright secured. All rights reserved.

Representative works found at the Library of Congress consist of those published by C. F. Peters for orchestra: *Agamemnon, Baccanalia, Furies in Hades* (Ballet); by C. F. Peters for percussion: *Fantasia-tahmeel* (Derabucca), *Hindiyaat No. 1, Juxtaposition No. 1, Sonic No. 7, Sonic No. 10, Tablatahmeel No. 1, Tabla-dance* (with piano); *Mosaic No. 1* (double trap and piano); voice: *Lamentation de Pharaon* for baritone and soprano soli, *Pyramide, Pierre Jusqu' au Ciel* for male voice and orchestra; by Peters for piano, viola, and oboe; *Thulathiya*; manuscripts of electronic music produced at Columbia-Princeton Studio: *Diffusion of Bells* and *Electronic Fanfare* (with Otto Luening) and *Leiyla and the Poet*. Recording of *Spectrum No. 1* (electronic music) is found on Folkways FX6160, as well as on a filmstrip entitled "Electronic Music" for keyboard (Columbia-Princeton Electronic Music Center).

El-Dabh has composed well over 100 works for various media from African drums to the western piano. Of the African and western idioms, the music has not lost the flavor of his native Egypt. Seconds, clusters, octaves and unisons in simple combinations are placed against modal or tonal harmonies in short, rhythmic patterns. El-Dabh has composed the following works: *Mekta in the Art of Kita*, books I–III; *Thulathiya* (trio for viola, oboe, and piano); *Juxtaposition No. 1* for two timpany, xylophone and marimba; *Twenty-five Arabiyaats* (arabic forms); *Misriyaats* (Egyptian forms); *Ifriqiyatts* (African forms); *Clythemnestra*; and various pieces for African and western instruments.

ADAM FIBERESIMA (1926–)

Adam Fiberesima was born in Okrika, a town in the Rivers State of Nigeria. Having studied at Trinity College of Music in London, he received a fellowship in composition to further his education. After returning to Nigeria to head the music department of the Voice of Nigeria, in Lagos, he took his place as one of the many types of composers in Nigeria.

His style during the 1970s, though changing, was analyzed by Oscar Henry of Easter Michigan University as more like that of the nineteenth century than of the twentieth. His use of African and European mergers, however, made his music unique.

Among his compositions at the Library of Congress are *Concertos* Nos. 1 and 2 for trumpet and *Fantasia Origin* (on Broadcast Foundation recording N. 543.7/7), *Opu Jaja*, an opera reviewed for possible performance in the African and American Festivals of Art and Culture in 1972, and scored for voices and traditional Western and African instruments. Others are *Music for Brass Band, Concert Overtunes* for orchestra, *Symphonies* Nos. 1, 2, 3, and 4 for orchestra, *Buluwayo* (musical), and *Three Ballads* for voice and piano.

SAMUEL EKPE AKPABOT (1934–)

Samuel Ekpe Akpabot was born in Nigeria. Educated at King's College in Lagos, Nigeria, the Royal College of Music in London, England where he studied composition, organ, and trumpet, and the University of Chicago where he received a master's degree in musicology, Akpabot earned the Ph.D. from Michigan State University. He has worked as senior music producer at the Nigerian Broadcasting Corporation, as a senior research fellow in musicology at the Institute of African Studies, University of Ife in Nigeria, and while on leave from Nigeria, he was a faculty member in both the Department of Music and the African Studies Center at Michigan State University before returning to Nigeria around 1975.

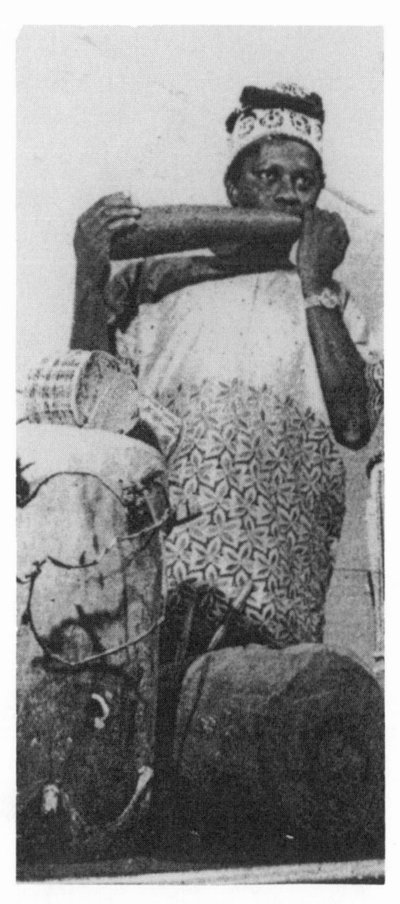

Samuel Akpabot. Courtesy of Michigan State News Bulletin.

Akpabot received grants from the Gulf Oil Corporation; he was a Fellow in Research at Trinity College until 1967; he received commissions from the American Wind Symphony Orchestra for *Nigeria in Conflict* and *Cynthia's Lament* and from the Ofala Festivals in 1963, 1965, and 1973. His works have enjoyed several performances in Michigan, Pennsylvania, Illinois, and other American states as well as in Nigeria. The Chicago Chamber Symphony performed his *Scenes from a Nigerian Ballet*, sponsored by the Chicago Park District and Music Performance Trust Funds. The University City Senior High School Orchestra performed *Three Nigerian Dances* and wrote favorable comments about the unusual rhythms and melodies as being effective in conveying the music.

Showcased in several newspapers such as the *Pittsburgh Courier* (June 30, 1973), the *Michigan State News* (January 25, 1974), the *Pittsburgh Post-Gazette* (June 2, 1973), and the *Michigan State News Bulletins*,Akpabot was favorably reviewed. His music consisted of African and Western instrumentations and he himself felt that his *Nigeria in Conflict* was the "connection" of similarities between "African music, progressive jazz and soul music of today." Originally trained in Western classical music, Akpabot returned to Nigeria in order to learn African music.

Among his compositions are *Nigeria in Conflict*, a seven-minute tone poem, with instrumentation for xylophone, flute, trumpet, trombone, bass trombone, horn, tympani, Chinese gong, rattle, wooden drum, and nkwong; *Three Nigerian Dances* for string orchestra and percussion; *Cynthia's Lament* for wind symphony orchestra and six African instruments; *Scenes from a Nigerian Ballet* for full symphony orchestra; *Overture for a Nigerian Ballet* for full symphony orchestra; and others, published by Oxford Press, 1972. He has published articles in *Presence Africaine*, Paris, 1959; the *Journal of the New African Literature*, Stanford University, California, Spring 1966; *African Arts*, University of California, Vol. V., No. 1, 1971, and Vol. VI, No. 2, 1972; *African Music*, Roodeport, South Africa; and in *Reflections on Afro-American Music*, Kent State Press, 1972.

AYO BANKOLE (1935–1976)

Ayo Bankole, recorded as one of Nigeria's front-running organist-composers of his day, worked at the Nigerian Broadcast Corporation before joining the faculty at the University of Nigeria. According to Eileen Southern's *Dictionary*, and the preface to his scores, Bankole was born in 1935 in Lagos and was educated at the Guildhall School of Music and Drama in London, at the Clare College of Cambridge University where he received his Master of Arts degree, and at the University of California at Los Angeles.

Among his works listed at the Library of Congress are *Fantasia, Sonatas* for piano, Nos. 1 (Christmas), 2 (Passion), 3 (Song from Stories), 4 (Winter Birds); *Toccatos* Nos. 1, 2, and 3; *Variations Liturgical; Jona* (Yoruba language text) for soprano solo, drum, and piano; and *Ten Yoruba Songs* for voice. *Three Songs* for baritone and piano are included on a 1976 listing from the University of Ife Press, Nigeria. Some of his music is recorded on Broadcast Foundation recordings N. 543.13/7 (3/7; 4/7; 9/7; 10/7; and 12/7).

AKIN EUBA (1935–)

Akin Euba, composer, ethnomusicologist and educator, was born in Nigeria. A graduate of Trinity College of London in piano and composition and of the University of Ghana at Legon, where he received the Ph.D. under J. K. Nketia, he became known for his work both in the United States and Africa and for his compositions containing elements of the Yoruba.

In the *Music Educators Journal*, January 1975, Euba wrote that the traditional concept of the African musician was lost to the Western culture's introduction of composing music meant just for listening. Posing questions about the future of the African music, he also offered solutions to documenting and studying traditional music so it would not be lost. In another article, he pointed out the Yoruba influences and background histories concerned with Yoruba music. In general, many of his lectures and writings have been presented in conjunction with the promotion, documentation, and preservation of African music as it met the more widespread Western music.

One of the front-runners of the Nigerian composers, Euba has served African music in the capacity of Director of Research and Music at the University of Lagos. He also served as senior research fellow in musicology at the University of Ife and as executive editor of the University of Ife Press, devoting himself to the problems encountered in publishing and generally promoting the study of African music.

Among his music compositions are those published by the University of Ife Press: *Six Yoruba Songs* for voice and piano, *Scenes from Traditional Life* for piano, and others. The Howard University Center for Ethnic Music and the Library of Congress listed his *Igi Nla So* for Yoruba drums and piano, shown in Example 95, whose unique instrumentation lent interest to the work and whose compositional techniques were of the contemporary vein, having sparse intervallic concepts. The Library of Congress listed no publishers for the following holographs: *Amici* (String Quartet); *Abiku* for orchestra; *Four Pictures* from *Oyo Cabashes; Six Yoruba Songs; Tortoise and the Speaking Cloth*; and the *Wanderer*, but did list Broadcast Foundation recording numbers on which they appear (N.543.18/7 and N.543.15/7).

Ex. 95. *Igi Nla So*, Euba. Used by permission.

Ashenafi Kebede, in his *Roots of Black Music* (Prentice Hall), listed Euba's other works as *Dirges* for speakers, singers, instrumentalists, and dancers; *Chaka*, the setting of a poem by Senghor; *Two Tortoise Folk Tales* in Yoruba, a musical drama for Nigerian instruments; and *Festac*, seventy-seven anthems for four-part chorus, jazz combo, and string bass with text excerpted from Margaret Walker's *For My People*. Euba and his works were also discussed in other books such as Eileen Southern's *Biographical Dictionary of Afro-American and African Musicians.*

ATO ALPHONSO TURKSON (1937–)

Ato Alphonso Turkson, a gifted young musician and composer of several works, has received his doctorate from Northwestern while on leave from the University of Ghana. He was educated at Achimoto College with Robert Kwamk, Philip Gbeho and J. Kwabena Nketia. He later accepted a composition fellowship to study in Hungary at the Franz Liszt Academy where he was a student of Kodaly's protégé, Rezso Sugar. His teaching experience was gained at the Winneba Secondary School and the University of Ghana, where he worked as a research assistant, and at Oregon State where he was a visiting Fulbright professor.

Ato Turkson.

Turkson's works show a refreshing approach to composition in general, and is representative of the contemporary era. A mixture of the African-western style, his works sometimes use common scales but primarily utilize twelve tone techniques. The most Africanized aspect of his music is the rhythmic interest, an intricacy of cross-rhythms, sporadic fragments and extended lines.

His *Sonata for Violin and Piano,* Op 16, and the *Three Pieces for Flute and Piano* display a mastery of skill and a natural affinity for the characteristics of each instrument. Both challenging and well constructed, they demand talent and control. The first measures of *Three Pieces for Flute and Piano,* Op. 14 (available from the University of Ife Press, Nigeria) are shown in Example 96, taken from each of the three movements.

Ex. 96. *Three Pieces for Flute and Piano,* Op. 14, Turkson. Used by permission of the African Institute, University of Ghana at Legon.

ASHENAFI KEBEDE (1938–)

An Ethiopian-born ethnomusicologist turned composer, Kebede, author, educator, and administrator, attended Teacher's Training Institute in Ethiopia, graduating in 1958. In 1962, he graduated from the University of Rochester with the Bachelor of Arts Degree, and in 1969 and 1971, from Wesleyan University with the Master of Arts and Doctor of Philosophy degrees, respectively.

Kebede has taught at the graduate school of the City University of New York, at the New England Conservatory of Music, and at the Brandeis School of Music. Since 1980, he has been on the faculty of Florida State University School of Music, where he also serves as director of the Black Studies Center for Black Culture and as executive director of the Florida Arts Council for Afro-American Affairs, Tallahassee. In 1963, he served as founder and administrator of the National School of Music in Ethiopia; in 1970, he coordinated Programs of World Music at Queens College in New York; and in 1978, he worked as UNESCO Consultant in Khartoum, Sudan. In Africa, he made giant strides, too, by writing the syllabi of the Institute of Music, Dance, and Drama for the government of Sudan.

Ashenafi Kebede.

Honors which distinguish him include the Diploma of Distinction from the International Biographical Center of Cambridge, England (1979), the designation as National Composer of Ethiopia, and the 1958 nomination for the Most Outstanding Ethiopian, which awarded him a four-year college grant to the United States. Kebede has also received support from the Haile Selassie I Foundation Grant for Outstanding Achievement in Musical Composition (1967), the Wesleyan Graduate Fellowship (1968), a UNESCO grant, Canadian Music Council Grant, American Council of Learned Societies Travel Grant to Germany, a National Endowment for the Humanities Grant, and a Florida Fine Arts Council Grant (1981–82). Kebede has been protocol guest of governments in Hungary, Bulgaria, and Iran.

Kebede has written articles published in the *Black Perspective in Music, Ethnomusicology, Music: An Appreciation* by Roger Kamien, the *Musical Quarterly, African Music, Cahiers D'Histoire Mondiale*, the *Ethiopian Observer*, and others. In addition, he is the author of *Roots of Black Music* (Prentice Hall, 1982) and is the co-author of *Ethiopie: Musique De L'Eglise Copte*. Kebede has lectured extensively at institutions both in the United States and in Ethiopia, discussing topics covering the sacred chant of the Ethiopian monotheistic churches, secular verse and poetry in Ethiopian traditional music, the musical culture of the Black Jews, and the styles of composition by contemporary African composers.

In music, Kebede edited, produced, and recorded the *Anthology of the World's Music* (Society of Ethnomusicology, Ethiopia, 1969); he conducted the Hungarian Orchestra on a recording in 1968; he edited and composed the text for *Music of Ethiopia* (from the Laura Boulton Collection of Columbia University, RCA Victor, Canada, 1966); and he wrote several compositions, recording some of them on *Pentatonism and Microtonality* (International Music, Newton, Massachusetts, 1979). Kebede also composed the following works used for the 1981 performance of his music at Florida State University's Center for Black Culture Presentation: *Soliloquy for Soprano, Japanese Koto, and Flute; Mot for Two Sopranos*, Japanese koto; and *Koturasia: Pentamelodic Exposition for Japanese Koto, Clarinet, and Violin.*

Kebede wrote about *Koturasia* thusly: "*Koturasia* is primarily a composition for the Japanese zither called *koto*, clarinet, and violin. The thirteen strings of the *koto* are tuned according to *Low Hira-joshi* scale, one of the most popular systems of tuning in Japan. Though basically pentatonic, the *Hira-joshi* system of tuning enables the composer to musically explore pentachordal, chromatic, and subtle microtonal sound inflections and ornaments on the *koto*. The name *Koturasia* is derived from the words koto-europe-asia; it refers to the intercultural blending of musical styles in a single composition, as is the case with *Koturasia*."

Koturasia was written especially for Fusako Yoshida, Master of Koto, who helped popularize Japanese koto music in New York City and Washington, D.C. *Koturasia*, measures 20–25 of which are seen below in Example 97 and measures 1–9 in Example 98, was premiered in Colden Auditorium, Queens College, on March 3, 1974, by Master Yoshida.

Ex. 97. *Koturasia* (Western notation), Kebede. Used by permission.

Ex. 98. *Koturasia* (Eastern notation), Kebede. Used by permission.

The score in the Japanese notation must be read from right (page 11) to left (page 10) and top to bottom.

Postscript VII: Other Composers

Still other songwriters and musicologists or composers of Africa are not discussed in detail here primarily because of limitations of correspondence, communications, time, travel, and other considerations. Among them are educators, collectors, and musicologists mentioned by Hare and others:

Nicholas J. Ballanta-Taylor, from Sierra Leone, whose compositions were performed in New York in 1923 and whose writing and lectures influenced his time.

Madikane Cele of Southeast Africa.

Kamba Simango of Portuguese East Africa, foremost among those who had "been able to give valuable information regarding African music."

Phillip Gbeho, composer of Ghana's national anthem, *Akinwumi.*

Anthony Okelo from Uganda, whose *Kyrie* from *Missa Maleng* for choir and African instruments are listed with the University of Ife Pressworks.

A. Twumasi-Ankra Ofori, the Ghanaian songwriter.

Emoka Meki Nzewi, listed in Eileen Southern's *Black Perspective in Music.*

"Third-stream" composers named by Kebede in his *Roots of Black Music* (Prentice-Hall, 1982): Akinola Akinyele, Wilberforce Echezona, Lazarus Ekwueme, Felix Nwebe, Alphonso Okosa, T. K. E. Phillips, and Joshua Uzoigwe, as well as ethnomusicologists N. Z. Nayo and Annan Mensa from Ghana. J. K. Nketia wrote that Nayo now works at the University of Lagos and that he "has written more works" and was invited by the University of Cologne for a term "so that his orchestral works could be read or performed." Nketia also noted that Atta A. Mensah is now at the University of Illorin.

Noel Da Costa (1930–), born in Nigeria and transplanted to America by age eleven, is discussed in earlier sections of volumes I and II with the North American composers.

A writer of Nigerian opera, found in the *Encyclopedia Britannica*: E. K. Ogunmola, composer of *The Palmwine Drinkard*, and *Love of Money*, which incorporate praise poetry, proverbs, and incantations.

Hubert Ogunde, composer of *Yoruba Ronu* (Yoruba, Think) and *Journey To Heaven.*

Duro Ladipo, composer of *Oba Ko 'So* (The King Did Not Hang), *Moremi, eda* (Everyman), of church music, and preserver of traditional arts, writer of cultural plays based on history, employing ritual drumming, chanting, and singing.

J. K. Nketia also referred to a young Ghanaian, Emmanuel Gyima-Larbi, who has just completed his Ph.D. in composition in the United States and has written several works which have been performed at the University of Illinois and elsewhere.

Certain other musicians are Mahmoud Ahmed (ca. 1945–), the Ethiopian-born singer-composer, whose new album of original songs, *Ere Mela Mela*, was said by Geoffrey Hines of the *Washington Post*, to be "Motown meets Islam";

The exciting Hugh Masekela, jazz trumpeter and band leader originally from South Africa, whose albums such as *Uptownship*, his conducting of the Mariam Mekeba album *The Voice of Africa*, his co-writing with Mbongeni Ngema of the score for the musical *Sarafina!*, his arrangements and/or co-composing of "Shihibolet", "Qhude", "Mayiguye", etc., confirm his solid place as a giant talent of the world; and

Hugh Masekela. Ca. 1970. Courtesy of Columbia Records.

The young Jonathan Butler, singer, composer and guitarist from South Africa, and 1990 Image Awardee for jazz rendition of "Deliverance", whose album *Heal Our Land* (Jive/RCA) contains originals (co-written with L. Siffre) include *Heal Our Land, Sing Me Your Love Song, All Grow'd Up, A Good Life*, and whose songs co-written with J. Skinner are *This Time Is Forever, Black & White in Colour, Scene of the Crime, I Stopped Believing and No Strings, No Ties.*

Jonathan Butler. Courtesy of VNCF.

Toumani Diabate (1965–), from Mali, an instrumentalist-composer billed by the Smithsonian as "Prince" and "master of the African Kora" who "performs an hypnotically beautiful concert . . . " and whose "sound is made familiar and compelling by (his) love of jazz, classical, rock and ethnic music from around the world".

Still more South African talent was exposed in *Sarafina!* program notes by composer-playwright Mbongeni Ngema in a discussion of the music of Kippie Moeketsi, Sandile Shange, Mankunku Ngozi, Gabriel Thobejane, Abdullah Ibrahim, and groups such The Soul Brothers, The Dark City Sisters, Mohottela Queens, Mahlatini, Izintombi Zesi Manje-Manje, and the South African group, Ladysmith Black Mombazo, has recently had exposure through joint performances and recordings with the American singer-composer, Paul Simon.

An article by Brian Cullman entitled "The Beat of Africa", (*Emerge*, June, 1990) revealed musician-composers from different African locales, some of whom have toured America in recent years: Mory Kante; King Sunny Ade, who play Nigerian "juju" music; Youssou N'Dour, Tabu Ley, and Baaba Laal from Senegal; Thomas Mapfumo from Zimbabwe; Cameroonian saxophonist Manu Dibango ("only African bandleader to have a bona fide American dance hit, *Soul Makossa* in 1973"); Ray Lema of Zaire; Salif Keita from Mali; Gambian griot Foday Musa Suso who now lives in

Chicago; and Fela Anikulapo Kuti of Nigeria. Cullman also pointed out that American musicians should follow the patterns of Quincy Jones (who worked with African musicians in producing music for the television series, *Roots*), Stevie Wonder (who "guested" on Brazilian, Caribbean, and on albums with King Sunny Ade to help popularize reggae and juju music, respectively) and of Herbie Hancock, who performed with Foday Musa Suso to make the *Village Life* album.

Conclusion

In the past, scholars have had to rely on oral tradition in order to pinpoint many of the talents discussed in various parts of this book. Or they have had to trust a hapless, chance association dictated by some mysterious force which draws truths together through intellectual interchange. In order to assemble data for the future, however, and particularly because of the bulk of information involved and in order to complete the musical contributions of the Pan-African realm, compilers and musicologists must do several things: (1) foreign languages must become more important—particularly French, Spanish, and Portuguese; (2) computers must be used in the study and aggregation of these neglected and lost composers of Pan-African music; and (3) the largest centers should develop a network of communication and exchange with the Afro-Creative Arts Center and the publishers of anthologies and reference works so that transcontinental research might be facilitated. Henceforth, worldwide identification must become the priority.

The flood of materials which have surfaced within the last ten years shows a definite progress toward a new era and a new intellectual acceptance of Pan-African music in the classroom and in the societies. Already a change has begun, but much more concentration should be placed upon those areas which have not been touched at all such as the Middle East where slavery was as real as elsewhere.

According to an article by Gerishon M. Manani of East Africa (published in East Africa's *Cultural Heritage* monograph number 4, 1966), Ghana and Nigeria were the first to have full governmental support for cultural projects in their countries by providing funds and other support. In assessing the state of affairs in East Africa and in encouraging East African countries to follow suit, he suggested that this would be a "very big step forward in African society." Since that time, the African-American Forum and other study programs have included the East African part of the continent in their seminars and exchange goals, exacting a progressively hopeful change in the further development and upgrading of the musical world in East Africa.

But more development and exchange is needed between the East and the West to inculcate new values, new life, and new views into educational systems steeped with simplistic caste and class divisions reflective of leftover remnants of enslaved continents. This will be the challenge of tomorrow: teaching must increase; learning must not surcease. Time will dictate the terms and talents of the composers of tomorrow whose futures rest upon the heritage of the past. Without question, the recent accelerating movements supporting the promotion, aggregation, and preservation of music by Pan-African composers suggest a far better plan for Pan-African affairs than ten years ago and a far better placement of priorities than ever before.

XVII

THE FUTURE: ART MUSIC VERSUS POPULAR MUSIC?

Society today not only poses some questions concerning the right to compose within certain forms and techniques, but also questions the best available medium of expression for this Black identity. Should Black composers be restricted to forms or techniques generally associated with traditionally African forms? Or should composers merge with the period in which they live and participate in all existing elements of music? Should music rise above the faction of society which debases or criticizes by types and people, or should music be left for all to enjoy? What is the future of Black music, and what was its past? Can this music be identified as that of Afro-Americans? Is there Black music at all? And finally, what music is representative of both the Afro-American whose heritage is African and whose citizenship is, by birth, American? The final chapter will ponder these questions and discuss the nature of survival of both the Pan-African society and its music.

Many have felt that Pan-African art musicians were traitors to a Black heritage. They knew nothing of Elizabeth Greenfield, Blind Thomas Bethune and George Bridgetower, or of Chevalier de Saint Georges or of the countless others who had pioneered in art music long before the era of jazz. On the other hand, few in art music knew of Tom Turpin, Jelly Roll Morton and Scott Joplin.

White Americans once voiced another opinion of the matter. Their actions stated that Black folk musicians were acceptable as entertainers, and that art musicians were almost acceptable as vocalists. They also showed that the work of such musicians could not possible be taken seriously and felt that they should simply restrict their activities to popular music. Whereas Black critics felt that Black composers should develop their own music such as jazz, Whites simply considered them too inferior to practice concert or art music. Blacks, they said, were designed to improvise, to make "fun music" for brothels. But to participate in composing, conducting or performing art music was unthinkable for the majority of Pan Africans. They became victims of this propaganda.

The social conditions and biased associations led to a frustration and ambivalence in the practice of both popular music and art music. Some practiced popular music because they wanted to; others, because they had to. While popular musicians worked continuously and received ready fame and fortune, art music composers were generally neglected. For the latter, publishers abandoned their causes, while promoting music by popular composers. Blacks led no orchestras, performed in no symphonies, performed no significant concerts at the institutions of higher learning, and produced few recordings of their works. No one realized the potential of these Pan Africans, not even they themselves.

Consequently, many composers became greatly disillusioned with America and traveled to Europe in order to seek a more respectable existence and an appreciation of their talents. Others trained in art music took up the practice of jazz and accomplished sound developments in the then non-established form. Significantly, still others remained in America and wrote in both types simultaneously.

The fact now, however, is that popular music and art music enjoy a healthy competition and are worthy of the accolades extended them. Never before has the world of art music given as much thought to popular music as today, and never more credit, study, and bold admission of the comradeship between the two. Popular music has even grown so strong as to boast superiority, particularly as far as jazz is concerned. This is especially true since trained musicians are not restricting their talents to one medium alone. It is now more common for musicians to practice professionally in both the academic and popular forms at once.

The contemporary period offers many choices, styles and philosophies concerning popular and art music forms. Many feel that jazz and other popular forms have reached parity with the traditional classical music, and that they will either merge in complexity or will become the epitome of simplicity. Others feel that jazz is the real classical music of Blacks, and of America. Based upon the traditional history related above, society, they say, has led them to seek a more separate art as approved by a Black definition. And even according to the definitions already established, some feel that jazz fits the concept of "classical music". For example, jazz has withstood the "test of time", concerning itself with decorum in performance, with ornamentation, improvisation and nuances common to the pleasant aesthetics and professional achievements of music. In addition, art music has benefited by its innumerable experiments from instrumental ranges and stamina to a compositional technique. Jazz has also abandoned the sole function of dance music, and has attained the rank of "music for listening" and analysis. Still others feel that both are so inbred that there is no need to separate them. They feel that the history of both classical and popular music has consisted of enough major contributions to allow them to claim any participation within any type of music. These musicians point to parallelism of techniques, evaluation in functions and plagiarism. In some cases, both types become inseparable and are not easily distinguishable. Both have evolved from Africa. Both have enjoyed active and passive participation from their listeners. Yet both are on the verge of becoming extinct unless a more definitive clarification evolves between third streamism, avant-garde, or some other concept. While art music and jazz are not the same, many characteristics and similarities are apparent. To further contribute to the confusion, many jazz performers have admitted to being impressed with Stravinsky, Bach and other classicists. Yet Stravinsky is reported to have been equally fascinated with jazz.

The real definitions and prognosis of popular music, art music or Black music are not easy, for there is a history of excellence in all types of music. Few can tell twelve-tone jazz from twelve-tone art music or without previous study, the music of Hale Smith from that of a White counterpart using the same compositional techniques. Few can distinguish whether a composer better loves his well-planned rock-opera or his classical opera since equal efforts are used to create both. Yet composers themselves have less trouble explaining the music around them (i.e., the style, type and future). To them, the future rests in any medium of expression which they choose. Their music is life itself—what they see and know, and what they experience and do. They demand the freedom to compose as they wish and demand the freedom for rivalry and coexistence among all musical forms. Most composers do not like restrictions, but relish versatility. One composer, Arthur Cunningham, who has written numerous works from orchestral pieces to rock, uses a descriptive poem to denote a general feeling among contemporary composers. His thoughts give a potential cue to the future of music.

LET OTHERS DREAM

What they Dream
I Dream
Music

I am a source person
My body
Its height width length and color
Is my house

The earth
My estate
The universe
My place

Call me what you will
Call my music
MUSIC

Arthur Cunningham
(Used by permission)

The future of Afro-American music is supported by its past, and depends upon this heritage for its future survival. Reflected in a long history of oral tradition, improvisation, harmonic variety and rhythmic perfection, this music enjoys a certain unique characteristic in its performance and acceptability of popular and folk forms. But never has the contribution toward such intellectual aesthetics been rewarded for its astuteness, practicality and beauty. Black composers have practiced their music in many types of compositions and philosophies, only now commanding the just respect which they deserve. Perhaps this knowledge of the past, this completeness of characteristic styles and a forward movement will guarantee an acceptance of individual talents, forms and ideas, and will render a new performance for tomorrow.

But knowledge and acceptance of this music, no matter what its definition, semantics and interchange, will not be effected without the benefit of concerned Americans. This music should be promoted, learned, studied, probed and considered as being American. All should invest in the enrichment of these compositions through performance and listening experiences. Publishers and recording industries must join with the public to support the heritage of a music which is interwoven with American tradition and whose message for all minds speaks of freedom now!

Map of modern Africa.

Map of America in the 1800's.

APPENDIX A
MUSICAL TERMS AND SELECTED WORDS

A cappella—unaccompanied vocal music.
Adagio—slow speed.
Ad libitum—at will of performer; freedom to interpret.
African-American—the most definitive reference to those born in America with African ancestral links.
Afro-American—shortened version of the above.
Air—simple melody or tune.
Allegro—lively speed; spirited.
Andante—"walking" or moderate speed.
Aria—a melody or air in an opera, oratorio, etc.
Arpeggio—broken chord tones.
Art music—classical music, whose history includes centuries of European development, but also encompasses African contributions; Bernstein felt, however, that "art music" was any which strove to achieve superb artistic or musical standards.
Art song—classical vocal piece in through-composed or strophic form, sometimes taken from larger cycle.
Atonal—music without key center.
Bambá—African handclapping and dance music, related to Puerto Rican bombé.
Bamboula—African dance similar to the habanera and later identified with the cakewalk rhythms of ragtime.
Banto—Bantu tribe of Africa.
Banza—Fiddle, guitar.
Ballet—music for dancers and orchestral accompaniment.
Bar—measure or frame containing specific number of notes equal to value of meter signature.
Bar line—vertical line used to separate measures.
Binary form—two-part piece, each section of which usually repeats.
Black—rather than color, a misnomer for Pan-Africans, preferred in 1960–80s for classifications of colored, darker, mulatto, Negro, negrito, nègre, negreiro, negrinho, schwartz, etc.
Black music—that composed by Pan-Africans as well as those smaller root forms handed down through oral tradition of Africans.
Blue notes—those lowered tones (such as 3rds, 7ths) found in jazz scales.
Break—instrumental interlude in jazz compositions.
Cadence—ending.
Cakewalk—dance associated with ragtime era, similar to bamboula.
Call and response—African performance idiom roughly equivalent to antiphony, which is characterized by the alternation of leader and chorus.
Cantata—large vocal work containing arias, etc., usually dramatic or religious.
Chamber music—that written for small ensembles such as trio sonatas, quartets, etc.
Chattel—personal property other than real estate.
Chord—two or more blending tones; harmonic.

Chromatic—distance of a half-step, or smallest distance between western tones.
Classic—traditional, standard, or "set" example such as "classic blues" with its 12-bar structure.
Classical—term describing both the music of the late 18th century, as well as a general type once based on intellectual affiliation with Greco-Roman traditions of the upper class status.
Combo—small ensemble, used mainly in popular vernacular.
Composer—one who writes and/or conceives music by originality and inspiration.
Concerto—large piece containing several movements of varying speeds, for solo and orchestral accompaniment (although Ulysses Kay has composed one for orchestra).
Consonant—agreement; chordal.
Contrapuntal—counterpoint, polyphony; melody against melody, such as seen in imitative inventions and fugues, or interruptive overlapping lines.
Creole—term defined according to locale and era. In Brazil, "crioulo" was "originally a native-born Negro", but is now "any Negro" (J. O. Taylor's *Portuguese Dictionary*); in other places, it meant mixtures of African with either French or Spanish, while in New Orleans, it included "black" *or* "white" creoles.
Dança, Danza—Brazilian, Spanish terms for dances, some of which were merengue, habanera, seis, and milonga.
Development—middle section of sonata-allegro form, from (usu.) first movement of a sonata, concerto, etc.
Diatonic—stepwise or scalewise movement.
Dissonant—harsh, non-traditional blendings.
Dynamics—symbols used to indicate loudness or softness.
Element—constituent or part; substance of music, such as the three main elements of melody, harmony and rhythm.
Ensemble—group of players such as combo, duet, trio, quartet, or quintet; togetherness.
Escola—School (Portuguese).
Etude—study piece emphasizing a technical difficulty; exercise.
Exposition—first section of Sonata-allegro movement, which exposes main themes.
Form—shape, structure or organization of composition.
Forte—loud.
Fortepiano—piano (the instrument so named because of its ability to render loud and soft music).
Fugue—imitative piece employing specific rules for linear, thematic entrances (Also see contrapuntal).
Glissando—gliding or sliding across several tones (a "zip" effect!).
Grave—very slow speed.
Half Step—smallest unit between two tones; chromatic.
Harmony—science of sound; agreement, togetherness, chordal; consonant.
Heritage—that handed down by one's ancestors, as culture, tradition or birthright.
Homophony—chordal, but having predominant melody, as in four-part hymns.

Imitation—repetition of theme by alternate voices or instruments.
Improvisation—spontaneous performance, but based upon a knowledge of the music at hand; to "improve" by additions, changes, etc.
Interval—distance.
Invention—smaller imitative piece, related to canons, fugues, etc.
Inversion—mirror-like exchange or "upside down" counterpoint; also rearrangement of harmonic tones, or even melody in reverse or retrograde order.
Jam Session—usually a jazz "improv" work-out, possibly related to history of the "jammette" bands in Caribbean masquerades.
Key—tone, note or scale.
Keynote—tonic or main tonal center.
Largo—very slow speed.
Lento—slow.
Lick—jazz term meaning phrase, melody or theme.
Linear—line, melody.
Lining out the Notes—Role of leader or cantor in call and response rendition of old Watts-type hymns, which involves singing the line of music usually from the poetic reference and which is followed by congregational singing in harmonized and improvised fashion.
Liturgical—of the church; sacred, religious ritual.
Long meter—illusive term to define, shrouded in various geographical traditions; some explanations imply slow tempo used in singing "Dr. Watts" type hymns; another possibility is simply a reference to the "longus" shape of old mensural notations, or common time, with "short meter" being a faster, "alla breve" execution.
Major scale—eight notes in succession, having half-steps between third and fourth tones, and seventh and eighth.
Maroons—Jamaicans who gained freedom from British during slavery and fled to mountainous Accompong near Montego Bay; some, originally blue-eyed, brown people.
Mass—Catholic liturgical order of worship in celebration of Last Supper.
Measure—quantity of metric equality, divided by bar lines.
Melody—tune, theme, subject, or motive; primarily linear or horizontal arrangement of single tones.
Mestizo—South American Indian.
Mestre—priest-teacher (Port.)
Medium—means by which musical sound is transmitted; i. e., either by instrument or voice, etc.
Meter—numerical signatures indicating rhythmic relationships of notes.
Microtones—see quarter tones.
Minuet—dance in three.
Mode—type of scale or quality of intervals such as major or minor; also liturgical scale, etc.
Modinha—Brazilian ballad.
Monody—single line; melodic; unison voices.
Motive—theme, main melody.
Movement—section of larger work, although complete entity within itself.
Mulatto—designation for person of mixed heritage, similar to octoroon, creole, etc.
Note—key, pitch, or tone.
Octet—piece for, or number of eight players

Opera—music drama, predominantly vocal with orchestral accompaniment.
Oratorio—large vocal work usually, but not necessarily, of religious theme; contains solo parts, choral sections, orchestral overtures, interludes and accompaniments.
Orchestration—compositional writing for instruments.
Overture—instrumental "opening" piece.
Padre—priest; father.
Pan-African—Brotherhood of Blacks in worldwide diaspora; related to Franz Fanon's theory of negritude and the precepts formulated by C. L. R. James, et al.
Parallel—similar motion of harmonic parts.
Phrase—musical sentence; "lick" (jazz).
Piano—soft (dynamics); keyboard, the modern type of which was popularized during ragtime era.
Polyphony—many sounds; melodies in overlapping or imitative counterpoint; contrapuntal music.
Polytonal—many keys (scales, chords, tones) used simultaneously within same piece.
Pitch—tone, note, sound.
Presto—very fast and lively speed.
Prelude—opening piece, sometimes akin to technical goals of an etude.
Quarter tones—microtones; smaller intervals than half-steps, used by blues singers, etc.; sometimes referred to as "singing between the cracks", because tones cannot be duplicated within western scalar concepts of major and minor modes.
Quartet—either any piece for four voices or instruments; also instrumental sonata-type piece usually containing several movements.
Quintet—piece for five performers.
Recapitulation—last section of a sonata-allegro movement; return of main themes in main key.
Rap—spoken verse accompanied by vocal and instrumental rock ensembles.
Reggae—popular Jamaican music with socio-political overtones, whose ostinato rhythm consists of two sixteenths and an eighth
Rest—symbol for silence equal to duration of corresponding note.
Requiem—mass for the dead.
Retrograde—crab motion or backward order of tone row.
Rhythm—pulsation or flow of music; movement, motion.
Row—atonal scale based on serial or twelve-tone technique.
Scale—successive, diatonic tones in special order; a row.
Scherzo—playful piece.
Score—written music; "full score"—orchestral music with all parts shown together.
Sextet—piece written for six.
Septet—piece for seven.
Seventh—chord composed of four consonant tones; interval or distance of seven note span.
Short meter—see long meter.
Solo—music for exhibition; one performer.
Sonata—in baroque period, "sound piece" for one several instruments; in

classical period, piece for one to three players; work consisting of several movements contrasting in mood, key, speed, and form.

Strophic—piece with different verses and chorus set to same music (hymn style).

Subject—see melody.

Suite—piece containing several movements with dance characteristics.

Syncopation—displacement of the expected rhythmic schemes; accentuation of second and fourth beats.

Symphony—piece written for orchestra containing several movements; sonata form.

Tempo—speed.

Theme—see melody.

Third—interval of three notes apart; combination of first and third scale tones, or other such alternates.

Timbre—tone color; characteristic quality of sound made by instrument or voice.

Time signature—meter found at beginning of composition indicating predominant note value.

Toccata—"touch piece" of baroque era, employing flashy technical idioms and fantasy-like features.

Tonal—music with definite key or tone center.

Tonic—keynote.

Triad—chord composed of three notes.

Trio—piece for three players, usually in sonata form if classical.

Tune—see melody.

Twelve tone—music with equal emphasis upon twelve tones of chromatic scale; loosely, also serial music.

Unison—same melody in all parts, using exactly the same pitch or octaves.

Vivace—quick and lively tempo.

Waltz—dance in three.

Whole step—scale-wise interval composed of two half steps.

Zambo—offspring of a "Negro man and an Indian woman".

APPENDIX B
READINGS, RECORDINGS AND RELATED RESOURCES

Chapter I: The Slave Era: Black Man in Colonial America

Historical

Aptheker, Herbert. *American Negro Slave Revolts*. New York: Columbia University, 1943.

Bennett, Lerone, Jr. *Before the Mayflower: A History of the Negro in America from 1619–1964*. Baltimore: Penguin Books, 1968.

Botkin, B. A. *Lay My Burden Down*. Chicago: University of Chicago Press, 1968.

Butcher, Margaret. *Negro in the American Culture*. New York: Alfred Knopf, 1969.

Davidson, Basil. *The African Past*. New York: Atlantic-Little Brown, 1964.

Diop, Cheikh A. *The African Origin of Civilization: Myth or Reality*. New York: Lawrence Hill, 1975.

Edey, Maitland et al. *The Missing Link*. New York: Time-Life Books, 1972.

Diffie, Bailey W. *A History of Colonial Brazil, 1500–1792*. Malabar: Krieger, 1987.

DuBois, W. E. B. *The Souls of Black Folk*. New York: Avon Books, 1965.

Elkins, Stanley. *Slavery: A Problem in American Institutional and Intellectual Life*. Chicago: University of Chicago Press, 1969.

Franklin, John Hope. "Brief History of the Negro in the United States". *American Negro Reference Book*. Englewood Cliffs: Prentice-Hall, 1966.

———————. *From Slavery to Freedom*. New York: Alfred Knopf, 1948, 1974.

Frazier, E. Franklin. *The Negro in the United States*. New York: Macmillan, 1957.

Graham, Gerald, ed. *McLean of the Gold Coast*. London: Oxford University Press, 1962.

Hayes, William. *Most Ancient Egypt*. Chicago: University of Chicago, 1965.

Hodges, Norman. *Breaking the Chains of Bondage: A History of the Black People*. New York: Monarch Press, 1971.

Jones, Leroi. *Blues People*. New York: Apollo, 1968.

Rawlinson, George, trans., and Manuell Komroff, ed. *The History of Herodotus*. New York: Tudor Press, 1928, 1943.

Snowden, Frank. *Blacks in Antiquity*. Cambridge: Belknap-Harvard, 1970.

Turner, G. C. *Pioneers of Long Ago*. Elementary school level. Washington D.C.: Associated Publishers.

Van Sertima, Ivan. *African Presence in Early America*. New Brunswick: Journal of African Civilizations, Africana Studies Department, Rutgers University, 1987.

Woodson, C. G. *African Heroes and Heroines*, Elementary. Washington D.C.: Associated Publishers, 1939.

———————. Charles Wesley and Thelma Perry, eds. *Mis-Education of the Negro*. Washington, D.C.: Associated Publishers, 1969.

———————. and C. H. Wesley. *The Story of the Negro Retold.* 4th ed. rev. Washington D.C.: Associated, 1959.

Work, Monroe N. *Bibliography of the Negro in Africa and America.* New York: Octagon Books, 1970.

Supplementary: Slave Narratives by Josiah Henson, Sojourner Truth, Frank Tannenbaum and Lunceford Lane.

Recordings

A Portrait of the Black Man, Sidney Poitier Reads. RCA Victor. (Also see Appendix D).

Chapter II: African Heritage

Historical

Bohsnan, Paul. *Africa and Africans.* New York: Natural History Press, 1964.

Bowdich, Edward. *Mission From Cape Coast Castle to Ashanti.* London; Reprinted in Mollien's *Travels in the Interior of Africa, Bowdich, T. E.* Biblo Publishers, 1967.

Coughlan, Robert. *Tropical Africa. New York*: Life World Library, Time, 1963.

Howard, C. and J. H. Plumb, eds. *West African Explorers.* London: Oxford University Press, 1951.

Jobson, Richard. *The Golden Trade.* London: Oxford University Press, 1623.

MacMichael, H. A. *A History of the Arabs in the Sudan.*, vol. 1. London: Frank Cass and Company, 1967.

Oliver, Roland, ed. *Dawn of African History.* London: Oxford University Press, 1968.

———————., ed. *The Middle Age of African History.* London: Oxford University Press, 1967.

Seligman, C. G. *Races of Africa.* New York: Oxford University Press, 1967.

Woldering, Irmgard. *The Art of Egypt.* New York: Greystone Press, 1963.

Musical

Aning, B. A. "Factors That Shape and Maintain Folk Music in Ghana." *Journal of International Folk Music Council*, Vol. XX, 1968.

Baines, A. *Musical Instruments Through the Ages.* London: Penguin, 1961.

Brandel, Rose. *The Music of Central Africa.* The Hague: Martinus Nijhoff, 1961, 1969.

Butcher, Vada. *Development of Materials for a One-Year Course in African Music for the General Undergraduate Student.* Washington D.C.: Howard University, 1970.

Chernoff, John Miller. *African Rhythm and African Sensibility.* Chicago: University of Chicago Press, 1979.

Coughlan, Robert. *Tropical Africa.* New York: Time, Inc., 1963.

Dietz, Betty and Michael Olatunji. *Musical Instruments of Africa.* New York: John Day, 1965.

Geis, Darlene and Glenn Kittler. *Nigeria and Ghana.* New York: Children Press, 1962.

Jones, A. M. *Africa and Indonesia: The Evidence of the Xlophone and Other Musical and Cultural Factors.* London: E. J. Brill, 1959.

Makeba, Miriam. *The World of African Songs.* Chicago: Quadrangle, 1971.

Nettl, Bruno. *Music in Primitive Culture.* Cambridge: Harvard University Press, 1956.

Nketia, J. Kwabena. *African Music in Ghana.* Illinois: Northwestern Press, 1963.

_______________. *Drumming in Akan Communities of Ghana*. Edinburg: Thomas Nelson and Sons, 1963.

_______________. *Folk Songs of Ghana*. London: Oxford University Press, 1963.

_______________. *Music of Africa*. New York: W. W. Norton, 1974.

_______________. *Music in Ghana*. London: Longmans Green, 1962.

_______________. "Musicology and African Music: A Review of Problems and Areas of Study." *Africa and the Wider World*. London: Brokensha and Crowder.

_______________. "The Problem of Meaning in African Music". *Ethnomusicology*, Volume IV, No. 3, 1960.

_______________. *Our Drums and Drummers*. Accra: Ghana Publishing House, 1968.

_______________. "The Hocket Technique in African Music." *Journal of the International Folk Music Council*. Volume XIV, 1962.

Opuku, A. M. *African Dances*. Legon: African Institute, University of Ghana, n. d.

Sachs, Curt. *History of Musical Instruments*. New York: W. W. Norton, 1940, 1960.

_______________. *Rise of Music in the Ancient World, East and West*. New York: W. W. Norton, 1934.

Wachsmann, Klaus. *Essays on Music and History in Africa*. Evanston: Northwestern University Press, 1971.

_______________. "The Trend of Musicology in Africa." *Institute of Ethnomusicology*., Volume I, No. 1. Los Angeles: University of California.

Wallaschek, Richard. *Primitive Music*. London: Longsman, 1893.

Warren, Fred and Lee. *The Music of Africa*. Englewood Cliffs: Prentice Hall, Inc., 1970.

Waterman, Richard. "African Influence on American Negro Music." *Acculturation in the Americas*. Chicago: University of Chicago Press, 1947.

Wilson, Margaret Welch, ed. *Our African Neighbors*. Gastonia: Brumley, c.1953.

Recordings and Strips

Africa: Man and His Music:. Nick Rossi. Keyboard Publications

Africa: Musical Instruments, Textiles, Jewelry and Architecture. Filmstrip with records. Warren Schloat Productions, Inc. Pleasantville, 1969.

African Society's Best Music for 1952. Decca LF 1171, No. 6.

Afro-American Music and Its Roots. Silver Burdett 74187747, 1976.

Anthology of Music of Black Africa. Everest EV 3254/3, Folkways, or Library of Congress.

Ghana Asuafo Reto Dwom. University of Ghana Chorus. Request Records.

Michael Olatunji and His Drums of Passion. Coumbia CS8210.

Miriam Makeba. RCA Victor LPM 2267, or Reprise 6274.

The Music of Africa Today. Universal Art, UAS 15556.

(Also see Appendix D).

Chapters III and IV: Early Folk Songs and Spirituals

Historical

Douglass, Frederick. *My Bondage and My Freedom*. New York: 1853.

Drimmer, Melvin. *Black History, A Reappraisal*. New York: Doubleday, 1968.

Glass, Paul. *Songs and Stories of Afro-Americans*. Elementary. New York: Grosset & Dunlap, 1971.

Herskovits, Melville. *The Myth of the Negro Past.* New York: Beacon, 1958, 1970.
Hughes, Langston and Milton Meltzer. *Black Magic: A Pictorial History of the Negro in American Entertainment.* Englewood Cliffs: Prentice-Hall, 1967.
Lincoln, Eric. *The Black Church in the African American Experience.* Chapel Hill: Duke, 1990.

Musical

Alen, W. F., Lucy Garrison and C. P. Ware. *Slave Songs of the United States.* New York: A. Simpson and Company, 1867; Reprint with accompaniments by Irving Schlein, Oak, 1965.
Bontemps, Arna. *American Negro Poetry.* New York: American Century and Long, 1963.
Burleigh, Harry T. *Minstrel Melodies.* New York: Schirmer, 1886.
———. *Negro Spirituals.* New York: Franco Colombo; Belwin Mills, 1984.
Courlander, Harold. *Negro Folk Music, U.S.A.* Chicago: Chicago University Press, 1963.
Epstein, Dena. "Slave Music in the U.S. Before 1960." *Notes.* Spring, 1963.
Fischer, Miles. *Negro Slave Songs in the U.S.* New York: Russell and Russell, 1968.
George, Zelma. "Negro Music in American Life." *The American Negro Reference Book.* J. Davis, ed. Englewood Cliffs: Prentice-Hall, 1966.
Hare, Maud Cuney. *Negro Musicians and Their Music.* Washington: Associated Press, 1936; Da Capo Reprint, 1974.
Hughes, Langston and Arna Bontemps. *The Book of Negro Folklore.* New York: Dodd, Mead and Company, 1958.
Hughes, Langston. *Famous Negro Music Makers.* New York: Dodd, Mead and Company, 1955.
Jackson, George. *Spiritual Folk Songs of Early America.* New York: Dover, 1937.
Johnson, James W. and John Rosamond. *The Book of Negro Spirituals, Volumes I and II.* New York: Viking Press, 1969.
Krehbiel, H. E. *Afro-American Folksongs.* New York: Schirmer, 1914.
Landeck, Beatrice. *Echoes of Africa.* New York: McKay and Company, 1969.
Locke, Alain. *The Negro and His Music.* New York: Arno Press and New York Times, 1969.
Lomax, Alan. *Folk Songs of North America.* Garden City: Doubleday, 1960.
Lomax, John and Alan. *Negro Folksongs.* New York: Macmillan, 1936.
Lowens, Irving. *Music and Musicians in Early America.* New York: W. W. Norton, 1964.
Lovell, John. *Black Song: The Forge and the Flame.* New York: Macmillan, 1972.
Marsh, J. B. T. *The Story of the Jubilee Singers.* New York: Negro University Press, 1969.
Nettl, Bruno. *An Introduction to Folk Music in the United States.* Detroit: Wayne State University Press, 1962.
Parrish, Lydia. *Folk Songs of the Georgia Sea Islands.* Hatboro: Folklore Associates, 1965.
Pichierri, Louis. *Music in New Hampshire, 1623–1800.* New York: Columbia University Press, 1968.
Standifer, James and Barbara Reeder. *Source Book of African and Afro-Ameri-*

can Materials. Vienna, Va.: Music Educators National Conference, 1972, CMP7.

Stevenson, Robert. "Afro-American Legacy to 1800". *Musical Quarterly*, October, 1968.

Toppin, Edgar. *A Mark Well Made*. Chicago: Rand McNally, 1967.

Walker, Wyatt T. *Somebody's Calling My Name*. Valley Forge,: Judson Press, 1975.

Work, John W. III. *American Negro Songs and Spirituals*. New York: Bonanza, 1940.

Supplementary: Collections by Dett, Bond, Jessye, C. C. White, Cook, etc.

Recordings and Film

Black Folk Music in America.. W. Stracke, O. Hurt, eds. Burton Munk and Co., 1970.

Five Centuries of Song, v.2. Roland Hayes. Vanguard VRS449.

Folk Music of the United States. Botkin, Lomax et al, eds. Library of Congress AAFS-L3, L4, L10, L30, L49.

Historical Interpretation of Negro Spirituals and *Lift Ev'ry Voice and Sing*. Dorothy Elan. Camden: Franklin Publishing Company.

Leontyne Price Sings Spirituals: Swing Low, Sweet Chariot. RCA Victor.

McHenry Boatwright Sings Spirituals. Atlantic RE7024

Negro Folk Music of Alabama, v. 1. H. Courlander, ed. Folkways.

New Born Again.. James W. Johnson. Film with selections from his *God's Trombones*..

Paul Robeson Sings Spirituals, Ballads. William Grant Still Music, 22 S. San Francisco St., Suite 422, Flagstaff, Arizona, 86001-5737.

Others: *Spirituals* by Tuskegee Institute Choir, Fisk Jubilee Singers, Hampton Institute, Virginia State College, etc..

(Also see Appendix D).

Chapters V and VI: Historical Background and Black Minstrels

Historical

Franklin, John H. *From Slavery to Freedom*. New York: A. Knopf, 1948, 1974.

Frazier, E. Franklin and Eric Lincoln. *The Negro Church in America/The Black Church Since Frazier*. New York: Schocken Books, 1963.

Johnson, James W. *The Autobiography of an Ex-Colored Man*. New York: Hill and Wang, 1960.

____________. *Along This Way*. New York: Viking, 1933; Funk and Wagnalls, 1964.

Lewis, David. *When Harlem Was in Vogue*. New York: Knopf, 1981.

Lynch, John Roy. *The Facts of Reconstruction*. Salem, N.H.: Ayer Co. Publishers, 1913; 1968.

Washington, Booker T. *Up From Slavery*. Williamstown, Mass: Corner House Reprint of 1900 ed., 1971.

Musical

Boni, Margaret. *Fireside Book of Folk Songs*. New York: Simon Schuster, 1974.

Burleigh, H. T. *Minstrel Melodies*. New York: Schirmer, 1886.

Burton, Jack. *The Blue Book of Broadway Musicals*. New York: Century House, 1962, 1965.

Callender's original Colored Minstrel Songster, 1882.

Daly, John. *A Song in His Heart*. Philadelphia: J. Winston, 1955.

Ewen, David. *History of Popular Music*. New York: Barnes and Noble, 1961.

______________. *The Life and Death of Tin Pan*. New York: Funk and Wagnalls, 1964.

______________. *Popular American Composers*. New York: H. W. Wilson, 1972.

Floyd, Samuel. *Black Music in the Harlem Renaissance*. Westport: Greenwood Press, 1990.

Goldberg, Isaac. *Tin Pan Alley*. New York: J. Day, 1930.

Haywood, Charles, ed. James Bland Album. New York: E. B. Marks, 1946.

Howard, John T. and George Bellows. *Music in America*. New York: Crowell, 1957.

Kingman, Daniel. *American Music: A Panorama*. New York: Schirmer Books, 1979.

Lomax, John and Alan. *American Ballads and Folk Songs*. New York: Macmillan, 1953.

Matfield, Julius. *Variety: Music Cavalcade (Musical-Historical Review 1620–1961)*. Englewood Cliffs: Prentice-hall, Inc., 1962.

Nathan, Hans. *Dan Emmett and the Rise of Early Negro Minstrelsy*. Norman: University of Oklahoma Press, 1962.

Niane, D. T. *Sundiata: An Epic of Old Mali*. Humanities Press, 1969; Longsman Trade, n. d.

Patterson, Lindsey. "The Negro in Music and Art." *Encyclopedia on Negro History and Art*, Volume IX. Washington D.C.: Associated Press; New York: Publishers Company, 1967.

Scarborough, Dorothy. *On the Trail of Negro Folk Songs*. Cambridge; Harvard University Press, 1925.

Scott, John Anthony. *The Ballad of America: The History of the United States in Song and Storm*. Carbondale: Southern Illinois University Press, 1983.

Southall, Geneva. *Blind Tom: The Post-Civil War Enslavement of a Black Musical Genius*. Minneapolis: Challenge Productions, Inc. (P.O. Box 9642, Minn. 55440), 1980.

Speath, Sigmund. *History of Popular Music in America*. New York: Random House, 1948.

Tinney, James S. *Spirit: A Journal of Issues Incident to Black Pentecostalism. Vol. 1, No. 1*. Washington D.C.: Howard University, 1977.

Wittke, Carl. *Tambo and Mr. Bones*. New York: E. B. Marks, 1829.

Recordings

Gentlemen Be Seated. Minstrel show arranged and conducted by B. Masingill. Epic Records LN 3596.

Golliwog's Cakewalk. Claude Debussy.

Leontyne Price: God Bless America.. Incl. *Lift Ev'ry Voice and Sing*. RCA ARL1-4528

Shuffle Along. E. Blake. On *Black Music: The Written Tradition*. Dr. S. Floyd, Center for Black Music Research, Columbia College, Chicago; or College Music Society.

Wild About Harry. J. Morris, soprano; W. Bolcom, E. Blake, pianists. Columbia 34504.

Chapters VII, VIII, and IX: Jazz Forms, Styles, and Composers

Historical

Aptheker, Herbert. *Documentary History of the Negro People in the United States*. New York: Carol Publishing Group, 1951.

Cotner, Robert, John Ezell and Gilbert Fite. *Readings in American History*, Volume II. Boston: Houghton Mifflin, 1952.

Frazier, E. Franklin. *The Negro in the United States*. New York: Macmillan, 1957.

Musical

Asch, Moses and Alan Lomax. *The Leadbelly Songbook*. New York: Oak, 1962.

Armstrong, Louis. *My Life in New Orleans*. New York: Da Capo Reprint, 1986.

Baker, David. *Jazz Improvisation*. Chicago: Maher, 1969.

Blesh, Rudi and Harriet Janis. *They All Played Ragtime*. New York: A. Knopf, 1960.

Boechman, Charles. *Cool, Hot and Blue: A History of Jazz for Young People*. New York: Simon and Schuster, No. 46555.

Bradford, Perry. *Born With the Blues*. New York: Oak, 1965.

Bruynoghe, Yannick. *Big Bill Blues*. New York: Oak, 1964.

Burt, Jesse and Duane Allen. *The History of Gospel Music*. Nashville: R & S Press, 1971.

Carey, Dave and Albert J. McCarthy. *Jazz Directory*. Fordingbridge, England, n. d.

Charters, Ann. *Ragtime Songbook*. New York: Oak, 1963.

Charters, Samuel. *Jazz; New Orleans*. New York: Oak, 1963.

———. *Robert Johnson*. New York: Music Sales Corporation, No. 000059.

Chilton, John. *Billie's Blues: The Billie Holiday Story 1933–1959*. New York: Stein and Day, 1975.

Clayton, Buck. *Buck Clayton's Jazz World*. New York; Oxford University, 1989.

Cole, Maria and Lovie Robinson. *Nat King Cole*. New York: William Morrow, 1971.

Coleman, Janet and Al Young. *Mingus/Mingus: Two Memoirs*. Berkeley: Creative Arts Book Company, 1989.

Colin, Sid. *Ella: The Life and Times of Ella Fitzgerald*. London: Elm Tree Books, 1987.

Copland, Aaron. "Jazz Structure and Influence." *Modern Music, 4:9–14*, January–February, 1927.

———. *The New Music*. New York: W. W. Norton, 1968.

Cornell, Jean Gay. *Mahalia Jackson, Queen of Gospel Song*. Champaign, Ill.: Garrard Publishing Co., 1974.

De Toledano, Ralph, ed. *Frontiers of Jazz*. New York: Unger, 1962.

Dexter, Dave, Jr. *Jazz Calvacade: The Inside Story of Jazz*. Criterion, 1946.

Dixon, Robert and John Godrich. *Recording the Blues*. New York: Stein and Day, 1970.

Edwards, A. and W. T. Marrocco. *Music in the United States*. Dubuque: William Brown, 1968.

Ellington, Edward (Duke). *Music is My Mistress*. Garden City: Doubleday, 1968.

Erlich, Lillian. *What Jazz is All About*. New York: Messner, 1966.

Feather, Leonard. *Encyclopedia of Jazz*. New York: Bonanza, 1962.

———. *Inside Bebop*. New York: Robbins, 1949.

Gershwin, George. "The Relation of Jazz to American Music." *American Composers on American Music*. Stanford: Stanford University Press, 1933.

Garland, Phyl. *The Sound of Soul*. Chicago: H. Regnery, 1969.

Goldstein, Richard. *The Poetry of Rock*. New York: Bantam Books, 1969.

Gray, John. *Blacks in Classical Music*. Westport: Greenwood Press, 1988.

Gridley, Mark. *Jazz Styles; History and Analysis*. Englewood Cliffs: Prentice-Hall, 1978.

Grissim, John. *Country Music; White Man's Blues*. New York: Paperback Library, 1970.

Groia, Philip. *They All Sang On The Corner: New York City's Rhythm and Blues Vocal Groups of the 1950s*. Sketaket, New York: Edmond Publishing Company, 1976.

Handy, W. C. *Father of the Blues*. New York: Collier, 1941.

Heilbut, Tony. *The Gospel Sound: Good News and Bad*. New York: Simon & Schuster, 1971.

Hentoff, Nat and Albert McCarthy. *Jazz: New Perspectives on the History of Jazz by 12 Critics*. New York: Da Capo Reprint, 1974.

Hillsman, Joan. *Gospel Music: An African American Art Form*. Washington D.C.: Middle Atlantic Press, 1990.

Hodeir, Andre. *Jazz: Its Evolution and Essence*. New York: Grove, 1956.

Horricks, Raymond. *Dizzy Gillespie*. New York: Hippocrene Books, 1984.

Keil, Charles. *Urban Blues*. Chicago: University of Chicago Press 1969.

Keepnews, Orrin and B. Graver. *A Pictorial History of Jazz*. New York: Crown, 1966.

Kliment, Bud. *Ella Fitzgerald: First Lady of American Song*. Los Angeles: Melrose Square Publishing Company, 1988.

Jasen, David. *Recorded Ragtime: A Discography (1897–1958)*. Hamden: Shoe String Books, 1973.

Kinkle, Roger D. *The Complete Encyclopedia of Popular Music and Jazz, 1900–1950*. New Rochelle: Arlington House, 1975.

Kirkeby, Ed. *Ain't Misbehavin': The Story of Fats Waller*. New York: Da Capo Reprint, 1975.

Kriss, Eric. *Six Blues Roots Pianists*. New York: Music Sales, No. 000144.

Leadbetter, Mike and Neil Slaven. *Blues Records: Encyclopedia to Recorded Blues*. New York: Music Sales, No. 000110.

Lomax, Alan. *Mister Jelly Roll*. New York: Grosset and Dunlap, 1950.

Lord, Albert. *The Singer of Tales*. Cambridge: Harvard University Press, 1960.

Mann, Woody. *Six Black Guitarists*. New York: Music Sales, No. 00135.

Martin, John and William Fritz. *Listening to Jazz*. Fresno: University of Fresno Press, 1970.

McCarthy, Albert. *The Dance Band Era (1910–1950)*. Radnor, Pa.: Chilton, 1971.

McDearmon, Kay. *Mahalia*. New York: Dodd, Mead & Company, 1976.

Megill, Donald D. and Richard S. Demory. *Introduction to Jazz History*, 2nd ed. Englewood Cliffs: Prentice Hall, 1989.

Mehegan, John. *Jazz Improvisation, Volumes I–IV*. New York: Watson-Guptil, 1962.

Meyer, Sheldon. *The Story of Jazz*. New York: Grosset and Dunlap, 1960.

Mezzrow, Milton and Bernard Wolfe. *Really the Blues*. New York: Random House, 1946.

Milhaud, Darius. "Jazz Band and Negro Music." *Living Age*, No. 323/1924, 169.

Montgomery, Elizabeth. *W. C. Handy's Father of the Blues*. Elementary. Champaign: Garrard Publishers, 1968.

Morath, Max. *Giants of Ragtime*. New York: E. B. Marks, 1971.

Oliver, Paul. *Story of The Blues*. Radnor, Pa.: Chilton Book Company, 1969.

Pleasants, Henry. *Serious Music and All That Jazz*. New York: Simon and Schuster, 1969.

Priestley, Brian. *Charlie Parker*. New York: Hippocrene Books, 1984.

Reisner, Robert, ed. *Bird: The Legend of Charlie Parker*. New York: Da Capo, 1962.

Rose, Al and Edmond Souchon. *New Orleans Jazz*. Louisiana: State University Press, 1967.

Sargent, Winthrop. *Jazz, Hot and Hybrid*. New York: Da Capo Press, 1974.

Schafer, W. J. and J. Riedel. *Art of Ragtime: Form and Meaning of an Original Black American Art*. La Stile: University Press, 1973.

Schuller, Gunther. *Early Jazz*. New York: Oxford, 1968.

Shapiro, Nat and Nat Hentoff. *Hear Me Talkin' to Ya'*. New York: Hinehart, 1955.

———. *The Jazz Makers*. New York: Grove, 1958.

Shaw, Arnold. *The Rockin' 50s: The Decade That Transformed the Pop Music Scene*. New York: Hawthorne Books, 1974.

Silverman, Jerry. *Folk Blues*. New York: Oak, 1958.

Smith, Willie the Lion, with George Hoefer. *Music on my Mind: The Memoirs of an American Pianist*. New York: Doubleday & Company, Inc., 1964.

Spencer, Ray and Arnold Laubich. *Art Tatum: A Guide to His Recorded Music*. Metuchen, N.J.: Scarecrow Press, 1982.

Stearns, Marshall. *The Story of Jazz*. New York: MacMillan, 1968.

Tanner, Paul and Maurice Gerow. *A Study of Jazz*. Dubuque: William Brown, 1964, 1973.

Taylor, William. *Jazz Piano: A Jazz History*. Dubuque: William Brown, 1983.

Terkel, Studs. *Giants of Jazz*. New York: Thomas Y. Crowell, 1975.

Ulanov, Barry. *A History of Jazz in America*. New York: Viking, 1952.

Walton, Ortiz. *Music: Black, White & Blue*. New York: Wllliam Morrow and Company, Inc., 1975.

Waters, Ethel. *His Eye Is on the Sparrow*. New York: Doubleday, 1951.

Whitcomb, Ian. *After The Ball: Pop Music From Rag to Rock*. Baltimore: Penguin, 1974.

Williams, Martin. *Jazz Masters of New Orleans*. New York: MacMillan, 1967.

Williams-Jones, Pearl. "Afro-American Gospel Music: A Brief Historical and Analytical Survey (1930–1970)." In Vada Butcher's *Development of Materials or a One Year Course in African Music for the General Undergraduate Student*. Washington D.C.: Howard University, 1970.

———. "Afro-American Gospel Music." *Journal of the Society for Ethnomusicology*, XIX, No. 3 (Sept. 1975), 373–385.

Witmark, Isidore and Isaac Goldberg. *From Ragtime to Swingtime*. New York: Lee Furman, 1939.

Work, John W. III. "Changing Patterns of Negro Folk Songs.". *Journal of American Folklore*. (April–June 1949), 136–144.

Recordings and Films

Amazing Bud Powell, The. Blue Note BLP 1598; also *Bud's Mood*, Verve MGV 8154.

Birth of the Cool. Miles Davis. Capitol DT-1974.
Charlie Parker. Fantasy 6011.
Caught in the Act. Bill Harris. Als E. Marcy 36097.
Dizzy Gllespie and His Band. Crescendo 23.
Duke Ellington and His Orchestra. Columbia 32160252, Decca 79224.
Early Erroll. E. Garner. Columbia J 1269; also his *Concert by the Sea,* CL883.
Ellington Era. CL 2046.
Essays in Ragtime. Folkways FG 3563.
Handful of Keys. Fats Waller. RCA Victor LPM 1502. Also see *Smashing Thirds.*
Hello Dolly and Weather Bird movies; Hot Five & Seven Albums. L. Armstrong.
Jazz. Folkways. (Vol. 11, FP 75 includes S. Joplin)
Jazz Concerto. L. Bernstein.
Jazz Omnibus. Columbia CL 1020.
La Creation. D. Milhaud. RCA Victor LD 2625.
Lady Soul. Aretha Franklin. Atlantic SC8176.
Monk's Music. Riverside RLP 12-242.
Piano Rags. Rifkin, pianist. Nonesuch H7 1248.
Ragtime for Eleven Instruments. I. Stravinsky.
Smithsonian Collection of Classic Jazz. M. Williams, ed. Smithsonian Institute.
Trio, vols. 1 & 2. Billy Taylor. Prestige 7015, 7016.
Zodiac Suite. Mary L. Williams. Verve VRS 6024.
(Also see Appendix D).

Chapters X and XIII: Art Music and Contemporary Forms

Historical

Adams, Russell. *Great Negros: Past and Present,* 3rd rev. ed. Chicago: Ebony Bookshop/Afro-Am Publishing Company, 1969.
Brawley, Benjamin. *The Negro Genius.* New York: Biblio and Tannen, 1966.
Frazier, Thomas R., ed. *Afro-American History: Primary Sources.* New York: Harcourt, Brace and World, 1970.
Rogers, J. A. *World's Great Men of Color, Vols. 1 & 2.* New York: Macmillan, 1972/

Musical

Abdul, Raoul. *Blacks in Classical Music.* New York: Dodd, Mead & Company, 1974.
Apel, Wllli. *Harvard Dictionary of Music.* Cambridge: Belknap Press of Harvard University Press, 1958, 1982.
Arpin, P. *Biographie de L. M. Gottschalk, Pianists Americain.* New York: Imprimerie du Currier des Etats Unis, 1953.
Arvey, Verna. *In One Lifetime.* Fayetteville, Ark.: University of Arkansas Press, 1984.
Bacharach, A. L., ed. *The Music Masters: The Twentieth Century,* Vol. 4. London: Cassell, 1948.
Baines, Anthony. *Musical Instruments Through the Ages.* Baltimore: Penguin Books, 1966.
Baker, Theodore. *Biographical Dictionary of Musicians.* New York: G. Schirmer, 1965.
———————. *Bibliography of African and Afro-American Music.* Vienna, Va.: MENC, No. 321-10460.

Brooks, Tilford. *America's Black Music Heritage*. Englewood Cliffs: Prentice-Hall, 1984.

Butcher, Vada. *Annual Report From the Center for Ethnic Music*. Washington D.C.: Howard University Press, 1970–71.

Chase, Gilbert. *America's Music: From the Pilgrims to the Present*. New York: McGraw-Hill, 1966.

Claghorn, Charles Eugene. *Biographical Dictionary of American Music*. West Nyack: Parker Publishing Co., 1973.

De Lerma, Dominique, et al. *Black Music in Our Culture*. Kent, Ohio: Kent State University Press, 1970.

Eagon, Angelo. *Catalog of Published Concert Music By American Composers*. Metuchen: Scarecrow Press, 1969.

Ewen, David. *American Composers Today*. New York: H. W. Wilson & Co., 1949.

______________. Composers Since 1900. New York: H. W. Wllson, 1969.

Faurot, Albert. *Concert Piano Repertoire*. Metuchen: Scarecrow Press, 1974.

Friskin, James and Irwin Freundlich. *Music for the Piano*. New York: Dover, 1973.

Garcia, William B. *The Life and Choral Music of John Wesley Work III*. Ph.D. thesis. Ann Arbor: University Microfilms, 1973.

Gottschalk, Louis M. *Notes of a Pianist*. Trans. by Robert Peterson. Philadelphia: J. B. Lippincott, 1881.

Green, Jeffrey. *Edmund Jenkins, The Life and Times of An American Black Composer, 1894–1926*. Westport: Greenwood Press, 1982.

Green, Mildred Denby. *Black Women Composers: A Genesis*. Boston: Twayne, 1983.

Grout, Donald. *History of Western Music*. New York: W. W. Norton, 1960.

Haas, Robert B., ed. *William Grant Still*. Los Angeles: Black Sparrow, 1972.

Hare, Maud Cuney. *Negro Musicians and Their Music*. Washington D.C.: Associated Press, 1936; New York: Da Capo Reprint, 1974.

Hinson, Maurice. *Guide to the Pianist's Repertoire*. Bloomington: Indiana University Press, 1973.

Hitchcock, H. Wiley, ed. *Music in the United States: A Historical Introduction*. Englewood Cliffs, N.J.: Prentice-Hall, Inc., 1969

Howard, John Tasker and G. K. Bellows. *A Short History of Music in America*. New York: Crowell, 1967.

Hyamson, Albert M., ed. *Dictionary of Universal Biography*. New York: E. P. Dutton and Company, 1951.

LaBrew, Arthur. *Studies in 19th Century Afro-American Music: Francis Johnson (1792–1844)*. Baton Rouge: Southern University, Author, 1974.

______________. *Elizabeth Taylor Greenfield:: The Black Swan*. Baton Rouge: Author, 1969.

Lang, Paul Henry, ed. *The Princeton Seminar in Advanced Musical Studies: Problems of Modem Music*. New York: W. W. Norton, 1962.

Machlis, Joseph. *Introduction to Contemporary Music*. New York: W. W. Norton, 1961.

McBrier, Vivian. *The Life and Works of Robert Nathaniel Dett*. Washington D.C.: Associated Publishers, 1977.

Miller, Hugh Milton. *History of Music*. New York: Barnes and Noble, 1968.

Moore, William. *The Cyclical Principle As Used in the Construction of Piano Sonatas*. Inc. George Walker's *Sonata No. 2*. Ph.D. thesis. Ann Arbor: University Microfilms, 1975.

Pavlakis, Christopher. *The American Music Handbook.* New York: Free Press, 1974.
Reis, Claire R. *Composers in America.* New York: Macmillan, 1947.
Rossi, Nick and Robert Choate. *Music of Our Time.* Boston: Crescendo, 1969.
Rublowsky, John. *Black Music in America.* New York: Basic Books, 1971.
Sablosky, Irving L. *American Music.* Chicago: University of Chicago Press, 1960.
Scholes, Percy A. *Oxford Companion to Music.* London: Oxford Press, 1970.
Seay, Albert. *Music in the Medieval World.* Englewood Cliffs, N.J.: Prentice-Hall, Inc., 1965.
Simmons, Otis. *Teaching Music in Urban Schools.* Boston: Crescendo, 1975.
Skrowronski, Joann. *Women in American Music: A Bibliography.* Metuchen, N.J.: Scarcrow Press, 1978.
Southern, Eileen. *Biographical Dictionary of Afro-American and African Musicians..* Westport, Conn.: Greenwood Press, 1982.
——————. *The Black Perspective in Music.* Cambria Heights: The Foundation for Research in the Afro-American Creative Arts, Inc., 1974.
——————. *Readings in Black American Music.* New York: W. W. Norton, 1971.
——————. *The Music of Black Americans.* New York: W. W. Norton, 1983.
Taylor, Camille and William A. Ballinger. *A List of Black Derived Music and Black Related Music Materials Submitted by Music Companies and Individuals.* Tne National Black Caucus of Music Educators National Conference, 1980.
Thompson, James C. *Music Through the Renaissance.* Dubuque: William Brown, 1968.
Thompson, Oscar, ed. *The International Cyclopedia of Music and Musicians.* New York: Dodd, Mead and Co., 1964.
Tishler, Alice. *Fifteen Black American Composers.* Detroit: Information Cooperative, 1982.
Trotter, James. *Music and Some Highly Musical People.* New York: Dillingham, 1881; Johnson Reprint Corporation, 1969.
Turner, Patricia. *Dictionary of Afro-American Performers.* 78 RPM & Cylinder records of opera, choral music, etc., c. 1900–1949. N.Y.: Garland Pub., 1990.
White, Evelyn. *Selected Bibliography of Published Choral Music by Black Composers.* Metuchen: Scarecrow Press, 1972.
Whiting, Helen A. *Negro Art, Music and Rhyme.* Washington D.C.: Associated, 1967.
Williams, Ora. *American Black Women in the Arts and Social Sciences.* Metuchen: Scarecrow, 1973.

Recordings

Black Composer in America. Desto DC 7107.
Black Music: The Written Tradition. (Address above).
Black Music Series. includes works by T. J. Anderson, George Walker, José White, Ulysses Kay, Olly Wilson, Roque Cordero et al. Columbia Records, now available from Still Music or College Music Society.
Dawson, William: *Negro Folk Symphony.* Decca DL 10077.
Kay, Ulysses: *Brass Quartet,* Folkways; *Choral Triptych,* Cambridge; *Round*

Dance and Polka, CRI 209; *Choral Works*, Cambridge CRM 416; *Serenade for Orchestra*, Louisville Orchestra Special, LOU 545-8.

Music of Black Composers. N. Hinderas, pianist. Includes Dett, Work, Still, Walker, etc.

Smith, Hale: *Nuances*. Sam Fox.

Still, W.: *Afro-American Symphony*, Columbia M 118; *Danzas de Panama*, Orion; order works from symphonies to suites from Still Music Company 22 San Francisco St., Suite 422, Flagstaff, Ariz.

Swanson, H.: *Night Music*, Decca DCM 3215; *Seven Songs*, Desto B 432; *Short Symphony*, American Recording Society ARS 7.

(Also see Appendix D).

Chapters XI and XII: Contemporary Jazz and Its Agnates

Historical

Addison, Gayle, ed. *The Black Aesthetic*. New York: Doubleday, 1971.

Brown, Claude. *Manchild in the Promised Land*. New York: Macmillan, 1978.

Carmichael, Stokely and Charles Hamilton. *Black Power*. New York: Random House, 1967.

Fanon, Frantz. *The Wretched of the Earth*. New York: Grave Press, 1968.

Kenyatta, Jomo. *Facing Mount Kenya*. New York: Random House, 1962.

King, Martin Luther. *Stride Toward Freedom*. New York: Harper & Row, 1958.

Lewis, David. *King: A Critical Biography*. Baltimore: Penguin Books, 1970.

Lincoln, Eric. *Martin Luther King, Jr.: A Profile*. New York: Hill & Wang, 1970.

Malcolm X. *Autobiography*. New York: Ballantine, 1987.

Musical

Buerkle, Jack and Danny Barker. *Bourbon Street Black: The New Orleans Black Jazz-man*. New York: Oxford University Press, 1973.

Bullock, Ralph. *In Spite of Handicaps*. Freeport: Books for Libraries Press, 1968.

Dexter, Dave, Jr. *The Jazz Story From the 90's to the 60's*. Englewood Cliffs: Prentice-Hall, 1964.

Hillsman, Joan, M. Warrick and A. Manno. *The Progress of Gospel Music*. New York: Vantage Press, 1976.

Ricks, G. *Some Aspects of the Religious Music of the U.S. Negro: Gospel Tradition*. Ann Arbor: University Microfilms, 1960.

Simosko, Vladimir and Barry Teppermann. *Eric Dolphy: A Musical Biography and Discography*. Washington D.C.: Smithsonian, 1976.

Spellman, A. B. *Black Music*. Inc. C. Taylor, O. Coleman et al. New York: Schocken Books, 1966.

Thomas, J. C. *Chasin' The Trane: The Music and Mystique of John Coltrane*. New York: Doubleday, 1975.

Welch, Chris. *Hendrix: A Biography*. New York: Flash Books, 1973.

Recordings

Coltrane, John: *A Love Supreme*. Impulse A 77.

Coleman, Ornette: *Art of the Improvisers*. Atlantic SC 1572; also *Free Jazz*, Atlantic.

Jones, Quincy: *Walking in Space*, AM 3023; also others on Mercury, Reprise, etc.

(Also see Appendix D, and supplementary resources for Chapters VII, VIII, etc.)

Chapters XIV and XV: Pan Africanism, Latin America, The Islands and Europe

Musical

Azevedo, Corrêa de. *150 Anos de Música no Brazil*. Rio de Janeiro: Univraria José Olympio Press, 1956.

Béhague, Gerard, Robert Stevenson and Isabel Aretz. "Latin Secular Song". *New Grove Dictionary*. Washington D.C.: National Press, 1982.

_______________. *Music in Latin America: An Introduction*. Englewood Cliffs: Prentice-Hall, Inc., 1979.

Braithwaite, P. A. and Serena, eds. *Musical Traditions, v. 2*. Paper. St Augustine: University of West Indies, 1975.

Cable, George W. *The Creoles of Louisiana*. New York: Charles Scribner's Sons, 1884.

Chase, Gilbert. *Guide to Latin American Music*. Washington D.C.: Library of Congress, Series 5, n. d.

Coleridge-Taylor, Avril Gwendolyn. *The Heritage of Samuel Coleridge-Taylor*. London: Dennis Dobson, 1979.

Coleridge-Taylor, Jessie. *Coleridge-Taylor: A Memory Sketch or Personal Reminiscences of My Husband, Genius and Musician*. London: Bobby and Company; New York: John Crowther, n. d.

Duncan, John. "Chevalier de St. Georges—Musician." *Negro Bulletin*. Washington D.C.: Associated, 1/1946.

Eaglefield-Hull, A., ed. *Beethoven's Letters*. Inc. George Bridgetower. New York: Dover Publications, 1972.

Elder, Jacob D. "Social Development of the Traditional Calypso of Trinidad." (From Congo Drum to Steel Band). Pamphlet. St Augustine: University of West Indies, 1968.

_______________. *Song Games from Trinidad & Tobago*. Port-of-Spain: National Cultural Council Publications, 1973.

Espinosa, Guillermo, ed. *Compositores de América, v. 2*. Washington D.C.: Union Panamericana, 1956.

Forbes, Elliot, ed. *Thayer's Life of Beethoven*. New Jersey: Princeton University Press, 1967.

Garcia, Juan Francisco. *Panorama de la Musica Dominicans*. Santo Domingo: Republico Dominicans, n. d.

George, Luvenia. *Teaching The Music of Six Different Cultures in the Modem Secondary Schools*. West Nyack: Parker, 1975.

Hooks, Rosie and Bernice Reagon, et al. *Black People and Their Culture: Selected Writings from the African Diaspora*. Washington D.C.: Smithsonian Institutioon, 1976.

Howard, Joseph. *Drums in the Americas*. New York: Music Sales, No. 00035.

Jablonski, Edward. *The Encyclopedia of American Music*. Garden City: Doubleday, 1981.

Luper, Albert. *The Music of Brazil*. Washington D.C.: Pan-American Press, No. 9, 1943.

Mattos, Cleofe Person de. *Catalogo Temático Das Obras do Pegro José Maurício Nunes Garcia*. Brazil: Ministerio da Educação e Cultura.

Mayer-Serra, Otto. *Música y Músicos de Latino América*. Mexico: Editorial Atlante, S. A., 1947.

Napoleão, Arthur Ltda., ed. *Catálogo de Obras Nacionais (1868–1968)*. São Paulo, Brazil: Ministerio da Educação e Cultura, 1968.
Paesky, Efraim. *Compositores de América*. Washington D.C.: Union Panamericana, 1979.
Roberts, John Storm. *Black Music of Two Worlds*. New York: Praeger, 1972.
Sayers, W. C. *Samuel Coleridge-Taylor, Musician: His Life and Letters*. Chicago: Afro-American Publishing Company, 1969.
Scherman, Thomas K. and Louis Biancolli. *The Beethoven Companion*. New York: Doubleday, 1972.
Sealy, John and Krister Maim. *Music in the Caribbean*. Great Britain: Hidder and Sloughton, 1982.
Simmons, Moody, J. "Samuel Coleridge-Taylor: Black Composer." *Crisis Magazine*, November, 1971.
Van Sertima, Ivan and Runoko Rashidoeds. *African Presence in Asia*. New Brunswick: Transaction Books/Rutgers University, 1988.
______________. *African Presence in Early Europe*. New Brunswick: Transaction Books/Rutgers University, 1988.
Vega Druet, Hector. *Some Musical Forms of African Descendants in Puerto Rico*. Ann Arbor: University Microfilms, 1969.

Recordings and Resources: See Appendix D

Chapter XVI: Pan-African Composers: Africa

Bebey, Frances. *A People's Art*. New York: G. Schirmer, 1965.
Herdeck, Donald E. *African Authors*. Washington: Black Orpheus, 1973.
Herskovits, Melville J. "The Significance of West Africa for Negro Research." *Journal of Negro History*. Washington D.C.: Associated, 1936.
Hyslop, Graham. "Music and Education in Kenya." *East Africa's Cultural Heritage*. Nairobi: The East African Institute of Social and Cultural Affairs Press, 1966.
Jahn, Janheinz. *Muntu: The New African Culture*. New York: Grove Press, 1961.
Manani, Gerishon. "Problems Facing East African Music." Nairobi: East African Institute of Social and Cultural Affairs Press, 1966.
Olaniyan, Richard, ed. *African History and Culture*. Nigeria: Longman, 1982.
Robinson, Wilhemena. *The Teaching of African History and Culture*. Washington D.C.: Associated Press.
Wachsmann, Klaus P., ed. *Essays on Music and History in Africa*. Evanston: Northwestern University Press, 1971.
Wright, Josephine. *Ignatius Sancho (1729–1780).: An Early African Composer in England*. New York: Garland Publishing Company, Inc., 1981.

Recordings: See Appendix D.

Other Magazines, Articles, and Books

AVMP. *Audio Visual Market Place (A Multi-Media Guide)*. New York: R. R., Bowker (Xerox Corp.), 1974–75.
Black Heritage Library Collection, The Compiled/Fisk University Library. New York: Books for Libraries.
Brazell, Troy. *Bibliography Series Number Two: Black American Musical Heritage*. Ypsilanti: Eastern Michigan Library, 1972.
Current Biography. New York: H. W. Wilson Company.

De Lerma, Dominique and Thomas, C. Edward. Minneapolis: *Afro-American Opportunities Association Newsletters.*
Ebony magazine. Chicago: Johnson Publications.
Etude: The Music Magazine. Vols. 1–75 (1883–1952). (35 mm; A21; $1075). Brookhaven Press or University Microfilms.
Floyd, Samuel. *Black Music Newsletter.* Nashville: Fisk University.
Henry, Oscar. *An Original Monograph on Samuel Coleridge-Taylor: Man Against Myth.* Delivered at University of Michigan for the Organization of American Historians, 1971.
Imagen de Haiti (Jamaica, del Brasil, Paraguay, El Salvador, Dominican Republic). Washington D.C.: Organization of American States.
International Buyers Guide. For more complete reference to publishers and records. New York: Billboard Publications, 1974–75.
Jet magazine. Chicago: Johnson Publications.
MENC Journal. Vienna, Va.: Music Educators National Conference.
Morgenstern, Dan. *The Jazz Story: An Outline History.* Free booklet. New York: Jazz Museum, 1973.
Music and Artists. Ron Eyer, ed. New York: The Music Journal, Inc.
NAJE Educator. Matt Betton, Sr., ed. Manhattan, Kansas, National Association of Jazz Educators Magazine. Washington D.C.
National Leader Newspaper, Philadelphia.
Negro Alamanac. Work, Monroe, ed. Alabama: Tuskegee Institute Press, 1912.
Negro Almanac, The. A Reference Work on the Afro-American. 3rd rev. ed. New York: Bellwether & Company, 1976.
Negro History Bulletin. Washington D.C.: Associated Publishers.
Osborne, Jerry. *Record Collectors Price Guide.* Phoenix: O'Sullivan, Woodside, 1976.
Roots of Jazz Series, The. (New York: Da Capo Reprints include *Waller's Story, Ain't Misbehavin'; Bibliography of Jazz; Bird: The Legend of Charlie Parker; Duke Ellington; The Country Blues; A History of Jazz in America; Jazz: A People's Music; Jazz; From the Congo to the Metropolitan; Jazz: Hot and Hybrid; Jazz: Its Evolution and Its Essence; Jazz: New Perspectives on the History of Jazz; The Jazz Life; The Jazz Scene; Music on My Mind; Shining Trumpets; The Story of the House of Witmark*; and Bechet's *Treat It Gentle*)
Smithsonian. *Glimmer of Their Own Beauty; Black Sounds of the Twenties.* Washington D.C.: National Portrait Gallery, Smithsonian Institution, 1971 (pamphlet).
West, Hollie. Review articles/jazz, etc., *Washington Post News.*

I. AFRICAN TRADITIONALISM: Scores, Strips, Films, and Records

Musical Scores:

Ajibola, J. O. *Orin Yoruba.* Ile-Ife: University of Ife Press.
Brandel. *Music of Central Africa.* Martinus Nijhoff.
Jones. *Studies in African Music.* Vol. 2. Oxford.
Kalanzi. *Bantu and You* (African Folksongs). Eulenburg.
Kalanzi. *Mysteries of African Music.* McM.
Landeck. *Echoes of Africa: Folk Songs of the Americas.* David McKay.
Makeba. *World of African Songs.* Quadrangle.
Nketia. *Folk Songs of Ghana.* Oxford.
Rashied. *Egyptian Folksong.* Music Sales.

Skiekh. *Folk Songs of Africa*. Lyons.
Williams, Maselwa and Seeger. *Choral Folksongs of the Bantu*. Schirmer.

Filmstrips/Films:

Adventures in Search of Early Man. National Geographic Society.
African Art and Culture. Schloat or Lorraine.
Africa's Cultural and Ethnic Heritage. National Geographic Society.
Africa: Man and His Music. Rossi, ed. Keyboard.
Africa: Instruments. Rossi, ed. Keyboard.
Africa. Rossi, ed. for elementary level. Keyboard.
African Dances. Les Ballet Africains with Instruments. McGraw-Hill.
Africa: Musical Instruments, Textiles, Jewelry and Architecture. Schloat or Lorraine.
Africa: Musical Instruments. Schloat.
African Musicians. MacMillan.
African Musicians. Bailey.
Baruka, People of the Congo. Bailey.
Music of Primitive Man. Educational Dimension.
Music of Africa (includes Sowanda), Indiana University/RS-741.

Recordings:

African East and West. University of California (Institute of Ethnomusicology).
African and Afro-American Drums. Lyons/LB7551.
African Drums (Watutsi and Yoruba). Courlander, ed. Lorraine/1151NH.
African Music. Lorraine and 1152NH.
African Music. Boulton, ed. Folkways/FW8852.
African Musical Instruments. Abdurahuram, ed. Lyons/LB7715.
African Politics—More (w/music and text). Nzomo, ed. Folkways and FW8502.
African Society's Best for 1952 (Music of Amu, etc.). Decca and LF1171.
African Story-Songs. Washington.
African Tribal Music & Dances: Senegal. Washington/CPT5513.
African Tribal, Ritual and Love Songs. Afro-Request/SRLP5033.
Anthology of African Music: Rwanda. UNESCO. Lorraine/1198NH-20005.
Anthology of Music of Black Africa. Everest and 3254/3.
Around Africa in Song. Silver Burdett.
Baijun Ballads (Somali Songs in Swahili). Skiekh, ed. Lorraine/1908.
Coptic Music. Folkways/FR8960.
Folk Music of Ethiopia. Folkways/FE4405.
Folk Music of Ghana. Folkways/8859.
Folk Songs of Africa. Lyons/LB7331.
Ghana Asuafo Reto Dwom. Afro Request/SLRP5027.
Ghana Ndwom: Songs of Ghana. Afro Request/SLRP5029.
Makeba Sings: Best of Makeba. RCA Victor/LSP3982.
Man's Early Musical Instruments. Sachs. Lyons/LB5760.
Master Drummer of Ghana. Lyrichord/7250.
Hi Neighbor Series, Introduction to African countries, musi UNESCO.
Morocco: Folk Music. Bowles, ed. Lyrichord/7229 and 7
Music of Morocco. Folkways/4339 and 4101.

Music From an Equatorial Microcosm: Gabon Bwiti or Cult Music. Folkways/4214.
Music From Mali. Folkways/4338.
Music of Africa Today. UN ART/UAS15556.
Music of Chad. Folkways/4339.
Music of Equatorial Africa. Dider, ed. Folkways/4402.
Music of Ghana (Kpanlogo Party). Lyrichord/7251.
Music of Zaire. Vol. 2. Folkways/FE4242.
Negro Folk Music of African and America. Folkways/4500 or Lorraine.
Nigeria: Drums of the Yoruba. Folkways/4441.
Nigeria Sings. Afro-Request/SRLP 5028.
Nigerian Music. Field records by Sowande. Broadcast Foundation N.543.42/7; N.543.43/7; N.543.40/7.
Olatunji and His Drums of Passion. Columbia/CS8210.
Ritual Music of Ethiopia. Folkways/4353.
Sierra Leone (Mende Music). Folkways/4322.
Somali Freedom Songs. Folkways/5443.
Songs of the Watutsi. Verwilghen, ed. Folkways/FE4428.
Songs and Sounds of Far-Away Places. Philharmonic/Pcc201.
Sounds of Africa. Verve/FT3021.
Voice of the Congo: Tribal Music of Central Africa. Washington/WLP703.
West African Highlife Scene. London/99498.
World Library of Folk and Primitive Music (East Africa) Lomax and Tracy, eds. Columbia/KL213.

II. MUSIC OF THE AMERICAS: Recordings and Scores

Recordings:

African Heritage Dances. Educational Acts.
Afro-Bahian Religious Songs from Brazil. Library of Congress/L13.
Afro-Hispanic Music From Western Colombia and Ecuador. Lorraine/4376.
American Indian Music For the Classroom. Ballard, ed. Canyon/C3001-4.
Authentic Afro-Rhythms. Educational Acts/K6060.
Bahamian Songs, French Ballads and Dance Tunes, Spanish Religious Songs and Game Songs. Lomax, ed. Library of Congress.
Children's Jamaican Songs and Games. Lorraine/1157NH.
Children's Jamaican Songs and Games. Folkways/FC7250.
Early Childhood Songs. Scholastic/SC7620.
Guiana Sings. Vesta Lowe. Cooperative Recreational Service.
Roots of Black Music in America. Charters, ed. Folkways/FA2694.
There's A Brown Boy in the Ring. (w/calypso). Lorraine/1173NH.

III. AFRO-AMERICAN MUSIC: Portraits, Scores, Films, and Records

Portraits:

Portraits and Profiles. James Bland, etc. (11) Barnell Loft.

Scores:

Fun Songs, Rounds and Harmony. Includes various languages. Challis, ed. Oak Pub.
Genesis Songbook. Young. Agape Pub.
Sing, Children, Sing. UNICEF.

Scores: Art Music (Also See Sketches of Composers)

Afro-American Sings. O. McFarland, compiler. Detroit Public Schools.
Anthology of Art Songs by Black American Composers. W. Patterson, compiler. E. B. Marks.
Anthology. Samuel Floyd, compiler. Contact at Columbia College.
Collected Piano Works of R. Nathaniel Dett. Summy-Birchard.
Negro Art Songs. Anthology. R. Clark, compiler. E. B. Marks. Out of print.
Twenty-Four Negro Melodies for piano. Samuel Coleridge-Taylor. Da Capo.

Scores: Spirituals, Songs

Album of Negro Spirituals. Burleigh. Belwin/FC1432 or 1433.
Album of Songs and Spirituals. Rupp. Includes arrangements by Boatner and Johnson. Schirmer.
Afro-America Sings. Detroit Public Schools. McFarland, ed.
American Ballads and Folk Songs. Lomax. Macmillan.
American Negro Songs. Work. Bonanza.
Book of Negro Spirituals. Johnson. Viking.
Folk Songs in American History. Lorraine/C501-510.
Negro Songs From Alabama. Courlander, ed. Music Sales or Oak.
Negro Spirituals. Johnson. G. Schirmer.
Road to Heaven. Logan. University of Alabama.
Slave Songs of the Georgia Sea Islands. Parrish. Folk Association of Choral Art Pub.
Slave Songs of the United States. Oak Reprint. Allen et al.
Songs of the American Negro Slaves. Lorraine/2017NH.
Spiritual Folk Songs of Early America. Jackson. Dover/250.
Spirituals for Children. Theodore Presser.

Scores: Minstrel Music, Blues, and Ballads

American Ballads and Folk Songs. Lomax. Macmillan.
Blues Bag. Traum, ed. Simon & Shuster/10341.
Country Blues Songbook. Music Sales.
Dan Emmiett and the Rise of Early Negro Minstrelsy. Nathan. University of Oklahoma Information Coordination Reprint.
Favorite Songs of the Nineties. Fremont. Dover Pub.
Folk Blues. Silverman. Music Sales/000113.
James Bland Album. Haywood E. B. Marks.
Leadbelly Songbook. Asch. Music Sales/00042.
On the Trail of Negro Folk Songs. Scarborough. Harvard University.
Treasury of the Blues. Handy.
Wake Up Dead Man (Worksongs). Jackson. Harvard University.

Scores: Ragtime

Collected Piano Works of Scott Joplin. New York Public Library.
From Rags to Jazz. Consolidated Music.
Giants of Ragtime. E. B. Marks.
Great Scott! Best of Ragtime. Hansen.
Piano Ragtime Classics. Hansen.
Ragtime Piano. Belwin.
Ragtime Songbook. Charters, etc. Music Sales/040157.

Ragtime (Vocal). Dover Publication.
Collected Vocal Works of Scott Joplin. New York Public Library.

Scores: Jazz

Amazing Bud Powell. Edmonds, trans. Patricia Music.
Blues and the Abstract Truth. Nelson, O. Marks/Belwin.
Errol Garner: Five Original Piano Solos. Criterion Music Corporation.
Faces of Jazz. Smith, H. Marks/Belwin.
Jammin' the Blues. Macmillan/1944-U.S.
Jazz for the Young Pianist. Peterson, O. Hansen.
Jazz Giants: Yesterday and Today. Hansen.
Jazz Improvisation. Vols. 1–4, Baker. Maher.
Jazz Piano Solos. Peterson, O. Hansen.
Origin of the Spiritual. McLin. Neil Kjos.
Saint Louis Blues. Bessie Smith in movie. Macmillan/1929.
Son House. Folkways.
Sun's Gonna Shine. Pyramid.
Tall Tales. Macmillan/1941 (w/Josh White).
Thirteenth Annual Monterey Jazz Festival. Including Ellington et al. National Geographic Society.
To Hear Your Banjo Play. Traces history of banjo made by slaves to present form. Macmillan/1947-U.S.A.

Recordings: Art Music (Also see Sketches of Composers)

Afro-American Music and its Roots. Includes Carman Moore et al. Silver Burdett.
Althea Waites Performs the Music of Florence Price. Cambria Records C 1027.
Art Songs by Black American Composers. Compiled by W. Patterson for use with his *Anthology*. University of Michigan Records.
American Concertos. Includes U. Kay. Remington Series, Varèse Sarabande.
Black Composers in America. Desto.
Black Music Series, Vols 1–8. CBS/College Music Society or Still Music.
Black Music: The Written Tradition. Dr. S. Floyd, Center for Black Music Research, Columbia College, Chicago.
Contemporary Black Images in Music. Trio Pro Viva. T & T Associates.
David Baker. Concerto for Violin and Jazz Band, etc. Laurel Records.
Natalie Hinderas Plays the Music of Black Composers. Desto.
Natalie Hinderas Plays Sensuous Music. Includes Saint Georges. Orion.
Choral Triptych. Ulysses Kay. Cambridge Records.
Kermit Moore. Includes *Music for Cello and Piano*. Cespico Records.
Marian Anderson, The Legendary. Lincoln Center Concert. Legendary Records.
New American Music, vols. I, II, III. Includes Hakim, Swanson, C. Moore, Mary Lou Williams et al. Folkways.
Raymond Jackson, Pianist. Includes Hall Johnson and Saint Georges. Cespico.
Richard Fields Plays Piano Music of William Grant Still. Orion.
Ruth Norman, Pianist. Opus One. Contemporary music includes Kay and Fax.
R. Nathaniel Dett: Piano Works. D. Oldham, pianist. New World.

Frances Walker, Pianist. Samuel Coleridge-Taylor and William G. Still. Orion.
Leon Bates. Music of G. Walker et al. Orion.
Samuel Coleridge-Taylor. Quintet. Spectrum/Uni Pro.
Six Dances for Strings. Kay. Includes Still. Turnabout.
Twelve Outstanding Singers. Includes spirituals. Legendary Recordings.
Works also listed in Patricia Turner's *Afro-American Singers*, CRI, Louisville, Orion, Folkways, etc.

Recordings: Historical and Musical

Afro-American Music. James. Lorraine/AA702.
American Negro Folk and Work Songs. Jenkins. Lorraine/1154NH.
American Negro Slave Song. Everest/2108.
American Negro Songs from Slavery Time. Larue. Folkways/FH5252.
American Sea Songs and Shanties. Lomax. Library of Congress/121.
Been in the Storm So Long. Folkways/FS 3842. Spirituals, shouts, game songs, and folktales.
Call and Response. Lyons/LB5921 or Lorraine/1095. Group singing for school children.
Evening with Jester Hairston. Custom Fidelity/CFS 2990. De Anza College Choir sings spirituals, other folk songs w/composer's comments.
Fisk Jubilee Singers, The. Lyons/LB5641 or Lorraine/1158NH.
Folk Music U.S.A. Folkways/FE4530.
Folk Music of the United States. Lomax. Library of Congress. Ballad Hunter AAFS-L3, Blues and Gospel Songs AAFS-L3; Blues and Game Songs AAFS-L4; Negro Blues and Hollers. Stearns/ASF-L59; Religious Work Songs and Calls. Lomax/AAFS-L8.
From Spirituals to Swing. Vanguard VSD-47 & 48.
Jambo and Other Calls and Response Songs and Chants. Jenkins. Folkways/FC7661.
Leadbelly Sings (Keep Your Hands Off Her). Verve/FV/FVS-9021. Blues, spirituals, work songs, and ballads.
Leontyne Price Sings Spirituals. RCA/LSC2600.
Long Time, A: Music of the Black Man. Jenkins and Sellers. Lyons/LB7714.
Marian Anderson.
McHenry Boatwright Sings Spirituals. Golden Crest/RE7024.
Memphis Slim: Favorite Blues Singers. Folkways/2387.
Music Down Home. Smith. Folkways/FA2691.
Negro Folklore from Texas Prisons. Elektra/7296.
Negro Folk Music of Africa and America. Folkways/4500.
Negro Folk Music of Alabama. Courlander. Folkways/FE4418, FE4473.
Paul Robeson Sings Spirituals and Ballads. Vanguard/VSD79193.
Play and Dance Songs and Tunes. Library of Congress/L9.
Railroad Songs and Ballads. Green. Library of Congress/L61.
Ring Games: Negro Children of Alabama. Courlander. Lorraine/1171NH.
Roland Hayes Sings Spirituals. RCA/VRS 494; also A1801 and RAL774.
Love Is A Many Splendored Thing. Cole, Nat King. Pickwick/S3046; P8-128; CS-128.
Music Down Home. Smith, D. C. Lorraine/1784. Intro. to Black folk music.
Music of New Orleans. Charters, Samuel. Folkways/FA24624, vol. 3; Blues, ballads.

My Fair Lady. Cole, Nat King. Capital/SW2117.
Nature Boy. Cole, Nat King. Pickwick/3249.
Negro Prison Songs. Lomax, Alan. Trad/TLP 1020.
Queen of the Blues. Washington, Dinah. 2-Roulete/RE117; 8045-117M.
Sings the Blues. Simone, Nina. RCA/LSP 3837.
Sleepy John Estes Legend. Estes, John. Del/9603.
They Sang the Blues. Blind Baker, Slue Foot Joe, etc. Historical/17.
Up, Up and Away. The Fifth Dimension (Soul City/SCM91000/SCS92000.
What A Difference A Day Makes. Washington, Dinah. Mercury/60158.

Recordings: Ragtime and Early Jazz

Best of the Big Band. RCA/P8S-8011.
Big Bands. Brown, Ellington, etc. 6-Capital/STGL-293.
Big Bands/1933. Ellington, Henderson. Prestige/S-&645.
Big Bands' Greatest Hits. Vol. 2. Hampton, Ellington. Columbia/G-31213; GA31214.
Central Avenue Breakdown. Vol. 2. Onyx/215. 40's on West Coast.
Classic Rags & Ragtime Songs. Anderson, T. J., conductor-arranger. Smithsonian.
Do That Guitar Rag. Broonzy. Y2200/200/L1035.
Encyclopedia of Jazz. (20's–50's). 4-Decca/DXS7140E.
Fifty-Second Street. Vol. 1. Onyx/217; Hawkins et al.; music of 30's, 40's.
Heliotrope Bouquet: Piano Rags 1900–1970. Includes Jopkin, Turpin, Roberts, Lamb, etc. W. Bolcom, piano. Nonesuch/H71257.
History of Jazz: New York Scene/1914–15. RBF/3 From Original Dixieland to Gillespie.
Hot Clarinets: 1924–29. Historical/25.
Hot Pianos: 1926–1940. Morton, Waller, etc. Historical/29.
Hot Trumpets: 1924–37. Beiderbecke, etc. Historical/28.
Jazz, Vol. 1–11: The South. Folkways/2801. *The Blues*. Folkways/2802. *New Orleans*. Folkways/2803. *Jazz Singers*. Folkways/2804. *Chicago #1*. Folkways/2805. *Chicago #2*. Folkways/2806. *New York*. Folkways/2805. *Big Bands Before 1935*. Folkways/2808. *Piano*. Folkways/2807. *Boogie Woogie, Jump and Kansas City*. Folkways/2810. *Addenda*. Folkways/2811.
Jazz Piano Anthology. Blake, Johnson, Waller. 2-Columbia/KG32355.
Jazz Odyssey. Vol. 3. J. P. Johnson, Bessie. Columbia/C3L-33.
Johnny Hodges: Ellingtonia. Onyx/216. 1946–50.
Jugs, Washboards, and Kazoos. Smith, Holiday, etc. RCA/LPV-540.
Kansas City Piano; 1936–41. Basie, Wm. Decca/9226E.
Live At Blues Alley. Smith, W. Chiaro/104.
Original Boogie Woogie Piano Giants. Columbia/KC32708 1938–41.
Ragtime Entertainment. Folkways/RBT 22.
Reunion in Ragtime. Blake, Jordan, etc. Stero/S1900.
Story of Jazz. Lyons/LB5922.
Swing and Bop 1945–53. Onyx/220. Rushing et al.
This Is The Big Band Era. RCA/VPM 6043.

Recordings: Transitional, Modern, and Contemporary Jazz

After Hours. Vaughan, S. CSP/JCL660.
Ahmad Jamal. Jamal, A. Cadet/602.

Amazing Bud Powell, The. Powell, B. Blue Note/81504.
At Duke's Place. Fitzgerald, E. Verve/64070; 8140-4070M.
Bebop Era, The. RCA/LPV5190.
Best of Ella. Fitzgerald, E. Decca/DXS-7156E; 6-1003.
Blacks and Blues. Humphrey, B. Blue Note/LA 142-G.
Blues in Modern Jazz. Atlantic/1337.
Cote d'Azur. Fitzgerald, E. w/Ellington. Verve/64072.
Count 'Em 88. Jamal, A. Cadet/610.
Cue for Sax. Strayhorn, B. Mast. Jazz/8116.
Dig This. Humphrey, B. Blue Note 84421.
Drums Unlimited. Roach, Max. Atlantic/S1467; 81467.
Earl Fatha Hines. Hines, E. Arc Folkways/246E.
Early Modern Jazz. Gillespie, Parker, and Young. Milestone/9035.
Echoes of an Era. Parker, Gillespie w/Coltrane, etc. 2-Roulette/120; 8045-120M.
Echoes of an Era. Vaughan, S. 2-Roulette/103; 8045-103M.
Ella Fitzgerald. Fitzgerald, E. Arc Folkways/276.
Encyclopedia of Jazz, The. Lyons/5274. Set covers 20s to 50s.
Encyclopedia of Jazz in the Sixties. Verve.
Gentlemen of Jazz. Lewis, R. Cadet/62 Giants. Taylor, C., Lewis, J. Gillespie, etc. Percep/19.
Giants of Jazz. Monk, Stitt, etc. 2-Atlantic/2-905.
Great Guitars of Jazz. Montgomery, W. etc. MGM/S4691.
Greatest Hits. Grant, E. Decca/74813; 64813; C73-4813.
Greatest Hits. Montgomery, W. and Friends w/Jackson, M. A&M/4247; 8T-4247; CS4247.
Greatest Jazz Concert War. Gillespie, Parker, Roach, etc. 2-Prestige/2404.
Gospel According Shirley, D. Columbia/GS9723.
Headhunters. Hancock, H. Columbia.
History of Ella. Fitzgerald, Ella. 2-Verve/68817; 8140-8817N.
Jay and Kai. Johnson, J. Say/12106.
Jazz at Massey Hall. Roach, Powell, Gillespie, etc. Fan/86003.
Jazz of the Sixties, Vols. 1 and 2. Ampex/2E8179, 80.
Jazz Piano. Decca/LPM3499.
Lift Every Voice and Sing. Roach, M. Atlantic/S1587; M81587; M51587.
Many Faces of Blues. Parker, Gillespie, MJQ, Davis, etc. Savoy/12125.
Master Jazz Piano. Vols. 1, 2, 3. Hines, etc. Mas. Jazz/8105; 1808; 8117.
Monty Alexander. BASF.
Saxophone, The. Hawkins, Carter, Byas, Stitt, Young, Parker, Coleman, etc. Ayuler-Imp/9253.
Ups and Downs. Powell, B. Mainstream/385; M8385; M5385.
Smithsonian Collection of Classic Jazz. Martin, Wm. ed.; inc. Taylor, C. Basie, Lunceford, Watter, etc. Smithsonian/P6-11891 (7 LPs).
Works by Oscar Peterson, Randy Weston, Cecil Taylor, Jimmy Smith, George Duke, Anthony Braxton, et al.

Recordings: Gospel

Abide With Me. Jackson, M. Harmony, 11 372.
Aretha Franklin w/James Cleveland and the Southern California Community Choir, Atlantic/SD2-906.
Best. Angelic Gospel Singers. Nashboro/7047E.
Bless This House. Jackson, M. Columbia/CS8761.

Bread of Heaven. Cleveland, J. Hob/1417.
Cleveland, Rev. J. w/Southern California Choir. Savoy/14284.
Cleveland, Rev. James and Voices of Tabernacle. Hob/264.
Free At Last. Cleveland, Jr. Savoy/14211.
Gospel In Song. Cleveland, J. Hob/211.
Great Getting Up. Jackson, M. Columbia/CS8153.
Hear My Call. Staple Singers. Pickwick/700 1LP.
House of the Lord. Hawkins, Singer. Pav/10001.
I Saw The Light. Thorpe, R. Pickwick/7005.
It's Time. Mighty Clouds of Joy. ABC.
Jesus Paid It All. Angelic Gospel Sing. Nashboro/7061.
Lord Help Me to Hold Out. Majestics. Savoy.
Move On Up Higher. Dixie Hummingbirds. Hob/296.

Recordings: Rock, Rhythm and Blues, and Soul

Aretha's Gold. Franklin, A. Atlantic/S82270; M88227; M58227.
Black Moses. Hayes, I. Enter/5003.
Curtis. Mayfield, C. Curtom/8005; M88005; M58008.
Fats Domino. Domino, F. Everest/FS280.
Floy Joy. Supremes, The. Motown/751.
Filthy. Creach, P. J. Grunt/1009.
Get It Together. Jackson Five. Motown/783.
Golden Sound. Cooke, S. Trip/8030-2.
Good Foot. Brown, J. Polydor/2-3004; 8F-2-3004.
Greatest Hits. Jackson Five. Motown/S741.
Greatest Hits. Gladys Knight and The Pips. Soul/723; S81723; S75723.
Greatest Hits. Little Richard. Epic/K18-10060.
Greatest Hits. Temptations, The. Gordy/S919; G81919; G75919.
History of Rhythm & Blues. Atlantic/S816/3E; M88161/4; M58161/4.
In the Still of the Night. Platters, The. Pickwick/S3120.
Innervisions. Wonder, S. Tamla/326.
Last Days and Time. Earth, Wind, and Fire. Columbia/KC31702.
Music of My Mind. Wonder, S. Tamla/S314.
Natural Man. Rawls, L. MGM/S3771; 8130-4771; 5130-4771.
Otis Redding Sings Soul. Redding, O. Atco/S33284.
Playing My Fiddle. Creach, P. J. Grunt/BFL1-0418.
Queen of Soul. Franklin, A. Harmony/11274.
Ray's Moods. Charles, R. ABC/S550; M8550.
Recipe for Soul. Charles, R. ABC/S465.
Salt of the Earth. Soul Searchers w/Buchanan, arr. Sussex.
Solid Gold Soul. Pickett, W., Redding, etc. Atlantic/SC8116.
Supremes. Supremes, The. Motown/756.
Talking Back. Wonder, S. Tamla/319, T319T.
That's the Way of the World. Earth, Wind, and Fire. Columbia/PC33288.
We the People. Soul Searchers. Sussex.

APPENDIX C
LIST OF COMPOSERS, PUBLISHERS, RECORD COMPANIES AND RESEARCH CENTERS

1729–1780 Sancho, Ignatius: (In Josephine Weight's *I. Sancho*, Garland Publishers).

1739–1799 Joseph Chevalier de Saint Georges: Peer-Southern/T. Presser.

1767–1830 Garcia, José Maurício: Schirmer; Brasileira do Produtores de Discos, MEC/Funart; Columbia Recordings.

1779–1860 Bridgetower, George Augustus Polgren: Score, Indiana University/B.M.C.

1839–1920 White, José: Schirmer; Columbia Recordings.

1848–1916 Lucas, Samuel: Oliver Ditson/T. Presser, Bryn Mawr, Pa.

1849–1908 Bethune, Thomas (Blind Tom): Schirmer, N.Y.; Hinshaw, Chapel Hill, N.C.

1854–1911 Bland, James: Schirmer, N.Y.

1866–1949 Burleigh, H. T.: Franco Colombo, N.Y.

1868–1917 Joplin, Scott: Stark; E. B. Marks/Belwin; N.Y. Public Library.

1869–1944 Cook, Will Marion: Schirmer, N.Y.

1869–1954 Freeman, Harry L.: Pace-Handy, N.Y.

1873–1958 Handy, William C.: Handy Brothers, N.Y.

1873–1954 Johnson, J. Rosamond: E. B. Marks/Belwin.

1873–1922 Turpin, Thomas: E. B. Marks/Belwin.

1875–1912 Coleridge-Taylor, Samuel: Novello; Augener; Schirmer; Hinshaw; Willis; Da Capo Columbia, Orion Recordings.

1880–1973 Charlton, Melville: Schirmer, N.Y.

1880–1960 White, Clarence Cameron: Summy-Birchard; Shomberg, Hackley Centers.

1881–1946 Brymn, J. Tim: Folkways Recordings.

1882–1943 Dett, R. N.: Summy-Birchard, Evanston, Ill.

1883–1983 Blake, Hubert (Eubie): E. B. Marks/Belwin; Biograph Recordings.

1883–1958 Dabney, Ford: Folkways Recordings.

1885–1941 Morton, Ferdinand (Jelly Roll): Folkways, Riverside Recordings.

1886–1969 Diton, Carl: E. B. Marks/Belwin.

1887–1982 Nickerson, Camille: Handy Bros., N.Y.; Leeds; Boston Music.

1888–1970 Johnson, Hall: Robbins; Fisher, N.Y.

1888–1953 Price, Florence: Affiliated; T. Presser; Summy-Birchard; Galaxy.

1890?–19--? Morgan, William Astor (Jean Stor): Handy Music, N.Y.

1891–1955 Johnson, James P.: Belwin Mills, N.Y. 1891–1962

1891–1962 Margetson, Edward H.: Belwin; Boosey; Boston Music.

1892– Garcia, Juan: Compositores de America, D.C.

1894–1967 Cohen, Cecil: E. B. Marks/Belwin.

1895– Jessye, Eva: Summy-Birchard; Robbins Engel; Belwin.

1895–1978 Still, William Grant: William G. Still Music, Flagstaff, Ariz.

1896–19--? Elam, Ulysses: Lawson-Gould, N.Y.
1898–1981 Boatner, Edward: Galaxy.
1898– Hall, Frederick: Summy-Birchard.
1898–1952 Henderson, Fletcher: Pace-Handy, N.Y.
1898–1965 Williams, Clarence: Folkways Recordings.
1899– Amu, Ephraim: University of Ghana; Afro-Request Recordings
1899– Dorsey, Thomas: Aberbach; Hill & Range; Columbia, Milestone, Nashboro, Smithsonian Recordings.
1899–1990 Dawson, William: Neil Kjos, Park Ridge, Ill. or Felder's Gift & Variety Shop, 1301-B Old Montgomery Rd., Tuskegee Institute, Ala. 36088.
1899–1974 Ellington, Edward (Duke): Mills Music, N.Y.
1900–1971 Armstrong, Louis (Satchmo): Melrose Bros., N.Y.
1900–1966 James, Willis Laurence: Schirmer; Remick.
1900–1939 Roldán, Amadeo: Peer-Southern/T. Presser.
1901– Hairston, Jester: Bourne Music, N.Y.; De Anza College Choir Recording.
1901–1967 Work, John W. Ill: Galaxy; Fisk University, Nashville, Tenn.
1902– Brown, Harold J.: Summy-Birchard, Evanston, Ill.
1904–1989 Moore, Undine: Augsburg, Minn.; Delta Fine Arts (Winston-Salem), Va. State Recordings.
1904–1943 Waller, Thomas (Fats): Schirmer; Santly-Joy, N.Y.
1905– Dorsey, James E.: Schirmer, N.Y.
1905–1987 Sowande, Fela: Chappell; Franco-Colombo; Broadcast Foundation Recordings.
1906–1984 Basie, William (Count): Decca Recordings.
1906– Merrifield, Norman L.: Handy; Richmond.
1907– Allen, Gilbert: Summy-Birchard, Evanston, Ill.; Row/Fischer, N.Y.
1907– Battle, Edgar: Gem, Cosmopolitan Music.
1909– Barefield, Edward E.: Charles Colin.
1907– Broadnax, Eugene J.: Galaxy.
1909– Jacobs, Clarence: Joli-Tinker; Columbia Recordings (on DePaur).
1909–1956 Mells, Herbert F.: Handy Music, N.Y.
1909– Miller, James: Galaxy.
1909–1978 Swanson, Howard: Weintraub, N.Y.
1910–1981 Williams, Mary Lou: Verve Recordings.
1910– Work, Julian: Shawnee.
1911–1975 Duncan, John: Alabama State University, Montgomery, Ala.
1911–1974 Fax, Mark: Howard University, D.C.
1913–1972 Bonds, Margaret: Mercury, N.Y.
1914– Perry, Zenobia: Composer, Wilberforce, Ohio.
1914–1964 Ryder, Noah: J. Fischer; Handy, N.Y.
1915– De Paur, Leonard: Lawson-Gould; Columbia, RCA Recordings.
1915–1988 Kerr, Thomas: Summy-Birchard, Evanston; E. B. Marks/Belwin; Desto Recordings.
1917– Cordero, Roque: Peer-Southern/T. Presser; Columbia Recordings.
1917– Gillespie, John (Dizzy): Crescendo Recordings.

1917–	Kay, Ulysses: C. Fisher; Pembroke; MCA, N.Y.; Desto, CRI, Columbia Records.
1918–	Lowe, Samuel: Jay & Cee Music; Arnell Music.
1918–1985	Billups, Kenneth M.: Choral Arts; Schirmer, N.Y.
1920–1991	Davis, Miles: Columbia Recordings.
1920–1955	Parker, Charlie: Verve Recordings
1920–	Lewis, John: Atlantic Recordings.
1920–1982	Monk, Thelonius: Charles Colin, N.Y.
1920–	Cooper, William B.: Dangerfield; Southern.
1921–	Bonnemere, Edward B.: Le Bon Music; Fortress Press.
1921–	El Dabh, Halim: C. F. Peters; Folkways, Columbia-Princeton Music Studio Records.
1921–	Nketia, J. Kwabena: University of Pittsburgh.
1921–	Taylor, William (Billy): Hansen; Belwin Mills, Melville, N.Y.
1922–	Eubanks, Rachel: Music Mart, Oakland, California.
1922–	Walker, George: General; MMB Music, St. Louis; Columbia, CRI Recordings.
1923–	Bebey, Frances: Ocora, Paris, France; Phillips, EMI.
1923–	Kennedy, Joseph: Hema Music, Mt. Vernon, N.Y.; Richmond, Va.
1923–	Russell, George: James Abersold; Robbins; Fuss-Hix Music & Records.
1924–1979	Perry, Julia: Peer-Southern/T. Presser; CRI Recordings
1925–	Peterson, Oscar: Hansen; BASF-MPS & Pablo Recordings.
1925–	Smith, Hale: Merion/T. Presser, Bryn Mawr, Pa.; Sam Fox, Columbia Records.
1926–	Coleman, Charles: Word, Detroit Public School.
1926–1967	Coltrane, John: Impulse Recordings.
1926–	Fiberesima, Adam: Broadcast Foundation Recordings, N.Y.
1926–	Lindsey, Roy H.: Tatlin Music; Choral Press.
1928–	Anderson, Thomas J.: ACA; Bote & Bock/Associated; Columbia, Nonesuch Recordings.
1928–	Cunningham, Arthur: T. Presser, Bryn Mawr, Pa.
1928–	King, Betty Jackson: Pro Art.
1928–	McLin, Edward M.: Red Band, Hansen, Pro Art Music.
1928–	McLin, Lena Johnson: Neil Kjos, Park Ridge, Ill.
1929–	Hancock, Eugene: H. W. Gray; McAfee Music.
1929–	Moore, Kermit: Rudmor Music, New York City; Cespico, CRI & Orion Records.
1930–	Banks, Robert: Belwin.
1930–	Coleman, Ornette: Atlantic Recordings.
1930–	Da Costa, Noel: ATSOC Music.
1930–	Tillis, Frederick: ACA; Southern; Hansen.
1931–	Baker, David: Abersold; T. Presser; Belwin; Decca, Silver Crest, Riverside, Golden Crest, Columbia, Silver Burdett Recordings.
1931–	Fox, Frederick A.: Seesaw; CMP; Galaxy.
1932–	Adams, Leslie: Lawson-G; Walton; Son-Key; Belwin.
1932–	Makeba, Miriam: Quadrangle Press; RCA Recordings.
1932–	Perkinson, Coleridge-Taylor: Belwin/Tosci (Frank).
1932–	Simpson, Eugene: Murbo.
1933–	Jones, Quincy: A&M Records.

1933–1975 Nelson, Oliver: E. B. Marks/Belwin, Melville.
1934– Akpabot, Samuel: Oxford.
1934– Dickerson, Roger: Peer-Southern/T. Presser.
1935–1976 Bankole, Ayo: University of Ife Press; Broadcast Music Recordings.
1935– Euba, Akin: University of Ife; Library of Congress; Broadcast Foundation
1935– Fischer, William S.: Cimino; Ready Productions, N.Y.; Arcana Recordings.
1935– Price, John: Slave Ship Press, Tuskegee Institute; Belwin. Records.
1936– Moore, Carman: Silver Burdett Recordings; Sweet Jam Music, N.Y.
1937– Carter, John: Southern Music, N.Y.
1937–1989 Furman, James: Hinshaw Music, Chapel Hill, N.C.
1937– Turkson, Ato: University of Ife, Nigeria.
1937– Wilson, Olly: Belwin; University of California at Berkeley; Columbia Records.
1938– Kebede, Ashenafi: CRI, Eastern, Louisville, Desto Recordings.
1940–1988 Hakim, Talib (Chambers); Bote & Bock; Columbia, Desto Recordings.
1940– Harris, Howard: Southern, San Antonio; DeMos Music, Houston, Tex.
1940– Jackson, Ambrose: Gerard Billaudot, Paris..
1940– Logan, Wendell M.: E. B. Marks/Belwin, Melville, N.Y.
1940– McDaniel, William F.: Stimuli, Cincinnati.
1940– Moore, Dorothy Rudd: Rudmor Music, New York City
1941– Hailstork, Adolphus: Belwin; Fema; Anglo-American Music; Hinshaw.
1942– White, Andrew: Andrew's Musical Enterprise, D.C.
1946–198-? Roxbury, Ronald: Walton Music.
1950– Wonder, Stevie: Jobete Music; Tamla Recordings.

Research

African Institute, University of Ghana at Legon.
African-American Institute, 866 United Nations Plaza, N.Y. or 1201 Conn. Ave., N.W., D.C.
Afro-American Museum, 1553 W. Grand Blvd., Detroit, Mich.
American Society of African Culture, New York, N.Y.
Amistad Research Center, 100 Esplanade Avenue, New Orleans, La.
Association for the Study of Negro Life & History; 1407-14th St., N.W., Washington D.C.
Atlanta University: CAAS-Afro-American Music Center, 223 Chestnut St., S.W., Atlanta, Ga.
Caribbean Cultural Center; 408 W. 58th St., N.Y.
Center for Black Music Research, Columbia College, Chicago, Ill.
D.C. Public Library: Martin Luther King Branch, The Black Studies Div.; 9th & G Sts., N.W., Washington D.C.
Detroit Public Library, The Azalia Hackley Room, 5201 Woodward Ave., Detroit, Mich.

Fisk University, Special Collections Room, Nashville, Tenn.
Fleisher Collection, Philadelphia Free Public Library, 19th & 20th on Vine, Phila., Pa.
Funn Consultant, 1214 Oronoco St., Alexandria, Va.
Hampton Institute, Hampton, Va.
Howard University, The Moorland Room, Washington D.C.
Indiana University, Black Music Center, Terre Haute, Ind.
Library of Congress, Washington D.C.
Maryland Historical Society, Baltimore, Md.
Morgan State University, Baltimore, Md.
Museum of African Art, Smithsonian Institute, Washington D.C.
Negro Bibliographic & Research Center, Inc., 117 R St., N.W., Washington D.C.
North American Black Historical Museum, 277 King St., Amherstburg, Ontario, Canada.
Rhode Island Black Heritage Society, One Hilton St., Providence, R.I.
Rutgers University Jazz Center, New Brunswick, N.J.
Smithsonian Institute, Constitution and 14th Sts., Washington D.C.
Southern Folklore Center, 1216 Peabody Ave., Memphis, Tenn.
Talladega University Library, Ala.
Tuskegee Institute Library, Ala.
Shomburg Collection, New York Public Library.
Talladega College, Ala.
Tuskegee Institute, Ala.
University of Ife, Ile-Ife, Nigeria
University of Ibadan, Nigeria.
Virginia State College, Black Music Center, Petersburg, Va.
Yale University, New Haven, Conn.

INDEX